£24-99

R A C

T I O N

This poster, found on a wall in Pamplona (Iruña in Basque) in March 2002, proclaims "All rights for all people." Pamplona is a hotbed of Basque nationalist activity, and this poster is a manifestation of that activity; yet, it proclaims its multiracial intentions. The figures in the foreground bear the physiognomies of the Andes and West Africa. In the crowd of Basque working people behind are an Asian and a Middle Eastern or North African man. The entire crowd stands across a map of Europe.

RACE AND NATION

ethnic systems in the modern world

EDITED BY paul spickard

ROUTLEDGE
NEW YORK AND LONDON

Published in 2005 by
Routledge
Taylor & Francis Group
270 Madison Avenue
New York, NY 10016
www.routledge-ny.com

Published in Great Britain by
Routledge
Taylor & Francis Group
2 Park Square
Milton Park, Abingdon
Oxon OX14 4RN
www.routledge.co.uk

10   9   8   7   6   5   4   3   2   1

Library of Congress Cataloging-in-Publication Data
    Race and nation : ethnic systems in the modern world / edited by Paul Spickard.
        p. cm.
    Includes bibliographical references.
    ISBN 0-415-95002-3 (hb : alk. paper) — ISBN 0-415-95003-1 (pb : alk. paper)
    1. Ethinicity. 2. Race awareness. 3 Group identity. 4. Nationalism. I. Spickard, Paul R., 1950-

    GN95.6R325 2004
    305.8—dc22   2004015905

To Roger Daniels

Also by Paul Spickard

Mixed Blood: Intermarriage and Ethnic Identity in Twentieth-Century America

A Global History of Christians (with Kevin M. Cragg)

Japanese Americans: The Formation and Transformations of an Ethnic Group

World History by the World's Historians
(with James V. Spickard and Kevin M. Cragg)

Colorism in Asian America
(with Joanne L. Rondilla)

as editor

Pacific Island Peoples in Hawai'i

Pacific Islander Americans: A Bibliography
(with Debbie Hippolite Wright and others)

We Are a People: Narrative and Multiplicity in Constructing Ethnic Identity
(with W. Jeffrey Burroughs)

Pacific Diaspora: Island Peoples in the United States and Across the Pacific
(with Joanne L. Rondilla and Debbie Hippolite Wright)

Revealing the Sacred in Asian and Pacific America
(with Jane Naomi Iwamura)

Racial Thinking in the United States: Uncompleted Independence
(with G. Reginald Daniel)

Affect and Power: Essays on Sex, Slavery, Race, and Religion in Appreciation of Winthrop D. Jordan
(with David J. Libby and Susan C. Ditto)

Contents

Acknowledgments ix

About the Authors xi

Race and Nation, Identity and Power:
Thinking Comparatively about Ethnic Systems 1
Paul Spickard

Part 1 Founding and Sustaining Myths

1 Guilty Pleasures: The Satisfactions of Racial Thinking in
Early-Nineteenth-Century California 33
Douglas Monroy

2 *Mestizaje* and the "Ethnicization" of Race in Latin America 53
Virginia Q. Tilley

3 Creating a Racial Paradise: Citizenship and Sociology
in Hawai'i 69
Lori Pierce

4 White into Black: Race and National Identity
in Contemporary Brazil 87
G. Reginald Daniel

5 Memories of Japanese Identity and Racial Hierarchy 115
Miyuki Yonezawa

Part 2 Colonialisms and Their Legacies

6 Ethnicity and Power in North Africa: Tunisia, Algeria,
and Morocco 135
Taoufik Djebali

7   Racial Frontiers in Jamaica's Nonracial Nationhood 155
     Violet Showers Johnson

8   Between Subjects and Citizens: Algerians, Islam,
     and French National Identity during the Great War 171
     Richard S. Fogarty

9   On Becoming German: Politics of Membership
     in Germany 195
     Elisabeth Schäfer-Wünsche

Part 3   Nation Making

10   Reinventing the Nation: Building a Bicultural Future
     from a Monocultural Past in Aotearoa/New Zealand 215
     Cluny Macpherson

11   Metaphors of Race and Discourse of Nation: Racial
     Theory and State Nationalism in the First Decades of
     the Turkish Republic 239
     Howard Eissenstat

12   The Fragmented Nation: Genealogy, Identity, and
     Social Hierarchy in Turkmenistan 257
     Adrienne Edgar

13   Becoming Cambodian: Ethnicity and the Vietnamese
     in Kampuchea 273
     Christine Su

Part 4   Boundaries Within

14   A Race Apart? The Paradox of Sikh Ethnicity and
     Nationalism 299
     Darshan Tatla

15   Race and Ethnicity in South Africa: Ideology
     and Experience 319
     T. Dunbar Moodie

16   Eritrea's Identity as a Cultural Crossroads 337
     Tekle M. Woldemikael

17   The Problem of the Color-Blind: Notes on the Discourse
     on Race in Italy 355
     Alessandro Portelli

Bibliography 365

Index 383

Acknowledgments

Seldom is a book written without the help of many hands; in the case of this book, the hands have been more numerous than is common. To an unusual degree, the authors of the various chapters have collaborated in revising each other's work and in creating the intellectual structure that is evident in the book's introduction and its outline. In that sense, we all share coauthorship. In addition to the chapter authors, Patrick Miller has been a collaborator on this project from its inception, took part in all the discussion sessions and planning meetings, read drafts of every chapter, and contributed wisdom and insight at every turn. It was he who boosted the poster that is the frontispiece and cover art. Eric Arnesen and Giulio Angioni contributed to our discussions as well.

The Collegium for African American Research provided the inspiration for the volume and the forum for our first interchange. The University of California, Santa Barbara, was the gracious host to our second working meeting and gave the editor many means of support as the book came into being. In particular, thanks are due to the UCSB Interdisciplinary Humanities Center, where Leonard Wallock and Theresa Peña worked hard on our behalf; to Chancellor Henry Yang; and to Dean David Marshall and former Dean Ed Donnerstein of the College of Letters and Science, all of whom provided financial support. The Oregon State University Center for the Humanities provided a fine place to prepare the final manuscript.

My students and colleagues at UCSB were generous with their skills and time, both during our working group meetings and as I was editing the manuscript. I am especially grateful to James Brooks, Marc Coronado, Jon Cruz, Kathleen Garces-Foley, Ann Greenwald, Anita Guerrini, Rudy Guevarra, Matt Kester, John Lee, Gurinder Singh Mann, Jeff Moniz, Sharleen Nakamoto, Chidinma Offoh-Robert, Mike Osborne, Ingrid Page, Luke Roberts, Catherine Salzgeber, Travis Smith, Gabriela Soto Laveaga, Michael Tucker, Isaiah Walker, and Stacey Ytuarte.

Bill Germano, Jaclyn Bergeron, Gilad Foss, and their colleagues at Routledge have been models of editorial wisdom, encouragement, energy, efficiency, and grace.

About the Authors

G. Reginald Daniel is Associate Professor of Sociology at UC Santa Barbara. While his research and teaching interests cover a variety of areas, he has been particularly active in the area of race and ethnic relations, as well as cultural analysis. Within these fields, he has examined a wide range of issues including general race and ethnic relations, multiracial identity and interracial relationships, and general cultural analysis. His books, *More Than Black? Multiracial Identity and the New Racial Order* (Temple University Press, 2001) and *Race and Multiraciality in Brazil and the United States: Converging Paths?* (Pennsylvania State University Press, in progress), are a culmination of much of his thinking on this topic.

Taoufik Djebali earned degrees in English and sociology from the University of Tunis and the Ecole des Hautes Etudes en Sciences Sociales, respectively, as well as a Ph.D. in American studies from the Sorbonne. He is Associate Professor in the Department of American Studies at the University of Caen. He has published many articles on racial and immigrant issues in the United States and is currently working on a book on Irish Americans.

Adrienne Edgar is Assistant Professor of History at UC Santa Barbara. Her degrees are from Oberlin College, Columbia, and UC Berkeley. She has published articles on ethnic nationalism in Turkmenistan, and was a postdoctoral fellow at Harvard University's Davis Center for Russian Studies. Her book, *Tribal Nation: The Making of Soviet Turkmenistan*, will be published by Princeton University Press in 2004.

Howard Eissenstat teaches Middle Eastern History at the University of Wisconsin – Stevens Point. He is currently completing his dissertation on competing narratives of the nation in the early Turkish Republic in the Department of History at UCLA.

Richard S. Fogarty is Assistant Professor of History at Bridgewater College in Virginia. He holds the M.A. from the University of Georgia and the Ph.D. from the UC Santa Barbara. He is coauthor of "Constructions and Functions of Race in French Military Medicine, 1830 to ca. 1920," in Tyler Stovall and Sue Peabody, eds., *The Color of Liberty: Histories of Race in France* (Duke University Press, 2003).

Violet Showers Johnson is Associate Professor of History and Chair of the Department of History at Agnes Scott College. She holds degrees from the University of Sierra Leone, the University of New Brunswick, and Boston College. She has written many articles on British West Indians in Boston, and has completed a book, *Black and Foreign in Brahminland: A History of the West Indian Experience in Boston, 1910–1950.*

Cluny Macpherson is Professor of Sociology, in the College of Humanities and Social Sciences at Massey University in Auckland, New Zealand. He teaches in the areas of ethnicity, development economics, health, and research design. His research interests and projects are focused on Aotearoa/New Zealand and the South Pacific. He is the author of many books and articles on ethnicity and Pacific Island peoples in Aotearoa/ New Zealand, most recently *Tangata o te Moana Nui: The Evolving Identities of Pacific Peoples in Aotearoa New Zealand* (Dunmore Press, 2002) with Paul Spoonley and Melani Anae, and *Tangata, Tangata: The Changing Contours of Ethnicity in Aotearoa/New Zealand* (Dunmore Press, 2004) with Paul Spoonley and David Pearson.

Douglas Monroy is Professor of History at The Colorado College. A native of Los Angeles and a graduate of Hollywood High School and UCLA, he presently lives in Colorado Springs. He is the author of *Thrown Among Strangers: The Making of Mexican Culture in Frontier California*, winner of the James Rawley Prize of the Organization of American Historians, and *Rebirth: Mexican Los Angeles from the Great Migration to the Great Depression*, both from the University of California Press. He is working on *In the Footsteps of Father Serra: Essays on California, Mexico, and America.* For the year 2004–2005, he is the Ray Allen Billington Distinguished Visiting Professor at the Huntington Library and Occidental College.

T. Dunbar Moodie is Professor of Sociology at Hobart and William Smith Colleges in Geneva, New York. He is the author of *The Rise of Afrikanerdom: Power, Apartheid, and the Afrikaner Civil Religion* and *Going for Gold: Men, Mines and Migration* both published by the University of California Press. Moodie has received grants from the United States Institute of Peace, the MacArthur Foundation, the Rockefeller Foundation, and the National Endowment for the Humanities. He has been a fellow at the Institute for Advanced Study in Princeton, the Southern African Research Program at Yale, the Center for the Humanities at Wesleyan, and the Annenberg School at the University of Pennsylvania. He was director of the Fisher Center for the Study of Women and Men, and served as a consultant for the United Nations Department of Peacekeeping Operations.

Lori Pierce holds degrees from Lake Forest College, Harvard Divinity School, and the University of Hawai'i. She has written several articles and book chapters on racial constructions and on Asian American Buddhism. She is Assistant Professor of American Studies at DePaul University.

Alessandro Portelli is Professor of American Literature at the University of Rome "La Sapienza." He is the author or editor of numerous books, articles, and essays on American, African American, and Italian literature, history, and culture, including *The Battle of Valle Giulia: Oral History and the Art of Dialogue* (University of Wisconsin Press, 1997); *La linea del colore: Saggi sulla cultura afroamericana* [The Color Line: Essays on African-American Culture] (Manifestolibri, 1994); *The Text and the Voice: Writing, Speaking, and Democracy in American Literature* (Columbia University Press, 1994); and *The Death of Luigi Trastulli and Other Stories: Form and Meaning in Oral History* (SUNY Press, 1991).

Elisabeth Schäfer-Wünsche teaches American Studies at the Rheinische Friedrich-Wilhelms-Universität Bonn. She received her doctorate from Heinrich-Heine-Universität Düsseldorf and is the author of a book on racial naming, *Wenn von Weißen die Rede ist: Zur afroamerikanischen Praxis des Benennens* (Stuttgart: Francke, 2004) and coeditor of *The Civil Rights Movement Revisited: Critical Perspectives on the Struggle for Racial Equality in the United States* (Hamburg: LIT, 2001). She has published articles and essays in the fields of American literature, African American studies, and cultural studies and is currently working on a book on American autobiography.

Paul Spickard is Professor of History at UC Santa Barbara. He holds an A.B. from Harvard University and an M.A. and Ph.D. from UC Berkeley. He has taught at twelve universities in the United States and abroad. He is the author or editor of twelve books and many articles on the comparative history and sociology of race and ethnicity and related topics. Among the books are *Mixed Blood: Intermarriage and Ethnic Identity in Twentieth-Century America* (University of Wisconsin Press, 1989), *Japanese Americans* (Twayne, 1996), *We Are a People: Narrative and Multiplicity in Constructing Ethnic Identity* (Temple University Press, 2000), *Revealing the Sacred in Asian and Pacific America* (Routledge, 2003), and *Racial Thinking in the United States* (University of Notre Dame Press, 2004).

Christine Su earned her Ph.D. in American Studies from the University of Hawai'i, her M.A. from Bowling Green State University, and her B.A. from the University of Notre Dame. The daughter of a Cambodian father and a Scottish mother, her major research interests include biracial and multiracial identity and Southeast Asian studies. She currently teaches anthropology and international studies at Hawai'i Pacific University.

Darshan Tatla, M.A. Cambridge University, Ph.D University of Warwick, is an Honourary Research Fellow, Department of Theology, University of Birmingham, United Kingdom. He is the author of several books, including *The Sikh Diaspora: The Search for Statehood* (University of Washington Press, 1998) and *Sikhs in North America* (Greenwood, 1991), and an editor of *International Journal of Punjab Studies*.

Virginia Q. Tilley is Associate Professor of Political Science at Hobart and William Smith Colleges. She holds a Ph.D from the University of Wisconsin–Madison and has written many articles on ethnicity and the state in Latin America and elsewhere, as well as the book, *Seeing Indians: A Study of Race, Nation, and Power in El Salvador* (University of New Mexico Press, 2005), and a book on the Israeli-Palestinian conflict, *The One State Solution* (University of Michigan Press, 2005).

Tekle M. Woldemikael is Associate Professor of Sociology and Anthropology in the University of Redlands, California. He received his Ph.D from Northwestern University and his B.A. from Addis Ababa University in Ethiopia. He has taught in several universities including the University of Gezira in the Sudan. He has published a book, *Becoming Black American: Haitians and American Institutions* (AMS Press, 1989), and numerous articles on ethnicity and nationalism in Eritrea, including "Language, Education, and Public Policy in Eritrea," in *African Studies Review* (2003).

Miyuki Yonezawa is Professor in the Foreign Language Center at Tokai University in Kanagawa-ken, Japan. She is the coauthor of *Young Japan and the World* (Tokai University Press, 1998). She has published articles on race, immigration, and the U.S. labor movement; U.S. immigration law; and relationships between American and Japanese labor leaders. Yonezawa has degrees from Aoyama Gakuin University, Tokyo, and San Diego State University, and she was a visiting scholar at UC Santa Barbara in 1999 and 2000.

Race and Nation, Identity and Power
Thinking Comparatively about Ethnic Systems

PAUL SPICKARD

The old man and I sat in the dust of the bazaar, our backs against a whitewashed wall, hiding from the sun in what little shade we could find. Radio Beijing blared from a loudspeaker on a pole nearby, unheeded by the people around us. Like my companion and 95 percent of the people in Turpan, this little oasis town in the Takla Makan Desert in China's far western borderlands, they were Uygurs.[1] Hawk-nosed with slanted eyes and tawny complexions, they spoke a kind of Turkic and very little Chinese. When they talked about their Chinese colonial overlords they spat with contempt and used words like "hate" and "kill."

To pass the time, the old man and I tried to make conversation using the few Chinese words we each could command.

"So you're Japanese," he declared.

"No, I'm American," I answered.

"What's that?" he asked. Aside from the radio playing overhead, there was no local means of learning about the outside world. No Uygur language radio, no television, no newspaper. Few outside visitors except for Chinese bureaucrats. No way of knowing about the United States, or much else outside Turpan.

I tried to describe my country to the gentleman. He wasn't buying it. No place like that existed, so far as he was concerned.

He knew about three kinds of people. There were *people* — that is, Uygurs of many tribes and lineages. There were Chinese, the hated colonizers, and, as it turned out, there were Japanese. Every two weeks a minibus brought about a dozen Japanese tourists to Turpan. Outsiders, in this man's worldview, people who were neither Uygur nor Chinese, were *ipso facto* Japanese. A White American like me was Japanese.

I expect that things have changed a lot in Turpan since that hot spring day in 1989. Probably today I would not be labeled Japanese. But that day I was not *mistaken for* Japanese; I *was* Japanese, in the language of the Turpan racial system of that time.

1

My encounter in Turpan suggests a few themes that reemerge persistently throughout this book. First, there are many kinds of racial and ethnic systems in the world: many ways that groups of people with different ancestries come into contact with one another, interact, and assort themselves into socially significant groupings. Second, these groups may initially see each other as simply ethnic or cultural groups, but at some point — I will call this *the racial moment* — they begin to see themselves as fundamentally and irrevocably different from one another. And third, at such times power is at issue between the groups, and there is a tendency to associate physical markers with racial difference. In short, *race is about power, and it is written on the body*. I will have more to say about each of these themes in the pages that follow.

In almost every place on earth where people live, there is more than just one kind of people. And in each such place, there is a system of ideas and a language describing the relationships between those peoples. Most often, those peoples arrange themselves in hierarchies. Theoretically, a system of difference might be articulated without hierarchy, but historically, I know of no situation where racial or ethnic difference has endured without some element of domination. Frequently, we use terms like "racial" or "ethnic" to characterize those hierarchies. According to the estimates of scholars and government agencies[2]:

- Afghanistan is 38 percent Pashtun, 25 percent Tajik, 19 percent Hazara, 6 percent Uzbek, and 13 percent various other ethnicities.
- Angola is 37 percent Ovimbundu, 25 percent Kimbundu, 13 percent Bakongo, 2 percent Mestico (mixed European and African), 1 percent European, and 22 percent others.
- Belgium is 55 percent Fleming, 33 percent Walloon, and 12 percent mixed and others.
- Bosnia and Herzegovina is 40 percent Serb, 38 percent Muslim, and 22 percent Croat.
- Brunei and Darussalam is 64 percent Malay, 20 percent Chinese, and 16 percent others.
- The Gambia is 42 percent Mandinka, 18 percent Fula, 16 percent Wolof, 10 percent Jola, 9 percent Serahuli, and 5 percent various others.
- Kazakhstan is 46 percent Kazak, 35 percent Russian, 5 percent Ukrainian, 3 percent German, 2 percent Uzbek, 2 percent Tatar, and 7 percent others.
- Malaysia is 59 percent Malay, 32 percent Chinese, and 9 percent Indian.
- Samoa is 92 percent Samoan, 7 percent Afakasi (people of mixed Polynesian and European ancestry), and less than 1 percent European.
- Serbia and Montenegro is 63 percent Serb, 14 percent Albanian, 6 percent Montenegrin, 4 percent Hungarian, and 13 percent others.
- Slovakia is 86 percent Slovak, 11 percent Hungarian, 2 percent Gypsy, 1 percent Czech, and smaller numbers of Ruthenians, Ukrainians, Germans, and Poles.

- Switzerland is 65 percent German-speaking, 18 percent French, 10 percent Italian, 1 percent Romansch, and 6 percent others.
- Trinidad and Tobago is 43 percent Black, 40 percent East Indian, 14 percent mixed, and 3 percent White, Chinese, and others.
- The United Arab Emirates is 19 percent Emiri, 23 percent other Arab and Iranian, 50 percent South Asian, and 8 percent other expatriates from the West and Asia.

In every one of these places, there are dynamics between peoples that observers would call "racial" or "ethnic."

As one can tell from this recital, what the relevant racial and ethnic groups are — and what one may mean by such terms as "race," "ethnicity," or even "people" — is quite different in different places. So too, there is substantial variation in the ways that peoples relate to one another in such diverse places.

The goal of *Race and Nation* is to address such questions as these: What is the nature of ethnic systems? Are they the same things around the globe, are they distinct but related things, or are they very different things in different places? We see enough similarity to call them by common terms such as "racial" and "ethnic"; are the similarities we perceive real? If so, what are the common issues in ethnic and racial systems around the globe? And what are the sources and shapes of the differences that exist in different places?

It is fair to say, whatever the differences may be, that nearly all the parts of the world have systems of hierarchy that most observers call "racial" or "ethnic." For example, Colombia lists its population as 58 percent Mestizo, 20 percent White, 14 percent Mulatto, 4 percent Black, 3 percent mixed Black and Indian, and 1 percent Indian. Peru reports its population as 45 percent Indian, 37 percent Mestizo, 15 percent White, and 3 percent other.[3] Does it mean that in these places great care is made to note fractions of mixed ancestry? Some would say that it represents an attempt on the part of individuals to flee association with Blackness or Indianness by emphasizing that they have some European ancestry. Others would say that the ideal of a Mestizo nation is an attempt to erase the Indian element entirely. Still others that the distinctions are primarily ones of class, not of ancestry at all — that "Indians" are just poor, rural "Mestizos."[4]

To take another example, consider Israel, where 82 percent of the population is Jewish. We all are familiar with the Jewish domination of the nearly 18 percent of the Israeli population who are ethnic Arabs. But we are probably less familiar with the complex dynamics among various groups we might call "ethnic" within the Jewish part of the population. Not only are there splits along lines of religious affiliation — secular Jews versus the ultra-orthodox, to take the two extremes — but there are also differences among Jews with respect to their origin — to simplify, those born in Israel (50 percent of the total population), immigrants who were born in Europe and the Americas (20 percent), the 7 percent who were born in North Africa, and so on. This is to say nothing of divisions along class and political lines. How all those groups and identities assort themselves in the Israeli nation (or is it the Israeli community?) is an incredibly complex affair.[5]

Myanmar is another polyglot place: 68 percent ethnic Burman, 9 percent Shan, 7 percent Karen, 4 percent Rakhine, 3 percent Chinese, 2 percent Mon, and 2 percent Indian. Outsiders are generally aware of the bloody dictatorship that has run Myanmar for a couple of decades now, but few of us know much about the ethnic character of some of that oppression. Karens, particularly, have a long history of suffering at the hands of ethnic Burmans.[6]

How is one to deal with all this variety in ethnic situations and systems? Is there any way to comprehend race and ethnicity as a global phenomenon — not all around the world at once, but in its particularity in various different places? There are many studies of racial or ethnic hierarchies in individual countries, such as the United States, Britain, China, Brazil, Zambia, Indonesia, and so on.[7] There are a few comparative studies of racial and ethnic systems in two or three places.[8] But almost never have scholars attempted to compare racial and ethnic systems across a wide range of countries in a single study.

The main impediment, I think, has been that it has been hard to gather expertise on enough places and organize it into a single, coordinated study. There also is the very real question of comparability. How are we to know that what we are calling "racial" or "ethnic" or "people" groups in one place are the same kinds of groups as those to which we are attaching similar labels in another place? Is there a common language we can use, a common set of concepts? Then there is the matter of choosing the right size frame for studying racial and ethnic systems in various places. I say "places" to be purposely vague, but, in fact, most of the authors assembled here and I have used the nation as their frame. Why would we necessarily choose that unit of view? Is there another that might work better? Should we compare regions? What is a "region," and how are we to make regions comparable to one another?

Our project: to write a comparative history of racial systems in the modern world

The subtitle of this book is *Ethnic Systems in the Modern World*. I am increasingly convinced that the way to write world history (at least the way that satisfies me most) is as widely comparative as practical, yet as specific as possible. Thinking of the history of the world's peoples in an integrated fashion has been one of the most prominent growing trends of the past few decades in the historical profession. Some, like Arnold Toynbee, Will Durant, and William H. McNeill, once approached world history from the angle of one grand theory or another.[9] More commonly in recent years, scholars like Oliver Cox, Immanuel Wallerstein, Andre Gunder Frank, and Janet Abu-Lughod have sought to understand world history primarily as a matter of large-scale economic systems.[10] Some others, such as Philip Curtin, Alfred Crosby, Jerry Bentley, and John Thornton, have sought to describe specific kinds of connections between very large regions — for instance, the slave trade or plantation economies.[11] Each of these approaches operates at such a very high level of abstraction, however, that it is very difficult to discern in them the lives of humans, or even the shapes of the experiences of quite large groups of people.

There are lots of theoretical studies of race and ethnicity. But, useful as they are, like the world histories of Durant and Wallerstein, most theoretical treatments seem remote from the everyday interactions of people on the ground, and so make concrete understanding of and comparisons between ethnic systems in different places impossible. This is no criticism, for that is not their purpose; they are promulgating theory.[12] Other theoretical studies, while each may be more grounded in a particular place and set of experiences, are bound to those places and do not lend themselves to cross-cultural or international comparisons.[13] Some scholars attempt to make more universal statements about race and ethnicity based on their analysis of racial and ethnic dynamics in a particular place — usually the United States or Britain — but fail genuinely to transcend those bounds. Insofar as they do make attempts to analyze dynamics outside the United States and Britain, they, nonetheless, merely apply the phenomena and categories of analysis they see in the United States or Britain to another place, rather than actually exploring racial or ethnic dynamics there in that place's own terms.[14]

In the present project, we are using a group approach to scholarship in order to gain something of a worldwide comparative perspective yet not completely sacrifice detail and the stuff of human lives. In putting together this working group, I have tried to foster a sense of the specificity of experiences in each of the various places; at the same time, I have tried to gather scholars from a wide enough set of places and disciplines to make some real comparisons work. The common questions we have all attempted to address should, I hope, provide some element of glue.

There are only a few people who have attempted anything like the kind of coordinated international study of racial and ethnic dynamics that I have in mind. George Fredrickson wrote a much-respected comparison of the development of White supremacy in the histories of two places: South Africa and the United States. He mainly used secondary sources in a single language (English), although he did consult some archives and read some documents in Afrikaans. Establishing some scholarly competence on two widely disparate countries might be about as much as one could expect of a single scholar. Michael Banton and Anthony Marx both wrote about the United States, Brazil, and South Africa, although they did so from, primarily, sociological rather than historical points of view, and without much recourse to archival sources or sense of change over time. St. Clair Drake adopted a scattershot approach in *Black Folk Here and There*. His geographical and temporal range was broader than Fredrickson's, but he dealt at even greater remove than Fredrickson, Banton, and Marx from the details of scholarly investigation, and operated solely from secondary and tertiary sources.[15] In the past few years, a few books have begun to look at African-descended peoples across a number of settings with some precision of comparison. As I have suggested, in order to explore a broader geographical range with any depth of expertise, these projects bring together many scholars who are specialists on African-descended peoples in particular places. *Blackness in Latin America and the Caribbean* harnesses the talents of three dozen anthropologists. It divides the Caribbean and Latin America into four geographical zones and presents a wealth of mainly ethnographic studies of local populations in each zone. It attempts only limited historical analysis, however, and the studies do not respond to a common set of analytical issues. *The African Diaspora* is a compendium of more than thirty literary and artistic analyses, organized by theme rather than geography or genre. The closest relative to the present volume is *Crossing Boundaries: Comparative History of Black People in Diaspora*. Editors Darlene Clark Hine and Jacqueline McLeod gathered twenty historians to address the commonalities, connections, and discontinuities between the experiences of African-descended peoples in various parts of Africa and the Americas over the past three centuries.[16]

These three works treat only one kind of racial or ethnic dynamic — that between African-descended peoples and European-descended peoples — although they do treat that dynamic in multiple settings. There is only one writer, Philip Mason (in *Patterns of Dominance*), who so far has done what we are attempting to do in *Race and Nation, Identity and Power*: compare the dynamics of ethno-racial interaction in several societies made up of various combinations of peoples. Mason's is as magisterial and wide-ranging a synthesis of scholarship as one can imagine. It wanders across India, Europe, Rwanda, South Africa, Brazil, Spanish America, and the Caribbean. It treats not just African-descended peoples but as many of the peoples as it can in each of those places. Although *Patterns of Dominance* is long out of date, it is a daring and prodigious work of scholarship. It asks the big questions in comparative ways and with some depth in each of the places it examines.[17]

Now, more than thirty years later, with a new generation of scholars asking a revised set of questions based on new data that have emerged over the intervening decades, we are collectively trying to do the kind of work that only Philip Mason has been able to do in the past. *Race and Nation: Ethnic Systems in the Modern World* is an attempt at a coordinated study of ethnic and racial systems in various parts of the globe. In 1999, I began to organize an international group of scholars via the Internet to talk about comparing racial and ethnic systems. We exchanged ideas about how to frame our project and what questions to address. In 2001, a dozen scholars who know about the ethnic systems in various places came together in Cagliari, Sardinia, at the biennial meeting of the Collegium for African American Research. We presented papers at a series of interlocking workshops, listened carefully and commented on one another's ideas, and mapped out plans for the remainder of the project.

In Sardinia, each author was asked to write about the racial or ethnic system of the part of the world about which he or she was knowledgeable. Each author selected a topic and angle of analysis that fit his or her own expertise. In addition, all the authors were asked to address these common questions:

- What is the history of the making of national identity in the place you study?
- What is the key period for understanding race in this place? Examine it in some detail.
- What are the racial or ethnic groups that currently make up the population of this place?
- What is the history of each of those groups in this place?
- What is the history of their interactions?
- What have been their relative structural positions in society?
- What has been the mutual imagery surrounding them and their interactions?
- Where do racial or ethnic relations seem to be heading in this place as we enter the twenty-first century?

Another cohort of six scholars was unable to attend the Sardinia conference, but, nonetheless, prepared papers and contributed to the Internet discussion. Some of them joined the discussion in person at a second meeting held in Santa Barbara in 2002. The scholars revised their papers based on comments from the Sardinia meeting. We printed and bound them. As the scholars came to Santa Barbara from around the world, some identified each other by the copies of The Green Book they clutched in airports and on inbound flights. In the Santa Barbara meeting, we spent many hours critiquing each other's chapters and trying to bring them into conversation with one another. One of the participants in the Santa Barbara conference likened our sessions to "intellectual slam-dancing," so intense were our discussions.

The key task in preparing this book has been to foster interaction among the authors. We come from several disciplines (history, sociology, anthropology, political science, literature, American studies, English language studies). We know about different parts of the world that conceive of their racial and ethnic systems in quite different terms. So, the key to making this book a success has been discussion among the authors. In Sardinia and again in Santa Barbara, we were surprised and pleased at the ways that our different perspectives contributed to each other's thinking.

After the Santa Barbara meeting, the authors retired to their studies to fashion third revised drafts. In addition to the questions that guided our writing from the beginning, we agreed to attempt to address these additional themes: gender, religion, historical change, migration, colonialism, class or economic location, access to political and military participation and power, legal and constitutional status (citizenship, membership, etc.), and family and lineage. The chapters that follow this introduction are the result of several months of interaction with the book's editor and publisher.

The structure of the book

Race and Nation is divided into four parts: "Founding and Sustaining Myths," "Colonialisms and Their Legacies," "Nation Making," and "Boundaries Within." Each of the book's parts highlights a particular angle of vision on matters of race, nation, ethnicity, and identity. These parts do not contain separate categories, as much as they express vectors along which analysis and interpretation flow. Many of the chapters could easily be placed in two or more parts. The placement of an individual chapter highlights certain issues that are embodied in it. However, each chapter also opens up to issues in several other parts of the book. The chapters in each section of the book are arranged with chronology in mind. The early chapters in each part focus mainly on the pre-twentieth-century era; later chapters deal mainly, but not exclusively, with the present. Thematically, the last chapter in each section and the first chapter in the following section form a conceptual bridge between the two.

Part One: Founding and sustaining myths

Part One highlights the myths that are built in various places regarding the making of nations and peoples, and the ways those myths facilitate particular kinds of ethnic hierarchy and domination. It offers a broad-based and deeply grounded conversation among scholars working on the nineteenth, twentieth, and twenty-first centuries in three continents and the mid-Pacific about the myths that societies make surrounding ethnicity and nationhood. The authors and the ethnic systems they examine are Douglas Monroy on race and citizenship in nineteenth-century California; Virginia Tilley on the concept of *mestizaje* in Latin America and its functions in nation-building and erasure of Indian identity; Lori Pierce on the discourse of aloha in Hawai'i; Reginald Daniel on the myth of multiracial democracy in Brazil; and Miyuki Yonezawa on the myths of racial purity and multiplicity that underlay the nation-building project in modern Japan.

Part Two: Colonialisms and their legacies

Part Two explores the legacies of various kinds of colonialism: Roman, French, German, British, and American in several parts of Africa and the Caribbean. It examines the effects of colonialism on both the colonizer and the colonized, and on the metropole as well as the periphery. The chapters in Part Two include Taoufik Djebali on successive waves of colonialism and ethnic divisions in North Africa; Violet Johnson on the legacy of British colonialism for race and nation making in Jamaica; Richard Fogarty on French colonialism and citizenship for North Africans; and Elisabeth Schäfer-Wünsche on colonialism, race, and the politics of membership in Germany.

Part Three: Nation making

One of the myths of modern thinking is that the nation-state is normative — that each political state naturally and ideally controls one people, race, or ethnic group, that ethnicity and national identity naturally reinforce one another. The chapters in this section highlight some very different dynamics. Not only in the cases studied here, but in most states, the task of government has been to forge some kind of political unity out of, not one ethnic group, but rather several disparate peoples. Described here are several attempts by class elites, dominant ethnic groups, and outsiders to make nations. Cluny Macpherson shows how Maori and Pakeha fought for control in nineteenth-century Aotearoa/New Zealand, and how they are now attempting to make a bicultural nation sometimes together and often at odds. Howard Eissenstat shows how, in the wake of World War I, an Ottoman elite defined by class and religion shaped themselves and the people around them into a nation defined by an ethnicity they created, the Turks, and how the idea of Turkishness took on the superstructure of European-derived scientific racism. Adrienne Edgar explores the Soviet attempt to create Turkmen nationality out of a complex web of identities, and to make it fit Soviet models of what ethnicity should be. Finally, Christine Su takes the reader on a harrowing tour of Cambodia where a nation is being made anew, and where ethnic Vietnamese occupy a precarious position.

Part Four: Boundaries within

Part Four emphasizes the relationships between majority and minority groups within states. Darshan Tatla details the Sikh call for elements of national self-determination and the response of the Indian state. Dunbar Moodie describes the creation of White, Coloured, Black, and tribal identities in the context of British colonialism and postcolonialism, and their new shapes and dynamics in the postapartheid state. Tekle Woldemikael explores the complex relationships between groups that some might (and some might not) call ethnic in Eritrea, especially the Eritreans' affinity for Arab identification and their shunning of connections with sub-Saharan Africa. Alessandro Portelli, in the book's concluding chapter, gives us a whirlwind tour of the racial and cultural dynamics that operate among the kaleidoscope of peoples who make up the new Italy.

Thoughts on race and nation, identity and power

The chapters in this book focus on racial and ethnic systems in eighteen different settings around the globe. Taken together, they raise a host of issues about racial and ethnic dynamics. Once upon a time, a book on race and ethnicity would attempt to come up with a set of more or less universal rules about how such systems work, everywhere and always — something like Robert Park's famous "race relations cycle."[18] I am not as convinced as the avatars of the social scientific paradigm once were that there is indeed a universal set of laws, stages, patterns, or processes that describes the ways in which all ethnic groups shape themselves or interact with one another in all times and places. But I do think there are tissues of similarity and webs of relatedness that may help us think productively about widely disparate ethnic systems alongside each other. That is the task of this book.

Ethnicity, Race, Nation, Identity, Power

This book is partly, but not primarily, about the nexus between race and nation. The nation is one of our concerns, but only one.[19] This book is more broadly about systems of relationships in various places that are most often called "ethnic" (less often called "racial"). In such systems, race, power, identity, and nation are all factors that shape the relationships between peoples. For our purposes in this book, one might suggest that identity is the issue at stake; power is the means; race (or ethnicity) is the interpretation; and nation is the usual frame of analysis. It is more complex than that, of course, and the factors always morph and interweave, but that will give the reader an idea where we are headed. Many studies of race or ethnicity — especially, but not only, those by political scientists — operate in a teleological mode. Starting with the geographically and politically convenient unit of the state, they search for the grounds of identity (by which they usually mean citizenship) in the nation that they assume to be the ethnic core of the polity.

For scholars of nationalism such as Ernest Gellner, the most important question is the nature of the nation. For Gellner, a nation more or less equals an ethnic group. Gellner sees a particular ethnic group — a specific people with a shared history, language, and ancestry — as the foundation of each nation. Multiethnic states, for Gellner, are conceptually incoherent and inherently unstable. His concern is the nation. He does not attend to the way that the ethnic group is constructed and maintained, what its processes and permutations are; he takes it as a given, and a near-synonym for the nation. Then he spends most of his attention on the relationship between the nation and the state. The state is the governing apparatus. The nation is a collection of people who see themselves as one and who aspire to be governed together as one people. Gellner sees an intimate connection in European history between the formation of particular ethnic groups and particular nations.[20]

Other nationalism scholars like Anthony D. Smith are open to more detailed exploration of the nature of the ethnic groups. But Smith's main concern (as much as Gellner's), is the nature of the nation. For him, as for Gellner, each nation is founded on an ethnic group. As Smith writes, "modern nations — a fusion of premodern ethnic identities and modern 'civic' elements — require the symbols, myths and memories of ethnic cores if they are to generate a sense of solidarity and purpose ... there is ... [an] inner 'antiquity' of many modern nations."[21]

The term "nation," then, implies aspirations to achieve political sovereignty or statehood, whereas an "ethnic group" is simply a people (more about that later).[22] For example, people who call themselves, and are called by others, Jews share a common identity and fellow-feeling; they are an ethnic group. By contrast, Zionists in the first half of the twentieth century expressed aspirations to achieve statehood; that is, they saw the Jewish people as a nation, the core of a potential state, something more than an ethnic group.

In *Race and Nation* we are interested in turning the angle of investigation the other way around. We are interested in the nation, but primarily as a frame for ethnic systems, or insofar as national dynamics may influence ethnic dynamics. Although all of our contributors attend to the question of nationalism, and some (particularly in Part Three) take nation building as a critical issue, as a group of scholars our main concern is about ethnic systems. We are interested in race and ethnicity, their relationships and interactions, and the various ways they have arranged themselves around the globe in the modern world. We are less interested in the ways that racial, ethnic, and national identities are put in the service of, or hinder, the projects of forming and maintaining states. For the most part, we use the nation to frame the scope of investigation, although there are exceptions: California in the period described by Douglas Monroy was a part of the Mexican nation first and then of the United States; Taoufik Djebali's analysis of North Africa and Virginia Tilley's of Latin America include several nations each; whether Hawai'i or the Punjab is a nation or a part of a nation depends a good deal on one's perspective.

Ethnicity and the racial moment

If ethnicity and race are the central concerns of this book, what then are they? At the broadest level, I see at least two ways that people tend to think about these matters. One way comes to us from the eighteenth- and nineteenth-century pseudoscience of Blumenbach, Gobineau, Cuvier, and their intellectual descendants (right down to Charles Murray and Richard Herrnstein, J. Philippe Rushton, and Jon Entine as the twentieth century turns to the twenty-first).[23] Their vision is the one that most lay people assume to be the way things are.

According to the pseudoscientists, there are big races (perhaps four or five of them) and smaller subsidiary ethnic groups. In this view, race is about biology, genes, phenotype, the body. It is physical, inherited, and immutable. The races are discrete from each other. Each race has not only specific distinguishing bodily features — skin color, hair texture, nose shape, and so forth — but specific character qualities that cannot be erased; they may be suppressed, but eventually they will come out. In this same mode of thinking, ethnicity is based on smaller human subdivisions of race. The members of various ethnic groups within a race look very much, if not completely, alike. Their differences are based on cultural or national divisions, such as language, citizenship, religion, child-rearing practices, food habits, clothing, and so forth. Ethnic differences, in this way of thinking, are mutable. Ethnicity derives from an ancestral group, but it can be changed by changing behavior.

An alternative view emphasizes the plasticity and constructedness of groups, whether we call them "races" or "ethnic groups."[24] It notes that groups that are often called races have cultures, and that there are average physical differences that can be observed among the peoples who are called ethnic groups, so the race/ethnic group dichotomy tends to break down pretty quickly. It emphasizes (as do several authors in this volume) that race is not a thing or a condition but a *process*. This alternative view further notes that the understanding of the pseudoscientists was created in a particular time and place (Europe and the United States in the late-eighteenth to early-twentieth century). It was created among a set of people who were trying to explain the varieties of peoples that Europeans and Euro-Americans were encountering as they made colonies around the globe. Some would say that they were trying to naturalize colonialism, to lay it onto the genes of people.[25]

I have argued elsewhere in favor of using "ethnicity" over "race" as a generic term for kinds of groups that operate on more or less the same bases.[26] Both are social and political constructs based on real or fictive common ancestry, which were generated in particular contexts and which have gone through particular histories. If one is focusing on internal group processes, they are much the same kinds of groups, whether one calls them "races," "ethnic groups," "ethno-racial groups," or some other common term. To distinguish between "race" and "ethnicity," I have contended, is to give in to the pseudoscientific racists by adopting their terminology. It is to conjure up visions of large, physical, immutable races and smaller, cultural subgroups that are ethnic.

In the United States, it is true that the markers of the largest social groups do, in fact, more or less correspond to pseudoscientific racial categories: red, yellow, black, brown, and white. Those are the meaningful racial formations in American society.[27] But elsewhere, it is other markers that make the big divisions. In Britain, at least for a time in the 1970s and 1980s, people whom Americans would call Asians and Africans, many Britons joined together under the single term "Black."[28] Taoufik Djebali in this volume argues that in North Africa throughout much of its history, it was religion that constituted the big divider. Religion is therefore, in power terms, a "racial" divider, in that people on either side of the religious divide see each other as fundamentally, immutably different from themselves. So too, Han Chinese and Tibetans, Japanese and Koreans have something like "racial" differences between them.[29]

Despite such evident similarities between "racial" and "ethnic" groups, there *is* nonetheless a critical juncture in relationships between peoples when they come to see each other, and are seen by outsiders, as fundamentally, essentially, immutably different from one another. At such a juncture, the differences they perceive are often laid on the body and the essential character. That is what I would call *the racial moment*. At such times, that racializing move is accompanied by at least an attempt by one group to exert power over the other, or to highlight its own disempowerment. It is worth noting that "race" is a term that seems static and essential, while "racialize" emphasizes agency and process: ongoing action taken to make hierarchy, to position oneself, and to create an Other.

Not to make too fine a point of it, I would claim that, at its point of origin and in its ongoing formations, race is about power, and it is written on the body. That is, the dividing into peoples has usually been done for reasons of asserting power vis-à-vis one another. Those with more power have frequently dictated the shape of the division: who would be in each group, what would be the criteria for group membership, what would be the relationships between the groups, and what members of each group would have to do henceforth. Subordinate groups may do some reflexive policing of their own, but the impetus comes from the powerful. The purpose of writing racial division onto the body is to naturalize it, to make it inevitable, and thus no one's fault.[30]

In the United States, for instance, much of race relations has depended on the one-drop rule: race relations have been defined as being between Black and White, and any person with any known African ancestry has been regarded as Black.[31] That was in order to keep the part-White sons and daughters of slave owners and slave women as slaves and to keep them from asserting any measure of Whiteness. Then subordinate status was written onto the Black body itself. Whites (and others) assumed that the people who were defined as Black had particular character qualities and life chances, and that people defined as White naturally, by virtue of their supposed biological inheritance, were blessed with more positive character qualities and better life chances.

Yet, for other groups in the United States, the one-drop rule does not apply, at least not in the same way and with the same pervasiveness. People who are part-Indian and part-White are sometimes reckoned Native American and sometimes White, depending on the degree of their connectedness to Native peoples, cultures, and institutions. People who are part-Indian and part-Black are generally reckoned Black. People who are part-Asian and part-something else have much more complex sets of ethnic possibilities and constraints.[32]

Race and religion

To what extent is the sense of difference between groups derived from one's sense of race, hence imputed to the genes and the body, and more broadly to ethnicity? Alternatively, to what extent is the sense of difference a derivative of the religious identity one may embrace? Douglas Monroy describes the dominance of Catholic Christianity in nineteenth-century California and the ways that converting to Catholicism allowed some Indians, if not to enter the dominant class, at least to elevate themselves from the ranks of the most despised class. My own research on Fiji suggests that the dominant group — ethnic Fijians — defines itself nearly as much by its Protestant identity as by its racial difference from the Hindu and Muslim Indo-Fijian subject class.[33] In similar fashion, chapters in this book speak of the power of adherence to Islam to make one Turkish, of commitment to Marxism to make one Turkmen, and of identification with Christianity rather than with Islam to make one French. There was also a religious aspect to the difference my Uygur Muslim acquaintance perceived between himself and the Chinese (and probably me).

But even in such situations, where religion is the label dividing peoples, race lurks not far away. For example, when French Catholics imputed a fundamental, immutable viciousness to Algerians who failed to convert, or when Spanish

Catholics expressed a similar assessment of Indians who were similarly reluctant, the conquerors were making something like a racial judgment.

Further, one cannot ignore the ways in which a dominating power's religion may be used as a weapon to destroy the cultural underpinnings of a dominated people, whether it be Spanish Catholics destroying Indian culture or Japanese conquerors imposing Buddhism and Shinto on Ainu in order to make of them Japanese subjects.

Among the societies surveyed in this volume, the encounter between the French people and North Africans is unique in that there the colonized people adhered to two distinct religious systems — Islam and Judaism. France defined their colonial underlings by these two religious identities and divided them in order to rule, favoring Jews over Muslims in the matter of limited access to French citizenship, education, and other benefits. Conversely, in the same region and the same colonial situation, religion was a unifying force — an international, panethnic bond asserting a common peoplehood among all Muslims, Arabs and Berbers alike.

Colonialism

The power dynamic that makes racial difference historically has been tied to colonialism. This is true not only in the case of European colonialism;[34] other peoples also make race. Over many centuries, people from the North China Plain expanded their power into surrounding territories and united them into the Chinese empire. Some they incorporated fairly fully, forcing the national language (or at least its writing system) on them and reckoning them Han, or members of the Chinese race. Others they kept at further distance, conceptually and socially, as conquered and colonized peoples: Uygurs in what became Xinjiang Province, Dai and Miao in the Southwest, Tibetans on the mountainous plateaus of Qinghai and Tibet. On these last, they wrote a story of immutable biological separateness and cultural unassimilability. And the Han Chinese's take on Tibetans is every bit as vicious as the most racist White American's take on Blacks. In fact, it has many of the same themes: Tibetans are supposed to be filthy, lazy, sneaky, dishonest, promiscuous, and intellectually incapable of higher orders of achievement. This discourse attributing primitivity to the less powerful is also found in the way that Khmer Cambodians talk about Vietnamese Cambodians, and the way Nordic Germans talk about Turkish Germans.[35]

There are lots of varieties of colonialism and they seem always to result in racialized hierarchies between the conquering people and the conquered. In this volume, we learn of the colonial conquests achieved and ethnic hierarchies created by the British in South Africa and India, the French in North Africa, Germans in Southwest Africa, Euro-Americans in California and Hawai'i, Soviet Russians in Central Asia, and Italians in Eritrea. In each of those places, the colonizers created a language of racial order with themselves at the top and the local peoples arrayed below.[36]

There seem to be some common elements in these colonial processes and some instances of conscious modeling going on. For example, as Miyuki Yonezawa explains in Chapter 5, the Japanese consciously modeled their treatment of the Ainu in Hokkaido after the U.S. treatment of native peoples in North America. They employed two strategies in alternating periods. At times they attempted to assimilate the Ainu, make farmers and citizens out of them, change their language and religion, force them to take Japanese names — in essence, to wipe out differences and make the Ainu into ordinary Japanese. On other occasions, they kept the Ainu separate, restricted them on reservations, kept their educational and economic level low, and settled ethnic Japanese onto their lands.[37] Similarly, White South Africans modeled their dominance of Black South Africans on U.S. racial policies: the "homelands" policy was a frank imitation of the U.S. Indian reservation policy; *apartheid* was a crude facsimile of Jim Crow segregation of Black Americans.[38] In this context, the Euro-American domination of peoples of color in the United States stands indisputably as a colonial process.

Colonialism brought many common items to the places that were colonized. One of the impacts of modern-era European colonialism in many places was the rapid decline of native populations. In this volume, we see massive destruction of human lives — of Hereros in Southwest Africa, of Hawaiians, of Maori in Aotearoa/New Zealand, of Indians in California — many by violence, more by disease. In each place, the colonizers mounted a discourse touting the inevitable extinction of the native people. Within these cultural frames, the local people were naturalized as part of the landscape, like beasts of the field and forest. The extinction of Hawaiians, of Indians, of Maori was seen as inevitable, like the sad disappearance of the buffalo from the Great Plains, a reminder of a bygone era that could be celebrated in iconic memory by the descendants of the people who had done the killing. Because it was inevitable, it was nobody's fault.

Colonial connections brought new ideas to the colonized places. Among the new ideas that the French brought to North Africa were "race," "nation," "citizenship," and "anti-Semitism" in the European meanings of those terms. As Taoufik Djebali and Richard Fogarty show in Chapters 6 and 8, the French created new racialized distinctions between Arabs (whom they characterized as oppressors, bad people, and lazy) and Berbers (whom they pictured as good people and noble sufferers at Arab hands) — all this as a means of dividing and ruling the conquered peoples.

Colonialism also brought new peoples, and not just the colonizers. European and American colonial enterprises brought Chinese workers to California; Indians to South Africa, East Africa, Fiji, and the Caribbean; and Chinese, Japanese, Filipinos, and Koreans to Hawai'i. In several instances, a key task for the colonizers was to turn these peoples or local minorities who could be separated off from the bulk of the native populace into middleman minorities. They formed a kind of local elite, working for the colonial governors and also in small business. This was the situation the French attempted to create with the

Jews in Tunisia and the Berbers in Algeria and Morocco; that the British created with Indians in Fiji, Uganda, and Jamaica; and that the Americans created with Northeast Asian immigrants in Hawai'i. There was no guarantee that such middleman minorities would always side with the colonizers; according to Djebali, the Jews did side with the French in North Africa but the Berbers did not.[39]

Nor is colonialism necessarily forever. In the fullness of time, as Dunbar Moodie describes in Chapter 15, Black South Africans overturned White hegemony and attempted to build a multiracial democracy. And in Aotearoa/New Zealand, as Cluny Macpherson relates in Chapter 10, descendants of Europeans and of Maoris are remaking their postcolonial society as a bicultural nation, 150 years after the colonial imposition.

Nationalism

Questions such as how the state is made up, what constitutes citizenship, and what is the common civic glue animate several of our chapters in this volume and also a lot of extant literature that relates to ethnicity. This is especially true among political scientists, but one finds it among historians and sociologists as well. Whether ethnic groups are taken to be primordial entities or "invented traditions" and "imagined communities," they seem fundamental to modern notions of the state, at least in Europe.[40]

The idea of one people corresponding to one nation is a powerful one. But as we have seen, most nations are in fact polyglot places. Moreover, ethnic processes are not bound by national borders. Pashtuns, Kurds, and Uzbeks live on both sides of several borders in Western Asia, as do Mongols and Koreans in East Asia. And what is one to make of the fact that the primordial tie of ancestry does not seem to unite into one people Japanese whose families have never left the home islands and their cousins who have recently returned after four generations in Brazil, only to find that you cannot go home again and still be regarded as Japanese?[41] There are perhaps several transnational dynamics at work here. So, it is unclear to me that the nation-state is necessarily the appropriate frame for investigation of ethnic questions. And I am fairly certain that questions of construction of the polity are not the most important ones when dealing with racial and ethnic issues.

I am aware that some of my esteemed colleagues in this book would perhaps not agree with me on this last point. Nor would some distinguished American scholars, such as Nathan Glazer and Arthur Schlesinger, Jr. Schlesinger and Glazer are former liberals who have spent a good portion of their respective careers writing about White ethnic groups in the United States. While they have shown interest in the lives, institutions, and cultures of various peoples within the United States, both have always had, as their overarching concern, how to create a single, harmonious American polity. Their bottom-line concern is essentially a civic one. Thus, in the last fifteen years or so, they have been criticizing people who advocate a multi cultural view of the United States and insisting on a high degree of homogeneity (which I read as demanding conformity — dare one say "submission?" — to Anglo-American culture and identity).

One of the questions that Douglas Monroy raises in Chapter 1 is the degree to which membership in the civic community will be based on *demos* (the idea of universal citizenship) deriving in the modern world from the age of democratic revolutions, versus *ethnos*, (membership in a particular core cultural, ancestral, or racial group). *Ethnos* emphasizes a common language and *leitkultur*, and goes beyond these to metaphors of blood and the body. It speaks of the spirit and the essence of the people who are believed to be central to the nation's life. *Demos* places the people, the citizenry, at the center, and insists that all are equally members on the basis of their common accession to the social contract.

France is perhaps the quintessential nation to operate on the *demos* idea. The French have long been proud of their commitment to the idea that, whatever one's ancestry, if one becomes a French citizen then one becomes French. And for the French, citizenship laws operate on the principle of *jus soli*: if you are born on French soil, you are French. Yet, one need look no further than Chapter 8 of this book to be reminded that even the French have had some ethnic hesitations about how far to extend membership. One need only read a newspaper account of the recent antics of Le Pen and the National Party to be reminded that, even in France, there is a counter-discourse of blood and belonging.[42]

Like the French, the Americans have long prided themselves on their ideology of assimilation. The large lady who presides over New York Harbor invites, "Give me your tired, your poor/Your huddled masses yearning to breathe free/The wretched refuse of your teeming shore/Send these, the nameless, tempest-tost to me/I lift my lamp beside the golden door."[43] The idea is — if you will change your clothes, your food, your language, and perhaps your religion, you can become fully an American. Well, as long as you are White. Formally, the United States recognizes both *jus soli* and *jus sanguinis*, right of birth by ancestry. They say that anyone who is born there, or anyone who has American parents, is a citizen. But for much of U.S. history, Americans denied citizenship to a large class of people — those of African descent — despite the fact that they were born in the United States. Not just slaves, but free people of color as well, were denied the right to vote, to bear arms, to testify in court, throughout the antebellum South.[44] Native Americans, likewise, have only intermittently been regarded as U.S. citizens. Native American citizenship rights have usually been predicated upon accepting individual land ownership and abandoning Native American culture, habits, clothing, and so forth — essentially, upon performing Whiteness.[45] And for most of U.S. history, the American majority chose, on a racial basis, to refuse to naturalize certain people: Asian immigrants could not become citizens.[46] Perhaps, more important, people of color have never been accorded full membership in the body social, whatever their formal citizenship may have been.[47] So, the United States is a mixed bag with regard to the question of the basis of membership in the nation. Other nations do this differently. China is a classic empire, with a vast congeries of peoples — with different histories, languages, and physiognomies — all calling themselves Han, and another array of peoples treated as domestic dependents, not quite full citizens.[48] In Germany, as Elisabeth Schäfer-Wünsche shows in Chapter 9, *ethnos* reigns. Modern Germany was born amidst images of shared blood among people who spoke a variety of languages that are vaguely commonly denominated as "German." It became a nation accompanied by a soaring hymn to the German *volk* and dedicated to modern science, which at the time highlighted pseudoscientific racism. Few Germans today dispute the granting of citizenship to so-called Volga Germans — people whose ancestors migrated into the Russian empire some centuries ago and who have themselves applied for German membership since 1989.[49] Meanwhile, Turkish Germans and other children of immigrants, even though they were born in Germany, have enjoyed less than the full blessings of citizenship (the government has recently indicated some new willingness to naturalize foreigners).[50]

Some of our writers address specific nation-building projects and the national moment. Darshan Tatla writes of "the route from ethnic group towards a nation-in-the-making" for Sikhs in Chapter 14. That implies there is a necessary instability and fragmentation in states that are multiethnic. Clearly, there is not such a direct route for minority peoples in places like the United States, Australia, and France. Perhaps, the difference is that minority peoples do not have their population concentered on particular land bases, as do Sikhs in the Punjab. Or perhaps, some nations are better able to maintain themselves as multiethnic entities.

In Chapter 6, Taoufik Djebali shows how Arabs and Berbers in Morocco and Algeria used the imported French idea of the nation and their own sense of commonality as colonized Muslims to forge a national idea. Yet, with independence achieved and with both the colonizers and most of the favored Jews having left, the Berbers again perceived themselves as a minority ripe for oppression and so withdrew from the coalition.

Miyuki Yonezawa describes Japanese attempts at state building through narrative. In the case of the Ainu, the Japanese drew on ancient stories of the Emperor Jinmu journeying to the east to unite the Japanese people to justify conquering and attempting to incorporate the indigenes. In the Ryukyu Islands, they made up the idea of a historical ethnic connection between Yamato Japan and the Okinawans in order to justify a power grab that reeks of *realpolitik*. In both cases, and within the mainstream Japanese population in Honshu, the government created a mythic sense of ethnic national homogeneity as one of the grounds for the modern Japanese nation-state. And it worked. People believed it, and Japan became one of the world's great powers.

Terms and concepts

Words matter. In the chapters of this book, and more often in the documents, books, and interviews on which they are based, one finds several terms and concepts that are used in different contexts. Sometimes, they seem to be describing much the same sort of thing in each case; other times, they may mean some very different things.

Settler

One finds the term "settler" used to refer to British people who came to Aotearoa to displace the local Maori; for Dutch people who came to South Africa to displace the local Xhosa; for Europeans who came to North America to displace the Native Americans; and (in the news recently, not in this book) for Jewish Israelis who went to the West Bank to displace the local Palestinians. This term implies that there was no one there before the "settlers" came, or that the people who were there were heathen barbarians — that it was a wild land in need of settling by civilized people like the British, Dutch, Europeans, and Israelis.

Tribe

One finds the word "tribe" used in different settings for very different types of people and social organization. "Tribe" does imply a group of people organized by lineage, but it also implies that the people to whom it refers are more primitive in cultural attainments and less civilized than the people who are describing them. It may imply that they are natural parts of the landscape, like rocks and trees and antelopes and cougars, and thus reasonable objects for removal or extinction. In European history, the Goths and Visigoths are often referred to as "tribes" in contradistinction to the more "civilized" Romans. In early California, "tribe" meant a very small group of people, at the level of the village with perhaps only a few hundred people and a simple social organization that depended on personal leadership.

Compare that with a "tribe" in South Africa, which might have hundreds of thousands of members and a complex, hierarchically stratified social organization. Dunbar Moodie says that "In Africa 'tribalism' trumps all other explanations." In South Africa, "race" is widely understood to be an idea imposed by Europeans, but "tribe" is supposed to be local and primordial. Yet, Moodie and most other scholars who study the peoples of South Africa disagree with this assessment. For them, "tribalism" is a European import, too. Before Europeans arrived, the modes of social organization were homestead and lineage groupings. Europeans brought the idea of the ethnic group with them, but they called it "tribe" in Africa. Europeans perceived — indeed, reified — language groupings and divided the people according to them. They installed "chiefs" when they found no existing leaders at the level they deemed appropriate. Mangosuthu Buthelezi and the Inkatha Party turned this idea of "tribe" to their own purposes in claiming all the Zulu peoples for their own leadership. Moodie points out that White South Africans had their own "tribes": British and Afrikaners. He also demonstrates that supposedly primordial "tribal" identities have, in fact, been quite fluid in cities and mining districts. In short, Moodie sees the idea of "tribe" as an outside imposition, a tool of racist, colonialist oppression.[51]

It is arresting that the sizes and kinds of social organization that Moodie describes as being called "tribes" in South Africa, students of the Russian empire, such as Adrienne Edgar, call "nationalities" in Central Asia. This is in accordance with Soviet ideology, which refused to regard what the Russians were doing in Central Asia as having anything to do with colonialism. So there, the peoples they dominated in many of the same ways that British and Afrikaners dominated Black Africans, went by the term "nationality" instead. But it was more or less the same thing. In Turkmenistan, as in South Africa and Fiji, the colonial power more or less created tribe and nationality out of many lineages and local chiefdoms. Unlike the British, the Soviets rejected racialist explanations, yet their actions led to racialized distinctions. In Eritrea, according to Tekle Woldemikael, similar groups are marked off by the government as "ethnic groups," again on the basis of language divisions decided upon by the governing class (Chapter 16).

Mestizaje

Few words have quite so much current intellectual cachet as "mestizaje." At its historical base, the term derives from the nation-building project of José Vasconcellos and other Latin American intellectuals of the 1920s. A Mexican politician and scientifico-mystic, Vasconcellos extolled his country people (and indeed all Latin Americans) as *la raza cosmica* — a people specially gifted to lead the world on account of their mixture of European and Native American bloodlines. In more recent times, Gloria Anzaldúa brought the issue to the United States in one of the most-cited pieces of cultural criticism of the late twentieth century, *Borderlands/La Frontrera: The New Mestiza*. Anzaldúa challenged all kinds of binary category constructions, from race to nationality to gender to sexuality to language. In the place of neat categories, she exalted mixedness, multiplicity, paradox, simultaneity, contrariness, and betweenness. Gary Nash followed with "The Hidden History of Mestizo America", his presidential address to the Organization of American Historians.[52] In the late 1990s and beyond, "mestizaje" and a cognate term, "hybridity," have come to be used promiscuously in literary and cultural studies, to the point that their meaning has eroded in a flood of self-conscious fashion-following.[53]

We see the idea of mestizaje addressed in four contexts in this book. In nineteenth-century California, as in Mexico, the idea embraced the blending of Spanish and Indian, but erased the African and Asian elements in the people's racial heritage. As Douglas Monroy writes, "How racial mixture and a concern for racial purity could exist congruously in the same society" is an issue in Chapter 1. The knowledge among the conquerors that they shared bloodlines with the people they dominated and feared lent force and vigor to their assertion of racial superiority. In Chapter 2, Virginia Tilley takes the discussion to

El Salvador in the twentieth century. There, in her interpretation, a hegemonic state discourse of mestizaje hushed public debate about discrimination toward Afro-Latinos and Indians. Further, by defining ethnic politics as atavistic and even anti-nationalist, the mestizaje doctrine legitimized repressive state measures against ethnic and racial minorities. Few Brazilians used the term mestizaje, but the issue of racial multiplicity and how to deal with the in-between statuses of multiracial people are at the heart of the dynamics which Reginald Daniel describes in Chapter 4. Finally, in Eritrea in Chapter 16, Tekle Woldemikael finds not a unifying force in mixedness, but rather a "triple marginality" for mixed people.

The flip side of mestizaje, of course, is the myth of racial purity. All populations are mixed,[54] but for some groups in some places, the fiction of purity played a critical role as social glue. Such was the case in pre-World War II Japan (but not during the earlier imperial period) and among Boers in South Africa, as we learn from Yonezawa and Moodie.

Blackness

There is an abiding fixation on the idea that race is something limited to, or generated from, the relationships between Black and White, and something found mainly in the United States. The scholarly literature on race in the United States is vastly richer than the literature on race or its analogues anywhere else in the world, and by far the majority of that literature is about Black and White.[55] There may be other racial groups in the United States and the world, but, in the words of one of African America's most accomplished scholars, "The Black–White relationship [in the United States] is the master narrative of racial studies."[56]

There are peoples called "Black" in several parts of the world studied in this book. Their Blackness is related, but it is not always exactly the same thing. The Black Consciousness Movement of South Africa in the 1960s had a specific content and meaning. It was a reaction formation against the White nationalist movement that had wedded Afrikaners and English descendants in creating the myth of White racial purity, the edifice of *apartheid*, and the oppressive fiction of Black "tribal" separate development in the Bantustans. That movement had only a tenuous place for many Coloureds, that is, people of mixed race.

There was also a Black Consciousness Movement in Brazil in the 1980s. It included echoes of its South African predecessor, but operated in a very different context. In Brazil, the movement also sought to undermine White domination, but there that domination took place through the myth of a raceless society, not through walling people off in separate and supposedly pure social boxes. The social situation in Brazil in the 1980s, in fact, looks much more like the situation in Hawai'i in the 1990s and 2000s. Those farthest down seek to unite with those in the middle against the Whites at the top, except in the Brazilian case it is dark people and racially mixed people, while in Hawai'i it is Hawaiians and Asians. In Hawai'i, Blackness plays no part in a thoroughly racial social structure.

All three of these racial situations are very far removed from though not totally uninfluenced by Blackness in the United States. In the United States, Blackness was not a self-generated panethnic category created for self-defense, but rather an oppressive imposition — the one-drop rule — though in the 1960s and after, the Black Power Movement did take on the form of positive self-assertion. In the United States, Blackness had no place for anyone who lacked African ancestors. Contrast that to political Blackness in Britain in the 1980s, which was an attempt to make common cause among many peoples descended from New Commonwealth countries, from Pakistan and the Middle East as well as the West Indies. Political Blackness in Britain for a time hid those differences and let West Indies-descended people dominate the Black agenda.

There was a Black nationalist movement in Jamaica too, identified with the person and ideas of Marcus Garvey. That movement influenced later U.S. Black consciousness movements, which in turn contributed to Jamaican Black nationalism. Another root of the Jamaican movement, however, was the idea of Ethiopia and the person of Haile Selassie, which made their influence felt through Rastafarianism and Reggae. All these racial movements were at least slightly affected by the pan-African ideas of Garvey, W.E.B. Du Bois, Kwame Nkrumah, Sékou Touré, and others. That is even true in the Hawaiian case (if one counts the 1990s popularity of Jawaiian music, a strange blend of Reggae and slack-key guitar), and among Turkish-descended hip-hop youths in Germany.

One place where outsiders regard the people as Black operated even more distinctly than these four — Eritrea. There, people separate themselves from sub-Saharan Africans and see themselves more as part of the culture of the Middle East. Within the region, Eritreans and Ethiopians have deep and abiding senses of identity and difference from each other, without recourse to an ideology of Blackness.

Finally, this book reports on profoundly racial dynamics in many places where Blackness (far from being the master narrative) is a complete nonissue — Japan, Hawai'i, Morocco, Tunisia, Algeria, Aotearoa, Cambodia, Turkmenistan, and the Punjab. Blackness and African-descended people are hugely influential in modern racial issues, but they are far from the whole story, nor even the main story.

Narrative

Among Pacific people, where I have spent a good bit of my adult life, before one speaks in public, one must chant one's ancestry. The story begins back in the mists of time and accounts for all the main lines of one's genealogy. Only after I have told who my people are and what is the land that gave me birth, can I speak of the matter of the day, for only when I have done so can you know who I am and judge my words. Stephen Cornell and others write eloquently of the power of narrative in ethnic identity. "We are the people who ..." and, by implication, "you are not," are narratives that lie at the core of ethnic self-assertion and racial hierarchy making.[57]

Again and again in this book, the reader will be impressed by the powerful role that is played by racial and ethnic narratives in creating social hierarchy and social glue. In Eritrea, it is the tale of descent from King Solomon and the Queen of Sheba. Among Afrikaners, it is the Great Trek and divine triumph over the Zulus at the Battle of Blood River. In Japan, the story of the Emperor Jinmu was used as a tool in the forcible remaking of Okinawans and Ainu into ethnic Japanese as part of "the emperor's family-nation" since time immemorial. In Hawai'i, on the Hawaiian side, it is the story of the *mahele* and the overthrow of the Hawaiian monarchy by haole colonizers that gives vitality to Hawaiian ethnic self-assertion. On the White side, the aloha story of the multiracial Paradise of the Pacific attracts more Whites to come to the islands and quiets native resistance.

These are examples of narrative's influence at the level of the group — as the most powerful sort of ethnic glue that holds a group together. But at the individual level, race is narrative too. Race is the story of what we think we know about a person, a story we write on that person's features. For example, in California I may meet a person with light brown skin, brown eyes, black hair, and a slim build, and I may assume on the basis of what I read on his features that he is a Filipino. On interacting with him and learning his personal story, however, I may find out that he is Chicano, or Samoan, or Lebanese, or mixed Japanese and White. The same person might in another context be taken for Egyptian or Rom. Once in 1989, far out of my usual context, I was even taken for Japanese.

Conclusion

These, then, are some of the themes and issues, topics and terms that emerged as our research team compared the systems of racial and ethnic hierarchy that existed in seventeen places around the world. It seems clear that there are some common dynamics. Wherever there are multiple peoples in one social space, there develops a language of hierarchy that one may call "racial" or "ethnic." Such hierarchy seems tied to colonialism and impositions of power by some groups over others, as well as defensive oppositions pursued by the less powerful. Racial thinking and signifying, then, are means to naturalize those oppressions and resistances. The formation of nations is often influenced by racial concerns, but nation making and the meaning of citizenship are not the primary objects of race making. Concepts such as "mestizaje" and "Black" that derive from particular racial contexts may be used in other contexts, but they do not necessarily mean the exact same thing in those other contexts. In fact, there is a host of different sorts of racial and ethnic systems in various places around the world. Each has its own configurations of peoples and issues; each generates its own language and hierarchy. Different systems may be related to one another, or they may not. There is no master narrative of racial and ethnic relationships. But there are fascinating accounts of complex racial and ethnic systems that await the reader in the pages that follow.

Notes

1. I follow the Chinese Pinyin spelling here; some use the spelling "Uighur."
2. Percentages in this section are taken from *Ethnicity and Race by Countries*, http://www.infoplease.com/ipa//A0855617.html, January 7, 2002.
3. *Ethnicity and Race by Countries*, http://www.infoplease.com/ipa//A0855617.html, January 7, 2002.
4. Marisol de la Cadena, *Indigenous Mestizos: The Politics of Race and Culture in Cuzco, Peru, 1919–1991* (Durham, NC: Duke University Press, 2000).
5. *Ethnicity and Race by Countries*, http://www.infoplease.com/ipa//A0855617.html, January 7, 2002.
6. *Ethnicity and Race by Countries*, http://www.infoplease.com/ipa//A0855617.html, January 7, 2002.
7. Just a few examples are: Yasmin Alibhai-Brown, *Imagining New Britain* (New York: Routledge, 2001); Tomás Almaguer, *Racial Fault Lines: The Historical Origins of White Supremacy in California* (Berkeley: University of California Press, 1994); Susan Bayley, *Caste, Society and Politics in India from the Eighteenth Century to the Modern Age* (Cambridge, U.K.: Cambridge University Press, 1999); Daniel R. Brower and Edward J. Lazzerini, eds., *Russia's Orient: Imperial Borderlands and Peoples, 1700–1917* (Bloomington: Indiana University Press, 1997); de la Cadena, *Indigenous Mestizos*; Nicholas B. Dirks, *Castes of Mind: Colonialism and the Making of Modern India* (Princeton, NJ: Princeton University Press, 2001); Mark C. Elliott, *The Manchu Way: The Eight Banners and Ethnic Identity in Late Imperial China* (Stanford, CA: Stanford University Press, 2001); Neil Foley, *The White Scourge: Mexicans, Blacks, and Poor Whites in Texas Cotton Culture* (Berkeley: University of California Press, 1997); Paul Gilroy, *'There Ain't No Black in the Union Jack': The Cultural Politics of Race and Nation* (Chicago: University of Chicago Press, 1987); Dru C. Gladney, *Ethnic Identity in China* (Fort Worth: Harcourt Brace, 1998); Michael A. Gomez, *Exchanging Our Country Marks: The Transformation of African Identities in the Colonial and Antebellum South* (Chapel Hill: University of North Carolina Press, 1998); Grace Elizabeth Hale, *Making Whiteness: The Culture of Segregation in the South, 1890–1940* (New York: Pantheon, 1998); Stevan Harrell, *Ways of Being Ethnic in Southwest China* (Seattle: University of Washington Press, 2001); Michael Hechter, *Internal Colonialism: The Celtic Fringe in British National Development, 1536–1966* (Berkeley: University of California Press, 1975); David Horrocks and Eva Kolinsky, eds., *Turkish Culture in German Society Today* (Providence, RI: Berghahn Books, 1996); Jeffrey Lesser, *Negotiating National Identity: Immigrants, Minorities, and the Struggle for Ethnicity in Brazil* (Durham, NC: Duke University Press, 1999); John Lie, *Multi-Ethnic Japan* (Cambridge, MA: Harvard University Press, 2001); Daniel T. Linger, *No One Home: Brazilian Selves Remade in Japan* (Stanford, CA: Stanford University Press, 2001); Neil R. McMillen, *Dark Journey: Black Mississippians in the Age of Jim Crow* (Urbana: University of Illinois Press, 1989); Gérard Noiriel, *The French Melting Pot: Immigration, Citizenship, and National Identity*, trans. Geoffroy de Laforcade (Minneapolis: University of Minnesota Press, 1996); T. Dunbar Moodie, *The Rise of Afrikanerdom: Power, Apartheid, and the Afrikaner Civil Religion* (Berkeley: University of California Press, 1975); Paul Spoonley, David Pearson, and Cluny Macpherson, eds., *Nga Take: Ethnic Relations and Racism in Aotearoa/NewZealand* (Palmerston North: Dunmore Press, 1991); Ronald Takaki, *A Different Mirror: A History of Multicultural America* (Boston: Little, Brown, 1993); Michael Weiner, ed., *Japan's Minorities* (London: Routledge, 1997).
8. For example, Michael Banton, *Racial and Ethnic Competition* (Cambridge, U.K.: Cambridge University Press, 1983); Frank Dikötter, ed., *The Construction of Racial Identities in China and Japan* (Honolulu: University of Hawai'i Press, 1997); Anthony W. Marx, *Making Race and Nation: A Comparison of the United States, South Africa, and Brazil* (Cambridge, U.K.: Cambridge University Press, 1998); Stephen Small, *Racialized Barriers: The Black Experience in the United States and England in the 1980s* (London: Routledge, 1994).
9. Arnold Toynbee, *A Study of History*, 12 vols. (London: Oxford University Press, 1935–1961); Will and Ariel Durant, *The Story of Civilization*, 11 vols. (New York: Simon and Schuster, 1935+); William H. McNeill, *The Rise of the West* (Chicago: University of Chicago Press, 1963).
10. Oliver C. Cox, *The Foundations of Capitalism* (New York: Philosophical Library, 1959); Cox, *Capitalism As a System* (New York: Monthly Review Press, 1964); Immanuel Wallerstein, *The Modern World-System*, 3 vols. (New York: Academic Books, 1974–1988); Andre Gunder Frank and Barry K. Gills, *The World System: Five Hundred Years or Five Thousand?* (London:

Routledge, 1993); Janet L. Abu-Lughod, *Before European Hegemony: The World System* (New York: Oxford University Press, 1989); L.S. Stavrianos, *Global Rift: The Third World Comes of Age* (New York: Morrow, 1981).

11. Philip D. Curtin, *The Rise and Fall of the Plantation Complex* (New York: Cambridge University Press, 1990); John Thornton, *Africa and Africans in the Making of the Atlantic World, 1400–1800*, 2nd ed. (New York: Cambridge University Press, 1998); Jerry H. Bentley, *Old World Encounters* (New York: Oxford, 1993); Alfred W. Crosby, *The Columbian Exchange* (Westport, CT: Greenwood, 1972). *See also* Wang Gungwu, ed., *Global History and Migrations* (Boulder, CO: Westview, 1997).

12. *See*, for example: Etienne Balabar and Immanuel Wallerstein, *Race, Nation, Class: Ambiguous Identities* (London: Verso, 1991); Michael Banton, *Racial Theories* (Cambridge, U.K.: Cambridge University Press, 1987); A.L. Epstein, *Ethos and Identity* (London: Tavistock, 1978); Emmanuel Chukwudi Eze, ed., *Race and the Enlightenment* (Oxford: Blackwell, 1997); Monserrat Guibernau and John Rex, eds., *The Ethnicity Reader* (Cambridge, U.K.: Polity Press, 1997); Kenan Malik, *The Meaning of Race* (New York: New York University Press, 1996); Marx, *Race and Nation*; William H. McNeill, *Polyethnicity and National Unity in World History* (Toronto: University of Toronto Press, 1986); Albert Memmi, *Racism*, trans. Steve Martinot (Minneapolis: University of Minnesota Press, 2000); Robert Ezra Park, *Race and Culture* (New York: Free Press, 1950); John Rex and David Mason, eds., *Theories of Race and Ethnic Relations* (Cambridge, U.K.: Cambridge University Press, 1986); R.A. Schermerhorn, *Comparative Ethnic Relations* (Chicago: University of Chicago Press, 1970); Werner Sollors, ed., *Theories of Ethnicity* (New York: New York University Press, 1996); Paul Spickard and W. Jeffrey Burroughs, eds., *We Are a People: Narrative and Multiplicity in Constructing Ethnic Identity* (Philadelphia: Temple University Press, 2000); J. Milton Yinger, *Ethnicity* (Albany, NY: SUNY Press, 1994).

    A subgenre of nonetheless useful books that do not address such cross-cultural possibilities is the literature on the biology of race. *See*, for example, Stephen Jay Gould, *The Mismeasure of Man*, rev. ed. (New York: Norton, 1996); Joseph L. Graves, Jr., *The Emperor's New Clothes: Biological Theories of Race at the Millennium* (New Brunswick, NJ: Rutgers University Press, 2001); James C. King, *The Biology of Race*, 2nd ed. (Berkeley: University of California Press, 1981); Jonathan Marks, *Human Biodiversity: Genes, Race, and History* (New York: Aldyne de Gruyter, 1995); Ashley Montagu, *Man's Most Dangerous Myth: The Fallacy of Race* (New York: World, 1964).

13. *See*, for example: Glenn C. Altschuler, *Race, Ethnicity, and Class in American Social Thought, 1865–1919* (Arlington Heights, IL: Harlan Davidson, 1982); Lee D. Baker, *From Savage to Negro: Anthropology and the Construction of Race, 1896–1954* (Berkeley: University of California Press, 1998); Robert Blauner, *Racial Oppression in America* (New York: Harper and Row, 1972); Kimberlé Crenshaw, Neil Gotanda, Gary Peller, and Kendall Thomas, eds., *Critical Race Theory* (New York: New Press, 1995); Richard Delgado, ed., *Critical Race Theory* (Philadelphia: Temple University Press, 1995); Gilroy, *"Ain't No Black"*; Matthew Pratt Guterl, *The Color of Race in America, 1900–1940* (Cambridge, MA: Harvard University Press, 2001); Milton M. Gordon, *Assimilation in American Life* (New York: Oxford, 1964); Nathan Glazer, *Ethnic Dilemmas* (Cambridge, MA: Harvard University Press, 1983); Henry Louis Gates, Jr., ed., *"Race," Writing, and Difference* (Chicago: University of Chicago Press, 1986); Reginald Horsman, *Race and Manifest Destiny: The Origins of American Racial Anglo-Saxonism* (Cambridge, MA: Harvard University Press, 1981); Michael Omi and Howard Winant, *Racial Formation in the United States*, 2nd ed. (New York: Routledge, 1994); Audrey Smedley, *Race in North America*, 2nd ed. (Boulder, CO: Westview, 1999); Werner Sollors, *Beyond Ethnicity: Consent and Descent in American Culture* (New York: Oxford, 1986); Stephen Steinberg, *The Ethnic Myth: Race, Ethnicity, and Class in America* (Boston: Beacon, 1981).

14. *See*, for example: Floya Anthias and Nira Yuval-Davis, *Racialized Boundaries: Race, Nation, Gender, Colour and Class and the Anti-Racist Struggle* (London: Routledge, 1992); Frank Dikötter, *The Discourse of Race in Modern China* (Stanford, CA: Stanford University Press, 1992); Paul Gilroy, *The Black Atlantic* (London: Verso, 1993); Robert Miles, *Racism After "Race Relations"* (London: Routledge, 1992).

15. George M. Fredrickson, *White Supremacy: A Comparative Study in American and South African History* (New York: Oxford, 1981); Banton, *Racial and Ethnic Competition*; Marx, *Making Race and Nation*; St. Clair Drake, *Black Folk Here and There: An Essay in History and Anthropology*, 2 vols. (Los Angeles: UCLA Center for African American Studies, 1987 and 1990).

16. Norman E. Whitten, Jr. and Arlene Torres, eds., *Blackness in Latin America and the Caribbean*, 2 vols. (Bloomington: Indiana University Press, 1998); Isidore Okpewho, Carole Boyce Davies, and Ali A. Mazrui, eds., *The African Diaspora: African Origins and New World*

Identities (Bloomington: Indiana University Press, 1999); Darlene Clark Hine and Jacqueline McLeod, eds., *Crossing Boundaries: Comparative History of Black People in Diaspora* (Bloomington: Indiana University Press, 1999).

17. Philip Mason, *Patterns of Dominance* (London: Oxford University Press, 1971).

18. Examples of this genre include Michael Banton, *Race Relations* (New York: Basic Books, 1967); Fredrik Barth, ed., *Ethnic Groups and Boundaries* (Boston: Little, Brown, 1969); H.M. Blalock, Jr., *Toward a Theory of Minority-Group Relations* (New York: Wiley, 1967); Abner Cohen, ed., *Urban Ethnicity* (London: Tavistock, 1974); Oliver C. Cox, *Caste, Class and Race* (New York: Modern Reader, 1970; orig. 1948); Roger Daniels and Harry H.L. Kitano, *American Racism* (Englewood Cliffs, NJ: Prentice Hall, 1970); Arnold Dashevsky, ed., *Ethnic Identity in Society* (Chicago: Rand McNally, 1976); Harry H.L. Kitano, *Race Relations*, 4th ed. (Englewood Cliffs, NJ: Prentice Hall, 1991); Martin N. Marger, *Race and Ethnic Relations* (Belmont, CA: Wadsworth, 1985); Robert Ezra Park, *Race and Culture* (New York: Free Press, 1950); R.A. Schermerhorn, *Comparative Ethnic Relations* (Chicago: University of Chicago Press, 1970); George Eaton Simpson and J. Milton Yinger, *Racial and Cultural Minorities*, 4th ed. (New York: Harper and Row, 1972).

19. Anthony Marx takes a sharp focus on that narrower question in *Making Race and Nation*.

20. Ernest Gellner, *Nations and Nationalism* (Ithaca, NY: Cornell University Press, 1983). *See also* E.J. Hobsbawn, *Nations and Nationalism since 1780* (Cambridge, U.K.: Cambridge University Press, 1990).

21. Anthony D. Smith, *The Ethnic Origins of Nations* (Oxford: Blackwell, 1986), back cover. *See also* Smith, *Nationalism and Modernism* (London: Routledge, 1998).

22. *See* Paul Spickard and W. Jeffrey Burroughs, "We Are a People," in *We Are a People*, 1–19.

23. Johann Friedrich Blumenbach, *The Anthropological Treatises of Johann Friedrich Blumenbach* (Boston: Milford House, 1973; orig. 1865); Joseph Arthur, comte de Gobineau, *The Inequality of Races* (New York: H. Fertig, 1915; orig. 1856); J. Philippe Rushton, *Race, Evolution, and Behavior*, 3rd ed. (Charles Darwin Research Institute, 2000); Richard J. Herrnstein and Charles Murray, *The Bell Curve: Intelligence and Class Structure in American Life* (New York: Free Press, 1994); John Entine, *Taboo: Why Black Athletes Dominate Sports and Why We're Afraid to Talk About It* (New York: Public Affairs, 2000); Emmanuel Chukwudi Eze, ed., *Race and the Enlightenment* (Oxford: Blackwell, 1997). Scholars such as Dinesh D'Souza and Thomas Sowell essentialize "culture" and use it to the same ends as the pseudoscientists use "race"; *see* D'Souza, *The End of Racism: Principles for a Multiracial Society* (New York: Free Press, 1995); Sowell, *Ethnic America* (New York: Basic Books, 1981).

   For correctives, *see* Jonathan Marks, *Human Biodiversity: Genes, Race, and History* (New York: Aldine de Gruyter, 1995); William H. Tucker, *The Science and Politics of Racial Research* (Urbana: University of Illinois Press, 1994); Steven Fraser, ed., *The Bell Curve Wars: Race, Intelligence, and the Future of America* (New York: Basic Books, 1995); Stephen Jay Gould, *The Mismeasure of Man* (New York: Norton, 1996); Patrick B. Miller, "The Anatomy of Scientific Racism: Racialist Responses to Black Athletic Achievement," in *We Are a People*, eds. Spickard and Burroughs, 124–141; Joseph L. Graves, Jr., *The Emperor's New Clothes: Biological Theories of Race at the Millennium* (New Brunswick, NJ: Rutgers University Press, 2001); Matt Ridley, *Nature via Nuture: Genes, Experience, and What Makes us Human* (New York: Harper Collins, 2003).

24. *See*, for example, the correctives noted in the previous footnote, as well as Paul Spickard, "The Illogic of American Racial Categories," in *Racially Mixed People in America*, ed. Maria P.P. Root (Newbury Park, CA: Sage, 1992), 12–23; Spickard and Burroughs, *We Are a People*; Miri Song, *Choosing Ethnic Identity* (Cambridge, U.K.: Polity Press, 2003); Michael Omi and Howard Winant, *Racial Formation in the United States*, rev. ed. (New York: Routledge, 1994); Stephen Cornell and Douglas Hartmann, *Ethnicity and Race* (Thousand Oaks, CA: Pine Forge Press, 1998).

25. Reginald Horsman, *Race and Manifest Destiny: The Origins of American Racial Anglo-Saxonism* (Cambridge, MA: Harvard University Press, 1981); Matthew Frye Jacobson, *Special Sorrows: The Diasporic Imaginations of Irish, Polish, and Jewish Immigrants in the United States*, rev. ed. (Berkeley: University of California Press, 2002), 177–216; Catherine Hall, ed., *Cultures of Empire: Colonizers in Britain and the Empire in the Nineteenth and Twentieth Centuries* (New York: Routledge, 2000); Robert J.C. Young, *Colonial Desire: Hybridity in Theory, Culture and Race* (London: Routledge, 1995).

26. Spickard and Burroughs, "We Are a People," 2–7.

27. Of course, there are meaningful differences between peoples within each of the U.S. races. Korean Americans and Vietnamese Americans are quite different from one another, much more so than are, say, Irish Americans and Italian Americans. For a critique of the intellectual

and political movement that would elevate differences among White people of different ethnic derivations to something like the level of racial differences, *see* Paul Spickard, "What's Critical About White Studies," in *Racial Thinking in the United States: Uncompleted Independence*, eds. Spickard and G. Reginald Daniel (Notre Dame, IN: University of Notre Dame Press, 2004).

28. Small, *Racialised Barriers*; Anthias and Yuval-Davis, *Racialized Boundaries*; Paul Spickard, "Mapping Race: Multiracial People and Racial Category Construction in the United States and Britain," *Immigrants and Minorities*, 15 (July 1996), 107–119.

29. On the former, *see* Paul Spickard and Rowena Fong, "Ethnic Relations in the People's Republic of China," *Journal of Northeast Asian Studies* (Fall 1994).

30. Virginia Tilley points out in Chapter 2 that in Latin America, masking what are manifestly racial distinctions behind an alternative language is also a power move.

31. F. James Davis, *Who Is Black? One Nation's Definition* (University Park: Pennsylvania State University Press, 1991); G. Reginald Daniel, "Passers and Pluralists: Subverting the Racial Divide," in *Racially Mixed People in America*, ed. Root, 91–107.

32. Circe Sturm, *Blood Politics: Race, Culture, and Identity in the Cherokee Nation of Oklahoma* (Berkeley: University of California Press, 2002); James F. Brooks, ed., *Confounding the Color Line: The Indian-Black Experience in North America* (Lincoln: University of Nebraska Press, 2002); Teresa Williams-León and Cynthia Nakashima, eds., *The Sum of Our Parts: Mixed Heritage Asian Americans* (Philadelphia: Temple University Press, 2001); Paul Spickard, "What Must I Be? Asian Americans and the Question of Multiethnic Identity," *Amerasia Journal*, 23.1 (Spring 1997), 43–60.

33. Michael C. Howard, *Fiji: Race and Politics in an Island State* (Vancouver: UBC Press, 1991); Brij V. Lal, *Broken Waves: A History of the Fiji Islands in the Twentieth Century* (Honolulu: University of Hawai'i Press, 1992); Stewart Firth and Daryl Tarte, eds., *20th Century Fiji* (Suva: USP Solutions, 2001); Deryck Scarr, *Fiji: A Short History* (Sydney: George Allen and Unwin, 1984); Victor Lal, *Fiji: Coups in Paradise: Race, Politics and Military Intervention* (London: Zed, 1990); Brij V. Lal, *Power and Prejudice: The Making of the Fiji Crisis* (Wellington: New Zealand Institute of International Affairs, Victoria University, 1988); Deryck Scarr, *Fiji: Politics of Illusion: The Military Coups in Fiji* (Kensington: New South Wales University Press, 1988); Jeremaia Waqanisau, "The Only Option: Fijian Coup Détat: A Product of Political Development" (MA thesis, Department of Politics, Cartmel College, University of Lancaster, UK, 1989); Robert T. Robertson and Akosita Tamanisau, *Fiji: Shattered Coups* (Leichhardt, NSW: Pluto Press, 1988); Robert T. Robertson, *Multiculturalism and Reconciliation in an Indulgent Republic: Fiji After the Coups, 1987–1998* (Suva: Fiji Institute of Applied Studies, 1998).

34. Here I disagree with my esteemed colleague Lori Pierce, who argues in Chapter 3 that race is "a specific Western derived or influenced model of social development." I see few traces of Western derivation in the power relations between Han Chinese and the peoples they conquered and racialized. Douglas Monroy may be correct in Chapter 1, where he argues: "racial thinking is gratifying because it is explanatory and thus comforting. But each of the situations it explains is local, contingent, and time-specific."

35. Spickard and Fong, "Ethnic Relations in the People's Republic of China".

36. For insights into this process, *see* Albert Memmi, *The Colonizer and the Colonized* (Boston: Beacon Press, 1967; orig. 1956).

37. For the parallel developments in U.S. Indian policy, *see* Francis Paul Prucha, *The Great Father: The United States Government and the American Indians*, abridged ed. (Lincoln: University of Nebraska Press, 1986); S. Lyman Tyler, *A History of Indian Policy* (Washington: U.S. Department of the Interior, Bureau of Indian Affairs, 1973).

38. Fredrickson, *White Supremacy*.

39. Edna Bonacich, "A Theory of Middleman Minorities," *American Sociological Review*, 38 (1970), 583–594; Jonathan H. Turner and Edna Bonacich, "Toward a Composite Theory of Middleman Minorities," *Ethnicity*, 7 (1980), 144–158; Walter P. Zenner, "Middleman Minority Theories: A Critical Review," in *Sourcebook on the New Immigration*, ed. Roy Simon Bryce-Laporte (New Brunswick, NJ: Transaction, 1980), 413–425; Maurice Freedman, "The Chinese in Southeast Asia," in *Race Relations in World Perspective*, ed. Andrew W. Lind (Honolulu: University of Hawai'i Press, 1955), 388–411; Candace Fujikane and Jonathan Y. Okamura, eds., *Whose Vision? Asian Settler Colonialism in Hawai'i*, special issue of *Amerasia Journal*, 26.2 (2000).

40. The intersection between ethnic questions and national ones can be read about in Eric Hobsbawm and Terence Ranger, eds., *The Invention of Tradition* (Cambridge U.K.: Cambridge University Press, 1983); Benedict Anderson, *Imagined Communities: Reflections on the Origin and Spread of Nationalism*, rev. ed. (London: Verso, 1991); Gellner, *Nations and Nationalism*; Anthony D. Smith, *The Ethnic Origins of Nations* (Oxford: Blackwell, 1986);

Smith, *Nationalism and Modernism*; Geoff Eley and Ronald Grigor Suny, eds., *Becoming National* (New York: Oxford, 1996); E.J. Hobsbawm, *Nations and Nationalism since 1780*, 2nd ed. (Cambridge U.K.: Cambridge University Press, 1990); John A. Armstrong, *Nations Before Nationalism* (Chapel Hill: University of North Carolina Press, 1982).

41. Linger, *No One Home: Brazilian Selves Remade in Japan*.

42. *See*, for example, *Profile: Jean-Marie Le Pen*, BBC News, April 22, 2002 (http://news.bbc.co.uk/1/hi/world/europe/1943193.stm). The phrase is Michael Ignatiev's; *see* his *Blood and Belonging: Journeys into the New Nationalism* (Toronto: Penguin, 1993).

43. Alan M. Kraut, *The Huddled Masses: The Immigrant in American Society, 1880–1921*, 2nd ed. (Wheeling, IL: Harlan Davidson, 2001), 2.

44. James H. Kettner, *The Development of American Citizenship, 1608–1870* (Chapel Hill: University of North Carolina Press, 1978); Ira Berlin, *Slaves Without Masters: The Free Negro in the Antebellum South* (New York: Random House, 1974); Eugene D. Genovese, *Roll, Jordan, Roll: The World the Slaves Made* (New York: Random House, 1974), 398–413; James Oliver Horton, *Free People of Color Inside the African American Community* (Washington: Smithsonian, 1993); Winthrop D. Jordan, *White Over Black: American Attitudes Toward the Negro, 1550–1812* (Chapel Hill: University of North Carolina Press, 1968), 122–128 and *passim.*; John H. Russell, *The Free Negro in Virginia, 1619–1865* (New York: Dover, 1969; orig. 1913); Arthur Zilversmit, *The First Emancipation: The Abolition of Slavery in the North* (Chicago: University of Chicago Press, 1967).

45. Robert Berkhofer, Jr., *The White Man's Indian* (New York: Knopf, 1978); Vine Deloria, Jr. and Clifford Lytle, *The Nations Within: The Past and Future of Indian Sovereignty* (New York: Pantheon, 1984).

46. Sucheng Chan, *Asian Americans: An Interpretive History* (Boston: Twayne, 1991); Lisa Lowe, *Immigrant Acts: On Asian American Cultural Politics* (Durham, NC: Duke University Press, 1996); Erika Lee, *At America's Gates: Chinese Immigration during the Exclusion Era, 1882–1943* (Chapel Hill: University of North Carolina Press, 2003).

47. For the enduring hierarchy of ethnic and racial groups in American social life, see Paul Spickard, "Who Is an American? Teaching about Racial and Ethnic Hierarchy," *Immigration and Ethnic History Newsletter*, 31.1 (May 1999).

48. Spickard and Fong, "Ethnic Relations in the People's Republic"; June Teufel Dreyer, *China's Forty Millions: Minority Nationalities and National Integration* (Cambridge, MA: Harvard University Press, 1976); Gladney, *Ethnic Identity in China*; Jonathan N. Lipman, *Familiar Strangers: A History of Muslims in Northwest China* (Seattle: University of Washington Press, 1997); Mette Halskov Hansen, *Lessons in Being Chinese: Minority Education and Ethnic Identity in Southwest China* (Seattle: University of Washington Press, 1999).

49. Noted historian Abraham Friesen contends that many of these people were not originally Germans at all, but Dutch and possibly Danes; private communication with the author based on a manuscript in progress. Recent news accounts report that Germany "grants all Jews from the former Soviet Union citizenship and automatic government benefits." Some Jewish organizations have questioned the Jewish *bona fides* of the immigrants, but "never again, officials said, would Germans sort out who is a Jew"; *Newsweek* (July 14, 2003), 34.

50. Horrocks and Kolinsky, *Turkish Culture in Germany Today*; Paul Mecheril and Thomas Teo, *Andere Deutsche* (Berlin: Dietz Verlag, 1994).

51. Nicholas Dirks sees caste in India in a related way, not as exactly created by the British but as codified in the Indian–British encounter; *see* Dirks, *Castes of Mind*.

52. José Vasconcellos, *The Cosmic Race/La raza cosmica*, trans. Didier T. Jaén (Baltimore: John Hopkins University Press, 1997; orig. Spanish, 1925); Gloria Anzaldúa, *Borderlands/La Frontrera: The New Mestiza* (San Francisco: Aunt Lute, 1987); Gary B. Nash, "The Hidden History of Mestizo America," *Journal of American History*, 82.3 (1995), 941–964.

53. Examples of the trend include: Juan E. DeCastro, *Mestizo Nations* (Tucson: University of Arizona Press, 2002); Ernst Rudin, "New Mestizos: Traces of a Quincentenary Miracle in Old World Spanish and New World English Texts" in *Cultural Difference and the Literary Text*, eds. Winfried Siemerling and Katrin Schwenk (University of Iowa Press, 1996), 112–129; Amy K. Kaminsky, "Essay, Gender, and *Mestizaje*: Victoria Ocampo and Gabriela Mistral," in *Politics of the Essay*, eds. Ruth Ellen B. Joeres and Elizabeth Mittman (Bloomington: University of Indiana Press, 1993), 113–130; Nelson H. Vieira, "Hybridity vs. Pluralism: Culture, Race, and Aesthetics in Jorge Amado," in *Jorge Amado: New Critical Essays*, eds. Keith H. Brower, Earl E. Fitz, and Enrique E. Martinique-Vidal (New York: Routledge, 2001), 231–251; Julie Brown, "Bartok, the Gypsies, and Hybridity in Music," in *Western Music and Its Others*, eds. Georgina Born and David Hesmondhalgh (Berkeley: University of California Press, 2000), 119–142;

Martha Cutter, "The Politics of Hybridity in Frances Harper's Iola Leroy," in *Unruly Tongue: Identity and Voice in American Women's Writing, 1850–1930* (Oxford: University Press of Mississippi, 1999), 141–160; Pnina Werbner and Tariq Modood, eds., *Debating Cultural Hybridity* (London: Zed, 1997); Avtar Brah and Annie E. Coombes, eds., *Hybridity and Its Discontents* (London: Routledge, 2000); Zipporah G. Glass, "The Language of Mestizaje in a Renewed Rhetoric of Black Theology," in *Racial Thinking in the United States*, eds. Spickard and Daniel. One wonders what might be the Finnish word for mestizaje, and what it might connote in that context. For a summary of the literature on multiraciality (a related flood of writing about mixedness and betweenness), *see* Paul Spickard, "Does Multiraciality Lighten? Me-Too Ethnicity and the Whiteness Trap," in *New Faces in a Changing America: Multiracial Identity in the 21st Century*, eds. Loretta I. Winters and Herman L. DeBose (Thousand Oaks, CA: Sage, 2003), 289–300.

54. Marks, *Human Biodiversity*.

55. I am well aware that there is a growing literature on other racial and ethnic groups in the United States. I have taught for many years in an Asian American studies department, and as I type these words I am looking at a wall full of books on Asian Americans; nearby are many shelves filled with books on Native Americans, Latinos, and multiracial people. Still, most scholars of race treat the encounter between Black and White in the United States as if it were the master narrative of race. It is not so.

56. Personal communication with the author.

57. Stephen Cornell, "That's the Story of Our Life," in *We Are a People*, eds. Spickard and Burroughs, 41–53; Liisa Malkki, "Context and Consciousness: Local Conditions for the Production of Historical and National Thought among Hutu Refugees in Tanzania," in *Nationalist Ideologies and the Production of National Cultures*, ed. Richard G. Fox (Washington: American Anthropological Association, 1990); Patricia Ewick and Susan S. Silbey, "Subversive Stories and Hegemonic Tales: Toward a Sociology of Narrative," *Law and Society Review*, 29 (1995), 197–226; Phillip H. McArthur, "Narrating to the Center of Power in the Marshall Islands," in *We Are a People*, eds. Spickard and Burroughs, 85–97.

Part 1

Founding and Sustaining Myths

1

Guilty Pleasures
The Satisfactions of Racial Thinking in Early-Nineteenth-Century California

DOUGLAS MONROY

Up and down the coast of California, there are monuments to the Indians, the Spanish, and those Mexicans who called themselves Californios. Few of those people remain in or around those monuments — the missions, the presidios, houses of elite rancheros, and an occasional Indian site — all imaginatively restored for the tourists and school children. These peoples appear on the landscape frozen in time, remnants of a distant past, though indeed more than a million Mexican and Mexican Americans — migrants of the twentieth century — live around California. The monuments have narratives that explain the different peoples' histories but mostly they deny, distort, or even disappear their experiences. But there are real stories haunting those places, ones that have so much to do with race and nation, identity and power.

It is a much more fascinating story than even the fanciful re-creations. People who looked distinct from one another, who organized production differently, and who asserted or defended singular customary ways to various degrees, all encountered one another on a fabled landscape. In ways we can think of California as a "frontier," first New Spain's far northern, then the United States' far western. And, in many ways, the frontier paradigm is useful: when two peoples each with deeply developed spiritual and cultural principles that give them their sense of being human, converge on a frontier, there is often barbarism. This was true in California in the eighteenth and nineteenth centuries, first for the calamitous encounter of the Catholic Spaniards and the tribal Indians, then for the violent confrontation of crusading Yankee Protestants with Mexican Californios and the remnant, but by then chaotic, native peoples. Those dramatic moments of Spanish soldiers capturing Indians who fled the missions and then lassoing Indian women to satisfy their lust, or of American men either lynching Mexicans who challenged Anglo supremacy or firing into helpless villages of Indians, stunningly reveal the horrible consequences of one people constructing other people in racial ways. It is these episodes, ones that condense and display people's racial thinking in frightful and dramatic moments, which have usually attracted, with good reason, those of us interested in what usually is called frontier California.

It may well be, though, that California throughout its postcontact history can be understood not only as a frontier but as a place where different people met and then shared the landscape together. In this context, the development of racial thinking becomes associated not only with expropriation of lands and exploitation of labor but with explanation. That is, it is a way people accommodate, however hierarchically, to the presence of strangers on the landscape, and the spectacles of their religious practices, dress, labor, and (in this case) social and cultural decay, on a day-to-day basis. Nineteenth-century California is particularly compelling in this context because so many different people have lived together in the cities, towns, and countryside for so long, and because there has been some fluidity for individuals and groups in the matter of their rank. And it is a place where people very different in appearance and belief systems have encountered one another, a process that continues profoundly to this day.

Indian peoples lived upon the landscape of what would become California in small tribes or even bands. While anthropologists may group people according to language families and culture areas, life revolved around the small villages and the spirits unique to each, and around their hunting and gathering by which they had achieved self-sufficiency and a delicate balance with nature. While there were some commonalities between the various peoples, they had few secure and faithful bonds between them; they lived in decentralized villages, which squabbled, exchanged, and fought with one another; indeed retributive warfare, but not conquest or empire as in ancient Mexico, prevailed.

The Spanish could not have been more different: they, too, were several peoples — Castilians, Catalonians, Mallorcans, even Basques — but they were united under one Royal Crown and by One True God. Having been conquered by Romans, Visigoths, and Moors, they themselves moved to conquer new worlds in 1492, the year in which not only did Columbus sail but the last of the Moors and Jews were expelled from the Iberian Peninsula. The cross and the sword would be the twin, but often antagonistic, means of conquest. With actually little to offer, the self-sufficient peoples of the Americas, the Spanish priests, and civil authorities could only extend the Word of God and the promise of unity under the Crown, or put another way, the destruction of the Indians' spirit world and village societies. The idea, though, was that the indigenous peoples would be Christianized and civilized such that they would become loyal subjects of his Catholic Majesty.

The Spanish not only conquered Indian peoples of the New World, but mixed with them. The blending of foods and of blood through concubinage and marriage brought forth in Mexico a profound racial and cultural *mestizaje*, or mixture, of the Spanish and Indian peoples. Oftentimes, it is hard for non-Latin Americans to understand how racial mixture and a concern for racial purity could exist congruously in the same society. Indeed, they could, as this essay will attempt to explain. While racial and caste tensions would inspire many troubles, the One True Faith would attempt to bind these diverse societies. Neither *demos* (the notion of the citizen) nor *ethnos* (the culture group) would bind this society because their ideas about membership in a community pre-dated the Age of Democratic Revolutions and because they were several ethnicities. It would be a corporate body politic, one patterned on the Church, a mystical body itself modeled on the body of Christ. The Church and the friars would lead this society much as if they were the head of the Holy Savior, and the rest — the Christianized Indians, mestizo settlers and soldiers, and civil authorities — would be integrated into the social hierarchy much like the feet and arms of the body of Christ.

Among these *mestizos* were many of the people who would call themselves *Californios*, a regional variety of the new Mexican nation that would win independence from Spain in 1821. Their lives revolved around their extended families, their faith, and simultaneously having some Indians work for them and then engaging in desperate warfare with others. California was part of this emerging Mexican nation that sought desperately to forge a national will out of a population divided by caste and regional allegiances, and which argued and fought over whether reason and democracy or faith and authority would guide it.

From the east would come the Americans to California, which was to them the golden prize of the Mexican American War (1846–1848). Their understandings of the peoples who differed from their own fair-skinned appearance had mostly to do with the fights with warrior Indians of their east coast and the Ohio and Mississippi River Valleys, not the missionized Indians of California or those who had avoided the missions and whom the Americans called "diggers," allegedly because they dug for roots. Or knowing these strange people would have to do with their experience with African slavery, which twisted into their minds all manner of ideas about non-White peoples and about the mostly repulsive, but sometimes attractive, practice of racial mixing. In contrast to the Spanish, the Americans (owing to their English Puritan history) only rarely contrived to convert indigenous peoples into dedicated citizens of the nation, but rather to rid the place of them so that White, republican families could assume their place on the landscape. The Spanish, the Californios, and the Americans all presumed that their activities fulfilled God's plan.

On the one hand, in nineteenth-century California, and most everywhere at most every time, racial thinking has been so easy to dissect and refute — and thus condemn — because of its logical contradictions, its lack of scientific evidence, or its gross misuse of science. But perhaps it is these very inconsistencies, its rejection of evidence and logical rigor, that provide so much of the guilty pleasure of racial thinking. Notions of race, now so facilely deconstructed in the postmodern academy, have compelling explanatory powers that enable people, like those of early California, to harmonize that which seems so incongruous to them, especially when encountered on a strange terrain.

My point here will be that racial thinking, a phrase I prefer over racism at this point in my analysis because I am first concerned with how people get certain ideas implanted in their consciousness, has been a way that people reconcile what they know to be right and true to the activities, beliefs, and conduct — in other words, the spectacle — of alien people they encounter either in their travels or when strange people come, voluntarily or under various forms of coercion, to their place. How, in other words, people experience one another at ground level. I will wrestle with the idea, scary in its implications, that what people look like, their dress or their phenotype, proved to be the most ready explanation for various nineteenth-century Californians' emotional and cognitive solutions to their disorienting and anxiety-producing encounters with people from different cultures and nations.

One cannot help but be struck with how the thinking of the Spanish priests changed as the native peoples they encountered did not cohere with their European Christian scheme of embracing the True Word of God. The Viceroy in Mexico City, Antonio María Bucareli, waxed optimistic in 1774 when he entertained "strong hopes of extending, among the many heathen tribes . . . , the dominion of the king and the knowledge of our true religion (which is the principal purpose of his Majesty . . .) by means of the missions." All boded well, for, as Father President Fermín Lasuén, successor to Padre Serra as Father President of the California missions, put it in 1771 "the country is most beautiful, the heathen very numerous and very docile, and by planting crops we may be able to replant our voices, with all assurance that with the favor of God the most abundant harvests for things both eternal and temporal may be reaped." The priests referred hardly at all to the Indians' phenotype, though, in the matter of appearance in the words of Father Zalvidea, that "they are much addicted to nudity," could hardly escape their gape.[1]

It should be apparent how, for these European men of the cloth, Indian people could become more fully human by two simple steps: they could adopt the True God and wear clothes. In the brilliantly revealing words of Cabeza de Vaca, garbed and screaming at naked Indians, "I am more human than you are. I have a God!" In California, Padre Lasuén put the matter more thoughtfully: "Here then we have the greatest problem of the missionary: how to transform a savage race such as these into a society that is human, Christian, civil, and industrious."[2] With that policy in mind about the qualifications for "being human," it is not difficult at all to imagine the incomprehension of the priests and the civil authorities about Indian intransigence about realizing their potential as human beings.

The priests, armed with faith, albeit lagging, in the equality of the souls of all of God's children, remained more sanguine about the missionizing project than the civil authorities for whom the natives seemed much like the detritus of an otherwise fruitful countryside. Yet, the more optimistic priests and the actually more pragmatic functionaries of the crown quickly came to similar understandings of the Indians' continuing with their familiar spirits and lack of dress. "The Indian by nature is apathetic and indolent," said Padre Narciso Durán, Father President of the missions from 1825 to 1827. "Their characteristics are stupidity and insensibility." Padre Venegas expatiated frankly: "want of knowledge and reflection; inconstancy, impetuosity and blindness of appetite; and excessive sloth and abhorrence of fatigue; an incessant love of pleasure, and amusement of every kind, however trifling or brutal; in fine, a most wretched want of everything which constitutes the real man, and renders him rational, inventive, tractable, and useful to himself and society." One of the grandees of southern Alta California, Don Juan Bandini, simply claimed that "The Indians are naturally dirty and lazy; their heritage is misery, ignorance, and stupidity, and their education is not calculated to develop their reason . . . and the *gálico más refino* [venereal disease] among them is very natural."[3] How else but to explain the obvious and abysmal failure of the missionizing effort but to say that there was something inherently wrong with the Indians? This was not a time when Catholic priests could know of the contingency of religious belief and practice, only of the mono Truth of the One True God and His transforming power. When the priests did not rely on the Devil as an explanation for Indian intransigence, then it was their "nature" that made comprehensible a notion that was otherwise as incomprehensible as the rejection of the Christian God.

There is another point to be made here: when these religious and governmental potentates expressed themselves, they did so in response to the actual condition of the native Indian peoples. Let us put aside for the moment the obvious and profound reality that the Indians' dreadful condition owed to the wreckage of their spirit world, the alienation of their lands, and especially the horrible, mysterious diseases that the Spanish brought. (It is utterly true that the syphilis and gonorrhea that the soldiers introduced proved the most terrible in terms of both physical and spiritual destruction of the Indians' bodies and souls.) Contact with the missions had succeeded not in Christianizing the Indians but in unraveling their societies and cultures, something about which most everyone commented with various degrees of incomprehension. Prefect Mariano Payeras noted in 1819 "that the majority of the Indians were dying exceedingly fast from dysentery and the *gálico*" and a year later that "they live well free but as soon as we reduce them to a Christian and community life they decline in health, they fatten, sicken and die. It particularly affects women." "They have at present *two* religions," observed a Scottish resident of San Gabriel, "one of custom and another of faith. . . . The life and death of our Savior is only, in their opinion, a distorted version of their own life." Said Father President Lasuén, "The majority of our neophytes have not acquired much love for our way of life; and they see and meet their pagan relatives in the forest, fat and robust and enjoying complete liberty. They will go with them, then, when they no longer have any fear and respect for the force, such as it is, which restrains them." What Padre Durán said about those who stuck around the Spanish outposts resonates throughout the historical record as an indictment of the Spanish soldiers and an description of Indian life: "It is said that prostitution, drunkenness and gambling with the Indians are continuous."[4]

In other words, the religious impulse of missionization, when it failed to create of the Indians *gente de razón*, Hispanicized Christians, that is, created instead the spectacle of a deracinated, disease-ridden, demoralized people. This display of cultural wreckage provided the spectacle upon which other people who traveled to, or stayed on in California would know the Indians and then base their understanding of Indian nature on. I wish to introduce now the idea of how contingent the formation of racial ideas can be: the mission Indians who the Spanish created out of the indigenous peoples, and then the Indians who resisted or fled the Spanish, were unique to California. They were not the great warriors of the plains like the Sioux or of New Mexico like the Apaches and Navajos, nor were they like the agricultural Pueblos of the Rio Grande Valley, nor were they as violent and intransigent in their rejection of the Spanish as the Yaquis, nor did they experience the calamitous fall from greatness and power to conquest and disease as did the Aztecs. Race, or at least what we call race these days, for the Californios, or those mestizo and creole peoples who settled Spanish and Mexican California from the interior of Mexico, took on a mix of meanings.

Let us return now to this issue of contingency and racial thinking and to the Californios. It must be said now that these Californios who encountered the Indians were not just any non-Indians, but ones who suffered the issue of the Indian without and the Indian within. In other words, like all mestizo peoples, the Californios were well aware of the fact that they were part Indian, or, if they weren't, how an unfortunate marriage could taint a family's blood. Recall, too, the particularities of the Indians with whom they lived: these were technologically rudimentary ones who had first been missionized, but who had since become fearsome.

And there can be no doubt that Indians who refused missionization, or who escaped it, increasingly terrorized California society in the early- and mid-nineteenth century. To give only one notable example for now — in February 1824, neophytes of the missions Santa Barbara, Santa Inez, and La Purísima revolted against the mission fathers and especially against the soldiers who putatively protected the missions. The soldiers, angry and incontinent given their imprudent neglect in the context of Spain's battling against Mexico's struggle for independence, responded against the rebels furiously and viciously; The Indians burned mission buildings, and, in the anguished words of Padre Ripoll, "separated the exchanged wives and returned them to their proper husbands," or, in other words and as confirmed by other observers, brazenly offended every precept of Christian morality regarding monogamy and chastity when "they exchanged their women for those of the gentiles without distinction as to married and unmarried women."[5]

It is not for us here to discuss matters of sexual virtue and vice or the consequences of involuntary sexual repression, but rather to emphasize the dread and trepidation with which the *gente de razón* would have seen such an episode. Think about how modern people armed with psychoanalytic theory or romantic notions about escaping the confines of bourgeois monogamy, or opponents of imperialism and monotheism, would think about such an episode, and then imagine exactly the opposite: that is how nineteenth-century Spanish Catholics would have thought about the event, this multi-faceted spectacle of rebellion against God and Christian morality. It's not only that they would have found the behavior of Indians abhorrent, which they did, it's that they were so concerned, as mestizo people — a mix of Spanish and Indian — that they were them. An interesting twist in our narrative of racial thinking, no doubt.

The cleaner the blood, the greater the distance from this sort of possible deportment. Thus, those without Indian blood, and indeed there were some few, strove to keep their families that way, and those *gente de razón* with Indian blood, quite apparent in even many of the leading families, sought to distance themselves from it in various ways. In 1777, on the day of her birth, the parents of María Antonia de Lugo promised her in marriage to Ygnacio Vicente Vallejo, and at the time of menarche, when she was fourteen, she married the ex-soldier who was forty years old. The reasoning behind such caution over marriage emerges when Vallejo, immediately after his marriage, petitioned for a decree of *legitimidad y limpieza de sangre*, or legitimacy of pure Spanish blood. The decree, granted after fifteen years, affirmed that the Vallejo name had been untainted by Jewish, African, Indian or any other non-Christian blood. The intense concern was not lost on the three daughters issued from this marriage, two of whom married Euro-Americans and the other a Frenchman. Similarly, the five legitimate daughters of the shamelessly womanizing and frequently besotted Governor Juan Bautista Alvarado all married Anglo Americans.[6] Procreation, in other words, was quite bound up with racial thinking; it was one way that racial ideology and ritual practice converged. Fearful of any association with putatively naked, licentious, and alcoholic Indians, Californio parents guided, or even determined, their children's marriage partners not only on account of property concerns but to guard closely "the blood."

Among other elite families, matters proved more difficult. That most prominent family of the south, the Picos, had running through their veins the blood of Africans and Indians, and quite apparently so. Another grandee of the south, Manuel Dominguez, in the American period could not testify in court because of his Indian phenotype, in spite of the fact that he was a signer of the new state constitution. In these cases, we are witnessing the other half of the Mexican raciological coin. In Monterey, for example, between 1773 and 1778, 37 percent of marriages were interracial — mostly soldiers and Christianized Indian women — something the Church encouraged. After that, the rate declined to about 15 percent.[7] What is so intriguing — in part because of its apparent contradictoriness — is that consciousness of "race purity," of being "pure

Spanish," existed side-by-side with the practice of officially sanctioned race mixing. The Spanish priests' famous disregard of Indian phenotype — usually attributed to the Iberian peninsula's history with the Moors — but huge disquiet over their nudity and idolatry, also figures in to this cognitive mix. (Another obvious contradiction must be pointed out here: Iberians, Celts, Romans, Visigoths, and Moors have all peopled the Iberian landscape making the notion of "pure Spanish" a curious one.)

Again, the historical record confronts us with the contingencies of racial thinking. Factors and tensions distinctive to specific historical moments, tensions, and peoples combine to create particular racial ideologies. These have provided satisfaction to peoples perplexed and conflicted not only about phenotype but about sexuality, nudity, and personal deportment, especially when their own behavior has shamelessly mirrored their objects of scorn. When there has been social and sexual race mixing as was the case in California, then these dispositions towards racial thinking are diversified and intensified.

The concept of *shame* is crucial here: part of what made the native people of California *indios* was the fact that they were *sin vergüenza*, or shameless, and part of what made the Californios *de razón* was that they did have *vergüenza*, shame. And, thus, it was that mestizo and creole Californios, apprehensive about the Indian within and the Indian without, came to re-make the Indian peoples in ways that were quite particular to this place, in ways that were quite soothing of their tensions, and in ways that would make reconciliation between the two peoples impossible — indeed create scenarios that would play out in fire and blood.

This matter of shame, moreover, expressed itself in the appearance and activities of all Californians' bodies. As with African slaves in the American South, so much of people's ideas about one another formed in their close proximity, in the spectacle of their bodies and quotidian activities. "In those times," Juana Machada could not help but remember forty years later, "female Indians did not clothe themselves except for a cover of rabbit skins that covered their shameful parts (*partes vergonzosas*)." Apparent in this statement are several matters: the difference in dress of the two people, obviously (Californios prided themselves and were renowned for their sartorial splendor); that how the body was displayed manifested so much about what was considered civilized; and what about God's creation was considered shameful in the minds of the Catholic Californios.[8] In this spectacle of deportment, what people *saw* was what informed them about who and what these other people were.

What everyone who visited or lived in California saw was that Indians did all the work. Padre Narciso Durán noted with disgust in 1831 that

> If there is anything to be done, the Indian has to do it; if he fails to do it, nothing will be done. Is anything to be planted: The Indian must do it. Is the wheat to be harvested? Let the Indian come. Are adobes or tiles to be made, a house to be erected, a corral to be built, wood to be hauled, water to be brought for the kitchen? Let the Indian do it.

"The Indians," concurred Richard Henry Dana in 1834, "do all the hard work, two or three being attached to the better house; and the poorest persons are able to keep one at least."[9]

But, this same spectacle displayed yet more about the Californios: "But what about the other class that calls itself 'gente de razón'?" Durán continued indignantly. "Nothing. With them it is walk about, play the gentleman, eat, be idle." Priests, travelers, and merchants repeated this description over and over. This display of Indian labor achieved not only production of goods and services but Californio graciousness and more Indian disgrace. José del Carmen Lugo verified the legendary hospitality of the Californios: "The traveler could go from one end of California to the other without it costing him anything in money, excepting gifts he might wish to make to the Indian servants at the missions or on the ranchos."[10] Again, what people saw as they traveled the nineteenth-century California landscape generated their knowledge of who Indians were. They were heathen, naked (or, when they adopted the White man's clothes, laughed at), disorganized, and living in a state of servitude.

Recent writing about the history of California in the years after Mexican independence has added an important emphasis on everyday life — the threat of violence. It's not that there hadn't been bloody resistance against Spanish religious imposition in the years previous, but by 1820 so much of the Indians' traditional lands had been subsumed by the missions, and then yet more of them by the granting of ranchos to ex-army officers, that Indian peoples — some of them ex-neophytes, many of them simply those who refused missionization — had come to understand the missions and the ranchos as fair game for their simple subsistence. Thus, Indians, once the "the heathen very numerous and very docile," had become powerfully threatening.

At first, and really before very many settlers had come to California in the decades when Spanish settlement centered around the mission, the Indians had become, by European standards, quite utterly disgraced. That is, their men had usually been defeated by the Spanish military when they resisted missionization, and their women had been violated. These "soldiers," in the famous description of Father President Serra in 1773, "clever as they are at lassoing cows and mules, would catch an Indian woman with their lassos to become prey for their unbridled lust. At times some Indian men would try to defend their wives, only to be shot down with bullets." There is the horror for Indian families revealed here — "even the boys who came to the mission were not safe from their baseness" — but also the Indians' infamy, their civil death, their lack of any legal or moral standing.[11]

"During part of 1823 the Indians from the missions in the middle of the mission chain plotted an uprising with unexpected discretion," chronicled Antonio María Osio. "The ultimate goal was to kill the *gente de razón*, those who did not belong to the Indian race." Exactly what the Indians' goal was — the restoration of their old cultural ways, rebellion against the outrages of the soldiers and mission discipline, the affirmation of sexual desire — will remain ambiguous.

What is clear though is that *indios*, whether neophytes, or still "in the wild," or most menacing, in league with each other, had effected a new place upon the physical and psychological landscape of California. No longer infamous, they had become notorious, that is their new presence resounded in the imaginations of the Californios, not as docile heathens but as fearsome barbarians.[12] Another point must be made here: the new Republic of Mexico could not mount sufficient military violence against first these Indians who threatened its domestic tranquility, and then later, against the Americans, who attacked them from without in 1846. There is more than mere *will* to nation building: violence, or at least its credible threat, must be able to subdue threats both internal and external.

The complexities of historical contingency are writ large here and so too are their consequences for racial thinking. Recall here what had happened with the native peoples of coastal Alta California: many became reduced to Christianity and dependent on the missions for their simple subsistence by disease and the concomitant dissolution of their spiritual world. Indians outside the missions simultaneously adapted their old foraging grounds — now the pastures of the Californios or of the missions and each full of horses and mules — and pillaged these animals. Some they ate and others they used to engage in modern ways of free trade with Hispanic New Mexicans and Anglo Americans — ever desirous of marketable goods, even ones which Indians had harvested from the ranchos and missions. This made them seem all the more brutish and ominous. Our postmodern perspective might be helpful here. The same people, the same historical context, the same acts can been seen in different ways: savages refused civilization and resorted to crime instead; native people resisted their expropriation through fighting back; the Indians inventively did what was necessary to adapt to the new conditions of hoofed beasts on their old lands and a market for them. Neither Indians, nor missionaries, nor Californios, nor arriviste Americanos would articulate the situation in any of these ways, but there can be little doubt but that Californios and Americanos, the divide of the events of 1846–1848 notwithstanding, were similarly in a state of confusion, bewilderment, and aggressive tizzy about the Indians.[13]

Again, we see the possibilities and satisfactions of racial thinking. The immense complexities of such a situation could be reduced to ideas about peoples' innate qualities. "The Indians are so utterly depraved," stated *síndico* Vicente Guerrero in 1840 "that no matter where they may settle down their conduct would be the same, since they look upon death even with indifference, provided they can indulge in their pleasures and vices." The Los Angeles *Star* in 1852 referred to "the most degraded race of aborigines upon the North American Continent," while Indian agent T. Butler King reported to the Secretary of State that "They use the bow and arrow, but are said to be too lazy and effeminate to make successful hunters," and "seemed the lowest grade of human beings." The Indians' spectacular and unsettling degradation — a very particular creation of missionization, European disease and alcohol, and military conquest — was explained with racial thinking.[14]

What I am arguing for here — the importance of seeing the ways in which the spectacle of people functioned much like ritual drama, that is the dynamic of the interaction between performer and viewer — produced racial thinking that was both peculiar to this region of the world and likely generally illustrative of the ways in which racist ideas have been generated. This is not to say that Indians, in their animist beliefs, relative nudity, and subsistence ways; Californios, in their Roman Catholicism, sartorial splendor, or their rituals of generosity and feigned leisure; or lower class *cholos* were culpable for the nasty ideas that would be generated about them, only that interlopers would see their display and react and create comforting ideas that would make these troubling behaviors explainable.

Indian men could hunt quite well — witness their ability to appropriate horses from the Californio and American ranches. It's just that it was called "stealing" by those others. That their presence should be undermined necessitated this reconfiguration of their manliness. Since it is men's actions that foreigners usually judge, their activities had to be construed in a particular way. Similarly, Indian women had to be contrived, but since it is usually their appearance that is most meaningful, how they looked figured most importantly in the Americans' eyes.[15]

The Indians, in their cultural and productive ways, displayed themselves in contradictory ways to the Euro-Americans. There were those few who remained around the missions and usually farmed and worshiped in the Faith. Others hung around the towns, largely in disarray. Then there were those who provided the labor force in California everywhere from Sutter's Fort to the ranches of the southern and central counties, to the agricultural fields, to households north and south, and who lived in close proximity to Californios and Americans. Then, too, there were those in the interior and San Diego who had never been missionized or otherwise integrated into the Spanish or Mexican systems, or who had resolutely rejected the ways of the intruders, and who proved to be fearsome raiders. Each group suffered disease and alcoholism, though to varying degrees.

What sense the Americans, who began arriving in significant numbers after 1840 and who conquered the place in 1846–1848, would make out of this contrasts remarkably with the Spanish. Yes, the priests imperiously and consistently referred to the "*conquista espiritual*"; they reviled the Indians' nudity and marshaled soldiers against the practice of their religious ceremonials. Then, when Father Zalvidea, that earnest fisher of men at Mission San Gabriel, journeyed to the village of Talihuilimit he told how he "baptized 3 old women, the 1st of 60 years, who had lost the use of one of her legs. To her I gave the name Maria Magdalena." You see, the Spanish had compassion for those they understood to be inferior: Zalvidea gave this decrepit woman a revered name, one indicative of his hope for her. As I have pointed out elsewhere, *passion*, in Spanish *pasión*, derives from the Latin *pati*, "to endure" or "to suffer," as Christ did on the cross. *Compassion* thus means "to endure with," which is often how the priests saw their task. They "endured with" the Indians in their lack of knowledge of the Word of God. But, the Indians would come to know God. They would come to be "civilized." Thus, the Indians were the future of, the key to "civilization," as the Spanish understood that now all-too-well deconstructed notion in California.[16]

To the Americans, the Indians, especially those still less affected by the Spanish and the Mexicans and still occupying lands in the interior, represented an impediment to civilization. This is because of the fact that they occupied lands that White American farmers, those most closely associated with the "march of civilization," should be free to occupy. Both thought the Indians groveling, heathen, dirty, and potentially lethal, but they construed their relationship to European civilization entirely differently. From Cuzco to Tenochtitlan to the Río Grande Valley to California, the Spanish — in the form of priests and single men — sought to change the peoples of the New World to *gente de razón*, "people of reason," hispanicized Indians who would be bound to the land and loyal to the Crown of Castile and the Holy Faith. And they had faith that this civilizing process, one that would hold these lands forever for the Crown, could succeed. From New England to the Great Plains to California, the English settlers — mostly in the form of families — sought not to populate the lands with transformed indigenous peoples, but to hold those lands for either the English crown or the American republic by sending their own people there, a strategy that necessarily entailed the ridding of those lands of Indians. In some cases, they were family farmers and in others they were slave holders, but certainly they knew that only White Europeans could bring civilization to the landscape of North America.

California Indians appeared to the Americans to be darker in color than those of the Plains. This put them closer to Blacks than to those who were occasionally categorized as noble savages, that is, the defeated warriors of the places the Americans had already conquered. Yet another source of racial thinking about the native peoples, thus, presents itself: White Americans' cognitive baggage about race predisposed them to apply many of the ideas about race already twisted into their minds to the aboriginals of the Golden State. James Rawls quotes the following two: "Their complexion is a dark mahogany, or often nearly black, their faces round or square, with features approximating nearer to the African than the Indian," said one traveler in 1850. Another, arriving at Monterey at the end of the Mexican American War, saw them as "the most hideous-looking creatures that it is possible to imagine. They are very dark, indeed I may almost say black, with a slight tinge of copper colour; the features are, in all other respects, as purely African in their cast." As we might expect, comments about "a fair supposition of a brain . . . [were] miserably small." That this observer referred so quickly to their *color* reveals much about the quickness with which people with white-tinged skin jumped to conclusions based upon their notions of more customary dark-skinned people, and that he was British.

It is remarkable indeed how many different people saw the same thing: the German Georg Von Langsdorff observed some decades earlier that

> These Indians [in the San Francisco Bay area] are of middling or rather short stature, and their color is of such a dark brown that it approaches black. This color is owing very much to their filthy mode of living, to the power of the sun's rays, to their custom of smearing their bodies with mud and ember dust, and their slovenly way of wearing their scanty covering.

Seemingly inevitably it followed that "we were all agreed that we had never before seen the human race on such a low level." Each, in other words, jumped to conclusions; each illustrates our points here about *seeing*. And each reiterates a previously made suggestion about racial consciousness: it is the continual ingression of the new implanted upon the received wisdom, foolishness, nastiness, intelligence, or, most often, simply bequeathed presuppositions of the old.[17]

The values of family and civilization (always associated with race), then, expressed themselves in what many Anglo settlers in California at mid-century called all too chillingly and frankly "extermination." While the Spanish frankly sought the extermination of the Indians' abhorrent culture and devilish hearts, their clothed and disciplined bodies and converted souls would become the basis for civilization in California. The Americans were different: "To place upon our most fertile soil the most degraded race of aborigines upon the North American Continent," railed the Los Angeles *Star* in 1852, "to invest them with the rights of sovereignty and to teach them that they are to be treated as powerful and independent nations, is planting the seeds of future disaster and ruin." In the north of California, near Humbolt, the leader of a local militia unit, William Kibbe, claimed in 1860 that his guards had killed over 200 Indians, and that "Some twenty-five families of this year's immigration have already taken up claims in these valleys. And this is the country which has been hitherto almost exclusively occupied by Indians."[18]

What, though, counted for civilized behavior constituted another dilemma for both Anglo and Hispanic Californians. Readers of this essay should already be taken aback at the putatively indiscriminate murder of Indian peoples living on their own lands. Even if we consider the raids and the counter-raids of Indians and militias over horses and mules something of a fair fight, Indian men's defense of their wives and daughters, on the other hand, against the attacks of drunken, single White men — the riff-raff of the Gold Rush mostly — can only be understood within the realm of "family values." The dispossession of Indian farms, often as not tended by Christianized natives, would seem utterly contradictory. Yet, these are the things that happened. Helen Hunt Jackson's monumental and unprecedented novel *Ramona* revolves around the actual dispossession of the lands of Christian, ex-mission Indians. During her research for the novel and her dramatic exposé, *Century of Dishonor*, an Indian agent told Jackson about a White man who filed a claim for some land which ex-mission Indians of San Luis Rey had been farming: "He owned, the agent says, that it was hard to wrest from these well-disposed and industrious creatures the homes they had built up; but, said he, 'if I had not done it somebody else would; for all agree that the Indian has no right to public lands.' " Albert Hurtado quotes a San Francisco *Bulletin* of 1856 telling how "some of the agents, and nearly all of the employees" in charge of some reservation Indians were "daily and nightly . . . kidnapping the younger portion of the females, for the vilest purposes" and that the "wives and daughters of the defenseless Diggers" were "prostituted before the very eyes of their husbands and fathers, by these civilized monsters, and they dare not resent the insult, or even complain of the hideous outrage."[19]

In each case here, there is positive acknowledgment that certain elements of American society acted not in accord with precepts of civilization; that there is some degree of guilt or remorse about such behavior; and, through professed powerlessness over the actions, that the legal or rational system of justice — Max Weber's distinction between civilized and tribal justice — would not be brought to bear upon the transgressors. Readers may need to be reminded here that the California Constitution of 1851 barred Indians from testifying in court, a provision which, obviously, precluded their use of the law for redress. Perpetrators used racial thinking to commence their deeds, and authorities used racial thinking — referring to "Diggers" and "creatures"— to neglect prosecution. Helen Hunt Jackson has Aunt Ri, a character who comes to love Ramona and accept the Indians as persecuted and worthy, say after Ramona's and Alessandro's land had been swindled from them: " 'Why, they take folks up, 'n' penetentiarize 'em fur life, back'n Tennessee, fur things thet ain't so bad's thet!' " A brilliant comment on the ability of racial thinking to efface the rule of law and justify actions that violate one's cultural norms indeed.

This sort of racial thinking on the part of the Americans had now evolved into full-fledged racism: ideas about the nature of Indians now accompanied their horrific treatment. Again, these sorts of ideas derived mostly from White peoples' lived experience, anxieties, and what they saw of Indians in California. To state the obvious, Indians looked and acted different. And not only did these new imperialists arrive on the scene with different cultural baggage about racial thinking than their Spanish predecessors, the Americans encountered Indians in California who had been undergoing dramatic cultural changes; they ranged from alcoholic dregs to rugged, desperate warrior raiders. As our present narrative has only hinted at, an immensely complicated series of human actions had created this perplexing situation for the Indians, but it could not be complexity that the Americans would appreciate. They needed, and then opted for, simplicity and reference to what was already known about people who looked different to explain the Indians' baffling condition. And to vindicate their actions against them.

Matters of the Americans and race continue on in California, of course, and this issue of appearance takes on new dimensions when the Americans start to process those who do, and do not, "look" like them. And, importantly "look" takes on two meanings here: first, it refers to what (post)modernists would refer to as the signified — that is those who are looked at — but also to the signifiers — that is those whose gazes fall upon the same peoples (yes, Indians here). To give away the point of this part of the present narrative, to the Americanos some Californios "looked" Indian, many of them "looked" somewhat European in their phenotype and especially their dress, but they all "looked" to be different in their deportment. But, second, the Californios and the Americanos evidently "looked" at Indians in some very similar ways.

As we have already noted, Californios' treatment of the race question varied from family to family. Some affirmed and protected their *limpieza de sangre*, others arrived already mixed, others mixed in California, and yet others endeavored to marry their daughters to the *ojos azules*, as the Yankees and British businessmen were often called. The Americans (almost exclusively men), then, often found the Californios strange in their ways; these were pastoralists who aspired to gentility and leisure, and who gave away rather than saved to affirm their status. Yet, the Americans could not always racialize the ways in which they differed owing to these two peoples' shared disdain for Indians, lower class Mexican *cholos*, and Anglo trappers, and the fact that many of the young Californio women had become their wives and the patriarchs their fathers-in-law.

The most famous of American commentators on the Californios, the Boston Brahmin Richard Henry Dana, attributed the differences to environmental factors. In his widely and continuously read *Two Years Before the Mast*, a book published in 1840 and read by California public school students through the 1960s, Dana asserted how "in their domestic relations these people are not better than in their public. The men are thriftless, proud, extravagant, and very much given to gaming: and the women have but little education, and a good deal of beauty, and their morality, of course, is none of the best." Mostly, though, he attributed these characteristics, ones with some truth to them — they used generosity to affirm status, raced horses, and exuded pride in their seigneurial status — to environmental factors, something he called "California fever." "Indolence" proved the inevitable outcome of this malady with the further consequence that those upon this "soil in which corn yields from seventy to eight-fold," in "climate than which there can be no better in the world," wasted their opportunity. In a stunning prediction of things to come, he concluded his comments with, "In the hands of an enterprising people, what a country this might be!"[20]

Like most Americans, Dana had an ambivalent attitude toward the upper class Californios; he could be alternately drawn to their genteel ways and condemning of their quotidian gratifications. And, most certainly, this conjecture about the men being proud and the women beautiful reveals much about his standards. Other Americans — men such as Abel Stearns, Alfred Robinson,

John Temple to name only a few — intermarried with the daughters of the Californio dons. Elite men shared not only bloodlines, but notions of hierarchy. They all disdained Indians — both those who did all the work in the towns and on the ranchos and those with whom they fought over cattle and horses — and they spurned the unwashed lower classes of both cultures, be they the crude cast-offs of the United States or of Mexico.

Meanwhile, though, Dana's antecedents on the prolific landscape, with help of debt, drought, and the market, proceeded to dispossess the Californios — regardless of what they looked like — of their bounteous lands. But it was the lower class of Mexican Californians, those most likely to be mestizo, those "hungry, drawling, lazy half-breeds," as Dana (and plenty of others) called them, who would most experience the racial violence of the conquering Americans. This is a complicated and difficult story, one rooted in the conquest of the Mexican American War (1846–1848), the chaos and degradation of those overpowered that virtually inevitably accompanies such defeat, the need to secure the land and labor of the vanquished, the resistance to conquest and transfer of economic opportunity, and racial thinking that justified and motivated the whole endeavor.[21]

Let us consider an illustrative moment, one both dramatic and frighteningly common. In February 1857, a group of Anglo vigilantes captured a Mexican robber in the vicinity of Mission San Gabriel and summarily killed him. Then, according to an eyewitness and reported in the Mexican newspaper, *El Clamor Público*, "when they brought the body, a justice of the peace of the mission took out his knife and cut off the head and rolled it around with his foot as if it were a rock; then he thrust the knife into his chest several times, with a brutality rarely seen even amongst these very barbarians." The well-armed lynch mob had pressed a good part of the modest and mostly unarmed Mexican population of the vicinity into witnessing the spectacle, and then executed two of the innocents; they were, as the paper put it, "hanged as suspects."[22]

We have here in the decade of the 1850s something beyond mere racialization, something *El Clamor Público* called "la guerra de las razas." What happened between the Spanish and the Indians was a conquest, no doubt: the sincerity of the intent to bring the Indians something as sublime as everlasting salvation cannot obscure the coercion, guns, and disease that brought the Indians under the culturally calamitous rule of the Franciscans and the soldiers. The Americans had not such exalted intent: the "civilizing" of California, with the exception of the acceptable members of the Californio populace, would entail a mixture of removal, the sequestering in forgotten enclaves or reservations, and rugged discipline of the lower orders — read more "colored" — of that society. Naked force — something the Americans had in large measure, in contrast to the Mexicans, for their process of state building — would be the means to this end.

That the Mexicans of California, and everywhere in the newly conquered lands, looked like, and were, a mixed race people captured the imaginations of

Americans. In one of the nastier expressions of racial thinking about them, D.L. Phillips explained in 1877 how

> The fruits of the intermarriages between the converted Indian women and the Spanish soldiery had given here, as in New Mexico, a class far more vicious than the Indians, and without a redeeming trait of the pure Spaniard. Ignorance, laziness, indolence and vice, were and are the characteristics of the moribund race, the fruits of an experiment which has failed in all the past, and will in the future.

We see here that a people's race insinuated certain attributes, and that, actually, the mixed races emerged as the most faulty because they tended to combine the worst traits of the original two. This notion derived from Americans' thinking about the miscegenation that took place within slavery and between lower class Whites and free Blacks. Then, too, such thinking facilitated the expropriation of the Mexicans' land, the appropriation of their labor, their general criminalization (like what we saw in a previous paragraph), and their general exemption from equal treatment under law.[23]

"About one-fifth of it [Los Angeles] is occupied by that part known as 'Sonora,' the home of the genuine Mexican. . . . This mixed Spanish-Mexican-Indian race are [sic]," continued our Illinois commentator who seriously undercounted the indigenous population, "for all industrial purposes — male and female — about utterly worthless. They are poor, lazy, ignorant, vicious and drunken. The Americans are enterprising, intelligent, and in the main prosperous." Indeed, such Protestant American sojourners and settlers saw a pastoralist, conquered people upon the land of California, ones who sought continuity of their family ways, who worshipped in a fundamentally medieval and folk Catholicism, who enjoyed wine and dance, and who in some few numbers took to brigandage for some combination of sustenance and revenge — and whose any other ambition for political or economic advancement vigilante groups would thwart. Emblematic of such a situation were those who took reprisal against the Americanos — the great bandidos, such as Joaquin Murieta and Tiburcio Vásquez — who may have gained a measure of vengeance and given their country people a modicum of satisfaction. In the end, though, these fighters only further convinced the Americanos of Mexicans' criminal tendencies and brought down more meanness at the hands of official and unofficial enforcers of the law. Thus, when Anglo Americans saw a Mexican Californian of the lower class, they "saw" someone whose mixed-race looks betrayed an idolater, an indolent and unclean idler, and someone whose deportment ranged from dishonest to criminal. "The men, as a rule, are greasy, black-haired, moustachoed fellows that one would not want to meet in the dark — fellows who would make you feel that it would be proper for a Christian to be well armed with carnal weapons." Again, comments about character follow in the same sentence as observations about appearance. And most apparently and powerfully so does a justification for preemptory violence.[24]

That, as another Anglo traveler noted, the "large Mexican population, but semi-civilized at best . . . as a class, hate the Americans with an inveterate hatred," should not be surprising. As a consequence of all this violence and animosity, Mexicans and Indians in the decades after the Mexican American War sequestered themselves, the former in small towns and urban barrios, and the latter on reservations and in the mountains. Each emerged on occasion to work, owing to their loss of other means of subsistence. Yet, they could not even come close to meeting the labor needs of the expanding Anglo economy, especially in the north where the violence against the Indians was most intense and from which most Mexicans had fled in those brutal years during and right after the Gold Rush. In other words, the Americans had fewer and fewer people to work for them: the Indians were dying, the Mexicans were scared of the Americans and did not like them, and both preferred their familiar and safe enclaves. Thus was the stage set for the subsequent and massive immigrations of Filipinos, Chinese, Japanese, and more Mexicans.

The sources of racial thinking are many and particular to time, place, and the people involved. Upon the same landscape, and upon the same people, different imperial Christians — Americans and Spaniards — evolved entirely different ways of creating what they called civilization as regards the natives. Then too, those that came in between, the criollo and mestizo Californios, contended with Indianness in remarkably unique ways.

What we have here — and this may be the contribution of this particular essay to theories of racism — is that racial thinking is gratifying because it is explanatory and thus comforting. But each of the situations it explains is local, contingent, and time-specific. If, then, racial thinking is about satisfying tension and wonder about the conduct of those others whose relationship to pleasure, work, the body and its functions, dirt, and the spirit world, then the origins of such racialization will always differ from place to place, from conquest to conquest, from anxiety to anxiety.

Reading the Americans' geographic and verbal expatiations in which they can only analyze others in terms of their putative likeness to those they already know who differ in looks, I was reminded of Herodotus' *Histories*. He continually reflects upon the new people he meets in his travels only in relation either to his people or to those strangers he has already met. This prompts me to think that we of the modern, even postmodern world are not so different from our predecessors who have taken guilty pleasures when they wandered in their travels and then ruminated about what they saw. Indeed, the whole comparative effort of this volume may speak to our need as human beings to make troubling human interactions and strange people understandable by establishing their resemblances (however superficial, but profound in their consequences) to things we have already observed. We understand those who are new based upon what we know about ourselves and those near us. Thus, we must know ourselves and our neighbors much better.

Notes

1. Antonio María Bucareli to (Juan) Arriaga, Mexico City, January 27, 1773, in Herbert Eugene Bolton, *Anza's California Expeditions*, Vol. 5, *Correspondence*, 53; Fray Fermín Lasuén to Fray Pangua, April 23, 1774, in Bolton, *Anza's California Expeditions*, Vol. 4, *Font's Complete Diary of the Second Anza Expedition*, 141; Zalvidea is quoted in E.B. Webb, *Indian Life at the Old Missions* (Los Angeles, 1951), 43.
2. Cabeza de Vaca, Producciones Iguana in co-produccion with Instituto Mexicano de Cinematografia; screenplay, Guillermo Sheridan, Nicolás Echevarria; producers, Rafael Cruz, Jorge Sánchez, Julio Solórzano Foppa, Bertha Navarro; director, Nicholás Eshevarria; Fermín Lasuén, *Writings of Fermín Lasuén*, (Washington DC, 1957) 2: 202.
3. Durán is quoted in Irving Berdine Richman, *California under Spain and Mexico, 1535–1847* (Boston, 1911), 254; Venegas is quoted in Alexander Forbes, *California: A History of Upper and Lower* (London 1839), 184; Juan Bandini to Eustace Barron, December 8, 1828, Stearns Papers, Huntington Library, Box 4.
4. Payeras' first statement is quoted in Zephyrin Engelhardt, *San Gabriel Mission and the Beginnings of Los Angeles* (San Gabriel, Calif., 1927), 109 and the second in Robert Archibald, *The Economic Aspects of the California Missions* (Washington DC, 1978), 157; Sherbourne F. Cook, *The Conflict between the California Indian and White Civilization* (Berkeley and Los Angeles, 1976), 28. Hugo Reid, letter to the *Los Angeles Star*, no. 22 (1852), appended in Susanna Bryant Dakin, *A Scotch Paisano: Hugo Reid's Life in California, 1832–1852* (Berkeley, 1939); Lasuén to Fray Antonio Nogueyra, January 21, 1797 in Lasuén, Writings, 2: 6; Durán is quoted in Cook, Conflict, 106
5. José María Amador, "Memorias," Bancroft Library ms., 1877, 74; Maynard Geiger trans. & ed., "Fray Antonio Ripoll's Description of the Chumash Revolt at Santa Barbara in 1824," *Southern California Quarterly*, LII (December, 1970), Padre Ripoll is quoted on page 354 from his letter to Father President Vicente Francisco Sarría, Santa Barbara, May 5, 1824; "Testimony, June 1, 1824," De la Guerra Documents, quoted in Cook, *Conflict*, 108; Hubert Howe Bancroft, *History of California* (San Francisco, 1886), II: 527–537; Webb, *Indian Life*, 51; Angustias de la Guerra Ord, *Occurrences in Hispanic California*, eds. Francis Price and William H. Ellison (Washington DC, 1956), 7–9; George Harwood Phillips, *Indians and Intruders in Central California, 1769–1849* (Norman, Okla.), 65–67.
6. Antonia I. Castañeda, "Engendering the History of Alta California," in Ramón A. Gutiérrez and Richard J. Orsi, *Contested Eden: California before the Gold Rush* (Berkeley and Los Angeles, 1998), 241–242; Robert Ryall Miller, *Juan Alvarado: Governor of California, 1836–1842* (Norman, Okla., 1988), 181.
7. Helen Tyler, "The Family of Pico," *Historical Society of Southern California Quarterly* 35, No. 3 (September, 1953), 229–236; Castañeda, "Engendering the History of Alta California," 241.
8. Juana Machado, "Los Tiempos Pasados," Bancroft Library ms., 1877, 16; on the sartorial splendor the Californios, *see* Monroy, *Thrown among Strangers*, 138; much of this discussion of shame derives from Ramón A. Gutiérrez, *When Jesus Came, the Corn Mothers Went Away: Marriage, Sexuality, and Power in New Mexico, 1500–1846* (Stanford, CA, 1991), 208–221.
9. Durán is quoted in William Marvin Mason, "Indian-Mexican Cultural Exchange in the Los Angeles Area," *Aztlán*, 15, no. 1 (Spring, 1984), 129; Richard Henry Dana, *Two Years Before the Mast* 1845 (New York, 1963), 63.
10. José del Carmen Lugo, "Life of a Rancher," *Historical Society of Southern California Quarterly*, 32, (September, 1950) 223–224; Monroy, *Thrown among Strangers*, 144–149.
11. Serra to Antonio María Bucareli, May 21, 1773, in Junípero Serra, *Writings of Junípero Serra*, ed. and trans. Antoine Tibesar (Washington DC, 1966) I: 359–363; Gutiérrez, *When Jesus Came*, 180–206.
12. Antonio María Osio, *The History of Alta California: A Memoir of Mexican California*, Rose Marie Beebe and Robert M. Sankewicz trans. (Madison, 1996), 55, 268–269; "Fray Antonio Ripoll's Description of the Chumash Revolt at Santa Barbara in 1824," ed. and trans. Maynard Geiger, *Southern California Quarterly*, 52 (December, 1970); Sandos; Monroy, *Thrown among Strangers*, 94–95.
13. This is one of the main points of the entire Phillips, *Indians and Intruders*.
14. Vicente Guerrero is quoted in J.M. Guinn, *Historical and Biographical Record of Southern California*, (Chicago, 1902), 67; Los Angeles, *Star*, March 13, 1852; T. Butler King, *Report on California*, (Washington DC, 1850), 16.

15. John Berger, *Ways of Seeing* (New York, 1977), 45–47.
16. Monroy, *Thrown among Strangers*, 22–24; Diary of José María Zalvidea, July 19–August 14, 1806, Santa Barbara Mission Archives.
17. James Rawls, *Indians of California: The Changing Image* (Norman, Okla., 1984), 196–198, credibly discusses Anglo Americans' association of Africans with Indians, and the quote is on pp. 196–197 and is from Ryan, Personal Adventures 1: 73, 92–93; Nicolai Petrovich Rezanov and Georg Von Langsdorf, "The Rezanov Voyage," in Joshua Paddison ed., *A World Transformed: First Hand Accounts of California Before the Gold Rush* (Heyday Books, Berkeley, 1999), 111–112.
18. *Los Angeles Star*, March 13, 1852; William C. Kibbe, *Report of the Expedition Against the Indians in the Northern Part of the State*, 6, 8, 10 quoted in Rawls, *Indians of California*, 179; on "extermination" *see* Robert F. Hizer and Alan T. Almquist, *The Other Californios: Prejudice and Discrimination under Spain, Mexico, and the United States to 1920* (Berkeley, 1971), 26–44.
19. Helen Hunt Jackson, *A Century of Dishonor: A Sketch of the United States Government's Dealings with Some of the Indian Tribes*, new ed. (Boston, 1893) 459–460, 495; Hurtado, 181 but he gets it from Hizer, *Destruction*.
20. Dana, *Two Years Before the Mast*, 135–137.
21. Leonard Pitt, *The Decline of the Californios: A Social History of the Spanish-Speaking Californians, 1846–1890* (Berkeley and Los Angeles, 1966), 83–119; Robert Glass Cleland, *The Cattle on a Thousand Hills: Southern California, 1850–80* (San Marino, Calif., 1975), 33–50, 102–137; Monroy, *Thrown among Strangers*, 222–232.
22. *El Clamor Público*, February 14, 1857.
23. D.L. Phillips, *Letters from California: Its Mountains, Valleys, Plains, Lakes, Rivers, Climate and Productions*. Springfield Ill. 1877; Pitt, *Decline of the Californios*, 148–167; Monroy, *Thrown among Strangers*, 205–219; Rodolfo Acuña, *Occupied America: A History of Chicanos* (New York: Harper and Row, 1988), 112–129.
24. Phillips, *Letters from California*, 119; Pitt, *Decline of the Californios*, 148–180; Monroy, *Thrown among Strangers*, 214–219. The present author, himself a native born Californian of Mexican descent, does not attend church on Sundays but instead usually plays tennis and does not shave in honor of the day. After a match that last description may well apply.

2

Mestizaje and the "Ethnicization" of Race in Latin America[1]

VIRGINIA Q. TILLEY

In discussing our worldwide range of case studies, the authors of this volume sometimes confronted the typological question of whether a case constituted a racial conflict or an ethnic one (which would, therefore, reside outside the scope of comparative racial studies). These debates engaged the often murky distinctions between race and ethnicity that Paul Spickard discusses at length in the Introduction. But taken in historical perspective, a more expressly political dimension of this question also emerged. The *ethnicization* of racial groups — public redefinition as *ethnic* those groups formerly understood as *racial* — has been a strategic discursive maneuver by governments seeking to mitigate the political tensions associated with racial politics. Such maneuvers have fed powerfully into mass popular perceptions and beliefs regarding racial and ethnic identities. They have also impressively influenced the knowledge of scholars, who — accepting hegemonic (originally state-sponsored) definitions less critically than might be wise — have weighed in on related and politically sensitive questions: for example, of whether Turkey's Kurdish population endured a true genocide in 1917 or something more appropriately described as "ethnic cleansing"; or whether Latin America's indigenous peoples still suffer from racial discrimination or only from lingering marginalization as "ethnic groups."

State interests in "ethnicizing" groups formerly understood as racial reflect the historical importance of both concepts to nation-building projects as well as states' international profiles. As traced below, nation-building in the late-nineteenth century became highly concerned with race, as seemingly incontestable European racial "sciences" affirmed its determinative role in shaping mental characteristics and, therefore, national cultures, and ultimately each nation-state's capacity for growth and "higher" civilization. The same ideas suggested that a nation-state's international relations (most baldly, its capacity to resist colonial takeover) would depend partly on how its racial character was perceived by European imperial powers. Inserted into the nation-building doctrines of political elites, these ideas indicated that national security itself required the government to craft racial unity where it was lacking, preferably centered on one of the racial types positioned as high as possible on European charts ("Anglo-Saxon" high, "Negroid" low). By the early twentieth century, these ideas had been translated into a range of local solutions: from deliberate diffusion of a preferred racial type throughout a territory (e.g., Javanization in Indonesia) and "whitening" strategies (e.g., Latin American efforts to promote the mass immigration of Europeans) to outright removal or extermination campaigns (e.g., of Jews and Gypsies and Slaves during Nazi rule, as well as genocidal policies toward native North Americans, Australian Aborigines, and Amazonian indigenous peoples).

After the traumatic experience of Nazism, however, western European and North American doctrines shifted to reject racial nationalism and promote ethnic pluralism. Reconceiving racial division as ethnic diversity provided a way to reconceptualize groups in less rigid ways, permitting recognition of culture, custom, and worldview as valued group experiences without locking individuals into any predestined set of life chances. It also allowed governments to disavow older racial systems and launch public education campaigns to mitigate lingering racial effects. But this normative shift had mixed effects on groups. Affirming that racial groups were actually ethnic ones was obviously a key step toward delegitimizing and dismantling racial hierarchies, setting the political stage for antiracist legislation and pluralist politics. But the claim also granted states the moral advantage of endorsing an enlightened doctrine whether those hierarchies were dismantled or not. Indeed, given the advantage to economic elites of enduring racial hierarchies (such as cheap labor systems), the *conceptual* evaporation of race tended to absolve states of politically onerous projects to ameliorate such (now putatively nonexistent) hierarchies. Ethnicization also repositioned racial groups far more comfortably within the national fold by eroding the political viability of minority claims to peoplehood and ethnonationalism, which many racial hierarchies (reflecting settler-colonial or other forcible-absorption legacies) tended to sustain. (Hence Turkey's move to redefine Kurds via the politically disabling ethnic formula, "mountain Turks.")

The Latin American doctrine of *mestizaje* was such a strategic discursive maneuver. In Latin America, *mestizaje* is the claim — both scientific and ideological — that racial mixture throughout the continent has affected both genetic and cultural blending to the point where any racial distinction has become meaningless. The claim has embedded in popular discourse, naturalizing the omission of racial and ethnic identities from policy and academic consideration (e.g., from census counts). Not incidentally, the belief in complete racial mixture also conveniently casts any claim of enduring racism or related group needs (e.g., by indigenous peoples) as wrong-headed and atavistic. *Mestizaje* has seeped into North American political science scholarship as well by removing race from consideration as a central political question; hence, for most of the late-twentieth century, North American political scientists boldly theorized on such desperately important questions as "democratization" and regime "transitions" while entirely omitting consideration of entrenched, and often bitter, racial and ethnic divisions.[2] That such omission was mistaken became glaring when in-depth studies of Mexico, Guatemala, Peru, Ecuador, and Bolivia by political scientists (and other social scientists) in the 1960s through 1980s entirely failed to anticipate, or even theoretically account for, the wave of indigenous uprisings and mass insurrections that shook the foundations of national politics in those countries in the late-1980s and 1990s.[3]

That upsurge of open rebellion revealed, with new clarity, the character of *mestizaje* as a political doctrine strategically developed to complement nationalist projects as well as a larger "Latin American" identity discourse. To understand that broader scope, we need to consider *mestizaje's* historical emergence: in this chapter, by exploring its older debates centered in Mexico.

The "Indian problem"

Policy debates about Indians proceeded for three centuries under Spanish rule, and by the 1920s, racial ideas about the Indian's role in the modernizing nation had been under extensive debate in Mexico for at least half a century.[4] By the late nineteenth century, nationalist intellectuals throughout Latin America had joined economic and political elites in trying to analyze and further urgent nationalist agendas of trade, development, and security. With better communication and travel infrastructure, these discussions became increasingly transnational, as intellectuals shared ideas through extensive writings, visits, European tours, and regional conferences. Among these debates were extensive discussions about what scholars perceived as urgent problems facing their nations, including endemic social problems among the working classes (like crime, drunkenness, promiscuity, vagrancy, and "morality" in general). National economic development was indeed universally understood to be obstructed by the poverty and political marginalization of the vast ranks of the poor.[5] Indians were clearly part of that problem: deemed ignorant, backward, and possibly racially inferior, the indigenous communities seemed ominously to impede both national unity and national economic development.

Debates about how to handle the "Indian problem" were, however, far from a solely American affair. They were increasingly informed by respected European writings about race (supported by impressive statistical and photographic studies of nostrils, earlobes, and the like), which seemed to confirm not only the scientific reality of racial division but its reliability as signals of mental and cultural capacity. Not incidentally, the same sciences also expounded the racial — and, hence, cultural — superiority of the "Caucasian" or "Anglo Saxon" relative to darker races.[6]

When incorporated into Latin American debates about modern nation-building, these European sciences presented an obvious policy dilemma. Latin

American nations could hardly aspire to European achievements while composed of a racially mixed and darker population that "science" had determined was racially and, therefore, culturally inferior. While the Indian might simply disappear over time (as a weak and disadvantaged race, doomed to dissolve by natural extinction and miscegenation), Indian miscegenation would only further degrade (darken and hybridize) the national gene pool. (The continent as a whole was variously estimated, by contemporary observers, as 60–75 percent indigenous.[7]) As noted above, one obvious answer was to "whiten" Latin American nations through mass white European immigration. "Whitening" did seem viable in countries like Argentina (where "cleansing" of the Pampas was largely completed by the 1890s), but elsewhere, as in Mexico, "whitening" loomed difficult or impossible, given heavily Indian demographics. In any case, no amount of "whitening" would ever make the continent as white as Europe. European scientific authority, therefore, seemed to confirm Latin America's future, in international affairs as in its nations' domestic growth potential, as permanently inferior and subordinate. Both policy solutions and European theory itself were, therefore, under hot debate.[8]

Although everyone involved in these debates used the term "race," discussion labored under extensive confusion as to what a "race" actually was. Especially, people questioned whether race was more a biological fact or a social identity, and so whether the miserable situation of the Indian communities could be redeemed through educational and hygienic programs or was somehow fixed biologically, confirming their degenerated state as hopeless. Some celebratory currents were visible: some "indigenist" ideologists believed that Latin American countries should find their true character and inspiration in the original indigenous cultures.[9] But the tone of most authors was prescriptive: to find some way to make moral and scientific sense of the Indian's abysmal poverty and isolation in order to arrive at some set of remedial policies. Given the conflation of "Indian" with poverty, ignorance, superstition, and crime, and elite desire to turn Indians into productive capitalist units, for many writers the "Indian problem" was actually the need to *eliminate* "Indian-ness" through policies consistent with a moral framework.

The nationalist dimension of the "Indian problem" was equally clear, for many recognized that Indians did not seem *interested* in the nation. Andrés Molina Enríquez, for example, recognized that the Indians were a plethora of peoples (*patrias*), whose own lack of unity prevented their obtaining any larger political vision or loyalty:

> In particular the indigenous element, comprised of tribes and peoples very different among themselves, completely lacks unity. . . . The multiplicity and confusion among the traditions of origin, the differences of type, the divergences of customs, the diversities of language, and the evolutionary distances that distinguish and separate among them, are so evident as to belong to the range of public and well-known facts. . . . Each

indigenous group is consequently a special *patria* and the units of them are considered so in reality. Only in exceptional cases of great danger, do those groups count on the others; generally they keep each to their own forces, and when they are attacked, if they cannot win, they resign themselves to death. They have, however, multiple and small indigenous *patrias*, that are autonomous. These are complete *patrias* and not fragments of *patrias*. They do not have, therefore, any external orientation. The Indians will never be deliberate traitors to their own *patria* to the benefit of an external *patria*.[10]

Molina Enríquez was equally pessimistic about Mexico's creole elite, whose class snobbery and cosmopolitan ties to their European home countries (he argued) precluded their identifying with (mixed-race, impoverished) Mexico. Rather, he believed, the *mestizo* — the mixed-race and mixed-cultural population — provided the foundation for Mexican nation-building:

> The fundamental and inevitable base of all future labor undertaken for the good of the country, must be the continuation of the *mestizos* as the preponderant ethnic element and as the directive political class of the population. . . . In them truly exist a unity of origin, unity of religion, unity of type, unity of language and unity of desires, goals and aspirations. . . . All those circumstances of unity compose and translate into a firm, ardent and resolute patriotic love.[11]

Molina Enríquez was not alone in this view. The concept of the *mestizo* as the racial foundation of the nation was increasingly seizing the imagination of the emerging cadre of post-Revolutionary Mexican nation-builders. Yet, celebrating the *mestizo* raised, again, the dilemmas posed by European racial theory (cited above). "Anglo" racial superiority theory cast Indian blood as a pollutant that adulterated and degraded white blood. To redignify the *mestizo* as the nation vanguard race, its Indian component had to be redefined as a positive contribution.

A key voice toward that crucial project was provided by Manuel Gamio, a Boas-trained anthropologist and one of the most influential Mexican social scientists of his day.[12] Manuel Gamio published his famous *Forjando Patria* ("Forging the Fatherland," 1916), a powerful argument for a more systematic, pragmatic, and scientific approach to racial divisions, seven years after Molina Enríquez detailed his arguments for a nationalism built on the *mestizo* core. His preface was a poetic celebration of the *mestizo* as the veritable racial incarnation of the continent's epic history:

> In the great forge of America, on the gigantic anvil of the Andes, virile races of bronze and iron have battled for centuries and centuries . . . When the brown arm of the Atahualpas and the Moctezumas reached the moment of mixing and confusing peoples, a miraculous link was

consummated: the same blood swelled the veins of the Americans and their thought flowed in the same paths. . . . Today it is for the revolutionaries of Mexico to take up the hammer and gird themselves with the blacksmith's apron in order to bring forth from the miraculous anvil the new patria made of mingled iron and bronze.

There is the iron . . . There is the bronze. . . . Strike, brothers![13]

Gamio concluded his book with a phrase in uppercase letters:

FUSION OF THE RACES, CONVERGENCE AND FUSION OF CULTURAL PRACTICES, LINGUISTIC UNIFICATION AND ECONOMIC EQUILIBRIUM OF THE SOCIAL SECTORS, are concepts that summarize this book and indicate conditions which, in our opinion, must characterize the Mexican population so that it will constitute and incarnate a strong Patria and a coherent and defined Nationality.[14]

Gamio's re-imagining of an ennobled (Spanish-Indian) *mestizaje* galvanized imaginations not only in Mexico but throughout those parts of Latin America where "whitening" appeared hopeless: especially, the middle Isthmus and the Andes. Intellectuals, politicians, journalists, and literati in Guatemala, Lima, Costa Rica, Caracas, and Havana found it compelling.[15] His formula enabled a quantum leap toward what I will term *indo-mestizaje*: a concept of racial mixture that celebrated Indian blood for its attached mythic history and romanticized values, and overtly called for an end to racial discrimination. The idea rapidly assumed hegemonic proportions in Mexican thought as well as in El Salvador, Nicaragua, and Honduras.[16] In all these states, *mestizaje* conceptually incorporated the Indian heritage as a mark of national distinction — "we all have Indian blood." The same project would enfold the larger indigenous heritage into the national *mytho-moteur* by appropriating the art of pre-Columbian indigenous societies — even of indigenous heroic resistance to Conquest — as iconographic referents to the national origins and character.[17]

Indo-mestizaje might well have offered a framework of values — and a national identity discourse — through which societies could begin to address racial bias in more substance, as Gamio clearly intended. But the anti-Indian (and anti-Black) penchant in contemporary popular thought was instead reinforced by a second and equally compelling doctrine: a different version of *mestizaje*, invented to conceptualize "Latin America" itself as a geostrategic bloc in the international community. For Latin America's nationalist intellectuals were also well aware that domestic nation-building was dependent on their nations' *foreign* trade and security relations, and that those relations were dangerously vulnerable. Their solution — to re-imagine Latin America itself as a glorified mixed-racial presence on the international stage — would set the doctrinal conditions for patterns of racial denial, ethnic violence, and continued Indian marginalization.

Mestizaje as a foreign relations discourse

By the late nineteenth century, Latin America as a region was facing new international pressures. Economic trade had always been dependent on primary product export to Europe and to the United States but, with the exponential expansion of commercial export agriculture, the domestic impact of that dependency rapidly intensified. El Salvador was, of course, an exemplar of this pattern; by 1910, all domestic railroad traffic was controlled by the (United States) United Fruit Company, and all ocean shipping was controlled by a U.S. monopoly. By the 1920s, coffee accounted for 95 percent of Salvadoran exports and many of the local coffee processing plants were owned by foreigners, especially North Americans and Germans. Predictably, this dependency also transformed the sociology of the Salvadoran political elite; by the 1920s, the Salvadoran government was almost entirely dominated by sugar and coffee growers with, of course, strong social and commercial ties to North American and European business sectors.[18] Similar patterns characterized the other Central American states.

Viewing the economic risks inherent in such a scenario, Latin American nationalist intellectuals had long worried about the vulnerability of Latin American economies to foreign monopoly prices and to frequent and unpredictable fluctuations in the international market. But the political risks were also apparent, especially the region's concomitant vulnerability to growing U.S. political and military leverage. Intellectual debates became more urgent after the Spanish–American War, with a series of U.S. military invasions to support U.S. trade interests; for Central Americans, the occupation of Nicaragua (1911–1933) was particularly alarming.

Given their military and economic vulnerability to Europe and especially the booming United States, solidarity among Latin American states was, therefore, an obvious agenda. One dimension of transnationalist intellectual debates was, therefore, an effort to conceptualize and consolidate "Latin America" itself as a "security community,"[19] whose innate cohesion and solidarity could be proposed from its common history of colonialism and independence and its emerging common character — which had to be defined. Enlisted in this definitional project were racial ideas of a quite different order from those argued by Gamio, cited above. Instead, racial conceptualization of "Latin America" built on European and U.S. polemics about "Anglo" superiority, by re-imagining Latin America as a similarly large racial and civilizational bloc.

Inventing "la Raza" and undefining Indians

In the project to re-imagine "Latin America" as an identity community, intellectuals had to challenge European theory itself. As noted above, European racial sciences seemed to clarify that a nation's racial qualities would determine its political accomplishments. As each country's political accomplishments would, in this logic, prove its intrinsic racial qualities, British imperialism and U.S. territorial expansion seemed to indicate the clear superiority of the "Anglo-Saxon" or "white" race. By contrast, the relative political and economic decline of Spain (Britain's long-time imperial rival) in the same period suggested Spanish "racial" flaws like "languor," "laziness," and "arrogance." From such precepts, it followed that the relative weakness of Latin American countries derived from the heritage of Spanish racial flaws coupled with the inherently inferior "negro" and "indio" components.

Still, the Anglo-Saxon racial discourse inspired a counter-maneuver by Spanish intellectuals. A century after Latin American independence, Spain was indeed the crippled core of its former imperium, greatly weakened relative to both Britain and the United States. The 1898 Spanish–American War had deprived Spain of its last major imperial holdings, Cuba and the Philippines. Spanish ambitions to reaffirm a lasting link — political, therefore cultural, therefore racial — to its former colonies inspired the doctrine of "la Raza": the concept of a single Spanish–Latin American "race" historically born of American fusion with Spanish "blood." In 1912, Spanish ideologues building on this doctrine gained state backing officially to launch Dia de la Raza (Day of the Race), an annual holiday commemorating the arrival of Columbus in the Americas and still celebrated throughout Latin America.

Resonating so well with Latin America's nervousness about the U.S. imperialism, "la Raza" was immediately popular. By the early 1920s, it was of growing importance to anti-imperialist nationalist discourses throughout the continent. Influential elite advocates included Enríque Jose Varona in Cuba, Leopoldo Lugones and José Ingenieros in Argentina, and poet Gabriela Mistral in Chile. But its scope was not confined to elite discourse; it rapidly became a popular holiday down to the village level. As Salvadoran intellectual and humanitarian Albert Masferrer observed somewhat cynically in 1923:

> If one gives attention to our journalistic literature and in belligerent and nationalistic poetry — so prolific in Hispanoamerica — one will find that hardly a day passes without an article, a harangue, an ode, a sonnet, dedicated to celebrating the merits of la raza, the defense of la raza, the future of la raza; which, veiled or openly, always allude to the United States of the North. The governments and towns contribute every year, the 12 of October, with discourses, artillery salvos and glasses of champagne to wish strength, breadth, prominence and splendor to the prestige of la raza, a continental idol.[20]

In this receptive terrain, Vasconcelos published his key works. His most famous articles, "The Cosmic Race" (1925) and "Indology" (1926) detailed his assessment of Latin America's predicament and his prescription for resisting U.S. pressure.[21]

The cosmic race

The core message of "The Cosmic Race" was that the American continent was fundamentally divided between two races: the northern *"sajones"* (Saxons) or

"Whites," and the southern "*latinos*" — the Spanish–French amalgam that had settled the tropical regions (a category that tacitly absorbed the Portuguese).[22] Even as these two races had fought for centuries, so their rivalry persisted in Saxon ambitions to control the hemisphere, and only in this racialized context could the Latin American predicament be understood.[23] (Again, Spain's geostrategic interests are apparent here.) The Saxons had the advantage, partly because they had sustained their racial and cultural identity in league with Europe (White/Saxon England). As a consequence, the "Saxon" United States now enjoyed a fine political unity over a vast swath of territory, rendering it a hemispheric colossus. By contrast, the creoles had made the fatal error of cutting themselves off from European (Spanish and French) mother culture(s) in wrenching their independence from imperial Spain, and, consequently, had lost track of their glorious common heritage and had broken up politically into degenerated state fragments. (Like Gamio and many others of his time, Vasconcelos viewed the modern Latin American states as the products of *caudillos*, whose self-interest had disgracefully betrayed the glorious potential for *latino* unity sought by the independence heroes.)

And yet, Vasconcelos proposed a solution. In bold contradiction to European "pure-race" theory, Vasconcelos argued that the Whites had erred badly in so fiercely preserving their racial purity and in disdaining miscegenation with Negros and Indians. Purity ultimately meant inbreeding, and weakening; moreover, pure races were inevitably betrayed by their own hubris, and would be swept aside by history when their historic moment had passed. Nonracist *latinos*, on the other hand, had "out of love" interbred freely with Negros and Indians, and so the continent was now a vast homogeneous mixture of all the immigrant European races. Such a synthesis was unique, marvelous, and the foundation for the next great stage of human history: a single united World. "What will come," wrote Vasconcelos, "is the definitive race, the synthesis race or integral race, made of the genius and blood of all the peoples, and moreover, more capable of true brotherhood and of a truly universal vision."[24]

Vasconcelos's "cosmic race" concept had, however, little or nothing to do with Indians. Although citing the admixture of indigenous and black blood, he saw the true value of la Raza in its European Spanish and French — hence, "Latin" — cultural (racial) roots. In *La Raza Cósmica*, his tone about Indians was indeed dismissive; those Indians not already "Spanishized" (*españolizados*) had "no other door to the future than the door of modern culture, nor any other future than the road already cleared by the *latino* civilization." His goal was to eliminate "Indian-ness" by turning "Indians" into *latino-mestizos* through cultural change, rather than truly to obviate and eliminate anti-Indian bias.

Indeed, *La Raza Cósmica* actually sustained and reinforced such bias, by arguing that the Indians, Africans, and Chinese were still distinct races, and that racial defense against them was still necessary, if problematic to world peace. The need of "civilized races" was to prevent the "lower breeds" from "multiplying madly," a brute practice that secured their poverty, which then sent them clamoring to the civilized races for succor. The high road to world peace was accordingly to help such races advance in wealth and "culture" to the point where such pressures would recede. All races could then naturally interbreed as equals, creating a world system of mixed races and, finally, one world Race. At one North American conference, Vasconcelos diplomatically lauded this future (based on biological, cultural, and "spiritual" fusion) as the ultimate road to for harmonious global relations:

> If we do not wish to be overwhelmed by the wave of the Negro, of the Indian, or of the Asiatic, we shall have to see that the Negro, the Indian, and the Asiatic are raised to the higher standards of life, where reproduction becomes regulated and quality predominates over numbers. Instead of the competitive manner of life advocated by the defenders of the pure-race civilization and by the imperialists and conquerors, we shall have to adopt, then, the co-operative, collaborating manner of interracial organization.[25]

But when speaking to Latin American audiences, Vasconcelos assumed a much more combative tone, much more illuminating of the Indian's conceptual place in his vision. He was adamant that the immediate task for Latin America was to consolidate a "Latin" racial consciousness to oppose the "Saxons" or "Whites" of the North. Any premature adoption of "internationalism," he argued, would only secure Latin America's ultimate subordination. His geostrategic vision of world racial politics is clear:

> So as not to have to renounce the patria at some time it is necessary that we live in conformity with the highest interest of *the race*, even when this is still not the highest interest of Humanity. It is clear that the heart alone conforms to a perfect internationalism, but, in the actual circumstances of the world, internationalism would only further the triumph of the most powerful nations; it would serve exclusively English ends. . . . It would be, then, infantile for weak peoples like ourselves to reject all that is ours in the name of propositions that will not crystallize in reality.[26]

In this defensive logic, the indigenous peoples' marginalization became essential to the racial project essential to "Latin America's" *international* security and standing. The region's geostrategic interests rested on the construction and celebration of a *Latin* American identity because the region's principal racial conflict was not domestic — Whites or creoles against Indians — but external: *latinos* against "Saxons." Hence, the "*mestizo*" to be celebrated was "Latin."

This *latino-mestizaje* was, therefore, distinctly divergent from Gamio's *indo-mestizaje*: still Euro-centric in its values and orientation, subsuming indigenous peoples only on conditions of their utter ethnic dissolution and effective disappearance. Indeed, in the global racial confrontation it imagined, "Indians" were merely atavistic outliers of the "great synthetic race." *Indo-mestizaje* had already assumed that indigenous people could not be allowed to sabotage Latin

America's solidarity and growth, whether by retarding Latin America's national economies or by stubbornly sustaining indigenous *patrias*. But *latino-mestizaje* proposed more: that the very presence of "Indians" had to be defined as insubstantial, irrelevant to the region's character and future. Thus, while their disappearance was considered inevitable, the Indians' forced assimilation, or even violent repression of any recalcitrant ethnic resistance, could be granted nationalist sanction. . . . and would be, in the violence and struggles of subsequent decades.

Mestizaje: interweaving doctrines

Thus, in the writings of these two prominent theorists, Gamio and Vasconcelos, we see two threads of *mestizaje*, both deploying ideas of racial mixing yet grounded in antithetical precepts. Gamio's *indo-mestizaje* called for (at least rhetorical) celebration of Indian blood as a dignified element of the national racial stock, and set the terms for celebrating or at least accepting indigenous communities as (politically innocuous) ethnic groups. Vasconcelos's *latino-mestizaje* disparaged and rejected Indians, admitting them into "la raza" only on terms of their effective ethnic disappearance through complete assimilation to *latino* norms. *Indo-mestizaje* was rooted in biological and anthropological theories of race, rejecting racism in the interest of justice, social welfare, and national unity. *Latino-mestizaje* was rooted in a global geostrategic competition conducted in racialized terms, rejecting racial division only in affirming its own superior fused-race character. Both doctrines took their urgency from an understanding that racial fusion was essential to the integration of Latin American states, and that the unassimilated Indian was a drag on Latin America's racial-cultural competition with the "Saxon" United States. But one made some ideological room for indigenous peoples as living ethnic communities; the other did not.

As these two currents interplayed in *mestizaje*, they allowed state elites and many nationalist intellectuals sincerely to reject the social salience — even the existence — of racial division. Those indigenous peoples who remained clearly distinct (marked by language, dress, and discrete communities) were now recast as ethnic groups (*etnias*). Yet, this apparently enlightened shift actually provided cover for states. First, indigenous needs were, thus, pleasantly divorced from unwelcome questions of enduring racial discrimination — not to mention questions of indigenous ethnonationalist rights as unjustly conquered peoples with prior claims to sovereignty. Second, Latin America's anti-imperialist goals that infused *mestizaje* sustained an ambition to rival European standards of civilization, and so consolidated *mestizaje's* value-orientation toward "Latin" civilization and a hearty antipathy to present-day (backward, non-European) indigenous cultures.[27] Yet, by appropriating "Indian" ethnicity for nationalist rhetoric, song, and historical monuments, governments could obscure this orientation. Indeed, *mestizaje* has seemed to absolve whole societies from confronting otherwise glaring racial hierarchies.

Indigenous peoples could be promoted for their ethnic color, denatured into nationalized forms like a national Ballet Folklorico, or sometimes even rhetorically recognized as disadvantaged ethnic relics of colonial abuses. But any serious indigenous demand for group rights can manifest as not only retrograde but seditious, because such demands revive the ghost of racial division, impugning both the nation's "civilized" status and its very (racial/cultural/political) unity.

These xenophobic and rejectionist implications of *mestizaje* did not escape other contemporary thinkers. One such critic was Salvadoran intellectual and humanitarian Alberto Masferrer, cited above, who found the whole "la raza" discourse overblown and disturbing. On its face, Masferrer was impressed by *mestizaje's* empirical flaws. As Gamio had done, he observed that the real-life *mestizo* was still far more Indian than White, and so did not accord with the largely White imagery that pervaded "la raza" discourse.

> . . . when they speak of defending and cultivating the race, they are referring vaguely and immediately to a white or almost white nucleus; something almost Spanish or almost French, which they designate with the adjective *latino*. The fact is as false as the name. That *latino* nucleus is, in the realm of reality, and if we refer to the vast Hispanoamerican assembly, a small minority, barely noticeable.[28]

Masferrer's view of the Indians' logical fate in the new "la raza" discourse was prescient:

> . . . if our vision and our criteria are *la raza* . . . then we are hindered by the thousands of Mexican and Central American Indians; we are hindered by the broken mixed-Araucano Chilenos and the Indians of diverse denominations in Venezuela and in Colombia, in Ecuador and in Bolivia; we are hindered by all that is not white, or *mestizo* with mostly white blood, not aboriginal; that is to say, we are hindered by, at least, half the population of the Indo*latino* [sic] continent.
>
> And as they hinder us, to be logical we would try to annihilate them, or at least *continue treating them as we have up to now*, as an inferior race, good only to be exploited . . . left in ignorance and in misery, and given up to Time, with the tacit and hopeful wish that we are getting rid of them.[29]

The answer to this dilemma, he argued, was not to base the continental identity on specious ideas of a unified race, but rather to launch a continent-wide program to create a unified culture, one that could indeed bring all races together within a common set of progressive ideas and spiritual values.

Yet, we must note that, scarcely four years later, Masferrer was a convert. If the continent had not yet actually achieved racial unity, he wrote in his 1927 essay *Now and in You* (1927), "la raza" was nevertheless emerging, infused with spiritual and nationalist mission. In *Battle Cry*, also in 1927, he reproduced the "cosmic race" discourse of Vasconcelos almost intact: "American has complete territorial unity, and *a unity in formation of race and of language* that gives it a capacity to attempt the work of fusion that no other Continent can realize."[30] Gone entirely from his discourse was any mention of "Indians"; the only "peoples" were now the state-nations themselves, forged into the "continental" unity that was its "supreme need" through racial fusion:

> In other Continents the mountain ranges separate. In America they unify. The Andes are the granite thread that connects twenty peoples. . . . A hundred million whites, twenty million blacks, seventy million *mestizos* and two million Asians, that mix their blood and their souls, clothing their spirit in two unique languages that will blend into one, form the elements of the NEW RACE, of the *cosmic race* that will forge America.
>
> . . . And so, while by birth and coming together the sum of Humanity is formed, we are forming of ourselves a consciousness, a *Continental Consciousness,* that is our supreme need: and the *new race* is forming that we must purify and refine, so that it answer the desires of a *New and Unique Consciousness.*[31]

Thus, the discourse of *mestizaje* diffused into nationalist doctrines, wedding contradictory threads into a compelling fabric. Yet, those contradictions were not a handicap. Rather, they provided crucial flexibility, as a synoptic glance at Mexico and the Central American context suggests. In Mexico, *mestizaje* grappled with heavily indigenous demographics by adopting an ostensibly enlightened ethnic pluralism. Yet, in the state's national discourse, the indigenous "ethnic" presence remained a watered-down, folkloric image denuded of any political force, a matter of colorful costume and handicrafts. This "ethnicized" indigeneity even entered North American political science scholarship, converting "Indian-ness" into an incidental quality sometimes worth noting in studies of a (conceptually de-ethnicized) peasantry. But the inadequacies of this ethnicization for both Mexican policymakers and scholars would eventually show as widening cracks in the hegemonic facade (most dramatically, with the Zapatista revolt in 1994), for it abysmally failed to ameliorate enduring racial hierarchies, indigenous political marginalization and poverty, and indigenous resentment.

By contrast, in both El Salvador and Nicaragua, *mestizaje* faciliated the dominant claim that "Indians" had vanished altogether. In both countries, *mestizaje* emerged in periods of violent racial strife and provided cover for continuing land alienation by ladinos — Jeff Gould (1998) has traced related upheavals in Nicaragua in the 1910s; elsewhere, I have explored the "race war" dimension of El Salvador's infamous 1932 *Matanza.*[32] In both countries, *mestizaje* subsequently embedded as a "commonplace notion," yet remained a poor fit with enduring racial tension. In the 1980s, it would feed a Sandinista attempt forcibly to integrate the indigenous peoples on the Atlantic Coast into the

Sandinista's revolutionary program, triggering a bloody and painful conflict leading to establishment of an (still much contested) autonomy zone.[33] In the 1990s, indigenous movements would also arise in the Nicaraguan Pacific Coast and in El Salvador.[34] Seen as contrived by a population steeped in the *mestizo* myth, these movements have refused to evaporate and have gained a toe-hold in transnational networks and the public national stage.

In all three countries, as *mestizaje* took hold in the 1920s, its embedded racial logics manifested in racial rejection. All fostered rabid Sinophobia and state policies to expel the Chinese population; all rejected the idea of Black intermixture, yet obviated public consideration of endemic popular anti-Black bias; and all redefined all rural communities as "peasants," converted indigenous communities into politically innocuous ethnic groups — and so cast any revived indigenous politics as ignorant, obsolete, and artificially created by foreigners.[35]

Guatemala offers still another variation of *mestizaje's* interweaving logics. For many decades, official doctrine followed *latino-mestizaje* values in assuming (and being satisfied with) the "Indian's" cultural obsolescence and imminent ethnic demise. At the same time, threads of *indo-mestizaje* inspired token gestures like "Conquest Indian" monuments of Tecun Umán — a fig-leaf over continued rampant exploitation of the indigenous labor caste. The inadequacies of these claims were clear from their inability to obscure racist state policies and social practice, extending even to genocidal violence against the indigenous peoples. When explicitly indigenous challenges to state policies were raised in the 1980s, the state attempted a confined ethnic accommodation (through such public measures as approving the Guatemalan Academy of Mayan Languages). In 1995, state recognition of indigenous needs was gained in the Peace Accord on Indigenous Identity and Rights. Yet, implementation lags in a new climate of denial. Mayan ethnic revival stimulated a ladino rhetorical re-entrenchment, expressed as Gamian *indo-mestizaje*: that Indian and Spanish races had long ago been "forged" into one, and that collective Mayan protest was, therefore, nonsensical and specious, even racist.[36]

Conclusion

The claim that racial division and prejudice has been transcended in Latin American societies cannot be entirely dismissed as "false consciousness." Racial identities are social constructions, and are not gainsaid by outside authority. If the obvious divisions or biases within Latin American societies (e.g., continuing biases toward whiter skin) are not understood as racial in nature, then it is dangerous or even imperialist for North Americans to affirm that they actually are. Nevertheless, enduring social hierarchies, political exclusion, and discrimination — and especially the language in which these practices are legitimized and pursued — reveal little substantive difference between the older racial and the newer ethnic epistemes.

For scholars, the interplay of ethnic (behavioral) and racial (somatic) factors in shaping "groupness" will always be an important question for study. But that interplay cannot be accepted *prima facie* — that is, through attitude surveys — without some attention also to the history of these terms: how and when they emerged, the role of the state in endorsing and promoting them, and the context of internal and/or external political stress in which such state campaigns were launched. Ethnicization may seem a positive trend in general, and surely often is one. But, it can also be a tool for states and societies to evade and obscure (for outsiders and for themselves) ongoing patterns of conflict that are racial in all but name. Certainly comparative racial studies should not exclude cases solely on the basis of their terminology. An "ethnicized" racial conflict may be one of the most insidious forms that racial politics can take.

Notes

1. Sections of this chapter are drawn from my *Seeing Indians: A Study in Race, Nation, and Power in El Salvador* (Albuquerque: University of New Mexico Press, 2005). I thank Paul Spickard and all authors of this volume for their comments and insights on this chapter, and especially for inspiring its principal thesis.
2. *See*, for example, the collected articles in David Collier, ed., *The New Authoritarianism in Latin America* (Princeton, NJ: Princeton University Press, 1979); Guillermo O'Donnell and Philippe C. Schmitter, *Transitions from Authoritarian Rule: Tentative Conclusions about Uncertain Democracies*, Vol. 4 (Baltimore: Johns Hopkins University Press, 1986); Larry Diamond, Juan J. Linz, and Seymour Martin Lipset, eds., *Democracy in Developing Countries: Latin America* (Boulder, CO: Lynne Reiner, 1989).
3. For an insightful critique of anthropology on this failure, *see* Orin Starn, "Missing the Revolution: Anthropologists and the War in Peru," *Cultural Anthropology*, 6.1 (1993), 65–93.
4. For English language reviews of these early debates, *see* especially Martin S. Stabb, "Indigenism and Racism in Mexican Thought: 1857–1911," *Journal of Inter-American Studies*, 1 (1959); T.G. Powell, "Mexican Intellectuals and the Indian Question, 1876–1911," *Hispanic American Historical Review* (1969); David A. Brading, "Manual Gamio and Official Indigenismo in Mexico," *Bulletin of Latin American Research*, 7.1 (1988), 75–89; Alan Knight, "Racism, Revolution and *Indigenismo*: Mexico, 1910–1940," in *The Idea of Race in Latin America*, ed., Richard Graham (Austin: University of Texas Press, 1990); Alexander S. Dawson, "From Models for the Nation to Model Citizens: *Indigenismo* and the 'Revindication' of the Mexican Indian, 1920–40," *Journal of Latin American Studies*, 30 (1998), 279–308.
5. *See* the "Minutes and Antecedents," Vol. 7, Seventh International Conference of American States (Montevideo, 1933). For an analysis of this focus on social ills, *see* Robert Buffington, "Forjando Patria: Criminology and Citizenship in Modern Mexico" (unpublished book manuscript, 1997).
6. For a history of these studies, *see* especially Stephen Jay Gould's *The Mismeasure of Man* (New York: Norton, 1981).
7. For instance, in 1916 Manuel Gamio estimated the indigenous population of Mexico at 8–10 million, and the population "of European origin" at 4–6 million; *Forjando Patria* (Mexico Porrúa, 1960; orig. 1916), 9. Chilean writer Guillermo Feliu Cruz later described the Chilean population in the early nineteenth century as "about three quarters constituted of Spanish-indigenous *mestizaje*, neither barbarian nor civilized"; *Un Esquema de la Evolución social en Chile en el Siglo XIX* (Santiago: Editorial Nascim Ugarte, 1941), 6.
8. For example, Argentinian José Ingenieros viewed Spanish mixture with Indian (and Arab) blood as having "retarded the formation of new nationalities of white race [in the southern cone] by a century"; "La Formación de una Raza Argentina," *R. de Filosofia*, 11 (1915), 471. Both Chilean and Argentinian sociologists, with a few notable exceptions like Manuel Ugarte (*The Destiny of a Continent* [New York: Knopf, 1925]), leaned toward "whitening" as a solution to resulting backwardness.
9. On these debates, *see* also Stabb, "Indigenism and Racism"; Dawson, "From Models for the Nation to Model Citizens"; and Powell, "Mexican Intellectuals and the Indian Question."
10. Andrés Molina Enríquez, *Los Grandes Problemas Nacionales* (Mexico: Ediciones Era, 1978; orig. 1909), 380.
11. Enríquez, *Los Grandes Problemas Nacionales*, 357, 393. For a contradictory interpretation of indigenous political thought, *see* Florencia Mallon, "Constructing *Mestizaje* in Latin America: Authenticity, Marginality, and Gender in the Claiming of Ethnic Identities," *Journal of Latin American Anthropology*, 2.1 (1995).

12. On Gamio's role, *see also* Stabb, "Indigenism and Racism"; Powell, "Mexican Intellectuals and the Indian Question"; Knight, "Racism, Revolution and *Indigenismo*"; and Brading, "Manuel Gamio and Official *Indigenismo*."

13. Gamio, *Forjando Patria*, 5–6.

14. Gamio, *Forjando Patria,*, 183; emphasis in original.

15. The idea that racial fusion in Latin America constituted a unique and glorious meld, and the image of a forge predates Gamio; *see*, for example, Francisco Gavida, "El Porvenir de la América Latina," *La Quincena*, 1.1 (1903), 330, who considers that the various ethno-racial groups in Latin America "are the brotherhood, synthesis of all History, they are the liberty proclaimed with the heroic gesture of the wars of Independence, and of a thousand revolutions, the divine forge on which the paladión has been revitalized, of everlasting metal, of Democracy and Republic. The rest of the nations are races. Latin America, sir, is humanity."

16. The Ecuadorean state also resorted to *mestizaje* when under pressure by indigenous collective protest: for an example from the 1970s, *see* Robert G. Whitten's classic account, *States and Social Evolution: Coffee and the Rise of National Governments in Central America* (Chapel Hill: University of North Carolina Press, 1976), chapter 9.

17. Hence "Conquest Indian" monuments are a ubiquitous totem in most Central American capitals. Such mythologized figures include Moctezuma in Mexico, Tecún Uman in Guatemala, Lempera in Honduras, Atlacatl in El Salvador, and Nicarao in Nicaragua.

18. On the sociology of the Salvadoran elite in comparative context of Central American economic development, *see* especially Williams, *States and Social Evolution*; and Erik Ching and Virginia Tilley, "Indians, the Military, and the 1932 Rebellion in El Salvador," *Journal of Latin American Studies*, 30 (1998).

19. A security community, in the writings of Karl Deutsch, is a group of states that "possess a compatibility of core values derived from common institutions, and mutual responsiveness — a matter of mutal identity and loyalty, a sense of 'we-ness,' and are integrated to the point that they entertain 'dependable expectations of peaceful change'" (Emanuel Adler and Michael Barnett, *Security Communities* (New York: Cambridge University Press, 1998], 7). The concept has recently been revived in international relations theory to explain new alliance patterns and identity politics among states in the post-Cold War era.

20. Alberto Masferrer, *Paginas Escogidas* (San Salvador: Ministerio de Educación Departamento Editorial, 1961; orig. 1923).

21. José Vasconcellos, "La Raza Cósmica," in *José Vasconcellos*, ed. Justina Sarabia (Madric: Ediciones de Cultura Hispánica, 1989); Vasconcellos, "Indología," in *José Vasconcellos*, ed. Sarabia.

22. The relation of race to climate was a contemporary theme: *see*, for example, Argentinian nationalist José Ingenieros, "La Formación de una Raza Argentina," *R. de Filosofia*, 11 (1915), 471.

23. Vasconcelos also sometimes uses the term "ethnic groups" but primarily in reference to White European differences: for example, "Indología," 46.

24. "La Raza Cósmica," 38.

25. José Vasconcelos and Manuel Gamio, *Aspects of Mexican Civilization* (Chicago: University of Chicago Press, 1926), 100–102.

26. "La Raza Cósmica," 33, emphasis added.

27. On "civilization" as a discourse related to empire-building, *see* Gerrit W. Gong, *The Standard of "Civilization" in International Society* (Oxford: Clarendon Press, 1984).

28. Masferrer, in "Todavía no existe la raza" [As yet, the race does not exist], in *Paginas Escogidas*, 253.

29. Masferrer, in "Todavía no existe la raza," 255, emphasis in original.

30. Masferrer (1927), "El Grito de Batalla," in *Paginas Escogidas*, 262, emphasis added.

31. Masferrer (1927), "El Grito de Batalla," 263, emphases in original.

32. *In the Shadow of the Nation: Being Indian in El Salvador* (Pittsburgh: University of Pittsburgh Press, forthcoming), Chapters 6 through 8. *See also* Ching and Tilley, "Indians, the Military, and the 1932 Rebellion."

33. Charles R. Hale, *Resistance and Contradiction: Miskitu Indians and the Nicaraguan State, 1894–1987* (Stanford, CA: Stanford University Press, 1994).

34. For an ethnic analysis of highland violence in the 1980s, *see* Timothy C. Brown, *The Real Contra War* (Norman: University of Oklahoma Press, 2001). On the Salvadoran movement, *see* especially Mac Chapin, *La Población Indigena de El Salvador* (San Salvador: Ministerio de Educación, Dirección de Publicaciones e Impresos, 1990).

35. On Mexican Sinophobia, *see* Knight, "Racism, Revolution, and *Indigenismo*."

36. *See* especially Kay Warren, *Indigenous Movements and Their Critics* (Princeton, NJ: Princeton University Press, 1999). On the Maya movement, *see* Santiago Bastos and Manuela Camus, *Entre el Mecapal y el Cielo: Desarollo del Movimiento Maya en Guatemala* (Guatemala City: FLACSO and Cholsamaj, 2002).

3

Creating a Racial Paradise
Citizenship and Sociology in Hawai'i

LORI PIERCE

Race, an ideological imperative that ranks people according to Eurocentric norms, imposes a specific kind of order on the creative chaos of identity. Racial hierarchies were created in the wake of the expansion of capitalism and the political systems required to sustain markets. States competing for scarce resources exerted their control over land and natural resources and the cultural assets of communities. The migrations of peoples between states created multiple narratives of belonging and conflicting visions of identity. Mythologies, facts, theories, scholarly frameworks, fantasies, and desires inflect the history of a place. These competing historical narratives impede our ability to analyze how racial ideologies function in a particular place or historical moment.

Hawai'i provides an example of the confluence of these forces and the complexity of comprehending race, ethnicity, identity, and citizenship. Over the course of only a few hundred years, Hawai'i was re-invented many times over; for people indigenous to Hawai'i, *kānaka maoli*, the *'āina* (land) gave birth to the people; for European explorers, the Sandwich Islands were discovered at the height of the expansion of global imperialism; for the descendants of the chiefs known as Kamehameha, Hawai'i comprised the chiefdoms as far north as Kaua'i and as far south as Hawai'i. For New England missionaries, moved by the plight of men and women living in primitive darkness, Hawai'i became an outpost of Christian civilization, capitalist enterprise, and American democratic ideals. For post-Christian Hawaiians, Hawai'i was no longer just the land and the legends of their community, but the *aupuni*, the governing authority, a constitutional monarchy. For the thousands of migrant workers who were brought to Hawai'i to labor and create profit, Hawai'i was a foreign land — *Tan Heung San* ("Sandalwood mountains") for the Chinese; for their children, it was home. For the White missionary descendants who fomented the overthrow of the monarchy, Hawai'i was a frontier whose resources were traded to the U.S. government in exchange for military and economic protection.

All of these stories make alternative claims to the truth. The facts can be shaped in a variety of directions and still remain stubbornly twisted. This chapter will provide a brief analysis of the meaning of race and the construction of racial and ethnic identities in Hawai'i by examining the question of citizenship and race in the nineteenth century and the representation of race and ethnicity in the work of sociologists in the early twentieth century. The racial ideologies imposed on Hawai'i originated in the United States. White Americans in Hawai'i created laws, social bureaucracies, and cultural theories that protected them — physically and metaphysically — from the non-White majority population.

Foreign and native in the kingdom of Hawai'i

The questions of who was foreign and who was native, of what it meant to be Hawaiian, are central to untangling the complicated history of race and ethnicity in Hawai'i. The fact that the Hawaiian term for White Europeans and Americans, *Haole*, means "foreigner" is telling. The fact that the term is still used is even more revealing. The gradual incursion of Haole into Hawai'i and the gradual insinuation of western values (which implicitly promoted White supremacy) into Hawaiian culture set the terms for the racial discourse that was to follow during the Territorial period (1900–1959). As a minority community, White Americans established laws and institutions designed to protect themselves. Using the language of democracy and equality, they were able to assert a form of White supremacy that relied not on oppressing the majority non-White population, but on insuring their own protection by the promotion of racial equality.

Understanding race in Hawai'i requires an awareness of how Hawaiians recognized their own identity and how they dealt with the growing encroachment of foreigners. Hawaiian *mo'olelo* recorded their origins from the land and from the sea: Hawaiians knew that their ancestors had migrated to Hawai'i from *kahiki*, a word that can refer to Tahiti, but also means "foreign country." But Hawaiians also understood themselves to be descended from the land in a very fundamental, even a metaphysical way. Papa and Wakea were the progenitors of the Hawaiian Islands and people. Papa and Wakea gave birth to a daughter, Ho'ohokulani. After mating with her father, Ho'ohokulani gave birth to a stillborn child, Haloa, who was planted in the earth where *Kalo*, the taro plant, grew. Ho'ohokulani gave birth to a second child, also called Haloa, who was the progenitor of the Hawaiian people.[1] Hawaiians, then, were blood relatives to *kalo*, the life-sustaining root crop that when cooked and kneaded becomes *poi*. Hawaiians were kin to *kalo*, to the land and all that sustained life. The people existed in a reciprocal relation to their environment, a relationship that was mediated by *akua*, superior beings who sometimes took human or animal forms.[2]

The hierarchy that existed between people, both *ali'i* (chiefs) and *maka'āinana* (commoners), and the gods was replicated in day-to-day life. The *ali'i* who ruled Hawai'i did so because they possessed *mana* or power. *Mana* could be expressed in a number of ways — through an auspicious genealogy, personal charisma, or by excelling at war.[3] *Ali'i*, like *akua*, were responsible for maintaining the good order of the worlds by protecting the people from harm. This they did by maintaining a strict order in society so that crops, fishponds, and natural resources were maintained. In exchange for regulating the overall functioning of society, the *maka'āinana* gave their *ali'i* allegiance, loyalty and, above all, *aloha*.

On the eve of contact with Westerners, Hawaiian society had developed a complex, logical set of social relationships geared toward maintaining the production of food through *mālama 'āina*, care for the land. Each island was divided into large districts, *ahupua'a* that ran from the mountains to the shoreline and into the sea. *Ahupua'a* were subdivided into smaller districts, each with a *konohiki* (chief) who oversaw lesser chiefs, *kaukau ali'i*. The highest chiefs could eventually garner enough power to rule an entire island. Internecine warfare was not uncommon as success in war was an expression of *mana*. By the time of Captain Cook's arrival in Hawai'i in 1778, it had endured a series of battles that resulted in the consolidation of rule under one chief, Kamehameha.

Since Hawaiians understood themselves to exist in a kinship relationship to their food and land, naturally, they cared for the land in a most diligent fashion. The earliest Western accounts and observations and the archaeological evidence suggest that this was indeed the case. Archibald Menzies, the naturalist who sailed with Captain Vancouver to Hawai'i in 1792, was impressed with Hawaiians' agricultural cultivation and conservation:

> Every step we advance . . . plantations became more and more interesting as we could not help admiring the manner in which the little fields on both sides of us were laid out to the greatest advantage and the perseverance and great attention of the natives in adapting to every vegetable they cultivate as far as lays in their power, its proper soil and natural situation by which their fields in general are productive of good crops that far exceed in point of perfection the produce of any civilized country within the tropics.[4]

The basis of Hawaiian religious belief was this relationship to the land, which was, in turn, an expression of their identity. Hawaiians believed that their lives would be sustained as long as they were *pono* — balanced or righteous. The gods would continue to supply fish, food, and water so long as the people acted in right relationship to one another, to the lands, and to the gods. Taking care of the land, then, was not only a rational act, but also a religious one. Activities and behaviors that would result in the pollution of water or the exploitation of resources, for example, were *kapu*, or restricted. In that way, the religious, economic, and social values of Hawaiian culture were holistically integrated. To be Hawaiian was to be a part of these relationships.

Much of this changed with the arrival of foreigners. Before Captain Cook, foreigners who arrived in Hawai'i from other Pacific Islands either returned to where they had come from or were gradually incorporated in the Hawaiian society. In 1778, however, foreigners arrived in a different way — in ships that did not resemble the familiar double-hulled canoes, speaking languages that were not familiar. They also came in greater numbers and, to the consternation of Hawaiians, brought diseases and refused to leave.

Initially, the presence of foreigners was limited: White sailors traded metal, cloth, and other Western manufactured goods with Hawaiians. Because these foreigners were perceived to be powerful people, possibly even *akua* of some kind, they were approached with deference. Their persons and the material goods they carried would have possessed some of their *mana*. The chiefs of the islands visited by Cook quickly made the ships and Western goods *kapu*, reserving these goods for themselves. But, some Hawaiians violated the *kapu*, making the trinkets even more powerful.

One particularly powerful means of contact with this *mana* was available to women in the form of sexual intercourse with the men of Cook's crew. The White sailors were, from their point of view, taking part in a purely sexual encounter. Cook's crew was well aware that in some Pacific Island cultures, sexual mores were quite a bit freer than those in England. In Hawai'i, they encountered women who seemed to be especially eager to engage in sex with them. Although we have little to no understanding of these encounters from the point of view of Hawaiian women, feminist historians and anthropologists have questioned some of the traditional judgments about these women. Marshall Sahlins argues that, at least initially, these women did not deserve to be characterized as prostitutes because they did not demand money in return for their sexual favors.[5] Caroline Ralston contends that even when Hawaiian women began to ask for metal, cloth, and other goods they were not, strictly speaking, prostituting themselves — terminology which implies a Christian Eurocentric judgment of Hawaiian women's sexuality.[6] What were these women doing? Sahlins contends that if these men were perceived to be *akua* or men with a great deal of *mana*, one way to gain access to that *mana* was through pregnancy. A Hawaiian woman could advance the rank of her family by having a child by a chief or a man of higher rank than herself, thus, giving her access to a higher status. *Maka'āinana* women who eagerly sought sex with White sailors were not lascivious, but were using sex as a means to elevate the status of their families. This interpretation is substantiated by an event that must have struck the sailors as peculiar: As they were leaving Kaua'i in March of 1779, several canoes pulled up to the ships. The Hawaiian men boarded and placed the detached umbilical cords of babies into the cracks of the ship's deck. Historian Mary Kawena Pukui says: "Cook was first thought to be the god Lono, and the ship his floating island. What woman wouldn't want her baby's piko there?"[7]

There is no evidence to confirm whether or not the children born of these encounters did, in fact, elevate the status of their mothers. They may not have survived or perhaps, by the time they were born, there was a changing sense of what kind of *mana* these foreigners carried. What is known is that very soon afterward, Hawaiians began to die of the diseases brought by the Haole.

Epidemic disease became a fact of life in Hawai'i after 1778. Historians have recorded at least ten major epidemics including influenza, mumps, cholera, and leprosy — throughout the course of the nineteenth century. These epidemics and the rapid spread of venereal diseases had a devastating effect on the fertility of Hawaiians and the health of their children for generations.[8] The debilitation of Hawaiian fertility combined with epidemics that killed thousands caused a population collapse of over 90 percent between 1778 and the end of the nineteenth century.[9]

What effect disease had on the lives of ordinary Hawaiians can only be imagined. Mass deaths and the arrival of foreigners as traders and missionaries caused a great deal of confusion and perhaps a loss of faith in traditional social structures. Foreigners were both a blessing and a curse. Clearly, their diseases were dangerous and unwanted. But, foreigners helped to establish Hawai'i as a modern nation-state with laws and treaties that Europeans were bound to respect. In that way, British and American settlers in Hawai'i attempted to shield it from economic and political exploitation by other Europeans. The members of the Kamehameha dynasty clearly trusted and relied on the advice and counsel of European foreigners, many of whom become a part of Hawai'i, a part of *aupuni* (government) if not *lāhui* (the people).[10] However, other foreigners — traders, merchants, beachcombers, and sailors — who lived alongside of but not among Hawaiians, did not necessarily enjoy such high regard. Many White men took Hawaiian women as mates, but had a tendency to abandon them. Laws established in the 1830s required foreign men to swear to become citizens before they could marry Native women.[11]

The foreign community played an increasingly important role in Kingdom of Hawai'i. British and American advisors to the *ali'i* gradually established a form of government in which Hawaiian values were grafted onto a constitutional monarchy. Jonathan Osorio demonstrates that, in addition to being converted to Christianity, Hawaiians also had to be converted to ideologies of Western law and government. This conversion entailed, among other things, creating categories of citizenship that clashed with Hawaiian understandings of identity and what it meant to be part of *lāhui*. Citizenship and ethnic identity clashed in most unfortunate ways. For Hawaiians, leadership meant that it was the responsibility and duty of the *ali'i* to make decisions about issues that protected the entire community. But, Hawaiians were not merely retainers on the land, doing the bidding of chiefs. Chiefs were considered temporary residents because they could be dismissed in the wake of war or other political upheavals. Further, *maka'āinana* were free to leave an *ahupua'a* if they did not like the way they were being treated. Although traditional Hawaiian government was not democratic in the modern sense of the word, Hawaiians certainly had recourse to change their political and social circumstances.

The shift to a constitutional monarchy had unforeseen repercussions. Hawaiians who were elected legislators were reluctant to interfere in some forms of decision making because this form of shared power was so antithetical to traditional models of leadership. The constitutional monarchy and legislative process "turned the traditional notion of authority and rule on its head through a legal chain in which, first, traditional authority was subsumed beneath the law, and second, the power to compose that law was appropriated by an institution declaring itself to represent the interests of the people."[12] Further, when Hawaiians were dissatisfied with taxes or other laws passed by the legislature, they used a very traditional means of protesting, — petition. They trusted that if their voices were heard, the chiefs would remedy the situation. Under the constitutional system, their voices were noted, but often their concerns were ignored.

One of the most difficult questions that had to be dealt with by the government of Hawai'i throughout the nineteenth century was how to manage the foreign community and create laws that accommodated both Hawaiians and Haole. Since Hawaiians and Haole had fundamentally different approaches to the basic concepts of law, democracy, land, and citizenship, conflict was inevitable. For example, in 1848, the Kingdom established the laws and bureaucracies needed to effect a Western-style land tenure system (the Māhele), enabling individuals to own land. Foreigners saw the Māhele as a great opportunity for Hawaiians, because they believed that land ownership was the key to liberating Hawai'i from its "feudal" social structure. When Hawaiians became "independent" of their chiefs, able to work the land to their own satisfaction, then Hawai'i would become a civilized as well as a Christianized nation. Individual effort and participation in a capitalist economy was crucial to creating a modern Hawai'i.

The reluctance of Hawaiians to take advantage of the Māhele mystified the Haole, especially the missionaries who believed that hard work was a sign of God's blessing and the key to earning God's grace. In their eyes, land ownership was the future of Hawai'i and the failure of Hawaiians to cultivate their lands could only be seen as laziness. Minister of Education, Richard Armstrong, put it this way: "If you now continue poor, needy, living in disorder in miserable huts, your lands lying waste and passing into other hands, whose fault will it be? Whose but yours?"[13]

Eventually, foreigners began to press for the right to own land themselves. If Hawaiians were not going to cultivate the land and make it a productive part of the capitalist economy, why should not foreigners be able to take advantage of the situation? In 1850, the Legislature gave foreigners the right to own land in fee simple. This act provoked an outcry from Hawaiians who sent dozens of petitions to the Legislature. Hawaiians had a visceral reaction against foreign land ownership; if foreigners could own and control the land, not only were they acting like the *ali'i* but they were becoming part of Hawai'i in an unnatural way. After all, to be Hawaiian meant existing in a kinship relationship to the land. How could a foreigner actually *be* Hawaiian?

Land ownership brought the question of citizenship to the fore. The laws of citizenship and naturalization in Hawai'i were unusually generous, but designed to protect the rights of Hawaiians from foreigners who might take advantage of them. The first laws that regulated foreigners were those aimed at beachcombers and ship-deserting sailors who came to the port towns of Honolulu and Lahaina. In 1822, foreigners were required to post a bond of $60 if they wanted to come ashore, to be forfeited if they caused trouble or were responsible for any damage. Foreign men who wished to marry Hawaiian women had to obtain permission from the governor of the island, post a bond, and swear allegiance to the King.[14]

Taking an oath of allegiance to the King, required of those who wished to own and operate businesses in Hawai'i, vote, or serve in public offices, was offensive to many foreigners. British and Americans were particularly reluctant to give up their native citizenship. Some foreigners preferred to retain their rights of inheritance in their native lands; Americans seemed philosophically opposed to swearing allegiance to a King or Kingdom. As foreigners became more influential and as Hawaiians continued to die, laws regarding citizenship and voting were gradually loosened to favor foreigners. Soon, a foreigner was allowed to become a naturalized citizen after less than a year, providing that she or he was not a fugitive from crime and was a person of good character. The law also allowed foreigners to apply for denizenship, which effectively gave them all the rights to citizenship without having to swear allegiance to the King or give up their native citizenship. The King or the Privy Council even had the right to confer "[l]etters Patent of Denization upon any alien resident abroad, or temporarily resident in this Kingdom . . . conferring upon such alien, without abjuration of native allegiance, all the rights privileges and immunities of a native."[15] By 1854, an act that removed all disabilities from aliens was passed by the legislature. This act "meant that the foreign residents were only one step below the natives in their rights, and that naturalization meant but little. Foreign influence had again broken down one more barrier against aliens."[16]

By the middle of the nineteenth century, foreigners, whether naturalized or temporary residents, enjoyed the same rights as Hawaiians. In the eyes of the law, according to the American democratic tradition, all parties were equal. But, from the point of view of Hawaiians, there was something fundamentally offensive about equality, which threatened to supplant the basis of Hawaiian identity. If, in the eyes of the law, it meant the same thing to be a resident of Hawai'i as it did to be a Hawaiian, then who was the government representing?

In spite of objections by Hawaiians, foreign entrepreneurs began buying and leasing large plots of land and pursued the production of sugarcane on large plantations. Chinese, Japanese, Koreans, Portuguese, Filipinos, Puerto Ricans, Norwegians, Germans, and Swedes were brought, or encouraged to come, to Hawai'i as laborers from the 1840s until the 1920s.[17] In 1900, the year the American annexation of Hawai'i became official, nearly 60 percent of the population of Hawai'i was foreign-born.[18] Chinese were the first to be recruited and indentured; between 1851 and 1864, a few hundred Chinese were brought to Hawai'i as plantation workers on three-to-five-year contracts. After the sugar planters secured a Reciprocity Treaty with the United States in 1876, the industry expanded. "In 1878, some 2,464 Chinese, nearly all men, arrived. . . . An additional 3,812 . . . landed in 1879, then 2,505 in 1880, then 3,924 in 1881."[19] By 1900, some 46,000 Chinese resided in Hawai'i.

After Chinese immigrants worked out the terms of their contracts, many farmed rice or taro, or opened their own dry-good stores and *poi* factories. Planters then turned to Japan and in spite of its initial reluctance to allow its citizens to migrate, the Japanese government relented. In 1882, Chinese workers were 49 percent of the workforce on the plantations. By 1892, Japanese workers represented 63 percent of the total workforce. By 1902, they were 73 percent of all plantation workers.[20] Between 1890 and 1930, the Japanese population of Hawai'i jumped from 12,610 to 139,631 — an increase that reflected immigration as well as natural growth.[21] On the eve of World War II, the Japanese community represented nearly 40 percent of the total population.[22]

Filipino immigration to Hawai'i was a late development, peaking well after the annexation in 1898. Filipino workers began coming to Hawai'i in relatively small numbers in the early 1900s; by 1940, they were 12 percent of the total population. Koreans also migrated during these years, forming a community of roughly 6,000 before World War II. Nearly all the other immigrant groups represented experiments on the part of planters to secure a reliable, cheap supply of labor. European immigrants, who were more likely to bring families, proved to be prohibitively expensive. What is more, White plantation owners seemed to believe that White men were racially "unsuited" for grueling labor in the tropical heat.[23] Other Euroamericans who worked on the plantations were supervisors or managers. Ronald Takaki noted that the Hawai'i Sugar Planter's Association (HSPA) made this their official policy in 1904: "[T]he HSPA trustees adopted a resolution that ... [stated] that all skilled positions should be filled by 'American citizens, or those eligible for citizenship.' The restrictions had a racial function, for it excluded from skilled occupations Asians or immigrants regarded as not white' according to federal law and hence ineligible to become naturalized citizens."[24] The 1890 census depicted Hawai'i in this way: 89,990 people lived in Hawai'i; about a third of the population lived on O'ahu. Of the 31,000 who lived on O'ahu, 22,000 lived in Honolulu. The next largest city in the Kingdom was Hilo, which had a population of just over 9,000. The majority of the population, then, lived in rural areas. In 1890, just over 40,000 were Hawaiian or part Hawaiian; 6,220 were Haole; 12,719 were Portuguese; 16,752 were Chinese; 12,610 were Japanese. Roughly 53 percent of the population was born in Hawai'i. On the eve of annexation to the United States, Hawai'i was a rural, agricultural, Hawaiian and Asian-immigrant community.[25]

The complex political rivalries that led to the overthrow of the monarchy are more thoroughly discussed elsewhere.[26] Suffice it to say that as White foreigners gained control over the political economy of Hawai'i, they became more dissatisfied with the monarchy. In 1887, after a series of scandals, they foisted a new constitution on King Kalakaua. He signed it under duress and it became known as the Bayonet Constitution. From the point of view of Hawaiians, the Bayonet Constitution undermined the power and authority of the King; he was no longer allowed to appoint or dismiss his ministers, and any official act of the King had to be validated by the cabinet. The constitution also consolidated the power of White foreigners by disfranchising naturalized citizens of Hawai'i from China. This constitution, meant to address what White foreigners saw as corruption and rule by fiat, became the signal issue in the overthrow of Kalakaua's sister and successor, Lili'uokalani.

In 1900, when Hawai'i became an official territory of the United States, the census depicted Hawai'i in this way: 154,001 people resided in Hawai'i, 58,504 on the Island of O'ahu, 39,306 in Honolulu. The next largest town of Hilo had a population of 19,785. Roughly 75 percent of the population lived outside of the only urban area of the Territory. 39,656 of the residents of the territory were Hawaiian or part Hawaiian; 8,547 were White; 25,767 were Chinese; 61,111 were Japanese. Approximately 41 percent were foreign born. In 1900, of 90,172 workers gainfully employed, 55,931 were employed in agriculture. In 1900, Hawai'i remained, a rural, Asian immigrant, and Hawaiian community. [27]

The Organic Acts, the legal structure that reconciled the laws of Hawai'i to the laws of the United States, provided United States citizenship to anyone who had been a citizen of the Republic of Hawai'i. This included over 700 Chinese and three Japanese.[28] Chinese who were not citizens of the Republic were denied American citizenship. Hawai'i became a complicated mix of race and ethnicity, citizens and migrants, *maka'ainana* and "Americans."

The racial laboratory: studying race in Hawai'i

By the 1920s, Hawai'i was a community fraught with racial tensions. The legacy of the overthrow left many Hawaiians politically alienated and economically marginalized. The growing Asian workforce meant that Hawaiians were gradually being replaced in their own land. By 1930, Hawaiians were only 13 percent of the population. Euroamerican Whites were, by all measures, a minority community — about 12 percent in 1930; however, they were over-represented as the heads of all the major businesses in Hawai'i.[29] The non-White labor force of Asians and Hawaiians organized unions and struck the plantations, wharves, docks, and other industries repeatedly, fighting for higher wages and better living conditions.[30]

It was into this complicated cultural mix that Romanzo Adams entered in 1920. Although he had no special expertise in race relations, by the time of his death in 1942, Adams was one of the foremost authorities on race in the Territory. Romanzo Adams arrived at the newly incorporated University of Hawai'i in the spring of 1920.[31] Adams was a senior scholar arriving at a decidedly junior university, a campus whose buildings were still in the process of being built, and which was plagued by flies.[32] The university shared classroom facilities with McKinley High School and library of Bishop Museum until their own library was completed in 1925.[33]

Adams earned his Ph.D. in Sociology from the University of Chicago in 1904. He was particularly adept at demography and statistics and within a few years applied his expertise to the Territory. With the help of his students who became his research partners, Adams began to write popular and scholarly works that became the authoritative studies of race, ethnicity, and immigration in Hawai'i for more than a generation. His seminal work, *Interracial Marriage in Hawai'i*, is still a definitive study of the demography of race and ethnicity in Hawai'i.

Under Adams's leadership, Hawai'i briefly became an important outpost in the development of the sociological theory of race in the United States. Diverse populations living in close proximity in a relatively uncomplicated social environment, made Hawai'i a perfect "laboratory" for the study of race and immigrant assimilation. Robert Park, the University of Chicago sociologist, was a contemporary of Adams and came to the University of Hawai'i as a visiting scholar in 1931–1932. Park's student, Andrew Lind, would go on to become one of Adams's successors at the University of Hawai'i. Bernhard Hormann, Emory Bogardus, William Carlson Smith, Jitsuichi Masuoka, Margaret Lam, and Clarence Glick — all known for their work on race relations or early Asian American studies — wrote about ethnicity in Hawai'i. These social theorists found Hawai'i to be a perfect laboratory — it was a term they liked to use — for testing their theories of race and assimilation.

What made Hawai'i even more attractive as a racial laboratory was the fact that it seemed not to have a race problem. There were no Jim Crow statutes barring non-Whites from schools or public accommodations; there was little *de facto* segregation in housing and the social life of Honolulu appeared to be integrated. Most importantly, there was little public sentiment or legal barrier to interracial dating, sexual relations, or marriage. The children of such unions were seemingly a well-accepted and well-adjusted part of the local community. Adams, who was always careful to maintain scholarly objectivity in his work, was clearly fascinated by the situation in Hawai'i. Although he recognized that the plantations maintained rigid racial hierarchies, which determined work assignments and wages, and that individuals in Hawai'i were as capable of bigotry as any other American, he noted that the social mores were open and tolerant enough to encourage interracial marriage. By understanding the factors that made interracial marriage acceptable, he argued that it was possible to understand race and ethnicity in Hawai'i.

In 1925, Adams' *The Peoples of Hawai'i* opened with this astonishing paragraph: "There is abundant evidence that the peoples of Hawai'i are in process of becoming one people. After a time the terms now commonly used to designate the various groups according to the country of birth or ancestry will be forgotten. There will be no Portuguese, no Chinese, no Japanese, — only American."[34] At a time when Asian immigrants and their children were being systematically excluded from political and social life in the United States,

Adams seems to be suggesting something unprecedented: Asian immigrants and their children in Hawai'i were not only adapting to the United States, they were well on their way to being assimilated. Contrary to the beliefs of most White Americans, Asians assimilated, and did so successfully. For sociologists of race concerned with Asian immigration and assimilation, this was a remarkable assertion. If Adams could prove that Asians in Hawai'i were capable of being fully assimilated, his work would demonstrate that the sociological theories of race relations were sound and that Hawai'i had somehow gotten it right.

Two theoretical premises are illuminated in Adams's study of Hawai'i: the race relations cycle and the theory of social distance. Robert Park is credited with the theory of the race relations cycle, which described what happened to groups as they encountered each in the modern, urban settings. Park used this model to describe how immigrants went from being foreigners to fully assimilated Americans. He theorized that immigrant groups moved through several stages — contact, competition, accommodation, and assimilation — a process that was inevitable and irreversible. In the first stage, immigrant groups had limited contact with the mainstream community, living isolated lives in ghettos or ethnic enclaves. In the realm of employment, they faced competition, sometimes literally true but more often it was merely the perception of competition for scarce jobs or access to other economic resources. Eventually, as immigrants dropped their language, institutions, and other practices, which made them objectionable to the outside community, they were accommodated by the larger society. Once their behavior changed, once they assimilated, they would no longer be subject to discrimination. Discrimination and racism were understood to be the natural by-products of the race relations cycle, an inevitable but temporary result of group interaction. Left alone and without any outside interference, immigrants would naturally assimilate.[35]

The race relations cycle is premised on an understanding of the concept of "social distance."[36] Social distance, according to Park, was a measure of "race consciousness." Another contemporary of Park's, Emory Bogardus, a sociologist at the University of Southern California developed a survey designed to measure social distance by monitoring individual's reactions to various ethnic groups. In order to assess "social distance," participants were asked questions such as, "Would you willingly admit members of another race to your street or to your workplace?" The social distance scale measured how close someone would allow a member of another race to move into her or his life. From exclusion from the country altogether, at the extreme, to marriage and kinship, at the most intimate, the social distance scale tracked the gradual assimilation (or lack thereof) of Armenians, Filipinos, Greeks, Irish, Italians, Japanese Jews, Mexicans, Blacks, Scots, and Finns. Whereas Park speculated on the idea of social distance, Bogardus devised "racial distance quotients," 1.00 being as close as kinship and 7.00 being as distant as exclusion from the country.[37]

Both of these theoretical models for understanding the social process of assimilation influenced Adams's work. In fact, *Interracial Marriage*, both the text and the social text, prove the soundness of these theories and ultimately showcase Hawai'i as a place where race relations worked. If marriage were a barometer of a lack of social distance between ethnic groups, then high rates of intermarriage should indicate a high rate of social assimilation among ethnic groups in a diverse society.

In *Interracial Marriage*, Adams gives a full account of race relations in Hawai'i, using marriage as a barometer of social distance. Adams' argument was founded on four central ideas: first, equality had been an esteemed social value in Hawai'i since first contact with Europeans. Second, this value of egalitarianism was publicly enacted and symbolized. Third, the diversity of groups that came to Hawai'i adopted this set of values, and enjoyed relatively close social contacts. Fourth, close social contacts and a preexisting code of egalitarianism led to a high rate of interracial marriage, resulting in a large class of hybrids or mixed-race people.

Adams argued that the pattern of stable race relations in Hawai'i was premised on a "historic accident"— the precedent set by the encounter between Hawaiians and Haole beginning in 1778. "Why, in Hawai'i, did the people of British and American origin fail to set up obstacles that are so commonly found where English-speaking people have established contacts with the darker races?"[38] He described Hawaiian cultural values that dictated the terms of this first interethnic encounter. Hawaiians, he suggested, had a relatively more relaxed view of marriage and family relationships, enjoying a tradition of free marriage that enabled Hawaiian women to choose to be with White men. These pairings resulted in the first generation of mixed-race children who were accepted within the Hawaiian community, not cast out or ostracized. The pattern of race relations, then, was established within the context of sexual relations. Because Hawaiian women had sex and children with Haole men, Adams argued that this determined the pattern of interethnic relations from that point forward.

Once the pattern of egalitarianism in sexual relations had been set, Adams argued that everyone who subsequently migrated to Hawai'i moderated their own cultural values in order to harmonize with Hawaiian values. Here, Adams stressed the public nature of racial mores. The initial encounter between Hawaiians and Haole, and the continuation of the alliance between these two groups in ruling Hawai'i for many generations, meant that racial segregation of any type was never legislated. There could be no segregation in Hawai'i because Hawaiians would not allow it. This lack of legal racial discrimination, along with a pre-established sense of egalitarianism, led to a set of public mores to which all groups subscribed. No matter what their private sentiments, they were tempered by public actions that symbolized equality. "A man of any race is addressed as 'Mister' in Hawai'i . . . [I]n Honolulu a Chinese man or a man of any other race may be entertained in any hotel and white men may sit at the table with him."[39] Adams drew a sharp contrast to the segregation that was the norm in American cities. He reiterated the importance of this public, ritualistic enactment of racial equality. No matter what a person or a community believed in private, if the community values dictated a certain kind of equal treatment this eventually would affect the nature of race relations. "He may not accept all the implications of the ritual [of equality] . . . he may profess doctrines of a contrary character. But, the existence of these contrary sentiments and beliefs is a matter of second-rate importance. The really important thing is the general body of tradition that inhibits the open and constant avowal of such attitudes. In the conflict between antagonistic mores, the sentiment that cannot be openly avowed, that cannot be expressed in slogans, and that cannot influence civil law or the social code is ineffective."[40]

This public code is crucial to Adams' explication of Hawaii' race relations. They symbolized a value of egalitarianism, but they also led to closer social contact between the various ethnic groups in Hawai'i. Public schools, for example, were not legally segregated because they *could not* be. Racial segregation would be a violation of this public ethos. Therefore, children of all groups mixed and socialized, decreasing the social distances and leading to a greater chance of interracial marriage. The chances of interracial marriage in Hawai'i were also increased by the fact that plantation owners imported a large number of unmarried men who married local women, and because they imported laborers from so many different places in so short a period of time.

In *Interracial Marriage*, Adams carefully examined the rates of intermarriage for all the ethnic groups in Hawai'i, determining that not all groups intermarry at the same rate. The Japanese and Haole, for example, had relatively low rates of intermarriage when compared to other ethnic groups. But overall, Adams predicted that interracial marriage would continue apace in Hawai'i. "If marriage across racial lines is permitted it will take place, and, through such marriage, there will gradually come into existence a more or less homogenous mixed-blood population."[41] Because of the value of egalitarianism, Adams believed that this homogenous class could play a special role in defusing any possible source of racial tension. "The mixed-bloods have an especial role in relation to the further process of cultural assimilation of the parent groups and in relation to further amalgamation."[42] Because Hawai'i had none of the problems of a caste-based society, mixed-race children were not consigned to an inferior status, but were free to move about the society and establish contacts across ethnic lines. As members of two ethnic groups, in a society where public antagonisms between groups were disallowed, the mixed-race population did not feel pushed to identify strongly with either parent group. Over time, this led to a diminution of tension between groups and a decline of private prejudices.

Adams discussed the history of Hawaii's various ethnic groups in *Interracial Marriage*, describing the degree to which they had assimilated and the factors that led to or impeded cross-racial mixes. For example, he considered Hawaiians to be "an amalgamating race," because they experienced the highest rates of interracial marriage. In addition to the historical precedent set by early interracial marriage between Hawaiians and Haole in the early nineteenth century, Hawaiian women, he argued, were more inclined to marry White and Chinese men because those men proved to be better providers than Hawaiian men. White and Chinese men also provided Hawaiian women with access to greater social prestige and economic advantages. The children of these unions were influenced by their fathers' cultures to work hard and get a good education, leaving them in a position to assimilate fully into Americanized Hawai'i. All of these elements, working in concert with the natural social process of immigrant groups assimilating to a new culture, helped to explain Hawaii's unorthodox race relations. Race relations in Hawai'i worked because they had always worked and were constantly improving. The unique historical circumstances established a pattern of behavior that other groups adopted. The lack of legalized discrimination created a public sentiment that Adams believed would, in time, affect private belief. Interracial marriage, facilitated by the natural social process of assimilation, created an emergent class of mixed-race people who would eventually replace distinct ethnic communities and the exclusive loyalties they demanded. Hawai'i truly could be the model for race relations for the United States, perhaps the world.

Adams' vision of Hawaii's unorthodox doctrine of race based on its history and social conditions was whole-heartedly embraced by the local community and by sociologists of race relations. Adams presented Hawai'i with a vision of itself that, while not perfect, was flattering and optimistic. The racial tensions that the community was experiencing on the plantations, for example, would not be a permanent blot on the Territory. The plantations themselves were an aberration in the history of race relations. Plantations, according to Andrew Lind, introduced racial distinctions to Hawai'i: "Prior to the plantation era, the only important distinction with any clear resemblance to race observed in Hawai'i was between the natives and the foreigners and this distinction was primarily cultural and did not necessarily imply a difference in status or class."[43] Because Hawaii's leaders had established and remained committed to American democratic traditions, race relations would move smoothly along. Immigrants would continue to assimilate so long as barriers to their success were not erected. Instances of prejudice and discrimination were not structural but were part of the larger race relations cycle and would abate over time.

This was a very reassuring vision based on a pragmatic assessment of the facts of demography and a hopeful vision of the future. But, there are several sources of tensions between the texts — the written text of *Interracial Marriage* and the social text Adams studied. For example, the assimilation model of ethnicity operates on three premises: first the model was built around the movement of immigrants through the social process. Second, it is a model that was based on the experiences of immigrants in urban settings. Finally, it was a model based on the experiences of White European immigrants. These premises were only partly applicable to the case of Hawai'i. The majority of Hawaii's population was immigrants, but Hawaiians were not. Did the assimilation model of race relations pertain to indigenous people? Was the process of assimilation the same? If so, into what were Hawaiians being asked to assimilate?

Adams' work pertains primarily to the urban setting of Honolulu in the early twentieth century. He was examining how immigrants adjusted once they had moved off the plantations and into urban Honolulu and Hilo. But, between 1900 and 1930, more than 70 percent of Hawaii's population lived in rural areas of the Territory, largely on the plantations. Adams argued that the rates of intermarriage were the same in rural and urban settings of Hawai'i, but he speculated on the future of Hawai'i based on the actions of a small percentage of the population. The trend Adams saw moved toward the collapsing of social distance to the point where "nationalities" no longer mattered. Ethnic identity would fracture to the point where it was meaningless.

However, what was happening on the plantations was not the fracturing of ethnicity, but the gradual consolidation of ethnicity around class lines — "locals" versus. Haole. Working-class plantation laborers living in close quarters in the rural areas gradually coalesced, creating political, economic, and social alliances to stand against the elite class of Whites who ran the plantations and social bureaucracies. "Local" as a pan-ethnic identity based on class distinctions between Asian and Hawaiian workers on the one hand and Haole owners and managers on the other, emerged in rural Hawai'i and was reinforced through language and the common experiences of Hawaii's working-class majority.

The race relations cycle, based on social theories derived from the experiences of White European ethnic groups in Chicago, New York, and other metropolitan areas, were ill-equipped to deal with race, racial ideologies, and the entrenchment of institutional racial discrimination. Park argued that "prejudice against the Japanese in the United States is merely the prejudice which attaches to every alien and immigrant people."[44] Adams acknowledged that there were numerous instances of racial prejudice in Hawai'i, but they were exceptions to the rule. For example, Adams described the discrimination Chinese workers faced as they moved off the plantations in the late nineteenth century:

> The literature of this period abounds in expressions of fierce hatred. There were no words in the English language too strong to express the disapprobation of the publicists of the time. . . . But in all this anti-Chinese movement the language of hostility was not in terms of color. Public sentiment was directed to their behavior, not to them as representatives of the non-white race. White propagandists did not use their color or other physical traits to symbolize things that were held to be mean and contemptible in Chinese character.[45]

Instances of racial discrimination were considered to be exceptional. The Chinese faced discrimination not because of their race, but because of their behavior, which would change as they assimilated according to the race relations cycle.

Adams also insisted on the importance of distinguishing between private versus public displays of racial attitudes. Private actions were less important because the public ethos was so strongly opposed to bigoted attitudes that their public expression was not tolerated. But what of private acts with public consequences? The plantations, for example, were private enterprises. The White men who ran these plantations relied on a racial hierarchy in order to determine hiring and wages. Asian workers rarely rose to the level of management or to jobs out of the fields. Those jobs were reserved for White immigrants. The Haole owners' views were clearly antithetical to the racial egalitarianism that Adams described as the rule, not the exception, in Hawai'i. And yet, because these men had the power guaranteed to them as privileged members of a racial hierarchy, their private views had very serious public consequences.

Our understanding of race in Hawai'i is mediated through a variety of lenses. The romantic vision of the islands and the promotion of tourism invented the image of the hula maiden, the beach boy, the warm and welcoming Natives of Paradise. The sociological vision of Hawai'i as a place where race relations worked, the racial laboratory in which immigrants were studied as they made their way through the social process. As with any stereotype, there are kernels of truth, or at least fact in these visions. Hawaiian culture provided a framework for the encounters, between all the foreigners who came to call Hawai'i home and the indigenous Natives. And, for sociologists, race relations in Hawai'i were remarkable and noteworthy. In the early twentieth century when Tulsa, St. Louis, Chicago, and other cities in the continental United States were plagued with riots, when Black men and women were lynched for crimes as simple as failure to adhere to the strict codes of Jim Crow segregation, Hawai'i did not just *seem* like a racial paradise; by comparison it might well have been.

Hawai'i was not a racial paradise, but there was a deep desire to believe that it was so. If it was so, then the imposition of Western language, culture, religion, and government in Hawai'i was not an assertion of White supremacy, but the natural progress of a nation from the primitive to the modern. If it was so, then the overthrow of the monarchy was not racially motivated crime, but the natural result of good government wresting out bad. Proving that racial diversity did not necessarily lead to oppression clearly demonstrated that the American experiment could be successful even in such a remote location. At a time in American history when White supremacy clearly meant the forceful subjugation of non-Whites and those who refuse or who were unable to assimilate, Hawai'i was held up as an example to the nation of what was possible if Euroamericans conducted themselves with a sense of noblesse oblige.

Notes

1. David Malo, *Hawaiian Antiquities*, 2nd ed., trans. Nathaniel Emerson (Honolulu: Bishop Museum Special Publications #2, [1898] 1951), 244.
2. *See* David Malo, *Hawaiian Antiquities*; Samuel Kamakau, *Ka Po'e Kahiko* (Honolulu: Bishop Museum Press, 1991); John Papa Ii, *Fragments of Hawaiian History*, trans. Mary Kawena

Pukui, ed. Dorothy Barrere (Honolulu: Bishop Museum Press, 1959); and Martha Beckwith, *Hawaiian Mythology* (Honolulu: University of Hawai'i Press, 1970).

3. *See* Lilikalā Kame'eleihiwa, *Native Land and Foreign Desires: Pahea Lā E Pono Ai?* (Honolulu: Bishop Museum Press, 1992).
4. Quoted in Gary Best and Mary Best, eds., *Glimpses of Hawaiian Daily Life and Culture, 1778–1898* (New York: American Heritage, 1994), 37, 38.
5. Marshall Sahlins, *Historical Metaphors*, 39.
6. *See* Caroline Ralston, " 'Polyandry,' 'Pollution,' 'Prostitution': The Problems of Eurocentrism and Androcentrism in Polynesian Studies," in *Crossing Boundaries: Feminism and the Critique of Knowledges*, eds., Barbara Caine, E.A. Groz, and Marie de Lepervanche (Sidney: Allen and Unwin, 1988); Karina Kahananui Green, "Colonialism's Daughters: Eighteenth- and Nineteenth-Century Western Perceptions of Hawaiian Women," in *Pacific Diaspora*, eds., Paul Spickard, Joanne L. Rondilla, and Debbie Hippolite Wright (Honolulu: University of Hawai'i Press, 2002), 221–252.
7. Sahlins, *Historical Metaphors*, 41.
8. *See* O.A. Bushnell, *The Gifts of Civilization: Germs and Genocide in Hawai'i* (Honolulu: University of Hawai'i Press, 1993).
9. *See* Jonathan Osorio, *Dismembering Lāhui: A History of the Hawaiian Nation to 1887* (Honolulu: University of Hawai'i Press, 2002); David Stannard, *Before the Horror* (Honolulu: Social Science Research Institute, 1989) and O.A. Bushnell, *The Gifts of Civilization: Germs and Genocide in Hawai'i*.
10. For an extended description of how Hawaiians were literally and metaphorically incorporated into the Hawaiian government, *see* Kame'eleihiwa, *Native Land and Foreign Desires*.
11. Osorio, *Dismembering Lāhui*; *See also* Maude Jones, "Naturalization of Hawai'i 1795–1900" Manuscript, University of Hawai'i Archives, 1934.
12. Osorio, *Dismembering Lāhui*, 86.
13. Osorio, *Dismembering Lāhui*, 49.
14. Jones, "Naturalization in Hawai'i," 2.
15. Jones, "Naturalization in Hawai'i," 14.
16. Jones, "Naturalization in Hawai'i," 20
17. The first sugar plantation was established in 1835, but the 1848 gold rush and American Civil War in 1861 created a demand for sugar. Many Hawaiians worked on plantations, but because many resisted the backbreaking low-wage labor, planters looked elsewhere for laborers. *See* Edward Beechert, *Working in Hawai'i* (Honolulu: University of Hawai'i Press, 1985); Ronald Takaki, *Pau Hana: Plantation Life and Labor in Hawai'i 1835–1920* (Honolulu: University of Hawai'i Press, 1983); and Gary Okihiro, *Cane Fires: The Anti-Japanese Movement in Hawai'i, 1865–1945* (Philadelphia: Temple University Press, 1991).
18. Robert Schmitt, *Demographic Statistics of Hawai'i, 1778–1965* (Honolulu: University of Hawai'i Press, 1965), 121 [table 27].
19. Clarence Glick, *Sojourners and Settlers: Chinese Immigrants in Hawai'i* (Honolulu: University Press of Hawai'i/Hawai'i Chinese History Center, 1980), 15.
20. Takaki, *Pau Hana*, 28.
21. Paul R. Spickard, *Japanese Americans: The Formation and Transformations of an Ethnic Group* (New York: Twayne Publishers, 1996), 162.
22. Andrew Lind, *Hawaii's People* (Honolulu: University of Hawai'i Press, 1967), 28.
23. The Portuguese seemed to be the exception to this racial rule. In some other contexts they might have been considered "White. In Hawai'i the Portuguese existed in a separate racialized ethnic group and were rarely considered as part of the same race as White Europeans and Americans who occupied the upper and middle classes. Some suggest that these Portuguese may have come to Hawai'i mainly from the Azores rather than the Iberian mainland, and so have been racialized even among Portuguese.
24. Takaki, *Pau Hana*, 76.
25. Statistics drawn from Robert Schmitt, *Historical Statistics of Hawai'i* (Honolulu: University of Hawai'i Press, 1977).
26. *See* Ralph Kuykendall, *The Hawaiian Kingdom: Vol III 1874–1893* (Honolulu: University of Hawai'i Press, 1967); Gavan Daws, *Shoal of Time: A History of the Hawaiian Islands* (Honolulu: University of Hawai'i Press, 1968); William Russ, *The Hawaiian Republic* (Snellingsgrove, Pa.: Susquehanna University Press [1961], 1998). A contemporary journalistic account of the overthrow is Tom Coffman, *Nation Within: The Story of America's Annexation of the Nation of Hawai'i* (Kane'ohe, Hawai'i: Epicenter, 1999). For an account of Native Hawaiian resistance to the Overthrow, *see* Noenoe Silva, *Ku'e! The 1897 Petitions Protesting Annexation* (Honolulu: 'Ai Pohaku Press, 1998).

27. Statistics drawn from Schmitt, *Historical Statistics of Hawai'i*.
28. *U.S. Statutes at Large*, 31 (1900) Stat 141 "Organic Act: An Act to Provide a Government for the Territory of Hawai'i."
29. Five major companies "controlled 75 percent of the sugar crop by 1910, and 96 percent by 1933. By a kind of inevitable extension they came to control as well every business associated with sugar: banking; insurance; utilities; wholesale and retail merchandising; railroad transportation in the islands and between the islands and California." Daws, *Shoal of Time*, 312.
30. *See* John Reinecke, "Labor Disturbances in Hawai'i, 1890–1920," Manuscript, University of Hawai'i Archives (1966).
31. The University of Hawai'i succeeded the College of Agriculture and Mechanic Arts, founded in 1907. Kwai Fong Yap, a bank clerk with 12 children, whom he wished to see educated in Hawai'i, single-handedly lobbied for the establishment of a full fledged University in Hawai'i. *See* William Kwai Fong Yap, *The Birth and History of the University of Hawai'i* (Shanghai: Kwong Hsueh Publishers, 1933). *See also* Robert Kamins and Robert Potter, *Malamalama: A History of the University of Hawai'i* (University of Hawai'i Press, 1998).
32. A headline from the student newspaper succinctly states the problem: "Flies in lecture hall are cause of student and faculty dementia," *Ka Leo O Hawai'i*, October 15, 1931.
33. *See* Kamins and Potter, *Malamalama*, and Arthur L. Dean "Historical Sketch of the University of Hawai'i," Commencement Address, June 7, 1926 (Honolulu: University of Hawai'i Occasional Papers #5).
34. Lind, *The Peoples of Hawai'i*, 5.
35. *See* Robert Park, "Racial Assimilation in Secondary Groups with Particular Reference to the Negro," *American Journal of Sociology*, 19.5, 606–623.
36. *See* Philip Ethington, "The Intellectual Construction of Social Distance: Toward a Recovery of Georg Simmel's Social Geometry" *Cybergeo*, refereed electronic edition of *European Geography Journal* (posted September 1997 at http://www.cybergeo.presse.fr).
37. *See* Ethington, "Intellectual Construction of Social Distance."
38. Romanzo Adams, *Interracial Marriage in Hawai'i: A Study of the Mutually Conditioned Processes of Acculturation and Amalgamation* (New York: Macmillian, 1937), 44.
39. Romanzo Adams, "The Unorthodox Race Doctrine of Hawai'i," in *Comparative Perspectives on Race Relations*, ed., Melvin M. Tumin (Boston: Little, Brown, 1969), 82.
40. Adams, "Unorthodox Doctrine," 83.
41. Adams, *Interracial Marriage*, 45.
42. Adams, "Summary Statement," *Social Process in Hawai'i*, 1 (1935), n.p.
43. Andrew Lind, *Last of the Magic Isles* (London: Oxford University Press, 1969), 21.
44. Quoted in Eliot Grinnell Mears, *Resident Orientals on the American Pacific Coast* (Chicago: University of Chicago Press, 1928), 3.
45. Adams, *Interracial Marriage*, 59.

4

White into Black

Race and National Identity in Contemporary Brazil[1]

G. Reginald Daniel

Neither Black nor White: the Brazilian racial order and the ternary racial project

A Comparative-historical perspective

The Brazilian order has been contrasted with that in the United States by virtue of its history of pervasive racial and cultural blending and the validation of this process by maintaining a ternary racial project that differentiates its population into Whites (brancos), multiracial individuals (pardos), and Blacks (pretos). These dynamics have been accompanied by fluid racial and cultural markers and the absence of legalized barriers to equality in both the public and private spheres. Correspondingly, it has been argued that class and cultural, rather than racial, signifiers determine identity and status in the social hierarchy. This image was popularized in anthropologist Gilberto Freyre's monumental study of Brazilian race relations (*The Masters and the Slaves*, 1933; *The Mansions and the Shanties*, 1936; *Order and Progress*, 1959).

Brazil's "racial democracy" stands out in stark contrast to the U.S. racial order. European Americans have sought to preserve their cultural and racial "purity," as well as their dominant status, by enforcing the one-drop rule of hypodescent that designates as Black everyone of African descent. The U.S. racial order has thus supported a binary racial project that not only renders racial identification as either Black or White, but also has precluded any notion of choice in self-identification and ensured that African American ancestry has been passed on in perpetuity. Moreover, it has maintained both legal and informal barriers preventing Blacks from having contact with Whites as equals in most aspects of social life — both public barriers (e.g., political, economic, educational) and private ones (e.g., residential, associational, interpersonal). At the turn of the twentieth century, these restrictions reached drastic proportions with the institutionalization of Jim Crow segregation.[2]

Despite the absence of legalized barriers to racial equality in Brazil, as compared with the United States, data collected since the last half of the twentieth century indicate that physical appearance, if not ancestry (as in the United States), working in conjunction with class and cultural factors, significantly impact social stratification. Furthermore, the divide between haves and have-nots primarily coincides, respectively, with the racial divide between Whites (brancos) and the African Brazilian masses (negros), including both the Black and multiracial populations. These findings have not only challenged Brazil's image as a racial democracy, but also have moved conceptualization of Brazilian race relations in a direction similar to the binary racial project typified by the U.S. racial order. Examining these changes as they relate to ongoing racial formations of "Blackness" and "Whiteness" is particularly meaningful given the history of African slavery, and the unique attitudes, discourse, policy, and behavior that have crystallized around individuals of African descent in the formation of Brazil's national identity.[3]

The colonial foundation

In Brazil, where Whites were greatly outnumbered by Blacks from the early colonial era to well into the nineteenth century, multiracial individuals occupied an intermediate position in the social structure. Mulatto slave offspring were often assigned tasks that symbolized greater personal worth and required greater skill (e.g., domestics and artisans). The scarcity of White women mitigated opposition from the legal wife and enhanced the likelihood that these offspring would receive socially tolerated demonstrations of affection, as well as economic and educational protection. Furthermore, mulattoes were given preferential liberation over Blacks, who overwhelmingly were slaves. This made it possible for them in the early colonial period to enter the free classes, where they filled interstitial roles in the economy — particularly in the artisanal and skilled trades — due to a shortage of European labor and for which the use of slave labor was considered impractical.

Free Colored urban artisans, long before abolition, advanced from these interstitial positions into the arts, letters, and liberal professions (including medicine, engineering, law, and the civil service). However, they were barred from holding public office, entering high status occupations in the clergy and governmental bureaucracy, experienced limitations on educational attainment, and were denied a variety of other rights. In addition, Free Coloreds did not achieve vertical mobility through direct competition in the open market, but rather through the support of White elite patrons, who always controlled their advancement. Not surprisingly, these mulattoes feared that the end of slavery would threaten their social position. Thus, they were reluctant to oppose slavery, tended to eschew alliance with slaves, and were valuable allies in preserving the racial order.

In fact, mulattoes were so reliable that the distant Portuguese monarchs viewed Free Colored militia as a balance wheel against independence-minded

Whites. Both the Portuguese Crown and Brazilian slaveholders, as early as the seventeenth century, relied on Free Coloreds to help expel Dutch invaders, to secure Brazil's territorial borders against foreign interlopers. The planter class also utilized their services in local militia to protect their property, suppress slave uprisings, as well as capture and return fugitive slaves. European Brazilians, by granting mulattoes a social location superior to that of Blacks and Native Americans but significantly inferior to that of Whites, won their loyalty in an effort to exclude Blacks and Native Americans from power, at the same time without undermining White domination and control. The process of abolition signed and sealed this racial contract, enabling Whites to continue to rely on mulatto support long after slavery. As long as Blacks were retained in the least remunerative sectors of the secondary labor force — as agricultural, industrial, and service laborers — mulattoes settled for token integration into the skilled trades, the petty bourgeoisie, intelligentsia, and the primary white-collar labor force.

Multiracial individuals have thus been allowed token vertical mobility through a window of opportunity that historian Carl Degler calls the "mulatto escape hatch." The masses of mulattoes do not, however, gain access carte blanche to the ranks of Whites because they are mulatto as opposed to Black. Indeed, the social positioning of individuals designated as "multiracial," while intermediate in the Brazilian racial hierarchy, collectively speaking is closer to the subordinate Blacks than to the dominant Whites. Rather, Degler argues that the escape hatch is an informal social mechanism by which select "visibly" multiracial individuals — for reasons of talent, culture, or education — have been granted situational Whiteness in proportion to their phenotypical and cultural approximation to the European ideal. In its broadest sense the escape hatch has made it possible over time for millions of Brazilians with African ancestry who are phenotypically White, or near-White, to become officially White. This aspect of the escape hatch, which is best captured in historian Skidmore's *Black Into White*, indicates that the social construction of Whiteness — and the extension of White racial privilege — is more inclusive in Brazil as compared with the United States, where the one-drop rule can transform into Black an individual who appears otherwise White.

The myth of racial democracy

Brazil's history of miscegenation, and its absence of legalized barriers to equality, should not obscure the linking of Whiteness with superiority and Blackness with inferiority. The ruling elite is overwhelmingly of European descent and European in manners. It also has implemented covert and overt forms of discrimination that have kept the African Brazilian masses in a de facto subordinate status, both before and after the abolition of slavery. Though miscegenation has made the line between Black and White imprecise, and become central in the twentieth-century evolution of Brazil's concept of racial democracy, racial and cultural blending were not posited on egalitarian integration. In other words, there was not a random blend of European, African, and Native American traits, seeking its own "natural" equilibrium. In this scenario equal value would have been attached to each of these racial and cultural constituents through a reciprocal *transracial* and *transcultural* process (Figure 1a), which Gilberto Freyre referred to as "metaracial brunettism."[4] It was rather a process of inegalitarian integration (or *assimilation* in disguise), an unnatural contest between unequal participants, artificially manipulated to purify the Brazilian pedigree and culture of its "inferior" African (and Native American) traits, with the goal of *perpetuating* only European traits (Figure 1b).[5]

This "Whitening" ideology, in part a reflection of the indigenous toxins of Brazil's own racial ecology, was also Brazil's compromised response to

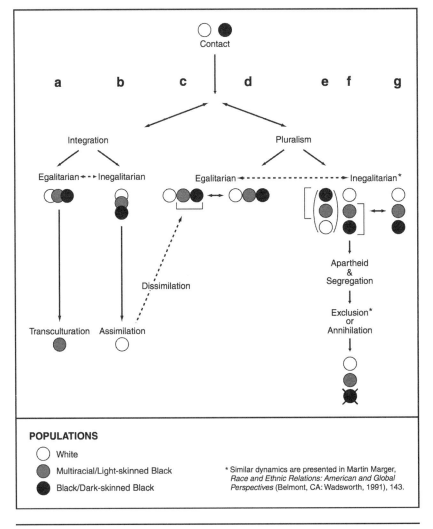

POPULATIONS

○ White

● Multiracial/Light-skinned Black

● Black/Dark-skinned Black

* Similar dynamics are presented in Martin Marger, *Race and Ethnic Relations: American and Global Perspectives* (Belmont, CA: Wadsworth, 1991), 143.

Fig. 1 Pluralist and integrationist dynamics.

nineteenth-century European and European American theories of the evils of miscegenation. In order to understand this ideology, consider that by the latter half of the nineteenth century, the majority of Brazilians, despite official claims to the contrary, were de facto *mulato claro* (clear[light]-skinned mulatto), or *claramente mulato* (clearly mulatto) in terms of ancestry and phenotype.[6] Not even the most phenotypically and culturally European elite individuals could be certain that their genealogy was free of African ancestry and, therefore, insulated from the stigma of slavery and the "evils" of miscegenation.

If miscegenation was the disease, Whitening through miscegenation became the cure. Thus, the Brazilian state encouraged European immigration, particularly from Germany, and passed legislation restricting the immigration of Blacks. This was matched by the tendency of many individuals to seek a spouse more culturally and phenotypically European than themselves, and the desire to assimilate anything (from ideas to cultural artifacts) that tasted of Europe, and by extension, the United States. At the same time, the majority of Blacks and mulattoes were excluded de facto from having contact with Whites as equals. This informal inegalitarian pluralism was envisioned as the final solution that eventually would eliminate African Brazilians through the "laissez-faire genocide" of sharply lower levels of education and higher rates of poverty, malnutrition, disease, and infant mortality (Figure 1f).[7]

Brazil's image as a racial democracy began to erode under the weight of massive data compiled in the 1950s by both Brazilian and foreign social scientists. These scholars used the latest research techniques to reveal complex correlations between physical appearance, culture, and class in determining social stratification. Comprehensive data were lacking, important regional variations existed, and opinions varied on how phenotype might affect future social mobility. The data did indicate that Brazilian race relations displayed fluid racial markers, such that Blackness and Whiteness represented merely polar extremes on a continuum. There was a general consensus, however, that Brazilians who were phenotypically more African were disproportionately found at the bottom of society in terms of education and occupation.[8] Journalists soon followed with anecdotal evidence that confirmed the existence of a subtle, yet unmistakable, pattern of racial discrimination in social relations. Though discrimination had never been codified since the colonial era, and Brazilians could still argue they had avoided the United States' violent urban uprisings and its distorted White supremacist ideology, the growing body of evidence made the Brazilian elite cautious about discussing their society's race relations. Moreover, the myth of racial democracy became an even more crucial official ideology. It was staunchly defended by Brazil's ruling elite, and reinforced by the series of military dictatorships that dominated the Brazilian political scene between 1964 and 1985.[9]

During this time period, further research and discussion on the problem of racial inequality was severely censored by claims that no such problem existed. In 1969, this resulted in the "involuntary" retirement of university faculty branded as subversives for doing research on Brazilian race relations. The political machinery of the state also decreed that efforts to mobilize along racial lines were "racist," "subversive," a threat to national security, and punishable by imprisonment. Individuals who were inclined to address a problem that the state declared did not in fact exist were therefore themselves viewed as creating a problem, and accused of having been infected with a contagion imported from the United States. Many individuals were imprisoned; others became voluntary exiles or were forcibly deported.[10] The intense censorship of public discussion on racial issues was paralleled by the fact that no racial data were collected on the 1970 census. The principal explanation for the decision was that previous data had been notoriously unreliable, because definitions of racial categories lacked uniformity. In actuality, government officials sought to promote the notion that racial criteria were insignificant in determining the distribution of societal wealth, power, privilege, and prestige — and were thus meaningless statistical categories. Part of their strategy for achieving this was to deprive researchers (and therefore the public and politicians) of nationwide figures that would make it possible to document the deplorable conditions endured by African Brazilians in terms of education, jobs, income, and health.[11]

Either Black or White: the Black consciousness movement and the binary racial project

The politics of Black culture

The veil of silence on the discussion of racial inequality in Brazil was lifted in the 1970s and 1980s during the gradual liberalization of the sociopolitical ecology — the *abertura democrática*, or democratic opening. Under military rule political organizing went underground and existed primarily in the form of social clubs and cultural centers. During the democratic opening in the early 1970s, Black consciousness thus first emerged in "cultural" phenomena, which were less threatening to military authorities. This was evident in the formation of "study" groups and cultural associations.[12] Many of these entities initially styled themselves "research centers" in order to avoid repression by the military. They organized lectures, debates, and exhibits to enlighten African Brazilians and the public-at-large on Brazil's African heritage. More importantly, they provided forums for meetings among activists and intellectuals to discuss racial issues.[13] Also, by the 1980s there was an upsurge in African Brazilian literature, much of which has been published in modest editions at the authors' expense.[14]

Other vehicles for Black consciousness in the 1970s included the urban "Black Soul" movement, composed of large numbers of underemployed working class African Brazilian youth — mainly in Rio de Janeiro and Salvador — who crowded into all-night clubs to dance to the "soul music" of African American singers such as James Brown, Isaac Hayes, and Aretha Franklin, and filled movie theaters to see "Black" American films such as "Wattstax," "Claudine," "Superfly," and "Shaft."[15] They adopted English-language phrases such as "soul" and "Black-power kids," as well as colorful clothes, elaborate handshakes, and "Afro" hair styles, as part of an emergent culture of opposition that rejected traditional African Brazilian culture (e.g., samba). The latter had been co-opted by European Brazilian society and had become central to maintaining the myth of racial democracy.

The same period that gave rise to "Black Soul" also witnessed a rebirth (or "re-Africanization") of traditional African Brazilian cultural expression such as samba through the formation of carnival groups such as *blocos afros* (Olodúm and Ilhê Aiyê). Beginning in the 1970s, samba schools began dealing explicitly with the issue of racial inequality, and were no longer willing to use racial democracy as a theme. The music, dance, and lyrics of samba, as well as African themes, along with *capoeira* — an African Brazilian martial art now stylized in dance form — became important conduits of Black consciousness, and served to affirm a "culture of opposition" — particularly among African Brazilian workers.[16] African Brazilian religious practices, such as *candomblé* and *umbanda*, became another important vehicle for Black consciousness. In fact, *umbanda* became one of the fastest-growing religions in Brazil in the 1980s and 1990s across groups. Yet, *umbanda*, much like samba, had been co-opted as a symbol of racial democracy in action.[17]

Despite the significance of African-derived religious expression, most Brazilians are practitioners of Christianity. Networks of religious groups and leaders have issued official position statements on racial inequality and encouraged grassroots activism. Catholicism and Pentecostalism, in particular, have provided support for Black consciousness in the form of African Brazilian martyrs and saints. One of the most popular symbols is Anastácia, an eighteenth-century African Brazilian slave, with a large following among older African Brazilian women.[18] The Catholic Church's *prevestibular* courses (college entrance exam preparatory courses) have provided instruction in professionalization, education, and consciousness-raising in poor and working-class communities. The African Brazilian Pastoral movement (Agentes de Pastoral Negro, APN), which was founded in 1983, has been a prominent religious organization involved with assisting in implementing religious, social, and political teachings while advancing efforts emphasizing the need for African Brazilians to learn more about and appreciate their heritage. In addition, the APN has sought to create a celebration of the Eucharist that incorporates elements of African culture as vehicle for raising popular consciousness about the value of African Brazilian culture. Practicing Catholics have tended to view this popular Christianity negatively. The response of the more secular branch of the Black consciousness movement has ranged from ambivalence to outright hostility, which may have marginalized a large number of potential sympathizers.[19]

From cultural politics to political culture

More explicit political expressions of Black consciousness emerged in the late 1970s with the formation of organizations such as the Unified Black

Movement (O Movimento Negro Unificado, MNU). The MNU was an outgrowth of protests in May 1978 (during the celebration of the abolition of slavery), which African Brazilians organized in several major cities (primarily in the industrialized Southeast) in response to the murder by police of an African Brazilian taxi driver named Robson Luiz, and the expulsion of three African Brazilian youth from a yacht club where they were playing as part of a volley ball team. None of these events was unusual in themselves. Nevertheless, growing covert racial tension, continuing mistreatment, the lifting of authoritarian rule, and the U.S. Civil Rights movement, combined to set the stage for the formation of the Unified Black Movement. In addition, exiled African Brazilian activists, such as Abdias do Nascimento and Guerrero Ramos who left Brazil after the military coup in 1964, returned and assumed leadership positions in the MNU. African Brazilians thus rekindled the militancy that the MNU's predecessor, the Black Front (A Frente Negra), had exhibited during the 1930s before having reached its nadir during the repressive dictatorship of Getúlio Vargas (1937–1945).[20]

The MNU comes the closest to being a national civil rights organization and has been estimated as having as many as 25,000 members. It is part of a broader Black consciousness movement composed of hundreds of organizations active in almost every state in Brazil that explicitly emphasizes struggling against racism and building a positive African Brazilian identity (although these organizations are neither unified nor speak in a singular voice). The MNU's methods in the struggle against racism have ranged from demanding recognition of important historical events involving African Brazilians to calling for political structural reforms. Despite its centrality in the Black consciousness movement the MNU was only one of many organizations that emerged since the late 1970s. The United Blacks for Equality (União de Negros pela Igualidade, UNEGRO) and other similar groups have focused on the antiracist struggle in judicial, labor, and legislative arenas. Since the late 1980s, a growing number of organizations like Criola in Rio and Geledés in São Paulo have focused on the specific concerns of African Brazilian women, and are distinguished from traditionally male-dominated organizations like the MNU.[21] Some cultural groups such as the Institute of Afro-Brazilian Research (Instituto de Pesquisas Afro-Brasileiras, IPEAFRO) have emphasized an African Brazilian identity rooted in an African cultural and racial lineage.[22] Others such as Rio de Janeiro's Afro-Reggae Cultural Group (Grupo Cultural Afro-Reggae) have focused on an African Brazilian identity rooted in the New World experience. Still others such as the Center of Afro-Asiatic Studies (Centro de Estudos Afro-Asiáticos, CEAA) have traditionally been composed primarily of middle-class professionals and intellectuals.[23] Another group is the Center for Marginalized Populations (Centro de Articulação de Populações Marginalizadas, CEAP).[24]

The MNU was originally antagonistic towards many African Brazilian cultural organizations, which activists accused of being not only apolitical but also reactionary and co-opted. Yet, the MNU has itself been the target of some criticism. One criticism has been that the organization is rigid, ideologically narrow, and too leftist in its orientation. In addition, the MNU has been criticized for being too aggressive in pushing Black consciousness. For many African Brazilians, Black identity is simply a fact of life. Consequently, identity politics are secondary to day-to-day economic survival. Many do not see the connection between their daily struggle for socioeconomic survival and the larger issue of structural racism. Others do not necessarily see a causal relationship between assuming a Black identity and eradicating racial inequality.[25]

Beginning in 1988, the MNU initiated a task of self-criticism, prompted in part by the rift between the "cultural" and "political" trajectories of the Black consciousness movement. Another factor was the increasing popularity of carnival groups, or *blocos afros*, as well as Pentecostalism and other forms of popular Christianity at a time when the MNU's effect on the African Brazilian masses was minimal. By the 1990s, the MNU had recognized that a combination of "cultural politics" and "political culture" articulate African Brazilian demands from the strength of their culture, as well as from class-based politics.[26]

The MNU's vision of Brazil diverged from the official assimilationist ideology (Figure 1c). Activists challenged the notion that social stratification is determined primarily by socioeconomic and cultural criteria that are potentially alterable in one's lifetime through personal achievement. Rather, they argued that social inequality is largely determined by ascribed, and thus essentially immutable, characteristics such as race. The illusion of racial democracy is maintained, however, through token inclusion of a few multiracial individuals (and some rare Blacks) into the middle class, while the African Brazilian masses are retained on the periphery of society in the manner of de facto, if not de jure, apartheid (Figure 1f). In addition, a multiracial identification brings with it the expectation, though not the automatic achievement of increased social rewards, and a concomitant rejection of any association with being African Brazilian in order to escape the social stigma attached to Blackness. Consequently, one of the MNU's goals has been to get Black and particularly multiracial individuals to assume an identity as African Brazilian.

The MNU met with hostility from sectors of the political and cultural establishment. Although African Brazilians mounted massive public demonstrations against racism during the centennial for the abolition of slavery in the spring of 1988, a barrage of academic papers and civic ceremonies extolling Brazil's genius in having allegedly liquidated slavery without such upheavals as the U.S. Civil War, largely overshadowed their protests.[27] Their goal of achieving a more equitable society by mobilizing an African Brazilian plurality was termed as "un-Brazilian" and a mindless imitation of the U.S. civil rights movement. Others described the MNU's tactics as a reverse type of apartheid (Figure 1e).[28] African Brazilian activists have received warmer, if somewhat tentative, support from intellectuals, students, progressive sections of the church, and workers committed to political and social change. Many of these individuals, however, have socialist leanings, and view African Brazilians as part of a larger transracial proletariat. They consider racism to be an epiphenomenon of class inequality, and argue that one automatically addresses the former by addressing the latter. They agree that racial prejudice and discrimination directed against African Brazilians has led to gross inequalities in educational, socioeconomic, and political attainment. However, these activists have focused primarily on the poor, the unemployed, and nonliterate. They believe that singling out African Brazilians for special treatment would deviate from the main course of social reform.[29]

The MNU enjoyed a significant amount of publicity in the late 1970s and early 1980s but received greater attention from academics abroad than in Brazil. Since its inception, it has been dominated by individuals from the urban bourgeoisie and plagued by class divisions. These factors prevented the MNU from garnering broad support from other urban, and (in particular) rural sectors of the African Brazilian community that remained largely unaware of its existence. Although more successful in electoral politics than their predecessors of the Black Front in the 1930s, contemporary African Brazilian activists confront the obstacles presented by a national political culture that still discourages, if not thwarts, mobilization around specific racial identities. Consequently, African Brazilians continue to be dramatically underrepresented as elected governmental officials compared to their proportion of the national population.[30]

Notwithstanding the MNU's lack of success in gaining broad support for a race-specific political agenda, or organizing a large race-based electorate, African Brazilian politicians have nevertheless organized formally and informally within political parties and government institutions. They have encouraged White political actors to address racism and racial inequality, or support of race-conscious public policies (e.g., introducing African and African Brazilian history into the public schools, award reparations to the descendants of slaves, and severely penalize acts of racism and racial discrimination, etc.).[31] In fact, the 1988 Constitution, for the first time in Brazilian history, outlawed racism, declaring that "the practice of racism constitutes a crime that is unbailable and without stature of limitation and is subject to imprisonment according to the law."[32] Yet, the antiracist article in the 1988 Constitution, like the Afonso Arinos Law of 1951 (which outlawed racial discrimination in public accommodations), is more rhetoric than commitment. Even with the passage of the necessary enabling law (the Lei Caó), Brazilian civil rights lawyers have found it difficult in practice to establish a legal basis for their criminal complaints.[33]

Quantifying racism and the quality of life

Previously, discussion on Brazilian race relations relied heavily on "qualitative" data, and was primarily framed in the context of historical and anthropological discourse. Historians focused on laws, traveler's accounts, memoirs, parliamentary debates, and newspaper articles in which anecdotal accounts remained the standard source of information. They generally neglected researching police and court records, health archives, personnel files, and other sources from which they might have constructed time series analyses. When such sources were consulted, it was generally to study slavery. Historians did not hesitate to draw conclusions about the historical nature of race relations, but rarely studied contemporary race relations. Anthropologists generally studied African-derived religious and linguistic systems, and artistic expression. When they did examine race relations, their focus was primarily on the ambiguity and situational nature of racial markers. They provided little analysis of the role of race in determining larger structural issues (e.g., education, income, and occupation).[34]

Since the 1970s, a new generation of sociologists, however, have provided activists with the necessary quantitative data to wage their struggle for social change at the level of unions, courts, employers, and the media. These researchers (most of whom are White) not only helped get the race question reinstated on the 1980 census, but also received funding from the Ford Foundation to provide a rigorous analysis of official data from such sources as the 1940, 1950, and 1980 censuses, and the National Household Surveys of the 1970s and 1980s.[35] Much more data on health, housing, education, family structure, etc., was needed, yet census forms are designed to collect only the most basic information. Furthermore, it was difficult for researchers to gain access to data already gathered: most of the important information has never been published. The data was available only on tapes, and researchers were denied access to them for years. When the tapes were released, they were made available only at great expense to users. A group of researchers, responding to these obstructionist procedures, pressured the Census Bureau to release future data on a timely and accessible basis.[36]

That said, these researchers verified glaring disparities in health, income, and education between Whites, who make up approximately 54 percent of the population, and African Brazilians, who make up approximately 46 percent.[37] For example, analyses of 1980 census data indicate that while overall school attendance had increased for all Brazilians, *preto* and *pardo* children tended to start school later, leave school earlier, and at all ages displayed a lower probability of attending school. In terms of employment, *pretos* and *pardos* are concentrated in less skilled and lower-paying jobs. Moreover, wage differentials persist among *pretos, pardos,* and *brancos,* even when controlling for education and job experience. These findings underscored the significance of race, quite apart from culture or class, in determining social inequality. More important, they clearly indicated that, in terms of overall socioeconomic stratification, the racial divide is primarily located between Whites and the African Brazilian masses, and only secondarily between mulattoes and Blacks.[38] Further analyses have emerged that support these findings.[39]

It is true that mulattoes have been able to enter the primary occupational tier as schoolteachers, journalists, artists, clerks, or low-level officials in municipal government and tax offices, and get promoted more easily. They also earn 42 percent more than their Black counterparts.[40] It is equally true that rates of intermarriage and residential integration among mulattoes and

Whites are comparatively higher than between Whites and Blacks, illustrating an intermediate position for the multiracial population in the Brazilian racial hierarchy.[41] Indeed, the credentials distinguishing someone who is White from someone who is multiracial are ambiguous, as African ancestry and African phenotypical traits does not preclude a White social designation. Nevertheless, Whites earn another 98 percent more than mulattoes.

Thus, the intermediate positioning of most of those 40 percent of Brazilians who are considered multiracial is much closer to Blacks than Whites. They are all but excluded from professions in medicine, law, academia, upper-level government, and the officer and diplomatic corps. Even entry-level jobs in the primary labor force that require a "good appearance," such as receptionists, secretaries, bank tellers, or even minimal authority, such as entry-level federal employees, are effectively closed to the majority of mulattoes. The multiracial population, along with the 6 percent of African Brazilians who are designated as Black, remains disproportionately concentrated in the secondary labor force (including agricultural and industrial workers, service employees, day laborers, and domestic servants), or in the ranks of the underemployed and unemployed. Moreover, Black and multiracial individuals in the proletariat, as both children and adults, are routinely subjected to police harassment, often resulting in murder.[42]

Whites and African Brazilians do experience similar disadvantages at the bottom of society, giving credence to the notion that social inequality is based primarily on class. Data indicate, however, that Whites receive higher rates of tangible returns once they have made educational gains. Whites are not only seven times more likely than African Brazilians to be college graduates, but African Brazilian professionals such as physicians, teachers, and engineers also earn 20 to 25 percent less than their White counterparts.[43] Furthermore, if the achievements of individual African Brazilians can be pointed to as examples of meritocracy in action, they also divert attention from the greater difficulty Blacks and mulattoes encounter breaking out of the proletariat, and the increasing disadvantages they suffer with vertical class mobility. Whites are more successful at intergenerational transferal of their achieved status given the same starting point. African Brazilians are handicapped by the cumulative disadvantages of previous, as well as persistent, racial discrimination. These factors hamper and erode, if not preclude, their ability to pass on their achieved status from generation to generation. This is precisely due to the superordinate and subordinate ascribed racial status, respectively, assigned to Whites and African Brazilians.[44] In short, these findings highlight the primacy of race, apart from culture or class, in determining social inequality.

White into Black: a "new" African Brazilian identity

Dismantling the escape hatch

Given that racial formation in Brazil exists on a continuum, which has historically supported the racial democracy (and Whitening) ideology, activists have faced the challenge of implementing cultural (or discursive) initiatives aimed at mobilizing Blacks (pretos) and mulattoes (pardos) under a politicized identity as African Brazilian (negro).[45] Activists frequently complain that the African Brazilians mass are not receptive to their message of positive Black identity and mobilization against racism, which is often attributed to the latter's ambiguous or vague awareness of racial identity and racial prejudice. Yet, anthropologist Burdick found in interviews conducted since the 1990s that most "lifelong Black" informants had no difficulty identifying racial prejudice. In addition, he found that minimal direct involvement in Black political organizations does not always mean ignorance or indifference toward the Black consciousness movement. In fact, his informants displayed a wide range of awareness of the movement and a variety of reasons for their lack of involvement. More neutral reasons given included a "lack of time." Those who gave more negative reasons posited the movement was more interested in self-promotion than in actually benefiting African Brazilians. To the extent that the leadership and social base of political organizations such as the MNU is disproportionately composed of and commandeered by individuals whose socioeconomic status (urban, middle-class, and professional) differ significantly from that of most of their targeted constituency, and who emphasize "assuming Blackness," may alienate the potential larger constituency of "life long" Blacks.[46]

This may include self-identified *negros* who express sympathy for fighting discrimination and valorizing an African Brazilian identity, but who view the objective of building a unified African Brazilian identity as personally less appealing. They may see little benefit in "assuming Blackness," which they consider to be of greater concern for the identity ambiguities of elite (often lighter-skinned) African Brazilians. They often accuse the latter of being more concerned about reclaiming an identity that may have been lost in the journey through the escape hatch, than with addressing the everyday problems of racism faced by people without such identity ambiguities. Burdick acknowledges that this claim is deeply polemical. Yet, he suggests that there is a relatively large and untapped constituency of movement sympathizers; to politically reenroll these individuals may require overcoming ideological barriers *within* the Black consciousness movement itself.[47] Whatever the case may be, at present it seems unlikely that large numbers of individuals actually will join African Brazilian political organizations. Yet, many more appear willing to embrace the idea of a distinct African Brazilian culture and experience. Several popular magazines targeting African Brazilians have been launched: *Black People* (English title, with Portuguese text) appeared in 1993, and *Raça: A Revista dos Negros Brasileiros* (Race: The Magazine of African Brazilians) in late October 1996.[48]

In addition, activists believe that the absence in Brazil of the original negative factor of legal discrimination typified by the United States — which was buttressed by the one-drop rule — along with pervasive miscegenation, and the greater fluidity and ambiguity of racial identities and markers, have resulted in a less unified voice against the brutalities of racial discrimination and undermined the social progress of African Brazilians collectively. Since the 1970s, a major portion of the Black consciousness movement's energy has thus been devoted to forging an African Brazilian plurality and political consciousness. Their tactic for achieving this goal has been to shift focus away from the color designations of *pardo* and *preto* and instead, sensitize individuals to the idea of ethno-racial origins (i.e., African ancestry) and assign positive value to the term *negro*.[49] Accordingly, activists have rearticulated a "new" African Brazilian identity based on the dichotomization of Whiteness and Blackness as two distinct categories of experience (or more specifically, that expands the boundaries of Blackness and contract those of Whiteness) to challenge the hierarchical relationship of Whiteness over Blackness. Indeed, many activists believe that the U.S. one-drop rule and binary racial project should be adopted in Brazil as a form of "strategic racial essentialism." This tactic so the thinking goes would enable the mass mobilization of African Brazilians, just as it has mobilized African Americans.[50]

Similar binary racial projects were deployed by the Black Front (Frente Negra Brasileira, FNB) in the 1930s and Black Experimental Theater (Teatro Experimantal do Negro, TEN) in the 1940s. Yet, racial pluralism was generally viewed as a temporary tactic to mobilize against social inequities. The goal was to fulfill Brazil's ideology of racial democracy by achieving integration of Blacks and mulattoes as equals into the racial order, rather than maintain them as a distinct African Brazilian plurality. At best, these tactics contested the ternary racial project, and succeeded in partially closing the escape hatch. Neither the Black Front nor the Black Experimental Theater actually dismantled these phenomena because African Brazilians lacked a significant power base to mount strategic incursions into the mainstream political process.[51]

The gains of the 1970s and 1980s, however, provided the diverse institutional and cultural terrain upon which more radical oppositional political projects could be built. Compared to previous strategies, pluralism is considered more as a strategy for dismantling (rather than fulfilling) the national ideology of racial democracy as well as a means of recognizing and maintaining a distinct African Brazilian racial and cultural plurality. Pluralism is now considered an integral and legitimate aspect of the Brazilian racial order, compared with the traditional image of integration. In addition, activists have sought to contract the boundaries of Whiteness and break its association with both miscegenation and national identity. Activists do not consider Brazil to be a racially and culturally integrated (i.e., Whiter) society, but rather composed of distinct pluralities of racial and ethnic groups. They envision a mosaic of mutually respectful and differentiated, if not mutually exclusive, African Brazilian and European Brazilian racial and cultural centers of reference. Yet, contemporary strategies of resistance, much as previous ones, seek to achieve structural integration of African Brazilians as equals into the racial order in terms of occupation, income, education, political representation, etc. Both Whites and Blacks would have equal access to all aspects of the public sphere, with the option of integrating in the private sphere. In this case, the selective pattern would be voluntary, rather than mandated by Whites, such that if and when African Brazilians choose to integrate, they do so as equals.[52]

The law of the excluded middle

The Black consciousness movement defines as *negro* (or African Brazilian) anyone of African ancestry and requires de facto that active participants in political organizations identify themselves. This in turn has resulted in a strong ideological rejection of terminology referring to racially intermediate phenotypes and experiences.[53] Burdick has noted that in political gatherings Black consciousness movement participants have been chastised when they inadvertently use one of the intermediate terms (e.g., *mestiço, mulato*).[54] Given the programmatic effort to prevent the formation of a radical African Brazilian subjectivity, or plurality, the strengths of the movement's identity politics are undeniable: the fostering of pride, group solidarity, and self-respect. Also, there can be no denying that one-drop rule was implemented to deny equality to Blacks, but also had the unintended consequence of forging group identity accordingly. This, in turn, enabled African Americans to organize and eventually culminated in the civil rights movement of the 1950s and 1960s, which dismantled Jim Crow segregation and achieved the passage of historic legislation that dissolved legal racial discrimination and inequality.

That said, the effectiveness of the one-drop rule when applied to the Brazilian terrain poses serious logistical problems and is inherently fraught with irreconcilable contradictions. It precludes acknowledging potentially legitimate differences between the experience, and therefore, identities of Black and multiracial individuals. Such thinking also perpetuates a rather pernicious racial essentialism premised on the belief that these differences are inherently invidious distinctions and precludes considering a "new" multiracial identity formulated on egalitarian or antiracist premises. Ultimately, this may keep at bay individuals who are sympathetic to the aims of the Black consciousness movement, who genuinely wish to valorize their African slave ancestry, and unequivocally acknowledge they are the descendents of slaves, but who honestly cannot translate these sentiments into adopting *negro* as an appropriate means of self-identification.[55] Some researchers suggest that disconnection from the term *negro* may originate in the awareness that their social experiences have been qualitatively different from those darker-skinned African-descent Brazilians. In addition, it is unclear as to whether the term *negro* can include individuals who generally would be considered "phenotypically White," but who have African ancestry and choose to identify as African Brazilian.[56] Although self-definition is apparently utilized to resolve this contradiction, tension has arisen over who is "authentically" African Brazilian.[57]

Black identity and the decennial census

The Black consciousness movement seeks to bring about social structural change by challenging institutions, policies, and conditions directly and indirectly based on the ternary racial project and the mulatto escape hatch. Activists have sought to forge a "new" African Brazilian identity that replaces the previous "Black into White" mentality with a "White into Black" one by contracting the boundaries of racial Whiteness and expand those of racial Blackness. The movement's cultural initiative is an interpretation, representation, or explanation of racial dynamics by means of identity politics; its political initiative is most evident in appeals for changes in official racial classifications, as in the census, and the collection of racial data.[58]

As part of their strategy for achieving this goal, activists have called upon the state to implement a *negro* identifier in the federal standard for collecting and presenting data on race as in the census.[59] By questioning the legitimacy of and demanding changes in extant racial categories, activists have forced recognition and discussion of the role the state plays in not only buttressing certain ideas about race and displacing others but also maintaining racial categories and the formation of identities.[60] The Brazilian state has historically neither made explicit definitions of racial categories and membership via the judicial system nor actually enforced institutionalized racially discriminatory polices as has the United States. Nevertheless, from its very beginning the Brazilian state, through the implementation of public policy, has been concerned with the politics of race and has sustained an identifiable racial order. This has linked the system of political rule and social inequities to the racial classification of individuals and groups.[61]

In 1980, based on its own analysis of the 1976 Household Survey (PNAD) and 1980 census, and responding to demands and recommendations by activists and social scientists, the Brazilian Institute of Geography and Statistics (IBGE), specifically its Department of Social Studies and Indicators, began documenting social inequities between Whites and the African Brazilian masses when it started analyzing and publishing racial data in binary form.[62] Yet, this change in procedure actually had broader implications. Previously, the IBGE had advanced policy decisions to serve the national project aimed at unifying Brazil's three parent racial groups — European, African, and Native American — to project a more integrated, albeit Whiter, national image. Although IBGE had not abandoned the traditional three-category concept of color (or four, if one includes the category of "yellows," *amarelos,* used to designate individuals of Asian ancestry) in the actual collecting of data, it had moved toward a conceptualization of Brazilian race relations similar to the U.S. binary racial project, in which both the *preto* and *pardo* populations were combined as a single nonWhite racial group.[63]

Activists place a great deal of emphasis on this data, as it confirms their argument that the socioeconomic status of *pretos* and *pardos* is similar. In 1990, they concentrated on changing procedures for collecting official data on race — particularly on the decennial census. The goal was to replace the color categories of *preto* and *pardo* with the single racial category of *negro.* This is directly related to the movement's strategy to identify its constituency as a numerical majority.

Individuals who identify themselves as *preto* on the census have never surpassed 10 percent of the population. Yet, if this 10 percent is combined with the roughly 42 percent who identify as *pardo*, the total would exceed 50 percent. Indeed, activists claim that the percentage of African Brazilians ranges from 50 to as much as 80 percent, based on their expanded ancestral definition of Blackness.[64] In addition, activists argued that the tendency of individuals to identify themselves on previous surveys with a lighter color (racial) category than their "actual" phenotype might warrant has led to a "distortion" of racial demographics. Consequently, Blacks numerically have lost much and gained nothing; multiracial individuals have gained more than they have lost, and Whites have made substantial gains.[65]

Beginning in 1990, African Brazilian organizations, along with nine non-governmental agencies (including development groups and research centers), gained the support of Instituto Brasileiro de Análisis Sociais e Económicas (IBASE) in mounting a joint publicity campaign with funds from the Ford Foundation and Terra Nuova (an Italian agency for cooperation), directing all Brazilians to be more "conscientious" in filling out the racial question on the 1990 census. The spirit of the campaign was captured best in its poster and brochure slogan — "*Não Deixe sua Côr Passar em Branco. Responda com Bom C/Senso,*" ("*Don't let your color be passed of as White. Respond with good [census] sense*), which utilized a play-on-words between census (*censo*) and sense (*senso*).[66]

The census was canceled in 1990 because of problems between the Ministry of the Economy and the Census Bureau. Although the census was finally taken in 1991, strikes by census staff short-circuited dialogue between campaign organizers, the Bureau administrators, and enumerators concerning changes in the wording on the census questionnaire from *branco* (White), *pardo* (multiracial), and *preto* (Black), to reflect the *branco* (White) and *negro* (African Brazilian) distinctions.[67] Color data for the 1991 census (released in 1995) are consistent with previous censuses, which indicate a progressive decline in the percentage of individuals identifying as *preto* and *branco*. Yet, the percentage of Brazilians identified as White still remained more than half of the population (52 percent), whereas those who identified as *preto* decreased slightly from 5.9 percent in 1980 to 5 percent in 1991. The percentage of individuals identifying as *pardo* increased from 38.8 percent in 1980 to 42 percent in 1991.

These data are in keeping with previous trends and is unlikely attributable to the census campaign.[68] Indeed, the data suggest that the campaign had little or no impact on racial identification. The campaign was constrained by a limited staff and inadequate financial resources. Despite its national aspirations, the campaign activities were largely centered in the city of Rio de Janeiro. It thus remains unknown how the masses of Brazilians would have responded to the campaign's slogan had they been aware of it.[69] Yet neither the lack of significant change in 1991 census data nor the failure to persuade the Census Bureau to use *negro* as an official designator on the census weakened activists' resolve in pursuing their campaign goals for the 2000 census. As was the case in 1991, they were unsuccessful in getting the term *negro* added to the 2000 census. The term has a political connotation that officials of the racial state did not wish to encourage. Nonetheless, the IBGE considered retaining the term *pardo* with a sub-option that would allow Brazilians to acknowledge African ancestry. *Branco*, *preto*, *amarelo*, and *Indigena* (Native American) would be retained. (Traditionally, the Native American population was listed under the color category *pardo*, which essentially translates as "brown." However, a separate "Indigenous" category was added beginning with the 1990 census.) More important, President Henrique Cardoso requested that the IBGE continue its policy of grouping *pretos* and *pardos* together as nonWhites for the purposes of public presentation (and certain statistical work).[70]

That said, the 2000 census figures indicate that 6.2 percent of the respondents identified as *preto*, which is a slight increase over the 5 percent on the 1991 census. At the same time, there was a decrease in the number of individuals who were identified as *pardo* (42.6 percent in 1991 to 39.1 percent in 2000). In the state of Bahia, which contains the largest number of *pretos* and *pardos* (75.7 percent), the increase in the proportion of *pretos* was even more significant. The proportion of *pretos* increased from 10.2 percent in 1991 to 13.1 percent in 2000; the proportion of *pardos* fell from 69.3 percent in 1991 to 62.5 percent in 2000. The *pardo* population is largest in the north (63.5 percent) and northeast (59.8 percent), whereas the central west region indicates a relative balance between Whites and African Brazilians, including both *pretos* and *pardos*. Yet, the census indicates that the majority of Brazilians (53.7 percent) still identify as *branco*, 39.1 percent identify as *pardo*, 6.2 percent as *preto*, 0.5 percent as *amarelo*, and 0.4 percent as *Indigena*. As expected, the majority of those who consider themselves White live south (84.2 percent) and southeast (62.4 percent) regions, where there was a significant influx of European immigrants mainly from Italy and Germany. In the southeast, 62.4 percent of the respondents identified as *branco*, 30 percent as *pardo*, and 6.6 percent as *preto*.[71]

If the small increase in the numbers of *pretos* on the 2000 census can be attributed to the census campaign, the Black consciousness movement nonetheless has a difficult task of consolidating its actual and potential constituents into a politically conscious collective subjectivity. Claims of representing an African Brazilian majority (or a large plurality) based on census data and actually mobilizing individuals into a collective subjectivity as *negros* are entirely separate, if related, tasks. Consequently, the Black consciousness movement will need to convince vast numbers of individuals who self-identify as *pardo* (or even as *brancos*) to view themselves as part of a larger African Brazilian (*negro*) constituency, or even as partners in a common cause with Blacks. The movement's calculated African Brazilian (*negro*) majority of approximately 73 million people (half of Brazil's population), which it claims as its constituency, is still an abstraction that exists only on paper.[72]

From racial denial to racial affirmation

Since the 1990s, there has been discussion of compensatory measures like affirmative action although such tactics have often been viewed with suspicion, or as "reverse discrimination," aggravating, rather than providing a solution to racial inequality.[73] Some have argued that it is difficult to determine the cause-and-effect relationship between racial discrimination and the marginalization and the poverty of African Brazilians (and Native Americans).[74] That said, some entities have established certain modest percentages (or quotas) of positions that must be reserved for African Brazilians (e.g., The Ministry of Agrarian Development (MDA), the Ministry of Social Security, the Labor Ministry, the Superior Federal Tribunal, the Ministry of the Chamber of Deputies, etc.).[75] In May 2002, President Cardoso announced outlines for affirmative action programs, mandating that 20 percent of all federal government jobs would be reserved for African Brazilians. None of these changes were accompanied by the necessary federal legislation and implementation of public policy to achieve political, economic, and social redistribution. Also, race did not appear to a priority for most candidates in the 2002 election campaigns for president, state governors, senate, and state and federal representatives. Yet, José Serra, who was the candidate for the government-backed Brazilian Social Democratic Party (PSDB), promised to expand the Cardoso government's small affirmative action programs. (Cardoso, meanwhile, was barred from running again by term limits.) In addition, the leftist Workers' Party (PT) candidate Luiz Inácio Lula da Silva, who was expected to garner more than 50 percent of the votes, presented a vague outline of his policy concerning racial matters. Lula promised to target African Brazilians for more jobs and educational opportunities. He also reportedly planned to promote to Cabinet level government agencies dealing with hunger, security, and racism. At his close-of-campaign rally, Lula introduced African American activist Jesse Jackson to the crowd.[76]

That said, the implementation of affirmative action in Brazil is complicated by the fact that only a few agencies have historically tracked race or color. This is compounded by the absence of a clearly defined racial (or color) categories, along with the uneven geographical distribution according to race within Brazil (itself giving rise to regional nuances in the way race is conceptualized). Critics also argue that racial "quotas" have no place in a multiracial society like Brazil. On June 23, 2003, the conservative and prestigious *Estado de São Paulo* newspaper called racial miscegenation "one of the nation's greatest sources of anthropological and cultural wealth." It was difficult to determine with precision "to which race each Brazilian belongs," the paper added.[77]

Correspondingly, opponents of race-based affirmative action argue that the most egregious racial inequalities could be reversed with universalist class-based policies aimed at eradicating poverty. They argue that policies supporting mass education, basic sanitation, universal medical and dental care, affordable housing, basic infrastructure, increased employment, land distribution, and the civic participation of the poor would proportionally benefit more African Brazilians than Whites given that most of the former are poor. On the other hand, race-based affirmative action aimed mainly at expanding access to university education, job promotion, contracts for materials or services, and so on, would benefit individuals in the African Brazilian middle class — who have the skills and qualifications to attend college, run a company, or supply needed goods or services — far more than the majority of African Brazilians.[78]

Other concerns focus on the legality of affirmative action in terms of provisions set forth in the Brazilian constitution (article 3, subsections III and IV) that protect the universalist and individualist principle of merit.[79] This provision is the new democracy's primary weapon against the personalistic and clientelistic practices that still dominate Brazilian public life. The main objective has been to strengthen universal mechanisms for rewarding merit, thus broadening democratic access to resources. From this standpoint, affirmative action policies do seek to expand universal civil rights. Consequently, there is no legal basis for the claim that affirmative action policies are unconstitutional. Indeed, some experts have argued that positive discrimination in the manner of affirmative action would further the egalitarian integration of all individuals as equals into Brazilian society. Yet, sociologist Guimarães argues that the issue is not simply whether to purse either universalist class-based or race-based affirmative policies. The challenge is whether African Brazilians should wait for the expansion of civil rights and social opportunities for the poor, or immediately demand race-specific measures that would enhance their access to both public and private universities, as well as expand and strengthen their business relationships, to enlarge the African Brazilian "middle class."[80]

What is equally problematic for the implementation of affirmative action in Brazil is that racial discrimination is linked to forms of status-based discrimination, that is, discrimination based on the assumption of natural privileges for certain groups and classes of people designated as "minorities." Guimarães argues there are at least three reasons for this. First, there is no strong tradition of protecting the rights of social minorities: to identify one's group as a "minority" effectively dooms it to political exclusion. Second, there is a strong influence on the left of the discourse of majorities, inherited largely from the Communist party's discourse of majority rule by workers. Finally, in the United States it is historically plausible for African Americans to share with European Americans the claim to have physically "built the nation." Yet, in Brazil the historical reality is that the wealth and infrastructure of the nation were built by the labor of the African Brazilian slave majority and a sizeable plurality of low-wage laborers in the postslavery era. Of course, this does not mean that being a numerical majority (or large plurality) precludes being a "minority" in the sense of lacking of institutional power and being excluded from the political sphere. Yet, in the United States there is no tension (at least conceptually) between identifying African Americans as a "minority" and having "contributed" to the building of the nation. In Brazil it is conceptually, discursively, and politically difficult for many individuals to reconcile the absolute dependence on African Brazilian slave and low-wage labor with the identity of "minority."[81]

If affirmative action has come under attack in the United States this policy has gained support in Brazil in terms of university admissions, government employment, and public contracts, and perhaps eventually in private companies. The state's sympathetic response to advocates of affirmative action has led to an intense parallel debate over what percentage should be designated for African Brazilians in affirmative action programs. According to census figures, about 45 percent of Brazil's 175 million people consider themselves to be Black and mulatto. But many of the strongest supporters of affirmative action argue that the ceiling should be set, at least for the moment, at 20 percent. Others contend that quotas should vary from state to state, based on the percentage of the population that is Black and mulatto. For example, more than 80 percent of people in the northeastern state of Bahia identify as Black and mulatto, compared with 10 percent of the population in southeastern states.[82]

In May 2002, the UERJ (Rio de Janeiro State University) began complying with recent state legislation requiring the university to reserve a 40 percent affirmative action quota in its 2003 entering class for all applicants declaring themselves on admission forms to be African Brazilian, that is, "of African descent" (or "Afrodescendentes"). Yet, the potential for abuse in this area is very real, considering that, technically speaking, the term "African Brazilian" includes anyone who identifies as such. To complicate matters, a significant number if not a majority of White-designated and White-identified individuals have African ancestry, that is, are "of African descent." In fact, in a recent *vestibular* examination (college entrance examination), two candidates who were White-designated and White-identified indicated they were "Afrodescendentes," which increased their chances of admission.[83] As a result of this debate, Brazilians are being forced to define who is African Brazilian, a process that is perplexing and alien to Brazilian racial thinking. As in the United States, White-identified students who were not admitted despite scoring higher on the entrance examination have challenged affirmative action in the courts. They contend that they are being denied the "equality of access to schooling" guaranteed by Brazil's 1988 Constitution.[84]

Because of the university admissions dispute, the Supreme Court has been asked to rule on the constitutionality of affirmative action racial quotas. Since the Chief Justice himself imposed a hiring quota for court employees last year, civil rights advocates expect a favorable decision, which they say could have an impact comparable to that of *Brown v. Board of Education* in the United States. Yet, they predict that the debate is likely to intensify and become even more acrimonious as a result of a sweeping Racial Equality Statute now before Congress. That bill, supported by the administration of newly elected President Lula, would make affirmative action obligatory at all levels of government, and required even in casting television programs and commercials.[85]

But critics say the state is making a difficult problem worse by turning to what they consider to be a solution imported from the United States, a nation where racial definitions and relations are very different. Critics were emboldened by the U.S. Supreme Court's June 23, 2003 split ruling in two affirmative action cases involving admissions to the University of Michigan Law School and undergraduate admissions. That ruling allowed race to be only one factor used in admissions decisions but banned quotas and systems based on points. The United States experience could foreshadow challenges ahead for Brazil as notions of racial identity change.[86]

Conclusion: a new Brazilian racial order?

During the first half of the twentieth century the Brazilian racial order sustained a national ideology of racial democracy (and Whitening) both implicitly and explicitly. By the 1970s and 1980s, the public and political debate increasingly included discussions about the importance of race, quiet apart from questions of class, in determining social stratification. Since the 1990s, there has been a gradual yet unmistakable decline in support of the racial democracy ideology in academic circles, official discourse, as well as national public opinion. Many Brazilians still hold on tenaciously to the racial democracy ideology; some consider this ideology an unfilled potential that may be realized in the future; others have cast aside the ideology for a more critical focus on contemporary racial inequality. State officials — including respectively the previous and present heads of state Cardoso and Lula — have publicly challenged that ideology. In addition, after taking office, President Lula took a number of steps, both practical and symbolic, to stress his commitment to racial equality. His cabinet included four African Brazilians, among them the minister of a newly created secretariat for the promotion of racial equality. In addition, Lula appointed the first African Brazilian justice to the Supreme Court.[87]

Also, attitudes, discourse, policy, and behavior surrounding race and national identity increasingly include references to Brazil's "racial diversity" and "multiculturalism" (egalitarian pluralism) as compared with the traditional reference to its "racial unity" (egalitarian integration), both of which are inextricably intertwined with census categories.[88] Indeed, the publication of color data in binary form, the debate over census categories, as well as the implementation of affirmative action and other initiatives to monitor and eradicate patterns of racial discrimination indicates a new racial project in Brazil. This project challenges the ternary racial project and the mulatto escape hatch by contracting the boundaries of Whiteness and expanding those of Blackness. Furthermore, it is clear that this change places increased emphasis on the White and nonWhite dynamic and is moving Brazil in a direction similar to the binary racial project traditionally associated with the United States. Whether and to what extent this "binary racial project" will actually lead to a new "binary racial order" in Brazil, underpinned by the one-drop rule, remains to be seen.

Notes

1. This chapter borrows on my chapters "Either Black of White: Race Relations in Contemporary Brazil," in *Latin America: An Interdisciplinary Approach*, ed. G. Verona-Lacey and J. Lopez-Arias (New York: Peter Lang, 1998); "Multiracial Identity in Brazil and the United States," in *We Are a People: Narrative and Multiplicity in Constructing Ethnic Identity*,

ed. Jeffrey Burroughs and Paul R. Spickard (Philadelphia, PA: Temple University Press, 2000); Multiracial Identity in Global Perspective: Brazil, South Africa, and the United States," in *New Faces in a Changing America: Multiracial Identity in the 21st Century*, ed. L. Winters and H. DeBose (Thousand Oaks: Sage Publications, 2002).

2. It should be pointed out that the emergence of the multiracial consciousness movement in the United States since the dismantling of Jim Crow segregation, including the last laws against racial intermarriage, has moved U.S. racial formation closer to the ternary racial project that has historically typified Brazil (G. Reginald Daniel, *More Than Black? Multiracial Identity and the New Racial Order*, Philadelphia, PA: Temple University Press, 2001).

3. Michael Omi and Howard Winant, *Racial Formation in the United States from the 1960s to 1990s* (New York: Routledge Press, 1994). Native Americans were a major component in discussions on Brazil's national identity in the nineteenth century. Indeed, they became the symbol of the "Noble Savage" so popular at the time in Romantic literature and the other arts as well as Brazil's anticolonial struggle against the Portuguese. This romanticization of Brazil's indigenous population was made possible by the fact that the Native American threat to continued Brazilian territorial expansion had been sufficiently neutralized by disease and the ravages of colonization afforded Brazilians the luxury of viewing aboriginal ancestry as a source of pride. African ancestry continued to be viewed as a serious liability and the source of great shame, a sentiment that was exacerbated by the very visible presence of millions of slaves.

4. Abdias do Nascimento, *Mixture or Massacre?: Essays on the Genocide of a Black People*. trans. Elisa Larkin Nascimento (State University of New York at Buffalo, Puerto Rican Studies and Research Center, 1979), 74–80. It should be pointed out, however, that Brazilian popular culture and the physiognomy of the Brazilian people remain strongly indebted to and influenced by the African component despite attempts by the elite to ignore and disguise, if not wipe out, its presence.

5. Anani Dzidzienyo, *The Position of Blacks in Brazilian Society. Minority Group Rights Reports*, no. 7 (London: Minority Rights Group, 1979), 2–11; Abdias do Nascimento, *Mixture or Massacre?*, 74–80; Thomas A. Skidmore, *Black into White: Race and Nationality in Brazilian Thought* (New York: Oxford University Press, 1974), 64–77.

6. Afrânio Coutinho, "El Fenómeno de Machado de Assis," *Brasil Kultura*, XIV, 63 (1989), 8–12.

7. David T. Haberly, "Abolitionism in Brazil: Anti-Slavery and Anti-Slave," *Luso-Brazilian Review*, 9, 2 (1972), 30–46.

8. Thomas A. Skidmore, "Race Relations in Brazil," *Camões Center Quarterly*, 4 (Autumn and Winter, 1992–1993), 49–57; Charles H. Wood and José Alberto Magno de Carvalho, *The Demography of Inequality in Brazil* (New York: Cambridge University Press, 1988), 135–153.

9. Skidmore, "Race Relations in Brazil," 49–57.

10. Skidmore, "Race Relations in Brazil," 49–57.

11. Nascimento, *Mixture or Massacre?*, 79–80; Peggy Lovell-Webster, "The Myth of Racial Equality: A Study of Race and Morality in Northeast Brazil," *Latinamericanist*, 22, 2 (May 1987), 1–6.

12. These organizations have included the Centro de Cultura e Arte Negra, the Grupo Evolução, the Grupo Negro, the Bloco Afro Ilhê Aiyê, the Sociedade de Intercambio Brasil-Africa, the Instituto de Pesquisas de Culturas Negras (IPCN), the Centro de Estudos Afro-Asiáticos (CEAA), the Grupo de Trabalho André Rebouças. Luiz Claudio Barcelos, "Struggling in Paradise: Racial Mobilization and the Contemporary Black Movement in Brazil," in *Race Relations in Contemporary Brazil: From Indifference to Equality*, ed. Rebecca Reichmann (University Park, PA: Pennsylvania State University, 1991), 160; John Burdick, *Blessed Anastácia: Women, Race, and Popular Christianity in Brazil* (New York: Routledge, 1998).

13. Observations of public behavior in Rio de Janeiro 1977–1978; Barcelos, "Struggling in Paradise," 155–177.

14. Skidmore, "Race Relations in Brazil," 49–57; Lelia González, "The Unified Black Movement: A New Stage in Black Mobilization," in *Race, Class, and Power in Brazil*, ed. Pierre-Michel Fontaine (Center for Afro-American Studies, University of California, Los Angeles, 1985), 120–134; George Reid Andrews, *Blacks and Whites in São Paulo, 1888–1988* (Madison, WI: University of Wisconsin Press, 1991), 211–244; John Burdick, "Brazil's Black Consciousness Movement," *North American Congress on Latin America Report on the Americas*, 25, 4 (February 1992), 23–27; Luiz Silva, "The Black Stream in Brazilian Literature," *Conexões*, 4, 2 (1992), 12–13.

15. Observations of public behavior in Rio de Janeiro 1977–1978; Pierre-Michel Fontaine, "Transnational Relations and Racial Mobilization: Emerging Black Movements," in *Ethnic Identities in a Transnational World*, ed. John F. Stack (Westport, CT: Greenwood Press, 1981), 141–162; John Burdick, "Brazil's Black Consciousness Movement," 27; Michael Hanchard,

Orpheus and Power: The Movimento Negro of Rio de Janeiro and São Paulo, Brazil, 1945–1988 (Princeton, NJ: Princeton University Press, 1994), 111–119; Sheila S. Walker, "Africanity Versus Blackness: The Afro-Brazilian/Afro-American Identity Conundrum," in *Introspectives: Contemporary Art by Americans and Brazilians of African Descent*, ed. Nancy McKinney (Los Angeles, CA: California Afro-American Museum, 1989), 17–21.

16. Walker, "Africanity Versus Blackness," 17–21; Observations of public behavior at Carnival in Rio de Janeiro, 1977–1978.

17. Burdick, "Brazil's Black Consciousness Movement," 27.

18. As recounted by these women, the jealous wife of a slave owner unjustly accused the virgin slave Anastasia of seducing her husband, and forced her to wear an iron mask for the rest of her life as punishment. Anastácia's legend represents a sharp critique of the master class, and refutes the traditional image of the kind and paternal Brazilian slave master. Burdick, *Blessed Anastácia*, 55–57.

19. Burdick, *Blessed Anastácia*, 55–57.

20. George Reid Andrews, *Blacks and Whites*, 146–156; Hanchard, *Orpheus and Power*, 104–129; Michael Mitchell, "Blacks and the Abertura Democrática," in *Race, Class and Power in Brazil*, ed. Pierre-Michel Fontaine (Center for Afro-American Studies, University of California, Los Angeles, 1985), 95–119. Although the Black Front had several successors in the 1940s and 1950s (Teatro Experimental do Negro, União dos Homens de Côr, Associação Cultural do Negro), none of these organizations achieved its level of prominence.

21. Burdick, *Blessed Anastácia*, 3–4; Hanchard, *Orpheus and Power*, 119–129; Observations of public statements made by Lélia Gonzalez at Center for Afro-American Studies 1980 symposium, Race and Class in Brazil: New Issues and New Approaches, University of California, Los Angeles.

22. Other representative organizations have included the National Center of Africanity and Afro-Brazilian Resistance (Centro Nacional de Africanidade e Resistancia Afro-Brasileira, CENAREB); Burdick, *Blessed Anastácia*, 3–4.

23. This has been typified by the Research Institute of Black Culture (Instituto de Pesquisa de Culturas Negras, IPCN) and the Center for the Support of Enterprise (Centro de Estudos e Assessoramento de Empreendedores, CEM); Burdick, *Blessed Anastácia*, 3–4.

24. Burdick, *Blessed Anastácia*, 3–4.

25. John Burdick, "The Lost Constituency of Brazil's Black Movement," *Latin American Perspectives*, 98, 25, 1 (January 1998): 150–152.

26. Barelos, "Struggling in Paradise," 155–177.

27. Skidmore, "Race Relations in Brazil," 49–57; Carlos Hasenbalg, "Race and Socioeconomic Inequalities in Brazil," in *Race, Class and Power in Brazil*, ed. Pierre-Michel Fontaine, 25–41; Rebecca Reichmann, "Brazil's Denial of Race," *North American Congress on Latin America Report on the Americas*, 28, 6 (May/June), 35–42; Burdick, "Brazil's Black Consciousness Movement," 23–27; Andrews, *Blacks and Whites*, 218–233.

28. Skidmore, "Race Relations in Brazil," 49–57.

29. Skidmore, "Race Relations in Brazil," 49–57; Reichman, "Brazil's Denial of Race," 35–42.

30. Ollie A. Johnson, III, "Racial Representation and Brazilian Politics: Black Members of the National Congress, 1983–1999," *Journal of Interamerican Studies and World Affairs* 40, 4 (Winter 1998): 112–113.

31. Johnson, "Racial Representation," 112–113.

32. Skidmore, "Race Relations in Brazil," 55.

33. Skidmore, "Race Relations in Brazil," 49–57; Hasenbalg, "O Negro nas Vésperas do Centenário," *Estudos Afro-Asiáticos*, 13 (1987), 79–86.

34. Skidmore, "Race Relations in Brazil," 49–57.

35. Silva's "White-Nonwhite Income Differentials: Brazil, 1960," Hasenbalg, "Race and Socioeconomic Inequalities in Brazil," 25–41.

36. Reichmann, "Brazil's Denial of Race," 35–42; Skidmore, "Race Relations in Brazil," 49–57.

37. Mac Margolis, "The Invisible Issue: Race in Brazil," *Ford Foundation Report*, 1, 2 (Summer 1992), 3–7; Reichmann, "Brazil's Denial of Race," 35–45; Regina Domingues, "The Color of a Majority Without Citizenship," *Conexões: Africa Diaspora Research Project, Michigan State University*, 4, 2 (November 1992), 6–7; Hasenbalg, "Race and Socioeconomic Inequalities in Brazil," 25–41; Lovell-Webster, "The Myth of Racial Equality," 1–6; Peggy Lovell-Webster and Jeffery Dwyer, "The Cost of Not Being White in Brazil," *Sociology and Social Research*, 72, 2 (1988), 136–138; Nelson do Valle Silva, "Updating the Cost of Not Being White in Brazil," in *Race, Class and Power in Brazil*, ed. Pierre-Michel Fontaine, 42–55; Anani Dzidzienho, "Brazil," in *International Handbook on Race and Race Relations*, ed. Jay A. Sigler (New York: Greenwood Press, 1987), 23–42.

38. Melissa Nobles, *Shades of Citizenship: Race and the Census in Modern Politics* (Stanford, CA: Stanford University Press, 2000), 160–161; Peggy A. Lovell and Charles H. Wood, "Skin Color, Racial Inequality, and Life Chances in Brazil," *Latin American Perspectives* 25, 3 (May 1998): 90–109; Nelson du Valle Silva and Carlos A. Hasenbalg, "Race and Educational Opportunity in Brazil," in *Race Relations in Contemporary Brazil: From Indifference to Inequality*, ed. Rebecca Reichmann (University Park, PA: Pennsylvania State University, 1991), 55–57; Edna Roland, "The Soda Cracker Dilemma," in *Race Relations in Contemporary Brazil: From Indifference to Inequality*, ed. Rebecca Reichmann (University Park, PA: Pennsylvania State University, 1991), 197; Burdick, *Blessed Anastácia*, 1–2. The glaring nature of these inequalities in terms of postsecondary education is most dramatically displayed at the Federal University of Bahia in the city of Salvador. For example, roughly 50 percent of the students enrolled at the university are white although they compose only one fifth of the city's population, which is a majority Black and multiracial. "Brazil's Unfinished Battle for Racial Democracy," *Economist* 335, 8167 (April 22, 2000): 31.
39. This research includes Pierre Michel Fontaine, ed. *Race, Class, and Power in Brazil* (Center for Afro-American Studies, University of California, Los Angeles, 1981); George Reid Andrews, *Blacks and Whites in São Paulo Brazil, 1888–1988* (Madison, WI: University of Wisconsin Press, 1991); Michael Hanchard, *Orpheus and Power: The Movimento Negro of Rio de Janeiro and São Paulo, Brazil, 1945–1988* (Princeton, NJ: Princeton University Press, 1994) and *Racial Politics in Contemporary Brazil* (Durham: Duke University Press, 1999); Howard Winant, *Racial Conditions: Politics, Theory, Conditions* (Minneapolis, MN: University of Minnesota Press, 1994); France Winddance Twine's *Racism in a Racial Democracy: The Maintenance of White Supremacy in Brazil* (New Brunswick, NJ: Rutgers University Press, 1997); Anthony Marx's *Making Race and Nation: A Comparison of the United States, South Africa, and Brazil* (New York: Cambridge University Press, 1998); Rebecca Reichmann, *Race in Contemporary Brazil: From Indifference to Equality* (University Park, PA: Pennsylvania State University, 1999); Larry Cook and Randall Johnson, ed. *Black Brazil: Culture Identity, and Social Mobilization* (Los Angeles, CA: Latin American Studies Center, University of California, 1999); Darien Davis, *Avoiding the Dark: Race and the Forging of National Culture in Modern Brazil*, 1999; G. Reginald Daniel, "Multiracial Identity in Brazil and the United States," in *We Are a People: Narrative and Multiplicity in Constructing Ethnic Identity*, ed. Jeffrey Burroughs and Paul R. Spickard (Philadelphia, PA: Temple University Press, 2000); Melissa Noble, *Shades of Citizenship: Race and the Census in Modern Politics* (Stanford, CA: Stanford University Press, 2000); Charles V. Hamilton, Lynn Huntley, Neville Alexander, Antonio Sergio Alfredo Guimarães, and Wilmot James, ed., *Beyond Racism: Race and Inequality in Brazil, South Africa, and the United States* (Boulder, CO: Lynne Reinner Publishers, 2001); Robin Sherrif's *Dreaming of Equality: Color, Race, and Racism in Urban Brazil* (New Brunswick, NJ: Rutgers University Press, 2001); Livio Sansone, *Blackness Without Ethnicity: Constructing Race in Brazil* (New York: Palgrave Macmillan, 2002); Jerry Dávila, *Diploma of Whiteness: Race and Social Policy in Brazil, 1917–1945* (Durham: Duke University Press, 2003); Edward Telles, *Racismo à Brasileira: Uma Nova Perspectiva Sociolgica* (Rio de Janiero: Relume Dumará, 2003).
40. Burdick, "Brazil's Black Consciousness Movement," 23–27; Silva, "Updating the Cost," 42–55.
41. Much as the United States, the vast majority of marriages in Brazil (approximately - 80 percent) are racially endogamous. Although multiracial individuals appear to intermarry with Blacks and Whites in about equal proportions, Black and White intermarriage is comparatively rare. Carlos A. Hasenbalg, Nelson do Valle Silva, and Luiz Claudio Bracelos, "Notas Sobre Miscegenação Racial no Brasil," *Estudos Afro-Asiáticos*, 16 (1989), 189–197; Edward E. Telles, "Racial Distance and Region in Brazil: Intermarriage in Brazilian Urban Areas," *Latin American Research Review*, 28, 2 (Spring 1992), 141–162.
42. Dzidzienho, "Brazil," 23–42.
43. Burdick, "Brazil's Black Consciousness Movement," 23–27; Hasenbalg, Silva and Bracelos, "Notas Sobre Miscegenação no Brasil," 189–119; Hasenbalg, "Race and Socioeconomic Inequalities in Brazil," in *Race, Class and Power in Brazil*, ed. Pierre-Michel Fontaine, 25–24; Laurie Goering, "Beneath Utopian Facade, Brazilians Uncover Racism," *Chicago Tribune*, (December 20, 1994), 1, 11; Marlise Simmons, "Brazil's Blacks Feel Prejudice 100 Years After Slavery's End, *New York Times* (May 14, 1988), 1, 6; Edward E. Telles, "Residential Segregation by Skin Color in Brazil," *American Sociological Review*, 57, 2 (April 1992), 186–197; Lovell-Webster and Dwyer, "The Cost of Being NonWhite," 136–138; Silva, "Updating the Cost," 42–55.
44. Silva, "Updating the Cost," 42–55; Hasenbalg, "Race and Socioeconomic Inequalities," 25–41.
45. Barcelos, "Struggling in Paradise," 164.

46. Burdick, "The Lost Constituency of Brazil's Black Movement," 150–152.
47. Burdick, "The Lost Constituency," 150–152.
48. Burdick, *Blessed Anastácia*, 3; Nobes, *Shades of Citizenship*, 124; Burdick, "The Lost Constituency," 136.
49. *Pardo*, in particular, has been considered meaningless because it includes all possible types of blended backgrounds. Nobles, *Shades of Citizenship*, 152; Robinson, "The Two Faces of Brazil," 38–42; Skidmore, "Race Relations in Brazil," 49–57.
50. Gayatari Spivak, "Strategies of Vigilance: An Interview with Gayarti Chakrovorti Spivak," in *Block* 10 (1985), 8.
51. Kim Butler, *Freedoms Given, Freedoms Won: Afro-Brazilians in Post-Abolition São Paulo and Salvador* (New Brunswick, NJ: Rutgers University Press, 1998), 25, 28–39; Andrews, *Blacks and Whites in São Paulo*, 150; Quintard Taylor, "Frente Negra Brasileira: The Afro-Brazilian Civil Rights Movement 1924–1937," *Umoja* 2, 1 (1978), 30; Darien Davis, *Avoiding the Dark: Race and the Forging of National Culture in Modern Brazil* (Brookfield, VT: Ashgate Publishing Co.), 184–185.
52. Nobles, *Shades of Citizenship*, 152; Andrews, *Blacks and Whites*, 250; Oliveira, "Dia Nacional Elvira Oliveira, "Dia Nacional da Consciencia Negra, *Nova Escola*, (November 1993), 23–25; Lori S. Robinson, "The Two Faces of Brazil: A Black Movement Gives Voice to an Invisible Majority," *Emerge*, (October 1994): 38–42; Skidmore, "Race Relations in Brazil," 49–57.
53. Burdick, *Blessed Anastácia*, 3, 112–113; Burdick, "The Lost Constituency, 150–152.
54. Burdick, "Brazil's Black Consciousness Movement," 23–27; Domingues, "The Color of a Majority Without Citizenship, 6–7; Oliveira, "Dia Nacional," 23–25; Jerry Michael Turner, "Brown into Black: Changing Attitudes of Afro-Brazilian University Students," in *Race, Class and Power in Brazil*, ed. Pierre-Michel Fontaine, 73–94; Ana Lúcia E. F. Valente, *Política e Relações Raciais: Os Negros e As Eleições Paulistas de 1982* (São Paulo: Fundação de Amparo a Pesquisa do Estado de São Paulo, 1986), 35–40. Some individuals use *mestiço* (which connotes a general multiracial background) in place of *mulato*, due to the derogatory connotations that have sometimes been associated with the latter.
55. Burdick, *Blessed Anastácia*, 5; Burdick, "The Lost Constituency," 150–152.
56. Werner Sollors, "The Idea of Ethnicity," in *The Truth About the Truth: De-Confusing and De-Constructing the Postmodern World*, ed. Walter Truett Anderson (New York: A. Jeremy P. Tarcher/Putnam Book, 1995), 58–65; Ali Rattansi, "'Western' Racisms, Ethnicities and Identities in a 'Postmodern' Frame," in *Racism, Modernity and Identity: On the Western Front*, ed. Ali Rattansi and Sallie Westwood (Cambridge: Polity Press, 1994), 57
57. Burdick, "The Lost Constituency," 150–152.
58. Omi and Winant, *Racial Formation*, 55–56.
59. Omi and Winant, *Racial Formation*, 55–56, 71–75.
60. Omi and Winant, *Racial Formation*, 55.
61. Nobles, *Shades of Citizenship*, 115–120.
62. Nobles, *Shades of Citizenship*, 115–120; Andrews, *Blacks and Whites in São Paulo*, 250.
63. Andrews, *Blacks and Whites*, 250; Oliveira, "Dia Nacional," 23–25.
64. Andrews, *Black and Whites*, 250; Oliveira, "Dia Nacional," 23–25.
65. Margolis, "The Invisible Issue," 3–7; Nascimento, *Mixture or Massacre?*, 74–80; Oliveira, "Dia Nacional," 3–25; Robinson, "Two Faces of Brazil," 38–42; Wood and Carvalho, *The Demography of Inequality*, 135–153. In 1890, *pardos* comprised 41.4 percent of the population. Their apparent decline from 41.4 percent to 21.2 percent between 1890 and 1940, and the growth of the White population from 43.97 to 63.5 percent during the same period is more related to the massive immigration of Europeans to Brazil than to increased miscegenation or racial self-recoding. Census figures make clear, however, that between 1940 and 1990, the *pardo* population was Brazil's fastest growing racial group, rising from 21.2 percent to 38.8 percent (±48 million) of the national population. During the same period Whites declined from 63.5 percent to 54.2 percent (±86 million) and *pretos* from 14.6 percent to 5.9 percent (±6 million). Hasenbalg, Silva, and Bracelos, "Notas Sobre Misçegenação," 189–197. This does indicate a progressive "lightening" of the population. It would be less appropriately described as a Whitening, however, and more as a "browning." If upwardly mobile African Brazilians have been moving out of the *pardo* category into the *branco* category, it, therefore, has not been in numbers sufficient to reverse this trend. Andrews, *Black and Whites*, 252.
66. Margolis, "The Invisible Issue," 3–7; Nascimento, *Mixture or Massacre?*, 74–80; Oliveira, "Dia Nacional," 3–25; Robinson, "Two Faces of Brazil," 38–42; Wood and Carvalho, *The Demography of Inequality*, 135–153.
67. Burdick, "Brazil's Black Consciousness Movement," 23–27; Domingues, "The Color of a Majority Without Citizenship," 6–7; Oliveira, "Dia Nacional," 23–22; Turner, "Brown into

Black," 73–94; Nobles, *Shades of Citizenship*, 120–122. A significant portion of Whites have African ancestry and display varying degrees of African phenotypical traits. If we were using the Anglo-North American rule of hypodescent, multiracial individuals would completely vanish, as would a large portion of Whites. Combining the figures for the approximately 40 percent of Brazilians who are designated as *pardos* with the 6 percent designated as *pretos*, rather than counting them as separate categories, brings the total of African Brazilians (negros) to roughly 46 percent.

68. Nobles, *Shades of Citizenship*, 160.

69. Nobles, *Shades of Citizenship*, 160.

70. Nobles, *Shades of Citizenship*, 123, 172.

71. Instituto Brasileiro de Geografia e Estadísticas. *Censo Demográfico 2000*. Tabulação Avaçado.-Tablas de resultados preliminares. Rio de Janeiro, Brazil; Francisco Neves, "Two Brazils," *Brazzil*, Society, (May 2002) <http://www.brazil-brasil.com/index.htm.>

72. Burdick, "Brazil's Black Consciousness Movement," 23–27; Nobles, *Shades of Citizenship*, 125–126, 171.

73. Andrews, *Blacks and Whites*, 218–233. Skidmore, "Race Relations in Brazil," 49–57. *See* Margolis, "The Invisible Issue," 3–7. Reichmann, "Brazil's Denial of Race," 35–42.

74. Reichmann, "Introduction," 23, 34, 21–22.

75. Marta Alvim, "Mixed Race, Mixed Up Feelings," in *Brazil*, "Society" (March 2002) <http://www.brazzil.com/pages/cvr02.htm>; Nobles, *Shades of Citizenship*, 123–124; Kevin G. Hall, "Brazil Program Will Set Aside Jobs for Blacks Government Plans to Address Inequities," *Detroit Free Press* (June 21, 2002) <http://www.freep.com/news/nw/ nbrazil11_20011001>; Patrice M. Jones, "Brazil Debates Affirmative Action," *Chicago Tribune*, Section 1, 9.

76. Larry Rohter, "Racial Quotas in Brazil Touch Off Fierce Debate," *New York Times* (April 5, 2003) <http: www.nytimes.com/2003/04/05/international/Americas/05BRAZ.html>; Tom Gibb, "Brazil's black-and-white poll," Front Page, Americas (October, 6 2002) *BBC News World Edition* <http://news.bbc.co.uk/2/hi/americas/2303059.stm>. In the October elections Lula easily beat Serra in the first round of voting, but since he failed to get 50 percent of the vote, the two top candidates met in a runoff in which Lula garnered 61.5 percent as compared with Serra's 38.5 percent of the vote. This marked a historic shift to the left for Brazil, which has never actually elected a leftist president. Indeed, the last leftist head of state João Goulart was a vice president who assumed power in 1961 when the centrist president resigned. He served 2 1/2 years and was deposed by a right-wing military coup.

77. Pueng Vongs, "Affirmative Action in Other Countries" *Pacific News Service* (July 11, 2003) <http://news.pacificnews.org/news/view_article.html?article_id=3e26118fcdf4fba57da467 da3eeb43d0>.

78. Guimarães, "Measures to Combat Discrimination and Racial Inequality in Brazil," in *Race in Contemporary Brazil: From Indifference to Equality*, ed. Rebecca Reichmann (University Park, PA: Pennsylvania State University, 1999), 143–153.

79. There are III: "eradicate poverty and marginalization and reduce social and regional inequalities" and IV: "promote the well-being of all, without regard to origin, race, sex, color, age, or any other form of discrimination." Guimarães, "Measures to Combat Discrimination and Racial Inequality in Brazil," 146, 6.

80. Guimarães, "Measures to Combat Discrimination," 143–153.

81. Guimarães, "Measures to Combat Discrimination," 143–153; Burdick, "The Lost Constituency," 150.

82. Rohter, "Racial Quotas in Brazil."

83. College admission in Brazil is highly competitive, with many more applicants than available places, especially for prestigious public universities. Of the 1.4 million students admitted to universities each year, only 3 percent identify themselves as African Brazilian and only 18 percent come from the public schools, where most African Brazilians study. Rohter, "Racial Quotas in Brazil Touch Off Fierce Debate"; Janer Cristaldo, "Spare Me Quotas," *Brazil* (March 2003) <http://www.brazil-brasil.com/p112mar03.htm>.

84. Rohter, "Racial Quotas in Brazil."

85. Rohter, "Racial Quotas in Brazil."

86. Pueng Vongs, "Affirmative Action in Other Countries."

87. Rohter, "Racial Quotas in Brazil."

88. Reichmann, "Brazil's Denial of Race," 35–42; Guimarães, "Measures to Combat Discrimination and Racial Inequality in Brazil," 143–153.

5
Memories of Japanese Identity and Racial Hierarchy[1]

MIYUKI YONEZAWA

Modern Japan is "a nation in a kind of trance about its past, unable to remember it distinctly and yet unable to forget — living in 'a floating world' "[2]

Since World War II, Japan has had a vague belief that it is a homogeneous country without any racial or ethnic conflicts. Most Japanese do not recognize the existence of minorities within their country; even the political leaders succumb to this prevailing belief. As a result of such a mentality, minorities living within Japan have been virtually ignored. Many Japanese today may be confused about their identity. This chapter discusses race, ethnicity, and the formation of a national identity in the making of Japan.

The chapter focuses on two minority groups: the Ainu and the Okinawans. These groups turned out to be the prototypes for the Japanese government's policy-making of their physical and psychological boundaries of the Empire of Japan. Later, Japan used the same tactics to include, and to exclude, other minorities such as Koreans and Taiwanese. While I explain about the inclusion of the minorities, I will discuss how Japan adopted the European ideas of race and social Darwinism. At the turn of the twentieth century, the Meiji government used these ideas to conceptualize its own identity in a national and international scene, while recreating the Japanese mythology in the national polity and strengthening Japan in a Western way.

Demography of Japanese minorities

"Race" is a concept originating from Europe categorizing people into distinct human types.[3] The Japanese have been put into a single division of the Yellow race, or Mongolian race, or some such category. In that interpretation, Japan is not a country with a variety of races living together as in the United States; they would appear homogeneous. However, the meaning of race connotes more than skin color. Racial connotation signifies some innate marking of a person, which segregates "Self" from "Other." It implies an imagined or real biological difference to a person in a social context, which in turn creates a hierarchy. In fact, the newest studies about race and ethnicity reveal that the seemingly scientific concept of race is largely a social construct.[4] Theories of racial thinking constructed in the West to understand outwardly different people around the world influenced Japan in the nineteenth and twentieth centuries in the face of the threat of Western colonialism and imperialism in Asia.

According to historian Michael Weiner, a mainstream group "racializes" or racially discriminates against other groups for the mainstream's socioeconomic and political benefit.[5] "Racialized" here refers to the fact that a group of people acknowledge differences (anything like skin color, posture, attitude, discourse, etc.) in a certain other group, no matter how vague the differences are to a third person. Differences are sometimes imaginary or sometimes real, and usually the group with greater benefits draws a line between "Self" and "Other." From this perspective, in Japan there are some "racialized" minority groups such as the Ainu, Okinawans, Korean and Chinese residents, *Hisabetsu* Burakumin,[6] a recently growing number of foreign laborers, especially Brazilians of Japanese descent, and others. If a Japanese person doesnot belong to one of these "racialized" minority groups, then one usually identifies him- or herself simply as Japanese or Yamato, the latter term used more for boosting jingoism during World War II.

Today, mainstream Japanese are the overwhelmingly largest portion of the total population of approximately 125 million. They are about 95 percent, while the total minority population is only about 5 percent. The population data of each group is not decisive, since the identity issue involves the group's political and social positioning. Below is a rough estimate from various sources.[7]

The Ainu are the smallest in number, somewhere around 24,000 or more.[8] They live mainly on the northern island of Hokkaido, and they are considered to be a different "race" from the mainstream Japanese people. The Okinawans are more than 1.1 million, living mostly in the southern islands, old Ryukyu — now called Okinawa. Korean residents are estimated to be more than 680,000. They are descendants of Koreans who voluntarily or involuntarily came to Japan before and during Japan's occupation of the peninsula (1910–1945). They live mainly in the Kansai region, which is the western area of mainland Japan. Chinese residents living in Japan number around 200,000.

Hisabetsu Burakumin are said to be descendants of outcasts called *Eta* (extreme filth) or *Hinin* (non-human) in the Tokugawa feudal period (1600–1868).[9] They are said to be from the same stock as mainstream Japanese (although some say that they were Korean descendants, which mainstream studies deny).[10] *Hisabetsu* Burakumin cannot be physically distinguished from mainstream Japanese. They can "pass" as being mainstream. With the history of strong social stigma and the liberating movement after World War II, the number of *Hisabetsu* Burakumin is not clear. Some sources report their number at three million right after the war.[11]

In recent years, there has been a new minority group forming: foreign laborers, especially Brazilians of Japanese descent. Their number increased during Japan's bubble economy period of the 1980s, and especially after 1990. Japanese Brazilians today number upward of 200,000.[12]

Early making of Japanese togetherness

Japanese history goes as far back as the Jōmon period (10,000 B.C.–400 B.C.), Yayoi period (400 B.C.–A.D. 300), and Kofun (Ancient Tomb) period (A.D. 300–A.D. 700). In the Kofun period, a unified nation called "Yamato" was established and developed around the area near Kyoto (called the Kinai area in western Honshu, the main island of Japan). From the Yamato dynasty until today, a Japanese imperial line is said to have continued. There were times when the imperial line lost their governing power from the twelfth century to the late nineteenth century, and then again later, after the end of World War II. However, the imperial line was and still is at the heart of Japanese culture. The reason can be attributed to the existence of a Japanese mythology that was written in order to authorize Yamato emperors' rule.

Around the early eighth century, Yamato emperors and their followers authorized officials to compile a national history book, which resulted in two national history-mythologies — *Kojiki* and *Nihon shoki*, edited respectively in A.D. 712 and A.D. 720.[13] The *Kojiki* and *Nihon shoki* are commonly referred to as *Ki-ki*, and they are filled with descriptions about the beginning of the universe — chaos; separation between Heaven and Earth; appearance of gods (*kamigami*), and the creation of the land of Japan by a pair of gods who gave birth to various gods including Amaterasu Ōmikami (a sun goddess); and Amaterasu's grandchild's descent to Japan. Also included in the *Ki-ki* is the legend of Emperor Jinmu,[14] an offspring of the god descended from Heaven, who conquered rebels in the wild "Eastern Land (*tōdo*)," unified the country, and established the Yamato government in the Kinai area on the mainland.[15]

Whether the *Ki-ki* constituted an allegory for Japanese history based on actual facts, or were entirely fictionalized epics or mythology, has been invariably controversial. It is not to be discussed further here. Rather, it is to be noted that the Yamato dynasty used the *Ki-ki* mythology as a way to declare its right to rule its own people and its legitimacy to other, outside powers, especially the strong neighbor, China. From around A.D. 400 to A.D. 600, before the *Ki-ki*'s history-myth was written, early Yamato emperors and their political supporters had already imported much from Chinese, ranging from their writing system and bureaucratic organization to their legal theories. Even a foreign religion, Buddhism, was imported. However, Yamato government leaders maintained their *Ki-ki* mythology, which became a foundation for the Japanese native religion and ideology called Shinto (literally translated as "Way to God"). Popular

Shintoism coexisted alongside Buddhism. In the Meiji Era (1868–1912), this popular Shintoism became more institutionalized as State Shinto and almost became the nation's appointed religion; however, this movement eventually failed because of pressure from the Western powers who demanded freedom of religion (what they actually wanted was freedom for Christian missionary activities).[16]

Throughout Japanese history, *Nihon shoki*, part of the *Ki-ki*, was formally lectured and widely read in the court and among bureaucrats.[17] Thus, in later centuries, even when the rulers of Japan changed from the Yamato dynasty to samurai lords, the ruling class was familiar with the stories of the *Ki-ki*, and used the stories to authorize their actions. For instance, in the twelfth century, a samurai lord, Minamoto-no Yoritomo, established his government in Kamakura, east of Kyoto, after he pacified the "Eastern Land." His rebels in the "Eastern Land" were the Fujiwara clan, northeast of Kamakura. Yatsuki Kunio, a scholar of Japanese ethics and ideas, points out the deep symbolical implications of pacifying the "Eastern Land" in Japanese history.[18] In other words, Minamoto-no Yoritomo intended to embody the legendary Emperor Jinmu in order to demonstrate his righteousness to rule the country. It was important for a ruler of Japan to pacify the wild East and rule the country.

The *Ki-ki* mythology as such had been a shared memory carried from generation to generation especially among the rulers of Japan throughout Japanese history even until World War II. The mythology created a feeling of togetherness among the Yamato. Because of this background, modern Meiji founders could succeed in leading the Japanese to draw a clear line between themselves, the Yamato, and "Others."

Ainu living at "the North Gate for the Empire of Japan"[19]

The *Nihon shoki* tells about the *Emishi*, a group rebelling against the Yamato emperor.[20] Modern scholars assume the term *Emishi* refers to the Ainu. The Ainu lived on Ezo — a pre-1869 name for the present-day northern island of Hokkaido — as well as in the Tohoku region in the northeastern part of Honshu, Sakhalin, and the Kurile or Chishima Islands. These areas were cold, crude, and undeveloped.

Unlike the Yamato Japanese farmers, the Ainu were hunter-gatherers. They had their own language, religious customs, and habits. Because of their features — with "hairy" and "clear-cut faces" resembling Caucasians — some old anthropologists even suggested that the Ainu were originally Whites.[21]

The Ainu came to be spotted more often in Japanese history during the rule of the Tokugawa Shogunate after the seventeenth century. A small feudal domain (*han*) made of Matsumae clan, was established in Hokkaido and they ruled the Ainu. In 1799, the Tokugawa Shogunate itself started to rule the Ainu directly when Russia began to proceed south and entered some islands where the Ainu were living. The Tokugawa government stationed security guards there, and encouraged the Ainu to be assimilated into Japanese society. In fact, the Tokugawa built Buddhist temples out of fear of encroachment by Russian

Christianity.[22] However, the Tokugawa did not do much financially to help the Ainu to be assimilated. After the Russians stopped their threat to move into Hokkaido for a while, the Matsumae clan again took control of the Ainu. However, after the end of the Tokugawa period in 1868, Japan once again confronted Russia about the northern borders.

Now, the newly established Meiji government had to negotiate with Russian representatives about the nation's border. In the negotiations, the Japanese government urgently insisted that Ezo land belonged to Japan because the Ainu were their subjects.[23] For Japan, Hokkaido was an important northern fortress to protect the mainland — it was "the North Gate for the Empire of Japan." The strategy was used again later with the inclusion of the Ryukyu Kingdom (later called Okinawa) in the south, as the "South Gate for the Empire."

Like Native Americans in the United States, the Ainu were segregated and did not enjoy full citizenship. The Meiji founders saw the United States as an example with its policies toward Native Americans. In May 1869, the Meiji government officials declared they would develop Ezo (now Hokkaido) and start the assimilation of the Ainu into the mainstream, from language and customs to education. The Meiji government took their land and gave it to thousands of Japanese colonists. In 1899, the Meiji government passed the Hokkaido Former Aborigine Protection Law. It aimed to transform the hunting Ainu into farmers on plots of land. The law gave the governor of Hokkaido the power to manage the Ainu's communal assets. Thus, the Ainu's life was uprooted.[24]

The Ainu were registered as Japanese commoners when a family register system was established in 1870. When registering, the Ainu were forced to change their names to Japanese. Also, their education opportunities were limited. Their schools were built in the Ainu's area, segregated from the mainstream Japanese children. The Ainu's compulsory education was shortened to 4 years with less subjects taught than the mainstream Japanese who got 6 years of education.[25] In the same way, later history shows that the Ainu were not treated equally as mainstream Japanese in the fields of politics, education, employment, marriage, and other civil rights.

Myth of pacifying the "Eastern Land"

Why was the inclusion of the Ainu accepted so easily even if Japan needed Hokkaido for their security interest? A clue to this lies in ancient Japanese mythology, which says that Japan will complete its unification under a strong leader after conquering rebellious "savages" in the wild "Eastern Land." The *Ki-ki* tells about rebelling groups called *Emishi* (often interpreted as Ainu), *Tsuchigumo*, and *Kumaso*, who were not thought to be Yamato people. Thus, conquering the Ainu, rebellious "savages" in the northeastern area,[26] follows the traditional *Ki-ki* myth.

Japanese ethics scholar Yatsuki Kunio points out the significant trips by Emperor Meiji for embodying Emperor Jinmu. Around 1873, Sanjō Sanetomo, an influential political leader, encouraged Emperor Meiji to travel to the northern land, Hokkaido, in order to show his authority. Because, even with the Meiji Restoration, the "imperial virtue" did not fully reach eastern Japan (*tōdo*), still less the marginal area of Hokkaido, Sanjō stressed how important and urgent it was to let people know of the Emperor's existence.[27]

When Sanjō submitted this to the Emperor, it was a politically uneasy year for the weak Meiji government. The Emperor was very young (only 15 years old on the day of the Restoration). The Meiji founders issued reforms for dissecting the *han*, or feudal domains, to help establish prefectures in 1871; and in 1873, they brought about the introduction of both a military draft and a land tax reformation. Ex-samurai lost several material privileges; in addition, they lost their status as warriors because of the proclamation of the new military draft that allowed all men to be drafted as soldiers. Around Japan, discontented ex-samurai caused riots. The largest riot was the unsuccessful coup d'etat of 1877 led by Saigō Takamori, one of the Meiji founders. Many peasants also were uneasy with the changes brought about by the Meiji government, including the land tax, and some even rioted.

Suspicion among Japanese people against the Meiji government's rapid open-door and Westernization policy was so high that there was even a rumor circulated in the newspaper that the Emperor was going to be converted to Christianity. The rumor began after the Meiji government dispatched a political mission to Europe and the United States with former court noble Iwakura Tomomi as delegate, from November 1871 through September 1873.[28]

Why did the Meiji Emperor take six trips all over Japan during the tumultuous years 1872–1885 — even twice to the Tohoku region and Hokkaido (all acknowledged as *tōdo*) in 1876 and later again 1881? Japanese ethics scholar Yatsuki contends that going to Hokkaido meant the Emperor was embodying Emperor Jinmu, the traditional mythological figure ruling Japan after pacifying the "Eastern Land."[29] The trips were significant in a mythological way.

The mythology was not just a fantasy in the minds of the Meiji founders. They needed a strong moral backbone to appeal to the public about the righteousness of their destroying the Tokugawa establishment by supporting young Emperor Meiji. For that reason, Iwakura formally put the name of legendary Emperor Jinmu of the *Ki-ki* into the Proclamation of the Meiji Restoration (*ōsei fukko no daigōrei*) on December 9, 1867. The proclamation declared that Japan would restore the monarchy "established by Emperor Jinmu (*Jinmu sōgyo no hajime ni motozuki*)." Without inclusion of such an ideologically powerful name, the Meiji founders could have just been rebellious traitors who set out to destroy the Tokugawa government and manipulate the young Emperor.[30]

Utilizing the *Ki-ki* myth, the Meiji founders started a grand but ambiguous project — trying to reconcile two opposites by transforming Japan into a modern nation-state like the Western powers, and at the same time trying to restore a nation living with the emperor as a divine leader in a traditional, and anachronistic way. It was a modern plan for building up "a rich country with a strong army" (*fukoku kyōhei*). Simultaneously, it was a plan for making "a divine country" where, based on the national Shinto, the emperor, a living god in "an unbroken line of sovereigns" (*bansei ikkei*) should rule his loyal subjects forever. The latter plan was called *kōminka*, and it forced the different ethnic groups into using the Japanese language, changing their names to the Japanese way, and adopting Shintoism, among other things. The Meiji founders started to create a strong nation-state built on Yamato ethnic solidarity.

Okinawans living at "the South Gate for the Empire of Japan"

Like the Ainu, the Okinawans were forced to be included into Meiji Japan. Okinawa, the former Ryukyu Kingdom, is located in the far southwestern part of the Japanese archipelago.

Ryukyu's history became connected with Japan directly in the late sixteenth century when a Japanese warlord, Hideyoshi Toyotomi, ruled Japan and attacked Korea. Because Ryukyu was reluctant to help his attack, the Satsuma clan, one of the influential domains (*han*) in southeast Kyushu, took the opportunity to "punish" the kingdom by invading them. Ryukyu came under Satsuma's control after that; it had to pay an annual tax to the Satsuma clan from then on, but it was also allowed to continue its tributary relations with China. This dual subordination continued until the annexation of Ryukyu by Meiji Japan.

In 1872, Japan forced Ryukyu to become a Japanese domain (*han*), and in 1879, formally annexed it into imperial Japan as one of the prefectures (*ken*). Because Ryukyu was an independent kingdom, because it had a dual relationship with China and Japan, and because the Western powers were ready to intervene, it was not easy for Japan to include Ryukyu, compared with the inclusion of the Ainu. Their excuse, that the Ryukyuans were ethnic Japanese, required a far-fetched logic even among Japanese political leaders.

In order to justify the annexation of Ryukyu, the Meiji government presented myths and legends as actual history when former U.S. President Ulysses Grant came to Japan to play an intermediary role between China and Japan about the Ryukyu issue in July 1879.[31]

One mythology Japan incorporated was about Shunten-ō, the Ryukyu king whose reign started in 1187. It says that he was supposed to be the son of a Japanese warrior-hero named Minamoto-no Tametomo. According to the Japanese historical record, Minamoto-no Tametomo killed himself or was murdered as a rebel against the Yamato emperor; however, as the legend puts it, he escaped from his pursuers, went to Ryukyu, and married the daughter of one of the influential rulers there. This story began to spread, especially after Takizawa Bakin, a popular novelist in the Tokugawa Era, wrote from 1807 through 1811, twenty-eight volumes of stories about Tametomo's life.[32]

In 1879, the Ryukyu Kingdom was forced to disappear, and Ryukyu became Okinawa-*ken*, part of the Empire of Japan. Even though there were different opinions among the Japanese about whether Ryukyuans or Okinawans were ethnic Japanese, the Meiji government's main concern was that they needed

Okinawa as "the South Gate of the Empire of Japan." Okinawa was merely a "gate lock" (*sayaku*) for the Yamato people's benefit, a buffer against Western colonization. To be sure, the fear of the Japanese proponents of Ryukyuan annexation was proven in 1886 when England inquired about leasing land in Okinawa for a military base in the midst of the growing conflict between China and Japan over the issue of Korea. The military value of Okinawa was more important to the Meiji government than ambiguity about the ethnic identity of Ryukyuans or Okinawans as Japanese. In this sense, the more the government thought that the Ryukyuans were different, the more it hastened its steps to make them Japanese through education in order to develop their loyalty to Japan.[33]

Language education was especially important because the Okinawans had their own language. In just three years after the annexation, fifty-one schools were built in Okinawa — from elementary schools to junior high and even teachers' schools. Interestingly, the Meiji government collected an elementary school fee from other new prefectures, whereas it gave subsidies for Okinawa school children to encourage education. Also, Okinawa was the first prefecture to place pictures of the Emperor Meiji in its schools. These pictures were called *goshin-ei* and they were considered to represent the sacred body of the emperor.[34] Thus, Okinawans were forced to become citizens of Japan for the benefit of the national narratives — the emperor's family-nation.

The Meiji founders' institutional control of the national identity encouraged the Japanese people along with Okinawans to support imperialist Japan. For example, from 1882 through 1884, the Meiji government made a collection of ninety-one nationalistic songs for elementary school children.[35] In addition, the first elementary school textbook of Japanese history, published in 1903, described the nation-making mythologies of Imperial ancestral goddess Amaterasu Ōmikami and the legendary Emperor Jinmu.[36] Moreover, well up until the end of World War II, geography and history textbooks described stories from the *Ki-ki* mythology and imperial virtues in order to develop narratives for the making of a nationalistic Japan.

Who are the Japanese? — discussion from Meiji through World War II[37]

Were the Yamato people of pure blood or of mixed blood in the "family" country? Such a proposition was fiercely discussed when Japan included a different race/ethnic group such as the Ainu or the Okinawans. Even before the Meiji Era, however, the proposition was examined by Japanese and Western scholars; this ran on into a wartime argument about the Japanese national identity.

For this section, I borrow extensively from Eiji Oguma's analysis of heterogeneous vs. homogeneous theorists because of its clarity and precision. According to Oguma, in the early eighteenth century, the two main representatives of the group of scholars perceiving heterogeneity of origin were Arai Hakuseki and Fuji Teikan. After examining the remains of shell mounds and stone tools, Arai, a Confucian scholar and politician, speculated that Japanese ancestors came from Korea. Also, Confucianist Fuji said that Susanō-no Mikoto, Amaterasu Ōmikami's brother god in the *Ki-ki* mythology, was originally from Korea, and that Emperor Jinmu, who is told to pacify the "Eastern Land," from China.

Against these theorists of heterogeneity, one of the strongest theorists of homogeneity was Motoori Norinaga. Motoori was a scholar and founder of the school called *kokugaku*, or the study of ancient Japanese thought. An ethnocentrist, Motoori said that "the stories about the gods depicted in the *Ki-ki*'s were true stories of miracles."

In the pre-Meiji and Meiji Era, Western researchers also started to investigate Japanese identity and race. Similar research conducted by Philipp Franz von Siebold, Erwin von Balz, and Edward Sylvester Morse suggested that the Japanese people were a mix between indigenous people living in the archipelago and people from the Asian continent.[38]

Early in the twentieth century, Japanese anthropologists backed up the Westerners' conclusion that the Japanese were of mixed races. Two anthropologists in particular, Tsuboi Shōgorō, the first president of the Tokyo Anthropology Association (*Tokyo jinrui gakkai*), and Torii Ryūzō, were advocates and advertisers of the mixed-race theory of the Japanese. They indirectly contributed to a national imperial policy of expansionism. When Japan stretched its national boundaries to Taiwan in 1895, to Korea in 1910, and to Manchuria in 1932, their theory of a heterogeneous nation lent support to the aggressive national political policy.

Kida Sadakichi also spread the theory of Japan as a heterogeneous nation. His scholarly work in many fields of study, including archaeology and ancient history, supported the contention that the Ainu and *Hisabetsu* Burakumin were not a different *minzoku*, or race/ethnic group, from other Japanese.[39] This philanthropist's main concern was to "save" these discriminated groups; however, his activities as a theorist of heterogeneity ironically backed up the imperial foreign policy of expansion.

Historians, linguists, magazine publishers, and influential politicians such as Ōkuma Shigenobu joined the group of theorists of heterogeneity, and the heterogeneous theory was increasingly supported in political circles. In contrast to Kida's perception of the different groups as equals with Japanese, however, the Japanese politicians and expansionists usually thought that the Koreans and Taiwanese, as well as the Ainu and Okinawans, were not equal to them, but should become subordinates under a "greater" Japanese Empire.

Against the heterogeneous theorists, there were national polity (*kokutai-ron*) theorists, eugenic scholars, some anthropologists, and historians. These theorists of homogeneity were not as well supported politically, especially during the Japanese expansionist period. As Oguma demonstrates, the idea of a homogeneous nation was not mainstream before World War II. Usually homogeneous theorists stressed the uniqueness of the Japanese among all the peoples of the world. *Kokutai-ron* is a theory that was firmly molded together with the promulgation of the Imperial Rescript on Education (*kyōiku chokugo*) in 1890. The Rescript, an attempt at a national moral guide with a tint of Confucianism, was closely interconnected with the Meiji Constitution. Roughly speaking, *kokutai-ron* aimed at creating a nation-state on the idea of a family writ large, with the emperor as its head. The implication was that the relationship between the governing and the governed should never be a forced one. The emperor and his subjects were related by natural *jō*, or emotions and affections, in a family nation. This national polity was the ideal for *kokutai-ron* theorists, some of whom were Katō Hiroyuki, President of Tokyo Imperial University (now University of Tokyo), Hozumi Hassoku, scholar of law, and Inoue Tetsujirō. Inoue was known for writing a government-sponsored guidebook for *kyōiku chokugo*. Homogeneous theorists' ideas did not mesh with the national heterogeneous policy in the nation's aggressive expansion resulting in the inclusion of different ethnic groups. They developed an idea of "adoption." If a family can adopt a child, then, too, can a family state "adopt" different *minzoku*, or races/ethnic groups.

On the other hand, eugenic theorists claimed that the Japanese should maintain pure blood, blaming the fall of the Roman Empire on its inclusion of different *minzoku*. They warned against racial mixing with Koreans. Anthropologist Hasebe Kotondo emphasized the uniqueness of the Japanese, especially after the start of the Pacific War. To him, the Ainu, Koreans, and others were completely different races from the Japanese. The Japanese were descendants of people of the Stone Age in the archipelago, who were very rarely mixed with people from the Asian continent after that period. In that sense, non-Yamato who were described in the *Ki-ki* mythology, such as *Tsuchigumo, Kumaso*, and *Emishi* were not the Ainu or some other different *minzoku*, but ethnic Japanese rebels against the imperial army. Historian Tsuda Sōkichi, famous for his hatred against the Chinese and Koreans, denied that the *Ki-ki* were national history books based on actual facts; rather he declared them imaginary fiction. According to him, *Nihon minzoku* — the Japanese race/ethnic group — had been living in the archipelago and the Ainu were later intruders.

Thus, as Oguma illustrates, the Japanese see two reflections when they look in the mirror at their own identity. One is the idea that the Japanese are originally a homogeneous people; the other is that the Japanese are a product of a mixture of different races and ethnicity. These two threads are spun into one yarn of Japanese society.

Racial thinking and social Darwinism

Japanese racial ideas also had some Western roots. Comparative law and politics scholar Yamamuro Shin'ichi provides two examples of how Japan developed its racial identity from a Western constructed mirror after the beginning of the Meiji Era. First, in 1869, Fukuzawa Yukichi, an influential opinion-leader and educator representing the Meiji Era, described five races all over the world in his book entitled *Shōchū bankoku ichiran*. Yamamuro points out that the description of races was probably based on an American high school geography textbook by Samuel Augustus Mitchell. Second, in 1870, the racial category of humans according to German racial theorist Johann Blumenbach was introduced and these categories were put into Japanese elementary school textbooks.[40] Thus, a Western ideology of racial hierarchy was adopted by a Japan that was on the verge of joining the colonizing movement in the world.

An imperialistic competition for supremacy took place in the late nineteenth century, involving European nations, the United States, and finally Japan. A key intellectual prop was a popular Western ideology — social Darwinism. The survival of the fittest doctrine became a social and political principle. Hierarchies of wealth, power, status, and even health were not moral or policy issues; they were simply the inevitable products of natural selection. Japanese intellectuals of the time imported this Western way of thinking. If the Ainu or Okinawans lived in poverty, it just proved their inherent inferiority in a struggle for survival. In the early twentieth century, England and the United States were proven to be "superior" because they flourished, whereas Spain was proven to be "inferior" because they lost their power in the Americas. Thus, Katō Hiroyuki, a national polity theorist, utilized the notions of "struggle for survival" and "survival of the fittest" as an analysis of the contemporary conflicts between Japan and Russia. Concerning the Russo-Japanese war, he declared that Japan's victory over Russia was a natural result of the superiority of his country's homogeneous polity.[41] Social Darwinism had the dangerous potential to transform Japan into an imperialist nation, as well as to appeal to the uniqueness of Japan in a competition with the then powerful England and America. The winner of the competition would prove to be superior, according to this principle.

With Japan's victory in wars against China (1894–1895), and then again against Russia (1904–1905), the discussion over race reached a point that some politicians and intellectuals thought the Japanese would be racially improved by intermarriage with Westerners. Even Prime Minister Itō Hirobumi asked for a second opinion from Herbert Spencer about the idea. Spencer advised negatively, saying "hybridization between disparate 'races' would produce disastrous consequences for both" and cited Latin America.[42] The idea of improving the Japanese "racially" soon lost support because it meant the extinction of the Japanese *minzoku*.[43]

From 1919 through the 1920s, several incidents aroused anger among the Japanese in terms of racial identity. First, in the discussion on the peace treaty in Paris after World War I, Japan proposed to add a new article abolishing racial discrimination in the international community in the Articles of the League of Nations. It was voted down. The motives for Japan's action stemmed from a Japanese immigration issue in the United States. Racists in the United States were against Japanese immigrants. This culminated when the U.S. Congress passed an immigration law banning Japanese immigrants in 1924. The Japanese media denounced the action as a "disgrace."[44]

This "disgrace" encouraged the homogeneous theorists to boast of Japanese homogeneity, ignoring the Koreans and Taiwanese who were in the country. The heterogeneous theorists were more enthusiastic in praise of their family nation-state, which was made of many *minzoku* from "the South Sea, China, Mongolia, Korea, and Siberia" compared with racist America. The Japanese "mission" was to lead Asia and regain Asia for the Yellow race (*ōshokujin*), taking it back from the White race (*hakujin*).[45] The mission culminated in "the Great East Asia Co-Prosperity Sphere" in 1940. The Pacific War was psychologically "a race war," especially from the Japanese point of view.[46]

Emperor Shōwa (1926–1989) inherited the Meiji's ideology and maintained it until the end of World War II. During the war, the Yamato spirit (*Yamato damashii*) was taught in schools. This spirit encouraged the racial superiority of Yamato *minzoku*. The Shōwa Era's pro-war leaders encouraged Japanese to believe the Yamato spirit was so sublime and so unique that they should sacrifice their lives for the country and the emperor.[47] If one died for the emperor in war, his loyal subjects' souls would be deified in the Yasukuni (Shinto) Shrine in Tokyo.[48]

Aftermath of minorities' inclusion

We need to discuss the Okinawans and the Ainu when the government-sponsored narratives collapsed after Japan's defeat in World War II. The United States occupied Okinawa until 1972 and maintains a dominating military presence to this day. Right after the occupation, there was a movement for the independence of Ryukyu, backed up by the Okinawans' trust in the United States as a liberator from Japanese rule. Soon, however, the Okinawans became disappointed because it became clear to them that the United States mostly intended to use their land for military bases. Also, they were discouraged that the U.S. military government treated them "racially" as lower people. This disappointment with the United States led the Okinawans into a movement to reunite with Japan.[49] Ironically, the process and idea of power relationships between the governing and the governed was almost similar to the former sovereign nation, Japan. In 1972, Okinawa was returned to Japan.

On the other hand, the Ainu remained in the same position before and after the war. They were Japanese citizens who were discriminated against socially. The only difference was that those Ainu who had been living in Sakhalin and the Kurile Islands (Chishima Islands) were compelled to move to Hokkaido by the former Soviet Union. After that, the Ainu issue was mainly left alone until quite recently.

In the 1930s, the first Ainu organization for the purpose of improving the Ainu's welfare was created. Also, right after the end of World War II, there was a movement among the Ainu, their Japanese supporters, and Christian missionaries represented by British John Batchelor, aimed at liberating the Ainu from Japanese exploitation and regaining their assets and their ethnic pride. In the 1960s and 1970s, there was a heightened Ainu movement demanding social equality corresponding to the worldwide movement for human rights.[50]

In 1997, the Hokkaido Former Aborigine Protection Law of 1899 was finally repealed and replaced with one designed to promote the Ainu culture. Also, under the new law, the office of the governor was supposed to return all assets to the Ainu people. However, because the Ainu's small population is limited to Hokkaido, their uprooted condition and their movement is almost forgotten or ignored by Japanese at large. Witness the following example: In 1998, Prime Minister Obuchi Keizō was visiting an exhibit of Ainu artifacts in the Smithsonian Institution's Natural History Museum in Washington, DC, and he reportedly asked if there were still Ainu in Hokkaido.[51] And in 2001, a congressman from Hokkaido is reported to have said that "the Ainu were totally assimilated"[52] as if they had lost their "Ainu-ness." Such naiveté and ignorance towards minorities is shared by the majority of Japanese.

Conclusion: illusion of a homogeneous Japan

Before World War II, the government-sponsored idea of Japan as a heterogeneous country prevailed, as part of the drive to build an empire in Asia. Postwar Japan aspired to portray itself as a homogeneous nation. This trend continues today, and is still criticized by scholars who study Japanese minority groups, as well as members of minority groups themselves. Postwar Japan began to be comfortable retrogressing into the old narratives of a peaceful and happy family nation-state with a single, homogeneous *minzoku* (forgetting the Ainu and Okinawans) after it lost its Korean and Taiwanese subjects because of the war. As sociologist Oguma contends, after the war, the intellectual circles started to support the idea of Japan as a homogeneous country.[53]

Shortly after the war, led by the U.S. Occupation Headquarters (GHQ), Japan dissected the totalitarian Meiji Constitution, the national moral guide (*kyōiku chokugo*), and State Shintoism, all of which had legitimized the power of the emperor. Instead, Japan adopted a new democratic Constitution, under pressure from GHQ, that declares that the emperor is "the symbol of the State."[54] Education reforms were taken to erase the *Ki-ki* mythology and other ultranationalistic descriptions from school textbooks. Since then, talking about the national mythology, the emperor, loyalty, patriotism, and wartime history in detail has become taboo to most Japanese. Japan's guilt for aggression in neighboring countries (as expressed in the word, "the collective repentance by the 'hundred million' Japanese" (*ichioku sōzange*)[55] affected the education system. Such issues are treated with near silence in the schools. The younger generations do not learn much, intentionally or unintentionally, about twentieth century wartime history.[56] All of this results in people's ignorance about and indifference to an idea of a national identity and issues about minorities.

Since the late 1960s, theories on Japan (*Nihon-ron*) and theories on Japanese (*Nihonjin-ron*) have blossomed. After the Japanese economy rose from the late 1970s through 1980s, and Japan regained confidence, more *Nihon-ron* were written by people outside Japan. The *Nihon-ron* publications mostly focused on the "unique" Japanese business and political system. [57] Naturally, these *Nihon-ron* and *Nihonjin-ron* described the Japanese as one solid, homogeneous group. In the process of describing a national homogeneous identity, the cultures and traditions of minority groups have been buried.

On the other hand, in recent years, there are changes both in how mainstream Japanese look at minority groups, and in how minorities see themselves. Briefly, some minority groups have assimilated into the mainstream, whereas others have worked to establish their identity outside of the mainstream. For example, some of the Ainu want to distinguish their ethnic difference with pride, and they did this by airing a radio show in the Ainu language in 2001.[58] At the same time, other Ainu want to assimilate into the mainstream.[59] For Okinawans, some are comfortable being accepted as Japanese, while others are still uncomfortable about sharing cultural and political identity with Japan even though since the late 1990s, the mainstream media has been celebrating Okinawa's exotic culture. In the case of the *Hisabetsu* Burakumin, liberation activists, as well as financial support from the government, has greatly lessened the discrimination against *Hisabetsu* Burakumin in the postwar era. Some have been merged into the mainstream; however, social discrimination against them still exists.[60] For Koreans in Japan, the general image of Korean culture has been improved after the 2002 World Cup, co-hosted by South Korea and Japan. There are other minority groups within Japan, but there is limited space for discussion here.

These illustrations of minority groups do not, of course, mean that Japan is becoming a multiethnic, multiracial society. Quite the contrary, Japan is still in a daydream that it is a homogeneous nation. Even though scholars of race and ethnicity have pointed out the multiethnic elements of the country, most Japanese are unaware of them. The image of a homogeneous nation has been so rooted in Japanese culture for the last 50 years that mainstream Japanese hardly notice the minorities' existence.

The 1990s witnessed a growing generation of leaders who were born after the war. They are somewhat free from the guilt of the war, history compiled by imperial ideology, and nationalist theories about the polity and the emperor. It is not by accident that there have been numerous publications recently concerning Japan as a nation-state and about the emperors of the last 100 years.[61] Nor is it unexpected to see a rise of ultranationalistic historians who wrote biased history textbooks for junior high schools.[62] The Japanese people born after the war thirst for an understanding of an identity of their own, as well as for an understanding of their country, for they are generations with dim memories and defunct narratives about the country's recent past. Thus, they have half-forgotten, or ignored, racialized minorities inside Japan.

Notes

1. For this chapter, I owe a great deal to John Lanning for both discussions and his continuous academic support that gave me insights to understand human, world and racial thinking; and to Tina Ferrato for her precise advice and editing for the clarity of my ideas in the chapter.

I would like to acknowledge their support at first. This chapter limits itself to draw a rough sketch about a Japanese identity and racial thinking from the late nineteenth century until the present. An enormous amount of historical descriptions and argument had to be omitted in order to avoid incoherence.

In this chapter, I write Japanese names in Japanese order: last names first and first names last. However, I followed the English order in the Notes. Other familiar words and place names are written in their Anglicized forms, for example, Tokyo, not Tōkyō.

2. Fareed Zakaria, "Why the Past Still Haunts Japan," *Newsweek* (Asian version), August 27, 2001, 7. A phrase quoted from a novelist, Kazuo Ishiguro. The article responded to Japan's ambiguous attitude — both regret on the expansionist Japan and seemingly bold acceptance of the nightmare which is seen in the Japanese Prime Minister's attempt to visit Yasukuni (Shinto) Shrine on August 15, 2001.

3. *See* Audrey Smedley, *Race in North America: Origin and Evolution of a Worldview* (Boulder, CO: Westview Press, 1999), 158–167. In the late eighteenth century, a German professor of medicine, Johann Blumenbach, classified humans into four, later five groups: Caucasian, Mongolian, Ethiopian, American, and Malay. His classification was widely accepted, and still is by some.

4. On ideas on race and ethnicity, I referred to the following scholars among others: Stephen Cornell and Douglas Hartmann, *Ethnicity and Race: Making Identities in a Changing World* (Thousand Oaks, CA: Pine Forge Press, 1998); Michael Omi and Howard Winant, *Racial Formation in the United States* (New York: Routledge, 1994); Michael Weiner, Ed., *Japan's Minorities: The Illusion of Homogeneity* (London: Routledge, 1997).

5. Weiner, *Japan's Minorities*, xi–xvii.

6. Burakumin is a taboo word in Japan now. Instead, *Hisabetsu*, or discriminated Burakumin, is used. I followed today's usage in Japan, although most works in English use the term Burakumin.

7. *See* the following estimation of each population in 2001: John Lie, *Multi-ethnic Japan* (Cambridge, MA: Harvard University Press, 2001), 4; On the estimation, *see also* Tony Laszlo, "Japan's Homogeneous Diversity," January 20, 2002: available from http://www.japantimes.co.jp.

8. The Ainu's population was 23,767 in 1999, which appears in Hokkaido government web pages: available from http://www.pref.hokkaido.jp; however, the Ainu Association of Hokkaido (Hokkaido Utari kyōkai) says that the number is not valid because it is underestimated: http://www.ainu-assn.or.jp.

9. Tomohiko Harada, *Hisabetsu Burakumin no rekishi* (Tokyo: Asahi Shinbunsha, 1975), 90–91. According to Harada, in the class system which the Tokugawa Shogunate made, *Eta* and *Hinin* were the outcasts outside the group of four — samurai on top, peasants next, artisans third, and merchants last. The authorities used a rigid class system in order to control the governed by arousing animosity among the classes, especially among the largest number of peasants and those outcasts.

10. Ian Neary, "Burakumin in Contemporary Japan," in Weiner, *Japan's Minorities*, 53.

11. *See* Harada, *Hisabetsu Burakumin*, 371–372. The Taisho Era (1912–1926) witnessed a Buraku community liberation movement with slogans liberating "6000 Buraku, or 3,000,000 people."

12. Daniel Touro Linger, *No One Home: Brazilian Selves Remade in Japan* (Stanford, CA: Stanford University Press, 2001), 6.

13. *See* Masaaki Ueda, *Nihon no shinwa o kangaeru* (Tokyo: Shōgakukan, 1994), 10, 28–29, 192. The *Kojiki* is the oldest government-sponsored history of Japan, and it consists of three volumes. The *Nihon shoki* is the second oldest history sponsored by the government. It is made up of 30 volumes besides one volume of the imperial line record.

14. Some English writers refer to Emperor Jinmu as "Emperor Jimmu," but I followed the popular Romanized Japanese citation.

15. *See* Takamitsu Kōnoshi, *Kojiki to Nihon shoki* (Tokyo: Kōdansha, 1999). There are slight differences in the stories of the gods between the *Kojiki* and the *Nihon shoki*. Kōnoshi compares their differences.

16. Yoshio Yasumaru, *Kamigami no Meiji ishin: shinbutsu bunri to haibutsu kishaku* (Tokyo: Iwanami Shoten, 1979), 196–211. Meiji founders put various kinds of local and village animist shrines under the authority of the great Ise Shrine of State Shinto. In the process, the Meiji founders attempted to destroy Buddhist temples; this tactic later failed. Article 18 of the Constitution of the Empire of Japan (or the Constitution of Meiji as it is commonly known) declared "freedom of religion"; Meiji founders obstinately insisted that State Shinto was not a religion but only customs and rites.

17. *See* Ueda, *Nihon no shinwa*, 195.

18. Kunio Yatsuki, *Tennō to Nihon no kindai, jō: kenpō to arahitogami* (Tokyo: Kōdansha, 2001), 37.

19. Terms such as Ezo (Hokkaido) as "the North gate" and Okinawa as "the South Gate for the Empire of Japan" that are discussed later, were quite popular terms among Japanese opinion leaders from the Meiji Era through 1945. Concerning the term "the North Gate (*kitamon*)," *see* Isao Kikuchi, *Ainu minzoku to Nihonjin: Higashi Ajia no naka no Ezochi* (Tokyo: Asahi Shinbunsha, 1994), 274. According to Kikuchi, an idea of Hokkaido as "the North Gate" went around before the Meiji Era. In 1834, Lord Nariaki Tokugawa, of the Mito clan, presented his opinion paper to a member of the Shogun's Council of Elders (*rōjyu*), suggesting the importance of developing Ezo (Hokkaido) as this place was "a lock of the North Gate." Five years later, he also presented a paper entitled "*Bojutsu fūji*," to the Shogun, saying that, since Japan, "a divine country" was threatened not only by a national famine but also by the encroachment of Christianity, it should prohibit "Dutch studies" (*rangaku*), and Buddhism as a foreign religion, and that it should strengthen the security of Ezo from Russian aggression.

20. For a discussion over whether the Ainu are *Emishi*, *see* Kikuchi, *Ainu minzoku*, 31–34.

21. *See* Kazurō Hanihara, ed., *Nihonjin no kigen* (Tokyo: Asahi Shinbunsha, 1984), 210; also Yōtaro Sawada, *Okinawa to Ainu: Nihon no minzoku mondai* (Tokyo: Shinseisha, 1996), 154–157.

22. Kikuchi, *Ainu minzoku*, 204. He says that three Buddhist temples were built in Higashi Ezochi in 1804, mainly for early Japanese colonists but also for assimilating the Ainu.

23. For more details about the discussions on the negotiations, *see* Eiji Oguma, "*Nihonjin*" no kyōkai [*The Boundaries of the Japanese*] (Tokyo: Shinyōsha, 1998), 51.

24. *See* George A. De Vos and William O. Wetherall; updated by Kaye Stearman, *Japan's Minorities: Burakumin, Koreans, Ainu, and Okinawans*, ed. Ben Whitaker, new 1983 edition (London: Minority Rights Group, 1983), 12–13. For a more recent description of the Ainu, *see* Richard Siddle, "Ainu: Japan's Indigenous people," in Weiner, *Japan's Minorities*, 17–49.

25. Oguma, "*Nihonjin*," 69; Sawada, *Okinawa to Ainu*, 181–182.

26. When Yamato emperors and other leaders of Japan talked about "the Eastern Land," it referred to somewhere east and somewhere uncivilized from their designated place. It was a vague notion; Yatsuki contends that the east does not have to be an actual geographical direction. Although the Ainu geographically lived in northeastern Tohoku and the northern frontier in Hokkaido, they were living in "the Eastern Land" in the sense in which the Japanese leaders spoke.

27. Yatsuki, *Tennō to Nihon*, 29.

28. Yasumaru, *Kamigami no Meiji*, 130.

29. Yatsuki, *Tennō to Nihon*, 27–40.

30. Isao Inoue, *Ōsei fukko* (Tokyo: Chūō Kōronsha, 1991), 333–341. Iwakura agreed with ideas of Misao Tamamatsu, a scholar of Japanese studies (*kokugaku*), that restoration declaration should be based on the authority of Emperor Jinmu. *See also* Yasumaru, *Kamigami no Meiji*, 3–4.

31. Oguma, "*Nihonjn*," 31–34.

32. For more details about the discussions on the mythology and ethnic identity of the Okinawans and Koreans, *see* Sawada, *Okinawa to Ainu*, 28–30; Shuzen Hokama, *Okinawa no rekishi to bunka* (Tokyo: Chūō Kōronsho, 1986), 35; Oguma, "*Nihonjn*," 197. Sawada contends that the Tametomo legend is based on *Chūzan sekan*, one of the official Ryukyuan history books edited in 1648. He suggests that Shunten was probably a Yamato descendant even if the Tametomo legend is suspect. However, Hokama says that *Chūzan sekan* and other Okinawa history books might have some parts which were embellished. Oguma also points out the Japanese government's similar use of the mythology for the inclusion of Koreans. He says that even Japanese confidential papers in *Naimushō*, or the Ministry of Home Affairs, said that one of the gods, Susanō-no Mikoto in the *Ki-ki*, is related to an ancestor of a Korean king. This "connection" that Japan and Korea shared the same ancestry was called *nissen dōso ron*. The idea of the connection was used as an excuse for Japanese expansionism.

33. Oguma, "*Nihonjin*," 37.

34. Oguma, "*Nihonjin*," 35–36; Sawada, *Okinawa to Ainu*, 49–50; *see* the details for Japanese language education for the Okinawans, Fujisawa Ken'ichi, *Kindai Okinawa kyōiku no shikaku* (Tokyo: Shakai Hyōronsha, 2000), 192–197.

35. Quoted in Yatsuki, *Tennō to Nihon*, 110.

36. Quoted in Kōnoshi, *Kojiki to Nihon shoki*, 201–202. Kōnoshi cited some lines of the first chapter of the history textbook which says: "Amaterasu Ōmikami is Your Majesty's ancestral goddess . . .."

37. Eiji Oguma, *Tan'itsu minzoku shinwa no kigen* [*The Myth of the Homogeneous Nation*] (Tokyo: Shinyōsha, 1995). As my intention here in this section is to make a rough outline of the

discussion among homogeneous versus heterogeneous theorists, I made a short summary of Oguma's book, but I had to omit many arguments by Japanese opinion leaders described by Oguma.

38. Oguma, *Tan'itsu*, 19–24. Siebold, a German doctor and naturalist, studied stone implements and wrote that the Ainu were a native people in Japan, later replaced by people from Mongolia. He also said that the Ainu and Rykyuans were the same race. Another German doctor Balz who taught medicine at Tokyo Medical School said that the Ainu were different from the Yamato. Morse, an American biologist as well as a follower of Darwinism, discovered the Ōmori shell mound, and made the hypothesis that before the Ainu an unknown native group had lived in Japan and left the mound.

39. *"Minzoku"* can be translated as people, race, nation, or ethnic group. There is a term, *jinshu* for race; however, like the English usage, the meaning of *jinshu* and *minzoku* is sometimes overlapping; and it was especially so during the periods from the Meiji Era to the end of World War II. I translated *minzoku* as race/ethnic group for its racial implication in this chapter.

40. Cited from Shin'ichi Yamamuro, *Shisōkadai toshite no Ajia* (Tokyo: Iwanami Shoten, 2001), 56, 663.

41. Michael Weiner, "The Invention of Identity: 'Self' and 'Other' in Pre-War Japan," in Weiner, *Japan's Minorities*, 6.

42. Weiner, "The Invention of Identity," in Weiner, *Japan's Minorities*, 7.

43. *See* Oguma, *Tan'itsu*, 172–179. Even the theory that Japanese were Whites from Judah, Babylon, Assyria or other places, appeared. Oguma contends the theory was not Japanese but from Westerners' ideas. A Spanish Jesuit priest, Pedro de Morejon (who is probably the one to whom Oguma refers — Oguma's citation is not clear here), wrote *Nihon Shina kenbunroku* published in 1621. Morejon contended that the Chinese and Japanese were a mix of Oriental indigenous races with people from Babylon.

44. See the details of the racially biased process on the U.S. immigration law of 1924 in John Higham, *Strangers in the Land: Patterns on American Nativism 1860–1925* (New York: Antheneum, 1978; orig. New York: Rutgers, 1963); and Roger Daniels, *The Politics of Prejudice: The Anti-Japanese Movement in California and the Struggle for Japanese Exclusion* (Berkeley, CA: University of California Press, 1962).

45. Oguma, *Tan'itsu*, 167–169.

46. Japan, needless to say, had discriminated against the Ainu, the Okinawans, the Taiwanese and Koreans. *See* John W. Dower, *War Without Mercy: Race and Power in the Pacific War* (New York: Pantheon Books, 1986), 4. He is one of a few Western historians who clearly says that "To scores of millions of participants, the war was . . . a race war."

47. Concerning Yamato spirit, *see* Herbert P. Bix, *Hirohito and the Making of Modern Japan* (New York: HarperCollins Publishers, 2000), 52.

48. Kazutaka Yamaguchi, *"Nihon bunkaron" to Yasukuni kyōiku* (Tokyo: Azumino Shobō, 1988), 13. Concerning a history of Yasukuni Shrine, *see* Yasumaru, *Kamigami no Meiji*, 63–64. Yasukuni Shrine was replaced by Tokyo Shōkonsha in 1877. Before Tokyo Shōkonsha of 1869, there was Shōkonsha held by the influential Chōshū clan around the end of the Tokugawa period, which enshrined the souls of those who died in duty to their country. The Meiji government adopted the ideology of Shōkonsha. During World War II, the Japanese were taught it was an honor to die for the Emperor as his royal subjects and that their souls would be gods (*kami*) enshrined in Yasukuni. At Yasukuni in order to ease the souls of the dead, the Emperor as a living god as well as a high priest of State Shinto, would bow to them.

49. Koji Taira, "Troubled National Identity," in Weiner, *Japan's Minorities*, 160–161.

50. Siddle, "Ainu," in Weiner, *Japan's Minorities*, 27–40; Sawada, *Okinawa to Ainu*, 186–188.

51. Mick Corliss, "Ainu Law Fails to Address Grievances," *Japan Times*, June 9, 2000. Ken'ichi Kawamura of Ainu descent, who manages the Ainu Memorial Museum in Asahikawa, Hokkaido, said that he happened to hear Obuchi's remarks about the Ainu at the Smithsonian.

52. "Keisanshō ni shitsumonjō," *Mainichi Shinbun* 6 July, 2001, 25. The statement was made by Congressman Muneo Suzuki; *see also* "Ainu Blasts Minister Over Racism," *Mainichi Daily News*, July 3, 2001, 1. Ainu activists were angry with the statement of Economy, Trade, and Industry Minister Takeo Hiranuma that Japan is a land inhabited by "a single race" (*tan'itsu minzoku*).

53. Oguma, *Tan'itsu*, 349–357.

54. For the text of Article I, the Constitution of Japan, *see Nihonkoku kenpō no subete* (Tokyo: Yomiuri Shinbunsha, 1997), 277–278. The Article declares: The Emperor shall be the symbol

of the State and of the unity of the people, deriving his position from the will of the people with whom resides sovereign power." The Constitution of Japan was promulgated on November 3, 1946. The text is also available from the Homepage of the House of Representatives of Japan, http://www.shugiin.go.jp. Compare with Article I, the Constitution of the Empire of Japan promulgated on February 2, 1889, which declares: "The Empire of Japan shall be reigned over and governed by a line of Emperors unbroken for ages eternal." (quoted in Yatsuki, *Tennō to Nihon*, 199).

55. John W. Dower, *Embracing Defeat: Japan in the Wake of World War II* (New York: Norton/New Press, 1999), 496–501. Dower explains that the term, "*ichioku sōzange*" was used by Prime Minister Naruhiko Higashikuni and that the catch line, "one hundred million" was an exaggerated figure of the Japanese population. The actual postwar population was around 70 million because Japan included Koreans and Taiwanese in the total population before the war.

56. As far as I researched, there are no statistics about how much the generations born after the war learn about the details of World War II. However, whenever I asked my classes (20 to 30 students each) about this question in the last few years, a very few, two to three each class usually responded that they did. As a person born after the war, I am positive that this personal survey reflects the whole social attitude about this question.

57. A handy summary on theories on Japan and the Japanese is: Yasuharu Ishizawa, *Nihonjin-ron, Nihon-ron no keifu* (Tokyo: Maruzen, 1997).

58. "Ainugo de jōhō hasshin," *Mainichi Shinbun*, April 8, 200l. Concerning the Ainu's ethnic activities, *see* Katsuichi Honda, *Senjyū minzoku Ainu no genzai* (Tokyo: Asahi Shinbunsha, 1993).

59. Concerning the mixed feelings of minorities' ethnic identity, *see*: "Kataru: jōmon ni manabu," *Mainichi Shinbun*, September 17, 2001, 22. Iizuka Toshio, a documentary film director, mentioned in an interview that many Ainu people are hiding their Ainu origins, and that the staff of a town hall mumbled about the number of the Ainu's population, saying, " There are some but . . . " when asked of their population. *See also* "The Plea of the Ainu," *Time*, January 6, 1992, 65. The article introduces a statement from an Ainu person, the manager of a tourist office in Nibutani (which has the highest density of the Ainu population) that [the Ainu's] "customs died because they were no longer needed."

60. John Toler, "Law or No, the 'Burakumin' Live," *Japan Times*, February 24, 2002, 18. A letter from a Rinzai zen monk talks about the discrimination against *Hisabetsu* Burakumin in Nara prefecture where he lives. *See also* "Effort to Erase Discrimination should Take Broader Approach," *Japan Times*, April 2, 2002, 22.

61. Ken'ichi Matsumoto, "Tennō-ron no genzai," *Mainichi Shinbun*, March 7, 2001, 8. Matsumoto suggests that the Japanese began to be free from the prewar national polity theory, that is, the totalitarian and apotheosized emperor-system ideology. It can be seen in many recent publications about Japanese emperors as follows: Akira Yamada, *Shōwa Tennō no sensō shidō* (Tokyo: Shōwa Shuppan, 1990). Ken'ichi Matsumoto, *Shōwa Tennō densetsu* (Tokyo: Kawaide Shobō Shinsha, 1992). Yutaka Yoshida, *Shōwa Tennō no shūsenshi* (Tokyo: Iwanami Shoten, 1993). Norihiro Kato, Daizaburō Hashizume, and Seiji Takeda, *Tennō no sensō sekinin* (Tokyo, Kai Shobō, 2000). Besides those mentioned above, two American scholars published the following: Donald Keene, *Meiji Tennō* (Tokyo: Shinchōsha, 2001), trans. by Yukio Kakuchi; Bix, *Hirohito*. One more biography was published about Emperor Taishō, who had a brief reign: Takeshi Hara, *Taishō Tennō* (Tokyo: Asahi Shinbunsha, 2000).

62. "Disputed History Text Approved," *Japan Times*, April 4, 2001, 1, 2. Some new junior high school history textbooks to be used in the spring of 2002 have ultranationalistic descriptions which made the neighboring countries, China and Korea, protest for corrections.

Part 2
Colonialisms and Their Legacies

6
Ethnicity and Power in North Africa
Tunisia, Algeria, and Morocco

TAOUFIK DJEBALI

In the beginning were the Berbers

The first known inhabitants of North Africa were the Berbers. However, very little information exists about their origin except that their language is derived from Hamito-Semitic. The controversy about whether they immigrated from Europe or from the Arabian peninsula is still not settled. It is true that they do not constitute a racially homogeneous group. Their blending of European, African, and Middle-Eastern peoples makes it difficult for the Maghreb[1] Berbers to claim a racial identity of their own. Anthropologists classify the Berbers into several distinct groupings: Mediterranean, Kurd-type, European, Nordic, and Negroid. This racial diversity, a logical consequence of migrations as well as a tumultuous history of conquest and occupation, has given rise to a situation in which language, and not race, is the Berbers' major ethnic marker.

Such Berber diversity is made even more complex because of the presence of Arabs whose identity is not only linguistic but also religious. It is estimated that Arab invasions brought about 150,000 people to North Africa during the early conquest of the seventh century and approximately 250,000 in the eleventh and twelfth centuries.[2] Thousands of other Arabs immigrated into North Africa separately and mingled with the existing populations. It is therefore unsurprising that a significant proportion of Berbers have adopted Arabic, whereas the number of Arabs who have adopted Berber has remained negligible (Figure 1).

The history of the Maghreb is largely one of invasions, conquests, and resistance. The first historically attested group to have invaded the Maghreb region were the Phoenicians, who, by 1100 B.C., had gained a limited presence in Tunisia. With the foundation of Carthage in 814 B.C., the grip of the Phoenicians was strengthened over much of North Africa. Not only did they reach the

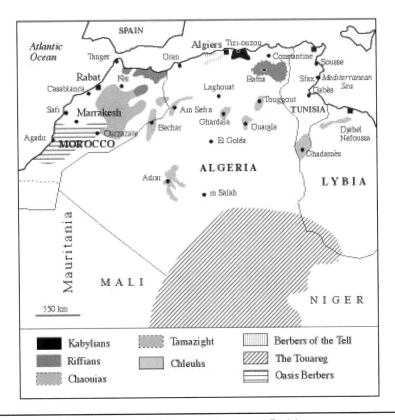

Fig. 1 Map of North Africa showing Morocco, Algeria, and Tunisia.

Moroccan west coast but they contributed to the founding of an urban embryo in many coastal areas from Tunisia to the south of Spain and France. Their influence on the Berber agricultural system and social structure was paramount. Indeed, the Phoenicians prompted the Berbers to modify their social and political systems by moving away, for example, from the tradition of kin-based solidarity. The impact of the Phoenician culture was to be felt even after the defeat of Carthage by the Romans in 146 B.C. Paradoxically, the Romans did not try to wipe out the Phoenician linguistic and religious presence in North Africa.

Between 146 B.C. and 100 B.C., the Romans dominated the Maghreb, imposing their grip on a wider area than did the Phoenicians. Their collaboration with the Berber chiefs led to the incorporation of about 270,000 Berbers in the Roman army in North Africa.[3] The reliance of the Roman army on Berbers, the emergence of a wealthy North African class, and the persistence even in cities of a Berber-speaking majority confined the role of Latin to an administrative function. Even the ubiquitous Latin inscriptions and Roman sites, still visible today in North Africa, translate more the social order and hierarchy of North

African society than the linguistic impact and pattern of Latin in the region. The most important symbolic influence was the Christianization of a significant part of the Berber population, in particular the upper classes, from the third century onward. However, the focus of the Romans was not on the conversion of the indigenous populations but on the economic exploitation of the conquered area. This exploitation, characterized by the quasi-enslavement of a significant portion of the Berber rural population, resulted in the emergence of a major Berber resistance movement. Rebellions, general discontent among the Romanized and non-Romanized populations, and cultural distinctiveness were the main political features of this period.

As long as the Romans were provided with wheat and other agricultural products, relations between the Romans and Berbers were relatively peaceful. As soon as internal conflicts within the Berber population began to affect the flow of agricultural products to Rome, the Romans decided to confiscate the land and expel the Berber owner-class.

Maghreb society was plagued by a rigid hierarchy. Supervising and controlling this hierarchy were the Romans. The Berber group was composed of the dispossessed Moors and the Numid agricultural and seasonal workers. Both groups were united in their hatred for the Romans and their rejection of the economic and social order imposed by the Romans. Roman oppression and the marginalization of the Berber populations generated a feeling of humiliation and exclusion among the latter, resulting in rebellion and revolt. The controversy about whether these rebellions resulted from the emergence of a national or social consciousness is still unresolved. However, the likelihood is that the quasi-enslavement of part of the Berber population and the confiscation of the land of another part set the collective feeling in motion. For the historian Jean-Paul Brisson,

> It is not because they were Berbers that they were the most underprivileged section of the population, but firstly with regard to the nomadic tribes, the natural resources had become increasingly restricted, and secondly there were those who, within the framework of an intensive development of the country, had accepted a more or less complete settling process, and so suffered from the general crisis of the time.[4]

Whether the Berber resistance emanated from the repressive nature of Roman policy in North Africa, the inability of the Christian Church (allied to the Roman landowner class) to federalize the Romans and the Berbers, or the rise of Berber nationalism, the result was the weakening of the Roman empire in the Maghreb and ultimately its defeat. Subsequently, with the invasion of the Vandals, of German origin, who had already conquered Spain, North Africa came under the influence of another "race." The Vandals (439–533), who inherited a particularly unsettled situation, were at first able to rally only the clergy and the landed class. These two non-Berber classes were soon, however, alienated by the new conquerors. The Vandals had to face external attacks on their empire and, on a larger scale, internal strife. The religious opposition started to become organized. It was coupled with a continuous resistance by the Berbers.

It was in this context that the Church pressed the Byzantine emperor to conquer the Maghreb. The conquest was carried out rather easily and put an end to a century of Vandal rule. The Byzantines (533–647) turned out to be like their predecessors: ruthless rulers whose aim was the exploitation of this part of the Mediterranean basin. High taxes, slavery, exploitation, and political marginalization were the lot of most Berbers who came under their domination.

The ethnic fabric of the Maghreb did not change radically under these successive invasions and the apparent changes partly concealed a surprising regularity and continuity as regards the social structure — Berber marginality, failed resistance, and the preponderance of ethnic perceptions. In other words, the masters' "race," religion, language, and background had changed, but not the social structure nor the Berber identity of North Africa.

The Arab invasion and the transformation of the ethnic structure

Political instability, persistent economic schism, ethnic rivalry, and religious persecution in the Maghreb under the Byzantines gave the Arabs, who had already conquered Libya in A.D. 642–643, the desire to conquer this area, unknown to the Muslims in the Near East and isolated by the sea and the desert.

Determined to revive Roman prestige through territorial expansion and economic domination, the Byzantines intensified their exploitation of the indigenous populations and attempted to destroy the Berber kingdoms and expand their influence to Tripolitaine (Libya). The Berber leaders, though eager to admit the symbolic domination of the Byzantines, were unwilling to surrender the reality of their sovereignty. They wanted the invaders to be confined to Carthage. However, their ambitions were thwarted by the growing hostility of the Byzantines and their determination to expand Christian influence. As a result, religion became another issue that deepened ethnic strife.

The Jews, persecuted by the Byzantines, took refuge in the Berber-dominated areas. Some Berbers were even converted to Judaism. Historians still debate the extent of monotheistic religions among the Berbers, but it seems that even if Christianity had made progress among the Berbers, the Berbers made a distinction, whether consciously or unconsciously, between Christianity and the imperial power. In other words, they maintained a certain autonomy vis-à-vis the official Church, which was in their minds much too closely linked to the central authority. According to Paul Balta,

> If they converted to Christianity, it was in opposition to imperial Rome. From the fourth century they embraced donatism, an egalitarian schism which set the impoverished farmers against the wealthy Roman colonists, inspired the revolts in the countryside which arose against Roman Christianity, the religion of power and cities.[5]

This context explains why the Islamization of the Berber populations was relatively easy. Indeed, the Arab invaders, brandishing the Islamic banner, first arrived in Tunisia via Libya. Unlike the preceding conquests that were carried out mainly by sea-borne incursions, the Arabs, with no maritime tradition, avoided the coastal areas, more sedentary and potentially more dangerous. Kairouan, founded in 670, was the first Muslim capital city in the Maghreb. It was originally a military camp in the middle of an arid area. The choice of this place showed that the Arabs, unfamiliar with North African cities, tried to avoid them.

As usual, the Berbers refused to submit to the new invaders. It took the Arabs more than 50 years to create a separate province in North Africa. We can easily imagine Islam as having been perceived by the dominated and enslaved Berbers as a form of salvation, as a religion that was at least more tolerant than Byzantine Christianity. Nonetheless, the centuries of invasions, intrigues, and short-lived alliances that had characterized this area complicated the situation for the Arabs in the Maghreb. Though many Islamized Berbers were integrated into the invaders' army, and despite the fact that the Arabs tried to give a positive image of themselves and of their new monotheistic religion, defiance persisted. The Arabs found in North Africa a complex society, composed of a variety of ethnic groups, tribal kingdoms, and social classes. In Arabic literature of that period, we find a reference to the *Rum* (Byzantines), in whom were concentrated military and administrative power; the *Afranj* (Romans and Romanized), who held the economic power by being the landed class; the *Afariqua* (Africans), who were Christianized and sedentary but situated at the bottom of the social ladder; and finally the Berbers, who constituted a majority. They were basically rural, and were inclined to rebellion.

This ethnic and social diversity made the conquest of North Africa difficult for the Arabs. Two Berbers represented this resistance: Kusayla, who took Kairouan from the Arabs in 682, and El Kahina, a Judaized woman who was able to unite the Berber tribes and inflict major losses on the Arab conquerors before being killed herself in 698.

Though the Arab conquest constituted a turning point in the history of the Maghreb, there were some patterns of continuity in the way the Arabs dealt with North Africa: after the end of the conquest, settlements were established in the cities, while Berber rural zones were neglected and left to the control of tribal chiefs. And when in 711 the Maghreb became an official province of the Arab empire, it began to provide the caliph (Muslim king) in Damascus with soldiers, slaves, and significant funds. Islam thus succeeded where Christianity had failed. Needless to say, the nature of ethnic encounters between Berbers and Arabs was a determining factor in this outcome. Indeed, physical similarities between Berbers and Arabs, the closeness of their cultural traits (rurality, nomadism), and the quasi-absence of an Arab settlement policy that would have resulted in land confiscation and the disturbance of the established social order mitigated Berber resistance to Islam. Additionally, the conquest of Spain in 711 by Tariq Ibn Ziad, a Muslim Berber, opened a new economic and social perspective for marginalized Berbers.

The apparent paradox between the opposition to the Arabs and the relatively easy conversion to Islam reveals an interesting cultural and political evolution. The Maghreb was not totally Islamized before the eleventh century, and complete Arabization has never in fact occurred, which is evidenced by the fact that Berber is still spoken by a significant minority in the Maghreb. However, the massive arrival of Arab tribes (Al Hilalyin) in the eleventh and twelfth centuries reinforced the presence of Arabic in the Maghreb. Indeed, in a short period of time Arabic replaced Latin as the language of the administration and the army. But in order to succeed, Arabic had to replace Berber, which was not an easy task despite the fact that Arabic is the language of the Koran.

We might assume that because of the linguistic diversity in the Maghreb, Islam was to play a homogenizing and pacifying role among the different ethnic groups. In fact, however, the Islamized Berbers were to lead one of their most important revolts in the name of Islam (740–780). Unable to foment rebellions on linguistic or economic grounds alone, the Berbers embraced *Kharijism* (Islamic puritanism) as a doctrine. Therefore, the military conquest and the disappearance of Christianity did not solve the Berber "problem" in the Maghreb. After a period of tolerance and inclusion, an Arab aristocracy appeared. Like their predecessors, the Arabs maintained their grip on the economic, political, and social institutions in the Maghreb. Moreover, the army was no longer an institution of social mobility for the Berbers and the ideological conflicts that plagued the central power in Damascus and then Baghdad led to the autonomy of the Maghreb vis-à-vis eastern Islam.

For centuries, the Maghreb was to be afflicted by wars, rivalries, and tribal dynasties. Only under the Almohades (1147–1269) was the Maghreb unified politically. Therefore, under this dynasty, a Maghreb culture and identity began to emerge for the first time. This was what historians called the last "gilded age" of the Maghreb. This cultural, religious, and political unity disappeared with the disintegration of the Almohade dynasty and the region again entered a period of turmoil and agitation. Under the Almohades, who constituted the first autonomous Maghrebi government, Berbers were integrated into the different political and social spheres. They were advisors to the caliph, doctors, military leaders, and the like. However, the Arabization and Islamization of the Maghreb continued, on a faster scale, under the influence of a powerful Sufi movement.

Since then, the Maghreb has gone through a long period of decay, conflicts, and wars that has ultimately destroyed such political and social unity. Dominated by three distinct socio-ethnic groups (Moors, Arabs, Berbers), the Maghreb has long endured competition for power and privilege. The urban crisis was intensified by the economic decline, and the central power was further weakened by the combined effects of the antagonism between city and countryside and the emergence of local leaders and enclaves. More than ever before, the Maghreb was left to the economic, political, and military ambitions of the Turks and the Spaniards. Only the independent Sherifian dynasty in Morocco was more or less immune to such endeavors.

The Arab defeat in Spain, followed by the Inquisition, compelled a considerable number of Muslims and Jews to flee to the Maghreb. Additionally, in order to counter Spanish expansionism, Turkey sent a significant number of Janissaries (Islamized European soldiers) and officials to defend the Maghreb. And to keep a hold on this part of Africa, the Ottoman sultan imposed a Turkish ruling class whose main task was to limit the expansion of the Spanish empire that was threatening the interests of Istanbul.

The Maghreb became an astounding ethno-linguistic mosaic. Arabic was consolidated as the official and national language. It was the language used by the administration and the *Madrasas* (Islamic teaching institutions) that began to proliferate all over the Sherifian kingdom and the Ottoman province of the Maghreb. In fact, the complete Islamization of the Maghreb and the association between Arabic and Islam attenuated the rivalries and the antagonisms based on linguistic identification and crystallized the conflicts around religious distinctiveness. Repelling the Christians henceforth became a priority for Muslims, whether Arabs or not.

French colonization and the metamorphosis of the ethnic structure

French colonization of North Africa, which began in the nineteenth century, was faced with strong resistance symbolized by the rebellion orchestrated by Abd-el-Kader, who was ultimately defeated in 1847. His national resistance movement used Islam as a unifying force. Islam, the major identifier of North Africa for many centuries, became the fundamental motive for North African mobilization. For many North Africans, what separated them from the French was nothing more than a separation between Islam and Christianity.

From the beginning, the French understood that to attenuate Muslim resistance to their presence, mainly in Algeria, they had to resort to the "divide and rule" doctrine. The most obvious divide that could be instrumentalized in this perspective was the ethnic one. North Africa, though Islamized and partially Arabized, still included a significant Berber minority and a rather important Jewish community.[6] The French began to orchestrate a campaign to denigrate Islam and portray it as the main source of North African troubles and backwardness. Religion therefore began to be utilized astutely as a dividing factor in North African inter-ethnic relations.

The first group to be the focus of French policy in North Africa was the Jewish community. Their history and presence had been associated with North Africa since the Phoenicians, and they became an integral part of ethnic North Africa after the Arab defeat in Spain and the Inquisition that followed. They found refuge and protection in Muslim countries, especially in the Maghreb. In fact, Islam guarantees free religious practice only to the two other monotheistic religions. However, any Jew or Christian under Muslim jurisdiction and protection had to pay *El Jizia*, a special tax.

There is no denying that the mistreatment of Jews was a common practice in North Africa before the arrival of the French in 1830, but their integration into the political, economic, and cultural spheres of North Africa was concrete. The Jews did not hesitate to fight alongside the Muslims to repel the Spanish invaders in the sixteenth and eighteenth centuries, and the legacy of the Inquisition reinforced the ethno-religious bonds in North Africa. However, the reaction of North African Jewry to French colonialism was to mark and define the Muslim–Jewish relationship for decades.

Accordingly, French colonization in Algeria was hailed by Jews as a liberating event. Indeed, the values of liberty, freedom, and solidarity defended by the French had nothing to do with the ideology and methods of the Inquisition. However, this reaction might not necessarily have turned into a "collaboration" with the French had Jews enjoyed equal rights and citizenship in the Maghreb. The arrival of the French at a moment of economic, political, and social decay in the Arab world marked, at least theoretically, the end of ethnic marginalization and religious oppression for the Jews.

Though the Muslim population was also the victim of this anarchy and general decadence, its reaction, motivated by national and religious pride, was hostile to the French. After all, in pre-colonial North Africa, the Arabs had constituted, even in this chaotic context, the privileged majority, and therefore had far too much to lose. The Jews, who certainly thought that their socioeconomic conditions could not be worse under the French, were enthusiastic about the French arrival:

> The Jews who were in the streets knelt down and kissed the hands and feet of the [French] soldiers–proud and triumphant, they walked through the streets in vivid clothes, beating the Turks who they met, and crying "Viva les Franchais!" to the accompaniment of ironic cheers from the crowd.[7]

From the beginning, and even before the total control of the French over Algeria, the Jews sided with the French and linked their destiny in Algeria with that of the French. When, for example, the French army had to abandon Blida, an Algerian city, in 1830, Jews had to follow in order to avoid Muslim vengeance, and when Oran was besieged by Muslim forces in 1833, Jews participated in the defense of the city alongside the French soldiers.[8] In order to reinforce the ethnic divide and isolate the Muslim community, the French tried to redefine the notion of nationhood in Algeria. In the act of capitulation of July 1830, one can read, "The liberty of the inhabitants of all classes, their religions, their properties, their trade, their industry, will not be violated; their women will be respected."[9]

At the heart of this replica of French law, we find a disguised attempt to reassure the Jews and break the traditional link between them and the Muslims. However, the French did not aim at unifying North Africans under the same laws and abolishing institutionalized racism. The distinction between Muslims and Jews was to be maintained not on the basis of religion, which had been the case in precolonial North Africa, but on the basis of nationality. Indeed, the Jews, after having been incorporated into the "Muslim nation," were considered by the new colonial system as members of the Jewish nation, having the right to a separate administration (schools, rabbinical justice, and so on), but subject to French rule. In this context, Jacob Bacri, a rich Algerian merchant, who was partly responsible for the French–Algerian conflict,[10] was designated by the French as head of the "Jewish nation," invested with special powers to supervise the Jewish community in Algiers. In other words, by replacing the Muslim *Sheikh* or the Jewish *Caid El Yhud* (Jewish chief), Bacri derived all his power and legitimacy from the French administration.

Following the "divide and rule" policy, which they had implemented from the start, the French made every possible effort to separate the Jews from the Muslims. Beginning in 1833, a process of integrating the Jews into French citizenship had begun. Hence, the autonomy of the "Jewish nation" was finally abolished in two separate ordinances in 1841 and 1842. By these ordinances, for example, judicial powers concerning Jews were entrusted to French courts, but Jews continued to be judged in those courts according to Jewish law. In November 1845, a new ordinance laid down the foundations of a new French policy for the Jews of Algeria. An Algerian consistory sat — a system modeled upon that of France but supposed to be independent from it. Nevertheless, the creation of the consistories in Algiers, Oran, and Constantine marked the end of the traditional model of Algerian Jewry and the ultimate division between Algerian Muslims and Jews.

The emancipation of Algerian Jewry and the end of their old lifestyle created a situation of confusion and a veritable identity crisis. Deprived of an independent identity, Jews were marginalized by the French and completely separated from Algerian Muslims. They considered any decision taken to reinforce their "Frenchness" as a positive step that further reinforced and clarified their identity. When, in 1860, Jews became eligible for compulsory military service, they regarded this symbolic action as an honor and a mark of confidence on the part of the French authorities.

It seems, then, that for Jews, their ethnic identity could only be enforced and protected by distancing themselves from Muslims and relating their future to the fate of the French in Algeria. Therefore, they continued to struggle for a long time for full French citizenship. In 1865, a petition signed by the majority of the heads of Jewish households in Algeria was presented to the French emperor, Napoleon III, who was visiting Oran in Algeria. It called explicitly for a collective naturalization of all Jews.

Only in 1870 did Algerian Jews become French citizens by virtue of the famous Crémieux decree, named after the French minister of justice, Adolphe Crémieux, himself a Jew. The decree read,

> The Jews indigenous to the departments of Algeria are declared citizens of France. In consequence their civil status and their personal status will be

regulated according to French law, effective with the promulgation of the present decree: all rights acquired to this day remain inviolable.

Every legislative provision, decree, rule or ordinance contrary to this decree is hereby abolished.[11]

The Crémieux decree, which was supposed to bring emancipation, freedom, and prosperity to the Jews, turned out to be a source of anxiety, insecurity, and fear for them. French, Spanish, and Italian *colons*, as well as Muslims, began to wage an anti-Jewish campaign that turned into violent action, especially around election times. Anti-Semitism, unknown before 1870, emerged not as a temporary phenomenon but as an unabated ideology. However, overall, the Muslims of Algeria refused to be drawn into anti-Jewish manifestations and riots, consequently ruining the hopes and expectations of anti-Semitic European ideologists in Algeria.

There is no denying that, since the early nineteenth century, ethnic relations in North Africa had been shaped by the economic, political, and social situation in France. By eagerly accepting French citizenship, Jews could no longer be outside the spheres of the intrigues and machinations that plagued French society. It goes without saying that in a situation of colonization, ethnic relations are not simply defined by factors intrinsic to the colonized society but by the colonizer–in the form of perceptions, alliances, and oppression.

Tunisian Jews, for example, were better integrated into mainstream society than their counterparts in Algeria or Morocco. Indeed, Tunisia had been exposed to a much greater extent to international influence and thus easily moved away from traditional Islamic laws regulating the status of the *dhimmis* (non-Muslims). With the treaty of September 10, 1857, Tunisian subjects of the Beylicate (the Husaynid dynasty) were permitted to practice their rites freely, and any constitutional distinction between Tunisian Muslims and Tunisian Jews was removed. In this context, French colonization in 1881 did not revolutionize ethnic relations. It merely resulted in an increase of the number of Europeans — Christians and Jews.

Despite the hospitality toward Jews for which Tunisian society was known, many Muslims were not ready to accept total equality with the *dhimmis*. By and large, the Jews still felt themselves to be second-class citizens. They began a series of public campaigns, not for collective naturalization, which could have been a problematic decision in a protectorate, but for extending to the Jews of Tunisia the right, allowed to foreign residents, to acquire French citizenship. It was not until 1923 that Tunisian Jews qualified (under the Morinaud Law) for French citizenship, and then only on a case-by-case basis.

Contrary to the nineteenth-century dews in Tunisia, those in Morocco were desperate in the nineteenth century. Confined to the status of *dhimmis*, they remained excluded from the political and social spheres. Living in a very traditional society that was impermeable to any Western influence, Moroccan Jewry was certainly the poorest as well as the most closed-in community in the

Maghreb. Still the subjects of the Sherifian sultan, Jews found themselves excluded from the French and Muslim communities even under the French protectorate (1912–1956). They failed to improve their lot under the French protectorate, and were unable to get the protection and guarantees enjoyed by their counterparts in Algeria and Tunisia. Ultimately, for Moroccan Jews liberty and equal rights existed in name only.

For centuries, there was no such thing as Moroccan "nationality." There were Muslims and Jews. Only foreign intervention in the internal affairs of Morocco, especially beginning with the international convention in Madrid in 1879, gave rise to this concept.[12] Indeed, foreign intervention resulted in the superimposition of a Western notion of nationality and citizenship on the traditional notion of "*umma*" (Muslim nation) in which the *dhimmis* were the protégés of the Muslim state. The basic notion of equal rights and duties, inherent in the Western philosophy of the eighteenth century, and the concept of citizenship did not exist in Morocco. Therefore, the Jews had no real ties or obligations to the Muslim state. From the late nineteenth century, the Jews, identifiable by their religious affiliation and their cultural particularity, were perceived as outcasts by Muslims and as Moroccan subjects by foreign observers.

Affiliation to Islam, then, became the fundamental criterion upon which the notion of "nationhood" was based in precolonial Maghreb. Almost all other criteria were dismissed. Only under direct or indirect foreign influence did the Maghreb move away from a religious definition of the "nation" to embrace the notion of universal "citizenship." With the rise of the nationalist movements in North Africa in the 1920s and 1930s, the rift between Muslims and Jews became wider. These movements accused the Jews of being the privileged group in the colonized Maghreb, at the expense of the Arab and Berber populations. For Muslims, who had for centuries found a kind of consolation in having an institutional superiority over the Jews, the colonial period relegated them to the bottom of the social and economic ladder.

Therefore, many Arabs and Berbers found satisfaction in the significant deterioration of the status of the North African Jewry with the rise of anti-Jewish propaganda that culminated in the Nazi occupation of France and later Tunisia. Other factors contributed to Muslim antagonism toward the Jewish community. Among these, the Palestinian question that surfaced in the 1930s was certainly the most important and the most symbolic. Fuelled by anti-Semitic European propagandists, anti-Jewish riots erupted in different cities in North Africa.

When France came under German occupation, Jewish anxiety reached its peak in North Africa. Having lost support from the Muslims, the Jews were now facing an uncertain future provoked by their supposed protectors. Many publications have documented the situation of North African Jews under the pro-German Vichy government.[13] Forced labor, heavy taxes, exclusion from certain categories of jobs, and humiliation were the lot of North African Jewry during that period. In October 1940, Philippe Petain signed an edict abrogating the Crémieux decree of 1870, thereby putting the Jewish "race" in a perilous position.

The end of the Vichy government and the defeat of the Germans put an end to a disastrous situation for North African Jewry. However, the creation of the state of Israel in 1948 and the strengthening of the nationalist movements in the Maghreb persuaded the Jews that Israel was a better place for them. Those Jews whose ancestors were part of the North African cultural, religious, and ethnic heritage came to regard themselves as the pariahs of the Maghreb.

Contrary to non-Muslim Arabs in the Middle East (Christians in such places as Lebanon, Syria, Egypt, and Iraq), who participated actively in the nationalist movements and sometimes sparked them off, North African Jews, willingly or otherwise, alienated themselves from the Muslim majority and sided with the colonizer.

The quasi-disappearance of Jews from the Maghreb remodeled the ethnic structure of Tunisia, Algeria, and Morocco where only a handful of them decided to stay. Hence, the Maghreb has become religiously more homogeneous than any other part of the Arab world. But a question remains: will Islam be sufficient as a unifying force for the Maghrebi people?

France and the Berber question

It was only in the mid-nineteenth century that ethnographic studies enabled the French to understand better the inherent differences between Berbers and Arabs. However, contrary to its inclusionist and protective policy vis-à-vis the Jews, particularly in Algeria, France did not seek to defend the Berber minority.

Both anti-Arab and anti-Muslim images and stereotypes had been widespread in France, as in every Western country since the Crusades.[14] However, dissociating the intellectual and ideological histories of two Muslim groups (Arabs and Berbers) who share geographical continuity and religious unity demanded a sophisticated process. At a time when ethnographic studies became ubiquitous and theories about race were rather popular, the division of North African populations on the basis of language was an attractive colonial strategy.

From this perspective, the French developed and defended a set of negative ideas about the Arabs, portraying them as ruthless, savage, and bloodthirsty nomads. Without shaping a totally positive image of the Berbers, the French portrayed them as a victimized group, forced to embrace Islam and pushed into mountainous areas by the Arab aggressors. These blatantly opposed images (bad Arab versus good Berber) constructed by the French were translated into a series of oppositions such as between ignoble and noble, sedentary and nomad, Semitic and Nordic, tyrannical and democratic, subjugation of women and freedom of women, religious fanaticism and religious tolerance, laziness and hard work.

Such ideas, created by certain ethnographers, military generals, and the officials of the Bureau of Indigenous Affairs, were used to define French policy in the Maghreb and more particularly in Algeria. In the long run, they influenced the Berbers' perception of themselves and of the Algerian Arabs.

Berber assimilability in the minds of the French was translated into a considerable investment in schools and religious missions to Christianize and to educate the Berbers, whom they considered less hostile than the Arabs. It is obvious that this "Berber Policy" did not intend to preserve and protect Berber culture and identity but was intended to divide the North African population, united by religion, history, and geographical continuity. This is clearly demonstrated by the fact that investments in the economic infrastructure of the Berber regions were minimal (which was not surprising for a colonial power) and education was promoted only in French and Arabic, never in Berber.[15]

The ethnicization of the Berbers by the French began as early as 1857, when the colonial army in Algeria created a separate administration for the Kabyle Berbers and implemented a preferential tax policy in their favor between 1858 and 1918. Throughout the colonial period, the Kabylians, who were at the heart of the French Berber policy, had an autonomous judicial system, and internal affairs were submitted to tribal and customary laws. Many Berber and French scholars today deny that preferential treatment of the Berbers ever existed.[16] Adding to this confusion is the fact that France has never admitted the existence of such a policy in Algeria. However, the discriminatory policy in Morocco could not be denied, especially with the promulgation of the Berber *Dahir* (decree) of 1930. This law tried to establish a system of customary law tribunals for Berbers separate from other Muslims. The enactment of this law was followed by an unprecedented Berber and Arab uprising and the creation of the first nationalist party. Interestingly enough, North Africans were mobilized against this decision not only because it endeavored to separate Arabs from Berbers, but mostly because it attempted to separate Berbers from Islam. Although the policy of "divide and rule" used against Arabs and Berbers was obvious in Morocco, in Algeria it clearly favored the Kabyle Berbers over the other Berber groups (Mzabs, Chaouia, Touaregs).

The "ethnic" policy of France in the Maghreb (Algeria and Morocco) as far as Berbers and Arabs were concerned aimed first at isolating the Arab majority, socially, economically, and politically, and second at forming a French-like (approved) intellectual elite in the Maghreb.[17] It would also facilitate and precipitate the assimilation of a part of the Maghrebi population into French cultural patterns.

This policy yielded spectacular results. An influential Berber (mainly Kabylian) elite, impregnated with French culture and language, has emerged. Famous authors such as Mouloud Feraoun, Jean Amrouche, Mouloud Mammeri, and Kateb Yacine wrote in French, but they were mostly admired, from Tunisia to Morocco, by North Africans, Arabs and Berbers alike. Ironically, the French schools that proliferated in Berber regions, instead of creating an alienated French-like elite, forged a virulent and determined nationalist group in Morocco, and brought the Berbers together with the Arabs in Algeria in their fight against the colonial system.

The major cultural impact of France on the Berbers did not deter the latter from their nationalist objectives. But it gave them a privileged position compared with the Arabs. Indeed, a relatively educated Berber diaspora came to include an important segment of merchants, farmers, and white-collar professionals. Between 1891 and 1950, nearly all of the state-recruited teachers for Algiers were of Berber origin.[18] Most importantly, this French policy gave Berbers an important place in the political apparatus. But this "privileged" position and the resulting economic success of Berbers were never perceived by the Arabs as a betrayal. They reserved such a judgment for the Jews. Obviously, although they enjoyed the benefits of the French policy, North African Berbers have never sided collectively with the colonizer. Whether this reaction was the result of the Berber nature of challenging authority and colonization, or the influence of Islam, it demonstrates that the ethnic divide — Arab/Berber — that plagued Algerian society afterwards finds its roots largely in colonial policy. It is also obvious that in the Arab world, non-Muslim minorities try to stress themes of Arab nationalism that transcend the borders of the nation-state as a common ground for unity, whereas non-Arab ethnic minorities tend to focus on patriotism.[19] This was the case for North African Berbers under French colonization.

When, in 1949, some Berber leaders raised the ethnic question within the nationalist movement, they were accused of promoting "Berberism"[20] and were immediately excluded. Most Berbers admitted that Algerian identity, with its ill-defined patterns, was articulated around the ideas of territory, religion, and affiliation to the Arab world. However, it is obvious that the absence of an "ethnic" debate in the nationalist movement was an indication that diversity, differences, and dissent were completely ignored by Algerian leaders, whether Berbers or Arabs. This attitude was used to define the nature of the ethnic question in the Maghreb after independence. Islam, which constituted the bond that united the nationalist factions and allowed Algerians, Tunisians, and Moroccans to distinguish themselves from Christian or Jewish "infidels," also helped the Maghreb build an independent identity.

As opposed to Algeria and Morocco, Islam played a minor role in the nationalist movement in Tunisia. In the early 1930s, the nationalist party, the Neo-Destour, took a secular turn. The absence of an ethnic question in Tunisia may explain in part why the nationalist movement did not resort to religion as a unifying force.

Generally speaking, the French certainly misunderstood the sociological patterns that allowed North Africans to have a strong belief in Islam and in the larger community of "believers." With the end of their colonial presence and the emergence of the concept of the nation-state, a redefinition of the ethnic question took place.

Arab hegemony and Berber ethnic revival

With the independence of Tunisia and Morocco in 1956 and Algeria in 1962, it was obvious that the Maghreb was heading toward a novel political and social situation. The European *colons* and the Jews left in great numbers, and the Maghreb found a religious homogeneity for the first time in its history. Nevertheless, the role that Islam was playing in reducing the ethnic conflict in the Maghreb, and accentuating the religious rift between Muslims and non-Muslims, could no longer be played out. With the achievement of independence, the Berbers, who had not been able to question the Arabism of the Maghreb for fear of being accused of collaborating with the French, had every reason to defend ethnic pluralism and the distinctive nature of their own identity.

Algeria is certainly the country in which political and cultural life has been the most seriously colored by Arab–Berber rivalries. Immediately after independence, the Algerian Berbers in their territorial stronghold (Kabylia) launched an insurrection against the newly created government dominated by Arabs and Arabized Berbers. The insurrection failed and its instigator, Hocine Aït Ahmed, was arrested in 1965.

It is important to avoid perceiving the emergence of the ethnic question in the Maghreb simply as a legacy of French colonization or French manipulation.[21] The Berber language and traditions are deeply rooted in the North African cultural mosaic. For centuries, Berber culture has survived conquests, repression, and exclusion; hence, it was clear that the formation of the nation-state in Algeria or Morocco would not wipe out Berberism as a culture or as an ideology. However, in the early stages of Algerian independence, most Berber leaders were opposed to a radical and extremist orientation of Berberism. Their ethnic identification was not strong enough to overshadow other social and political priorities such as national unity and economic progress.

Like any ethnic group that becomes conscious of the dangers that threaten its identity and specificity, the Berbers became aware of the political and ideological implications of Arabism as defended by successive governments. The irony of the Algerian situation is that from very early on, the political regime emphasized the Arabic and Islamic nature of the country to promote national integration and unity. This attempt in fact strengthened a collective Berber consciousness of their differences and particularities. In other words, the Algerian case showed that ethnic cultural oppression stimulated what Anthony Smith called a process of historical reappropriation and vernacularization of political and cultural symbolism.[22]

The political rhetoric of Algerian leaders symbolized by President Ben Bella's phrases "Nous sommes tous des Arabes" (We are all Arabs) and "l'Algérie est arabe, arabe, arabe" (Algeria is Arab, Arab, Arab) was associated with the rigid and undiscussed implementation of a radical Arabization program. For the Berbers, this policy initiated a double challenge: cultural and material. Berber had no place in the educational system in independent Algeria, and

Berber public officials, who had previously been over-represented in public service, had to adapt themselves to a new bureaucratic situation.

The Algerian government maneuvered by promoting economic growth in Kabylia and imposing at the same time an Arabo-Islamic identity on the country to assert its legitimacy. At a time when Arab nationalism was at its height with Nasser in Egypt, and an Algerian independent identity was being built for the first time, events in Algeria began to take a radical turn. Torn between an Arab nationalism that found in the Israeli–Palestinian conflict a *raison-d'être* and a popular mood highly influenced by the French cultural legacy, Algerian authority chose to impose the cultural traits of the new social identity that gave prominence to Arabic as a language and Islam as a religion. This process was in line with the authoritarian regimes that emerged with independence in the Maghreb, and that dealt with the masses as immature and irresponsible. It is thus clear that the nature of the political regime is responsible in a significant way for the nature of ethnic relations. Indeed, an authoritarian political and ideological stand concerning national identity and culture can succeed in obscuring diversity for a time. But national unity becomes superficial and artificial under these conditions.

In this context, the reassertion of Kabylian identity began as an intellectual militant movement in schools, universities, and popular songs. Indeed, Kabylian popular songs that had praised Kabylian resistance under the protectorate became hymns to Kabylian culture and identity in the newly independent Algeria. In 1974, when Arab singers abusively replaced Berber singers at the annual Cherry Festival in Laiba-Nait-Iraten, they received a hostile welcome that turned into an ethnic riot. More significantly, in 1977, the final game of the national soccer championship pitting a team from Kabylia against one from Algiers turned into an Arab–Berber conflict. The national anthem in Arabic was overwhelmed by the shouting of Berber anti-Arab slogans such as "A bas les Arabes" (Down with the Arabs) and "Vive la Kabylie" (Long live Kabylia). More recently, after the September 2001 attack on the World Trade Center in New York and the Pentagon, some Kabylian demonstrators brandishing the American flag denounced "Arab and Islamic terrorism." Hence, modern Berber ethnicity seems at once a reappropriation of the cultural heritage and symbols of the Berber group and an appropriation of some Western values.

A gradual radicalization began to emerge in Algeria and among the hundreds of thousands of Berbers in France who had been the spearheads of the Berber cultural movement. The yet ill-organized Berber movement has begun to focus its activities on a certain number of issues: the multicultural character of Algerian society, opposition to compulsory Arabization in the educational system, and the political recognition of Berber as an official language.

Berber demands were thus confined to culture. No ideological or political radicalization was allowed until 1980, when the opposition between the Berbers and the authorities broke forth in open confrontation. These events, commonly known as *le Printemps Berbère* (the Berber Spring), are certainly the most significant political incident that has taken place in Algeria since independence. Most importantly, the immediate reason that caused these disturbances was a government decision to reform the educational system from elementary school to university. Arabic and religious teachings were to be introduced and rein-forced, and French banned from school except for teaching math and science. At the same time, a lecture on Berber poetry, which was to be delivered on March 10, 1980, by the well-known Kabylian intellectual Mouloud Mammeri at the University of Tizi-Ouzou (Kabylia), was banned and severe riots followed. The regime spoke of a colonialist plot (a reference to France) and began a crackdown on Berber workers and students that resulted in a death toll of between thirty and fifty people.

Unable to draw the proper conclusions from these events, the regime hard-ened and remained insensitive to the ethnic rift and to Berber demands. In the 1980s, the economic downturn badly affected the population and the govern-ment was quickly overpowered by the enormous dislocation that destabilized the social fabric. Besides, a fundamentalist movement began to emerge with the complicity of the government, which was maneuvering to weaken the Berber and the leftist movements.

The general revolt in 1988 that shook the political regime ended in total con-fusion and the emergence of a "semi-democratic" system. The traditional Berber party, the Front des Forces Socialistes (FFS), was legalized, and in 1989 some militants of the Berber cultural movement founded the Rassemblement pour la Culture et la Démocratie (RCD). More significantly, the feud between different Berber associations and political parties has not overshadowed the Berbers demand for the preservation of their rights. These two parties, with an exclusively Berber base and leadership, have never admitted their eth-nic ideological orientation. Their discourse has always focused on national issues.

The attempts of Berber leaders to de-ethnicize the Berber question reflects the ambiguity of the social and political situation in the Maghreb. Both in Algeria and Morocco, Berbers are attached to their national identity. And for fear of being accused of fomenting trouble and division, they have restricted their demands to preserving their culture and identity and implementing a Western-like democracy. The Berber movement, whether in Algeria or in Morocco, remains free from any nationalist demand. Given the rising tide of ethnic assertion and separatism worldwide, this is a surprising development.

Cultural separateness, which is very popular among the Berbers, may have an explanation and a sociological basis. The Berber language is at the heart of the ethnic problem in the Maghreb. However, in order for the Berber move-ment to change into a nationalist one, other elements are needed: linguistic unity, a well-organized intelligentsia, an influential urban concentration, and a written language. Many of these factors are still lacking.

It is true that in the Maghreb, Berber exclusion and marginality are cultural rather than political. The different governments from the early days of independence have integrated a great many Berbers into the political machine. Some of them have reached prominent positions. For example, the three major Algerian presidents since independence (Haouari Boumediene, Chedli Ben Jedid, and Lamine Zeroual) were of Berber origin, and a great many Berbers have been part of the Moroccan government. Therefore, ethno-political oppression is so rare in the Maghreb that opposition to the hegemony of Arabic and Islam has taken a cultural rather than a political turn.

Additionally, these politicians, by being fervent partisans of Arabization, have damaged Berber ethnic solidarity and retarded the emergence of a Berber nationalist movement. It is an irony to see that in some nondemocratic states, it is possible to depoliticize ethnic demands. However, there is no reason to suggest that this paradox between strong cultural demands and the absence of a nationalist movement will last long. The most recent riots to occur in Kabylia and Algiers (April 2001) show that the radicalization of the Berbers is under way. Even if the origin of the unrest seems to be economic and not ethnic, there is no doubt that the ethnic divide, exacerbated by social factors, is becoming a major feature of the North African political landscape.

Conclusion

For historical and geographical reasons, Tunisia seems to be the most ethnically homogeneous country of the Maghreb. Berbers have almost disappeared from the southern enclaves where Berber was spoken until recently. Algeria, on the other hand, still has a significant Berber minority of between 20 and 30 percent of the population. Among the main Berber groups, the Kabylians are the most numerous and the most active in defending their culture and identity. They have maintained all the cultural and social attributes of a modern ethnic group. The solidarity between the Kabylian masses and their elite and diaspora has reinforced the cohesion of the group and highlighted the particularities of Kabylian culture in opposition to Arabic culture. However, this militant elite has failed to bind all Algerian Berbers and transcend the borders of the Algerian nation-state.

Indeed, Moroccan Berbers have never developed a strong sense of identity and consciousness. Though the Berber language has been excluded from official educational programs, there is a common perception that Berbers are better integrated into mainstream Morocco. Since independence in 1956, Moroccan kings have acted astutely to avoid any ethnic rift, and have emphasized their religious roles as "commanders of believers." Their subjects are not Berbers and Arabs but Muslims, first of all. And any attempt by Berber activists to stir the ethnic question in the Sherifian Kingdom had been faced with a severe crackdown. For example, a number of Berber activists were imprisoned in 1995 for publicly calling for the recognition of Berber as an official language. Only recently (July 2001) has King Mohamed VI admitted the necessity of preserving the Berber culture and language. In a speech to mark the second anniversary of his accession to the throne, he promised to set up a Royal Institute the aim of which would be to strengthen the Berber culture by integrating Amazigh (Berber) into the educational system.

Compared with Algerian Kabylians, Moroccan Berbers do not feel threatened by an overwhelming majority of Arabs. The fact that they constitute approximately half of the Moroccan population limits their concern about their ethnic survival in a national community that shares with them a strong patriotic feeling and a common religion.

The nature of the French colonization in these two countries is also an important factor in shaping Berber consciousness and militancy. The French colonization of Algeria for more than 130 years and the preferential treatment in education that benefited Berbers (mainly Kabylians) set up a French-created elite, unequaled in Morocco, where the French remained for fewer than 50 years. Access to the French language and cultural heritage has led Algerian Berbers to impregnate their identity with French values and modern ethnicity. Defending their ethnic specificity is thus integrated into a wider philosophical and ideological pattern. The influence of French culture and values is also perceptible through the Kabylian diaspora. Indeed, a considerable number of Kabylians who work in France have maintained a strong attachment to their homeland through a sophisticated tribal and family network. In this way, Kabylian ethnic consciousness is closely related to the French concept of freedom and human rights. For Berber leaders, the democratization of the political system is the only way to guarantee their ethnic rights within the spectrum of the Algerian nation-sate.

Notes

1. The word "Maghreb" (of Arabic origin), designates the north-west of Africa: Tunisia, Algeria, and Morocco. A political definition would include Libya and Mauritania.
2. Philippe Marçais, "Peoples and Cultures in North Africa." *The Annals of the American Academy of Political and Social Science*, 298 (March 1955), 22.
3. Abdallah Laroui, *L'Histoire du Maghreb: un essai de synthèse* (Paris: Maspero, 1975), 48.
4. Jean-Paul Brisson, *Autonomisme et christianisme dans l'Afrique romaine* (Paris: E. de Boccard, 1958), 28.
5. Paul Balta, *Le Grand Maghreb: des indépendances à l'an 2000* (Paris: Découverte, 1990), 15.
6. We exclude in this study the Black minority.
7. Claude Martin, *Les Isrélistes algériens de 1830–1902* (Paris: Editions Herakles, 1936), 42.
8. André Chouraqui, *Between East and West. A History of the Jews of North Africa*. Trans. Michel M. Bernet (Philadelphia, PA: Jewish Publication Society of America, 1968), 143.
9. Chouraqui, *Between East and West.*
10. Bacri, who was a resident of Algeria, was involved in selling Algerian agricultural products to France. Unable or unwilling to pay the 7 million francs they owed him, and encouraged by the "undiplomatic" behavior of the Algerian Dey in favor of Bacri, the French invaded Algeria.
11. Chouraqui, *Between East and West*, 150.
12. Chouraqui, *Between East and West*, 177.
13. See Juliette Bessis, *Maghreb: la traversée du siècle* (Paris: l'Harmattan, 1997); Michael Laskier, *North African Jewry in the Twentieth Century: The Jews of Morocco, Tunisia, and Algeria* (New York: New York University Press, 1994); Chouraqui, *Between East and West.*
14. Edward Said, *Orientalism* (New York: Pantheon Books, 1978).
15. Salem Chaker, *Berbères aujourd'hui* (Paris: L'Harmattan, 1989), 85.
16. Jeanne Favret, "Relations de dépendance et manipulation de la violence en Kabylie." *L'Homme*, 8 (1968), 18–44; Slimane Hachi, "Note sur la politique berbère de la France." *Tafsut*, 1 (1983), 29–33; Chaker, *Berbères aujourd'hui.*

17. Alain Mahé, *Histoire de la Grande Kabylie: XIX–XXe siècles* (Paris: Editions Bouchène, 2001), 156.
18. Bruce Maddy-Weitzman, "The Berber Question in Algeria: Nationalism in the Making?" In *Minorities and the State in the Arab World*, ed. Ofra Bengio and Gabriel Ben-Dor (London: Lynne Reiner, 1999), 35.
19. Gabriel Ben-Dor and Ofra Bengio. "The State and Minorities toward the Twenty-first Century: An Overview." In *Minorities and the State in the Arab World*, ed. Bengio and Ben-Dor, 191.
20. Berberism as an ideology started life in the 1940s. It is based on the idea that Algeria includes a significant minority that is not Arabic in language, history, tradition, and identity.
21. During the Berber riots that hit Algeria in 2001, Boutaflika, the Algerian president, did not hesitate to accuse "foreign nations" (a reference to France) of manipulating the Berbers.
22. Anthony Smith, *Nations and Nationalism in a Global Era* (Cambridge: Polity Press, 1995), 65–67.

7

Racial Frontiers in Jamaica's Nonracial Nationhood

VIOLET SHOWERS JOHNSON

In the twentieth century many of the postcolonial nations of Africa and Asia amply demonstrated the artificiality of nationhood as constructed largely through the political, social, and economic engineering of the former European colonial powers. Colonialism carved out nations from disparate ethnic groups separated by language, religion, and traditions. Conversely, it also severed through national boundaries peoples who shared a common ethnicity, language, religion, and historical experiences. The follies of such arrogant, arbitrary demarcations, long apparent since the colonial era, contributed in no mean measure to some of the most deadly upheavals of postindependence.[1] In the Caribbean, the nations, though they were also constructs of European engineering, seemed not so artificial, given their physical boundaries. After all, they conformed to the natural, island, geographical demarcations. However, in reality, they too, are complex amalgams of races and ethnicities, drawn together from the repercussions of conquest, slavery, colonialism, and migration.

The modern nation of Jamaica is one such amalgam. At independence the population consisted of 76.8 percent Black, 16.9 percent Mixed Race, 0.9 percent White, 0.6 percent Chinese, 1.7 percent Indian, and 3.1 percent others.[2] Although the numerical preponderance of Blacks was glaring, it could not subsume the presence of the other races, whose roles and niches in the society had been firmly carved by the time of independence. In essence, then, the new nation was multiracial. But from the onset, the architects of Jamaica's nationhood intended to drastically reduce or obliterate racial consciousness as an essential, defining trait of the nation. This resolve is encapsulated in the motto adopted, "Out of Many, One People." This was meant to be more than rhetoric. It was to be at the heart of the spirit of an ideology for nationhood. What is this ideology? Who were the proponents and what were their motives? What mitigating factors threaten the literal application of this ideology? What is imagined in this case, a Jamaican nonracial nationhood or the racially defined affinities within its national boundaries? These are questions that frame the analyses in this study.

The ink on the agreement with Britain that vacated colonial power had hardly dried when scholars began to analyze and assess the experimental feat of a nonracial nationhood. In fact, most of the reviewers were already poised for such a task. The complex dynamics of race, ethnic, and class relations in Jamaica — and indeed, the whole Caribbean region — have always held an appeal for scholars, from M.G. Smith's classic 1965 study, *The Plural Society in the British West Indies*, to more recent works by David Lowenthal, Adam Kuper, Rupert Lewis, Carl Stone, Derek Gordon, and Rex Nettleford.[3] These studies, through varying approaches, investigate and assess the evolution of the diverse groups that constitute the Jamaican population, the dynamics of race, ethnic, and class relations, and the meanings of nationhood. Therefore, the present study is not an attempt into virgin terrain. Instead, it seeks to contribute to an ongoing discourse on race, identity, and nationality in postcolonial Jamaica. I come into this work not as a Caribbeanist but as an immigration historian and scholar and teacher of the African diaspora. Because of this background, I intend to enter the discourse by examining Jamaica's nationhood within three contexts: the African diaspora, the Afro-Caribbean diaspora, and transnationalism. This approach will emphasize the agency of blackness in shaping the realities of Jamaica's nationhood. It is instructive to note here, at the outset, that this approach does not deny other racially based influences like Chinese expressions of ethnicity, for example. It singles out Black nationalism because that phenomenon provides the best insights into the enduring racial ramifications of the construction of a Jamaican people.

The premise of this study is that Jamaican nationhood has not proceeded and will not proceed without profound influences from outside currents. Most of these are couched in its long history of slavery and migration. These historical realities put Jamaica within a configuration that transcends national boundaries. This entity is one that is defined by a black collectivity born out of the African diaspora and aptly labeled the Black Atlantic by social and cultural historian Paul Gilroy.[4] According to Gilroy, the Black Atlantic serves as a useful tool for understanding the development of modern black societies:

> The history of the black Atlantic . . ., continually crisscrossed by movements of black people — not only as commodities but engaged in various struggles towards emancipation, autonomy, and citizenship — provides a means to reexamine the problems of nationality, location, identity, and historical memory.[5]

The Afro-Caribbean diaspora[6] has served to reinforce the sense of global Blackness already established by the African diaspora. In other words, the Afro-Caribbean diaspora, though a more modern phenomenon, like the African diaspora, is one of the underpinnings of the Black Atlantic. The crisscrossing within the Black Atlantic underscores the process of transnationalism,[7] a major ingredient of the Afro-Caribbean diaspora. Roy Simon Bryce-Laporte, one of the authorities of the Caribbean diaspora, emphasizes that migrations are not simple processes that divide people of African descent. On the contrary, they serve as a unifying force.[8] Ultimately, then, migration profoundly affects not only those emigrants who physically leave the homeland but also those who remain and the society in general. Through the crisscrossing, the migration process directly and indirectly alters and shapes the institutions of both the sending and receiving societies. Jamaican immigrants and their descendants, whose experiences in their new locations in the Black Atlantic, among other things, "ethnicize" and "racialize" them, continue to influence numerous aspects in their homeland, including the meanings and expressions of nationhood.

The main thrust of Jamaica's national ideology is summed up in the national motto.[9] It acknowledges the multiplicity of the new nation's racial and ethnic composition. But the crux of the Jamaican ideology is, as Milton Vickerman emphasizes, how "the ideology of multiracialism verges into one of non-racialism."[10] According to this rationale, the various groups, though many and diverse, coexisted amicably enough to render racial factors irrelevant. Who are these racial/ethnic groups? At independence did they really coexist amicably? In other words, what are the preindependence antecedents of race relations?

The story of race relations in Jamaica, as in other parts of the Caribbean, began with genocide. The invading Europeans wiped out the indigenous inhabitants, the Taino "Indians."[11] On the heels of genocide came slavery, with the introduction of Africans. The "two Jamaicas," "White and Black," began to emerge during the Spanish colonial era. English White Jamaica, as a distinct European variant, began with the British take over of Jamaica in 1655. The British colonial government inherited a Black population of 1500, which it consciously and steadily increased to sustain its plantocracy. People of African descent rose from 25 percent of the total population under the Spanish regime in 1655 to 96 percent of the population after emancipation in the census of 1844.[12] The evolution of this most distinct segment of the population is couched in the painful and complex history of slavery and resistance, too rich to recount here. Most germane to this discussion is the creation by emancipation of a Jamaican Black ethnicity. The Africans brought to the island were vastly diverse, from Yoruba to Asante to Fon to Bantu. But within a context of racial oppression, from this highly pluralistic composition was born a Black ethnicity, a situation not quite unlike that of other regions of the diaspora.[13]

This Black ethnicity had been well established when an Asian presence was infused into the Black–White Jamaican society. After emancipation Blacks moved *en masse* as far away as possible from the plantations, the most enduring reminder of bondage. In the search for an alternate source of cheap labor, the colonial government set its sights on India and China after efforts directed at Europe, North America, and Africa failed.[14] Between 1845 and 1914, about

36,400 East Indians were brought to Jamaica under the indentureship program agreed upon by both the colonial governments of Jamaica and India. Although, theoretically, both governments agreed to ensure the fair treatment of the workers, the evidence reveals that most of the Indian families could only get deplorable housing and worked under exploitative employment conditions.[15] In spite of these difficulties and the repatriation provisions built into the agreement, the East Indians did form a permanent community on the island. Their "alien" religions (80 percent Hindu and 20 percent Muslim) along with their initial inability to understand English set them apart. The colonial government, for its part, exploited the situation, pursuing deliberate policies designed to segregate the Indians from the Africans. This, of course, was principally to forestall any concerted Indian–African resistance.[16] The African Jamaican often displayed the same contempt for the Indians as White Jamaicans. Additionally, they resented those Indians who succeeded and, thereby, threatened their place in the economy. The Indians, for their part, quickly grasped the established racial stratification, which put Blacks at the bottom. Moreover, as Sherlock and Bennet point out in *The Story of the Jamaican People*, the Indians' fixed caste system, in which skin pigmentation partly determined social status, caused them to view the darker-complexioned African Jamaicans as socially inferior. Some of them openly referred to Blacks as Kafari or infidel. Even into the twentieth century some Indians would not allow their children to attend the same schools with Black children.[17]

The Chinese, the other Asian postemancipation immigrant group, came a little later than the Indians. The first waves of Chinese migration to Jamaica in the second half of the nineteenth century occurred within the wider context of a Chinese diaspora, which also took them to other destinations, including Brazil and the United States.[18] The first arrivals came via Panama, where they had been recruited to help construct the railroad. Almost 500 Chinese laborers, who were faring badly under the harsh Panama conditions, were exchanged for Jamaican labor. As shortages of Black labor on the plantations continued and Indian labor also began to prove unreliable, successive waves of Chinese immigrants were welcomed. These immigrants were farmers, originally from Guangdong province in southeast China. They did not come directly from there, however, as they were recruited from Hong Kong, Trinidad, and British Guiana. Chinese immigration to Jamaica continued into the twentieth century, by which time the established Chinese Jamaicans were beginning to send for relatives through a discernable chain migration process.[19]

Like the Indians, the Chinese experienced tremendous hardships. As a non-English speaking, non-Christian group, they faced similar contempt and bigotry. Although the majority of the migrants were farmers, in Jamaica, once they fulfilled their contracts they moved out of the estates and away from agriculture. Many found their niche in the retail grocery business. They were so successful in this economic arena that by 1910, "grocery store" and "Chinese shop" had become synonymous.[20] This success elicited resentment from other groups in the society. The resentment was violently demonstrated in the labor riots of the 1930s, when protesters attacked some Chinese and destroyed their property. The colonial government, too, partial to the interests of the White economic elite, resorted to policies aimed at restricting the entry of Chinese immigrants and monitoring the activities of those already resident on the island. Reaction to official and unofficial discrimination contributed to the building of a viable and permanent Chinese Jamaican community. Since they had no consular representation on the island, the Chinese built their own institutional support through benevolent, mutual benefit associations, and *fusee chen* (rotating credit association). Partly through these reactive processes, the Chinese Jamaicans were able to sustain a distinct community in spite of their relatively small number.[21]

Also present in the racial/ethnic tapestry were peoples of the Middle East. The Jewish presence actually began in the Spanish colonial era. Jews first arrived as indentured servants who helped to establish the sugar industry. In spite of initial discrimination against them as a non-Christian group, they made phenomenal progress, moving from the plantations into commerce. As prosperous merchants they came to exert a strong element of control over the Jamaican economy. This put them on a par with the privileged White planters who were known to seek financial help from Jewish enterprises.[22] The other groups from the Middle East — Palestinians, Lebanese, and Syrians (collectively more commonly referred to simply as "Syrians") — followed similar economic paths, moving their way up from peddlers to merchants and traders.[23]

So, by independence, there were the "two Jamaicas" — "Black" and "White" — and in the middle were the immigrant minority groups of East Indians, Chinese, Jews, and "Syrians." Because of this intermediary position, these groups have also been labeled "Middleman Minorities."[24] Undeniably, then, Jamaica's racial pluralism was clearly established by the late 1930s, when the struggle for self-government and independence got underway. Was there a sense of community, of peoplehood in spite of this pluralism? Historian Edward Braithwaite advanced his thesis of Creoledom as support for the existence of such a unified community. According to him, a Creole society that was neither European nor African had emerged by the nineteenth century, giving the Black, White, and colored inhabitants of the island a sense of being distinctly Jamaican.[25] But reviewers of Braithwaite's interpretation point out that it is improbable, under the existing acrimonious relations, that slave and master shared common values that could be channeled into forging a sense of being one people. Indeed, the planters often appealed to the island's distinct culture, but specifically in their struggles with England. Therefore, as Gordon Lewis points out, the "Jamaican sense," was opportunism rather than real Creole patriotism and it remained an ideology of narrow interest.[26]

Creolization, in its simplest sense of mere mixing of diverse peoples, intensified in the late nineteenth and early twentieth centuries with the arrival of the non-White and non-Black groups. While Creolization manifested itself clearly in some of the evolving hybrid cultural forms, sharp distinctions among the various racial groups persisted.[27] So, at independence, the attempt to foster a "one people" national ideology was not uncalled for. Such an ideology was essentially to serve as a tool of conflict control. Like everywhere else, the Jamaican "nationalizing elites" were inventing nation and national tradition. In this task, understanding the workings of "political affinities" and "cultural affinities" was crucial. Unlike in the new African nations, the two party system that evolved in Jamaica was not fiercely reflective of cultural affinities. The dominant parties, the People's National Party and the Jamaican Labor Party, essentially transcend race, color, and class in their membership, leadership, and agenda. Furthermore, as many Jamaicans, most especially the nation-building elites, are quick to point out, since independence, questions of race have seldom been raised explicitly in Jamaican politics.[28] This is seen as a major indicator of the viability, in fact the success, of the national ideology. According to this assessment, the inventors of the Jamaican nation successfully created a non-racial framework for nationhood. But how unqualified is this success? While it is true that only a few times have questions of race surfaced explicitly in post-colonial Jamaican politics, the fact that they are asked at all reveals salient racial fractures. The impingement of race on Jamaica as a nonracial invention will always be a factor because the African diaspora, the Afro-Caribbean diaspora and transnationalism aggregately have created a Black collectivity as a rival framework for understanding nationhood.

The salience of Black collectivity goes all the way back to the era of slavery. While there are many indices for this, perhaps the most pointed is the Maroon factor. A community of runaway slaves, Jamaica's Maroons, even though they were eventually "defeated" by the British colonial government, demonstrated the workings of a Black community within a larger White-dominated entity.[29] According to John Henrik Clarke, renowned scholar of the African diaspora, the Maroons must be recognized as pioneers of Black nationalism in the African diaspora.[30] Indeed, twentieth-century Black nationalist movements have tapped into the legacy of the Maroons to formulate their ideologies and strategies. One such beneficiary is Rastafarianism, which emerged in Jamaica in the 1930s. The movement was inspired by the pan-African efforts to rescue Ethiopia from the devastating Italian imperialistic assault. The Jamaican supporters of the Ethiopian emperor, Haile Selasie, also known as Ras Tafari, built a whole movement around their support for Ethiopia, which quickly came to include their counter assault on a more universal domination of Black people. This movement became clearly recognizable through its name, Rastafarianism; its adherents, Rastafarians or Rastas; their physical appearance, especially their dreadlock hair; and their music, reggae.[31] While too often critics emphasize distinguishing traits like ganja smoking to dismiss Rastafarianism, this movement is in fact one major expression of pan-Africanism. Pan-Africanism itself is a product of the African diaspora and for the purposes of this chapter, I must stress, is one of the forces that contribute to the rival framework that threatens the literal application of Jamaican nonracial nationhood.[32]

Marronage, Rastafarianism and, certainly not to be omitted, Garveyism[33] are all antecedents of postcolonial Black nationalism. The unrest of the 1960s, almost immediately after independence, provided the first glimpse into the enduring viability of race consciousness. The short-lived People's Political Party (PPP), led by Black lawyer Millard Johnson, presented the first significant attempt to incorporate Black protest into Jamaican postcolonial politics. Together with Rastas of the urban areas, the PPP protested the economic closure experienced by blacks; contested the dominance of the economy and society by Whites and ethnic minorities; advocated Black ethnic nationalism; and actually advanced the idea of Black supremacy.[34] The PPP did not survive in the political arena — not surprising, since its main support base, the Rastas, boycotted elections, which they branded Babylon politics.

The demise of the PPP did not mean the end of a Black indictment of a nonracial Jamaica. The Black Power Movement of the late 1960s and early 1970s underscored the continuation of Black nationalism. Black Power adherents focused substantially on the nation's economy by vigorously denouncing the workings of the major sectors — bauxite alumina and tourist industries. These were controlled by huge multinational companies which were mostly based in Canada and the United States. So, on one level, significantly, the Black Power Movement was an anti-imperialist movement aimed at neocolonial forces. As Jamaican scholar Rex Nettleford explained:

> . . . Many Jamaicans see this [bauxite-alumina industry] as the colonial industry par excellence, controlled as it is from multinational bases situated outside of the country. They know that decision-making does not rest with Jamaicans and seldom with white functionaries who reside on the island.[35]

But the Black Power Movement was more than a Jamaican nativist movement against foreign exploiters. Even as they pounded on foreign elements, Black Power protesters saw the racial implications of the Jamaican economy. Simply put, according to Nettleford, "the Jamaican economy did not live up to the expectations of an ex-slave society struggling to give full meaning to emancipation and freedom."[36] From this perspective, the Black Power Movement vented some of its most vehement resentment at the very internal economic structure of the nonracial nation. At the height of the movement the protesters released a pamphlet attempting to show "intensified white economic power in Jamaica." The list included over one hundred commercial businesses controlled by White families. The term "White" is loosely used here. As Carl Stone points out, by the time of the Black Power Movement "dominant economic power had shifted from the [White] rural-based planter class to the urban-based intermediary ethnic groups (Jews, Syrians, Chinese, and Browns), who reconstituted a new and powerful capitalism, which included the whites but eliminated the latter's ascendancy and dominance."[37] Similarly, Walter Rodney, one of the prominent pioneers of Black Power in Jamaica, consistently emphasized the extensive connotation of "Black" in the movement. As he put it:

I maintain that it is the white world which has defined who are black. However, it is obvious that the West Indian's situation is complicated by factors such as the variety of racial types and racial mixtures and the process of class formation. We have, therefore, to note not simply what the White world says but also how individuals perceive each other. Nevertheless, we can talk of the mass of the West Indian population as being black — either African or Indian, Portuguese or Chinese.[38]

For Rodney, as for most Black Power adherents, the power, influence and control exercised by the Black majority should reflect their numbers and immense contributions to the society. The Black Power Movement begged serious questions about non-White ethnic minorities, including "should their property be expropriated so as to accommodate control by the 90-odd percent black Jamaicans?"[39] While nothing so drastic ever materialized, Black Power adherents made it clear that their attack of existing economic arrangements did not stop at foreign exploiters. For emancipation and independence to be realistically meaningful, Blacks must exert economic as well as political control.

Admittedly, Black Power activists were not unanimous in their choice of an agenda for or approaches to protest. Nevertheless, even as they acknowledged class and international dependency theories, all of them forcefully raised matters of race and racism operating within their officially nonracial national boundaries.[40] If the economic targets of Black Power did not denote Black nationalism clearly, its adherents and their strategies screamed Blackness. In the forefront were Rastas, neo-Garveyites, and return migrants who were mostly young radical intellectuals embittered by racism in Canada, the United States, and the United Kingdom. Their composition and rhetoric clearly revealed the workings of pan-Africanism and transnationalism born out of both the African and Afro-Caribbean diasporas. Rasta and reggae icon Peter Tosh underscored the premise of Black Power in one of his hits: "No matter where you come from, as long as you are a Blackman you are an African. No matter your nationality you have got the identity of an African." According to this premise, Blacks of Jamaica are strongly connected to Blacks elsewhere in the diaspora and Africa. Clearly, then, such reasoning upheld the salience of race and underscored the impracticality of a truly nonracial nation.

Along with the racially charged reggae lyrics were attempts at aesthetic re-Africanization. Black Power supporters in Jamaica began to wear the dashiki and the big Afro hairstyle almost rivaled dreadlocks as a symbol of Blackness. These trends, undoubtedly, were imported from the United States, where the Black Power Movement had started earlier. As was the case in the United States, the efficacy of such aesthetic Africanization became a subject of debate. For example, a letter to the editor of the *Jamaica Daily Gleaner* of June 7, 1969, called such trends "black stupidity." A letter responding to this attack explained: "Wearing an African dress is a silent and dignified statement by a Jamaican of African origin that he belongs to one of the clearly defined, and I should like to think, great races of the world."[41] The *Gleaner* also reprinted an article by Kenyan activist Tom Mboya, which had first appeared in the *New York Times*. Entitled "Back to Africa Desire Unrealistic," Mboya questioned the usefulness of Black diasporic protest that, not fully understanding Africa and Africans, delved indiscriminately into various aspects of "African culture" in search of support. It is because of this kind of concern that some Black Power advocates pressed for a meaningful study of African history. Convinced that collective memory was an essential tool for sustaining Black collectivity, they stressed the necessity of learning "good African history." But even this more laudable form of re-Africanization provoked questions, the major one being: Would African history subsume West Indian, Jamaican history? The firing of Walter Rodney, Guyanese historian and self-proclaimed Marxist, hired to teach African history at the University in Mona, Kingston, is emblematic of the tension. Aesthetic or intellectual, Africanization propagated Black nationalism and threatened Jamaican nationalism.

Remarkably, the architects of nationhood also sought to tap into history for rationalization, believing as they did that a nation's identity is defined by the past. Norman Manley, one of the founding fathers of modern-day Jamaica, declared: "those who are daring . . . to talk about a national being must never forget that the history is the living garment of a nation."[42] But Manley and other state builders were more interested in a garment that clad the new nation in its finest, one that denoted historical unity and racial harmony. The Morant Bay Rebellion of 1865[43] appealed to both the nation builders and the Black nationalists as a significant landmark. But their emphases diverged in the interpretation of the roles of the protagonists of that historical event. While the Black nationalists held and projected the view that the most significant role was played by the Black rebel leader Paul Bogle, Manley and the "non-racialists" were attracted to George William Gordon as the premier protagonist. Gordon embodied many of the ingredients for their vision of a Jamaican national spirit. He was the son of a slave woman and a White planter. Even though he married an Englishwoman and rose to a position of power and influence in the society, he maintained a strong affiliation with the Negroes, to whom he was related by birth. Furthermore, his commitment to that race was underscored by his involvement in Morant Bay, a tenacity that led to his execution. So, his identity and career were reflective of how racial distinctions can be subsumed for the common good of the nation, and how national and racial loyalties can overlap and reinforce one another.[44]

As was the case in the United States, Black Power as a movement in Jamaica waned. But it would be erroneous to conclude that Jamaican nonracial nationhood triumphed. Transnationalism within the Afro-Caribbean diaspora would continue to interplay with pan-Africanism and loom over nonracialism. The

Afro-Caribbean diaspora has resulted in Afro-Caribbean communities mostly in three areas of the Black Atlantic: namely, the United States, Canada, and the United Kingdom. These communities, far from being detached, are closely linked through the crisscrossing of people and ideas.

The carnival provides a good example of the basis for interaction. Increasingly, West Indians, including Jamaicans, view the annual carnival celebrations in New York, Toronto, and London as significant points of contact. These celebrations, which are clearly far more than entertainment and merriment, provide insights into the evolution of the politics of diasporic nationalism. In all these connecting points in the Black Atlantic, the experiences of the Jamaicans abroad are shaped in no small measure by their encounters with race and racism: in the United States, from racial profiling, which goes as far as singling out "Jamaican posses," to police brutality against blacks; in the United Kingdom, from increasing racial residential segregation to widespread racism in the police force; and in Multicultural Canada, from the insidious practice of arbitrarily streamlining Black students into lower standard classes and programs to "police racism."[45] Black Jamaicans abroad, invariably then, have to deal with their Blackness. And because of the ongoing transnational connections within the Black Atlantic, the discourses engendered are transmitted across national boundaries, including those of the homeland, Jamaica. As Paul Gilroy describes it in his study of Blacks in Britain, culture develops in "complex, dynamic patterns of syncretism in which new definitions of what it means to be black emerge from raw materials provided by black populations elsewhere in the diaspora."[46]

The Black Bookshop Movement in England exemplifies this transnational process within the diaspora. In the late 1960s and 1970s, jolted by the increasing blatant expressions of racism in Britain and influenced by the Civil Rights and Black Power movements in the United States, Black British activists established Black bookshops to carry pertinent literature and organize activities and projects to combat White racism. Mostly from the Caribbean — Jamaica, Barbados, Trinidad, St. Lucia, and Antigua — they teamed up with African activists living in Britain to develop a whole movement around the bookstores. As Colin Beckles explains, "as politicized entities, the bookshops functioned as Pan-African sites of resistance."[47] The main objectives of the movement revolved around the quest to resist the dominant group's arbitrary imposition of their own perceptions of Black identities and propensities on Blacks in Britain. The publications that were produced and sold, as well as the activities that were organized, were geared toward creating and disseminating alternative definitions of their identity and interpretations of the Black experience. Their efforts led to a Black counter hegemonic discourse.[48]

This counter hegemonic discourse went well beyond the English shores to the United States, Canada, and the Caribbean. Through the vital contacts still maintained by the Caribbean principal activists, bookshop materials were distributed in large quantities in that region.[49] Herein lies the point most germane to the present study. The materials, representative of the counter hegemonic tradition, asked questions like: What does it mean to be Black in White-controlled societies? What can and should Black people do to reclaim their history and occupy more prominent niches in their societies? In sum, the discourse was mostly about keeping Black consciousness alive. And it was being brought into Jamaica, a nation striving to minimize race consciousness, by its citizens who had been racialized abroad.

As political as the bookshop counter hegemonic struggle was, a substantial amount of materials and activities were about culture, a crucial underpinning of Black diasporic nationalism. It is impossible to meaningfully consider culture in the Black diaspora without looking at music, which has always featured as one of the principal elements in Black diasporic counterculture. In Jamaica, as in other slave societies, from the work songs in the fields to the chanting in the slave quarters and houses of worship, music was used to express identities, protest and a reaffirmation of self and group worth. At the turn of the twentieth century, music still featured as a prominent conduit that funneled black identity into the parameters of a Jamaican nonracial nation. In the 1970s, especially, there was no question that reggae music was that conduit. From Bob Marley to Peter Tosh to Jimmy Cliff, the appeal to Black consciousness was clear. Significantly, reggae, even though vehemently denounced by some, touched almost every corner to the point that it became one of the hallmarks of the new nation. So solid is reggae's place in Jamaican history and society that its centrality was being invoked in far away New York. On July 30, 2002, speaking to a group of Jamaican immigrants on the occasion of the country's 40th independence anniversary, Bishop Charles Dufour explained the essence of reggae: "Reggae is a music of inspiration, pulsing with the struggles of a people . . . to talk about Jamaica without talking about Reggae music is like eating ackee [Jamaican national dish] without salt fish."[50]

While reggae continues to be prominent, with the new breed of second-generation Rastas still "chanting Babylon," hip-hop artists are making a rapid ascent as the cultural Black nationalists of the twenty-first century. Significantly, hip-hop owes some of its beginnings to the Giant Speaker Sound system of the Jamaican immigrant community of the Bronx in the late 1960s and early 1970s.[51] Fundamentally, a significant part of the message of both reggae and hip-hop is collective Black consciousness. Therefore, whether to celebrate the life of late reggae icon Bob Marley or to film a hip-hop music video in Moore Town, a historically renowned Maroon territory, the artists, blast their racial ideology.[52] Usually, their audiences are big, filling soccer stadiums and other such arenas. While many in the crowd would uphold one official standard and vigorously deny the salience of race in their nation, they find a comfort zone at these events, where they equally affirm a cultural Black nationalism, believing perhaps that this did amount to a coup against political, nonracial, Jamaican nationalism. This scenario could be illustrative of Molefe Asante's point about the connection between Black aesthetics and Afrocentrism.

According to him, even when entertainment was the *raison d'etre*, it could be couched in nationalism and could become Afrocentric and transformative.[53]

While Blackness is fundamental to African diasporic nationalism, it does not negate nation or nationality. In the multiple identities projected by immigrants from Jamaica, one very important one is Jamaican. Many immigrants have even invoked that identity as foreigners to counter racism in their new homes. So, simultaneously as they grapple with what it means to be Black in the United States, Canada, or the United Kingdom, they also attempt to articulate nonracial identities based on their homeland nationality.[54] By the late 1980s, these nationality-based identities had evolved further and had become even more complex. True transnational identities that grew out of the immigrants' feelings of dual citizenship in both Jamaica and their new homes in North America and Europe emerged. Jamericans (U.S.), Janadians (Canada), and Janglish (U.K.), by the close of the twentieth century, had been added to their lexicon of identities.

These new labels, depicting viable transnational identities and existence, were not around during the initial formulation of a modern Jamaican nation. Their existence, therefore, in many ways, demonstrates the reality of the charging external currents, which must be considered in understanding the evolution of nationhood in Jamaica. Present-day transnational identities and existence constitute one component of what Jamaican British Cultural Studies scholar Stuart Hall would call a "conjuncture:" a "contingent historical moment defined by the reorganization of an existing configuration of questions and answers."[55]

Anthropologist David Scott is one of the scholars looking into this conjuncture in Jamaica. He concluded:

> There is scarcely a postcolonial society today that is not in fundamental crisis . . . what these crises share — in places as distant and distinct from each other as, say, Sri Lanka and Jamaica — is the pervasive sense of a breakdown not merely in a few discrete areas of development policy or constitutional arrangement or political organization, but of the modern nation-state project as a whole. What is in crisis, in other words, is not simply the coherence or otherwise of rival ideological positions, but the conceptual and institutional bases themselves upon which the secular-modern project of building "new nations" was undertaken and sustained.[56]

Scott examined the upheavals of the close of the twentieth century to underscore the limitations (actually the obsolete state) of the established vocabulary of politics in Jamaica. Importantly, he pointed out that the so-called "lawlessness" was an expressioin of disillusionment among the "*black* [my emphasis], poor and urban, who have felt not only disempowered and disconnected from the political process of the postcolonial state, but also systematically disregarded and disrespected by the governing elite."[57]

The present chapter is also about this conjuncture in Jamaican nationhood. But while Scott focuses on the internal sources of the need for reorganization, this study has attempted to locate the centripetal forces emanating from the African diaspora, the Afro-Caribbean diaspora, Pan-Africanism, and transnationalism. What impact do the enduring legacies of the slave trade, slavery, and a Black collective have on the interpretations of nationhood in Jamaica? What are the implications for the home society of the existence of distinct peoples now known as Jamericans, Janadians, and Janglish, who are drawn together by shared experiences as Blacks in predominantly White societies, the carnival outside the Caribbean, reggae and hip-hop, and chatrooms in cyberspace?[58] How does their transnational crisscrossing within the diaspora and between their North American or European homes and Jamaica affect the course and realities of nationhood? These are viable questions, which, today, feature in the conjuncture or the reorganization of the existing configuration of what is the modern postcolonial state of Jamaica. These questions in actuality ask one question — is it correct to call Jamaica a nonracial nation?

Notes

1. The examples are legion, from military coups to secessions which culminated in deadly, protracted civil wars. In Africa there are a host of examples, from the Biafra war in Nigeria to the Rwanda and Burundi genocide. In Asia, the vicissitudes of the subcontinent, including the unending struggle over Kashmir, are exemplary.

2. Colin Clarke, *Kingston, Jamaica: Urban Development and Social Change 1692–1962* (Berkeley: University of California Press, 1975), 152.

3. M.G. Smith, *The Plural Society in the British West Indies* (Berkeley, CA: University of California Press, 1965); David Lowenthal, *West Indian Societies* (London: Oxford University Press, 1972); Adam Kuper, *Changing Jamaica* (London: Routledge and Kegan Paul, 1976); Rupert Lewis, "Black Nationalism in Jamaica in Recent Years," in Carl Stone and Aggrey Brown eds., *Essays on Power and Change in Jamaica* (Kingston: Jamaica Publishing House, 1977); Derek Gordon, "Race, Class and Social Mobility in Jamaica," in Rupert Lewis and Patrick Bryan eds., *Garvey: His Work and Impact* (Trenton, NJ: African World Press, 1991); Rex Nettleford, "Race, Identity and Independence on Jamaica," in Hilary Beckles and Verene Shepherd eds., *Caribbean Freedom: Economy and Society from Emancipation to Present* (Princeton, NJ: Markus Wiener, 1993).

4. Paul Gilroy, *The Black Atlantic: Modernity and Double Consciousness* (Cambridge, MA: Harvard University Press, 1993).

5. Gilroy, *The Black Atlantic*.

6. Often described as "migration-oriented," the societies of the Caribbean offer a vivid illustration of a diaspora within a diaspora. While, admittedly, the migration waves have been made up of the diverse ethnic and racial groups, the diaspora is predominantly Afro-Caribbean. Since immediately after emancipation in 1833, Blacks have been moving in varying volumes within and outside the Caribbean, motivated by the desire to move away from the physical and psychological torment of the legacies of slavery and lured by economic and other prospects in North America and Europe. For more on the Caribbean "migration tradition," *see* Dawn Marshall, "Toward an Understanding of Caribbean Migration," Mary M. Kritz, ed., *United States Immigration and Refugee Policy* (Lexington, MA: D.C. Heath, 1983).

7. Broadly speaking, Transnationalism is the complex ongoing connections of people, ideas and activities between nations. It is expressed in diverse political, economic, social, and cultural forms. For insights into the definitions of and discussions on that phenomenon, *see* Steven Vertovec, "Conceiving and Researching Transnationalism," *Ethnic and Racial Studies*, 22.2 (1999). Good case studies of transnationalism can be found in Peggy Levitt and Mary C. Watters, eds., *The Changing Face of Home: The Transnational Lives of the Second Generation* (Thousand Oaks, CA: Russell Sage, 2002). Chapter 14, "Second-Generation West Indian Transnationalism" by Milton Vickerman, is particularly useful.

8. Roy Simon Bryce Laporte, in the Introduction of Aubrey W. Bonnet and G. Llewellyn Watson, eds., *Emerging Perspectives of the Black Diaspora* (New York: University Press of America, 1990).

9. *See*, for example, Kathleen Norris, *Jamaica: the Search for an Identity* (London: Oxford University Press, 1962); Nyamayro K. Mufuka, "The Jamaican Experiment," *Current History*, 74, 434 (1978); Rex Nettleford, *Identity, Race and Protest in Jamaica* (New York: William Morrow and Co., Inc., 1972); and Anthony Payne, "Jamaica's Approach to Independence," *Caribbean Review*, XVI, 1 (1988).

10. Milton Vickerman, *Crosscurrents: West Indian Immigrants and Race* (New York: Oxford University Press, 1999), 37.

11. For more on the indigenous peoples and their extermination, *see* Irving Rowe, *The Tainos: Rise and Decline of the People Who Greeted Columbus* (New Haven, CT: Yale University Press, 1992).

12. Philip Sherlock and Hazel Bennett, *The Story of the Jamaican People* (Princeton, NJ: Markus Wiener, 1998), 77; G.W. Roberts, *The Population of Jamaica* (London: Cambridge University Press, 1957), 65.

13. For more on the dynamics of the evolution of a black ethnicity in Jamaica, *see* Don Robotham, "The Development of a Black Ethnicity in Jamaica," in Rupert Lewis and Patrick Bryan, eds., *Garvey: His Work and Impact*, 23–38.

14. Soon after emancipation the government recruited indentured servants from Germany, Scotland, England, and Ireland. This, the government hoped, would serve the dual purpose of providing labor and balancing the ratio between black and white. However, a number of factors, including antiemigration sentiments in Europe, the white workers' disdain of plantation work, tropical diseases, and the lure of other destinations like the United States, put an end to the project.

    Although between 1841 and 1867 thousands of Africans were recruited from Sierra Leone, West Africa, the African alternative was abandoned because it was unpopular, especially in Britain, where the Colonial Office feared that it could be seen as a continuation of African enslavement.

15. H.S. Sohal, "The East Indian Indenturship System in Jamaica 1845–1917," Ph.D. Thesis, University of Waterloo, 1979.

16. Sherlock and Bennet, *The Story of the Jamaican People*, 321.

17. Sherlock and Bennet, *The Story of the Jamaican People*, 321

18. For more on the Chinese diaspora, *see* Lynn Pan, *Sons of the Yellow Emperor: A History of the Chinese Diaspora*, Vol. 1 (Boston, MA: Little Brown & Co., 1990); Laurence Ma, Carolyn Cartier, eds., *The Chinese Diaspora: Space, Place, Mobility, and Identity* (Lanham, MD: Rowman and Littlefield, 2003); and Sharon Hom, ed., *Chinese Women Traversing Diaspora: Memories, Essays and Poetry* (New York: Garland Publishers, 1999).

19. Unfortunately, there is still paucity in the history of the Chinese in Jamaica. Detailed accounts in the *Daily Gleaner* and other such written sources, as well as oral sources, are still to be fully tapped.

20. For more on the Chinese and the grocery trade in Jamaica, *see* Jacqueline Levy, "The Economic Role of the Chinese in Jamaica: The Grocery Retail Trade," *The Jamaican Historical Review*, 15, (1986):117–138.

21. For more on the evolution of the Jamaican Chinese community, *see* Lee Tom Yin, *The Chinese in Jamaica* (Kingston: Chung San News, 1963).

22. For more on the history of Jews in Jamaica, *see* Stephan Alexander Fortune, *Merchants and Jews: The Struggle for British West Indian Commerce, 1650–1750* (Gainesville: University of Florida Press, 1984); C.S. Holzberg, *Minorities and Power in a Black Society: The Jewish Community of Jamaica* (Maryland: N.S. Publishing Co., 1987).

23. *See* David Nicholls, "The Syrians of Jamaica," *The Jamaican Historical Review*, 15 (1986).

24. One of the classic analyses of this phenomenon is Edna Bonacich, "A Theory of Middleman Minorities," *American Sociological Review*, 38 (1973).

25. Edward Braithwaite, *The Development of Creole Society in Jamaica, 1770–1820* (Oxford: Claredon Press, 1971).

26. Gordon K. Lewis, *Main Currents in Caribbean Thought: The Historical Evolution of Caribbean Society in its Ideological Aspects, 1492–1900* (Baltimore, MD: Johns Hopkins University Press, 1983), 321–322.

27. By the 1950s, many of the festivals and celebrations demonstrated the cultural creolization that had occurred. For example, the hosay and divali Hindu festivals and the Chinese Lion dance and prominence of fireworks in celebrations.

28. For example, Norman Manley, one of the architects of the nation, declared that "nowhere in the world has more progress been made in developing a non-racial society in which colour is not significant." Cited in Sherlock and Bennett, *Story of the Jamaican People*, 386.

29. Jamaica, like Guyana, Surinam and Brazil, has a rich history of marronage as a form of slave rebellion. A good study of Jamaica's Maroons is Mavis Campbell, *The Maroons of Jamaica 1655–1796: A History of Resistance, Collaboration and Betrayal* (Granby, MA: Bergin & Garvey, 1990).

30. John Henrik Clarke, "The Caribbean Antecedents of Marcus Garvey," in John Henrik Clarke, ed., *Marcus Garvey and the Vision for Africa* (New York: Vintage Books, 1974), 23.

31. For more on the history of Rastafarianism (from the perspective of a Rasta), *see* Bones Jah, *One Love: Rastafari History, Doctrine and Livity* (London: Voice of Rasta Publishing House, 1989). For a more objective view, *see* Joseph Owens, *Dread: The Rastafarians of Jamaica* (Exeter, NH: Heinemann Educational Books, 1976).

32. Since the introduction of the term, there has been an endless debate about the "correct" definition of Pan-Africanism. Internationally renowned Black activists have advanced some noteworthy pronouncements based in their experiences. Trinidadian and pioneer Pan-Africanist George Padmore saw Pan-Africanism as a manifestation of fraternal solidarity among Africans and peoples of African descent. Civil Rights and Black Power Movement activist Stokley Carmichael defined it as the total liberation and unification of Africa under Scientific Socialism. Rupert Emerson defined Pan-Africanism as "the sense that all Africans have a spiritual affinity with each other and that, having suffered together in the past, they must march together into a new and brighter future." Kwame Nantambu, critiquing the myriad of earlier definitions, emphasizes that Pan-Africanism must be understood in terms of revolutionary, historical struggle instead of couching it in emotional and politico-cultural platitudes. *See* Kwame Nantambu, "Pan-Africanism versus Pan-African Nationalism: An Afrocentric Analysis," *Journal of Black Studies*, 28.5 (May, 1998), 561–574. Also *see* George Padmore, *Pan-Africanism or Communism: The Coming Struggle for Africa* (New York: Anchor, 1972); and Rupert Emerson, "Pan-Africanism," I.L. Markovitz, ed., *African Politics and Society* (New York: Free Press, 1970).

33. Jamaican Marcus Garvey was an internationally known black nationalist. His Universal Negro Improvement Association, which he first formed in Jamaica in 1916, spread to other parts of the Caribbean, South America, Africa, and the United States, where he moved the headquarters in 1918. Though highly controversial, few deny his lasting impact on pan-Africanism and Black nationalism.

34. Carl Stone, "Race and Economic Power in Jamaica," in Lewis and Bryan, eds., *Garvey*, 251–252.

35. Rex Nettleford, "Race, Identity and Independence in Jamaica," in Hilary Beckles and Verene Shepherd, eds., *Caribbean Freedom: Economy and Society from Emancipation to the Present* (Princeton, NJ: Markus Wiener, 1996), 521.

36. Beckles and Shepherd, *Caribbean Freedom*, 520.

37. Stone, "Race and Economic Power in Jamaica," 251.

38. Walter Rodney, *Groundings With my Brother* (London: Bogle, 1968), 6.

39. Nettleford, "Race, Identity and Independence," 519.

40. For a concise and analytical study of the Black Power Movement in the West Indies, *see* Bert J. Thomas, "Caribbean Black Power: From Slogan to Practical Politics," *Journal of Black Studies*, 22.3 (March 1992), 392–410.

41. *Daily Gleaner*, June 16, 1969.

42. From one of Norman Manley's speeches, cited in Rex Nettleford, ed., *Norman Washington Manley and the New Jamaica: Selected Speeches and Writings, 1938–68* (Trinidad and Jamaica: Longman Caribbean, 1971), 113.

43 On October 11, 1865, a clash between police and protesters over the execution of arrest warrants led to violence in Morant Bay. The week-long bloody fighting that ensued was actually the culmination of a long confrontation between activists and the Jamaican colonial authorities. Led by mulatto George William Gordon and Black Paul Bogle, the protesters had been attempting to negotiate with an intransigent Governor Eyre for improved conditions and justice for the underprivileged masses. Failing to get any encouraging response from the government, they extended their protest directly to the courts, the very symbol of injustice. The disturbance was ruthlessly quelled only after a few days and the principal protesters, including Gordon and Bogle were executed.

44. For more on Jamaican history and nation-building, with particular reference to the Morant Bay Rebellion, *see* Karina Williamson, "Re-inventing Jamaican History: Roger Mais and George William Gordon," Sandra Courtman, ed., *The Society for Caribbean Studies Annual Conference Papers*, 3, 2002, http://www.scsonline.freeserve.co.uk/olvol3.html.

45. For good case studies of the evolution of economically and politically marginalized Black communities in the United Kingdom, *see* Mark Christian, "An African-Centered Approach to

the Black British Experience: With Special Reference to Liverpool,: *Journal of Black Studies*, 28.3 (January, 1998), 291–308; and Alfred B. Zack-Williams, "African Diaspora Conditioning: the Case of Liverpool," *Journal of Black Studies* 27.4 (March 1977), 528–542. In May 1990, for example, an amalgamation of Black organizations issued a protest document entitled "The Precarious Situation of Blacks in Ontario." A good introduction to the history of West Indian communities in Canada is Dwaine Plaza, "Migration and Adjustment to Canada: Pursuing the Mobility Dream 1900–1998," Courtman, ed., *Annual Conference Papers*.

46. Paul Gilroy, *There Ain't No Black in the Union Jack: The Cultural Politics of Race and Nation* (Chicago, IL: University of Chicago Press, 1987), 13.

47. Colin Beckles, "'We shall not be Terrorized out of Existence': The Political Legacy of England's Black Bookshops," *Journal of Black Studies*, 29.1 (September, 1998), 51.

48. Beckles, "We shall not be Terrorized out of Existence," 52.

49. Beckles, "We shall not be Terrorized out of Existence," 63.

50. "Jamaicans in New York Attend Service to Mark 40th Anniversary of Independence," http://www.jis.gov.jm/JA40/JIS%20NEWS%20releases/Jamaicans%20in%20NY.html.

51. Werner Zips, *Black Rebels: African Caribbean Freedom Fighters in Jamaica* (Princeton, NJ Markus Wiener, 1999), 220.

52. Zips, *Black Rebels*, 232–236.

53. Molefe Asante, *The Afrocentric Idea* (Philadelphia, PA: Temple University Press, 1987); Henderson, "Black Nationalism," 314.

54. For more on the development and complex articulation and manipulation of identities among West Indians in the United States, *see* Violet Johnson, "Black Immigrants," Paul Spickard and Jeffery Burroughs, *We are a People: Narrative and Multiplicity in Constructing Ethnic Identity* (Philadelphia, PA: Temple University Press, 2000), 57–69; and Vickerman, *Crosscurrents*, particularly chapters 3–5.

55. From David Scott's analysis of Stuart Hall, in David Scott, "The Permanence of Pluralism," Paul Gilroy, Lawrence Grossberg, and Angela McRobbie, eds., *Without Guarantees: In Honour of Stuart Hall* (London: Verso, 2000), 283.

56. Scott, "Permanence of Pluralism," 282.

57. Scott, "Permanence of Pluralism," 286. The so-called "tribal wars" rocked Jamaica in the 1990s, especially areas in Kingston. Communities rallied around area leaders known as "dons" or "dads" to vent their frustration at both the political parties and government. In his article, Scott uses the case study of Donald Phipps, "Zeeks" and his Mathews Lane community.

58. *See*, for example, Ja Web — the Web Yard for Jamericans, Janadians, and Janglish: http://www.pacificnet.net/~jaweb/.

8

Between Subjects and Citizens

Algerians, Islam, and French National Identity
during the Great War

RICHARD S. FOGARTY

It is for France an obligation to seek to compensate the *indigènes* who fight for her, or who, simply but loyally, have fulfilled their military duty. The highest, noblest recognition that France can perceive is to offer what she considers as the most precious, that is to say French nationality.[1]

This statement, from a 1915 legislative proposal designed to facilitate the naturalization of North Africans who served in the French army, was revealing not only of the supreme value of citizenship in French political discourse, but also of the strong links between that citizenship and service to the state in the military. This linkage, and France's commitment to its republican traditions, were tested after 1914 when the French began to recruit hundreds of thousands of colonial subjects to help fight the Great War in Europe. Though these men (known as *troupes indigènes*) were fighting and dying for their "adopted fatherland," making the sacrifices that the state routinely demanded of its citizens, they remained colonial subjects, without the rights of French citizens. Powerful republican traditions and the need to attract more recruits prompted French officials to attempt to address this anomaly with measures such as the 1915 legislative proposal. However, such efforts were not uncontroversial, and the debates they provoked among French officials and politicians highlighted the place of religion and culture in French conceptions of national identity, citizenship, and colonial ideology.

Revolutionary France was the birthplace of a new concept of national identity that linked closely the idea of citizenship with service to and defense of the state in the military. Thus, when France made extensive use of its colonial subjects on European battlefields to save the metropole from destruction at the hands of the

Germans, it was entirely in keeping with traditional republican ideology that these men be offered the rights of French citizens. Yet opposition to this idea was considerable, and many argued that it was not necessary at all to reward these soldiers in such a manner, that military service was a just price for the colonized to pay in return for the benefits of French imperial rule, and that, in fact, such an idealistic approach to the question ran very grave risks for the future of the French colonial empire. A crucial question, to be sure, was how France would maintain imperial control over naturalized and enfranchised colonial peoples, but another concern took on special importance during the war. Many in France wondered if members of these "other" peoples, with cultural practices very different from those of the French, were worthy and capable of exercising the rights of French citizens. The issue that most clearly revealed these anxieties was the naturalization of Muslim soldiers from Algeria. This was in part because Algerians made up a large percentage of the overall numbers of *troupes indigènes*, and because Algeria was more closely integrated into the administrative structure of the metropole than any other colony. But the contentiousness of the issue also had a great deal to do with the religious identity of these soldiers. Debate crystallized around Muslims' traditional customs and the special legal status that preserved them, the *statut personnel*. Muslims in Algeria were in many ways subject to French law, but in matters not of direct or urgent concern to the colonial administration (property or personal disputes between Muslims, laws regarding the family, inheritance, and other issues), they were subject to Koranic law administered by local religious authorities. In this *statut personnel*, many French officials saw an insurmountable obstacle to the acquisition of French citizenship. On the other hand — and this was what made the issue so difficult to resolve — how could the men who ran the Third Republic deny, in good conscience, the benefits of citizenship to those who had sacrificed so much for the defense of France?

Many scholars, and many French people themselves, consider understandings of nationhood in France to be "assimilationist," in contrast to more ethnically centered concepts of national belonging prevalent in other countries. As such, France is supposed to be relatively open to the political and social integration of immigrants and other outsiders, no matter what their ethnic or cultural origins, who choose to embrace French law, traditions, and culture. In this sense, France's "ethnic system" is, technically, not based upon ethnicity at all. It is a system, in theory, in which political and cultural assimilation override ethnic and racial differences. Yet, France's use of Algerian Muslims as soldiers in the Great War put its assimilationist impulses to the test, and confronted the French with acute ethnic, cultural, and religious questions. Putting republican assimilationist theory into practice turned out to be very difficult indeed. The most vexing of these questions for authorities were those involving customs and practices that authorities regarded as "uncivilized" and that they believed were linked with Islam. This was especially true of customs associated with the family and the rights of women, such as polygamy. That these fears were often more apparent than real did not lessen their importance in preventing the government from enacting any meaningful citizenship reform for Algerian Muslims. Such reform would have brought French policy into accordance with the republican ideology linking citizenship to military service, and with liberal traditions of assimilation that justified French colonialism by making indigenous peoples the targets of a "civilizing mission" designed to raise them up to the technological, intellectual, cultural, and eventually legal status of their colonial masters. However, despite the power of this ideology and these traditions, French officials were unable to integrate Islam into their conception of French national identity. In the final analysis, French assimilationist principles often gave way before what many French people regarded as insoluble ethnic, cultural, and religious differences. The limited access to naturalization in the colonies after the war brought into stark relief the ultimate weakness of the republican ideal of assimilation when it came to transforming colonial subjects into French citizens.

The relevance of these events extends beyond the Great War, and understanding them can help us understand the ethnic system that governs French politics, culture, and society today. In recent years, France has faced dramatic difficulties with the political and social integration of the millions of non-European immigrants who now reside in France, many of whom come from the same former colonies that provided the army with *troupes indigènes* between 1914 and 1918. During the 1980s and 1990s, vigorous debates over immigration often included discussion, and eventually modification, of citizenship and naturalization laws as they applied to immigrants and their children. Then as today, Algerians stand at the center of these debates, and it is their identity as Muslims that many non-Muslim French people see as the most important barrier to their full integration into French life, further indicating that today's problems have much in common with those that arose nearly a century ago. Even more recent debates over the official place of Islam in French life, embodied in the creation of a national Muslim council that is designed, in part, to transform French Muslims into good republican citizens, highlight even further the durability of arguments over the compatibility between Islamic religious identity and French national identity. These contemporary controversies and similar debates over the status of *troupes indigènes* reveal the limits of the republican ideology of assimilation when faced with difficult ethnocultural questions. Ultimately, what might appear as fairly new pressures on the egalitarian ideals of republican France, in response to large-scale immigration and heightened concerns over religious extremism and terrorism, turn out to be well within French historical traditions of citizenship policy. Understanding the debates over naturalizing Muslim soldiers who served France in the Great War, then, reveals important and enduring aspects of French conceptions of national identity.

Citizenship, military service, and *troupes indigènes*

Revolutionary France was the birthplace of the modern idea of national citizenship as a legal state of belonging to a political entity that derived its power and legitimacy from its expression of the will of a sovereign people, not from God and the king. The Revolution of 1789 removed the mediated, indirect relations that characterized interactions between the individual and the state under the Ancien Régime and introduced the modern idea of citizenship as membership in the national community on an equal basis with other citizens, with shared privileges and obligations.[2] The Revolution gave legal and ideological shape to the distinction between citizens and foreigners, a distinction that would become sharper as the nineteenth century wore on and that would characterize thinking about nationality in the modern era. The French revolutionary government invented or at least institutionalized many of the trappings of modern citizenship, such as passports, a state bureaucracy devoted to defining and monitoring citizens, and strict legal requirements for the acquisition and proof of national belonging.[3]

Ideas about nationality took on a special character in France. As they have developed from their origins in the Revolution, French understandings of nationhood have stressed allegiance to the state and willing integration into national political and cultural life as signs of nationality, while many other modern nations have stressed ethnic identity, blood ties, language, and shared cultural history as important components of national identity. Rogers Brubaker has illuminated this difference by contrasting the state-centered and assimilationist ideal in France with Germany's ethnocultural and "differentialist" model of national identity. His work reveals not only the importance of the Revolutionary heritage, but also the instrumental role that the Third Republic (1870–1940) played in solidifying this heritage and enshrining the assimilationist ideal in French consciousness and in law.[4] It was Ernest Renan, a leading intellectual figure in the early life of the Third Republic, who in 1882 made the celebrated and oft-quoted pronouncement that the French nation was a "daily plebiscite," reflecting the conscious will of citizens to join freely together under a common government. It is the official republican embrace of this rhetoric since 1870 (excepting, of course, the attitude of the Vichy regime during the World War II) that has led Maxim Silverman to characterize the French model of the nation as "contractual," as opposed to competing "ethnic" models.[5] These contrasting approaches are particularly evident in the historic embrace in France of the *jus soli* legal conception of citizenship, which accepts as members of the national community those who are born within national borders or those who reside there and meet certain other legal requirements. In other words, if a child is born in a nation operating under this principle, then he or she is automatically a citizen, regardless of race, religion, ethnicity, or other inherited characteristics. The individual becomes part of the national "daily plebiscite." An alternative definition of citizenship that prevails in many countries is known as *jus sanguinis*, which requires true members of the national community to have blood ties with the dominant ethnic group. Under this system, the nationality of a newborn child is entirely dependent upon the ethnic identity of the parents, and membership in the national community is thus restricted, even largely closed.

Yet, the French universalist and assimilationist model, rooted in *jus soli* conceptions of citizenship, is neither unconditionally open to outsiders, nor is it immune from seemingly particularist restrictions and exclusions. In the first place, the requirements of integration and assimilation can be absolute and unyielding. Those wishing to become French citizens must embrace French laws and customs, and this often requires sacrificing signs of ethnic and cultural difference. This has been especially true for Muslim Algerians. During the Great War, the most contentious debates revolved around how much of their distinctive cultural practices they could retain and still meet the requirements of French citizenship. In short, many officials doubted that Muslims could become truly French while retaining their religious identity. So France's "open" conception of nationality, while theoretically not limited by factors such as ethnicity, race, or religious belief, can be intolerant of diversity, of any deviation from prevailing notions of cultural identity. The use of *troupes indigènes*, however, posed particular difficulties because these men were carrying out one of the most sacred duties of modern citizenship, taking up arms to defend the nation.

The French Revolution was not only the birthplace of the modern idea of citizenship, but also the origin of a view of citizenship tied explicitly to the performance of military service.[6] On August 23, 1793, the National Convention adopted the *levée en masse*, declaring that "the French people are in permanent requisition for army service," in order to defeat the invading armies of Europe's monarchies. Empowered by this decree, the state conscripted thousands of young men, establishing the principle of the "Nation in Arms" that would over the next century transform European armies and the nature of modern war.[7] The *levée en masse* resulted from a transformation in the idea of citizenship. The measure rested upon the assumption that the state, as an expression and instrument of the popular will, could legitimately require all citizens to take up arms in defense of the nation. Now that all people had a stake in their government, they were obligated to protect its existence. If not all French citizens perceived the logic and justice of this obligation and failed to volunteer for military service, the state would rightfully resort to conscription. In fact, official documents such as passports were originally most important for administering the new system of conscription.[8] Thus, the first French republic established the enduring ideal of obligatory military service as "both the badge and moral consequence of citizenship," and the Third Republic embraced and extended this the ideal of the citizen-soldier.[9]

Thus, history and republican ideology prepared the ground for the linkage of military service and citizenship for colonial subjects in the French army during the World War I. This link was particularly strong when it came to conscription — which French officials used to fill the ranks in several colonies, most extensively in Algeria — as the draft was one of the more specific and onerous demands that the state made of its citizens. How could France conscript colonial subjects without offering them naturalization? In a 1918 address

to Parliament, the Minister of the Colonies offered the orthodox and idealistic republican answer that France could not deny *troupes indigènes* the opportunity to acquire French citizenship:

> These populations must . . . understand that, by the very call that she addresses to them, France raises them up to her [level]. In the metropole, it is an honor as much as a duty to be a soldier, and our laws have always excluded from the national army indigenous citizens [i.e., colonial subjects]: to fight in the first ranks of the French army is, for our African subjects, to stand forever on the side of civilization, threatened by our enemies. But, if she makes the *indigènes* a partner in her defense and demands of them their share of the sacrifices that she also imposes upon herself, France, in return, must take care to prove to them her spirit of justice and her recognition.[10]

Not everyone, however, agreed with this argument. Many military and political officials preferred to avoid conscription, and thus the problem of compensation in the form of naturalization, altogether. In 1915, Senator Henri Bérenger, though he urged the French government to make greater use of *indigènes* in the army, explicitly rejected conscription as a means of recruitment. He argued that obligatory military service was not a practice that the French could export to the colonies because,

> such as it functions today in French democracy, it is the complex work of time and liberty. It is the statut of a nation of citizens, it cannot be the regime of several races of subjects. Such sublime servitudes can be imposed by law only if they have first been consented to by the intellect and the heart. Conscription cannot be improvised any more than can the fatherland. We cannot require of our *indigènes* the same military obligations we require of ourselves, while we have not conceded them the same civil rights.[11]

The Senator did not envision according *indigènes* these civil rights, and so cautioned against conscripting men "who fight neither for their traditions, nor for their homes."[12] Bérenger suggested that the government make use of volunteers, or mercenaries fighting for material benefits, and perhaps offer limited access to naturalization to those who volunteered for military service and met certain requirements. This vision was far from the maximal republican ideal linking service to the state in the military with the right to citizenship.

Claims that colonial subjects were not fighting to protect their own homes were objectively true, but in fact the republican ideology of assimilation allowed many to argue that *indigènes* were defending their own immediate interests by serving in the French army. The 1918 address by the Minister of the Colonies was in this tradition. Colonial assimilationist ideology was similar and related to the assimilationism of French citizenship policy, but specific to the colonial context.

As it related to military service, the doctrine dictated that France would raise the colonized peoples up to its own elevated level of civilization, and so it was proper that France conscript *indigènes* to fight alongside native Frenchmen to defend their common interests, in this case to expel the Germans from French soil. Men like Senator Bérenger favored a competing vision of the colonial relationship known as association, which advocated allowing colonial subjects to develop within their own cultures and social institutions while the French associated local indigenous elites with the colonizing project. Association seemed to abandon, at least in part, the republican ideal of "civilizing" and assimilating indigenous peoples, and to recognize an irreducible difference between the French and their colonial subjects. Subjects would remain associated with the colonial project, not assimilated into an expansive French national community. Bérenger's colleague in the Senate, Etienne Flandin, made this point explicit in a 1917 critique of the use of conscription in Algeria. He believed it a mistake to force ill-prepared *indigènes* to assimilate to French practices and ideals, in this case obligatory service in the French army. A more prudent approach, he argued, would be to pursue a policy of association in military matters, which in this case amounted to a militia system based upon local tribal organization, to allow "the *indigène* to evolve not in our civilization, but in his own."[13]

The ideal of assimilation seemed to offer more hope for the eventual naturalization of colonial subjects, once they had achieved a certain level of cultural affinity and political maturity in the judgment of their colonial masters. Association, in contrast, did not seek such an allegedly utopian transformation of the mentality of *indigènes*, and seemed to maintain the political and cultural gulf that separated colonizers from colonized. Still, in practice, neither approach opened an easy path to French citizenship. Yet given the content of republican ideology and public discussion of military service for colonial subjects, *indigènes* themselves could be forgiven for being confused about the opportunities that existed if they joined the army. French officials routinely referred to France as the *indigènes'* "new" or "adopted" *patrie*. This term literally meant "fatherland," and implied an emotive, mystical bond between the nation and its "children." In 1914, Minister of War Alexandre Millerand, in an address to an important religious figure from Algeria who was touring France and visiting soldiers to improve their morale, gave his assurance that Algerians were defending "not only their adopted fatherland, but also the patrimony of liberty that they won nearly a century ago [i.e., in 1830 when France conquered Algeria] and which will not cease henceforth to increase."[14]

Such rhetoric raised the expectations of the soldiers. Reports on morale among troops from Algeria written very early in the war noted that the men "count entirely on the equity of France in order no longer to be treated, after the war, when they will have shed their blood without stinting, as pariahs in their country but as 'citizens.'"[15] One soldier, speaking of his hope for the future generation of Algerians, told a French official that "it would be generous to accord us certain rights, which France without doubt will not refuse to the survivors of

her Algerian children [many of whom] will have died contributing to her triumph over Germany."[16] In January 1915, the Ministry of War observed that there were numerous demands emanating from Algeria for the naturalization of all soldiers then in the army.[17]

Algerians, Islam, and Naturalization

However, from the French government's point of view, the religious identity of Algerian soldiers presented a serious obstacle to rewarding their service with citizenship. Wartime discussions about the naturalization of these men starkly illuminated the difficulties officials had in reconciling French citizenship with Islam. These problems stemmed from Muslims' *statut personnel*. This special "privilege" set Muslims apart from French citizens, who were subject to the Napoleonic Civil Code in all matters. Moreover, French and Koranic law were in direct contradiction in some areas, notably laws regarding the family. These contradictions raised grave concerns for many French officials when they contemplated the implications of naturalizing Algerian soldiers.

Though not the only group of colonial subjects to serve in the French army during the war, Algerians quickly became the focus of the debate over naturalization. In other areas of the French empire, powerful colonial interests were opposed to granting the rights of citizens to *indigènes*. These interests were no more powerful than those working in Algeria, but their objections carried more weight when they focused on Black Africans or southeast Asians, whose racial identity dramatically separated them from Frenchmen and North Africans, both "perfectible whites," in the words of Algeria's governor general.[18] Within North Africa, the status of Tunisia and Morocco as protectorates complicated plans for naturalization considerably, requiring that the French respect the nominal sovereignty of the indigenous rulers there. Converting those rulers' subjects into French citizens was hardly an effective way of doing so. Algeria, considered an integral part of France itself, was different. Unlike other colonies, it was a settler colony, and was divided into three administrative *départements*, which the French government treated on an equal basis with the other *départements* of mainland France. Moreover, according to the *sénatus-consulte* of July 14, 1865, legislation of Napoleon III's Second Empire that regulated the status of Algeria's Muslims, indigenous Algerians were "French," though they were not fully citizens because of their *statut personnel*. Since the early years of the Third Republic, the naturalization of *indigènes* in Algeria had been hotly debated. Liberal politicians had for years sought ways to improve and define more clearly the status of Algerian Muslims, trying to find an arrangement more appropriate to residents of an integral part of France and more in line with republican ideals of equality.[19] During the war, the issue of naturalizing Algerians also had special prominence because more of them were serving in the French army than any other group among the *troupes indigènes*: approximately 172,000 Algerians served, about one-third of all indigenous troops and nearly two-thirds of the 250,000 from all of North Africa.

If the *sénatus-consulte* of 1865 brought indigenous Algerians closer to French nationality, it also set the precedent of separation on religious grounds that would complicate the naturalization of soldiers during the Great War. As early as 1836, the French legal system no longer considered Algerians as foreigners. In 1862, the Court of Algiers declared that "while not being a citizen, the *Indigène* is French." But it was the 1865 legislation that formalized the opposition between French citizenship and Islam, stating that "The Muslim Indigène is French; nevertheless, he will continue to be subject to Muslim law."[20] Though some liberal officials and legislators explored the possibility of granting *indigènes* the political rights of citizens while allowing them to retain the civil rights of Muslim law, the majority ultimately decided that, in the words of one administrator, "the full exercise of the rights of a French citizen is incompatible with the conservation of the *statut musulman* and its dispositions, [which are] contrary to our laws and our customs on marriage, divorce, and the civil rights of children." As historian Charles-Robert Ageron has noted, this attitude and the resulting stipulations of the *sénatus-consulte* meant that, "Neither citizens, nor subjects, Muslims thus enjoyed instead a mixed position between that of foreigners and that of a citizen."[21] In order to escape this ambiguous status, a Muslim, once aged twenty-one or over, would have to reject formally the *statut personnel* and apply to the colonial administration for naturalization.

Yet it was clear from the beginning that the vast majority of Muslims were unwilling to meet this requirement. Though other factors besides religion were undoubtedly at work, as resentment toward the French conquerors had an important political aspect as well, fidelity to the tenets of Islam were crucial for many. For Algerian Muslims, to reject Koranic law was apostasy, "a kind of civil and moral death," which could lead to the legal dissolution of marriage and the confiscation of property. The apostate was excluded from the community of Muslims in this life and could look forward only to eternal damnation in the next.[22] Few Algerians were eager to make this sacrifice in order to obtain the rights of a French citizen: between 1865 and 1915, the government general in Algeria received a total of only 2,215 requests for naturalization.[23]

When the issue gained renewed prominence after 1915, Islam would remain the major impediment to gaining French citizenship, in the eyes of both the Muslims themselves and the French. Early in 1916, a French officer reported that some of the Algerian soldiers with whom he had contact had heard stories circulating in the press about a project for the naturalization of *indigènes*, and had expressed their unhappiness with the idea. The officer tried to explain to the men that the proposal was intended only to confer upon them the advantages of French citizenship, but they persisted in their belief that "our hidden motive was to suppress their *statut personnel* and to make them French only in order better to be able to subject them to obligatory military service, with the sole intention being to fill the gaps the war has created in the army."[24] Yet, if the soldiers were mistaken in thinking that the government was going to force Muslims to abandon their legal status in some sort of mass naturalization, they were justified in their suspicion that French authorities viewed French citizenship and the *statut personnel* as mutually exclusive. Ultimately, these views caused the most difficulty in drafting an effective plan to offer naturalization to Algerian soldiers.

Given these concerns, why then did the issue of granting French citizenship become so important to authorities? Paradoxically, it was their identity as Muslims that, in part, at first provoked efforts to reform naturalization procedures for soldiers. With Turkey allied with Germany in the war against France, the government in Paris sought ways to demonstrate to the *indigènes* that its commitment to furthering the interests of Muslims in Algeria was more than just rhetorical. Such a demonstration was all the more important as Germany and Turkey encouraged the spread of anti-French propaganda among France's Muslim subjects. In February 1916, the French seized a shipment of propaganda pamphlets, written in Arabic, intended for distribution in North Africa. Among these tracts was "Contempt for the Muslim Religion in the French Ranks," which, among its many charges against the French army, told readers that the French had coerced soldiers to fight for their so-called "second *patrie*." The author admitted that it was possible that Arabs would serve willingly, "on the condition that France confer on them all the rights which Frenchmen enjoy, both advantages and obligations." But they were fighting "without any compensation." The pamphlet asked readers if this was "glorious France, humanitarian France," which demanded blood and sacrifice and reduced Muslims to the "the last degree of servitude," working not only for the French but also Jews and other "thieves" to whom France had given the rights of citizens.[25] As for Muslim soldiers who served "this nation without honor," "ungrateful" for their sacrifice, "they must disobey the laws which force them to go into combat as into the abattoir, to fight against the allies of their religion, of their land, and of the green standard of the Prophet."[26]

The author of "Contempt for the Muslim Religion" skillfully exploited the evident gap between French demands for wartime aid from their subject populations and the republican ideal linking military service and the rights and duties of citizenship. It was precisely this gap, and the resulting vulnerability to anti-French propaganda, that efforts to naturalize Muslim soldiers sought to address. Many political authorities believed that charges of hypocrisy and bad faith threatened to undermine recruitment efforts, and as the war dragged on and France's manpower crisis deepened, naturalization seemed to offer a way to make enlistment more attractive and conscription more palatable to Algerians. Yet, despite the clear importance of military necessity in inspiring proposals to liberalize access to French citizenship, idealism also played a role. The various wartime legislative proposals emanated from the "liberal milieux" in French politics, and it is important not to discount the role of Revolutionary "Jacobin idealism" in stimulating lawmakers in their attempts to bring recruitment practices in line with republican ideology.[27]

This mix of pragmatic and idealistic motives was evident in the government's first consideration of naturalizing Algerian soldiers. In late 1914,

Minister of War Millerand began a serious examination of the issue, noting that up to then, Algerians' "moral and civil education" was insufficient for them to exercise the rights and fulfill the duties of citizens, but their service in France, and their courage, loyalty, and devotion to the French cause during the war rendered them "each day more worthy of acquiring the rights of French citizenship." Offering them the possibility of naturalization would also bring military and political benefits: it would, he hoped, stimulate voluntary enlistments, reducing the need to rely on conscription; and it "would further tighten the ties which unite our Algerian subjects with France," an objective ever more imperative given "the current situation in the Muslim world, agitated by the machinations of Turkey and Germany." The measure would also put an end to the complaints of the "Young Algerians," educated and assimilated *indigènes* who were clamoring for greater political rights, as naturalization through military service would permit them to acquire the same rights as Frenchmen by submitting to the same obligations.[28]

From the beginning, officials conceived of naturalization and the Muslims' *statut personnel* as mutually exclusive legal states, and *indigènes* would have to choose between their religious practices and French citizenship. Given this fact, these officials were aware from the beginning that the ostensibly generous measures they were considering were in fact largely symbolic when offered to Muslims little disposed to sacrifice traditional customs protected by the *statut personnel*. Millerand admitted that any measure would have very limited effects, as many of those in a position to obtain naturalization would prefer to retain their *statut personnel*.[29]

The representative of the Ministry of the Colonies on the *Commission Interministeriel des Affaires Musulmanes* (or CIAM, a group that included officials from the Ministries of War, Foreign Affairs, the Interior, and the Colonies), which took up the issue of the naturalization of North Africans at about the same time as the Minister of War, echoed this opinion, observing that many Muslims would reject naturalization, considering it "a sort of apostasy, because of the renunciation of the Koranic statut personnel." Colonel Jules Hamelin of the Ministry of War agreed that this was the case, but he thought the gesture was still worth making as a demonstration of French magnanimity. Another member of the Commission agreed, citing an obligation that arose directly from the republican coupling of military service and civic rights. "Do we not," he asked, "owe them a debt of recognition, and would this not be a means of paying it?"[30]

It was in this context that the CIAM worked on the issue and eventually reviewed various parliamentary proposals for the naturalization of *troupes indigènes*. The deliberations of this commission, in which the opinions of colonial administrators and members of the various governmental ministries were represented, offered some of the most revealing discussions of naturalization and French ideas about its incompatibility with Islam. Once the Commission took up the matter in early 1915, it heard immediately from the colonial administration in Algeria. That colony's governor general, Charles Lutaud, objected to plans for offering citizenship to Muslim soldiers, offering instead his own proposal on naturalization. His plan, however, was quite restrictive, and the president of the CIAM observed that the governor general's proposal seemed designed to give only "the appearance of satisfaction and to sabotage the reform."[31] Algerian officials were indignant at this characterization, but the practices of the colonial administration in the years before the war gave credence to the charge. Between 1865 and 1899, the administration had rejected the requests for naturalization of 178 out of 1309 applicants, or 13.6 percent. Between 1899 and 1909, the rate of rejection rose: 214 out of 551, or 38.8 percent. From 1910 to 1915, the rate fell somewhat: 101 applicants out of 355 were refused, 28.4 percent. Still, this last percentage was more than twice the rejection rate that prevailed during the nineteenth century, and this indicated an increased hostility in Algeria to the idea of *indigènes* gaining political rights.[32]

The idea that Islam and French citizenship were incompatible was implicit in all of these discussions. Ostensibly, naturalization did not require giving up one's faith, merely the special legal status of the *statut personnel*. Yet submitting to Koranic law was for many Algerians integral to their religious identity. But it was not just Muslims who regarded French citizenship and Islam as mutually exclusive; French officials too identified the *statut personnel* with a host of cultural practices that they considered synonymous with Islam. It was clear that religion was the primary problem that the French felt they had to solve in crafting a plan for the naturalization of Algerian soldiers. As Governor General Lutaud succinctly put it, "A great fact dominates the entire question of naturalization of Muslim *indigènes*: it is the Islamic fact."[33]

This "Islamic fact" ultimately revolved around one particular set of issues, Muslims' customs regarding marriage and the family. Lutaud was perhaps the most vociferous and eloquent on this point, but events would show that Parisian legislators and bureaucrats shared a similar outlook. Family life, especially the rights French law accorded to women, was a recurring theme in the discussions of naturalization that accelerated as 1915 wore on. In the spring of that year, legislators in Parliament took the initiative in offering proposals aimed at naturalizing *troupes indigènes*, introducing five proposals in six months. All were designed to ease the administrative process by which soldiers could become French citizens.[34] In response, Governor General Lutaud voiced his serious concerns about the dangers to French law and culture posed by Muslims' supposedly alien and incompatible practices, and he focused particularly on polygamy and other customs regarding women. In July, Lutaud pointed out several problems with reconciling common (he alleged) Muslim familial customs with French law. How could an administration governed by the French civil code allow a man to reclaim his wife's property when he divorced her (especially a problem if he had to repudiate polygamous unions contracted before the naturalization); to arrange his daughter's marriage without her consent, even if she was not "nubile;" to exclude his daughters entirely from inheriting his property? Lutaud suggested that this was only the tip of the iceberg, and allowing Muslims to retain traditional family customs would introduce into French law many "oddities," and even worse. He argued that France could not declare compatible with French law, "le droit de cité," practices which were in such flagrant contradiction with it, and that conserving such practices, "outmoded and often inhumane," would be to fail in the civilizing mission the French had set for themselves in 1830 when they began the conquest of Algeria.[35]

By the end of 1915, Lutaud had had an opportunity to consider all of the various proposals for naturalization, and he submitted a 63-page report laying out his arguments against them. He praised the *sénatus-consulte* of 1865, which did not allow naturalized Muslims to retain their *statut personnel*, for recognizing "the Islamic fact with its civil and religious consequences inseparably linked to each other, as one knows, by the Koran." Though the governor general conceded that Algerians were "perfectible whites," just like Frenchmen, he maintained that "there exists between them such a difference of culture that political equality is obviously not achievable for the moment." Assimilation, an integral part of the French "civilizing mission" and of the justification for republican colonialism, was a slow process that would have to await the subsidence of a stubborn adherence to the tenets of Islam. Lutaud went on at great length describing the contradictions between French law and Muslim customs, particularly with regard to polygamy, marriage rights, repudiation and divorce, and arranged marriages for very young women (a practice which he now called "legalized rape"). He adamantly rejected any compromise on the issue, such as a sort of "demi-naturalization," which would provide limited local electoral rights but allow the preservation of the *statut personnel*, because such a step "would risk crystallizing the *indigènes* in their laws and institutions, in a word in Muslim law, in Islam." What was needed, he argued, was "a wise assimilation, the gradual evolution of our subjects," so that France could open "progressively to the *indigènes* the doors of *la cité française*." Thus, any scheme for a hasty naturalization of Algerians was directly contrary to both French and indigenous interests.[36]

Despite Lutaud's arguments against "demi-naturalization," some officials and legislators considered such a measure as an acceptable compromise. Although work on the issue of naturalization had bogged down in the government and in Parliament by the end of 1915, this lull did not last long. On April 20, 1916, Deputy Henri Doizy introduced a new *proposition de loi* that offered Algerians "naturalization within the *statut personnel* and in a local capacity," an arrangement that increased *indigènes'* local political representation but allowed Muslims to retain their religious customs and avoided clashes with the French civil code.[37] This *proposition* also took direct aim at the colonial administration. Doizy quoted from a previous proposal (that of Maurice Viollette, Vice President of the Chamber of Deputies, which he had submitted on September 23, 1915) to support his assertion that the inertia and even ill will of colonial officials were blocking access to naturalization. Viollette had contended that, "One would like in the colonies" — "and," Doizy added, "this is particularly true in Algeria" — "the fewest possible French citizens. With subjects, the

Administration can deal with them on its own terms; with citizens, that would become more delicate, and such an arbitrary regime could no longer blossom so freely . . . A German would be naturalized more easily than would an Algerian . . . ." In view of the sacrifices of the *troupes indigènes*, "who give at this very moment a new and striking demonstration of devotion to the metropole," Doizy noted, it was appropriate to enhance the political rights of Algerians.[38]

Though all members of the CIAM did not fully share Lutaud's unbending hostility to the parliamentary projects for the naturalization of *indigènes*, neither did they fully endorse the liberal approach of men like Doizy. Ultimately, members of the commission, like most other officials who wrestled with the issue, had trouble accepting any plan that would give full citizenship to Muslims without requiring the sacrifice of their *statut personnel*. Such difficulties prevented any real reforms from getting beyond the proposal stage, so in 1917 the Chamber of Deputies charged the socialist deputy (and future Minister of the Colonies) Marius Moutet with reconciling the various previously submitted measures. In October, he presented the thirty-five articles of his new plan to the CIAM, and the subsequent discussions of this body were quite revealing of one of the issues that many French authorities felt most complicated the issue of naturalization: the practice of polygamy among Muslim men.

Moutet's proposal explicitly barred polygamists from becoming French citizens, and this issue provoked a lively discussion in the CIAM. In a November meeting, some of the members of the Commission foresaw problems with this stipulation. Edmond Doutté, professor at the madrasa of Tlemcen in Algeria, pointed out that polygamists were often important figures in Algerian society, whom the French had an interest in conciliating. But another member noted that the issue went right to the heart of a delicate question: whether or not the Muslim *statut personnel* was compatible with French citizenship. There was general agreement that an Algerian living in France could not have multiple wives, as preserving public order would dictate that he submit to French law on the matter. Also, the law would not permit an Algerian to contract multiple marriages after his naturalization, no matter where he lived. The real issue was what to do about applicants for naturalization who already had more than one wife. On this question there was much disagreement. Octave Depont, who represented the Algerian colonial administration in Paris, cited a study that showed many Algerians continued to practice polygamy even after naturalization. Others pointed out the legal nightmares that would result from naturalizing polygamists. Even if an Algerian broke his polygamous unions and kept only one wife upon his accession to citizenship, what rights would the former wives and their children retain? How could one have legitimate children with more than one wife? On the other hand, how could there be two sorts of French citizens, monogamous and polygamous? Depont then raised the objections that Lutaud had voiced earlier about many Muslim family customs, including polygamy, the right of *jabr* (by which, he alleged, fathers married off their prepubescent daughters without their consent and against their will), the "absolute and arbitrary" right to repudiate one's wife, the elimination of daughters from inheritance, and a host of other practices "as bizarre as [they are] inhumane." He painted a particularly lurid picture of the *jabr*, calling up the image of girls as young as eight or nine years old offered to their husbands, then "damaged for life, when they do not die from the effects of these legal rapes." These, he said, were the kinds of practices that French law would consecrate as legal if the government allowed naturalized *indigènes* to retain their *statut personnel*. How could these men be allowed to vote — one of the critical rights and responsibilities of citizenship — in effect making laws that would govern French people but not themselves? This was a particular danger given the large margin by which *indigènes* outnumbered Europeans in Algeria.[39]

In the end, some members of the CIAM were willing to allow men with multiple marriages contracted before the act of naturalization to keep them, a circumstance dictated no doubt by the desire not to offend the kind of prominent and wealthy *indigènes* who could afford to have multiple wives. However, the Commission ultimately rejected any measures that would preserve the *statut personnel* for those who became French citizens.[40] The two legal states were still mutually exclusive. In many respects, though increased access to French citizenship was supposed to reward soldiers who sacrificed so much for the defense of France, the direction of discussions on the issue of naturalizing Algerians ultimately tended toward tightening, not loosening, the restrictions of the 1865 *sénatus-consulte*. It was this fact that caused the human rights group *Ligue des droits de l'homme* to charge that Moutet's proposal fell short of its goal.[41] The *Ligue* favored, as the prominent left-wing historian Alphonse Aulard put it in April 1917, allowing "Algerians to retain their *statut musulman* when becoming French citizens," along with granting them representation in the French Chamber of Deputies, and would eventually even cite American President Wilson's appeal for national self-determination to argue for greater political rights for Muslims in Algeria.[42] On the other hand, the administration in Algeria remained adamantly opposed to Moutet's suggestions for reform, fearing the consequences of any increase in Muslims' electoral power.

When Georges Clemenceau came to power in late 1917, his government gave special priority to the reform effort in Algeria, as he saw in it an ideal means of achieving his overriding goal of increasing recruitment. As early as November 1915, Clemenceau, then chairman of the committee on foreign affairs in the Senate, had urged the government to make political reforms in Algeria in recognition of the loyalty and military service of the *indigènes*.[43] Now in power, the new Prime Minister recalled Lutaud, who was closely allied with the colonists and openly obstructing the reform efforts emanating from Paris, and installed Charles Jonnart as governor general in January 1918. By the end of that month, Jonnart had drawn up the government's plans for reform in Algeria. This modified some of the provisions of Moutet's plan, eventually replacing it, but the war ended before the new plan could become law. And when it eventually did, in 1919, the results hardly constituted a dramatic liberalization of access to French citizenship in Algeria. In the end, attempts to facilitate the naturalization of Algerians foundered on the incompatibility French officials believed existed between Muslims' religious identity, symbolized by the *statut personnel* and practices such as polygamy, and French national identity, which required absolute conformity to French legal and cultural norms.

Postwar reform and naturalization

By 1918, France had failed to close the gap that opened during the war between traditional republican ideology that linked defense of the nation in the military with the rights and duties of full citizenship, and the inferior civil status of *troupes indigènes* fighting and dying for France. This failure was particularly dramatic in the case of Algeria. Though the Jonnart Law, which passed in early 1919 and which would define French policy toward *indigènes* for the next twenty-five years, was ostensibly motivated by a desire to remove or lower obstacles to the naturalization of Algerians, it actually made the requirements and procedures more rigorous. An applicant would have to satisfy several preliminary conditions: to be aged twenty-five or older, to be monogamous or single, to have no convictions for serious crimes, and to have two consecutive years of fixed residence. In addition, he would have to satisfy one of seven secondary conditions: to be a veteran and in possession of a certificate of good conduct, to know how to read and write French, to be a settled and licensed farmer or businessman, to hold or have held elective office, to be a current or retired functionary in the colonial administration, to have received a French decoration, or to be the adult child of a naturalized father. The law represented the final rejection of the idea of naturalization with the retention of the Muslim *statut personnel*, and a repudiation of the colonial doctrine of assimilation as it applied to Algeria.[44] In addition to the new requirements for French citizenship, the law enacted a "special naturalization," demi-naturalization in fact, that provided a limited expansion of electoral rights for over 400,000 Algerians (43 percent of the adult male population) while allowing them to retain their *statut personnel*. In his address introducing the law to the Chamber, Jonnart claimed that this was an "intermediary status," a "stage between the status of French citizen and that of a French subject." He implied that this was a temporary state of affairs until Muslims evolved culturally and politically, but in reality this was more of a permanent condition for the vast majority of Algerians.[45] The *indigènes* had begun the war possessed of an ambiguous status between subjects and citizens, and despite four years of efforts to clarify this status and reward them for their military service, most ended the war in similar ambiguity. In an irony that many contemporaries did not fail to appreciate, the requirements for full naturalization under the new law were actually more stringent in many respects (e.g., in the minimum age for applicants) than was the *sénatus-consulte* of 1865.

The primary reason for this was the Algerians' religious identity. French government officials and legislators could not reconcile the practice of Islam with the obligations and privileges of French citizenship. One clear indication of this was the requirement in the Jonnart Law that applicants for naturalization be monogamous. This served to "mark" Muslims as polygamists, something that the 1865 legislation had not done explicitly (though in practice the colonial administration had refused the requests of polygamous applicants).[46] Polygamy was, in reality, in steep decline in Algeria. A Senate report of March 1918 revealed that between 1891 and 1911 polygamous marriages had declined from 149,000 to 55,427.[47] This was part of an even longer-term decrease in the frequency of polygamy: in 1886, 16 percent of married Algerian males had more than one wife, while in 1948 that figure had dropped to 3 percent, and the average age of these men was over 65.[48] Such men were unlikely to be interested in French citizenship after living into old age without it, and even if the age was somewhat lower in the years immediately following the Great War (though there is no reason to suppose that it was), polygamists were very unlikely to be recent veterans of the French army. Instead, polygamy was more important symbolically than as an actual practice among Algerians. It came to represent for the French all that was alien to and incompatible with French citizenship, particularly laws and customs relating to the family. This was hardly surprising, given French anxieties at home about gender roles during the first part of the twentieth century.[49] But the special mention of polygamy in the Jonnart Law also pointed to the difficulty the French had in accepting Islam as a component of French national identity.

The ultimate irony of the Jonnart Law was that it represented the failure of the French government to open up access to French citizenship for *troupes indigènes* who were fighting to defend France from invasion, and greater access was precisely what officials had been working for from the earliest days of the war. Though public figures in the government, legislature, and press had debated various measures designed to liberalize and simplify the naturalization process in the years before 1914, the new circumstances created by the war were clearly instrumental in stimulating the search for more dramatic ways to improve the lot of Muslims in Algeria.[50] That the service of Muslims in the army was the impetus for these efforts was clear even from the comments of opponents of reform. During the discussion of Jonnart's measure in the Chamber of Deputies on November 7, 1918, Algerian Deputy Gaston Thomson complained that reformers had allowed the sentimentality provoked by the presence of thousands of *indigènes* in the army to play too large a role in shaping their ideas.[51] Yet, opposition from colonists, the end of the war (which removed much of the urgency for the reforms, as recruitment was no longer a burning issue), and objections to sanctioning traditional Muslim customs under French law ensured that the end result of all the efforts at reform would fall far short of the ideal imagined by those who felt republican ideology demanded both the obligation of military service and the privilege of citizenship. As the 1919 measures governing naturalization actually represented a regression from those contained in the *sénatus-consulte* of 1865, it was unsurprising that Doizy, author of one of the more ambitious reform proposals in 1916, would sum up the Jonnart Law by saying, "I do not think that we have done anything important."[52]

Evidence of the failure of the reform efforts that culminated in the Jonnart Law of 1919 was clear in the postwar frequency of naturalizations. Between 1919 and 1923, the colonial administration received 317 requests for French citizenship under the terms of the new legislation, and denied 115.[53] The rejection rate of 36 percent was comparable to highest levels of the prewar years, due to the government general's suspicion and hostility to the naturalization of *indigènes*. Jonnart had intended his reforms, as he put it during his defense of the law in the Chamber, to make accession to citizenship a right for many Algerians, instead of a privilege or favor handed out by the administration to a select few.[54] Still, the governor general doubted that Muslims would or could abandon their customs in order to qualify for French citizenship, and he was in any case gone by July 1919, replaced by Jean-Baptiste Abel. In fact, Muslims were loath to sacrifice their *statut personnel* in return for naturalization, and so the law was flawed from the beginning. As one member of the Young Algerians put it, "Why, before according liberty to the Muslims and the improvement of their lot, require of them the cruel renunciation of their age-old traditions?"[55] In the end, the reform in the terms of accession to citizenship for Algerians, supposed to admit soldiers who had fought for France into the nation they had defended, remained a "dead letter."[56]

Conclusion

Despite the attempts of French officials to bring policy toward naturalizing Algerian soldiers more into line with republican traditions that linked military service with citizenship, the religious identity of these men — the "Islamic fact," as Governor General Lutaud put it — remained an insurmountable obstacle. The large number of *indigènes*, combined with a substantial European settler population fearful of the electoral consequences of naturalizing hundreds of thousands of unassimilated colonial subjects, prevented Algerians' accession to citizenship as long as they continued to observe their traditional and Muslim customs. Even the most assimilated among them, Lutaud argued in 1916, refused to sacrifice their religious identity in order to become truly French. Many whom the French had educated, and who had become lawyers, doctors, officers, or teachers, refused to sacrifice their *statut personnel* in order to obtain French citizenship. This refusal, he argued, stemmed from a mix of political and religious "fanaticism" which often resulted in subversion and even rebellion. He went on to say, in a blunt statement of the doctrine of association, that he preferred the "simple fellahs" who did not display a false assimilation but still remained in their own culture and loyal to their colonial masters, learning to "become truly friendly with us, often even to love us."[57]

It was not just the conservative Lutaud who viewed Islam as an insurmountable obstacle to naturalization, the highest stage of assimilation. The agreement on this point of even liberal republicans ultimately doomed the prospects for any measure granting French citizenship with the retention of the *statut personnel*. Gustave Mercier, a prominent lawyer who in fact favored reform in French policy toward Algerians, wrote in 1918 that it was dangerous to "make them electors before making them civilized human beings."[58] The liberal, socialist-sympathizing journalist Jean Mélia refused to entertain the idea of two groups of French citizens governed by two different statutes. Similarly the left-wing senator Raphaël Milliès-Lacroix, no friend to reactionary colonial interests, "quibbled constantly over the legal definition that it was proper to give to monogamy. The risk that the ballot of a monogamous Frenchman and that of a polygamous Frenchman might lie together in the ballot box filled him with dread."[59] And if the *statut personnel* stood for the *indigènes*' lack of civilization, then specific cultural practices (regardless of the extent to which Muslims really engaged in them), especially polygamy, dramatically symbolized the supposedly irreconcilable differences between the observance of Islam and the demands of French citizenship.

This state of affairs ran contrary not only to the republican tradition linking defense of the state in the military with citizenship, but also to the ideal of French citizenship itself. Indeed, the fundamental basis of this ideal was the proposition that membership in the national community was not limited by skin color, race, religion, or historical background, but only by the willingness to adopt French language, culture, and political authority. Yet when even the most assimilated of France's colonial subjects, many of whom fought in the French army during the Great War, applied for naturalization, the colonial administration often rejected them for reasons such as "morality," lifestyle, or doubts about their mastery of the French language. Usually, these justifications hid more important doubts on the part of officials that people from "primitive" cultures could or would ever really assimilate fully to French ways. In many respects, the ideology of association, especially as expressed by men like Governor General Lutaud, was an explicit denial of the possibilities of assimilation, a rejection of the republican ideal that justified France's possession of a colonial empire, and an excuse to maintain an essentially exploitative relationship with the colonies and their indigenous inhabitants.[60] One might argue that the resistance to naturalizing Muslims who retained their *statut personnel* was in keeping with the republican ideal of citizenship, as these *indigènes* were failing to accept French law and therefore undeserving of the benefits of citizenship. There was some truth in this, but it was more the idea that Muslims would remain Muslims, and not "civilized human beings," which prevented French authorities from facilitating their naturalization. In some respects this should not be surprising, as there is a religious component to French national identity — rooted in Catholic Christianity — that has coexisted with more secularized republican notions and that historians have often overlooked.[61] Moreover, as Pierre Birnbaum has shown, this religious heritage, along with Revolution's conception of the nation as an organic whole from which "autonomy and diversity are rejected; all manifestations of divergence are excluded as dysfunctional," has produced a sense of nationhood, which is often hostile to cultural and political pluralism.[62]

Recent controversies over the integration of immigrants, most of whom are from the former colonies, have highlighted the often intolerant side of French ideas about citizenship and national identity, but this intolerance has a long history, which includes the experiences of the *troupes indigènes* who fought for France in the First World War. Many immigrants in France today are discovering what many of their ancestors found out in the years after 1914: demands for cultural conformity, even within a supposedly relatively open assimilationist system of national identity based upon *jus soli*, can be as imperious and difficult to satisfy as are the more straight-forwardly ethnic requirements of systems based upon *jus sanguinis*.

In 1992, for instance, the *Haut Conseil à l'Intégration*, a government agency charged with studying ways to encourage the integration of immigrants into French society, declared that the French "concept of the nation as a cultural community . . . does appear unusually open to outsiders, since it regards an act of voluntary commitment to a set of values as all that is necessary." However, this same pronouncement criticized the idea of "multiculturalism" in no uncertain terms. Immigrants who wanted to become French citizens were to become truly French, legally and culturally: "Notions of a 'multicultural society' and the 'right to be different' are unacceptably ambiguous ... it would be wrong to let anyone think that different cultures can be allowed to become fully developed in France."[63] Muslim immigrants, especially North Africans, are often foremost in the minds of officials making such statements. An even more dramatic example of the limits of the assimilationist ideal in contemporary France occurred in 1993, when new legislation restricted the right of *jus soli*, making French citizenship less easily accessible to children born of foreign parents in France. Moreover, aspects of this legislation made it more difficult for Algerians, in particular, to take advantage of a liberal *jus soli* policy. Some aspects of this law were modified by new legislation in 1998, but immigrants and their children still faced greater difficulties becoming French citizens than they had prior to 1993. As Miriam Feldblum has shown, far from being a right-wing reaction against a rising tide of immigration, the new "constricted parameters of French [national] membership" had wide support across the political spectrum.[64]

More recent events have only heightened the visibility of difficulties with integrating Islam into French ideas about citizenship and nationality. Even before increased threats of terrorism and escalating violence in the Middle East magnified such issues in the first years of the new century, a majority of the French public expressed anxiety about the implications of large numbers of Muslims living in the country. In 1992, an opinion poll revealed that two-thirds of the population was fearful of the growing presence of Islam in France.[65] Such fears certainly influenced the findings of a March 2000 poll, in which over 60 percent of French people said there were too many people of "foreign origin" in the country, with 38 percent saying there were too many Blacks and 63 percent saying there were too many Arabs.[66] During the spring of 2003, the government held elections to create what Interior Minister Nicolas Sarkozy has called "an official Islam of France" by organizing a national Muslim council to regulate relations between the state and the nation's seven million Muslims. The government hoped, he said, to counter "the Islam of the cellars and garages that has fed extremism and the language of violence," and to that ensure Muslims become responsible citizens of the republic.[67] Yet, after a fundamentalist organization won an unexpectedly large number of seats on the council, Sarkozy warned that, "Any prayer leader whose views run contrary to the values of the French republic will be expelled." The views to which he was referring were any that would promote adherence to Islamic law, which he declared "will not apply anywhere because it is not the law of the French republic."[68] As was the case when French officials contemplated offering naturalization to Algerian soldiers of the Great War, a general uneasiness about the compatibility of Islam and French citizenship is often reflected in the specific fear that Muslims' beliefs and practices will undermine the law, one of the most sacred symbols of the one and indivisible republic.[69]

A genuine commitment to the liberal ideals of universalism and egalitarianism has led many in France to espouse an inclusive view of the nation that welcomes foreigners who want to become French, given that they demonstrate a willingness to accept republican political traditions and to integrate into social and cultural life. Yet, the process by which this transformation from foreigner to French occurs in practice is often complicated and difficult. The experience of Algerian soldiers during the Great War offers a particularly illustrative example, given their own difficulties transforming from subjects to citizens, despite the strong links in French republican tradition between military service and citizenship. That efforts to offer naturalization to these men were so controversial, and in the end unsuccessful, demonstrates the very real limits of the assimilationist ideal in the face of ethnocultural and religious differences. Demands for cultural conformity are well within the republican tradition, but such demands often stemmed from grave doubts that Muslims could ever truly be French, precisely because they were Muslims. Even Marius Moutet, the socialist deputy who labored so hard during the war to craft a reformed naturalization process in Algeria, worked from an extremely narrow premise and expressed skepticism about the ideal of assimilation, writing in 1918, "If one wants to accomplish anything practical, one must certainly renounce the illusion of the mystical unity of human beings, who could receive equally well the same laws and adapt themselves to them."[70] In the end, sentiments like these submerged the kind of universalism and republican idealism that stimulated reform efforts in the first place, setting Muslims and their laws outside the French nation. This ensured that many in France would continue to have difficulties integrating Islam into their conception of national identity.

Notes

1. *Centre des Archives d'Outre-Mer* (CAOM) AP534: Proposition de loi, no. 280, à faciliter l'accession des militaires et des militaires anciens Algériens, Tunisiens, et Marocains au statut

de citoyen français, Chambre des Députés, Albin Rozet, Georges Leygues, Louis Doizy, Lucien Millevoye, 1 avril 1915.

2. Renée Waldinger, Philip Dawson, and Isser Woloch, eds., *The French Revolution and the Meaning of Citizenship* (Westport: Greenwood Press, 1993).

3. John Torpey, *The Invention of the Passport: Surveillance, Citizenship and the State* (Cambridge: Cambridge University Press, 2000), 21–56.

4. Rogers Brubaker, *Citizenship and Nationhood in France and Germany* (Cambridge: Harvard University Press, 1992). On the construction of republican citizenship in the early years of the Third Republic, *see also* James R., Lehning, *To Be a Citizen: The Political Culture of the Early French Third Republic* (Ithaca NY: Cornell University Press, 2001).

5. Maxim Silverman, *Deconstructing the Nation: Immigration, Racism and Citizenship in Modern France* (London: Routledge, 1992), 19.

6. Alan Forrest, "Citizenship and Military Service," in Waldinger, Dawson, and Woloch, eds., *The French Revolution and the Meaning of Citizenship*, 153–165.

7. The classic study of the development of this principle in France is Richard D. Challener, *The French Theory of the Nation in Arms, 1866–1939* (New York: Columbia University Press, 1955). For a discussion of the *levée en masse* as the origin of mass armies, total war, and twentieth-century "industrialized killing," *see* Omer Bartov, "The European Imagination in the Age of Total War," in his *Murder in Our Midst: The Holocaust, Industrial Killing, and Representation* (New York: Oxford University Press, 1996), 33–50.

8. Isser Woloch, *The New Regime: Transformations of the French Civic Order, 1780–1820s* (New York: W. W. Norton, 1994), 130, cited in Torpey, 21.

9. Challener, *The French Theory*, 4. By the early years of the twentieth century, the Third Republic had instituted a system of truly universal and obligatory military service. *See* Challener, *The French Theory*, 10–90; and Douglas Porch, *The March to the Marne: The French Army, 1871–1914* (Cambridge: Cambridge University Press, 1981), 23–44, 191–212.

10. *Service Historique de l'Armée de Terre* (SHAT) 7N2120: Extract from the *Journal Officiel*, 17 janvier 1918, 677. The minister of the colonies was introducing new recruitment measures for West Africa, but his general point about the relationship between naturalization and military service held true for all of the *troupes indigènes* serving France in the war.

11. SHAT 7N2121: Bérenger, "Rapport sur le recrutement d'une armée indigène," 26 November 1915.

12. SHAT 7N2121: Bérenger, "Rapport sur le recrutement d'une armée indigène."

13. CAOM DSM6: "Rapport fait à la Commission de l'Armée sur la question de la conscription indigène en Algérie par M. E. Flandin," November 16, 1917. On assimilation and association, *see* Raymond F. Betts, *Assimilation and Association in French Colonial Theory, 1890–1914* (New York: Columbia University Press, 1961); and Martin D. Lewis, "One Hundred Million Frenchmen: The Assimilationist Theory in French Colonial Policy," *Comparative Studies in Society and History* 4, 2 (1962): 129–153.

14. SHAT 7N2103: Section d'Afrique, "Note sur le Chérif Si Brahim," November 15, 1915.

15. *Archives du Ministère des Affaires Étrangères* (AMAE) G1664: Report of Consul Général, Secrétaire Interprète Piat, December 27, 1914.

16. *AMAE*, Report of October 30, 1914.

17. SHAT 7N2081: Section d'Afrique, "Bulletin Politique," 1–15 January 1915.

18. Lutaud used this term in a letter to the Minister of Foreign Affairs. *See* AMAE G1671: CIAM, Séance 19, 20 January 1916. In addition to the 250,000 troops from North Africa, over 300,000 men from West Africa, Indo-China, and Madagascar served in the French Army during the war.

19. Lehning, *To Be a Citizen*, 128–154.

20. Charles-Robert Ageron, *Les Algériens musulmans et la France, 1871–1919*, 2 vols. (Paris: Presses Universitaires de France, 1968), 1: 343.

21. Charles-Robert Ageron, *Les Algériens*, 1: 344.

22. Charles-Robert Ageron, *Les Algériens*, 1: 344.

23. Charles-Robert Ageron, *Les Algériens*, 2: 1118 and 1120.

24. AMAE G1666: Minister of War to Ministers of Foreign Affairs and of the Interior, 13 février 1916, "Extrait du rapport de l'Officier Interprète Pons de la XIe Région."

25. In 1870, a decree sponsored by the Algerian Jewish jurist and politician Adolphe Crémieux granted French citizenship to all Algerian Jews. *See* Ageron, *Les Algériens*, 1: 13–17; and Daniel Amson, *Adolphe Crémieux: L'oublié de la gloire* (Paris: Éditions du Seuil, 1988).

26. SHAT 7N2104: "Mépris de la religion musulmane dans les rangs français," 1915.

27. *See* Gilbert Meynier, *L'Algérie révélée: La guerre de 1914–1918 et le premier quart du XXe siècle* (Geneva: Droz, 1981), 552–563.

28. AMAE G1664: Projet de lettre of Millerand, undated, but probably written sometime in December 1914.
29. AMAE G1664: Projet de lettre of Millerand, December 1914.
30. AMAE G1670: CIAM, Séance 3, December 31, 1914.
31. AMAE G1670: CIAM, Séance 6, January 25, 1915.
32. Ageron, *Les Algériens*, 2: 1118 and 1120.
33. AMAE G1671: CIAM, Séance 19, January 20, 1916, communication from Governor General Lutaud.
34. The first of these *propositions de loi* applied to all soldiers from North Africa, while the second, introduced at the end of May, aimed at soldiers from all areas of the French empire. But the three proposals which followed by the end of September narrowed the focus to the naturalization of Algerians. For details, *see* Ageron, *Les Algériens*, 2: 1191–1192.
35. AMAE G1665: Lutaud to Minister of Foreign Affairs, July 15, 1915.
36. AMAE G1671: CIAM, Séance 19, January 20, 1916.
37. For details, *see* Ageron, *Les Algériens*, 2: 1197–1198.
38. AMAE G1671: CIAM, Séance 28, June 10, 1916.
39. AMAE G1671^bis: CIAM, Séance 51, 13 November 1917.
40. AMAE G1671^bis: CIAM, Séances 53, November 29, 1917, and 59, Febraury 1, 1918.
41. *See* Ageron, *Les Algériens*, 2: 1201–1203; and Meynier, *L'Algérie révélée*, 555.
42. Ageron, *Les Algériens*, 2:1199; Vincent Confer, *France and Algeria: The Problem of Civil and Political Reform, 1870–1920* (Syracuse: Syracuse University Press, 1966), 100.
43. Confer, *France and Algeria*, 99.
44. Ageron, *Les Algériens*, 2: 1221–1223.
45. Confer, *France and Algeria*, 111.
46. Jeanne Bowlan, "Polygamists Need Not Apply: Becoming a French Citizen in Colonial Algeria, 1918–1938," *Proceedings of the Western Society for French History* 24 (1997): 113.
47. Bowlan, "Polygamists Need Not Apply," 111.
48. John Ruedy, *Modern Algeria: The Origins and Development of a Nation* (Bloomington, IN: Indiana University Press, 1992), 128.
49. Bowlan, "Polygamists Need Not Apply," 115.
50. As Vincent Confer has put it, "With the activities of Doizy and Moutet the reform movement had clearly entered a phase that carried it much beyond its demands of 1913." *France and Algeria*, 100. For the wider prewar context of reforms and policy toward *indigènes* in Algeria, *see* Confer, *France and Algeria*, 14–95 passim; Ruedy, *Modern Algeria*, 80–113; and Ageron, *Les Algériens*, passim.
51. Confer, *France and Algeria*, 110.
52. Meynier, *L'Algérie révélée*, 557.
53. Ageron, *Les Algériens*, 2: 1223. The administration also accepted 54 requests made under the old *sénatus-consulte* of 1865, as through a legislative quirk, both laws remained in place simultaneously.
54. Confer, *France and Algeria*, 111.
55. Ageron, *Les Algériens*, 2: 1222.
56. Confer, *France and Algeria*, 114.
57. SHAT 7N2104: Lutaud to Prime Minister/Minister of Foreign Affairs Briand, "A.s. d'une brochure allemande intitulée: L'Islam dans l'armée française, 'Guerre 1914–1915,' " 7 mars 1916.
58. Gustave Mercier, "Les indigènes nord-africains et la guerre," *Revue de Paris*, XXV, No. 4 (1 July 1918), 203–222, cited in Confer, *France and Algeria*, 98.
59. Meynier, *L'Algérie révélée*, 559. On Mélia's ideas, *see also* his *L'Algérie et la guerre (1914–1918)* (Paris: Plon-Nourrit, 1918).
60. Even though men like Lutaud argued that *indigènes* might be ready to assimilate in the distant future, even centuries, such an attitude still essentially represented a rejection, based upon assumptions about the inherent inferiority of non-Europeans, of the assimilationist ideal.
61. *See* Norman Ravitch, "Your People, My People; Your God, My God: French and American Troubles Over Citizenship," *The French Review* 70, 4 (March 1997): 515–527. David Bell's *The Cult of the Nation in France: Inventing Nationalism, 1680–1800* (Cambridge: Harvard University Press, 2001), also reveals the pre-Revolutionary and Catholic roots of French national identity.
62. Pierre Birnbaum, *The Idea of France* (New York: Hill and Wang, 2001); quote on page 65.
63. Quoted in Alec Hargreaves, "Multiculturalism," in Christopher Flood and Laurence Bell, eds., *Political Ideologies in Contemporary France* (London: Pinter, 1997), 184.
64. Miriam Feldblum, *The Politics of Nationality Reform and Immigration in Contemporary France* (Albany: State University of New York Press, 1999), 151. Among the many other recent

works that explore contemporary immigration and citizenship in France are Adrian Favell, *Philosophies of Integration: Immigration and the Idea of Citizenship in France and Britain*, 2nd ed. (Basingstoke: Palgrave, 2001); Tahar Ben Jelloun, *French Hospitality: Racism and North African Immigrants* (New York: Columbia University Press, 1999); Gérard Noiriel, *The French Melting Pot: Immigration, Citizenship, and National Identity* (Minneapolis: University of Minnesota Press, 1996); and Maxim Silverman, *Facing Postmodernity: Contemporary French Thought on Culture and Society* (London: Routledge, 1999).

65. Alec G. Hargreaves, *Immigration, "Race" and Ethnicity in Contemporary France* (London: Routledge, 1995), 119.

66. Suzanne Daley, "France's Nonwhites *See* Bias in Far Rightist's Strength," *New York Times* (April 30, 2002), 4.

67. Elaine Sciolino, "French Islam Wins Officially Recognized Voice," *New York Times* (April 14, 2003), 4.

68. Elaine Sciolino, "French Threat to Militant Muslims after Council Vote," *New York Times* (April 15, 2003), 3.

69. It is worth pointing out that France is not the only European nation to grapple with these fears. For the wider European context, *see* Talal Asad, "Muslims and European Identity," in Anthony Pagden, ed., *The Idea of Europe: From Antiquity to the European Union* (Cambridge: Cambridge University Press, 2002), 209–227; and Christopher T. Husbands, " 'They must obey our laws and customs!': Political Debate about Muslim Assimilability in Great Britain, France, and the Netherlands," in Alec G. Hargreaves and Jeremy Leaman, eds., *Racism, Ethnicity and Politics in Contemporary Europe* (Aldershot: Edward Elgar, 1995), 115–130.

70. Quoted in J. Merimée, *De l'accession des Indochinois à la qualité de citoyen français* (Toulouse: Imprimerie Andrau et La Porte, 1931), 74.

9

On Becoming German
Politics of Membership in Germany[1]

Elisabeth Schäfer-Wünsche

"Germany is an anachronism!" With these words, a participant of the International Women's University conducted in Hamburg in summer 2000 reportedly commented on the German unwillingness to acknowledge decades of immigration.[2] Indeed, one of the opening speeches further reinforced her judgment. As the article has it, the assembled scholars were somewhat jokingly assured in a welcoming address (the speaker not being a participant of the Women's University) that Germany was not really used to interculturalism, since it had hardly owned any colonies. The article does not elaborate on the women's reaction to the blunder, but it notes that the humor was not appreciated.

The apology for Germany's lack of intercultural competence repeats a still prevalent public narrative: Germany was no, or at least no real, colonial power.[3] If German colonialism is mentioned at all, it is often declared to have been of little consequence, since it was so short-lived.[4] It was the World Conference Against Racism in Durban, South Africa (August 31–September 7, 2001), that finally brought German media attention to the immense destruction caused by the slave trade and colonialism and to the fears of reparation claims on the side of the United States and European colonial powers. Breaking with a long tradition of denial, Secretary of State Joschka Fischer spoke of the necessity to accept guilt and responsibility for the German participation in the colonial scheme, while at the same time carefully avoiding any statement that might serve as a reference point for legal claims.[5] It remains to be seen whether this rhetorical gesture will have long-term consequences such as a general awareness of racial policies that precede National Socialism. In the heated debates on membership in German society, the colonial experience with its creation of a racial matrix still mostly speaks as an absence.[6]

Little more than a century ago, the importance of this phase was judged in dramatically different terms. "In these last days" an article in a German newspaper proclaimed on August 22, 1884, "we have been allowed to watch and to envision great and memorable times. We are experiencing the transition of our German *Reich* to a new and highly important stage of national development: Germany is making its first steps towards the creation of colonies."[7] "Under the African tropics," the article concludes, "the German may now be German and in the future will be able to remain German." Successful nation-building, the argument implies, is tied to ownership of territories beyond national borders. Envisioning the decisions made at the Africa Conference in Berlin (November 15, 1884–February 26, 1885), the article celebrates the official commencement of the comparatively short, but, I will argue, highly consequential phase of German colonialism.[8] Faced with colonialism's global scope, it is of course important to note that German colonies also included territories in the South Pacific, among them German New Guinea and parts of Samoa.[9] However, it is German policies in Africa (especially in the settler colony German Southwest Africa) that will provide a foil for my argument. Moreover, my focus on historical as well as current political and cultural developments will include an emphasis on the language that participates in and propels these developments.

With the rise of constitutional nation-states in Europe, the codification of citizenship laws became a necessity.[10] At the same time, these newly codified laws defined and brought forth the respective nations. Founded in 1871, the German *Reich* was considered a latecomer among European states, uniting smaller political units under the *de facto* leadership of Prussia — itself historically tied to colonial expansion in Eastern Europe. Significantly differing from but always intertwined with developments in France, specific notions of Germanness had historically preceded the nation-state. Idealist philosophy and nineteenth-century Romanticism had provided intellectual impulses that called for a state as the expression of a German spirit, an essential German *Wesen* (mentality).[11] Only partially synonymous with "people," the term *Volk* had already acquired its oscillating semantics, invoking mythical agelessness — an existence beyond time — as well as mythical history, a history with a telos. Rose-Marie Huber-Koller comments on the ideology of German statehood: "A *Volk* [is] declared a unified collective personality, [and] creates itself its own state."[12] Unlike the French Republic with its grounding in universalist principles, the modern German state was founded on the paradigm of descent, and the project of nationhood was tied to the achievement of an ethnonational identity.[13] Even before 1871, criteria for membership in the German principalities, in Prussia and in Bavaria had shifted from place of birth and residence (*jus soli*), to membership through descent (*jus sanguinis*), literally, "the law of blood."[14] Moreover, the establishment of a crucial distinction between *Inländer* (native born) and *Ausländer* (foreigner or resident foreigner), the quintessential nonmember within, was also prefigured in the legal practice of nineteenth-century feudal states. This distinction has remained a decisive and divisive force in German public discourse until the present and will inform my discussion.

"With the founding of the German *Reich*," William Barbieri argues, "a new era of nation-building as a concerted effort to homogenize the population and culture began."[15] Despite claims to an already existing Germanness, the early Kaiserreich was a rather heterogeneous society. It was the military and the civil service as well as mandatory education that greatly enhanced the process of political and, to a considerable degree, cultural homogenization.

As a consequence of the official ownership of African territory, the semantics of V*olk* took up the connotations of race in its twentieth-century manifestations. Germanness, mythically determined through blood and soil and through a language that was considered a conduit for a holistic essence, shifted towards scientific self-explanation. Drawing on biology, medicine, and anthropology, race sciences positioned the Aryan, more specifically, the Nordic race at the top of human evolution.[16] Mixture with inferior races was thus demonized as genetic contamination to be avoided at all costs.[17] Constitutional amendments in the United States, such as the emancipation and enfranchisement of former slaves were judged as "misunderstood humaneness" and "undignified cultural decline."[18]

Since Germany was a young colonial power, it was considered important to cultivate the instinct of race, which, the argument went, had had so much more time to develop in other nations.[19] Unlike in French or British colonial practice, access to membership in the *Reich* was highly restrictive vis-à-vis German colonial subjects. Even the patrilinearity of citizenship, deeply entrenched in German law, could be disrupted by race. In the *Schutzgebiete* — the official euphemism for colonial territories — children of German fathers and "native" women were rarely granted citizenship, even if the partners were married.[20] After 1905, "mixed marriages" were legally prohibited in German Southwest Africa, and existing marriages or openly lived relationships resulted in social exclusion from the White settler society for the German partner.[21] Other *Schutzgebiete* followed suit.

Philosopher Hannah Arendt is one of the early voices to emphasize the connectedness of European imperialism and the racial policies of National Socialism.[22] She explicitly claims that European experiences in Africa and the politics of expansion provided a basis for twentieth-century totalitarianism and genocide.[23] However, in the Cold War context that informed much of the reception of Arendt's work, her emphasis on race could be ignored. Interestingly, Arendt also mentions the tendency of ardent critics of National Socialism to consider the genocidal performativity of race a specifically German, that is, a National Socialist invention.[24]

Fatima El-Tayeb emphasizes another variety of German exceptionalism: "Historians often assume that Germans did not participate in the movement of scientific racism, at least where it was concerned with the 'black race,' that anti-Semitism was somehow Germany's 'substitute' to the racism prevailing in other countries."[25] Both kinds of exceptionalism imply a tendency to decontextualize and dehistoricize that is still present in public narratives. They have seriously limited discussions of race in the preceding decades, disconnecting the projects of Enlightenment and colonialism from the terror of National Socialism. Referring to German sociologist– philosopher Norbert Elias, Paul Gilroy asks: "How could Norbert Elias, the most subtle and perceptive of sociological minds, be unable to recognize in more than one lone sentence that Germany had possessed an empire at all, something made obvious by even the most cursory reading of *Mein Kampf*?"[26]

Very concretely, this partial historical amnesia has contributed to the often helpless reactions toward ethnicity- and race-based violence in the 1990s among otherwise highly critical segments of society. German reporting on the Durban World Conference Against Racism did mention the genocide of the Hereros and Nama in present-day Namibia committed by German troops in the war of 1904–1907. Yet, General von Trotha's rhetoric of the *Vernichtungsfeldzug* ("military annihilation campaign") and images of emaciated Hereros in chains and on cattle wagons, which from retrospect appear as a matrix for the rhetoric and images of the Holocaust, have barely started to enter public narratives and iconography.

In 1913, more than four decades after the founding of the *Kaiserreich*, a second codification of citizenship laws was considered necessary. The principle of *jus sanguinis* emerged even more firmly as the only basis of German citizenship. Inclusion of nonmembers was minimized. Barbieri concludes:

> Any notion of a right to naturalization was dispensed with; naturalization was identified as an exception made contingent on full cultural assimilation, expressed commitment to German constitutional values, repudiation of previous citizenship, and the presence of a pressing state interest in accepting the applicant. Through this legislation, the political community was limited to a culture- and blood-related group for which considerations such as long-term residence or place of birth were irrelevant.[27]

Barbieri also notes that the heated parliamentary debate about the citizenship laws of 1913 already contained many of the arguments raised in the 1980s and 1990s. There was even criticism of " 'racist' assumptions and the supposition of cultural homogeneity."[28] However, these critical voices from communist and some socialist members of the *Reichstag* remained a minority. The *Kaiserreich* kept legitimizing itself along ethnic and racial lines, and there was no catalog of natural or human rights, since this would have collided with the exclusivity of Germanness and the repressive policies within Germany. The citizenship laws of 1913 (*Reichs- und Staatsangehörigkeitsrecht*) were slightly modified after the founding of the Federal Republic in 1949, but basically remained unchanged in their trajectory until December 31, 1999. At the very *fin de siècle* they had literally prevailed in four different political systems.

German colonialism, which had *de facto* ended during World War I, was officially ended with the ratification of the Versailles Treaty of 1919. Experienced as highly oppressive, the treaty was resented not only within the conservative political spectrum. Its demands to redraw the nation's borders resulted in a substantial loss of territory, a loss that helped to provide a political platform for the rising National Socialist party. Moreover, the treaty called for an occupation of the Rhineland by troops of the Entente. It was the stationing of colonial troops — among them North Africans and Senegalese serving in the French army — that caused public outrage and became a theme of vicious racial propaganda.[29] Brochures and posters railed against the "*Schwarze Schmach am Rhein*" ("Black Disgrace on the Rhine") and showed monstrous Black soldiers, raped German, that is, White women, and a German population in shackles.[30] Even President Friedrich Ebert, a revered Social Democrat, in 1923 declared the Rhineland occupation an offense against the laws of European civilization for using "colored troops of the lowest cultural standing."[31] The German colonies had been lost, yet colonial subjects now entered German territory as an occupational force endowed with the power of the victors. As a result, the racial matrix became ever more deeply entrenched.

Denying the legitimacy of the Versailles Treaty, National Socialism spoke of the former colonies, especially of German Southwest Africa, as territories that rightly belonged to the *Reich*. The murderous conquests of 1884 led by colonial official Carl Peters in East Africa offered lore for myth-building and hero-worship. It was, thus, declared in 1938 that Carl Peters "was approaching National Socialist thinking already fifty years ago."[32] Peters who had actually lost his position as *Reichskommissar* because of continued accusations against the outrageous brutality of his land seizures and pacification campaigns, was declared a role model for the *Hitlerjugend*. Moreover, segregation patterns established in German Southwest Africa provided a platform for Apartheid in Namibia and South Africa. Patterns of exclusion and terror had been established in centuries of European anti-Semitism. However, the positioning of "the African" at the bottom of a racial hierarchy as well as genocidal colonial policies opened a political space for a scientifically reconceived anti-Semitism and the Holocaust.[33]

In 1937, the still existing German Colonial Society was assured by Hitler himself of the importance of a "new colonial front."[34] Despite the immense ruptures of World War I, continuity was thus claimed, even if these claims did not result in military efforts to reestablish any of the colonies.[35] Continuity with colonial law was, however, very concretely established in the Nuremberg Laws of 1935, consisting of a "*Reichs*-Citizen Law" and a "Law to Protect German Blood and German Honor." Those who could not claim Aryan descent lost their *Reichs*-citizenship, and racially mixed marriages were banned.[36] Moreover, in 1937, children of (North) African descent, brutally stigmatized as "Rhineland Bastards," were sterilized in a clandestine campaign for racial hygiene.[37] Along with other measures aiming at the achievement of health and purity of the German race as body, this measure preceded the industrialized genocide of non-Aryans in and beyond Germany.

With the upheavals of the 1960s, the near-extinction of Jewish as well as Sinti and Roma communities in German-occupied Europe finally emerged as a general topic of public debate. Germans of African descent and Africans residing in Germany, however, have only recently been officially recognized as heterogeneous groups with a history. One such public statement is a documentation on the African diaspora in Berlin published in 1995 and 2000 by the Commissioner for Foreigners' Affairs of the Berlin Senate. Clearly, the report follows in the wake of a highly influential anthology published by Katharina Oguntoye, May Opitz, and Dagmar Schultz with the loaded title: *Farbe bekennen* (*Showing Our Colors: Afro-German Women Speak Out*).[38] While the presence of individual Africans in the area that was to become Germany was already mentioned in medieval texts, one of the earliest documented African communities was a group of musicians who served in the Prussian military in the early eighteenth century.[39] It was in the 1920s and early 1930s that an African diaspora in cosmopolitan Berlin achieved cultural visibility on a larger scale. Yet, its members were heavily constrained by projections of primitivism and exoticism. Since racial thinking rigidly equated Blackness or Africanness with a lower- or rather an under-class existence, most members of the African diaspora had to either join variétés and traveling shows or work in menial positions. Only in recent years has the silenced history of the African diaspora in Germany become addressed in the media. Perhaps, however, the German translation of Hans-Jürgen Massaquoi's autobiography has done more to create public awareness of the implications of race for Black Germans than any officially authorized documentation.[40] Not surprisingly though, the reception of the book tended to focus on the author as an exceptional, if not exotic, figure. Even for an audience of the late 1990s, Germanness obviously still connoted Whiteness.

Despite its pathos of human rights, the German *Grundgesetz* (Basic Law) of 1949[41] carried on the semantics of *Volk* as defined through descent, not in openly racial meanings, but still as *ethnos* rather than *demos*.[42] Equality before the law and protection from discrimination because of ethnic or racial descent, emphasized in Art. 3(1) and 3(3), are counterbalanced in Art. 20(2): "*Alle Macht geht vom Volke aus*," usually translated as "All power emanates from the people."[43] The weight of ethnic descent and bloodlines for the term *Volk* was demonstrated when millions of refugees and expellees from the Eastern parts of the former *Reich*, from Poland, and from enclaves in Rumania and the former Czechoslovakia came to the Federal Republic after the end of World War II.[44] With claims to a German genealogy, they were members of the *Volk* and entitled to citizenship. If large-scale immigration is said to threaten the nation-state, these enormous demographic shifts did not. Institutionalized by a federal law of 1953, ethnic membership assured rights to citizenship for decades to come. Barbieri notes: "In many cases, these immigrants have little or no knowledge of German language and culture; nonetheless, by virtue of being related to a past member of the *Reich* they are entitled to receive citizenship status upon application."[45] As opposed to resident foreigners, ethnic Germans were offered language courses designed for integration into the labor market. The Law of 1953 also included the descendants of German emigrants who had followed the promise of land grants issued by Catherine II of Russia in the late eighteenth century. Having settled along the Volga, during the Stalin era, many were deported to Siberia and to the Soviet Republic of Kasachstan. While requirements of proof of German descent have become stricter in the last decade, even after German reunification, Russian *Spätaussiedler* ("late out-settlers") have made up a considerable proportion of the immigrant population.[46] Facing its historic responsibilities, the Federal Republic has also kept its borders open to Jewish Russians, who have contributed intensely to a reviving of Jewish communities in Germany.

In the early years of the Federal Republic, the reconstruction of war-devastated Germany tended to mean economic reconstruction only. Memory was silenced and, as a consequence, accountability denied in many realms of public life. Members of the N.S. elite were reinstalled, and some of the authors of the Nuremberg Laws served in high administrative or political positions. The Justice Department even reemployed those who had provided the legal basis for the sterilization programs of the 1930s.[47]

Especially in its first decade, the Federal Republic also kept up an explicit, scientifically authorized discourse of race in its treatment of Black Germans.[48] Those who had survived the Holocaust and reapplied for citizenship, a right granted to them by Art. 116(2) of the Basic Law, were confronted with an administration unwilling to put these laws into practice. If they succeeded, it was often after long struggles. Children of African American or African fathers and German mothers were still officially labeled *Mischlinge* ("mixed ones" or "mixed bloods"), a terminology anchored in race-based genetic research.[49] As in the 1920s, the presence of these children was associated with military occupation, and they were called *Besatzungskinder* ("occupation children"). Also, the 1950s still saw studies drawing on eugenics and racial anthropology that were conducted with *Besatzungskinder* who were taken from their mothers to be raised in state- or church-run institutions or given up for adoption into African American families. While the studies attempted to prove the general inferiority of children of mixed descent, they finally admitted that no such proof could be given. Still, the ascription of social deviance remained, a history chillingly recalled in Ika Hügel-Marshall's memoir.[50] Following debates in the *Bundestag* as to the status and the fate of *Besatzungskinder*, schools and other institutions were now called upon to deal with the presence of non-White Germans and non-Whites in general. The question became one of pedagogics: How to deal with those who are (categorized as) different. Huber-Koller thus speaks of pedagogical and administrative "non-membership."[51]

However, in the late 1950s and especially in the 1960s, West Germany's expanding economy experienced a serious labor shortage, and contracts with Southern European as well as, North African states (Tunisia and Morocco) and Turkey were signed, which regulated the hiring of foreign workers.[52] The official terminology, *Gastarbeiter* ("guest workers"), made it abundantly clear that these workers were supposed to leave and "go home" again after their limited term was over. While the early migrant workers and their families, many of them Italians, were heavily discriminated against, it was Turkish women and men who would eventually become the largest and the most socially visible group of *Ausländer*.[53] Religion, that is Islam, came to represent an unbridgeable, rigid difference, although Turkey is a secular state and by no means all Turkish families were practicing Muslims when they came to Germany.[54] Turkish migrant workers who turned into immigrants, one may argue, were raced, were positioned as the threatening, the unassimilable Other. If cultural difference was and is constantly called upon, culture kept up the hermetic determinism of race. The headscarves of (some) Turkish women and other women of Muslim faith — differences in the many ways scarves are worn are lost on most Germans — evolved into a perceived symbol of cultural backwardness, of potential fundamentalism and, more recently, of gender-oppression. In Germany and in France, the heated discussion has emerged as a space where both societies debate basic questions of cultural identity and difference and the political weight of religion.

Throughout the 1970s and 1980s, the historically loaded claim of *Überfremdung* (being overrun by foreign cultures or races) was taken up by German authorities. But, while they publicly deplored the rising number of foreigners, until the late 1990s, politicians of a wide spectrum categorically denied the reality of immigration. The slogan with a quasi-axiomatic status was: "Germany is no country of immigration." The lives of *Ausländer* in the Federal Republic were (and still are) regulated by the *Ausländergesetz*, the Aliens Act, and the central administrative institution that those without a passport from one of the countries of the European Union have had to cope with is the *Ausländeramt* ("Aliens/Foreigners Office"). Comparing the social ruptures of immigration in Germany to those of the United States Barbieri points out:

> The central feature defining the *Ausländer* population is its subordination or exclusion, which arises in the intertwined processes of nation-building, state-building, and *civitas*-building, in the interrelated forms of discrimination, socioeconomic inequality, and legal disadvantage. Characteristic problems falling under these three headings reflect the established status of the migrant worker population as a minority in the American sense, exhibiting all the social isolation and collective alienation that this term suggests.[55]

It is important to note that the descendants of *Gastarbeiter* make up only a part of the resident foreigner population in Germany. Until 1993, Art. 16, Basic Law, granted asylum to persons who were politically persecuted. The claim of political persecution had to be legally proven, however — in most cases a year-long struggle. Due to an economic recession and a growing number of political refugees, in the 1980s, the court rulings became more and more restrictive. Since the boundaries between political and economic motives for seeking asylum are often blurred, many who came to ask for asylum were considered "fake" asylum seekers, "*Scheinasylanten.*" They were accused of being economic refugees who abused the generous German social security system. In 1993, Art. 16 was amended with a modification that practically subverted the tenor of the initial statement. Moreover, the legal restrictions barring many political refugees from receiving work permits and thus forcing them to rely on state support has exacerbated the debate. (This restriction has been eased but not yet abolished.)

"Not surprisingly," Barbieri notes, "political parties in Germany have been leading participants in discussions concerning policy toward the foreign minority."[56] Moreover, there were major differences in the policies of Foreigners Offices in the different *Bundesländer* (federal states) and even on the administrative levels of communities.

> At the same time, the foreigner issue itself has played a major role in shaping the party–political landscape in Germany since the early 1970s. Thus 1988 saw the rise to political viability of the far-right Republikaner party on the basis of their opposition to the foreign presence and commitment to reducing it. At the other end of the political spectrum, the Greens have likewise made the equal treatment of foreigners a cornerstone of their platform. . . .[57]

In their attempt to appeal to voters, politicians of a broad political spectrum have kept metaphorizing the debate. Common figures of speech in the 1980s and 1990s were the trope of the "flood" ("*die Asylantenflut*") and the infamous boat metaphor — "The boat is full." Granted performativity through its official status, this language not only affirmed preceding acts of violence, but in turn called forth new strategies of exclusion. It also lent support to the ideological positioning of Jewish Germans as "foreigners," and anti-Semitic acts have resurfaced. One might even argue that, claiming to take the electorate's anxieties seriously, political rhetoric actually counteracted an emerging toleration of heterogeneity, especially in urban centers of West Germany.

If Turkish and, as a smaller group, North African immigrants were raced, race has been even more of an agent for those who have applied for political asylum. By now a large part of this group is from countries outside of Europe; many are from the African continent. Germanness may no longer imply a specified Whiteness — at the height of racial doctrine German was quasi-synonymous with Germanic[58] — but it still tends to anchor itself in a diffuse Whiteness, a self-positioning that is as unacknowledged as it is pervasive. Those who are visually recognized as non-White are, thus, in an especially vulnerable position.

"The turbulent postwar decades," Barbieri states, "witnessed the creation and dissolution of a competing German citizenship in the German Democratic

Republic. Yet citizenship in the Federal Republic has adapted to the new, postreunification scale of the state with a minimum of formal changes."[59] The German Democratic Republic (GDR) had also hired foreign workers, especially from Vietnam. After reunification, some were granted political asylum, but many were forced to return to Vietnam.

The demonstrations in Leipzig in 1989, which helped to bring down the entrenched power structures of the GDR, were accompanied by the call: "*Wir sind das Volk!*" Directed against the oligarchical SED ("*Sozialistische Einheitspartei Deutschlands*") this call should indeed be translated as "We are the people!" However, along with the insistence on *Volk* as *demos*, the semantics of *ethnos* resurfaced. The balance has remained precarious between a political community and an ethnic or cultural one that still has traces of *völkisch* (qualities of *Volk* as race) inscribed in it. There was a certain public awareness of the loaded meanings of *Volk*, when the inscription on the old building of the *Reichstag* — "*Dem deutschen Volk*" ("To the German *Volk*") — was critically questioned and a substitution of the word *Volk* with "nation" was suggested. The inscription has remained.[60]

The festive mood of German reunification of the years 1989–1990 was accompanied by shrill demands for a newly defined national identity, demands that made the redrawing of boundaries acceptable even to those who would situate themselves as the political middle. Not surprisingly, during the decade of the 1990s, a catalogue of place names came to connote chronologies and geographies of violence against *Ausländer*, ranging from Rostock in 1992 to Düsseldorf in 2000. The newly reunified Republic, it seems, was being mapped and marked through an enacted Germanness that either extolled, or at least tolerated, the exclusivity of bloodlines. Whenever acts of violence could no longer be denied and had to be publicly denounced, politicians and large parts of the media tended to be more concerned with Germany's suffering image abroad than with providing support to victims and questioning the postunification rhetoric of national identity.

Proclaiming that the Federal Republic had broken with the National Socialist past meant that the specter of race could be relegated to the past as well. There were of course voices of dissent — sometimes illustrious ones — who kept denouncing German neonationalism of the 1990s. Mostly, however, critical voices have focused on explicit acts of racism and xenophobia. Proclaimed to be pathological, these highly visible acts can be identified, isolated, and thus supposedly contained. But along with the strategies of denial and decontextualization mentioned above, this focus has kept race as a structural category from becoming a public issue. Also, the emphasis on cultural difference as an ontological, a static given, an emphasis that still informs concepts of multiculturalism in Germany, has tended to reinforce strategies of exclusion.

The citizenship laws of 1913 were finally rewritten in 1999 under a newly constituted coalition of Social Democrats and the Green Party. By that time about 9 percent of the population residing in Germany were resident foreigners.

To this percentage, a significant number of immigrants from Russia and Poland should be added who had only recently received their German passports and still tended to be unofficially labeled as *Ausländer*. The process of rewriting the laws included significant concessions vis-à-vis conservative demands. While the Green Party had demanded dual citizenship in order to avoid the legal severing of ties to the countries of emigration, Christian Democrats claimed that dual citizenship works against integration. Realizing that it could no longer successfully operate on a crude anti-immigration platform, the party made no secret of its concept of integration as uncompromising assimilation. Becoming a German citizen was supposed to exclude further membership, denying the "growing fluidity and multiplicity of political social and cultural ties" that large-scale migration has generated.[61] Since the beginning of the new century, German citizenship is automatically conferred to those who are born in Germany and who have one parent with 8 years of German residency. The new laws are still restrictive, and indeed, the number of resident foreigners applying for citizenship has been lower than expected. Ironically, eligible *Ausländer* are now accused of not wanting to become German, of not wanting to integrate. The current political project is one of legislating what has come to be labeled as *Zuwanderung* ("ad-migration"), a term signaling the unease which is still felt with the acknowledgment that membership in German society has become accessible for *Ausländer* from beyond the confines of the European Union. Like the rewriting of the citizenship laws, this legislation has been a topic of a prolonged and intense political and legal debate. The shift from *ethnos* to *demos* is still a precarious one.

Under pressure from employers' organizations, the government made an attempt to adopt U.S. policies and suggested to offer a Green Card to information technology specialists who were to be recruited primarily from India. The language used in a campaign against the Green Card launched by members of the Christian Democrats invites a close reading. The semi-public slogan of the campaign was: "*Kinder statt Inder!*" ("Children instead of [Asian] Indians!"). It is the semantic extension of "Kinder" which makes the rhyme vicious, since "Kinder" refers to White German children only. The statement, thus, implicitly calls for the birth of more White children who are then supposed to fill job vacancies, rather than bringing in non-White foreigners (whom the architects of the Green Card project indeed expected to come without children). When the Green Card was finally sanctioned by the *Bundestag*, it was meant to open German borders to a new class of privileged *Gastarbeiter* who were supposed to leave again after five years. Not surprisingly, the immediate results of these attempts at recruiting "wanted foreigners" were highly embarrassing. Rather few specialists were willing to come, and only a small percentage came from India. Openly, the media now quoted statements from potential recruits criticizing German toleration of violence against non-Whites. Ironically, while the public narrative of Germany as an "open society" still circulates, the Secretary of the Interior has kept emphasizing that immigration legislation does not invite immigration but above all effectively limits access to the territory of the nation-state. Still, compatibility of German legislation with immigration policies in other states of the European Union has become a necessity. With open borders among the states of the Union, the sovereignty of the nation-state will diminish, and with the consummation of a unified (and redefined) Europe, it is to be expected that national citizenship will at least be partially subsumed under European citizenship.

The intense ambivalence toward impending immigration legislation in Germany led to the coinage of a national neologism: German *Leitkultur* ("lead culture"). Immigrants, leading members of the Christian Democrats insisted, need to accept a normative German core culture. Since this rhetoric caused a heated debate and an outcry among intellectuals — it was also nominated as the "non-word" of the year 2001 — party leaders considered it necessary to define the term. Accepting a German *Leitkultur* means that immigrants should learn the German language, confess loyalty to the values of the Basic Law, and accept the traditions of a *christlich–abendländische Kultur* ("Christian–Occidental culture"). Especially the latter demand was denounced as *Kulturkampf* ("culture fight"), instrumentalizing a supposedly national culture for acts of political exclusion.[62] The term *Leitkultur* has faded from public rhetoric, yet many of its claims have remained part of the debate.

Stressing that life in Germany and, of course, throughout Europe, has been intensely impacted by immigration would be a truism. While the acquisition of citizenship is a singular act, cultural membership as active participation — and the previous discussion has made this all too clear — is a contested process.[63] I would like to suggest that it is in the interconnected realms of popular culture and language where the impact of immigration has truly been pervasive. Due to the enormous weight of a globally consumed American popular culture, a process of claiming spaces has been changing cultural life in Germany.[64] Since the 1980s, immigrant youth, especially those who carry the visual marks of being *Ausländer*, have been major participants in the creation of an urban culture that strongly relates to contemporary African American urban cultures.[65] Through the translation of media-disseminated sounds and advertised Black styles, specific diasporic cultures have emerged. This form of reinterpretation and appropriation is of course a highly eclectic, gendered process, always grounded in the shifting paradigms of class.

While blue-collar second– and third-generation immigrant youth have tended to claim the more transgressive versions of Hip Hop culture, ranging from graffiti and breakdance in the early 1980s to gangsta rap in the 1990s, satellite TV has resulted in a reimporting of popular music from the countries of emigration, especially from Turkey and North Africa. Some critics fear that this may result in a reethnicization, a process that would reproduce boundaries and threaten cultural membership in the larger society. However, the sounds emanating from Turkish and Algerian studios quite often clearly target the immigrant market in Germany and France, and thus already imply the shifts and hybridities migration produces. The last two decades have also seen groups that polemically defy any ethnic categorization, and with the manifesto of "Kanak Attack" (1999) a cultural or political statement by a collective of immigrants and nonimmigrants was made that not only demanded resistance to smooth assimilation, but also subverted romanticizing concepts of multicultural coexistance.[66] Moreover, as the success of Hip Hop, reggae, and dancehall scene with a nonimmigrant middle-class background demonstrates, Black New World sounds keep crossing borders and keep being retranslated to an Old World that is intensely reinventing itself. "It is exactly the Americanization of German popular culture" Christoph Ribbat points out, "which results in an increasingly multiethnic, broken, hybrid self-definition of German culture."[67] By now one may claim though that German or European popular culture is self-confidently pursuing its own agenda.

How much race as lived reality is acknowledged in popular culture, however, is shown in projects of Afro-German rappers, reggae, and dancehall artists who have emerged as highly visible cultural agents. Their explicit reaction to the fatal and near-fatal attacks on Black resident foreigners and on German citizens of African descent (at least temporarily) presented a strategy to counter the attractiveness of right-wing movements not only for East German youth but also for the younger population in urban centers of West Germany.[68] These musicians tend to focus on Blackness as resistance and, increasingly, on Blackness as success. With their rapid-fire lyrics and their staging of a diasporic culture, they at the same time shake the foundations of an inherently White Germanness. While this may seem to challenge the urban Black-inspired pose of young Turkish or Moroccon Germans (who are usually not included in the category *Black*), immigrant sounds and styles are constantly being recreated with shifting alliances. Clearly, German popular culture has been presenting itself as a fast-changing, sometimes highly politicized, contested cultural territory that has localized global migration and culture flow.

Germanness — some fear, others celebrate — has also been irreversibly affected in the linguistic domain. With a globalized American English reshaping the language of the economic sector and, of course, the language of popular culture in general, an increasingly hybrid colloquial German does not draw on American (and African American) English only. Out of the so-called *Gastarbeiterdeutsch* ("guest worker German") — linguistically a pidgin — creolized varieties have emerged. Heavily gendered, they are mostly spoken by blue-collar second-generation Turkish-Germans, by Moroccan-Germans, and also, with variations of course, by immigrants from Eastern Europe, for example from the former Yugoslavia, from Poland and Russia. Italian immigrants, I would like to suggest, provided a linguistic and a cultural matrix for this process. Strongly dependent on class affiliation, these ever-shifting varieties of German are stigmatized and connote marginalization. But combined with body language and clothes, they also connote a transgressiveness that has long claimed the status of an urban cool pose. It is this pose (together with some linguistic variables) that is also partially appropriated by nonimmigrant middle-class youth. If parts of the so-called margin have not yet moved to the center — and many have — they do send strong impulses and perhaps tend to disrupt the allocation of social spaces altogether.

As the debates on *Leitkultur* and immigration legislation have shown, claims of a hegemonic Germanness are still being made even by those who would publicly distance themselves from outright acts of racism and xenophobia. Worse, the mythical community of a bloodline-determined German nation as *Volk* — proclaimed by the extreme right — is still appealing to White youths across the country (and is quite often tolerated by the parents' generation). At the same time, neo-Nazi organizations increasingly cross national borders to cooperate with right-wing groups in surrounding European states. If Germany, despite the lure of neo-Nazi "Germans first" rhetoric, is no longer quite the anachronistic society the critical opening remark proclaimed it to be, questions of "thick citizenship," of cultural participation and cultural rights grounded in group membership are still among the tasks to be faced. In an expanding European Union, which, as Rainer Bauböck states, "has become a laboratory" for cutting and recombining "different strands of citizenship," this task is of course also a transnational one.[69] However, shifting political majorities within the member states may actually make the institutionalization of policies, which are not based on bloodlines and on authoritative national cultures, even more of a challenge for the decades to come.

Notes

1. I thank Carolina Asuquo-Brown and Danko Rabrenovic for sharing their insights on the political and cultural implications of immigration in Germany. Christoph Ribbat has been kind enough to provide his publications on Rap and Hip Hop in Germany, and Ellen Köhlings and Piet Lilly have generously shared their knowledge on adaptations of diasporic popular culture. All translations by the author.
2. Heide, Oestreich, "Clash der Kulturen als Methode," *die Tageszeitung, tazmag* (Oktober 7–8, 2000), iv.
3. In a similar vein, a London banker reportedly stated that Germany's problems with the Green Card (discussed below) simply resulted from the fact that it did not have enough colonies. *die Tageszeitung* (April 14, 2000), 3.
4. Cf. also Lewis H. Gann, "Marginal Colonialism: The German Case," in *Germans in the Tropics*, eds., Arthur J. Knoll and Lewis H. Gann (New York: Greenwood Press, 1987), 1–18. Fatima El-Tayeb critically discusses this position in the introduction to her monograph on Black Germans: *Schwarze Deutsche: Der Diskurs um "Rasse" und nationale Identität 1890–1933* (Frankfurt/Main: Campus, 2001).
5. The Herero Reparation Corporation filed reparation claims against the Federal Republic, the Deutsche Bank, and a German shipping line in September 2001. After the case was dismissed, claims were filed again under the Alien Tort Claims Act in August 2003 in New York.
6. Since orthodox Marxist analysis considered imperialism an outcome of capitalism, the readiness to critically discuss colonial/imperial policies of the German *Reich* may have been greater among historians in the German Democratic Republic than in the Federal Republic.
7. Quoted in Henning Melber, *Der Weißheit letzter Schluß: Rassismus und kolonialer Blick* (Frankfurt/Main: Brandes & Apsel, 1992), 35.
8. While this assessment is not generally shared by German historians and political scientists, there are, of course, authors who do emphasize the importance of German colonialism. Cf., for example, El-Tayeb's monograph and Rose-Marie Huber-Koller, "Schwarze Deutsche: Zwischen, 'Ethnos' und 'Demos' im historischen Spannungsgeld unterschiedlicher

Legitimationsgrundlagen und Techniken politischer Herrschaft," In *Vom Ausländer zum Bürger: Problemanzeigen im Ausländer-, Asyl- und Staatsangehörigkeitsrecht*. Festschrift für Fritz Franz und Gert Müller (Baden-Baden: Nomos Verlagsgesellschaft, 1994), 126–180. Cf. also Manfred O. Hinz, Helgard Patemann, und Arnim Meier, eds., *Weiss auf Schwarz: Kolonialismus, Apartheid und afrikanischer Widerstand* (Berlin: Elefanten Press, 1986); Katharina Oguntoye, May Opitz, und Dagmar Schultz, *Farbe bekennen. Afro-Deutsche Frauen auf den Spuren ihrer Geschichte* (Berlin: Orlanda, 1986); Ruth Mayer und Mark Terkessidis, eds., *Globalkolorit, Multikulturalismus und Populärkultur* (St. Andrä/Wördern: Hannibal, 1998); Paul Gilroy, *Against Race: Imagining Political Culture Beyond the Color Line* (Cambridge, MA: The Belknap Press of Harvard UP, 2000); Susanne Zantop, *Colonial Fantasies: Conquest, Family, and Nation in Precolonial Germany, 1770–1870* (Durham, NC: Duke University Press, 1997).

9. German colonies in the South Pacific included German New Guinea, also named "Kaiser-Wilhelms-Land," the Bismarck Archipelago, the Marshall Islands, Nauru, the Marianen, the Carolinas, the Palau Islands, parts of Samoa. Moreover, in 1898, Kiautschou was leased from China for 99 years.

10. Kay Heilbronner, Günter Renner, und Christine Kreuzer. *Staatsangehörigkeitsrecht. Kommentar* (München: Beck, 1998), 3.

11. Concerning the importance of Idealist philosophy and Romanticism for the process of German nation-building cf. also William Barbieri, Jr., *Ethics of Citizenship: Immigration and Group Rights in Germany* (Durham, NC: Duke University Press, 1998), 10–15. For the emergence of concepts of identity and culture as based on authenticity and originality cf. Charles Taylor's essay "The Politics of Recognition" in *Multiculturalism and The Politics of Recognition* (Princeton, NJ: Princeton UP, 1992), 28–32. As to Africanist traditions in German philosophy it is important to note that while G.F.W. Hegel's infamous positioning of Africa and Africans (Vol. 12 of his *Vorlesungen über die Philosophie der Geschichte*) is well-known among scholars focusing on constructions of race, general debates on the involvement of German idealism in the projects of race, and colonialism have barely left the niches of German academia.

12. Huber-Koller, "Schwarze Deutsche," 127.

13. My use of the term "ethnonation" is taken from Barbieri, *Ethics of Citizenship*, 32.

14. Cf. Barbieri, *Ethics of Citizenship*, 22.

15. Barbieri, *Ethics of Citizenship*, 13.

16. Cf. Huber-Koller and El-Tayeb for a more detailed discussion on the impact of race sciences.

17. Similar to U.S. - American regimes of race, such demonization of mixture either denied rape committed by the colonizers or refused to consider these acts of violence as crime.

18. Quot. in Huber-Koller, "Schwarze Deutsche," 32.

19. Huber-Koller, "Schwarze Deutsche."

20. Cf. Huber-Koller, "Schwarze Deutsche," 129. El-Tayeb notes that colonial law for Southwest Africa "defined each person as a 'native' that had an African ancestor, however far removed." *Schwarze Deutsche*, 159.

21. Texts do not dwell on the sanctions for African women or men.

22. Hannah Arendt names the three decades from 1884 to 1914 as the epoch of imperialism. I have subsumed this phase under colonialism. Hannah Arendt, *Elemente und Ursprünge totaler Herrschaft: Antisemitismus, Imperialismus, totale Herrschaft*, 1955 (München und Zürich: Piper, 2000).

23. Arendt, *Elemente und Ursprünge totaler Herrschaft*, 407. Another important aspect of Arendt's work is her emphasis on colonial bureaucracy for racial policies in Europe, cf. her chapter on "Rasse und Bürokratie," 405–408. There is a highly problematic aspect to Arendt's analysis though. Despite her demystification of race as a social construction and her scathing accusations of colonial atrocities, her own representation of Africa as inhabited by "worldless" people who remain mere extensions of a hostile nature literally reiterates the Africanist discourse of German Idealist philosophers. Cf. "Die Gespensterwelt des Schwarzen Erdteils," 408–428.

24. Arendt, *Elemente und Ursprünge totaler Herrschaft*, 351.

25. El-Tayeb, *Schwarze Deutsche*, 152.

26. Gilroy, *Against Race*, 79.

27. Barbieri, *Ethics of Citizenship*, 24.

28. Barbieri, *Ethics of Citizenship*, 177, annot. 21. Cf. also Melber, *Der Weißheit letzter Schluß*, 37 and Helmut Stoecker and Peter Sebald, "Enemies of the Colonia Idea," in *Germans in the Tropics: Essays in German Colonial History*, eds., Arthur J. Knoll and Lewis H. Gann (New York: Greenwood Press, 1987), 59–72.

29. While there were also soldiers from French colonies in South East Asia, their presence did not evoke the same outcry as the presence of North and West African soldiers.
30. An exhibit of propaganda writings calling for the "Befreiung des Rheinlands" ("The liberation of the Rhineland"), hosted by the main library of the University of Düsseldorf in May/June 2001, points toward a slowly growing awareness of the degree to which German politics were anchored in race during the Weimar Republic.
31. Quot. in Huber-Koller, "Schwarze Deutsche," 142.
32. Quot. in Oguntoye et al., Farbe bekennen, 55
33. In his article on the commemoration of resistance against German colonialism, Joachim Zeller states that the question of continuities between German genocide in Africa and the Holocaust currently "dominates historical debates." "Der totale Feldzug," die Tageszeitung, taz-dossier (January 10–11, 2004), 3.
34. Quot. in Oguntoye et al., Farbe bekennen, 57.
35. Wolfe Schmokel's work on colonial ambitions during the Third Reich argues that extensive plans "for the creation and administration of a new German overseas empire" actually existed. Wolfe W. Schmokel, Dream of Empire: German Colonialism, 1919–1945 (New Haven and London: Yale UP, 1964), vii.
36. Cf. Huber-Koller, "Schwarze Deutsche," 150 and Paulette Reed-Anderson, Berlin und die afrikanische Diaspora: Rewriting the Footnotes. Berlin and the African Diaspora (Berlin: Verwaltungsdruckerei, 2000), 54. Huber-Koller points out that the Nuremberg Laws, for reasons of international diplomacy, were not as explicit in their mentioning of "colored races" as had been initially demanded by adherents of racial science. Moreover, racial policies in Germany were inseparably tied to the construction of other forms of difference as deviance, of homosexuality, as well as mental illness.
37. Cf. Reed-Anderson, Rewriting the Footnotes, 56. In recent years, several documentaries have been shown on television, which thematized the sterilization campaign and the role of the film studios in Babelsberg/Berlin as a last refuge for some Black Germans.
38. The English version is Showing Our Colors: Afro German Women Speak Out (Amherst, MA: University of Massachusetts Press, 1992). The attention to histories and cultures of the African diaspora in Germany has dramatically increased, as any internet research will demonstrate. There has also been a special edition of the journal Calloloo, 26.2 (2003).
39. Ships from Brandenburg had landed on the West African coast in the late seventeenth century, and treaties were signed with African leaders. Already in 1682, the Brandenburg African Society had slaves shipped from the West African coast to Hamburg. Cf. Reed-Anderson, Rewriting the Footnotes, 8.
40. Hans J. Massaquoi, Destined to Witness: Growing Up Black in Nazi Germany (New York: Morrow & Co., 1999). There has been a controversy about the German title: Neger, Neger, Schornsteinfeger, a racist children's taunt mentioned in the narrative. A literal English translation of this rhyme would be: "Negro, Negro, Chimneysweep."
41. Cf. also the definition of who is German, Art. 116 Basic Law. The Basic Law was inspired by the UN Charter of Human Rights and by the U.S. Constitution.
42. Cf. the argument of Huber-Koller, "Schwarze Deutsche," and of Melber, Der Weißheit letzter Schluß, 157.
43. These articles are not subject to alteration.
44. Inhabitants of the Soviet-occupied parts of the German Reich of 1937, which later made up the German Democratic Republic, automatically held citizenship rights in the Federal Republic.
45. Barbieri, Ethics of Citizenship, 25.
46. Some older immigrants from Russia still speak an archaic version of German. Since language training for ethnic Germans has been curtailed, immigrants from Russia have come to be socially excluded and are represented in the media as prone to crime and violence. They have also become the target of Neo-Nazi attacks.
47. Cf. for example, Huber-Koller, "Schwarze Deutsche," 157 and Oguntoye et al., Farbe bekennen, 85–102.
48. Continuity was practiced not only with the upholding of racial hierarchies, but with the pathologizing and criminalizing of homosexuality, a practice that finally called forth an official apology in the Bundestag.
49. Hannah Arendt names the three decades from 1884 to 1914 as the epoch of imperialism. I have subsumed this phase under colonialism. Hannah Arendt, Elemente und Ursprünge totaler Herrschaft: Antisemitismus, Imperialismus, totale Herrschaft, 1955 (München und Zürich: Piper, 2000).
50. Cf. also Huber-Koller, "Schwarze Deutsche," 162ff and Oguntoye et al., Farbe bekennen, 85ff. Perhaps for reasons of marketing, perhaps also for the book's decidedly feminist stance, Ika

Hügel-Marshall's *Daheim unterwegs Eindeutsches Leben* (Berlin: Orlanda, 1998) has had less of an impact than Massaquoi's memories, but is still an important textual presence. This book too, has been translated into English as: *Invisible Woman: Growing Up Black in Germany* (New York: Continuum, 2001).

51. Huber-Koller, "Schwarze Deutsche," 161.

52. Since the beginning of the German *Reich*, foreign workers were employed in agriculture and in the expanding industries of the *Ruhrgebiet* (Ruhr Area). The largest group were Polish workers who received German citizenship and eventually became icons of German working-class culture. During WWI and WWII, a substantial part of the foreign labor force was made up of enforced labor. Cf. also Terkessidis, *Migranten* (Hamburg: Europäische Verlagsanstalt/Rotbuch, 2000), 10–15.

53. According to the official publication of the Federal Government's Commissioner for Foreigners' Issues, ca. 9 percent of the total population of Germany were resident foreigners in 1999, the largest group being immigrants from Turkey which made up 28 percent. *Facts and Figures on the Situation of Foreigners in the Federal Republic of Germany*. The Federal Government's Commissioner for Foreigners' Issues, 19th ed. (Berlin and Bonn: October 2000), 7.

54. Practices of discrimination and exclusion are said to have intensified the identification with more dogmatic versions of Islam among Turkish immigrants.

55. Barbieri, *Ethics of Citizenship*, 32.

56. Barbieri, *Ethics of Citizenship*, 42.

57. Barbieri, *Ethics of Citizenship*.

58. This semantic intersection still plays an important role in Neo-Nazi rhetoric.

59. Barbieri, *Ethics of Citizenship*, 25. To counter historical amnesia, a comparative study of citizenship laws of the German Democratic and the Federal Republic would be an important project.

60. This building now houses the Lower House of the German Parliament, the *Bundestag*.

61. Rainer Bauböck, *Recombinant Citizenship*, Institut für Höhere Studien (IHS), Wien/Institute for Advanced Studies, Vienna. Reihe Politikwissenschaft/Political Science Series, no. 67 (Vienna, 1999), 2. It is possible to retain dual citizenship until the age of 23. Dual citizenship may be retained during adulthood under specified conditions.

62. The reference is Bismarck's *Kulturkampf* (1871–1887), an unsuccessful attempt to destroy the political influence of the Roman Catholic church in the *Reich*. Interestingly enough, Samuel P. Huntington's *Clash of Civilizations* was translated into German as *Kampf der Kulturen*.

63. Cf. also Bauböck's basic distinction between "thin" and "thick" citizenship.

64. The consequences of importing American popular culture after WWII are discussed in Reinhold Wagnleitner and Elaine Tyler May, eds., *"Here, There and Everywhere": The Foreign Politics of American Popular Culture* (Hanover and London: University Press of New England, 2000). Cf. also Wagnleitner's essay, " 'No Commodity Is Quite So Strange As This Thing Called Cultural Exchange': The Foreign Politics of American Pop Culture Hegemony," *Amerikastudien — American Studies*, 46.3 (2001), 443–470. For a reflection on the semantics of the term popular culture and on the motives for its global popularity cf. Berndt Ostendorf, "Why Is American Popular Culture So Popular? A View from Europe," *Amerikastudien-American Studies*, 46.3(2001) 339–366.

65. Christoph Ribbat has focused on this process in two publications on popular culture in Germany: " 'Ja, ja, deine Mudder!' American Studies und deutsche Populärkultur," in *Kulturwissenschaftliche Perspektivenin den Nordamerikastudien*, ed., Friedirh Jäger (Tübingen: Stauffenburg, 2002), 145–160; "How Hip Hop Hit Heidelberg: German Rappers, Rhymes, and Rhythms," in *"Here, There and Everywhere": The Foreign Politics of American Popular Culture*, eds., Reinhold Wagnleitner and Elain Tyler May (Hanover, NH; University Press of New England, 2000), 207–216. In how far public youth centers have played a role in Turkish Hip Hop is another point of interest, cf. Terkessidis, *Migranten*, 80–83.

66. The term *Kanak* is a polemical resignification of the highly derogatory label *Kana(c)ke*, referring to *Ausländer* in general and Turkish immigrants in particular. While the colonial semantics of the epithet may not be known to most of its users, its resignification definitely follows the highly contested African American usage of *Nigger*. The reply to the term when used as an insult clearly draws the line: "Nazi!"

67. Christoph Ribbat, " 'Ja, ja, deine Mudder!' American Studies und deutsche Populärkultur," in *Kulturwissenschaftliche Perspektiven in den Nordamerikastudien*, ed. Friedrich Jäger (Tübingen: Stauffenburg, 2002), 8.

68. I have chosen to translate the label of self-reference "Afrodeutsch" as "Afro-German" rather than "African German."

69. Bauböck, *Recombinant Citizenship*, 2.

Part 3
Nation Making

10

Reinventing the Nation
Building a Bicultural Future from a Monocultural Past in Aotearoa/New Zealand

CLUNY MACPHERSON

Introduction

After 600 years of continuous residence, the worlds of the indigenous nations of Aotearoa were transformed by the arrival of colonists from Britain. From the early nineteenth century, colonists, promised a better life by English land settlement companies, arrived in search of land and opportunity. Over time, settlers used a legal treaty, and later, progressive legal imperialism, secular and religious argument and persuasion, deception, fraudulence and military force, to establish their economic and social dominance in the new land. This was won at the expense of the original inhabitants, Māori nations', social and economic well-being. By the late nineteenth century, the settlers had become a numerical majority and had established their cultural, religious, political, and economic dominance in the new "dominion."

Secure in their Eurocentric beliefs, derived from a combination of secular and religious ideologies, they set out to consolidate their position, and to establish a "nation" and "national culture," which was based on and re-affirmed these ideologies. As settler population and landholdings grew, Māori population and landholdings declined. As settler wealth and assurance grew, Māori wealth and assurance declined. As settler capitalism became established as the dominant mode of production, the Māori communitarian mode became marginalized. As a monotheistic *Pākehā* religion, that celebrated the virtues of the Protestant ethic and, albeit indirectly, those of capitalism became the dominant religion, a polytheistic Māori religion that stressed connectedness between humans and their natural and supernatural environments was labeled "primitive" and relegated to history. The demographic, cultural, economic, and religious grounds were set for the establishment of a largely uncontested and Eurocentric monoculture, which steadily marginalized the Māori population and worldview.

There is, on the surface, nothing remarkable about this sequence. Historians, such as James Belich[1] have noted parallels with sequences that occurred elsewhere as evolution of the capitalist world-economy sent core nations scrambling for sites for low-cost labor, inexpensive commodities, and raw materials, which their manufacturers transformed into higher value goods, and opportunities for high return investments for core capital. Britain, using various strategies, created "possessions" throughout the world to which it then sent settlers who, before long, dominated their polities and economies, turned them into peripheral parts of the world-system and integrated them into the world division of labor. These "white settler colonies" in Australia, Canada, the United States and Southern Africa, remained linked economically, politically, and ideologically to the core, which supplied much of their developmental capital and, in return, expropriated surpluses and profits.

Aotearoa/New Zealand was a typical case. It became a producer of low-cost timber, wool and hides, and later frozen meat and dairy produce for the "home" — that is, British — market. Once indigenous opposition had been quashed, and the indigenous nations had been consigned to the political and economic margins of the colony with whatever legal, quasi-legal, and extralegal means were necessary, it became a source of secure and profitable investment for British capital. It even became a source of low-cost military "assistance" as the British called on colonial "possessions" for support in various military adventures from the Boer War onward.

What makes the case of Aotearoa/New Zealand somewhat different is that less than 150 years after European, or Pākehā, settlers had dominated Māori and had put in place the foundations of an Anglocentric monoculture, their descendants are attempting to reestablish a bicultural nation founded on undertakings made in a treaty by their ancestors, which was largely ignored for some 130 years. Contemporary Māori and Pākehā are engaged in the conscious establishment of a political and social partnership of the type which was, paradoxically, envisaged by the founding document of the nation, the Treaty of Waitangi,[2] but never achieved. This reinvention is not simple. To constitute a new nation, both parties must overcome decades of social conditioning and admit to facts that had been deliberately and accidentally overlooked. But, difficult though this process may be, many involved believe that this process of acknowledgement of the past must occur before the future is secure. Like the Truth and Reconciliation Commission of postapartheid South Africa, the Waitangi Tribunal systematically investigates the claims of those who were, for decades, deprived of property and various rights, and recommends to the state ways of compensating those people. The hearing process and the findings are public, and expose all citizens to a new version of the nation's history, in which previously silenced voices are heard, and claims once ignored are verified and affirmed. This is the history that all must acknowledge to create a new bicultural nation.

This process is interesting because it has moved a relatively long way relatively quickly and with little of the political and social upheaval that often accompanies shifts in power relations within a state. Second, while much of the impetus for a "review" of the nation's history has always come from Māori elders and, more recently, Māori intellectuals, much of the momentum has been maintained by the Crown and the Courts of New Zealand. These institutions, which were once agents of colonial domination, have recently delivered a series of judgments that have validated Māori claims and have constrained the rights of the Crown to act without due regard for the rights of Māori. This chapter is about the social and political elements that make this case at once both similar and yet different from those of other White settler colonies.

Discovery and settlement of Aotearoa

Around 1200 A.D., Polynesian seafarers left Rarotonga, in what are now the Cook Islands, on a southerly voyage to a land they would call Aotearoa.[3] Why they left when they did remains a source of speculation, but that they explored, settled, named, and gradually populated that land is well-documented. The new land was significantly larger than their homeland, contained a wider range of flora and fauna, and a range of climates from the subtropical north to the cooler south. The new arrivals' principal challenge was to adjust their social organization and agricultural processes to these novel conditions and to harness the potential of the new natural resources. Large areas of fertile land, mature forests, productive rivers, and bountiful marine resources, allowed the newly arrived groups to grow without exerting significant pressure on the ecosystem.

The crews of each of the canoes founded tribes that settled around the coastline initially. Their descendants remained loosely affiliated groups known as a *waka*. These grew over time and divided into *iwi*, or tribes consisting typically of the descendants of various leaders of the original expedition. The *iwi* dispersed and settled around the point of arrival where their descendants remain today.[4] They became so closely associated with particular localities that they identified themselves by reference to a particular river, a mountain, and a chief. As *iwi* grew their day-to-day coordination became difficult. They split, in turn, into *hapū* or sub-tribes, which became the basic economic and social units that cooperated to undertake tasks which were beyond the capacity of the smallest units of Māori society, the *whānau*, or extended family.[5]

With land available for expansion there was, initially, little pressure on resources and little economic reason for tribes to come into conflict. This situation changed as tribal populations expanded and the control of certain valued natural resources generated increasing conflict between tribes. Intertribal wars became a significant feature of Māori society and involved even closely related *hapū*. Intertribal wars, while relatively frequent, were not hugely destructive. They typically involved small forces using a variety of wooden and stone weapons in close combat. The wars did, however, lead to the taking of slaves, property, and the occupation of land of the defeated parties. Social honor, *mana*, however, meant that acts that humiliated a tribe and its chiefs had to be avenged and led to retaliatory action, or *utu*. Thus, while no single action was necessarily destructive, ongoing retaliation could be. The political and economic risks of unchecked retaliation were recognized and "managed" through strategic marriages between senior members of the tribes or subtribes involved.[6]

Māori society developed efficient means of exploiting available resources. New means of creating and preserving food surpluses allowed it to support the development of specialist skills and knowledges that were transmitted by specialists, or *tohunga*, in schools known as *wānanga*. Protected by remoteness from introduced diseases, the population expanded steadily without significant pressure on its ecosystem by settling more remote inland areas and offshore islands. While some resources, such as the large flightless birds known as *moa* (*Dinornis maximus*), were extinguished by the Māori, others were protected by periodic conservation bans imposed to protect fisheries and forests. At the end of the eighteenth century, the ecosystem supported between 150,000 and 200,000 people. But this was soon to end.

The rediscovery of Aotearoa

The Dutch explorer Tasman "discovered" Aotearoa in 1642 and, without consulting its inhabitants, renamed it Staten Landt, and later, Nieuw Zeeland. James Cook visited in 1769 and again, without consultation, claimed it for England. Over three visits, he mapped the land and documented its economic potential. After Cook's expedition's record was published, the land's existence and economic potential became more widely known. Whalers and sealers began to settle around the South Island coast and, in a prelude of what was to follow, introduced the first major epidemic in the 1790s. Their reports stimulated further interest and, by the early nineteenth century, informal European settlement, drawn by whales and timber, had commenced in the North Island.

A mission was established in 1814 in the North to introduce the Gospel, and to protect Māori from the moral depredations of the European whalers, sealers, "traders," and escapees from New South Wales penal settlements who began to establish a presence.[7] The missionaries and Māori leaders became concerned about the destabilizing effects of these often-dissolute elements that introduced disease, liquor, and weapons, which threatened Māori society. In 1820, some northern chiefs acquired muskets and embarked on a series of punishing campaigns against their traditional enemies that lasted a decade and underscored the destabilizing potential of this new population and its technology.

The chiefs, and some missionaries, became increasingly aware of colonial powers' interests in annexing Aotearoa, and private companies' interests in acquiring land for large-scale, organized settlement. Of these companies, Edward Gibbon Wakefield's New Zealand Company was the most significant. Wakefield believed that organized settlement of New Zealand was "one answer to the massive problem of the condition of England."[8] As Miller noted,

> Wakefield concluded that there was little room in England for the profitable investment of any more capital, that intense competition among

investors tended to reduce profits to a very low rate, and that the small capitalist was less likely to survive that the large capitalist . . . Wakefield followed Adam Smith, the great master, in advocating an expanding economy as the best means of solving England's economic problems. New countries, Wakefield believed, had an important advantage over old countries in that they were not yet subject to the law of diminishing returns.[9]

Aware of the increasing support in England for Wakefield's scheme, and concerned about the possibility of a further influx of settlers, a group of twenty-four chiefs, encouraged by the British Resident, designed and adopted a flag as a symbol of their "national" identity in 1834.[10] A year later, thirty-four northern chiefs, aided and encouraged by missionaries, formally declared the independence of Nu Tireni, a Māori rendering of New Zealand, in the name of the United Tribes of New Zealand in 1835, in an attempt to establish their sovereignty and their right to regulate settlement and government in Aotearoa.[11]

When it became clear that these acts alone would not achieve their ends, some Church Missionary Society clergy promoted the idea of a compact with the British among their Māori followers. They then promoted "Māori" willingness to enter a compact with the British. However, their assessment of the Māori willingness to cede sovereignty rested on some significant misinterpretation of the bases of Māori interest in a compact.[12] The British government had, up until this point, resisted pressure to establish a colony on the grounds that,

Great Britain has no legal or moral right to establish a Colony in New Zealand, without the free consent of the Natives, deliberately given, without Compulsion, and without Fraud. To impart to any Individuals an Authority to establish such a Colony, without first ascertaining the consent of the New Zealanders, or without taking the most effectual security that the Contract which is to be made with them shall freely and fairly be made, would, as it should seem, be to make an unrighteous use of our superior Power.[13]

Confronted by what McHugh called "overwhelming necessity," the British government reluctantly agreed to establish British rule in New Zealand as long as the "free consent of Māori" was obtained as the consular instructions issued to Captain Hobson made clear,

As far as it is possible to establish such connexion with them, it is right that their title to be regarded as one independent Community should be observed in fact as well as acknowledged in theory. The Queen disclaims any pretension to regard their land as vacant Territory open to the first future occupant, or to establish within any part of New Zealand a sovereignty to the erection of which the free consent of the natives shall not have been previously given.[14]

British government representatives arrived in the country in the same year as those of the New Zealand Company arrived to acquire land for European settlements.

The Treaty of Waitangi

British representatives and some Māori chiefs negotiated a treaty, the Treaty of Waitangi, in which Māori ceded sovereignty[15] to the English crown in return for the rights of British citizens and were guaranteed undisturbed possession of all of their lands, fisheries, and other valued "assets" or *taonga*.[16] The Treaty was signed in the north in February 1840 and by some, but by no means all, other chiefs throughout the land in succeeding months. The apparent Māori support won the commitment of the British crown, whose agents could not have appreciated the complexities of Māori social organization. The second article of the Treaty was supposed to create an orderly land market by ensuring that Māori sold only such land as they chose, at times of their choosing and at an agreed price, and only to the Crown. The Crown would survey land, issue title, and resell it and would, in the process, improve relations between the Treaty "partners" that had deteriorated over earlier, unregulated land dealings.[17]

In these new, ordered circumstances, a set of policies known as "amalgamation" could be pursued, in which settler and Māori counterparts became legally and socially equal members of a new "amalgamated" colonial society. In the new society, Māori would live alongside European settlers in a bicultural society until they chose to opt for the advantages of "European civilization," as most Europeans simply assumed they would.[18] At that time, Māori would be free to enter and would be welcomed by European society.

While the Treaty and the policy of amalgamation was a genuine attempt to provide an honorable and just solution to a problem, it could not ultimately protect Māori interests for, as the historian Ward notes,

> In that these policies . . . assumed a high level of capability in Pacific People and stood ready to meet their desire to participate in the institutions of the new order, they were liberal and progressive. Their very great weakness was that they were underlain by undoubted convictions of the superiority of English institutions, and conversely by a disastrously limited appreciation of local values, of local peoples' possible preference for their own institutions and of the difficulties they would incur in adapting to new responsibilities and obligations. Though altruistically conceived, amalgamation policies could, in doctrinaire hands, become as oppressive as settler self-interest.[19]

Most Pākehā settlers had little doubt of their "culture's" superiority, as the historian Angela Ballara notes, Most European settlers coming to New Zealand assumed that theirs was a superior "civilized" race which could only have a beneficial effect on the Māori population. The settlers liked to see themselves as the harbingers of civilisation to the barbarian, and even maintained the fiction that this was the purpose of their coming.[20]

It is hardly surprising then that settlers resented the idea that Māori were their equals, the assignment of the rights of equals to the Māori, and in particular, the right to dispose of such land as they chose at times and at prices of their choosing.

The Treaty could not subvert the determination and greed of settlers who had been promised farmland, and who now sought more land to supply expanding, lucrative markets in Australia. While Māori sold some land, most were reluctant to alienate lands with which they were intimately associated, which were fundamental elements of their social identity, and on which some were making significant profits from supplying food to European settlements in New Zealand and Australia.[21] Settlers, jealous of Māori commercial success and hungry for land, increased pressure on the colonial government to secure more land. They pressed for abandonment of the policy of amalgamation, which assigned Māori the rights of equals, and the Treaty of Waitangi, which guaranteed these. The colony's newspapers served settlers' interests by pressuring colonial politicians. Their arguments were in some cases general ones, which challenged the assumptions of the policy of amalgamation. The editor of the *Southern Cross*, for instance, complained that "in the attempt to govern the natives we have made a false start. He was treated as if his mental constitution and moral nature were identical with our own race. The reverse being the case, we have signally failed."[22] Before long, these views were being echoed by colonial politicians, such as the influential J.C. Richmond who in 1851 wrote,

> I imagine that a day will come not long hence, when the preposterous Waitangi treaty will be overruled . . . and the ridiculous claims of the native to thousands of thousands acres of untrodden bush & fern will no longer be able to damp the ardour & cramp the energies of the industrious white man.[23]

The settler challenges to the policy also focused on the Māori reluctance to "use" all of their lands for commercial production and their reluctance to release it to those who would. They were offended by the Māori reluctance to embrace the *Pākehā* work ethic, and their open criticism of the European connection between work and moral improvement. As the *Auckland Star* observed,

> They ridicule the intense earnestness, the feverish anxiety and unrest, the sometimes bitter spirit of competition and rivalry, the grudgings and graspings of the *Pākehā* neighbours, who in this way live miserably that they may at last die comfortable.[24]

The Land Wars

The scene was set for a collision of Māori and *Pākehā* interests that would transform Māori society. In 1844, wars began in the north, in 1860 in Taranaki, and in 1863 in the Waikato. The wars broke out where Māori refused to sell land that settlers wanted. British forces confronted Māori ones in a number of areas.

Māori forces were accustomed to fighting in heavy bush and to constructing fortified hilltop settlements which could be occupied and defended against infantry attacks. Their military ability won the respect of the British military command, which was forced to bring in more forces and to enlist Māori allies[25] to gain advantage in the wars. The wars continued in various parts of the country until 1872, when one of the central figures, Te Kooti Arikirangi, retreated with his forces into the central region in the North Island and armed resistance ceased.

The Land Wars were represented as a series of European victories but recent research has shown that this was not generally true.[26] As Belich notes,

> Māori military achievement was mythologized into a more acceptable form. Māori which won most of the battles in the New Zealand Wars of the 1860s, usually at long odds in numbers and weaponry. Their courage and chivalry was often praised by Europeans, but the real key to their success was papered over. This key was the invention of trench warfare which negated European advantages. Such inventions were supposed to be another European monopoly.[27]

In fact, Māori "had to be defeated" for propaganda purposes, but Māori resistance, both active and passive, continued until long after the wars and impeded British settlement. The wars did, however, provide the *Pākehā* with two benefits: the apparent confirmation of their military, and, by implication, racial "superiority," and the "legal" excuse needed to engage in the systematic expropriation of such remaining Māori land as they considered "necessary." After the wars, land losses accelerated as an increasing range of "legal" devices, which Kelsey calls legal imperialism, were contrived to expropriate Māori land.[28]

As the historian Alan Ward noted,

> . . . the settlers wanted the land, and the law was continually framed to deny Māori more than a minor share in state power and control of resources. That most precious institution of British culture, the rule of law, was prostituted to the land grab, and brought into contempt in which many Māori today regrettably still hold it.[29]

Despite this, throughout the latter part of the nineteenth century, Māori leaders had also attempted to recover control of their situation by peaceful means. In an attempt to coordinate the activity of Māori, the idea of a Māori monarchy was canvassed in 1853 and, in 1858, the first king, Potatau I, was installed. Various Māori movements continued to attempt to resist European encroachment by active means, such as the formation of *Te Kingitanga* or King Movement in the Waikato, by passive resistance such as Te Whiti's community in Taranaki, and by forming religious movements such as the *Ringatu* and *Ratana* faiths.[30] Without a history of pan-tribal cooperation, and with difficult communication, establishing and managing pan-tribal movements was always going to be difficult. Limited success was attained when, in 1892, the first national Māori Parliament, the *Kotahitanga*, or Unity, assembled to take control of their political and social destiny.[31]

It was clear to some Māori leaders that they would have to press their political claims through the parliamentary process. However, although Māori political representation had been guaranteed since 1867, it was confined to four "Māori" seats out of eighty seats in the national parliament. As long as Māori could enroll and vote only in those four "Māori" electorates, their political impact in Parliament was bound to be limited. Despite Māori leaders' vision and their willingness to engage in national politics, the combination of declining population and continuing land loss meant that Māori, by then a minority in their own land and deprived of their traditional leadership and economic resources, were unable to assert an effective role in shaping their destiny.

The decline and marginalization of the Māori

Less than sixty years after signing of the Treaty of Waitangi, Māori had become a marginalized and demoralized people. For most Māori, the ideal of partnership between equals, to which they had signed on in the Treaty of Waitangi, had been betrayed by the European. Despite the Treaty's provisions, and the promises of those who promoted it to them, Māori had lost control of much of their land and of their lives. By the end of the nineteenth century, twenty million hectares, comprising almost the entire South Island and two thirds of the North Island, had passed to the Crown and private European owners. Māori had lost land as a consequence of military conquest and post-Land War confiscations by the Crown, and through a combination of sales, fraud, and legal imperialism.

Colonization depended on the individualization of title to land so that it could be surveyed and sold with clear title. The notion of land as a commodity and the consequences of new inheritance laws were new to Māori. Māori had not "owned" land: they had been assigned rights to use land that formed part of their tribal estate. Rights to use tribal land lapsed at death and were reassigned on the basis of need. The application of principles of English land tenure to Māori land, and of English inheritance laws to Māori estates by successive governments continued throughout the latter part of the nineteenth century. Few Māori realized that if they died intestate, their estate would be divided equally among their heirs. This process resulted in the fragmentation of Māori landholdings into many relatively small and separated lots that were uneconomic to farm and which were the subject of ongoing debate over ownership.

A population, estimated at between 150,000 and 200,000 in 1769, had declined to 100,000 at 1840, as a consequence of tuberculosis, typhoid, venereal disease, measles, and wars. By 1848, the Māori population had declined to 60,000 and by the 1860s, Māori had become a minority. The Māori decline continued until 1896 when it reached its nadir at 42,000 and prompted discussions about the possibility of "extinction of the race."[32]

The population decline was paralleled by its deteriorating social and mental health. The Māori health situation was made worse by the loss of tribal estates, with which Māori tribal and personal identity was so closely associated, and increasing landlessness, which deprived Māori of economic resources on which tribal viability depended. On top of these blows to Māori society, came systematic attempts to suppress Māori language, culture, and health practices through the "Native Schools" movement, which was chosen as the vehicle for the assimilation of the Māori into the European "culture." This was a consequence of growing support for the idea that Māori were, in Belich's words, "superior kind of inferior, a particularly European-like and convertible savage, destined to be honoured by full and equal assimilation into *Pākehā* society."[33] These ideas gained support from the publication of a book entitled, "Aryan Māori," by a civil servant, Edward Tregear, which "argued that Māori were not only European-like, but of European descent, the forgotten suntanned wing of and Aryan diaspora from the Orkneys to Stewart Island."[34] J.H. Pope, the architect of the Native Schools system, believed "that the Māori could be rapidly and painlessly Europeanized and that virtual identity between the people would be achieved and the Māori absorbed at no distant date."[35]

Not all *Pākehā* were, however, as sanguine as Pope about the future of the Māori population. But few were distressed by either its decline or its demoralized state, which was widely referred to as "degeneration." Indeed, many *Pākehā* regarded it as a "natural" consequence of Māori failure to adopt the advantages of "civilization." As Ballara notes,

> The causes of Māori population decline were widely discussed, but in popular opinion the favoured reasons for it were all ones which put the onus of depopulation on the Māori people themselves. . . . They did not recognise that this 'degeneration' was the outward symptom of a process in Māori society that was the direct consequence of their own activities. Landlessness, poverty, lack of opportunities to break out of poverty save through land-selling were the causes of dislocation, the most obvious symptoms of which were disease, drinking, and apathy.[36]

The early twentieth century

Early in the twentieth century, most Māori remained in rural areas in which they had traditionally lived. Land alienation continued: Māori farmers lost a further five million of their remaining eight million hectares and Parliaments continued to pass laws to secure access to the rest.[37] Widespread publicity of the decline of the Māori eventually had an impact on the Māori who came, in some cases, to accept the pessimistic prognoses of their future and saw little prospect of successfully obtaining justice and redress for injustice from an unjust and racist population, which was by then numerically, politically, economically, and socially dominant.

In the closing years of the nineteenth century and early years of the twentieth century, a generation of younger, well-educated, and politically aware Māori leaders, which included lawyers, doctors, warriors, and priests, united under the banner of the Young Māori Party and led by scholar and lawyer Sir Apirana Ngata began to promote a program designed to rebuild Māori society. Their task was a complicated one since it promoted engagement with, and the adoption of, certain ideas and forms from *Pākehā* culture, which many Māori blamed for their society's malaise. The historian Cox noted,

> Their philosophy . . . tended towards the emulation of *Pākehā* structures to strengthen and improve Māori society. Their task was further complicated by a desire not only to regenerate Māori society, but also to maintain the best of Māori cultural heritage and to preserve Māori spirituality.[38]

The movement's programs involved, first, public health initiatives, promoted by Māori physicians within the party, to improve Māori health status and to increase population growth. But, population growth and improvements in health status without parallel economic development were considered pointless and a second set of goals, promoted by leaders, such as Ngata, focused on using remaining Māori land more effectively to allow Māori to participate more actively in the growing economy. As a Member of Parliament, from 1905, he consolidated landholdings in his tribal area and developed large commercial farming and forestry operations, which generated new wealth and unity in his tribe. Later, as the Minister of Māori Affairs he advocated consolidating other tribes' fragmented landholdings and after 1930, with funding from government, bringing land into commercial production on the same basis as their *Pākehā* neighbors.

The Young Māori Party's political program had two elements. The first was to persuade Māori that withdrawal from national politics, which was advocated by some Māori leaders of the day on the grounds that Parliament was dominated by *Pākehā*, was futile. They argued instead that constructive engagement in national politics was the only viable route for Māori political and economic advancement. The second element of the strategy was to persuade *Pākehā* politicians to attend to the needs and rights of Māori, which they believed could be most effectively and publicly achieved by engaging in national politics. The success of members who entered national politics is credited with persuading Māori of the possibilities of constructive political engagement. As Cox notes,

> These men, building on the work of earlier Māori Parliamentarians like Sir James Carroll and Hone Heke, articulated Māori needs to *Pākehā* audiences. Through their work, *Pākehā* learned that Māori problems ought to be addressed by Māori and resolved through Māori customs and beliefs, albeit with significant modification to meet new times.[39]

The efforts of the new Māori leaders began to bear fruit. Despite earlier forecasts of the decline and demise of the Māori nation, improvements in public health and primary health care saw the Māori population began to grow again and, from 1896, the birth rate exceeded the death rate. Although it only reached its precontact levels again in 1945, 75 percent of the population remained in rural areas and, without access to some of their most productive lands, many were reduced to a combination of small-farming and laboring for *Pākehā* farmers and timber millers.

The later twentieth century

World War II was a watershed in Māori social history.[40] Māori women became involved in war-related industries in urban centers. After widespread opposition to serving in World War I, Māori men chose to participate in large numbers in World War II as members of a Māori Battalion, which served with great distinction in various European and North African theaters of war. The various companies, which comprised the Māori Battalion, were recruited from various *waka* areas and commanded largely by their own officers. The success and heroism of the Māori Battalion generated a new respect for Māori within New Zealand society. Amongst Māori, the proud record of the Battalion had a profound effect in rebuilding the self-esteem of the people.[41] At home, Māori united behind the war effort sought to organize in uniquely Māori ways to support their troops and to express their citizenship of the nation.[42] The growth of the Māori War Effort Organisation provided another site for the emergence of a new Māori leadership.

By 1945, the Māori had a body of men who had proven themselves as leaders in the 28th Māori Battalion and were ready and determined to play an active role amongst their people at home. There was also a group of Māori women who had worked in the city and had enjoyed the higher wages and greater range of options than had been available in the rural regions from which they had come. A third group who had been involved in the Māori War Effort Organisation had tasted autonomy and the pride that came with it. These men and women were not prepared to return to life as farm labor in depressed rural areas. Even if they had been, and if the land remaining in Māori hands had been converted into larger, more efficient farms, it would not have been able to support the steadily growing population. So, after the war, as politically aware Māori settled in the cities and sought more active roles in leadership, one of the most significant transformations of Māori society began.[43]

The increasing pace of Māori urbanization

Urbanization occurred because Māori wanted to move from rural areas and because new jobs were being created as the economy was being transformed from an agricultural to a more industrial one. By the 1950s, government had created a comprehensive scheme for Māori who wished to move to urban centers. Māori, drawn by higher wages, new career opportunities, better housing available on generous terms, moved in steadily growing numbers, and over a relatively short time, to the cities. In 1936, some 15 percent of the Māori population lived in urban centers; by 1945, this had risen to 26 percent; by 1956, this had risen to 37 percent; and by the mid-1960s, the figure had topped 61 percent.

The urban figure continued to rise and then flattened out in the mid-1990s at around 86 percent.

The urbanization transformed Māori social organization in several ways. Rural communities lost significant parts of their populations. The loss of youth to the cities caused a profound change in the rural societies where their energy was a vital ingredient of the economic and social organization of community life. The youth were the hunters, cooks, entertainers, gravediggers, and farmworkers for Māori farms. Many activities, which were the "glue" of rural social life, were more difficult to perform with smaller numbers of youth. Many *hapū*, for instance, found it increasingly difficult to accommodate and feed those who visited their rural *marae* for weddings, funerals, and meetings. Some of those young people who remained in rural communities became ambivalent about rural life as they compared their lifestyles with those of their urban cousins and waited for opportunities to follow them into the cities.

The steady loss of mature men and women who had proven themselves at war and in urban industries during the war, and their young families, was another serious loss to the social fabric of rural Māori society. Their leadership potential, and the future contributions of their children, were often lost to the communities as they drew steadily further from their communities as the demands of work and family reduced visits to their home *marae*. Other families were split as parents sent their young to the city and remained behind to look after their own ageing parents. Some of those who remained in rural areas did not stay back in those areas in which they had grown up and where opportunities for work were limited. Many became itinerant seasonal laborers dividing time between home communities and work on shearing and forestry gangs, and as fruit and tobacco pickers moving wherever there was work.

But, if the impact of the exodus on rural Māori tribal communities was serious, its impact on emerging urban Māori communities was even more serious. Those youth who left rural communities were separated from their language and traditions and, under pressure to assimilate, became progressively less proficient in these areas. Many Māori migrants had limited formal education, few job qualifications, and were victims of employer racism. These three factors confined the migrants to a narrow range of semi- and unskilled work. By 1976, 39 percent of all Māori were engaged in manufacturing and a further 29 percent of men were found in transport and communication.

Initially, the consequences of this pattern of occupational concentration were limited. Full employment in the booming postwar economy guaranteed relatively high incomes, which were protected by labor unions. The government housing programs ensured that urban Māori were well-housed, at least in comparison with rural housing to which they were accustomed, on very reasonable terms. Increasing numbers took advantage of employment training schemes and concessionary home ownership programs to acquire urban property and, in the process, became committed to a more urban lifestyle. Children too found a wider range of educational opportunities available in urban schools and more ready access to higher levels of education than was available in rural areas. Some commentators argue that Māori acceptance of this situation reflected a satisfaction with the new-found improvement in their situation. But this was not to last.

Cultural resurgence

A rapidly growing, better educated, and increasingly organized Māori population, which, from 1975 on, was able to enroll to vote in "general electorates" and increasingly did so, was able to exert more influence in both national and local politics. Leadership was provided by both individuals and urban political organizations, such as the New Zealand Māori Council, Māori Women's Welfare League, the New Zealand Māori Council, the Māori Graduates' Organisation, the Māori Organisation on Human Rights, Nga Tamatoa (the Young Warriors), the Māori branches of organized political parties, and the labor movement. These increasingly well-organized political forces began to develop and to articulate their social, political, and economic claims and objectives more clearly and more forcefully throughout the 1960s and 1970s.[44]

Their claims gained increasing moral force from the work of Māori scholars and academic historians who were beginning to locate, study, and publicize evidence of widespread illegal and fraudulent conduct by *Pākehā* in their dealings with Māori. In doing so, these scholars were beginning to deconstruct and challenge the central claims of the political ideology that had guaranteed *Pākehā* social and political dominance for over a century. In their place, Māori constructed a series of counter claims that pointed to the *Pākehā* failure to honor the Treaty, using evidence of deliberate, systematic abrogation of its provisions. These claims became embodied in a counter ideology that took a variety of forms.[45] Of these, one — entitled Māori *Sovereignty* — by Donna Awatere, a former opera-singer and psychologist, and a daughter of the former commander of the Māori Battalion, was arguably the most powerful and important. Donna Awatere took the government's own official data and showed that ever since contact with *Pākehā*, and despite the existence of guarantees contained in the Treaty of Waitangi, the psychological, social, economic, political, and epidemiological situation of Māori had deteriorated progressively.[46]

The success of Māori *Sovereignty* as counter ideology rested on its turning the commonly accepted explanation of the "Māori Problem" on its head. *Māori Sovereignty* argued that the contemporary situation of the Māori was, in fact, a "*Pākehā* problem." *Pākehā*, and not Māori, conduct was the cause of their marginalized situation. The *Pākehā* "justice system" had been used to deny Māori justice. *Pākehā* administration had made the Māori situation progressively worse because it had served the interests of *Pākehā* capital and had, in the process, denied Māori rights guaranteed by the Treaty. The remedy was deceptively simple. Nothing short of reclamation of Māori social, political, and economic sovereignty, *te tino rangatiratanga*, promised in and guaranteed by the Treaty of Waitangi could lead to the restoration of their rightful position as *mana* Māori *motuhake* with *mana tangata*, as a separate, autonomous, and sovereign nation within the nation. Similar, but more sustained and refined, arguments from Māori scholars, such as the anthropologist Dr. Ranginui Walker and linguist Dr. Pat Hohepa added intellectual momentum to the cause.[47]

These analyses gained increasing support among Māori and Ballara noted that,

> At many levels, and through many institutions, a reassertion of cultural integrity took place. This movement was achieved by different methods under different leaders, but all alike, from Sir Graham Latimer and the Māori Councils and Kara Puketapu and the Māori Affairs Department at one end of the established order, to the leaders of gangs and radical activists at the other had basically similar goals. . . .
>
> [T]he similarity of the aims of all Māori groups working for Māori cultural autonomy, is not always noticed. . . . But in 1980 there was no great difference, for example, between the expressed aims of *Mana Motuhake*, the newest Māori political party, and the views of the National Party's Māori Vice-President, M Searanke.[48]

In articulating these claims, the new Māori leaders were continuing, and extending, a long tradition started by earlier Māori leaders of seeking formal recognition and ratification of the Treaty of Waitangi and the investigation and redress of certain matters that were found to have violated either the letter or the spirit of the Treaty or both.[49]

The belated *Pākehā* response

The Labour Party, which had a long-standing political alliance with the Ratana Church and was generally considered more sympathetic to Māori interests, had promised statutory recognition of the Treaty of Waitangi in its 1972 election manifesto. In 1975, and spurred on by a march on Parliament by some 45,000 mainly Māori people led by a charismatic octogenarian who was to become known as the "mother of the nation," the government passed the Treaty of Waitangi Act, 1975. That legislation established the Waitangi Tribunal a quasi-judicial body, which was empowered to investigate claims for breaches of the Treaty from that date on and to advise government on appropriate forms of redress. The Act was an important one because, as the historian W.H. Oliver noted,

> The Waitangi Tribunal came into existence after a long period of 135 years during which the treaty that it was charged to apply to Māori grievances had already had a dual history. On the Māori side the Treaty had been consistently invoked and appealed to; on the *Pākehā* side it had been forgotten or ignored. In the mid-twentieth century these two traditions began to converge as, at length, the Māori viewpoint made an impact upon *Pākehā* awareness.[50]

But Māori immediately pointed out that the Tribunal, which could only investigate matters that had occurred since 1975, could do little to redress the most serious violations of the Treaty involving land alienation, which had occurred during the 1800s. In 1985, the government enacted amending legislation, which enlarged the Tribunal and allowed it to investigate claims, and to recommend to government, redress for all breaches that had occurred since the Treaty of Waitangi was enacted in 1840. This new Act led to the lodging of 86 new claims on behalf of tribes from throughout the country. Each claim had to be supported by evidence from research and the result was an explosion of interest in the historical record.

The research carried out for claims to the Waitangi Tribunal, the publication of the reports of the tribunal's hearings, and the growing body of historical and legal scholarship, exposed the nature and extent of *Pākehā* fraudulence and bad faith to all who could, and would, read them.[51] This undoubtedly led to a more widespread understanding and acceptance, by *Pākehā*, of the validity of Māori claims of systematic injustices committed over 150 years, and more general acceptance of the need to redress these acts. The Māori case did not, however, rest solely on *Pākehā* goodwill.

Legal scholarship was proceeding apace and a new generation of academic lawyers, well versed in international law, began to revisit the conventional interpretations of the legal status of the Treaty of Waitangi. A number argued, on the basis of a growing body of international legal scholarship on treaties, that an 1877 judgment by Chief Judge Prendergast, saying that the Treaty was a nullity, was wrong in law.[52] McHugh argued that because the original Prendergast decision had failed to take proper account of established colonial law, it was defective as were all subsequent rulings that had depended on it (McHugh 1994). These arguments gave new authority to the Treaty and challenged the government, and the society, to give substance to these realizations. In the event, the Waitangi Tribunal took the lead and argued as Sorrenson, drawing on the Tribunal decision, has noted,

> The Treaty was not to be regarded as simply a tract for its time, "A Māori Magna Carta. . . . It was not intended to merely fossilise a status quo, but to provide a direction for future growth and development." It was to be "the foundation for a developing social contract." That contract was not what Hobson had hoped, the formation of a single people, but rather the coexistence of two peoples within a single nation. "The Treaty was acknowledgement of Māori existence, of their prior occupation of the land and of an intent that the Māori presence would remain and be respected. . . . It established the regime, not for uni-culturalism but for bi-culturalism."[53]

The legal standing of the Treaty was soon tested. In 1987, Māori, concerned that the Crown proposed to dispose of land and assets, which could be used to settle claims against it, went to the Court of Appeal. In the case, *The Māori Council vs The Attorney General*, their claims were confirmed by the Court of Appeal. The Court asserted that a special relationship of ongoing partnership exists between Māori and the Crown requiring the partners to act reasonably and in utmost good faith to one another.[54] This bound the Crown in significant ways and prevented it from disposing of Crown assets that were the subject of Māori claims or which could be used in settlement of claims. The Court of Appeal also restated what Māori had believed since 1840, which was that the Treaty of Waitangi was the foundation of the modern nation within which Māori were equal partners, and in which their culture, language, and land rights were supposed to have been protected.[55] The formal, legal, and political recognition of the Treaty has reestablished its national significance.

Successive governments have, since 1975, moved to address some of the grievances and have acknowledged the necessity of addressing many more. Successive administrations have, since 1978, attempted to operationalize the principles of biculturalism in social policy with varying degrees of success. These efforts have attempted to identify and embody Māori aspirations in government policy and to involve Māori in the formulation and administration of "Māori policy."

The responsibility for the first attempts fell to the then Māori Affairs Department, which policy analyst Fleras noted was instrumental in devolving government programs to local Māori authorities.

> The success of this partnership thrust was reflected in programmes such as Kohanga Reo[56] and Matua Whangai,[57] in addition to various trade and employment training schemes. The inception of a community-based and culturally-sensitive development philosophy also sparked interest in the potential of whanau-hapu-iwi structures as viable channels for renewal. . . . By 1986, the Department had stepped up efforts to "de-institutionalise" Māori clients by devolving many of its community services and land administration functions to iwi structures. In spite of these reforms, the Māori Affairs' Department slipped into decline in part because it was unable to control the liberating forces it had set in motion.[58]

With steadily rising Māori expectations of greater autonomy, the government moved to restructure Māori Affairs in three stages around the newly defined role of the Treaty. The new Ministry or Māori Affairs, *Manatu Māori*, sought "To give substance to the principle of partnership embodied in the Treaty of Waitangi by generating an environment which encourages Māori people to express their *rangatiratanga* in ways that enhance new Zealand's economic, social and cultural life."[59]

The Ministry was to advise government on law and policy. The operations of Māori Affairs were to be transferred to the Iwi Transition Authority, *te Tira Ahu*

Iwi. The third part of the restructured administration was the Iwi Empowering Bill, which was to confer legal authority to recognized *Iwi* structures to allow them to contract with government to provide a range of services. As the Minister of Māori Affairs noted, "Underlying all Government policy for Māori development is devolution. This recognition of Iwi as equal partners in Government, and the participation of tribal organisations in the planning of Māori people's destiny, fulfils the guarantee of Rangatiratanga in the Treaty of Waitangi."[60]

In 1992, the Ministry for Māori Development, *Te Puni Kokiri*, was established and made responsible for advising the Crown on means of obtaining parity between Māori and non-Māori.[61] The Ministry has separate branches to advise government on Economic Development, Treaty Compliance, Social Policy, Regional Development, implications of Law Reform, and Monitoring and Evaluation of government agencies and programs.

Māori have demanded, and won, opportunities to define their own objectives and to be involved in design and administration of the processes designed to deliver these. They have also won the right to administer some government resources to provide services to Māori populations through "flax roots" organizations, such as tribal committees, or *rūnanga*, on the basis that they can provide more appropriate services more effectively and improve Māori outcomes in such areas as health, education, and welfare.[62] In this respect, Māori have won a much greater degree of autonomy over certain state activities than they have enjoyed since contact.

Māori have also founded independent, autonomous organizations to avoid both the fact and the appearance of dependence on the state. A national organization, the Māori Congress,[63] was formed in 1990 to find ways of advancing Māori interests. The Congress comprises representatives of forty-five tribes and provides a national forum for representatives to address economic, social, cultural, and political issues affecting Māori within a Māori cultural framework. The Congress promotes constitutional and legislative arrangements designed to enable Māori to control their development and reclaim their right to self-determination, or *tino rangatiratanga*, within New Zealand.[64] The recent adoption of a form of new proportional electoral system has significantly increased the level of Māori representation in the national parliament, and the growth of increasingly effective Māori political lobbies undoubtedly hastened this reform process. This success has produced its own changes. Much Māori political activity has moved from the *marae* and streets, into courtrooms, tribunals, Parliamentary Select Committees, professional associations, political parties, and trade unions where Māori increasingly believe their social and political objectives are most likely to be achieved.

There is now, ironically, also a prospect that further progress may be hindered by tension among Māori. Treaty settlements have resulted in return of significant amounts of cash and assets to properly constituted tribal authorities, which represent the descendants of the signatories to the Treaty. Many urban Māori have lost contact with their tribal roots and have become members of new, urban "pan-tribal" organizations, which represent their interests in negotiations with government and provide a range of social services. These urban Māori organizations are seeking, on behalf of their urban constituents, the right to share in the distributions of the resources that flow from Treaty settlements. The leaders of these urban Māori organizations argue that urban Māori are also descendants of the Treaty signatories and are entitled to share the benefits of settlements, and that the urban organizations are best placed to identify, understand, and to provide for their needs.

Part of the argument advanced in support of this claim is that these new urban Māori entities are the Māori tribes of the present. Their members live in, and identify with, particular locales, have a common history, have *marae* or tribal meeting places and *whare nui* or meeting houses, which both establish their connection with the place and embody their *mana*. These urban entities provide social and economic support for their members in the ways which tribes did earlier. On the other side of the debate are the leaders of traditional tribes who contend that only the tribal entities that existed at the time of the signing of the Treaty of Waitangi, can receive these resources since they are the descendants of the signatories to the Treaty.

It is, however, significant that the debates are no longer about whether Māori tribal structures will survive, but rather about the most appropriate form for these in the beginning of the twenty-first century, and that these debates are being controlled by Māori themselves. It is also significant that those involved on both sides of this debate are prepared to accept, sometimes reluctantly, that institutions created by the state, such as the court system and tribunals, may ultimately be trusted to resolve some of these issues. While progress is occurring, it is not proceeding as quickly as either government or Māori would like. But it may be too fast for many *Pākehā*.

The "Problem" for *Pākehā*

While recent governments' actions have combined to produce some reconciliation of Māori concerns, the Director of the Waitangi Tribunal, Buddy Mikaere, pointed out that the "Treaty cannot make a nation. To do that we need to be children of our country's past."[65]

This is where the problem, and the challenge, for the nation lie. The *Pākehā*, whose claims to dominate and manage a monocultural nation whilst ignoring the claims of Māori to equality within a bicultural one went largely unchallenged for 140 years, have now to confront their history. They have to accept that the legal and moral foundations of their domination of social, economic, and political life were, and remain, clearly shaky. They have also to acknowledge that the power and privilege that *Pākehā* have enjoyed were won at the cost of injustice to the Māori. Those *Pākehā* who have been accustomed to the benefits of dominance and who were, until recently, secure in the belief that their privileges were built on a history of solid pioneering endeavor on the part of their forebears, have huge problems in accepting that this version of history is probably not the truth.

This challenge to the place and authority of *Pākehā* within the nation has led to a body of scholarship in which the meaning of being *Pākehā* in postcolonial Aotearoa was explored.[66] For, as one of the leading writers, historian Michael King noted, "To be a citizen of Aotearoa in the 1980s, even a *Pākehā* one, is to inevitably affected by the enlarging Māori presence and the renaissance of Māori rituals and values — something my European ancestors never experienced (King 1985)."[67]

Others sought to go beyond statements of novelty, and to define what this new identity might embody. Schroeder, for instance, argued that being *Pākehā*, "means being prepared to acknowledge that the colonising values, procedures, priorities and structures were, and in many respects still are, unashamedly monocultural. To be a *Pākehā* in Aotearoa in 1986 means to begin taking seriously the prospect of sharing power and inevitably giving up power, and looking to a future which must involve a more equitable use of power."[68]

Since these early attempts to define the meaning of a *Pākehā* identity, the process has continued and the more recent formulations have refined both the concept and the conduct it implies.[69]

While some *Pākehā* find this reformulated identity relatively easy to accept, many more find it extremely difficult.[70] While some continue to reject this reinterpretation of the nation's history, denial has become increasingly difficult in the face of a growing body of evidence. This evidence of illegality of their forebears' actions, generated, ironically, by *Pākehā* academic historians and lawyers from the official record; affirmed in decisions from the *Pākehā*-dominated High Court, Court of Appeal, and Privy Council; and acknowledged by a succession of *Pākehā*-dominated governments is increasingly difficult to ignore or deny.

This dilemma for those individuals who would deny history is likely to remain a private one. While a few individuals and social and political movements have protested that the present generation should not be expected to pay for the shortcomings of their forebears, these claims have not enjoyed widespread public support.[71] The agendas of the major political parties in national politics focus on how, rather than whether, to redress the grievances of the past so that healing can commence, and how to produce a truly bicultural nation in place of an essentially monocultural one.

In the meantime, the education system, once the vehicle for the assimilationist policies of colonial governments, has become the vehicle for the re-education of a new generation of the nation's children. The myths, which sustained a history that "explained" the inevitability of a nation founded on the values and worldview of the *Pākehā*, have been quietly removed and relegated in their turn to history. In their place is "new" history, that starts with the Treaty of Waitangi and explains why a partnership between Māori and *Pākehā* must be the foundation for the nation. The new history explains why the nation's culture must respect and incorporate both societies' worldviews and practices. The history of the nation to which they are exposed is one that has the potential to make them "the children of the nation's past." Whether or not such a radical transformation can occur within a single generation has yet to be seen, but the early signs are promising.

Conclusion

The last two centuries have been turbulent ones for the Māori population. At one point, it seemed that they might lose their identity as population decline, intermarriage, and assimilationist policies of successive governments eroded their social organization and economic base to the point that governments were faced, at the beginning of the twentieth century, with charges of genocide. Since then, Māori have made a steady recovery and now constitute 16 percent of the total population. They are one of the fastest growing and most politically assertive segments of the population of Aotearoa. A combination of effective Māori political activity, growing electoral significance of Māori, and increasing *Pākehā* awareness of the need to redress the consequences of past has led to a transformation of the situation of Māori at the beginning of the twenty-first century.

The gaps between Māori and non-Māori populations are closing, and their future as a people is assured.[72] The Māori language has been reaffirmed as an official national language and a network of 690 language nests or *Kohanga Reo*, and bilingual programs in primary and secondary schools and tertiary institutions are reviving the language. Traditional tribal and subtribal entities are reestablishing and strengthening their leadership structures or *rūnanga* and looking to reclaim and redeploy tribal land and other assets for the benefit of their members, and to obtain funds from government to provide alternative, and more culturally appropriate, services for their members. Newer urban Māori authorities are establishing themselves as modern tribes and are contracting with government to provide a range of culturally appropriate educational, medical, employment, and advisory services to their urbanized Māori member clients. Māori identity is becoming a valued personal and social identity, and one which provides the basis for a widening range of claims against the state for recognition and redress of past injustices.

At the same time, many *Pākehā* face their own challenges as they come to comprehend and even accept the significance of a history that was conveniently obscured from them until some twenty years ago. They have now to acknowledge that the conventional explanations of their dominance with which they grew up were fundamentally flawed and that the legitimacy of their political, economic, and social domination is now contested. They are confronted with increasingly frequent challenges to their domination in a range of social spheres in the name of biculturalism. *Pākehā* are called on to acknowledge the centrality of the Treaty of Waitangi, to share their power in the name of bicultural partnership, and to accept the redistribution of part of the nation's resources to redress injustices of the past. Furthermore, this dramatic shift has all happened relatively suddenly.

In many places, such a challenge might have produced a determined backlash on the part of the dominant group. In this case, there is little evidence of such a backlash. Perhaps this is because so many New Zealanders have affiliations with both sides of the "divide." The long history of Māori–Pākehā intermarriage has blurred the boundaries and created linkages that reach across them. Intermarriage commenced early in the history of the nation, and gained momentum in the middle of the twentieth century when the urbanization of the Māori gained momentum. Many New Zealanders are, as a consequence, familiar with stories from both sides of their families. While most will tend to identify primarily with one or the other descent lines for purposes of social identity, few find it necessary to deny the other. Indeed, as the momentum for biculturalism increases, more may find it appropriate to recognize both. This reality may, ultimately, be the most important factor in designing and building the bicultural nation that most accept is both appropriate and inevitable.

Notes

1. James Belich, *Empire and Its Myth* (Washington, DC: Center for Australian and New Zealand Studies, Georgetown University, Occasional Papers April 27, 2000); Belich, "Māori and Pākehā, Past and Future," Waitangi Day Lecture, New Zealand Embassy, Washington, DC, February 4, 2000.
2. Named for the place where, on February 6, 1840, representatives of Māori nations and the British Crown first signed the treaty, which became the basis of the nation.
3. Aotearoa/NewZealand comprises two main and a number of smaller islands with a total area of 270,500 Km², which is similar to the area of Japan or the United Kingdom. The islands lie between 33 and 53° south latitude and between 160 and 173° west longitude.
4. Statistics New Zealand, "Māori Society," *New Zealand Official Yearbook 2000* (Wellington: Statistics New Zealand and David Bateman, Ltd., 2000), 150.
5. Peter H. Buck, *The Coming of the Māori* (Wellington: Māori Purposes Funds Board, 1958).
6. Bruce G. Biggs, *Māori Marriage: An Essay in Reconstruction*, Māori Monograph #2 (Wellington: Polynesian Society, 1960).
7. The missionaries, led by Reverend Samuel Marsden, also introduced sheep, cattle, horses, and poultry and instructed Māori in animal husbandry. These introductions allowed Māori to become involved in trade early and to produce food for sale to fledgling European settlements.
8. John Miller, *Early Victorian New Zealand: A Study of Racial Tension and Social Attitudes, 1839–1852* (London: Oxford, 1958).
9. Miller, *Early Victorian New Zealand*, 3.
10. J.O. Ross, "Busby and the Declaration of Independence," *New Zealand Journal of History*, 14 (1980), 18–39.
11. Alan Ward, *A Show of Justice: Racial "Amalgamation" in Nineteenth Century New Zealand* (Auckland: Auckland University Press, 1995).
12. Ward, *A Show of Justice*, 30–33.
13. Lord Glenelg, 1837, cited in P.G. McHugh, "Constitutional Theory and Māori Claims," *Waitangi: Māori and Pākehā Perspectives of the Treaty of Waitangi*, ed. I.H. Kawharu (Auckland: Oxford University Press, 1994), 31.
14. Cited in McHugh, "Constitutional Theory," 31.
15. There is considerable confusion and debate over what Māori agreed to cede. The English version of the Treaty contains the word sovereignty, but the five Māori versions, which circulated among and were signed by Māori, uses a word *kawanatanga*, which means administration. Scholars contend that it is unlikely that Māori would willingly have ceded sovereignty to a numerically small power in the circumstances.
16. From the outset, there were problems that stemmed from the coexistence of one English and five Māori versions of the Treaty — all of which had minor discrepancies. The most serious differences, however, existed between the English and Māori versions as Williams notes; David Williams, "Te Tiriti O Waitangi: Unique Relationship between the Crown and Tangata Whenua?," *Waitangi: Māori and Pākehā Perspectives of the Treaty of Waitangi*, ed. I.H. Kawharu (Auckland: Oxford University Press, 1989).
17. Ward, *Show of Justice*.

18. This supposition was underpinned by observation of the Māori willingness to adopt new agricultural crops, animals, practices, and technologies and to engage in trade for profit with Europeans. But it was also underpinned by the openly racist beliefs about the "obvious" superiority and attractions of "civilisation."
19. Ward, *Show of Justice*, 36.
20. Angela Ballara, *Proud to Be White? A Survey of Pākehā Prejudice in New Zealand* (Auckland: Heineman, 1986), 19.
21. As Ward has noted, around this time a number of chiefs and some pretenders did alienate land and without consultation with their kin who subsequently challenged the contracts for sale. One possibility is that the willingness rested on the mistaken view that they were selling rights to occupy rather than the freehold of the land which is a distinct possibility since Māori did not recognize the freehold of land.
22. Ward, *Show of Justice*, 18.
23. Ward, *Show of Justice*, 33.
24. Cited in Ballara, *Proud to Be White*, 21.
25. The Māori tribes who joined the British were known as "loyal Māori" by the British and *kupapa* or traitors, by other Māori. Their motives were complex: some joined to gain the upper hand over former enemies, some believed they would be treated better by the British whom they believed would eventually win, and some feared that defeated Māori would be heavily punished by British.
26. James Belich, *The New Zealand Wars and the Victorian Interpretation of Racial Conflict* (Auckland: Penguin, 1988).
27. Belich, *Māori and Pākehā*; Belich, *Empire and its Myth*.
28. Jane Kelsey, "Legal Imperialism and the Colonisation of Aotearoa," in *Tauiwi*, eds., Paul Spoonley *et al.* (Palmerston North: Dunmore Press, 1984).
29. Ward, *Show of Justice*, ix.
30. D.P. Lyons, "An Analysis of Three Māori Prophet Movements," in *Conflict and Compromise*, ed., I.H. Kawharu (Wellington: A.H. and A.W. Reed, 1975); M. Raureti, "The Origins of the Ratana Movement," in *Tihe Mauri Ora: Aspects of Maoritanga*, ed., Michael King (Auckland: Methuen, 1978), 42–59.
31. Lindsay Cox, *Kotahitanga: The Search for Māori Unity* (Auckland: Oxford, 1993).
32. Ballara, *Proud to be White*.
33. Belich, *Māori and Pākehā*; Belich, *Empire and its Myth*.
34. Belich, *Māori and Pākehā*; Belich, *Empire and its Myth*.
35. Ballara, *Proud to be White*, 92.
36. Ballara, *Proud to be White*, 84.
37. G. Asher and D. Naulls, *Māori Land* (Wellington: New Zealand Planning Countil, 1987); Ballara, *Proud to be White*.
38. Cox, *Kotahitanga*, 91.
39. Cox, *Kotahitanga*, 92.
40. I.L.G. Sutherland, "The Māori Revival," in *Yearbook of Education* (London: Evans Brothers, 1949), 213–221.
41. Tainui Stephens, "Māori Battalion March to Victory," *Television New Zealand Documentary Series*, Director and Producer Tainui Stephens, 1990.
42. *See*, for instance, Claudia Orange, "An Exercise in Māori Autonomy: The Rise of the Māori War Effort Organisation," *New Zealand Journal of History*, 21 (1987), 156–172.
43. Joan Metge, *A New Māori Migration: Rural Urban Relations in Northern New Zealand*, LSE Monographs on Social Anthropology (London: University of London, Athlone Press, 1964).
44. Evan S. Te Poata-Smith, "He Pokeke Uenuku I Tu Ai: The Evolution of Contemporary Māori Protest," in *Nga Patai: Racism and Ethnic Relations in Aotearoa New Zealand*, eds., Paul Spoonley, Cluny Macpherson, and David Pearson (Palmerston North: Dunmore Press, 1996).
45. Hauraki Greenland, "Māori Ethnicity as Ideology," in *Nga Take: Ethnic Relations and Racism in Aoteaaroa/New Zealand* (Palmerston North: Dunmore Press, 1991).
46. Donna Awatere, *Māori Sovereignty* (Auckland: Broadsheet Publications, 1984).
47. Ranginui Walker, *Ka Whawhai Tonu Matou: Struggle without End* (Auckland: Penguin, 1990); Pat Hohepa, "Māori and Pākehā: The One People Myth," in *Tihe Mauri Ora: Aspects of Maoritanga*, ed., Michael King (Auckland: Methuen, 1978), 98–111.
48. Ballara, *Proud to be White*, 163.
49. T. Lindsay Buick, *The Treaty of Waitangi: Or How New Zealand Became a British Colony*, 3rd ed. (New Plymouth: Capper Reprint, 1976; orig. 1936); Orange, "Exercise in Māori Autonomy."

50. William H. Oliver, *Claims to the Waitangi Tribunal* (Wellington: Waitangi Tribunal Division, Department of Justice, 1991), 3.
51. Oliver, *Claims to the Waitangi Tribunal*.
52. M.P.K. Sorrenson, "Towards a Radical Reinterpretation of New Zealand History: The Role of the Waitangi Tribunal," in *Waitangi: Māori and Pākehā Perspectives of the Treaty of Waitangi*, ed., I.H. Kawharu (Auckland: Oxford, 1994):158–178.
53. Sorrenson, *Waitangi*, 162.
54. Statistics New Zealand, "Māori," in *New Zealand Official Yearbook, 2000* (Wellington: Statistics New Zealand and David Bateman, Ltd., 2000), 136–140; idem., "Māori Society," in *New Zealand Yearbook 2000*, 141–150.
55. Augie Fleras, "Tuku Rangatiratanga: Devolution in Iwi Government Relations," in *Nga Take*, eds., Paul Spoonley, David Pearson, and Cluny Macpherson, 171–193.
56. A program known as "language nests" in which parents and guardians and their preschool children come together to learn the Māori language and protocols in preschool centers co-funded by government and users and managed by Māori.
57. A program under which Māori were made responsible for care and protection of Māori juvenile delinquents.
58. Fleras, "Tuku Rangatiratanga," 176.
59. Cited in Fleras, "Tuku Rangatiratanga," 177.
60. *Koro Wetere*, July 20, 1987.
61. *See* www.tpk.govt.nz.
62. *Te Puni Kokiri* (1998), 13.
63. The full name of the congress is *Te Whakakotahitanga o nga Iwi o Aotearoa*.
64. Statistics New Zealand, "Māori Society."
65. Oliver, *Claims to the Waitangi Tribunal*, 5.
66. Paul Spoonley, "Constructing Ourselves: The Post-Colonial Politics of Pākehā," in *Justice and Identity: Antipodean Practices*, eds., Margaret Wilson and Anna Yeatman (Wellington: Bridget Books, 1995), 29.
67. Michael King, *Being Pākehā* (Auckland: Hodder and Stoughton, 1985).
68. J. Schroeder, "Being Pākehā," *Canta* (1986), 3.
69. *See*, for instance, Spoonley, "Constructing Ourselves"; and Augie Fleras and Paul Spoonley, *Recalling Aotearoa: Indigenous Politics and Ethnic Relations in New Zealand* (Auckland: Oxford, 1999).
70. Paul Spoonley, "Pākehā Ethnicity: A Response to Māori Sovereignty," in *Nga Take*, eds., Spoonley, Pearson, and Macpherson, 154–170; Avril Bell, "We're Just New Zealanders: Pākehā Identity Politics," in *Nga Patai*, eds., Spoonley, Macpherson, and Pearson, 144–158.
71. Spoonley, 1987; Spoonley, "Pākehā Ethnicity."
72. *Te Puni Kokiri* (1998), 13.

11

Metaphors of Race and Discourse of Nation

Racial Theory and State Nationalism in the First Decades of the Turkish Republic

HOWARD EISSENSTAT

Introduction — Overlapping imaginings: race and nation

This essay examines the uses of race theory and metaphors of race in the for-mulation and elaboration of an official nationalist discourse in the first years of the Republic of Turkey. In the 1920s and 1930s, scientific racism was wide-spread, particularly in "the West." It should come as no surprise, therefore, that the Turkish elite was willing to adopt this sort of discourse for their own pro-gram of radical Westernization and state-building. What is surprising, given our association of race discourse with the policies of segregation in America or Nazi Germany, is that this discourse was fundamentally designed to act as an inclusionary (if aggressively assimilationist) rather than exclusionary discourse.

The blending of race and nation, two metaphors of shared identity, was a rel-atively common thing in the first decades of the twentieth century. The two terms have served mutually reinforcing notions of legitimacy in a wide variety of contexts. Nevertheless, a careful examination of the use of "race" in Turkish nation-building will not only serve to show a specific example of racial theory's role in nation-building, but, on a larger historiographical level, demonstrate the fluidity of both concepts in the hands of political elites who had to match ide-ology to messy political realities and create a viable language of legitimacy for their new state.

For the purposes of this chapter, racial thinking refers to the (erroneous) belief that humanity is divided into scientifically observable, homogeneous, and mutually distinct biological "types." Importantly, it assumes that these types exist transhistorically, that is, that these categories exist not as intellectual constructions, but as natural facts and that these categories existed throughout time, whether people in a particular era realized it or not.

Race and nation are both modern concepts that represent themselves as old, indeed timeless and natural. Like the term "race," the concept of nation has been so thoroughly accepted as a category that most lay people never question its validity. Indeed, it is only in the last twenty-five years or so that the literature on nationalism has begun to see it as an act of social construction rather than a process of awakening for a preexisting, organic social unit, called a nation.

At both the intellectual and political levels, racial theory and nationalist ideologies developed in tangent, reinforcing each other as they were elaborated. The overlap is not surprising. Both nationalism and racial theory take as their starting point the existence of distinct "peoples" with a common history and, presumably, a common destiny. Both are equally children of the transition to modern societies, nationalism meeting the modern state's demand for a more fully integrated — and thus "popular" — relationship between state and society and racial theory representing the Enlightenment's efforts to create rational, systematic categories to describe the world and the people in it.[1] Race theory allowed for an elaboration of the language of common identity, suggesting a blood tie which could correspond to common language, culture, territory, and heritage. "We are all brothers and sisters" could be taken almost literally and, moreover, obtain the imprimatur of natural science.

At the same time, the development of a seemingly scientific division of humanity often took the form of hierarchy, with some peoples more advanced, developed, or, indeed, noble than others. Moral qualities were ascribed to the races as well as physical characteristics and race often became yet another tool for rationalizing political, economic, and military dominance over other societies. Not surprisingly, intellectuals in societies under imperial control (whether direct or indirect) felt the need to answer these claims and show that they too were "fit" to rule and to control their own destiny. What needs to be stressed here, however, is that by the middle of the nineteenth century, both the concept of "race" and that of "nation" were coming to be widely agreed-upon signposts of people's intellectual worlds: race and nation had become "facts."

Ottomanism: a nationalism that failed

Before addressing the specific problem of nationalism in the early Turkish Republic and racial theory's place within it, a brief glance at the Republic's Ottoman legacy is in order. The Ottoman Empire was a prenational state *par excellence*, with a startling diversity of religions, languages, and local cultures represented among its subject peoples. By the late eighteenth century, however, it was clear to even the most myopic of observers within the Ottoman elite that the state was under increasing threat from both European competition and centrifugal forces within the Empire itself. First reluctantly and then with greater determination, this elite came to accept that only radical changes would serve to save the Empire.

The final decades in the history of the Ottoman Empire, starting in the second quarter of the nineteenth century and continuing through its destruction at the end of World War I, were marked by these radical changes, a long and bitter process of attempting to transform itself from a decentralized empire — based on negotiated arrangements and loose, local control — to a modern state capable of competing economically and militarily with both European incursion and control, on the one hand, and the growing threat of nationalist separatist movements within its own boundaries, on the other. To meet these twin threats, the Empire employed a variety of strategies: modernizing infrastructure and military efficiency through adoption of European strategies and technology, centralizing control of the state through the development of a modern and efficient bureaucracy, and shifting the nature of state legitimacy by developing a sense of citizenship and membership in a common "Ottoman" political identity.[2]

Traditionally, the beginning of this transformation within Ottoman governance is dated to the reign of Mahmud II (r. 1808–1839), who in 1826 destroyed the Janissary Corps and, with it, the main internal military threat to Ottoman modernization. Significantly, the most notable figures of the *Tanzimat* (generally translated as Reordering or Reform) Era which followed Mahmud's death were not Sultans but members of the expanding bureaucracy. As Feroz Ahmad has noted, the era of the *Tanzimat* saw a change in the relation of the bureaucracy to the state, in which loyalty to the state could supersede loyalty to a particular Sultan.[3] The development of a modern military and bureaucracy under Mahmud was extended after his death and combined with an elaboration of the concept of an Ottoman community (as opposed to a mere polity) under his successors. One of the earliest elaborations of this new conceptualization of Ottoman legitimacy, known in Western historiography as the Gülhane Rescript of 1839 (*Hatt-i Şerif-i Gülhane*), offered, in effect, a social contract:

> If there is an absense of security for property, and everyone remains indifferent to his state and his community; no one interests himself; no one interests himself in the prosperity of the country, absorbed as he is in his own troubles and worries. If, on the contrary, the individual feels complete security about his possessions, then he will become preoccupied with his own affairs, which he will seek to expand, and his devotion and love for his state will steadily grow and will undoubtedly spur him into becoming a useful member of society.[4]

In other words, good governance was assumed to be the requirement for loyalty to the state. More importantly, for our purposes, this suggestion of a social contract was extended to all subjects of the Empire, regardless of religion. Increasingly, lip service was paid to Islamic norms, while secularizing reforms continued apace. As Selim Deringil notes, the same Gülhane Rescript which formally initiated the Tanzimat era, "[stated] as its first principle that, 'it is evident that countries not governed by the şeriat [Islamic law] cannot prevail', even though much of what it decreed was indeed in contravention of the *Şeriat*."[5]

As religious institutions were secularized, the equality promised in the Gülhane Rescript slowly came into effect. From 1843 on, Ottoman courts recognized the equality of Muslim and non-Muslim subjects and as secular schools became the basis for entrance into the expanding Ottoman bureaucracy, non-Muslims found greater professional opportunities as well. An 1869 law defined Ottoman citizenship broadly, based on either residency or birth (through paternal descent).[6] This trend was further formalized in the Ottoman Constitution of 1876, which codified equal rights and responsibilities for all Ottomans and stated plainly that "Any individual who is a citizen of the Ottoman State, regardless of religion or sect, is without exception, [to be] called an Ottoman."[7]

In fact, however, the history of "Ottomanism" becomes significantly murkier rather than clearer after the proclamation of the 1876 Constitution. The chief question regarding membership in the "Ottoman nation" in the period up through 1876 was whether or not non-Muslims could share membership in a state that also made claims of Islamic legitimacy. In the face of national movements developing among the Christian populations in the rich Balkan provinces, a new language of legitimacy that would tie non-Muslims to the State was paramount.

Political realities shifted in a fundamental way after defeat in the Russo-Turkish War of 1877–1878; the peace treaty agreed to at the Berlin Congress meant the loss of approximately one third of Ottoman territory, with most of the losses occurring in the relatively rich Balkan territories. The Sultan, Abdülhamid II (r. 1876–1909), prorogued the newly established Constitution and quickly gathered the reins of political power into his own hands. For the first time since the beginning of the *Tanzimat*, the palace was the unquestioned center of power in the Ottoman Empire.

Traditionally, the historiography of the Ottoman Empire has argued the Hamidian period was marked by a shift from "Ottomanism" to "Islamism." This schema, based largely on Yusuf Akçura's 1904, *Üç Tarz-ı Siyaset* (Three Types of Policy), assumed that there were three distinct currents in Ottoman political thought — Turkism, Ottomanism, and Islamism. Abdülhamid's reign, it has been argued, meant the rejection of Ottoman nationalism or Ottomanism and a movement toward Islamic legitimacy. This framework, however, reifies these streams, suggesting that they represented mutually exclusive choices and assuming that the meaning of terms was static.

Ariel Salzmann is closer to the mark when she argues that, rather than abandoning Ottomanism, the Hamidian regime reinterpreted it to fit new demographic realities: with the loss of most of the Balkan territories, religious pluralism ceased to be a primary concern.[8] Instead, Ottoman citizenship was increasingly framed in ways that would maintain legitimacy among the remaining population. The Ottoman Empire, after 1878, had, for the first time in its history, an overwhelming Muslim majority and Abdülhamid's revision of Ottomanism reflected that by emphasizing Islamic legitimacy. Indeed, Muslim demographic dominance increased as time passed. Muslim populations in the Balkans were expelled or encouraged to leave the new states, causing a rapid influx of Muslims into the Ottoman Empire. Thus, in addition to losing Christian populations, the regions that remained within the Ottoman Empire became more Muslim as well.[9] Massacres of Christian populations, such as those perpetrated against the Armenians in 1894, along with sporadic inter-communal violence, precipitated increased migration among some of the Christian populations who remained. As the Empire became more Muslim, the symbols of legitimacy became more Islamic. Yet, as Selim Deringil makes clear, the Islamic elements of Abdülhamid's regime were not simply a return to past practice. Rather, Islamic symbols of legitimacy were reemployed to defend the modernization program of the Ottoman state.[10] The goal of creating a modern, cohesive Ottoman nation continued into the Hamidian period, while the content and form of that nation shifted dramatically.

The Hamidian regime was brought to a close in the Constitutional Revolution of 1908 (actually more military coup than revolution), though Abdülhamid remained on the throne as a figurehead until an attempted counter-coup in 1909. The CUP, or Committee for Union and Progress (*Ittihad ve Terakki Cemiyeti*), the so-called Young Turks, were generally junior level military officers and bureaucrats, convinced that Hamidian repression was to blame for the Empire's weakness. Their initial reaction was to attempt a return to the liberal path that Abdülhamid had ended in 1878. In the cities, Christians, Muslims, and Jews rejoiced together at the restoration of the Constitution. The territorial and constitutional metaphors of Ottoman identity initially formulated in the Tanzimat era were brought to the fore once again.

Whereas Abdülhamid had cloaked his nation-building and modernization programs in the garments of traditional and royal paternalism, the CUP was forthright in its intentions. Like the Tanzimat reformers, the Young Turks saw their hope in a liberal Ottomanism that would tie all citizens to a modernized and efficient state. The Young Turks had two important advantages over their Tanzimat predecessors, however: first, as relatively junior figures who came to power through armed revolt, they were less tied to the status quo; second, they had the very significant benefit of being able to take advantage of the steady development of education and infrastructure under Abdülhamid. Despite their acceptance of democratic opposition, the CUP position was further supported by the relative disorganization of potential opposition groups.[11] They enjoyed both the legitimacy of reasonably fair elections (in 1908) and — at least initially — a lack of serious opposition.

The goal of creating a sense of common Ottoman identity was pressed forward on all fronts. Military service was now required of non-Muslim as well as Muslim Ottoman males.[12] At the educational level, the state instituted citizenship classes to develop a sense of patriotism among its youth.[13] More controversially, the CUP instituted what has been referred to as a "Turkification" of the bureaucracy, attempting to make Ottoman Turkish more fully the language of state while increasing the level of Turkish-language education in the schools.

Many scholars have pointed to this as an example of a hidden Turkish nationalist agenda within the CUP. It seems more likely, however, that this policy was another example of the Young Turks attempting to rationalize the state and create a sense of shared Ottoman identity, an intensification rather than a break from long-term goals of the Ottoman state.[14] A common administrative language, after all, had long been an Ottoman goal. The Constitution of 1876 stated in Article 68 that, starting in 1880, knowledge of Turkish would be a requirement for members of Parliament (though in practice the question was moot: Parliament had been dismissed before this article came into effect).[15] The goal throughout this period was the integration of local elites into a unified, "rational," and modern state.[16] At the same time, Abdülhamid's policy of "Islamic Ottomanism" did not die in the Young Turk period and the CUP seems to have made active efforts to increase the economic power of Muslims over their non-Muslim countrymen.[17]

There is no question, however, that the decrease in local privileges, coupled with intensified foreign intervention, increased the inclination of local populations to contemplate a political future free of Ottoman rule and made political implementation of "national" imaginings more attractive. Among Muslim elites of the Ottoman Empire, the influence of national metaphors of identity, of an "awakening" to a linguistic and cultural past outside of political and religious identity were, despite their attractions, framed in the context of continued allegiance to the Ottoman political state. This was true even for Muslim regions that went into armed revolt. Albanians, who eventually gained full independence at the insistence of the Habsburgs in 1913, were initially resisting only taxation and military recruitment, the twin scourges of an increasingly efficient state, while the leadership in Yemen was satisfied with autonomy under an Ottoman umbrella.[18]

Among non-Muslims, the situation is murkier. Local Jewish populations seem to have placed their hopes in a liberal Ottomanism and remained deaf to the call of Zionism until quite late. Greeks and Armenians were more divided, with some following the Jewish model, while others hoped for European intervention that would offer them the opportunity for independent rule. Nevertheless, as late as 1913, significant numbers of non-Muslims fought alongside their Muslim fellow countrymen to defend Ottoman territory.[19]

The loss of many of the remaining Balkan territories at the end of the Balkan Wars (1912–1913) and the corresponding influx of Muslim refugees increased the inclination to frame Ottoman identity in Muslim terms. While the "citizen-based" framework of Ottoman nationhood did not completely die out after this time, the demographic realities made appeals to Muslim unity all the more vital, particularly after the Empire entered into World War I the following year (1914).[20] Under the strains of wartime, Christian populations were increasingly perceived as disloyal, a dangerous fifth column within the body politic.[21] One tragic result of this fear was, from 1915 on, the mass deportations and massacre of much of the Ottoman Empire's Armenian population.

Race and nation in the Turkish Republic: the search for a new discourse of self

The defeat of the Ottoman Empire in World War I shattered the old political order, creating new possibilities and constraints for the Turkish-speaking elite, which had most closely associated itself with the Empire and its preservation. Yet, while this period is typically framed in the historiography as a "Turkish War for Independence" the movement to resist the European-dictated peace terms and foreign occupation that followed the war was not specifically Turkish in nature.

During the War for Independence, the Parliament in Ankara used a variety of formulations to describe the nation; the most common by far was the phrase, "Turkish and Muslim." So frequent is this formulation, in fact, that it begins to resemble the doublets of Ottoman Turkish in which two words with more or less equivalent meanings are used together. Since the War for Independence was marked by intercommunal warfare between Muslim and non-Muslim citizens of the Ottoman Empire, as well as resistance to European imperial incursion, this conflation was natural.

Neither the idea of "Turkishness" nor the conflation of Turkishness with Ottoman Muslims was entirely new. The term, "Turk," of course, is ancient, but the idea of Turkishness as a politically meaningful term was something of a nineteenth-century innovation. For most of the Ottoman period, it had a descriptive quality, merely referring to those populations or individuals who spoke Turkish. In some contexts, the term even had a pejorative quality, suggesting a backward rural peasantry. Nevertheless, Ahmet Yıldız, overstates his case when he suggests that the term "*Türkiye*," or Turkey, was born with the republic.[22] Indeed, toward the end of the nineteenth century and increasingly in the first decades of the twentieth century, certain members of the Ottoman elite began to use this term, originally borrowed from European observers who had long conflated the language of the ruling dynasty with the state itself, as a synonym for Ottoman. Some of these individuals were intellectuals, trying to adopt and adapt European concepts of language-based "nations" for the Ottoman case. Others, however, seemed to have adopted the term more-or-less unproblematically, using the terms "Turkey" and "Ottoman Empire" interchangeably. For example, a member of the Ottoman Parliament from Muş stated in a debate on Ottoman identity papers that, "when a child is born in the Ottoman State, he is Ottoman. [This is because] he is born in Turkey."[23] Nor was this usage limited to Muslim Ottomans; Christian members of the Ottoman Parliament used the terms interchangeably as well.[24]

In a discussion of a proposed law to allow non-Muslim volunteers in the national army, for example, the terms "Turk" and "non-Muslim" are used mutually exclusively.[25] During a debate on education, the question was asked clearly by one member of Parliament, "Is not Turkish the same thing as Muslim (*Türk islâm değil mi?*)." Rasih Bey, the representative from Antalya, gave the accepted answer: "Sir, when one says Turkish one is saying Muslim. . . . Europe too refers to the World of Islam as Turkish."[26] Indeed, Bernard Lewis's observation that, at the popular level at least, the conception of a "Christian Turk is an absurdity and a contradiction in terms" reflects a conflation that seems to begin with the first suggestions of a Turkish nation in the nineteenth century and has largely continued to this day.[27] The success of Turkish nationalism has rested in large part on its ability to overlap a preexisting and deeply felt Islamic identity.

Nevertheless, even at this early stage there were fault lines evident within the framing of Turkish identity. The conflation of Turk and Muslim did not suggest a general Muslim rebellion against Western imperialism. Despite the preservation of the role of Caliphate through March 1924, there were no serious attempts at making common cause with other Muslim peoples. At best, the Turkish leadership tended to view themselves as leading by example, hoping that the Muslims of India and Iran would take the struggle in Anatolia as an example in their own efforts at gaining independence. The relation to the struggle of Muslims in the Soviet Union was more problematic, however. Many of the Members of Parliament were, after all, immigrants from these regions and their ties to their old homelands were strong. Nevertheless, while events in the U.S.S.R. were followed particularly closely, there were no real efforts to join with the Turkic peoples of the Soviet Union. The nationalist forces were already spread thin and the Soviet Union was the primary material support for the Turkish nationalists in Anatolia. A policy of union with the wider Turkic world at this stage would have been suicidal. As early as 1921, during a speech in Eskişehir, Mustafa Kemal rejected "Turanism" and stated that "the Government policy of the new Turkey is to consist in living independently, relying on Turkey's own sovereignty within her national frontiers."[28]

The linguistic and cultural diversity of Anatolian Muslims formed a logical challenge to the conflation of Turkish and Muslim identities. In a fascinating parliamentary debate on May 1, 1920, Emir Pasha, the representative from Sivas, challenged this verbal sleight of hand directly. Some among the delegates tried to shout him down, saying that "Turk" and "Muslim" were equivalent or that he should not "play with words," but he asked for their patience, arguing:

> There is a Caliphate founded in the name of Islam . . . I request that we not act only in the name of the Turks [*Türklük namına istimal etmiyelim*] because we did not gather here in only in the name of the Turks. If you please, it is more appropriate to say Muslims or even Ottomans not Turks. In our homeland there are Circassians, Chechens, Kurds, Laz, and other Islamic peoples. Let us not speak in a divisive manner that will leave [these groups] on the outside.[29]

While it is doubtful that Emir Pasha realized the ramifications of his comments, Mustafa Kemal certainly did and responded directly, so that, in his words, "this issue would not be brought up again."[30] In his response, he noted that not all Turkish populations were included within their declared national boundaries and stated that theirs was a movement of all the Muslims of their homeland, including Laz, Kurds, Turks, Circassians, and many others. What is striking about his response is that it did not particularly address Emir Pasha's concerns: why insist on the use of the word "Turk," if the goal of the movement was to defend the rights of "Muslims." It seems likely that Mustafa Kemal (later, Atatürk, the leader of the nationalist movement and eventual first president of the Republic) was engaging in a dodge, having already chosen an ethnic (if assimilationist) definition of Turkishness. However, the policies of assimilation of non-Turkic Muslim groups that would later be implemented by the Turkish Republic would have been self-defeating in the midst of the "national struggle." The vast majority of men and women engaged in this struggle after all were defending the "nation" of Islam, not an ethnic identity that had little political value to them.

At the same time, the Turkish aspects of the national movement could not be easily dismissed. The decidedly modernist military officers who formed the nucleus of the national movement were deeply affected by European thought and assumed, along with most European intellectuals of the time, that nations were the only legitimate means of organizing a state and that nations consisted of a people sharing a single language, territory, and culture. Even if their inclinations had been otherwise, there was no practical way to negotiate with the Europeans on equal terms other than by framing their struggle in terms of a nation as their Western adversaries understood the term. Russian nationalism and Muslim nationalism in the Russian Empire had both merged religion and linguistic group in their conception of the nation as had many of the Balkan nationalist movements as they defined their differences from the Catholic Hapsburgs and Muslim Ottomans. A similar fusion seemed the only possible solution for the Muslim national movement in Anatolia.

Demographically, victory in the War of Independence was a Muslim victory. The policy of the Turkish national movement toward immigration and in its negotiations at the Lausanne Conference was less one of Turkification than of creating a Muslim homeland in Anatolia. Framed in this way, it can be seen as the culmination of a nearly century-long process of religious homogenization in Anatolia. The relation of the Ottoman state to this process had not been entirely consistent: attempts at formulating a basis of Ottoman nationality that would appeal to the non-Muslim were frequent, as was the use of Islamic symbols to gird political legitimacy. As a matter of state policy, the revolutionary government in Ankara viewed the settlement of Muslim refugees as one of its highest duties while at the same time it facilitated the immigration of non-Muslims.[31]

In the treaty negotiations at the Lausanne Conference, the Turkish delegation fought for and received terms that would continue the trend of religious partition into the Republican period. During negotiations for the forced transfer of Muslim and Orthodox populations between Greece and Turkey, the Turkish delegation initially hoped for the transfer of the entire Greek Orthodox population, including those living in Istanbul and for the closure of the Orthodox Patriarchate in Istanbul.[32] While the other members of the commission did not accept this position, the results were nonetheless striking, with approximately 1.2 million Greek Orthodox moving to Greece and 500,000 Muslims emigrating from Greece to Turkey.[33] Presumably, as a means of precluding non-Muslims from converting to Islam and avoiding deportation, a decision on July 22, 1923 forbade non-Muslims from officially changing their religion until their status as citizens had been clarified.[34]

Although the Lausanne Conference is generally remembered as a Turkish diplomatic victory, the response of the Turkish Parliament to their returning delegation was cool. Goals that had been long fought for as holy ideals had been watered down in the process of hard negotiations. As Ayhan Aktar notes, the continued presence of non-Muslims was one serious source of disappointment.[35] Rıza Nur Bey, speaking for the delegation, defended the agreement, saying that the number of Armenians and Jews left was minimal and suggesting that 20–25 percent of the remaining Greek Orthodox would leave despite their protected status.[36] Indeed, Rıza Nur explicitly stated that during the negotiations, the Turkish delegation insisted on specifying the right of immigration for non-Muslims in the hope that those who could not be forced to leave would do so voluntarily.[37] At the same time, he agreed that "it would have been better if none remained," suggesting that the Turkish delegation had done the best they could in difficult negotiations.[38] Nevertheless, the discontent on this point was widespread and the topic of the remaining non-Muslim populations was brought up repeatedly in subsequent discussions.

For our purposes, however, the discussions of Muslim populations are more central. At this point, at least, there was a consensus regarding the non-Muslims. They were not part of the nation, even if they could not all be forced out of the national boundaries. The range of possibilities for Muslims was in greater dispute. Now that the Turks had won their independence, it remained to be decided who the Turks were.

Clearly the most important non-Turkish speaking population in the new Republic was the Kurds. In this light, Kurdish–Turkish brotherhood was stressed and attempts at the creation of an independent Kurdish state were attributed to English or Armenian intrigues.[39] Nevertheless, tensions regarding the geographic and ethnic borders of Turkishness occasionally emerged. In one heated exchange, when Hüseyin Avni Bey, the delegate from Erzurum, seemed to suggest that the Turkish Republic was betraying the Kurds by not fighting for Mosul, he was asked whether he was willing to sacrifice "another hundred thousand Anatolians" for those territories.[40] Defending himself, Hüseyin Avni responded, "Gentlemen, I too am a Turk, [but] when we outlined our national boundaries, we didn't distinguish between Turks and Kurds."[41]

The question of repatriating Turkish troops from Yemen precipitated a more freewheeling discussion. The term "Turkish" in this case was rendered as "*Türkiye'li*," a neologism which literally means "of" or "from" Turkey. "Whom," one delegate asked, "do we call Turkish [*Türkiye'li*]?"[42] Some proposed a strictly geographic definition, arguing that the term described officers "who had resided within our national borders."[43] Others worried that such a definition would prevent those of "Turkish blood" who had been raised outside the boundaries of the current Republic but who had, nevertheless, maintained their Turkish identity from being repatriated.[44] Could ethnic Albanians or Arabs be considered Turks? Should their loyalty to the Ottoman Empire be repaid with Turkish citizenship or should they be sent off to countries that now claimed to speak for them? As one member of Parliament stated, "Arabs and Albanians had served at the front; they had paid the tax of blood."[45] If Arabs and Albanians were to be rejected, then what of Bosnians and Circassians? Many, like Samih Rifat Bey, argued that blood had so far not been used as a determinant of nationality and that nationhood is properly defined by culture and religion.[46] Others worried of foreign elements sapping the unity of the Turkish nation. In the end, no real consensus was reached; tropes of blood, culture, territory, and religion all had appeal. But if these themes often converged, they also occasionally came into conflict. In the end, the Parliament seemed to accept that this was a question without a satisfactory answer.

The following year, a similarly heated and difficult debate occurred as the Parliament attempted to define citizenship. By this time, of course, the range of options was circumscribed by international law; the Treaty of Lausanne guaranteed the rights of non-Muslims within the Republic. Still, the inclusion of non-Muslims as Turks seemed counterintuitive. For most delegates, these groups might have Turkish citizenship, but they could not be Turks. Hamdullah Suphi (Tanrıöver) suggested that, at some point in the future, Jews and other non-Muslim groups might choose to enter into Turkish culture in the way that Jews had entered into French culture. However, he argued, that day had not yet come and these groups remained a foreign and potentially dangerous element.[47] Again, a satisfactory definition of the nation was sought; Celâl Nuri Bey stated that currently "the true citizen was a Hanefi Muslim and spoke Turkish," yet he noted that this definition did not take into account the ethnic and religious diversity of the new nation. In the end, he concluded, the only possible legal solution was for all the Republic's citizens to be included as Turks.[48]

As Kemal Kirişçi has noted, the acceptance of these non-Muslims was grudging and the practice of Turkish immigration reflects this: immigrants to Turkey were overwhelmingly Muslim regardless of their native language. The law was written broadly enough to give state officers a fair amount of latitude in accepting or denying applications for citizenship. As a general rule, individualsud would be accepted as immigrants if they were "tied to the Turkish race and culture."[49] In its implementation, most immigrants were Muslim from former Ottoman domains — primarily the Balkans. There were lesser numbers who fled from the Soviet Union and Iran and even some from further afield: Afghanistan, India, and China.[50] Nothing I have found in the archives, however, supports Kirişci's assertion that there was an anti-Shiite slant to Turkish immigration practice. Immigration from Azerbaijan was promoted in a decision of 28 May 1923[51] and examples of immigrants from Iran and Azerbaijan are relatively common.[52] In early 1925, a nineteenth-century law banning marriage to Iranian citizens was repealed.[53] If there was discrimination agains non-Hanefi Muslims in immigration policy, as Kirişci suggests, it was practiced only sporadically.

On the other hand, the continued presence of non-Muslim populations was one that the Turkish government had accepted grudgingly and the overriding concern seems to have been to make sure that those leaving in the population transfers did not return. Nevertheless, there was a certain number of non-Muslims who were accepted as Turkish citizens. Until at least the mid-thirties, all documents specifically state whether the individual to be accepted was Muslim or non-Muslim. Some non-Muslims were Europeans who worked as engineers or managers in Turkey. Another group included White Russian immigrants who had fled to Turkey after their defeat in the Russian Civil War. Later, German academics fleeing Nazi oppression were also accepted. The largest number, however, were former Ottoman citizens who had fled the country during World War I or the War for Independence and were accepted back as Turkish citizens. Of these, the vast majority were Jews, though it is unclear whether this reflects the preferences of the immigrants or of the state.

At the same time, there is evidence to suggest that the Turkish government used what legal leeway it had to remove citizenship from non-Muslims. There were a number of wedgest that the state had at its disposal: those who worked for other foreign governments without receiving permission from the Turkish government, those who accepted foreign citizenship, and those who did not serve in the national struggle and failed to return to Turkey before 1927 all were subject to loss of their Turkish citizenship. It should be noted that these laws are not, on their face, particularly discriminatory; indeed, a small number of Muslims lost their Turkish citizenship under each of these statutes. Nevertheless, it seems clear from the documents that the Turkish government recognized these laws as a means of ridding the nation of what it perceived as foreign elements. Non-Muslims and Muslims were listed separately in the decisions to remove citizenship and, by the late thirities, sheets explicit listing the total number of each ethnicity was attached to the orders for removal of citizenship.

Yet, one of the striking things about the decisions from the mid-and late thirities is that new definitions on non-Turkish ethnicity become evident. In addition to the various descriptions of non-Muslims, there are listings for Muslim groups such as Albanians, Gypsies, and Persians.[54] While their numbers would appear to be minimal, this trend points to a shift in the center of gravity of Turkish naitonlist discourse. During the early twenties, tropes of race had a decidedly secondary role within the discursive field of Turkish nationalism.

While always evident, religion and culture, far more than blood, were taken as the primary indicators of membership within the Turkish nation. Beginning in the late twenties, this balance began to shift so that race took on a greater role within discussions of national identity.

Tropes of race had always had an intellecutal potency for Turkish nationalist intellectuals. Race and nation were, after all, closely tied in much of nationalist thought in the late nineteenth and early twentieth centuries, and Turkish nationalism relfected this. The changing balance of emphasis within Turkish national discosure, however, seems rooted in practical politics as much as intellectual lineage.[55] The increasing secularism of the state and the reforms collectively known as the "Turkish Revolution" dramatically altered the relationship of the state to society and the nature of state ligitimacy. In the process, the state took an increasing interest in elaborating a definition of Turkish identity that would simultaneously act as a counter to Islamic symbols of political identity and yet still be able to incorporate the vast majority of the Republic's citizens.

Beginning in the late twenties, these trends began to take on the form of a state ideology. The First Turkish History Congress and First Turkish Language Congress, both held in 1932, represented a full and public elaboration of this process. The basic thrust of this new ideology was that Turks were the first and greatest of nations and that Turks brought civilization to the great civilizations of that past, including those of ancient China, India, and more importantly, Greece and Rome.[56] Through this historical fancy, Turkish appropriation of Western rooms and modes could be framed as a "return to its own roots" rather than a capitulation to a foreign culture. It would also place them squarely within Western (and White) civilization, a point that was of some importance for Atatürk, who detested reading studies, which included Turks among the "yellow" or "Asiatic" races.

A broad and colorful national mythology was developed and propagated "proving" the racial unity and continuity of Anatolia. Central to this was that the first civilizations of Anatolia — the Sumerians, Akkadians, and Hittites — were the products of Turkish migration from Inner Asia.[57] Perhaps the most notable example of this new racial scholarship was a broad survey of body and cranial types undertaken by one of Atatürk's adopted daughters, Afet İnan, in which she noted broad similarities between modern Turks and remains from ancient Anatolian peoples, particularly the Hittites.[58] A fair amount of cultural production was devoted to this historical myth-making as well. Novels, such as İskander Fahreddin's *Sumer Kızı*, which mixes Turkish names with heroic tales of Anatolia's ancient past, brought to life this new historical vision for the mass public.[59]

The most important reason for this shift was its utility in addressing the Republic's ethnic diversity. By claiming that the Turkish race had founded the ancient civilizations of Anatolia, the dilemma of how to place the sizable Kurdish population within the Turkish nation could be circumvented. In the aftermath of a series of violent upsprings in Eastern Anatolia, the firmer incorporation of the Kurdish minority became paramount. The Turkish History Thesis gave an easy solution. Kurds were Turks who had forgotten Turkish. As Turkishness became less tied to a popular Muslim identity, Kurdishness became more threatening.

Other Muslim groups also met with varying degrees of suspicion, however. Muslim gypsies are one important example. In his memoirs, Reşat Tesal notes that the gypsy population of Thrace was included in the population exchanges between Greece and Turkey and came into Turkey as Turks.[60] By 1934, however, "migrant gypsies" were among these, along with spies, anarchists, and individuals with no tie to Turkish culture, who were specifically forbidden to immigrate to Turkey.[61] As was (and still is) the case in much of Europe, gypsy communities within the Republic were treated as a foreign and inherently criminal element. A 1941 inspection report for the Zonguldak region, for example, complained bitterly of gypsies, who, it claimed, stole from and abused their Turkish neighbors.[62] Governmental reports on villages began to speak of "non-Turks," even when the populations were Muslim.[63] An inspectorate report of May 17, 1940 questions the propriety of having a man of Arab descent as local administrator in Çankir.[64] Another complained of the treasonous behavior and religious fundamentalism of Circassians and Abkhazians.[65]

Neverthless overall the state emphasized the need to assimilate these Muslim groups rather than force them out. With the exception of a radical fringe, represented by such figures a Nihal Atsız and Reha Oğuz Türkkan, the racial metaphor in Turkey — as it was applied to Muslim populations — was framed distinctly to include these groups under the rubric "Turkish" rather than reject them as foreign elements in the body politic. In most material of the day, the Turkish descent of non-Turkic Muslim groups was emphasized. Groups like the Kurds or Circassians always had the door of assimilation open to them. Such assimilation most often took the form of efforts to promote the use of the Turkish language and to de-emphasize religious or ethnic difference. Nevertheless, when resistance to such assimilationist efforts was widespread, as in the primarily Alevi Kurdish region of Dersim, the state was more than willing to employ the full force of its military strength ot impose its will.[66]

The relationship of state nationalism with non-Muslim Turkish citizens was more complex. One result of the new emphasis on race was that it had that potential to change the relationship of the Turkish state to non-Muslim Turkish-speakers. Thus, an article in the journal, *Ülkü*, the national publication of the state-sponsored People's Houses, speaks of Orthodox and Gregorian Turks in Anatolia.[67] In an fascinating — if unverifiable — quotation, Tanrıöver states that by the time of his death, Atatürk believed that the deportation of Turkish-speaking Christians in the population exchange with Greece had been a grave mistake.[68] By this time, of course, the question of Turkish Orthodox in Anatolia was largely moot: this group probably numbered no more than a few hundred in Turkey.[69]

This shift further manifested itself in a widely cited incident regarding the Gagauz — an Orthodox, Turkish-speaking population located primarily within the current boundaries of Moldova. At the time, this region was part of Romania, where Tanrıöer served as a diplomat after the closing of the Turkish Hearths. Tanrıöer, who had always been attracted to the idea of a Turkish race, took a lively interest in the Turkic populations in Romania and argued that they should all, Christian and Muslim alike, be "repatriated" to Turkey.[70] Indeed, after he returned to Istanbul, many Gagauz students were allowed to use his home as a make-shift dormitory.[71] A number of authors cite the case of the Gagauz as an example of the conflation of Muslim and Turkish identity and it is true that there was some high-level resistance to the idea of a mass Christian immigration. The Chief of the General Staff, Fevzi Çakmak, for one, was dubious of the plan.[72] This resistance was not universal, however. Tanrıöver, the architect of the plan, attributed its failure to the Soviet invasion of Romania and not Turkish resistance.[73] Indeed, government action was taken to list such immigrants as "Turkish Orthodox" rather than "Christian Orthodox" on their identity cards and a small number of Gagauz came over as students and eventually became citizens.

On the whole, however, non-Muslims were not included in the unifying metaphor of race. Kurds might be Turks who had strayed from their true identity, but non-Muslims maintained their foreignness. An inspectorate report from 1940 regarding the town of Ordu mentions a small community of perhaps 500 Armenians. While the author, Hilmi Kiliç, a member of Parliament from Kayseri, admits that this group had done nothing worthy of complaint, he concluded by saying that "this small minority's presence in Ordu is not positive."[74] Along similar lines, a letter to the Republican Party General Secretary from the Giresun Party Chief, Dr. Nuri Özkaya, complained of a group of several Jewish families who had immigrated there from Thrace and Istanbul. What particularly concerned Özkaya was that these Jewish families had officially changed their original names to what he described as "Turkish and Muslim" names. While he admitted that there was no obvious legal constraint on this, he worried that their children would also take on Turkish names and would, for all intents and purposes, be indistinguishable from what he described as "real Turks."[75] Suspicion often took the form of discrimination, the two most notorious examples of this being the forced relocation of the Jewish community of Thrace in 1934 and the targeting of non-Muslims for extraordinary taxes or Varlık Vergisi (Wealth Tax) in the mid-forties.

Nevertheless, the main thrust of racial discourse within official Turkish nationalism was always directed toward inclusion rather than exclusion. The use of scientific racism in Turkish nationalist discourse was the strengthening of state legitimacy by underlining the intrinsic brotherhood of Turkish citizens, their shared history, and long-standing ties to the Turkish Republic. The aim, in other words, was to create a metaphor that would unite a linguistically and culturally diverse population into a single nation. Although there were some flirtations with irredentism during World War II, these were limited and effectively repressed as the war came to a close. The defeat of fascism in Europe in 1945 changed the political landscape once more, severely limiting the political efficacy of racial tropes of nationhood.

While racial themes are still evident in popular discourse and very occasionally find their way into public policy, the use of race in Turkish nationalism has played a very different role from the policies of segregation most often associated with such terminology. In stark contrast to the American case (and with the important caveat that non-Muslims were consistently seen as outsiders), "race" in Turkey has primarily been utilized, at least in official ideology, as a metaphor of national unity. The ties of "blood," it was hoped, would combine with those of language, culture, citizenship, and religion to weld diverse communities into a single people. This did not preclude repression, including violent repression. As we have seen in the recent events in the former Yugoslavia, racial theory as assimilationist discourse (i.e., Bosnians are "really" Croats or Serbs who converted to Islam) can be as much a basis for ethnic cleansing as segregationist discourse.[76] In part, it is the very malleability of racial thinking that makes it attractive to nationalist projects.

Notes

1. Perhaps the most forceful argument for nationalism's relationship to the modern state structure can be in Ernest Gellner, *Nations and Nationalism* (Ithaca, NY: Cornell University Press, 1983). For extensive discussions of the roots of racial theory, *see* Miles; Ivan Hannaford, *Race: The History of an Idea in the West* (Washington, DC: The Woodrow Wilson Center Press, 1996); George L. Mosse, *Towards the Final Solution: A History of European Racism* (New York: Howard Fertig, 1978).
2. The Ottoman case, in many respects, runs parallel to a similar reformulation of political legitimacy in the Russian Empire. For a very useful examination of many aspects of Russian efforts, *see* Daniel R. Brower and Edward J. Lazzerini, eds., *Russia's Orient, Imperial Borderlands and Peoples, 1700–1917* (Bloomington: Indiana University Press, 1997).
3. Feroz Ahmad, *The Making of Modern Turkey* (London: Routledge, 1993), 25–26.
4. Quoted in Ahmad, *Modern Turkey*, 26.
5. Selim Deringil, *The Well-Protected Domains: Ideology and the Legitimation of Power in the Ottoman Empire, 1876–1909* (London: I.B. Tauris, 1998), 9.
6. Ariel Salzmann, "Citizens in Search of a State: The Limits of Political Participation in the Late Ottoman Empire," in Michael Hanagan and Charles Tilly, eds., *Extending Citizenship, Reconfiguring States* (Lanham, MD: Rowman and Littlefield, 1999), 45. Salzman provides in this essay perhaps the most succinct and useful overview of the recent literature on the changing sense of Ottoman legitimacy in the nineteenth century.
7. Füsün Üstel, "II. Meşrutiyet ve Vatandaşin 'İcad'ı" in *Cumhuriyet'e Devreden Düşünce Mirası: Tanzimat ve Meşruitiyet'in Birikimi*, Modern Türkiye'de Siyasî Düşünce Cilt 1 (Istanbul: İletişim, 2001), 166.
8. Salzmann, 50–51. Kemal Karpat refers to Abdülhamid's formula as one of an "Ottoman-Muslim" nation, *see* Karpat, "The *Hijra* from Russia and the Balkans," in Dale F. Eickelman and James Piscatori, *Muslim Travellers: Pilgrimage, Migration, and the Religious Imagination* (Berkeley: University of California Press, 1990), 147.
9. Karpat, 133.
10. *See*, especially, Deringil, 44–46.
11. Salzmann, 53.
12. Erik J. Zürcher, *Turkey: A Modern History* (London: I.B. Tauris, 1993), 105.
13. Üstel, 168–169.

14. This argument is made particularly forcefully by Hasan Kayalı, *Arabs and Young Turks: Ottomanism, Arabism, and Islamism in the Ottoman Empire, 1908–1918* (Berkeley: University of California Press, 1997), 79, 90–94.
15. *See* Suna Kili, *Türk Anayasaları* (Istanbul: Tekin Yayınevi, 1982), 18.
16. Kayalı, 92.
17. Salzmann, 54.
18. Zürcher, 109–112.
19. Salzmann, 54. The support of many non-Muslims for the Ottoman rule when they saw it as offering them opportunities for security and advancement were matched in the (rare) cases when the new government in former Ottoman territories gave Muslim citizens similar opportunities. In British-administered Cyprus (an Ottoman territory until 1878), for example, Muslims supported British rule in World War I against the Ottoman Empire and played key roles in the administration of the island (*see*, Nergis Canefe, "Türklük Tarihi ve Kıbrıs: Kıbrıslı Türk Kimliğin Hikâyelenmesinde Bir Yolağzi," in Esra Özyürek, ed., *Hatırladıklarıyla ve Unuttuklarıyla Türkiye'nin Toplumsal Hafızası* [Istanbul: İletişim, 2001], 54.).
20. Kayalı, 174–177.
21. Perception of Christian disloyalty were not completely unfounded. Many, though certainly not all, Ottoman Christians did see the turmoil of World War I as an opportunity to push forward claims of independence. Nationalism, coupled with still powerful memories of massacre and exile, has made the literature on this issue particularly prone to polemics and defensiveness.
22. Ahmet Yıldız, "*Ne Mutlu Türküm Diyebilene*" *Türk Ulusal Kimliğinin Etno-Seküler Sınırları, 1919–1938* (Istanbul: İletişim, 2001), 106.
23. Fevzi Demir, "Osmanlı Kimliği Üzerine Osmanlı'nın Son Tartışması: Osmanlı'nın Hüviyet Cüzdanı Nasıl Olmali?" in, *Kebikeç*, no. 10, 2001, 252.
24. *See*, for example, Demir, *Kebikeç*, 248.
25. TBMM, Zabit Ceridesi, Devre: 1 Cilt: 4, September 26, 1920, 312.
26. TBMM, Zabit Ceridesi, Devre: 1 Cilt: 4, October 4, 1920, 478.
27. Bernard Lewis, *The Emergence of Modern Turkey*, 2nd ed. (London: Oxford University Press, 1968), 15.
28. Quoted in Jacob M. Landau, *Pan-Turkism, From Irredentism to Cooperation*. (Bloomington and Indianapolis: Indiana University Press, 1995), 74.
29. TBMM, Zabıt Ceridesi, Devre: 1 Ciltz, May 1, 1920, 165.
30. TBMM, Zabıt Ceridesi, Devre: 1 Ciltz: ?, 165.
31. A *kararname* on December 14, 1922 gave permission for non-Muslims to leave the country for as long as they wished. BBA-CA: 030.18.01/6.41.02. Later non-participation in the War of Independence would be grounds for denying citizenship.
32. Kemal Arı, *Büyük Mübadele: Türkiye'ye Zorunlu Göç, 1923–1925* (Istanbul: Tarih Vakfi Yurt Yayınları, 1995), 17.
33. Arı, *Büyük Mübadele*, 177.
34. BBA-CA: 030.18.01/07.25.17.
35. Ayhan Aktar, *Varlık Vergisi ve "Türklestirme Politikaları"* (Istanbul: İletişim, 2000), 42.
36. TBMM Gizli Celse Zabıtları, Devre: 1 Cilt: 4, March 2, 1923, 8–9.
37. TBMM Gizli Celse Zabıtları, Devre: 1 Cilt: 4, March 2, 1923, 8.
38. TBMM Gizli Celse Zabıtları, Devre: 1 Cilt: 4, March 2, 1923, 8.
39. TBMM Gizli Celse Zabıtları, Devre: 1 Cilt: 4, March 4, 1923, 92–95.
40. TBMM Gizli Celse Zabıtları, Devre: 1 Cilt: 4, March 4, 1923, 95.
41. TBMM Gizli Celse Zabıtları, Devre: 1 Cilt: 4, March 4, 1923, 95.
42. TBMM Gizli Celse Zabıtları, Devre: 1 Cilt: 4, September 22, 1923, 265.
43. TBMM Gizli Celse Zabıtları, Devre: 1 Cilt: 4, September 22, 1923, 265.
44. TBMM Gizli Celse Zabıtları, Devre: 1 Cilt: 4, September 22, 1923, 265.
45. TBMM Gizli Celse Zabıtları, Devre: 1 Cilt: 4, September 24, 1923, 309.
46. TBMM Gizli Celse Zabıtları, Devre: 1 Cilt: 4, September 22, 1923, 271.
47. İlhan Unat, ed., *Türk Vatandaşlık Hukuku: Metinler, Mahkeme Kararları* (Ankara: Sevinç Matbaası, 1966) 39–41.
48. Unat, *Türk Vatandaşlık Hukuku*, 41–42.
49. Unat, *Türk Vatandaşlık Hukuku*, 136.
50. It is generally not possible to determine from names whether the immigrants from China were from the Turkic minority or some other Muslim group.
51. BBA-CA: 030.18.01/09.27.08.

52. *See*, for example, BBA-CA: 030.18.01/10.32.7; 030.18.01/12.67.07; 030.13.01/09.18.13; 030.18.01/30.16.13. Iran and Azerbaijan are both primarily shi'ite.

53. BBA-CA: 030.18.01/13.18.06.

54. BBA-CA: 030.18.01/88.95.15; 030.18.1.2/88.95.16.

55. In an extremely interesting article, Sam Kaplan has shown that race theory was employed as early as 1919, by both Armenian and Muslim intellectuals, to bolster their argument (to the occupying French forces) that the region of Cilicia was originally of "their" group. *See* Sam Kaplan, "Ortadoğu'ya Tutulan Fransız Aynaları: Ermeni ve Türk Belgelerinde Kilikya," in Özyürek, 19–47. This again suggests that racial discourse was long-available, but only put into practice as it intersected with state interests.

56. *See*, for example, *Türk Tarihinin Ana Hatları: Methal Kısmı* (Istanbul: Devlet Matbaası, 1931), 1–12.

57. *Türk Tarihinin Ana Hatları*, 8–9.

58. Afetinan, *Türkiye Halkının Antropolojik Karakterleri ve TürkiyeTarihi (Türk Irkının Vatanı Anadolu)*, Ankara: Türk Tarih Kurumu Basımevi, 1947. This work had been previously published in French under the title, *L'Anatolie, le Pays de la "Race" Turque: Recherches sur les Caractères Antropologiques des Populatins de la Turquie* (Geneva: Librairie de l' Université Genève, 1941) and represented research that Inan undertook under the direction of Eugène Pittard, again demonstrating the European origins of Turkish race science.

59. İskender Fahreddin, *Sumer Kızı, Tarihi Roman* (Istanbul: Akşam, 1933).

60. *Selânik'ten İstanbul'a: Bir Ömrün Hikâyesi* (Istanbul: İletişim, 1998), 27–28.

61. Unat, 156.

62. BBA-CA: 490.01.513.2061.2.

63. BBA-CA: 490.01.510.2048.01.

64. BBA-CA: 490.01.514.2062.2.

65. BBA-CA: 490.02.269.1073.2.

66. Nicole Watts, "Relocating Dersim: Turkish State-Building and Kurdish Resistance, 1931–1938," in *New Perspectives on Turkey*, no. 23 (Fall 2000), 5–30.

67. Hasan Fehmi, "Anadolu'da Gregoriyen ve Ortodoks Türkler," *Ülkü: Halkevleri Mecmuasi*, vol. 4, no. 21, November 1934.

68. *Mustafa Baydar, Hamdullah Suphi Tanröver ve anıları* (Istanbul: Menteş, 1968), 160–161. Özdemir Çobanoğlu ascribes a similar plan to Atatürk, saying that he planned to relocate the Gagauz to the Bursa region, but that after his death, the plan was forgotten; *see* Metin Akar and Acar Sevim, "Gagauz Yurdu'ndan Anayurda . . . ve Atatürk'ün Gagauz Türkleri'yle Ilgili Tasavvurları," in *Yesevi: Aylık Sevgi Dergisi*, year: 3, no. 27, March 1996, 25.

69. *See* Orhan Türkdoğan, "Anadolu'da Ortodoks Türkler," *Türk Dünyasi Tarih Dergisi*, no. 124, April 1997, 7–16.

70. *See* speech quoted in *Yıldırım Gazetesi*, Pazarcık, June 12, 1935 and reprinted in Baydar, 159.

71. Isenbike Togan, personal communication, October 16, 2000.

72. Halim Sevarslan, *Hamdullah Subhi Tanröver* (Ankara: Türk Kültürünü Araştırma Enstitüsü, 1995), 155.

73. Baydar, 159.

74. BBA-CA: 490.01.612.127.06.

75. BBA-CA: 490.01.611.120.06.

76. *See*, for example, Noel Malcom, *Bosnia: A Short History* (New York: New York University Press, 1996) and Tone Bringa, *Being Muslim the Bosnian Way: Identity and Community in a Central Bosnian Village* (Princeton: Princeton University Press, 1995), 12–36.

12
The Fragmented Nation
Genealogy, Identity, and Social Hierarchy in Turkmenistan

ADRIENNE EDGAR

In 1924, the Soviet regime redrew the map of Central Asia. Guided by the work of ethnographers and linguists, Soviet authorities dissolved the region's three multiethnic political entities and created a handful of "national" republics, each named for a single ethnic group. Within each new republic, Soviet policy called for preferential treatment for the "titular nationality" and the promotion of the indigenous language and culture. Imagining that this revolutionary policy would put an end to ethnic antagonism and permit rapid progress toward socialist internationalism, the Soviet state instead unwittingly laid the basis for the eventual emergence of independent nation-states in Central Asia.[1]

One of the republics created in the 1924 "national delimitation" of Central Asia was the Turkmen Soviet Socialist Republic. The Turkmen, like the other recipients of Soviet republics in Central Asia, appeared at the time to be poor candidates for nationhood. Traditionally pastoral nomads, the Turkmen population consisted of a number of genealogically defined groups — tribes — that lacked common political institutions, a unified territory, or a shared written language. Subethnic levels of identity had much greater significance than any overarching identification with "Turkmenness." Moreover, the territory that was to become Soviet Turkmenistan was ethnically diverse, with different peoples living side by side in a complex network of interdependent and hierarchical relationships. Yet, the Turkmen claimed a shared ancestry that provided a potential basis for unity. This genealogical structure, and the tribal customary law that went along with it, provided the basis for a Turkmen national identity.

It is a truism among historians of nationalism that states create nations.[2] Nowhere, however, was the creation of national identities carried out so consistently, deliberately, and aggressively as in the avowedly internationalist Soviet

Union.[3] In some ways, the impact of Soviet rule in non-European regions resembled that of colonial powers, such as France and Britain. With their obsessive need to classify and categorize, each of these modern states institutionalized and reified previously fluid indigenous identities.[4] Yet, the Soviet regime was far more ambitious in its efforts, seeking to create not just national territories and elites but also languages, cultural traditions, and histories for the non-Russian peoples under its rule.[5]

This Soviet "nationality policy" was not racial in nature; that is, it was not based on a belief in primordial, biologically determined differences between human groups. On the contrary, Soviet theorists explicitly rejected the racial ideas that legitimized colonial and nationalist movements elsewhere in Europe. In an important early work on Marxism and nationality, Joseph Stalin had written that the nation is "not racial, nor is it tribal." The Bolsheviks saw nations not as primordial entities with biological roots, but as historical constructs closely linked to modernity and capitalism.[6] In the 1930s, the Soviets vigorously disputed the ideas of race prevalent in Nazi Germany, which held that the characteristics of human groups were hereditary and immutable. The Soviets also rejected the notion that certain races or ethnic groups were inherently superior to others. Instead, Soviet theorists argued that all human groups were equal and that social and behavioral characteristics could change over time in response to external conditions and state policies.[7]

Although the Bolsheviks officially rejected a biological or racial definition of nationality, they were forced to contend with the existence of a primordialist view of nationhood among some of the peoples they ruled. Thus, Soviet ethnographers in the 1920s adopted the Turkmen definition of their own nation as a group defined by common ancestry. While communist officials maintained that the Turkmen were only a *potential* nation — a nation that would be constructed with the help of the Soviet state — they accepted genealogical claims as the basis for Turkmen identity. Moreover, Soviet nationality policy had the paradoxical effect of bringing about the primordialization of national identities over time. A number of historians have argued that the creation of national territories, elites, and languages in the Soviet Union in the 1920s ultimately led to the reification of these constructed nations among indigenous elites and communist officials in Moscow. In the late Stalinist and postwar periods, Soviet ethnographers increasingly described ethnic groups as primordial and unchanging entities. Soviet historians became masters of the teleological narrative, determined to prove that Soviet nations had lived on their current territories since time immemorial.[8]

In Turkmenistan, the Soviet promotion of Turkmen nationhood served to unify the scattered tribes and to produce a conviction that this newfound unity was natural and historically inevitable. At the same time, Soviet policy institutionalized and legitimized existing social hierarchies based on genealogy, reinforcing both the dominance of Turkmen over non-Turkmen and the elevation of "pure-blooded" Turkmen over those with less impressive genealogies.

Ironically, this primordialization of Turkmen nationhood occurred even as the national elite was moving away from a strictly genealogical definition of Turkmen identity. After 1924, many Turkmen learned to speak the Bolshevik language of nationhood, in which a common language and territory — not kinship or descent — were the most important components of national identity. Over time, genealogical, territorial, and linguistic criteria fused into a synthesis that continues to shape debates about Turkmen nationhood today.

Identity and power in Turkmenistan

In Central Asia, ethnicity and statehood were not historically linked. Due to the region's position as a frontier between nomadic and sedentary civilizations, Central Asia had long been home to a rich and complex mix of peoples, languages, and cultures. The demographic structure of the region had resulted from the encounter between successive waves of nomadic Turkic migrants and the sedentary Indo-Europeans they conquered. Diverse communities lived intermingled and interdependent, while sharing a common Turco-Persian Islamic culture.[9] Prior to the Russian conquest in the late nineteenth century, the prevailing model of statehood was the Muslim dynastic state ruling over a multiethnic population. The notion that a state should exist for the benefit of a single ethnic group was unfamiliar.[10]

The network of identities and loyalties that characterized Central Asia prior to 1917 was extremely complex. Ethnic labels, such as Turkmen, Kazakh, and Uzbek had little practical significance, coexisting with more compelling religious, dynastic, and kinship-based forms of identity. Sedentary Central Asians were more likely to consider themselves simply "Muslims" or to identify with the state or region in which they lived. Traditionally nomadic groups tended to base their social structure and identity on genealogy; for them, subethnic identities based on kinship were most salient.[11] Central Asian nomads were hardly unique in their conceptualization of identity in terms of descent, since most notions of ethnicity include at least an abstract notion of kinship or shared blood.[12] Among the Turkmen, however, genealogy was of unparalleled importance. All those who called themselves Turkmen traced their origins back to a single mythical ancestor named Oguz-Khan. Each of the major Turkmen tribes — Tekes, Salïrs, Sarïks, Yomuts, Chodïrs, and Ersarïs — was thought to descend from one of Oguz's grandsons. These tribes were divided into a series of ever smaller sections and subsections, each of which was also presumed to descend from a common ancestor. Individuals were obliged to know their genealogy back at least five to seven generations; those who could not name their ancestors were scorned as "kurama" or "mongrels."[13]

Prior to the Soviet creation of a Turkmen national republic, the broad genealogical category of "Turkmenness" had little political and economic significance. Even major tribes such as the Tekes and Yomuts had little practical unity. Smaller segments on the genealogical tree — tribal subsections, lineages, and extended families — were the main sources of loyalty and identity.

Members of smaller-scale kin groups were obliged to support each other politically and cooperate with each other economically.[14] Because kinship was so important as a way of conceptualizing relations among individuals and groups, kinship links were sometimes invented when unrelated groups maintained close relations over an extended period. Common ancestors were "discovered" so that outsiders — client tribes, former slaves, and others — could be assimilated to the Turkmen genealogical tree.[15]

Genealogy — whether real or invented — was also the main basis for social stratification in Turkmen areas. Social status depended on the purity and antiquity of one's lineage and on descent from "core" Turkmen tribes. Certain tribes and tribal segments enjoyed prestige because of the presumed purity and antiquity of their lineage. Groups of less august pedigree (often those incorporated into the tribe at a later date) were viewed as socially inferior and not fully Turkmen.[16] A distinction was made between "pure-blooded" Turkmen (*ig*) and those descended wholly or in part from slaves or captives (*gul* or *yarïmcha*). Prior to the Russian conquest, the Turkmen were known and feared for their involvement in the Central Asian slave trade. The neighboring rural villages of Persia and Afghanistan were the main victims of Turkmen raids, in which groups of armed men on horseback would carry away captives to be sold in the slave markets of Khiva, Bukhara, and Marï. Tradition permitted Turkmen men to take female captives as wives or concubines; when they did so, the offspring and their descendents were known as *yarïmcha* (literally "half"). Freed slaves sometimes formed their own lineages, which were eventually incorporated into the genealogy of the Turkmen tribe with which they were associated. Although these *gul* (slave) lineages had full economic and political rights as members of the Turkmen community, they were considered inferior and could not marry "pure-blooded" Turkmen.[17]

Apart from slaves and their descendents, certain other groups claimed Turkmen identity but were not considered to be full-fledged Turkmen. In most cases, these were non-Turkmen groups that had merged into the Turkmen genealogical tree in the distant past. For example, there were a number of small groups of non-Oguz Turkic origin that had been incorporated into larger Turkmen tribes. The Ahal region contained groups that called themselves Turkmen and spoke Turkmen dialects, but were believed to be descended from the original Persian inhabitants of the area. There were also groups living along the border with Uzbekistan who declared themselves to be Ersarï Turkmen although other Ersarïs did not recognize them as such.[18] In addition to these "marginal" Turkmen, there were groups that were not considered Turkmen at all despite their linguistic and cultural resemblance to Turkmen. These were the "saintly" tribes known as the Ewlad, who claimed descent from the prophet Muhammad or the early Arab caliphs. They played a special religious role in Turkmen society, serving as Sufi leaders, mediators between feuding Turkmen tribes, and caretakers of cemeteries and religious shrines.[19]

In addition to Turkmen and Turkmenized groups, a number of non-Turkmen lived in the future Turkmenistan. The Ahal-Teke region included

Kurds, Persians, and Baluchis. The regions bordering on the neighboring Uzbek and Kazakh republics were inhabited by numerous Uzbeks and Kazakhs. The cities of Turkmenistan were predominantly populated by Tatars, Russians, Armenians, and others.[20] The relationship between Turkmen and non-Turkmen varied by region. In historically stateless Transcaspia, where Turkmen were in the majority, ethnic minorities generally occupied an inferior position. Kurds often worked as servants and hired hands for the Turkmen, while Persians were "conquered peoples" and paid tribute to the dominant Turkmen groups.[21] In the Bukharan emirate and the Khivan khanate, Turkmen made up a minority of the population and often protested their ill-treatment at the hands of the Uzbek majority. Yet, they were hardly an oppressed minority. The Turkmen in Khiva constituted a special military caste and received tracts of land and other special privileges in exchange for their service to the khan.[22]

This, then, was the complex and diverse society into which Russian colonizers and Soviet modernizers would introduce a new and radical proposition — that the world is divided into distinct peoples or "nations," each with a right to self-determination in its own territorial state.

Ethnicity and identity under Russian and Soviet rule

For centuries before the Russian colonial conquest, Turkmen groups had extensive contact with sedentary peoples and states. They had traded with and preyed upon neighboring settled peoples, acknowledged sedentary rulers as their nominal sovereigns, founded dynasties, and been courted as military allies. Until the late nineteenth century, however, most Turkmen had not come under the effective control of any state. Instead, they lived in self-governing communities led by tribal elders and military leaders chosen by popular consensus.

By the end of the nineteenth century, the nominal Turkmen recognition of neighboring sovereigns had become more real. In the second half of the nineteenth century, the Russian empire steadily encroached on Central Asia, turning Khiva and Bukhara into vassal states in the late 1860s and early 1870s.[23] The southeastern Turkmen, including the Tekes in Marï and Ahal, were conquered by the Russians after fierce resistance in the 1880s.[24]

The Russian state's attempts to categorize the peoples under its rule helped to introduce new notions of identity. The tsarist regime had traditionally classified its subjects on the basis of religion.[25] In the late nineteenth century, Russians began to entertain new ideas about the relationship between language, descent, and ethnicity. Colonial ethnographers used criteria, such as physical type, language, and ancestry to divide the native population into distinct "peoples."[26] This work of classification anticipated the division of Central Asia along ethnic lines that would take place under the Soviets.

New notions of identity were also taken up by native Central Asians, under the influence of ideas circulating in Turkey and elsewhere in the Muslim world. In the early part of the twentieth century, Muslim reformers known as *jadids* began to question many aspects of traditional Central Asian culture, demanding reforms that would better equip their society to face the challenges of modernity and European colonialism. The *jadids* advocated a more rationalized, secular approach to education, the development of a written vernacular language, and changes in the status of women. Influenced by the Young Turk nationalists in the Ottoman Empire, they also began to promote Western-style conceptions of nationality, advocating a common Turkestani territorial identity and a single Central Asian Turkic language.[27]

The process of change begun under tsarist rule accelerated after the Russian revolutions of 1917. The Bolsheviks set out in much more deliberate fashion to transform and "modernize" Central Asia. Despite their ideological commitment to Marxist internationalism, the Soviets promoted ethnic nationhood in the non-Russian areas under their tutelage. Soviet authorities created nominally autonomous ethnoterritorial republics, promoted indigenous elites, sponsored the standardization of indigenous languages, and promoted native-language education and publishing. The Bolshevik commitment to promoting national cultures and national autonomy was based in part on a pragmatic calculation that this policy would win the support of the national minorities of the former Russian Empire.[28]

Along with pragmatic goals, the policy had firm ideological underpinnings. Lenin and Stalin believed that nations were objective entities, representing an essential stage of historical development through which every human group must pass. Moreover, the Bolshevik leaders were tolerant — at least in theory — of nationalism among the peoples of the non-Russian periphery, viewing such sentiments as an understandable response to past oppression suffered at the hands of tsarist colonizers.[29] Concessions to the national feelings of oppressed nations were, therefore, designed both to win their trust and to allow their more rapid progress toward socialism. Soviet ideology had little room for notions of racial difference or for a belief in the inherent inferiority of certain human groups; on the contrary, the Soviets insisted that all nations, no matter how poor or "backward," were equal and equally capable of progress. Nationhood was a temporary condition that could best be overcome, in true dialectical fashion, through the intensive promotion of national differences; eventually, all nations would attain the internationalist utopia of socialism.[30] Yet, the Soviet nations did not disappear or merge into one happy socialist family, as predicted; instead, the national differences institutionalized in Soviet republics only solidified over time.

Beginning in the 1920s and 1930s, the formative period of the Turkmen republic and the Soviet multinational state, the Bolshevik promotion of Turkmen nationhood had several important effects. First and most obviously, it reinforced existing social hierarchies by elevating the Turkmen over other ethnic groups within the republic. By according preferential treatment to the "titular nationality" and its language, the Soviet regime institutionalized the long-standing political and social dominance of the Turkmen within Turkmen-majority areas. Ethnic Turkmen received preferential treatment in hiring and were appointed to some of the republic's highest positions. In education, too,

Turkmen were favored; the largest quotas for university admission were reserved for Turkmen, while the Commissariat of Education placed a priority on establishing a network of Turkmen-language village schools. New laws mandated that the Turkmen language be used in educational institutions and offices throughout the republic. Moscow provided generous funding for the publication of Turkmen-language newspapers and textbooks and for the study of the Turkmen "national culture."[31]

In addition to reinforcing the preeminence of ethnic Turkmen, Soviet rule reinforced the dominance of powerful and high-status Turkmen groups. The Tekes, for example, had long been the largest and strongest Turkmen tribe. In the new Soviet republic, the Tekes' natural advantages were reinforced by their closeness to the levers of power.[32] Tekes occupied the core areas of Transcaspia, which had been under direct Russian colonial rule since the 1880s. Unlike the Yomut and Ersarï Turkmen of Khiva and Bukhara, the Tekes had experienced several decades of exposure to the Russian language and Russian officialdom. Their proximity to and familiarity with the Russian and Soviet authorities led to their recruitment into Soviet government and educational institutions in greater numbers than other Turkmen.[33] Because they were considered reliable, Tekes were often sent to non-Teke regions to take up important political positions. Turkmen of other tribes complained bitterly about "Teke hegemony" and "Teke arrogance," but to little avail.[34]

At the local level, too, Soviet rule reinforced existing Turkmen social hierarchies. Within each region, the strongest and most distinguished Turkmen lineages quickly came to dominate resources, such as Communist Party membership, access to higher education, and leadership of village soviets. The most influential citizens — often "pure-blooded" Turkmen or members of "saintly" tribes — got the best jobs in the Soviet bureaucracy. Even Koshchi, the Soviet-sponsored union of poor peasants, was dominated by influential community elders rather than by the poor and the dispossessed.[35]

Even as it reinforced the conviction that ethnic Turkmen and traditionally dominant groups should be preeminent in the republic, Soviet rule also fostered new conceptions of Turkmen identity. Beginning in the 1920s and 1930s, "Turkmenness" was transformed into something more closely resembling European understandings of nationhood. While presumed blood descent remained important for determining who was a Turkman, Soviet ideas about language and territory as critical components of identity also gained currency within the republic. Border disputes and language standardization became new arenas in which Turkmen elites could debate and solidify their embryonic sense of nationhood.

In Joseph Stalin's famous definition, a nation was a "historically evolved, stable community" sharing a "common language, territory, economic life, and psychological makeup manifested in a community of culture."[36] A national language and homeland were high on the Soviet list of defining attributes of nationhood. Yet, the Turkmen were geographically and linguistically fragmented, speaking a variety of dialects and scattered across the territory of at least five different states. Only with the acquisition of a national territory and a unified language, the Soviets believed, could the Turkmen be transformed from a *potential* into a *real* nation.

Throughout the Soviet Union, the Bolsheviks created "national territories" to fulfill the pledges of autonomy and cultural development made to non-Russian ethnic groups. For the Turkmen, a "national territory" was unprecedented. The boundaries of a Turkmen homeland had never been clearly defined because of the tribes' many migrations over the centuries and the fact that Turkmen-inhabited areas fell under the rule of a number of different states (Persia, Afghanistan, the Russian Empire, Bukhara, and Khiva, to name only the most important). Well into the Soviet period, Turkmen groups migrated regularly and freely across the region's supposedly inviolable sovereign borders. The existence of large Turkmen populations in neighboring countries meant that the new Soviet republic could not hope to include a majority of ethnic Turkmen within its boundaries. Equally problematic was the fact that Turkmen identification with territory was local and not "national"; each Turkmen descent group considered its land to be exclusively its own and not the property of the Turkmen people as a whole.[37]

Although the creation of a Turkmen national republic in 1924 represented a novel solution to the problem of Turkmenness, Turkmen elites for the most part welcomed this move enthusiastically. Exposure to the ideas of the *jadids*, Russian ethnographers, and Bolshevik nationality experts had persuaded some Turkmen that their "nation" deserved its own homeland and government. This piece of territory, however arbitrarily it might be defined, would henceforth become the focus of Turkmen national aspirations. The process of drawing national borders itself served to solidify incipient nationalist sentiments among Turkmen elites, encouraging them to pit the interests of their own future republic against those of other embryonic Central Asian nations. For each future republic, the Communist Party appointed a subcommittee made up mainly of members of the relevant nationality, who were expected to negotiate with representatives of other nationalities over the division of territory, cities, and populations. This process itself lent a competitive and acrimonious spirit to the delimitation, reinforcing a sense of common identity and destiny among the members of each ethnic group.[38]

The creation of national republics also had the effect of institutionalizing and "nationalizing" preexisting ethnic conflicts in Central Asia. Prior to the Russian conquest, Yomut Turkmen and Kazakh nomads in the northwestern part of Transcaspia had carried on a low-level war for decades over grazing lands for their flocks. In the Khivan khanate, Turkmen and Uzbeks had long clashed over access to land and scarce water resources. Under the Soviets, these communal and local feuds were transformed into "national" conflicts, requiring the intervention and mediation of republican governments and occasionally the Communist Party leadership in Moscow.[39]

Along with national territories, the Bolsheviks vigorously promoted language as an essential attribute of nationhood. The process of creating "national languages" faced special problems in Central Asia. Central Asia was dotted by a multitude of locally spoken Turkic dialects with subtle variations in pronunciation, vocabulary, and grammar, each shading into the next in a way that confounded any attempt to draw national borders between them.[40] Moreover, language generally had little to do with an individual's identity. In pre-Soviet Central Asia, especially among the urban and sedentary population, Muslims were often multilingual in Persian, Turkic, and Arabic, and language did not necessarily coincide with ethnicity. An individual of "Uzbek descent" might consider Tajik to be his or her native language, while Turkmen-speaking sacred tribes were considered to be Arabs.[41]

Because of the closeness of Turkic dialects, some pan-Turkic nationalists in Turkey and the Russian Empire called for the creation of a single Turkic written language to facilitate communication among the Turkic peoples. Central Asian *jadids* advocated a single Central Asian Turkic language.[42] The Soviets, however, favored the creation of a separate written vernacular for each Soviet Turkic "nation." Turkmen elites agreed wholeheartedly. Viewing the proposals of pan-Turkists as outright linguistic imperialism, they welcomed the idea that the Turkmen language should be developed as a distinct written vernacular.[43] The Turkmen dialects belonged to the Western or Oguz branch of the Turkic family, and were, therefore, more closely related to Azerbaijani and Anatolian Turkish than to the Turkic dialects of neighboring Central Asian peoples, such as Uzbeks and Kazakhs; this made it easier to argue against submerging Turkmen in a common Turkestani language.[44] Just as they had welcomed the unfamiliar notion that the Turkmen "nation" deserved a territorial entity of its own, Turkmen elites quickly adopted the Soviet emphasis on language as a critical component of "national" identity.

In the 1920s and 1930s, language became an immensely important symbolic arena for working out the meaning of Turkmen nationhood. A tremendous amount of time and effort was spent on combining elements of the diverse Turkmen dialects into a single "national" language — an exceedingly delicate task, since each tribe was determined to promote its own dialect. Like the preferential recruitment of Turkmen into Soviet jobs and educational institutions, moreover, language use became an arena of conflict between Turkmen and Russians. Turkmen intellectuals and communists insisted that Turkmen be used as widely as possible in schools, government offices, and the press, in accordance with the official Soviet policy of indigenization. Most Russians, however, viewed Turkmen as a barbarian tongue and did everything possible to avoid having to learn it. Because Russian-speakers continued to dominate Soviet institutions, Russian continued to be the lingua franca of the Soviet bureaucracy. The result was rising tension and mutual recriminations between Turkmen officials and their European colleagues.[45]

From Soviet republic to nation-state

Between World War II and the collapse of the Soviet Union, the promises of the early Soviet years were gradually fulfilled. Turkmen came to dominate the institutions of the Turkmen republic, which increasingly resembled a nation-state in all respects but the possession of actual sovereignty. Like many Soviet ethnic groups, the Turkmen became more rooted in and committed to their Soviet-demarcated territory over time. As Olivier Roy has argued, the existence of national-territorial institutions allowed Central Asians to develop a "habitus" of nationhood even in the absence of a nationalist ideology.[46]

The demographic dominance of ethnic Turkmen within the republic grew steadily in the last decades of the Soviet Union's existence. The proportion of Turkmen within the republican population rose from around 61 percent in 1959 to 72 percent in 1989, while the proportion of Russians, which had increased during the tsarist and interwar periods, declined from 17.3 to 9.5 percent. This trend was due both to high Turkmen birth rates and to the reluctance of most Turkmen to leave their home republic. Although the Soviet Union was a country of considerable geographic and social mobility, Central Asians tended to remain within their own republics, where the titular nationality had advantages in university admissions, employment, and other spheres. In addition, there was a net outmigration of Russians and other non-Muslims from Central Asia beginning in the mid-1970s.[47] The growth in the proportion of Turkmen living in cities has been particularly striking. At the time of the Russian revolution, the Turkmen population was overwhelmingly rural and made up only 7 percent of the urban population of Transcaspia. By 1989, Turkmen constituted 54 percent of the population of the republic's cities.[48]

The political preeminence of the Turkmen also grew in the later decades of Soviet rule. The proportion of Turkmen in leadership positions within the government rose, as did the numbers of Turkmen in the Communist Party.[49] While local officials in Central Asia naturally had to defer to Moscow on important questions, the considerable autonomy they enjoyed in local affairs was evident in the highly developed patronage networks and frequent corruption scandals of the late Soviet period.

In the early 1990s, the faux-nations of the Soviet Union acquired real national sovereignty. Along with the other Central Asian republics, Turkmenistan declared its independence from the Soviet Union in October 1991.[50] The republic's communist leaders rapidly refashioned themselves as nationalists, trading the hammer and sickle for symbols of Turkmen nationhood.[51] Yet, while the state's ideology has changed, many of its policies have not. Preferential treatment for the titular nationality and the indigenous language has continued, although the rationale is now explicitly nationalist rather than Marxist-Leninist.[52] No longer hindered by the ideology of Soviet internationalism, which forced them to share preeminence with Russians and other non-Turkmen, ethnic Turkmen can now dominate the republic as they please. Despite formal guarantees of equality for all ethnic groups, Russians and other minorities have been emigrating from independent Turkmenistan at a rapid pace.[53]

The once-novel association of language and territory with Turkmen identity is taken for granted today. Although concern with the Turkmen language was limited to a small literate elite in the 1920s, the spread of mass education during the Soviet period gave large numbers of people a vested interest in the widespread use of their native language. Since 1991, the Turkmen government has passed new laws declaring Turkmen to be the official state language and mandating its use in all official contexts. Russian-speaking government employees must learn Turkmen or lose their jobs; dissertations must be written in Turkmen and defended in front of a Turkmen-speaking committee.[54]

For this formerly nomadic people, the emphasis on the Turkmen "homeland" in state ideology is particularly striking. According to an old Turkmen proverb, a Turkmen's home was wherever his horse happened to stand.[55] Today, government officials and scholars spare no effort to prove that the Turkmen have occupied the current territory of the Turkmen state for millennia. As a speaker at a state-sponsored conference on Turkmen national identity put it, "the ancient historical roots of the Turkmen in the territory of Turkmenistan go back almost 4,000 years."[56] Turkmen living "abroad" (a majority of those who call themselves Turkmen) have been granted Turkmen citizenship and invited to return to their "historic homeland."[57] Since most non-Turkmen historians believe that the Turkmen migrated onto their current lands only within the last two or three centuries, the emphasis on the antiquity of Turkmen ties to the land has required some scholarly acrobatics. One approach has been to deny the nomadic history of the Turkmen by claiming that they are descended not from the Oguz tribes but from the Parthians, a sedentary Indo-European civilization that flourished on the territory of modern-day Turkmenistan from the second century B.C. to the third century A.D.[58]

For all the emphasis on the Turkmen language and homeland, genealogy remains an important component of identity among Turkmen. Some scholars have argued that Soviet rule reinforced kinship-based loyalties, in part because all other forms of independent social organization were suppressed.[59] In a survey taken on the eve of independence, 88 percent of Turkmen polled could name their own tribe and clan, while 57 percent said that people of their own tribe had a greater number of positive characteristics than Turkmen of other groups. Fifty-six percent of those polled predicted the fragmentation of the Turkmen people along tribal and regional lines; only 24 percent expected that the Turkmen would successfully unite into a single strong nation.[60] The Turkmen flag, which features carpet ornaments representing each of the main tribes, reflects these genealogical divisions. After more than seventy years in which the Soviets promoted the equality of all nations and tribes, genealogical hierarchies remain important. Most Turkmen still know which of their fellow Turkmen are former Persians or Uzbeks, which are *ig*, and which are *gul*. Sacred tribes are still regarded as being genealogically distinct and rarely intermarry with others.[61] The adoption of a nationalist ideology has also legitimized the dominance of "pure" Turkmen. In border areas near Uzbekistan, where Turkmenized Uzbeks once participated in local government, the administration has been taken over by members of core Turkmen tribes.[62] In July 2000, Turkmen President Saparmurad Niyazov declared that preference in university admissions should go not just to Turkmen-speaking applicants, but to those whose family pedigrees reveal them to be the worthiest.[63]

At the same time, genealogical issues are considered divisive and are little discussed in public. Although it is common knowledge that President Niyazov hails from the Teke tribe, the government avoids referring to his origins so as not to arouse the antagonism of non-Tekes. Officials insist instead that Niyazov is a "son of all the Turkmen" and above petty clan divisions. (This argument is facilitated by the fact that Niyazov grew up in a Soviet orphanage, having lost his entire family during a catastrophic earthquake in 1948.) As in Soviet days, the regime tries to appease other tribes by ensuring that they are represented in government institutions.[64] To emphasis his status as a supra-clan paternal figure, Niyazov is known by the honorific title Turkmenbashi, which means "head of the Turkmen." Niyazov has exploited popular concern about genealogical divisions to justify his dictatorial powers. He argues that a strong hand is needed to unite a divided nation, and that democratic institutions and a free press are dangerous because they may fuel tribal conflict.[65]

Conclusion

Over the past century, the Turkmen have been transformed from a stateless, fragmented population of seminomadic tribes into an independent, self-proclaimed nation-state. It would not be an exaggeration to say that the Soviet regime itself was responsible for this transformation. Yet, Lenin's belief that the promotion of nations would eventually lead to their disappearance proved misguided. The Turkmen, like other Soviet peoples, successfully internalized the Soviet conception of a nation as a group possessing its own language, territory, and history. This understanding of nationhood is embedded in the governmental, educational, and cultural institutions of contemporary Turkmenistan, most of which date from the Soviet period.[66] At the same time, certain features of the pre-Soviet ethnic system have remained in place and were even reinforced by Soviet rule — most notably, the importance of genealogy and the long-standing conviction that Turkmen are entitled to dominate others. Although the Bolshevik theorists of the 1920s officially rejected both primordial nationalism and ethnic hierarchy, their policies inadvertently helped to legitimize both in post-Soviet Turkmenistan.

Notes

1. This essay is based in part on research conducted for my book, *Tribal Nation: The Making of Soviet Turkmenistan* (Princeton: Princeton University Press, 2004).

2. E.J. Hobsbawm, *Nations and Nationalism Since 1780: Programme, Myth, Reality* (Cambridge: Cambridge University Press, 1990), 10–11.

3. The earliest and most influential proponent of the view of the Soviet Union as a "nation maker" was Ronald G. Suny. *See* his book, *The Revenge of the Past: Nationalism, Revolution, and the Collapse of the Soviet Union* (Stanford: Stanford University Press, 1992); *see also* Yuri Slezkine, "The USSR as a Communal Apartment, or How a Socialist State Promoted Ethnic Particularism," *Slavic Review* 53 (Summer 1994), 414–452, and Francine Hirsch, "The Soviet Union as a Work-in-Progress: Ethnographers and the Category *Nationality* in the 1926, 1937, and 1939 Censuses," *Slavic Review* 56 (Summer 1997), 251–278.

4. In non-European regions, colonial states created not just nations but also ethnic groups, castes, and tribes. *See* Donald L. Horowitz, *Ethnic Groups in Conflict* (Berkeley: University of California Press, 1985), chapters 2, 4; Nicholas Dirks, "Castes of Mind," *Representations*, vol. 37 (1992), 56–78. Dale Eickelman, *The Middle East and Central Asia: An Anthropological Approach*, 3rd ed. (New Jersey: Prentice Hall, 1998), 139–140; Thomas Hyland Eriksen, *Ethnicity and Nationalism: Anthropological Perspectives* (London/Boulder, CO: Pluto Press, 1993), 80–82.

5. Olivier Roy, *The New Central Asia: The Creation of Nations* (New York: New York University Press, 2000), vii.

6. Joseph Stalin, "Marxism and the National Question," in *Marxism and the National and Colonial Question* (London: Lawrence and Wishart, 1936), 5; Terry Martin, "Modernization or Neo-Traditionalism? Ascribed Nationality and Soviet Primordialism," in Sheila Fitzpatrick, ed., *Stalinism: New Directions* (Routledge, London and New York, 2000), 348.

7. Francine Hirsch, "Race without the Practice of Racial Politics," *Slavic Review* 61, no. 1 (Spring 2002), 30–43.

8. Martin, "Modernization or Neo-Traditionalism"; Yuri Slezkine, "N.Ia Marr and the National Origins of Soviet Ethnogenetics," *Slavic Review* 55.4 (1996), 826–861; Peter Blitstein, "Stalin's Nations: Soviet Nationality Policy between Planning and Primordialism, 1936–1953" (Ph.D. dissertation, University of California Berkeley, 1999), 9–10.

9. Beatrice Manz, "Historical Background." in Beatrice Manz, ed. *Central Asia in Historical Perspective* (Boulder: Westview Press, 1994), 4–7; Roy, *The New Central Asia*, 1–5.

10. Manz, "Historical Background," 12.

11. Adeeb Khalid, *The Politics of Muslim Cultural Reform: Jadidism in Central Asia* (Berkeley: University of California, 1999), 238–244; Hisao Komatsu, "The Evolution of Group Identity among Bukharan Intellectuals in 1911–1928: An Overview," *Memoirs of the Research Department of the Toyo Bunko*, no. 47 (1989), 117; Seymour Becker, "National Consciousness and the Politics of the Bukhara People's Conciliar Republic," in *The Nationality Question in Soviet Central Asia*, ed. Edward A. Allworth (New York: Praeger, 1973), 160–161; Timur Kocaoglu, "The Existence of a Bukharan Nationality in the Recent Past," in Allworth, ed., *The Nationality Question in Soviet Central Asia*, 154–155; On identity in Central Asia, *see also* John Samuel Schoeberlein-Engel, "Identity in Central Asia: Construction and Contention in the Conceptions of 'Ozbek,' 'Tajik,' 'Muslim,' 'Samarqandi,' and other groups" (Ph.D. dissertation, Harvard University, 1994).

12. On ethnicity and descent *see* Horowitz, *Ethnic Groups in Conflict*, chapter 2; Hobsbawm, *Nations and Nationalism since 1780*, 63–67; Robert Kaiser, *The Geography of Nationalism in Russia and the USSR* (Princeton: Princeton University Press, 1994), 11–14.

13. William Irons, *The Yomut Turkmen: A Study of Social Organization among a Central Asian Turkic-Speaking Population* (Ann Arbor: University of Michigan, 1975), 40–44. SSSR komissiia po raionirovaniiu Srednei Azii, *Materialy po raionirovaniiu Srednei Aziia. Kniga 1, territoriia i naselenie Bukhary i Khorezma* (Tashkent, 1926), 239. Genealogy commonly forms the basis for identity among pastoral nomadic groups, whose mobility precludes strong identification with a particular territory. A.M. Khazanov, *Nomads and the Outside World* (Cambridge, Eng., 1984), 138–139. On the role of genealogy in the construction of ethnicity in the Middle East and Central Asia, *see* John Armstrong, *Nations Before Nationalism* (Chapel Hill, 1982), chapter 2; Andrew Shryock, *Nationalism and the Genealogical Imagination: Oral History and Textual Authority in Tribal Jordan* (Berkeley and Los Angeles, 1997), 311–328.

14. Wolfgang König, *Die Achal-Teke: Zur Wirtschaft und Gesellschaft einer Turkmenengruppe im XIX Jahrhundert* (Berlin: Akademieverlag, 1962), 72–73.

15. Anthropologists have pointed out that genealogical systems are extremely malleable. Anatolii Khazanov, *Nomads and the Outside World* (Cambridge: Cambridge University Press, 1984), 142–143; König, *Die Achal-Teke*, 72–73, 78–79; Irons, *The Yomut Turkmen*, 56–58.

16. For this reason, the Bek subsection of the Teke tribe and the small Garadashlï tribe were particularly esteemed. König, *Die Achal-Teke*, 79–83.

17. Yu. E. Bregel, *Khorezmskie turkmeny v XIX v.* (Moscow: Izdatel'stvo vostochnoi literatury, 1961), 28, 161–164. The Russians outlawed the slave trade.

18. G.I. Karpov, "Turkmeniia i Turkmeny," *Turkmenovedenie*, no. 10–11 (October–November 1929), 39; König, *Die Ahal-Teke*, 84; *Materialy po raionirovaniiu Srednei Azii*, 241–242.

19. V.N. Basilov, "Honour Groups in Traditional Turkmenian Society," in *Islam in Tribal Societies: From the Atlas to the Indus*, eds. Akbar S. Ahmed and David M. Hart (London: Routledge, 1984), 220–243. F.A. Mikhaillov, *Tuzemtsy zakaspiiskoi oblasti i ikh zhizn: etnograficheskii ocherk* (Ashgabat, 1900), 38–39; Irons, *The Yomut Turkmen*, 65–66.

20. Gosudarstvennyi arkhiv Rossiiskoi Federatsii (henceforth GARF), f. 3316, op. 20, d. 156, l. 48; Shirin Akiner, "Uzbekistan: Republic of Many Tongues," in *Language Planning in the Soviet Union*, ed. Michael Kirkwood (London: Macmillan Press, 1989), 103. *See also* Rossiiskii gosudarstvennyi arkhiv sotsial'no-politicheskoi istorii (henceforth RGASPI), f. 62, op. 2, d. 286, ll. 13–16, 19–21.

21. RGASPI, f. 62, op. 2, d. 286, ll. 182–185, 164.

22. On the Khivan Turkmen, *see* Bregel, *Khorezmskie turkmeny* and G.I. Karpov and D.M. Batser. *Khivinskie turkmeny i konets kungradskoi dinastii* (Ashgabat: Turkmengosizdat, 1930).

23. Mehmet Saray, *The Turkmens in the Age of Imperialism* (Ankara: Turkish Historical Society, 1989), chapter 4. On the subjugation of Bukhara and Khiva, *see* Richard Pierce, *Russian Central Asia, 1867–1917: A Study in Colonial Rule* (Berkeley and Los Angeles: University of California Press, 1960), 22–34; Seymour Becker, *Russia's Protectorates in Central Asia: Bukhara and Khiva, 1865–1924* (Cambridge: Harvard University Press, 1968), 26–78.

24. Saray, *The Turkmens*, chapter 4; Karpov, *Ocherki po istorii Turkmenii*, 18–22; Pierce, *Russian Central Asia*, 40–41.

25. Michael Khodarkovsky, " 'Ignoble Savages and Unfaithful Subjects': Constructing non-Christian Identities in Early Modern Russia," in *Russia's Orient: Imperial Borderlands and Peoples, 1700–1917*, eds. Daniel R. Brower and Edward J. Lazzerini (Bloomington: Indiana University Press, 1997), 9, 15; John Willard Slocum, "The Boundaries of National Identity: Religion, Language, and Nationality Politics in Late Imperial Russia" (Ph.D. dissertation, University of Chicago, 1993), 54.

26. Daniel Brower, "Islam and Ethnicity: Russian Colonial Policy in Turkestan," in Brower and Lazzerini, eds., *Russia's Orient*, 115–116, 122–130. *See also* Slocum, "Boundaries of National Identity," 3–6; Peter Holquist, "To Count, To Extract, To Exterminate: Population Statistics and Population Politics in Late Imperial and Soviet Russia," in Ronald G. Suny and Terry Martin, eds., *State of Nations: Empire and Nation-Making in the Age of Lenin and Stalin* (Oxford: Oxford University Press, 2001), 111–144.

27. For more detail on the ideas and goals of the Central Asian *jadids, see* Khalid, *Politics of Muslim Cultural Reform*.

28. Suny, *Revenge of the Past*, chapter 3; Martin, *The Affirmative Action Empire*, 2–3.

29. Terry Martin, *The Affirmative Action Empire: Nations and Nationalism in the Soviet Union, 1923–1939* (Ithaca: Cornell University Press, 2001), chapter 1; Slezkine, "The USSR as a Communal Apartment," 418–421.

30. Slezkine, "The USSR as a Communal Apartment," 416; Martin, *The Affirmative Action Empire*, 2–8.

31. *See* Edgar, *Tribal Nation*, chapter 3.

32. RGASPI, f. 62, op. 1, d. 22, ll. 209–212; op. 3, d. 513, ll. 121–122. In 1927, the relative population strength of the major tribes was estimated as follows; Tekes, 270,254; Yomuts, 103,729; Saruks, 32,729; Salurs, 35,541; Göklengs, 20,899; Chaudirs, 24,077; Ersaris, 157,483. Karpov, "Turkmeniia i Turkmeny," 39–40.

33. RGASPI, f. 62, op. 1, d. 22, ll. 209–212; op. 3, d. 513, ll. 121–122; op. 2, d. 874, ll. ll. 19–31; d. 2818, l. 13. Examination of the backgrounds of a number of leading party officials in the 1920s and 1930s reveals that a majority were Tekes from Transcaspia. For lower-level positions, the evidence is mostly impressionistic and anecdotal; there is little hard data about recruitment by tribe, since this information, unlike information about recruits' national origins, was rarely included in *korenizatsiia* reports. The small amount of quantitative evidence that is available does support the picture of Teke dominance. *See*, for example, RGASPI, f. 62, op. 2, d. 1986, l. 20.

34. RGASPI, f. 62, op. 2, d. 874, ll. 19–21, 23–24, 31; d. 2818, l. 20.

35. RGASPI, f. 62, op. 2, d. 286, l. 107; RGASPI, f. 62, op. 2, d. 874; ll. 19–21, 23–24, 31.

36. I.V. Stalin, *Marxism and the National Question* (New York, International Publishers, 1942), 12.

37. The making of a modern nation-state requires a shift from a local conception of territorial belonging — the view that one's village is one's homeland, in effect — to a broader under-

standing of the "national territory." *See* Kaiser, *Geography of Nationalism*, 16–17. On "national" borders in non-European areas and their consequences, *see* Basil Davidson, *The Black Man's Burden: Africa and the Curse of the Nation State* (New York: Times Books, 1992); William F.S. Miles, *Hausaland Divided: Colonialism and Independence in Nigeria and Niger* (Ithaca: Cornell University Press, 1994).

38. For more detail on Turkmen elites and the delimitation, *see* Edgar, *Tribal Nation*, chapter 2.

39. GARF, f. 3316, op. 19, d. 39, ll 11, 15–17; op. 64, d. 46, l. 43; op. 64, d. 410, l. 32; op. 20, d. 1034, ll. 260, 269. A succession of committees under the auspices of the all-union Central Executive Committee was charged with resolving border disputes and other conflicts among new Central Asian republics. See GARF, f. 3316, op. 64, d. 410; also op. 19, d. 309.

40. Shirin Akiner, "Uzbekistan: Republic of Many Tongues," in *Language Planning in the Soviet Union*, ed. Michael Kirkwood (London: Macmillan Press, 1989), 100; William Fierman, *Language Planning and National Development: The Uzbek Experience* (Berlin and New York: Mouton de Gruyter, 1991), 69–71.

41. For a detailed analysis of language and identity in Central Asia, *see* Schoeberlein-Engel, "Identity in Central Asia," 19–23. *See also* Edward A. Allworth, *The Modern Uzbeks: From the Fourteenth Century to the Present, A Cultural History* (Stanford: Hoover Institution Press, 1990), 176–179. These circumstances produced interesting results during the Soviet census of 1926, when siblings would sometimes declare themselves to be of different nationalities. Becker, "National Consciousness," 160–161.

42. Khalid, *Politics of Muslim Cultural Reform*, 211–214.

43. Tagangeldi Tächmïradov, "Razvitie i Normalizatsiia Turkmenskogo Literaturnogo Iazyka v Sovetskuiu Epokhu," (Avtoreferat dissertatsii, Ashgabat, 1974), 10, 13; D. Chersheev, *Kul'turnaya revoliutsiia v Turkmenistane* (Ashgabat: Izdatel'stvo Turkmenistan, 1970), 46. *Tokmak*, no. 21 (1925), 3. M. Geldiev, " 'Türkmenistan gazetining dili ya ki bizde adalga (istilah) meselesi?" *Türkmenistan*, April 14, 1925, 2; A. Gulmuhammedov, "Shive chekishmesi yekebar diling bozulmasï meselesi?" *Türkmenistan*, January 19, 1926, 2–3.

44. On the origins of the Turkmen language, *see* A.P. Potseluevskii, *Dialekty turkmenskogo iazyka* (Ashgabat: Turkmengosizdat, 1936); A.M. Annanurov, *Razvitie turkmenskogo iazyka za sovetskii period* (Ashgabat: Ylym, 1972), 4–5.

45. RGASPI, f. 62, op. 3, d. 397, l. 109; d. 490, ll. 148–149; *Türkmenistan*, no 211 (September 16, 1928). Cited in RGASPI, f. 62, op. 2 d. 1641, l. 58. *Tokmak*, no. 31 (1927), p. 3; *Türkmenistan* no. 173 (August 3, 1927). Cited in RGASPI, f. 62, op. 2, d. 1185, l. 116.

46. Robert J. Kaiser, "Ethnic Demography and Interstate Relations in Central Asia," in Roman Szporluk, ed., *National Identity and Ethnicity in Russia and the New States of Eurasia* (Armonk, NY: M.E. Sharpe, 1994), 232; Suny, *Revenge of the Past*, chapter 3, 111–112; Roy, *The New Central Asia*, xiii–xiv.

47. Kaiser, "Ethnic Demography," 232–237, 240, 243, 250.

48. Ibid., 239–240.

49. Shokhrat Kadyrov, *Turkmenistan v XX Veke: Probely i Problemy* (Bergen, Norway, 1996), 184; Robert Lewis, ed., *Geographic Perspectives on Soviet Central Asia* (New York: Routledge, 1992), 52.

50 Michael Ochs, "Turkmenistan: The Quest for Stability and Control," in Karen Dawisha and Bruce Parrott, eds., *Conflict, Cleavage, and Change in Central Asia and the Caucasus* (Cambridge, Eng.: Cambridge University Press, 1997), 315–316.

51. On the "nationalizing" policies of the Central Asian states, *see* Graham Smith, Vivien Law, Andrew Wilson, Annette Bohr, and Edward Allworth, *Nation-Building in the Post-Soviet Borderlands: The Politics of National Identities* (Cambridge, Eng:: Cambridge University Press, 1998), 7–19, 139–163.

52. Ibid., 139, 142–143.

53. By 1995, Turkmen made up 77 percent of the population, while the Russian share had dropped below 7 percent. The remainder were mostly Uzbeks, Kazakhs, and members of other Central Asian ethnic groups. Ochs, "Turkmenistan," 333, 337–338. The alienation of Russians in a Turkmen nation-state has been tempered by government policies designed to prevent the departure of skilled workers and professionals, many of whom are non-Turkmen. John Anderson, "Authoritarian Political Development in Central Asia: The Case of Turkmenistan," *Central Asian Survey* 14 (4) 1995, 516.

54. Ochs, "Turkmenistan," 334, Jeren Sawyer, "Turkmen Nationalism and Higher Education," *Central Asia-Caucasus Analyst* (on-line version), Field Reports, November 22, 2000.

55. Kadyrov, *Turkmenistan v XX Veke*, 78.

56. B.O. Shikhmuradov *et al.*, eds., *Türkmen halkïnïng gelip chïkïshïnïng dünye yairaishïnïng we onung dövletining tarïkhïnïng problemalarï* (Ashgabat: Rukh, 1993), 12, 25.

57. Kadyrov, *Turkmenistan v XX Veke*, 76; Shahram Akbarzadeh, "National Identity and Political Legitimacy in Turkmenistan," *Nationalities Papers*, vol. 27, no. 2 (June 1999), 277–278.

58. Kadyrov, *Turkmenistan v XX Veke*, 70; Akbarzadeh, "National Identity," 280–289.

59. Anatoly Khazanov, *After the USSR: Ethnicity, Nationalism, and Politics in the Commonwealth of Independent States* (Madison: University of Wisconsin Press, 1995), 128; Roy, *The New Central Asia*, chapter 5.

60. Kadyrov, *Turkmenistan v XX Veke*, 87–88.

61. The Communist Party first secretary, Sukhan Babaev (1951–1958), who belonged to one of the small "Persian" tribes, was regularly attacked by political opponents for not being a "real Turkmen." Kadyrov, *Turkmenistan*, 152.

62. Kadyrov, *Turkmenistan*, 117.

63. "Niyazov suggests Revamping College, University Curricula," Turkmen Report, *RFE/RL Turkmen Service*, July 21, 2000.

64. Ochs, "Turkmenistan," 317.

65. Anderson, "Authoritarian Political Development," 514; Ochs, "Turkmenistan," 316–318.

66. On continuity between Soviet and post-Soviet institutions in Turkmenistan, *see* Akbarzadeh, "National Identity," 271–290.

13

Becoming Cambodian
Ethnicity and the Vietnamese in Kampuchea

CHRISTINE SU

In the midst of casual conversation, a close personal friend once told me that "it is *necessary* that we Cambodians hate the Vietnamese." The animosity, and furthermore, the exigency of such animosity expressed so succinctly in this statement will come as no surprise to the reader at all familiar with Cambodia, or Kampuchea, and more specifically, with the history of relations between Kampuchea and Vietnam. A level of enmity between the two nations, and subsequently, between Cambodians and Vietnamese, has its roots in centuries-old territorial conflict and is well-known to laypersons and scholars alike.[1] However, when I pressed my companion for an explanation as to why, in 1995, Cambodians necessarily *must* hate Vietnamese, he unhesitatingly responded, "There is no why — it's just a fact." Of significance here is the effortlessness with which my companion made the initial statement and subsequent response, both of which, I argue, would not be inconsistent with those of a significant number of Cambodians, both in Cambodia and abroad.[2] Cambodians are bombarded with anti-Vietnamese propaganda from a variety of sources on a regular basis, reminding them that the Vietnamese are the "hereditary enemy,"[3] the perpetual "threat to Khmerness."[4] They are thieves, gamblers, traitors, prostitutes. They are the antithesis of all that is Cambodian. The anti-Vietnamese response on the part of Cambodians is expected, and has become almost automatic.

What a Cambodian and "Khmerness" is forms the nucleus of many a debate. Still, there are recurring themes in how Cambodians, or *Khmer*, as they are known in their own language, define themselves. To be Khmer (1) is to be Buddhist; (2) is to speak the Khmer language[5]; (3) to be a descendant of the creators of Angkor Wat and the Bayon, massive temples in the north of Cambodia, and to acknowledge and respect that history; (4) to be the progeny of Kaundiya, an ancient Indian Brahmin prince, and Soma, the daughter of a *Naga* (sea-serpent) Princess; and (5) importantly, to be Khmer is to be flexible, to understand the impermanence of things and thus to readily adapt to changing situations. Narratives, such as the origin legend of Kaundiya and Soma, Buddhist *Jataka* tales, and folk stories help to explicate the Khmer worldview, unifying disparate complexities into an integrated whole. While there are different versions of the creation legend, for example, inherent in each is the blending of two different entities, foreign and native, human and animal, "culture" and "nature," and their attendant belief systems.[6] Cambodians stress that from their very origins, they incorporated and reconciled divergent worlds to form Khmerness. Geographically, as part of the crossroads that comprise what is now known as Southeast Asia, ancient Cambodia experienced individuals, ideas, practices, and materials from many countries, including India, Indonesia, Portugal, and China. Yet, rather than either rejecting or unreservedly accepting them, the indigenous inhabitants adapted and redrew exogenous concepts and rituals to accommodate local interests and predilections. No culture is static, but Cambodians stress that their culture expressed extraordinary flexibility.

This dynamism and elasticity seemed to reemerge in the last decade of the twentieth century. In 1993, after decades of civil war, during which Cambodia was isolated from nearly all of the outside world (under Communist rule from 1975 to 1979, and Socialist rule from 1979 to 1991), Cambodia held its first democratic elections, sponsored and overseen by the United Nations Transitional Authority in Cambodia (UNTAC).[7] While certainly not without numerous challenges, the elections ushered in a period of renewed optimism and interchange. Following UNTAC, Cambodia allowed and experienced a rush of outside economic investment by those who wished to explore a new Southeast Asian market. Young scholars found an increasing number of international academicians and courses at Cambodia's two universities. An unprecedented number of think-tanks, language institutes, and business schools opened, offering a multitude of opportunities for Cambodians to exchange ideas with French, Irish, Australian, Japanese, and Americans, among others.

Yet despite this renewed openness, anti-Vietnamese sentiment continued. Indeed, animosity escalated in the 1990s, often resulting in violent attacks — particularly against ethnic Vietnamese in Cambodia, many of whom had lived in Cambodia for decades and considered themselves Cambodian.[8] Post-UNTAC, as Cambodians sought to rediscover and redefine themselves, the Cambodia–Vietnam national conflict increasingly morphed into an internal ethnic conflict. For many, the definition of Cambodian became more specific: to be Khmer is to be *ethnically* Khmer — or at least, not ethnically Vietnamese.

Judy Ledgerwood, May Ebihara, and Carol Mortland note that Cambodians in the 1980s and 1990s commonly asserted that they no longer had a culture — any semblance of culture died with the Khmer Rouge aggression and subsequent years of despair. Furthermore, it is particularly bewildering for survivors that the Khmer Rouge were Cambodian.[9] The perpetrators of such horrific crimes were members of their own culture, their own society, their own "race" — to be Khmer is to be (albeit unwillingly) part of a holocaust. How could they reconcile this with all they had been taught about Khmer greatness? Certainly, in their search to comprehend such inexplicable realities, Cambodians might seek to locate a nonindigenous cause for such horrific suffering, and subsequently reinterpret history through that lens. Indeed, one possible explanation that various political groups wish to disseminate suggests that the Khmer Rouge took direction from an external impetus: the Vietnamese. While there are several powerful sources that may have contributed to Cambodians' political, economic, geographic, social, or personal upheaval, and despite the fact that Vietnamese forces deposed the Khmer Rouge, the overwhelming nemesis, as bolstered by propaganda and media and thus cited by Cambodians themselves, is Vietnam and the Vietnamese — and by extension, the ethnic Vietnamese Cambodians.[10]

In my brief discussion of Cambodian identity, notwithstanding popular opinion, I include ethnic Vietnamese in this intellectual category (Cambodians). I do not suggest that ethnic Vietnamese are or could possibly become ethnic Khmer. Nor do I suggest that tensions between the two are fabricated or unwarranted. I acknowledge these tensions and have discussed some of them in the subsequent paragraphs. However, I do suggest that ethnic Vietnamese are a part of the fabric of Cambodian society, and should be examined as such. I hope to provide insight into the extant lives and thoughts of Cambodians — including both ethnic Khmer and ethnic Vietnamese — as experienced on the ground. I rely heavily on the interviews I conducted in both urban and rural Cambodia in 1995 and 1996. During this time, I explored various areas with significant ethnic Vietnamese populations, including various districts in Phnom Penh City, the provinces of Kampot, Kratie, Kompong Cham, and Takeo.

The chapter is divided into two parts: first, I briefly discuss three areas in which Vietnamese are perceived to threaten Khmerness, and how these perceived threats have become integrated into Cambodian identity.[11] Second, I discuss the effects these perceived threats have on ethnic Vietnamese Cambodians, in terms of self-identification and reaction, at both group and individual levels. Both, moreover, contribute to the boundaries and centers of what it means to be Cambodian, to be Khmer.

The threat to Khmerness

Land

The front page of a late 1995 Khmer newspaper reported that Vietnam was formulating a plan to usurp a large portion of southern Cambodia. The report, complete with a map roughly outlining the scheme, suggested that "yuon"[12] planned to expropriate the Cambodian provinces of Prey Veng, Svay Rieng, Kompong Cham, Kratie, Rattanakiri, Mondulkiri, and Stung Treng, therefore extending Vietnamese territory and border to the Mekong River. The article even exposed the very hotel in which the plans allegedly were being formulated, although the perpetrators themselves were not mentioned by name or association with a particular organization. Arguably, these were unknown, making the story itself less plausible, but from a Khmer perspective, still very viable.[13]

The belief that Vietnam will overtake Cambodia is strongly held by ethnic Khmer, both in Cambodia and abroad. A Khmer newsletter published out of California, U.S.A., for example, stresses that Vietnam's aim "has always been to create an Indochinese Federation under its power."[14] They express pronounced distress about "shrinking" Cambodian borders, and report that in various provinces, namely Svay Rieng, Kompong Cham, and Prey Veng, the Vietnamese have extended their borders inside current politico-legal boundaries.

Khmer point to history to support claims of current impending confiscation of Cambodian soil. Historian Chou Meng Tarr notes, "quite clearly, forms of Cambodian racism toward the Vietnamese minority [in Cambodia] did not develop in a historical vacuum," but rather, in response to the " 'expansionist' tendencies of the pre-colonial Vietnamese imperial state."[15] Vietnamese movement into Cambodian territory began in the late sixteenth and early seventeenth centuries, and increasing numbers of Vietnamese moved into the Mekong Delta, eventually taking over Prey Nokor, now known as Ho Chi Minh City. Vietnam eventually came to control the southern area now known as Kampuchea Krom, where many ethnic Khmer still live.[16] (See Figure 1 and Figure 2). This history of encroachment, including highly unflattering stories of the surreptitious takeover of Kampuchea Krom, was taught openly in schools prior to the Khmer Rouge regime, and although less openly imparted today, the stories (and related attitudes) are passed down from generation to generation and ingrained in Khmer minds from a young age. They are reinforced regularly by the media; anonymous reporters warn of clandestine attempts to deceive Khmer.[17] Another 1995 article, for example, suggested that some ethnic Khmer may look to Southern Vietnamese (as opposed to Northern, "communist" Vietnamese) in their search for democracy. *Have you forgotten Kampuchea Krom?* the author asks, bewildered. Vietnamese are Vietnamese, he writes, and any Vietnamese who may seem kindhearted (or democratic) may easily change face (*trolop dae*). To trust Vietnamese is to forget the injustice of Kampuchea Krom: "The fact is that Yuon are Yuon. There are no good Vietnamese, from the South or the North. There are only those who are looking for the opportunity to take everything."[18]

Even in Phnom Penh, where land ownership is a complicated issue for all Cambodians,[19] Vietnamese have always been seen as trespassers. Khmer identify many of the squatter settlements that have sprung up around Phnom Penh since the early 1990s as "Vietnamese areas," despite their variegated ethnic makeup. Along the river Tonle Bassac in Phnom Penh, Vietnamese settlers have constructed a small village of floating houses. The area lies in front of two Khmer Buddhist temples, and the Vietnamese living there are so despised that even the temple monks have organized several attempts to expel them from the area.

Fig. 1 Current political boundaries of Cambodia.

Politics

In early December 1995, the Cambodian government arrested 38 persons allegedly associated with an anti-Communist group, which called itself "Free Vietnam," ostensibly planning to overthrow the Hanoi government in Vietnam. "Cambodia will not allow Free Vietnam to continue its activities here," stressed a police official in a newspaper interview. "Please go back to your country. We do not want to see bloodshed in Cambodia again."[20] On one hand, the government has asserted that the "new" Cambodia is a democracy, open to exchange of ideas and freedom of expression. On the other, in its actions it has communicated that this democracy does not apply to the ethnic Vietnamese. Vietnamese political concerns should not be played out on Cambodian soil, and thus officials have made valiant attempts to stop "Free Vietnam" and other political and even social activities associated with ethnic Vietnamese.[21]

Accompanying the threat of land takeover by Vietnamese is the threat of political takeover. If allowed to gather or demonstrate, the ethnic Vietnamese will soon dominate Cambodian politics. Again, this perceived threat has its

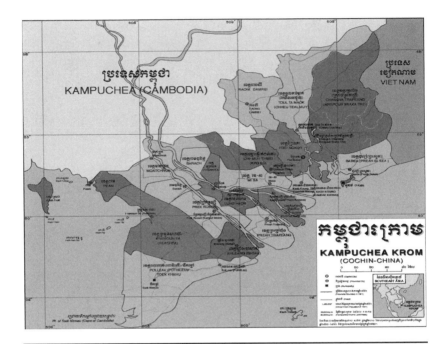

Fig. 2 Map of Cambodia showing Kampuchea Krom areas. The lighter shaded area indicates the southern boundary of the current political territory of Cambodia. The dark shaded areas delineate the various provinces of Kampuchea Krom, formerly part of the Kingdom of Cambodia, now part of the current political territory of Vietnam.

roots in history. Between 1835 and 1840, the Vietnamese emperor in Hue colonized Cambodia with Vietnamese criminals and prisoners of war from prior military engagements. During this time the Vietnamese, whose culture and ethos was Confucian, attempted a thorough "civilization" of "barbarian" Cambodian political culture and social customs. Cambodian provinces were given Vietnamese names, and Khmer officials replaced with Vietnamese administrators. In the absence of a sitting Cambodian monarch, the Vietnamese appointed a Cambodian queen according to Sino-Vietnamese, not Khmer, coronation ceremonies. In addition, the Vietnamese took away the Cambodian royal vestments and regalia thought by Khmer to be necessary for Cambodian monarchs to maintain and exercise their political legitimacy and moral authority.[22]

The perception of the Vietnamese as a political threat was exacerbated in the nineteenth and early twentieth centuries by French colonial policy. The French chose to "bypass Cambodians in favor of Vietnamese with the education and work experience" to serve in the colonial administration, convinced that Vietnamese were "technically more 'rational' than their more 'traditional' Cambodian neighbours and thus better-suited for administrative positions."[23]

The Vietnamese installation of the Heng Samrin regime following the overthrow of the Khmer Rouge in 1979, while appreciated for halting the genocide of Pol Pot, the leader of the Khmer Rouge regime, is criticized as yet another ploy by Vietnam to subjugate Cambodia politically. A young Khmer with whom I spoke extensively insisted that while the Vietnamese indeed stopped the horrors of Pol Pot, they only did so for their own purposes, in order to infiltrate and secure their hold on Cambodia, and continue to influence current leaders (see Figure 3). A Khmer newsletter from the 1990s reiterated that, during the Hun Sen regime, Vietnam "encouraged the Vietnamese 'settlers' to 'invade' the country and accept Cambodian nationalities." Extremists allege that even during the UNTAC-sponsored elections of 1993, Vietnamese soldiers entered Cambodia "in civil clothes," thus "endangering the future of Cambodia once the UN is gone."[24]

The UNTAC-supported Electoral Law of 1992 specified that any adult (person over 18 years of age) born in Cambodia, who also had at least one parent born in the country, was eligible to vote, regardless of other criteria. Because the elections were to be overseen by UN personnel, and not local authorities (who often assessed language ability, mannerisms, and dress to exclude the ethnic Vietnamese), anti-Vietnamese parties feared and circulated another takeover scare. Jay Jordens notes that although "by the time the elections took place, many of those [ethnic Vietnamese] who might . . . have voted had fled the country in terror," the suffrage issue became yet another facet of the alleged Vietnamese political threat.[25] In particular, the Buddhist Liberal Democratic Party (BLDP) suggested that "not content with occupying Khmer territory, [ethnic Vietnamese aim] to hijack the Khmer nation's future through the vote."[26] Under pressure, then-UN Special Representative of the Secretary General Yasushi Akashi organized Strategic Investigation Teams (SITs) to investigate allegations of the presence of foreign forces. By the end of the UN mission, SITs had "located and positively identified [exactly] three persons," who happened to be ethnic Vietnamese, "who qualified as members of a foreign force."[27] Rumors about throngs of Vietnamese loyalists present during the elections were unsubstantiated; however, Vietnam still loomed as a threat in some minds. "Perhaps there were only three," one of my respondents admitted, "but those three were Vietnamese."[28]

Culture

Perhaps most troubling for ethnic Khmer in terms of the perceived threat posed by the ethnic Vietnamese is the conviction that they denigrate Khmer culture. The Vietnamese are often described as the very antithesis of all that is Khmer, "offer[ing] cultural contrasts on almost every point."[29] "They don't know how to act Khmer" is a commonly held assertion. As one example, during the Water Festival (*Bon Om Tuk*) held in Phnom Penh in November 1995, a fight broke out between a woman selling drinks and festival officials. I was watching from

Fig. 3 Cartoon from *The Fighter*, November 1995. This illustration exemplifies Cambodians' common fear that their leaders, including Prime Minister Hun Sen, Prince Ranariddh, and King Norodom Sihanouk, operate under the influence of Vietnam, represented by the menacing caricature figure located behind them, wearing the stereotypical Vietnamese conical hat.

a third-floor window along the riverbank, and as the fight progressed news eventually reached me that the woman was Vietnamese. The woman had Khmer physical features, and later (in newspaper accounts) self-identified as Khmer, but because she was acting inappropriately and had attracted negative attention, the conclusion by those watching was that she must necessarily be Vietnamese. Ethnic Khmer believe ethnic Vietnamese occupy the lowest strata of Cambodian society. They are the undesirables: thieves, gamblers, and drunkards. Consider this anecdote, related by a university student in Phnom Penh:

> There is a house located near Union Hotel and the Pasteur Institute. It is a café style restaurant serving the Vietnamese. The owner is Vietnamese. He does not care about the hygiene and health of the people when he let[s] the water that is used to wash the dishes flood the street . . .[30]

The ethnic Vietnamese are described as dirty, backward, arrogant, and cruel.

Contrariwise, Khmer, specifically Khmer women, are described as exemplars of beauty, strength, and virtue, as reflected in the graceful Apsara figures sculpted both tangibly in the glorious Angkor monuments and symbolically in the minds of Khmer through folktales and legends. Thus, it was not surprising that when, in the course of determining where I should go to interview ethnic Vietnamese, quite a few acquaintances suggested that I investigate local brothels. I was told numerous times both that "all Vietnamese women are prostitutes" and that "all prostitutes are Vietnamese." A Khmer newspaper article in December 1995 claimed that Vietnamese in Cambodia make a better living for themselves than do Khmer for the following reasons: (1) any Vietnamese families coming to Cambodia which have daughters will employ them as prostitutes to earn money; and (2) Vietnamese with enough capital to buy or rent a house will immediately open up a brothel.[31]

Khmer cultural ideals dictate that "women are to walk slowly and softly, be so quiet in their movements that one cannot hear the sound of their silk skirt[s] rustling. While she is shy and must be protected, before marriage ideally never leaving the company of her relatives, she is also industrious."[32] Thus the behavior of prostitutes — notably, (1) standing or sitting quite visibly outside brothels (and thus neither within the sanctuary of the home nor diligently working in an acceptable way) and (2) loudly whistling at, catcalling, and even touching men as they pass by the brothels on motorcycles — stands in absolute contrast to the Khmer ideal.

There are a significant number of Vietnamese prostitutes in Cambodia. Yet, there are also prostitutes of other ethnicities, including ethnic Khmer. Still, the conviction that the Vietnamese presence will vilify Khmer culture by infiltrating the country with prostitutes is so strong that it alone is seen by some as reason enough to prohibit Vietnamese from entering Cambodia. Prostitution is one link in a chain of corruption, notes one Khmer student, and once entangled in such corruption, "a Khmer is no longer a Khmer."[33] Like the beautiful, seductive Cochinchine who caused Cambodia to lose Kampuchea Krom (see endnote 17), Vietnamese prostitutes threaten the integrity of the Khmer family unit and Khmerness.

Perhaps the most important manifestation of Khmer culture, moreover, is Theravada Buddhism, often said to be the foundation of Khmer society. The popular association of Vietnamese with Christianity, and often Catholicism, then, is another factor which identifies them as alien. Vietnamese are said to have no respect for either Khmer (Theravada) Buddhism or Khmer places of worship. An article in the *Nokor Phnom News*, a popular Khmer language newspaper, related that the Vietnamese government planned to construct a port along the Mekong River in southern Vietnam, in Kampuchea Krom lands. In order to construct the port, the report continued, they would first have to construct a road from the provincial capital to the river, which would require the removal of trees and relocation of houses inhabited by ethnic Khmer. It would also collide with the gates of a Khmer pagoda, which is very important to the Khmer living there. Vietnamese government officials will permit destruction of or damage to the gates, asserted the author of the article, proving that they fail to respect Khmer culture. Further, the author implored: "Don't take advantage of this development to formulate a *strategy of destroying heritages* which are integral to the identity of Khmer Kampuchea Krom."[34]

Disrespect for temples has also been cited as a culture-destroying stratagem by ethnic Vietnamese in Phnom Penh. In particular, representatives of two temples in Meanchey district, Wat Chrak Andre Leo and Wat Chrak Andre Krom, claim that the ethnic Vietnamese living on the adjacent river fail to respect the Wats and their monk inhabitants. An elder Khmer monk related,

> There are more than 100 houses of Vietnamese near the pagoda and they make trouble. The trample the pagoda area to cross to the big road [in front of the temple]. Sometimes children steal the fruit of the pagoda and uproot plants outside . . .. Some people sell sugarcane outside the temple and leave bags and trash all around. My thought is that I don't want the Vietnamese people to live here because the pagoda is a quiet, clean place for monks and people to follow Buddhism, but the people who live near here cause trouble. We [monks] don't have any place to wash — we used to wash in the river but now there are a lot of people here — noisy, dirty — oh!

Other city ills, such as the fires that plague crowded settlement areas, are attributed to the Vietnamese. When in August and October 1995 fires swept through "Bo Ding," a squatter settlement area near the Kabkor Market, rumors immediately surfaced that Vietnamese families had set them.

Finally, in several newspapers and propaganda pieces, as well as in common parlance, the Vietnamese have been compared to an HIV Virus which, following the metaphor, has infected Cambodia and is spreading like wildfire.

The threat to Vietnameseness

Loss of land and life

Although it has its basis in history, as described above, the fear that Vietnamese will take over Cambodian land became a major issue in the aftermath of UNTAC. The influx of UNTAC soldiers and workers greatly inflated prices of land and commodities, prices many Cambodians were unable to deal with after UNTAC left. Unable to purchase or lease land, many are forced to move frequently, relying on fishing and farming in random areas for their survival. There is a common perception that it is ethnic Vietnamese who live this gypsy-like existence, squandering natural resources, without concern for effects on the environment or the needs of others. As one Khmer fisherwoman told me,

> We Khmer only take the big [i.e., full-grown] fish, but the Vietnamese will take all of the small [i.e., young] fish, too. That leaves us with fewer fish. This is not good, not right.

Competition between ethnic Vietnamese and ethnic Khmer for scarce resources translates into perceived economic threat, once again linked to a perceived plan of usurpation. Khmer seem untroubled by the fact that Vietnamese are often targeted for taxes and fines in the marketplace by police to a greater extent than are ethnic Khmer. One Khmer publication stressed that

> the trade between Vietnam and Cambodia enables the Vietnamese to enter and leave Cambodia very easily. Every day, more and more Vietnamese come to Cambodia because it is easier to do business … the commerce between the two neighboring countries that allows the settlement of Vietnamese *will make Cambodia follow the fate of Kampuchea Krom.*[35]

Ironically, however, ethnic Vietnamese often find themselves being evicted from lands they supposedly have come to usurp. The Khmer Rouge in particular has never attempted to conceal its collective hatred for the Vietnamese, and their attacks on ethnic Vietnamese villages continued throughout the 1980s and 1990s. A small farming village I visited in Kampot province was attacked twice — once in 1985 and again in 1994. Small fishing villages in Kratie province were also targeted. One woman related that she returned from Vietnam in 1979 (having fled in 1975) and attempted to find her home village, but from that year on the Khmer Rouge entered the area three or four times, shooting at the people. After the fourth incident, she decided to relocate further downstream. Asked why she remained in the face of such danger, she commented, "Well, Vietnam is not 'home,' even though the real home is not so safe."

In many of the villages I visited, villagers (both Vietnamese and Khmer) have throughout the 1990s alternated between their villages in Cambodia and makeshift homes across the border in Vietnam to which they flee when an attack seems imminent. One Kampot woman related that before 1985 she had lived next to the village market. In that year, however, the Khmer Rouge attacked her village and burned her house. She moved to another house, but in 1994 there was a second assault, after which all of the villagers lived in fear of impending attacks. Thus ethnic Khmer and ethnic Vietnamese villagers alike, lived in the village during the day and crossed into Vietnam for the night, afraid to sleep in their own homes. "Only the village guard stayed here," she related. In Kompong Cham, an *ayd-jay* (scavenger-recycler), left her home village in 1973, yet returned as soon as she felt it possible in 1979. She found her village subjected to countless violent attacks, however, and so moved from village to village looking for another place to settle. Just before the UNTAC elections, she and her family fled to Vietnam in the face of more threats, but returned to Cambodia six months later.

It is not only the Khmer Rouge who participate in such violence. In a small fishing village in the Kampot province, inhabitants report that conflicts between local Khmer police (who ostensibly protect villagers from Khmer Rouge attacks), and ethnic Vietnamese fishermen have led to confrontations. They also report that the transport of lumber between the area and Vietnam by Vietnamese traders often leads to confrontations with Khmer "sea guards." In Phnom Penh, gangs of young Khmer men have attacked Vietnamese in known Vietnamese enclaves.[36] One family living outside Wat Chrak Andre Krom, for example, lived in Battambang until 1973 and the beginnings of Khmer Rouge harassment, after which they fled to Vietnam. In 1983, they attempted to return to Battambang, but continued attacks eventually led them to relocate to Phnom Penh, where they built a floating house along the river. Still, assaults, now by local authorities, continued. She related,

> Every day my husband goes to catch fish and I sell some cakes, candy, and cigarettes, but we don't earn enough to eat. Every year I've paid the pagoda commission [for permission to stay here], and now the commission has asked twice that the Vietnamese families leave anyway. But I'm waiting for the third time.

Her desire to stay in Cambodia did not stem from a desire to own (Cambodian) land, however:

> In Vietnam the government did give us some rice to eat and some land to plow rice fields, but the lands were not along the river. We are fishermen, so we came back to Cambodia to find a place to catch fish.

The ethnic Vietnamese have had to develop a certain degree of tolerance for the possibility of attack, and somehow subsist prepared to flee from their homes — and homeland. Facing loss of lives and land, the ethnic Vietnamese have responded by uprooting themselves innumerable times. Notably, however, the fact that so many respondents were able to relate stories of leaving *and returning* despite the threat of violence suggests both tenacity and incredible flexibility — and as has perhaps gone unacknowledged by some Khmer, a strong attachment to the sense of place that is Cambodia, lack of land ownership or claim to permanent homes notwithstanding.

Political powerlessness

On December 6, 1995, the Cambodian Council of Ministers approved a Nationality Law that was to take effect in 1996.[37] The impending institution of this law caused a great deal of concern for several reasons. First, Article 8 of the law stipulated that anyone who wished to apply for naturalization as a Cambodian citizen must have proof that he or she had been living in Cambodia continuously for 5 years since the "reception of a residential card which was granted within the framework of the Immigration Law." This proved problematic for the ethnic Vietnamese, who as noted above were forced to change places of residence frequently, and may have had to leave Cambodia several times. Additionally, even those who had lived in Cambodia since birth did not have this proof — that is, a paper or card testifying to their continuous residence — for as James Kanter and Ed Madra report, the Ministry of Interior admitted that "*no* residency cards had yet been issued under the Immigration Law."[38] Second, Article 19 of the law specified that naturalized Cambodians could be stripped of their nationality if found guilty of "insulting and contemptuous behavior towards the Khmer people." Gross indiscretions were likely executed as the result of Article 19, allowing those who dislike Vietnamese to randomly accuse them of acting inappropriately. The specifications of what constitutes "insulting and contemptuous behavior" are unclear, and thus open to a wide range of interpretation — certainly, in the eyes of some, simply *being* Vietnamese runs counter to all that is Khmer. Loyalty to Vietnam by ethnic Vietnamese in Cambodia is often assumed, whereas in most cases, the opposite is true: while they may be *chuncheat vietnam* (Vietnamese in ethnicity), they see themselves and wish to be seen as *sunhcheat khmaer* (Cambodian in nationality). They are, in fact, seen as Cambodian by officials in Vietnam. Hundreds of fishing boats were escorted down the Mekong River to the Vietnamese border in order to escape violent attacks in 1993, for example, but Vietnam rejected roughly the 4,000 ethnic Vietnamese on the basis that they were Cambodian citizens.[39] With the exception, perhaps, of the thirty or so participants in the "Free Vietnam" movement, most ethnic Vietnamese do not contribute to nor wish to be associated with a specifically Vietnamese polity.[40] Rather, they wish to be seen as Cambodians. Ethnic Vietnamese do attempt to vote; however, their desire to do so can hardly be construed as evidence of a takeover conspiracy. The UNTAC voting procedure was complex and, while in many ways it was fair, in the end it excluded many ethnic Vietnamese from participating in the electoral process. For various reasons, some did not have identity cards. Others, who had identity cards, either had them seized by police, or were denied voting privileges on the basis of either their physical appearances ("too Vietnamese") or Khmer language ability ("not clear"). Discussing the 1993 elections, a 44-year-old farmer in Takeo province stated,

> I tried to vote, but when I got there they told me I was Vietnamese, and when I told them I was born in Takeo they didn't believe me. So I didn't get to vote. In the village the next day some of the other Vietnamese people told me they voted, and I wondered, how come I didn't [get to]? I suppose I could have protested with the UNTAC officials, but I didn't want to make trouble.

Others who were part-Khmer, but Khmer matrilineally — that is, their mothers were Khmer but their fathers Vietnamese — were not allowed to vote. Ethnic Vietnamese communities view such denials of suffrage as terrible blows, verdicts by the international community that they are not Cambodian. One woman noted, "Think about Cambodians and what they think about the UNTAC. If UNTAC said we do not have the right to vote, people will say that means we are not Cambodians, and may be that we do not have the right to be here." Ethnic Vietnamese do seek to obtain political status as Cambodian citizens, but not in hopes of aiding Vietnam in taking over the country; but rather, so that they can participate in community affairs, send their children to local schools, and so forth. An elderly Vietnamese gentleman I met in the Kompong Cham province displayed at least ten different identification cards and letters, all different in terms of size, writing, and "official" stamps. "I'm an old man — I have a lot," he joked. More seriously, however, he noted that the police came to "control" him and other ethnic Vietnamese who fish along the Mekong on a regular basis. The police regularly asked for letters from the authorities permitting them to remain in their homes on the Mekong, but the type and style of letter required often varied. He related,

> Last year I made one but already this year I must make a new one, a different kind from last year. They say the old letter is not important and must be changed. Every time I make the letter I have to give money to the police . . . [but] I must have it . . . if I go to Phnom Penh or to another province I must carry it with me.

When I visited a Takeo village in 1995, a group of ten or so individuals, mistakenly thinking that I had come to "control" them, ran to retrieve identity cards from their homes to show me. Two to three months before my visit, police came into the village looking for "intruders." At their discretion, they informed some villagers that they would need to update their cards, since, they said, new cards had been issued. Reluctantly, some villagers relinquished their cards and awaited the arrival of the new ones; however, they received back neither the old cards nor new, but rather, letters indicating that they were now of "immigrant status," and thus without rights accorded to citizens.[41] The identity card issue is further complicated by the unofficial but widely acknowledged reality, particularly post-UNTAC, as the cost of living has risen exponentially, that almost any individual, regardless of nationality or ethnicity, can obtain one for the right price. Those who have legitimate claims may not be able to obtain cards if they cannot pay, whereas others with no legitimate claim but adequate resources can obtain them in a matter of days. The acceptance or rejection of an ethnic Vietnamese individual's claim to be a Cambodian boils down to his or her ability to produce a receipt for the circumstances of his or her birth, for his or her very existence.

Culturelessness

> Khmer citizens shall be equal before the law and shall enjoy the same rights, freedom and duties, regardless of their race, colour, sex, language, beliefs, religion, political tendencies, birth origin, social status, resources or any other position.

So reads Article 31 of the September 1993 Constitution of the Kingdom of Cambodia. The tenor of the article is optimistic, yet as evidenced above, for the ethnic Vietnamese equality and freedom in Cambodia are seemingly inconceivable concessions. The ethnic Vietnamese have faced physical intimidation and disenfranchisement. Moreover, on a regular basis they face the reality that to many they are "yuon," with all of the term's negative connotations. They have often been defined by what they are not — that is, that they are not Cambodian, and therefore not part of the greatness Khmerness represents. It is unfortunate, but not surprising, then, that one finds evidence that in wanting to continue living in Cambodia, the ethnic Vietnamese have made some "cultural" changes, away from Vietnamese and toward Khmer culture. One might concede that in the mid-1990s, the ethnic Vietnamese desired that their ethnic identity decline in importance, and thus acted in such a way that their distinct Vietnameseness would become less visible or disappear. One might conclude that they set out to break down the markers of ethnic identity in "an active self-formation in the direction of alien norms."[42]

Language and identity In their attempts to find acceptance in Cambodian society, some ethnic Vietnamese have changed their names, or adopted a second, Khmer name in addition to their Vietnamese name. While name changes as such were not mandated by law (as was the case with ethnic Chinese in Thailand), some believe that taking a Khmer name will make them more readily embraced. Names, moreover, do become important in dealing with authorities. An applicant for a passport, for example, arguably has a better chance of obtaining one if he or she has a Khmer name, rather than one typically identifiable as Vietnamese.[43] Some ethnic Vietnamese, whether they have married Khmer or not, give their children Khmer family names and first names. Even more important than one's name, however, in both social and political arenas, is one's use of Khmer language.

One of the most critical means of gaining acceptance into a culture is mastering that culture's language. As a Khmer of mixed ancestry whose physical appearance often prevented others from trusting my Khmerness, I personally witnessed the increase in the level of acceptance of me by other Khmer as I gained proficiency in Khmer language. The same held true for ethnic Vietnamese with whom I worked. Many times, when I asked Khmer about the relationship between ethnic Khmer and Vietnamese, if their feelings were positive they responded as did one village chief: "There are no problems — they live with us, *they speak Khmer like us*, their children study in school with Khmer children," and so forth, attesting to the importance of language as a part of Khmer cultural identity (emphasis mine). Police often used facility in using Khmer language as a gauge of Khmerness: if one could speak Khmer clearly (without discernible inflection or accent), he or she was more likely to believed in claiming identity as a Khmer — physical appearance, name, and other factors notwithstanding.

Not surprisingly, then, while many of the individuals with whom I spoke use Vietnamese in the home, many do not encourage their children to learn Vietnamese. One Takeo woman stressed that her children understand Vietnamese because they speak it at home, but they are not formally taught: "They learn Khmer in school and that is important because we are in Cambodia." Most individuals expressed little regret about the disappearance of their mother tongue among their children. A cake-seller in Kampot retorted,

> No, I'm not sorry if my child forgets Vietnamese language, because we are Cambodians and so we must know Khmer language.

The lack of regret is reinforced by fear of others' dislike. She continued,

> Some [Khmer] people say they don't like to hear Vietnamese language. Some people who went to Phnom Penh told me that if you speak Vietnamese there the police will penalize you, so I don't want to speak it.

One bilingual and bi-ethnic man noted that while he personally was glad that he knew both Vietnamese and Khmer languages, particularly because knowing both had helped him in business, others feel that because he can speak both he is untrustworthy. Khmer acquaintances who regularly spent time with him and his family, accused him of being the "enemy" when he speaks Vietnamese. A trader in Kampot, close to the Vietnamese border, reflected that

> We are near the border so really we must know all the languages — Vietnamese come here every day to trade so we must know Vietnamese — and some speak Chinese so it's good to know that, also.

But, he stressed,

> In my ideas we live in Cambodia, so we must know Khmer language. So my child goes to Khmer school.

Most of the children in the areas I researched go to Khmer schools if they attend school at all (and many do not). Even in areas where there are Vietnamese schools, such as in Phnom Penh, much of the stress is on learning the Khmer language, with only secondary emphasis on Vietnamese.

Religion and ritual Before the destruction of the Khmer Rouge regime, there were a significant number of Vietnamese Catholic churches throughout the provinces. To judge by the number of Catholic churches (or at least, the remains thereof), as well as by the testimony of those who lived in Cambodia before the Khmer Rouge period, there were a great number of Vietnamese Catholics. An elderly Vietnamese man in Kratie province fondly recalled a French missionary named David who attracted many followers and converts:

> We loved David! Many, many of the Vietnamese followed him to the Catholic church . . . I can remember him well . . . when he died we were all very, very sad.

Like most religious structures in Cambodia, most of the Vietnamese churches were defiled by the Khmer Rouge. And while many of the Vietnamese who had fled from these areas returned during the Heng Samrin regime, they rebuilt almost none of these. These and Vietnamese Buddhist temples similarly destroyed have been left to decompose. In Kompong Cham province, all that remains of what was a large Catholic church is a cluster of large stones from the church's foundation. Several families returning after the Khmer Rouge regime literally built their homes on top of them. In Kratie, a former Vietnamese pagoda is now used as a district hospital; a former Catholic church became a provincial and district government meeting-house.

Most of the Vietnamese with whom I spoke, moreover, claimed that the majority of Vietnamese in Cambodia now are Buddhists. With the exception of one large Catholic community in Phnom Penh, Catholic disciples seem few, or at least, they do not wish to be identified. A large Catholic charity organization refused to lead me to the several Vietnamese communities to which it ministers for fear of less-than-benevolent motives on my part. A Vietnamese man in Kratie noted that when he was single he was a Christian, but after he married, he "became" Cambodian, which meant becoming a Buddhist. A respondent in Kompong Cham noted that in the early 1990s, a Christian missionary came to Kompong Cham town in the hope of converting the ethnic Vietnamese population therein, but attracted no followers. He thus left the province, and, the respondent continued, "Now no one comes here and there is no Church."

Conclusions and reflections

Becoming Cambodian

Some Khmer insist that they can somehow intrinsically tell the difference between ethnic Khmer and ethnic Vietnamese, and even between Vietnamese and Chinese persons, by identifying certain key differences. Vietnamese women, Khmer say, wear pants, and in particular, wide-legged black pants. Khmer women wear skirts. Vietnamese wear conical straw hats; Khmer wear *krama* (checkered scarves). Apparently there are other indicators as well — one Khmer interviewee told me that even if someone spoke Khmer fluently and dressed like a Khmer, he would still be able to tell by the way that individual walked, sat, and moved that he or she was Vietnamese.

For those less astute at determining the differences, however, the lines between Vietnamese and Khmer, at least in terms of the more visible indicators, seem to have become more blurred. More Vietnamese women wear traditional Khmer silk skirts; many Khmer women wear pants. In the countryside, I saw ethnic Khmer wearing the typically Vietnamese conical straw hats. Intermarriage with Khmer over generations has led to a blurring of physical features, which in the past enabled one to differentiate between Sino- or Viet-Khmer and "pure" Khmer.[44] More and more Vietnamese can and do speak Khmer, adopt Khmer names, and follow Khmer customs. Some ethnic Vietnamese have even begun to subscribe to stereotypes about Vietnamese, despite the fact that many endured discrimination on the basis of these. A young woman in Kampot, pointed out as an ethnic Vietnamese by other villagers, described herself to me as Khmer, and made several unflattering comments about the Vietnamese. She remarked,

> Here in Cambodia most people dislike Vietnamese, and I don't blame them because some who come here are bad people — mostly prostitutes and thieves. I hate them. Yes, some people discriminated against me when I first came because they thought maybe I was a prostitute . . . but now I am married [to a Khmer man], and I don't have this problem anymore.

Both Khmer and Vietnamese residents of nearly all of the villages I visited attested that prior to the Khmer Rouge regime, these areas had many more Vietnamese than they did at the time of my interviews (1995–1996), thus belying a common stereotype that Vietnamese in Cambodia have only recently begun to settle there. One small farming village in Kampot referenced above, for example, had more than 100 Vietnamese families in the 1960s — now there are only ten. Notably, while many Vietnamese may have only recently come to Phnom Penh, many had previously lived in other Cambodian provinces for extended periods of time, migrating to the city in the hope of finding safety there. The long-time ethnic Vietnamese residents tend to make generational distinctions between themselves and those Vietnamese who have just arrived. As encapsulated in the words of one woman, speaking about herself and her husband,

> We are Cambodian. We have lived here our whole lives except for Pol Pot. We are not like the prostitutes who have just come. Compared to them, we are *Khmaer-sot* ["pure" Khmer].

Thus, in reviewing this research effort, the reader might, as I did, first identify a propensity for the ethnic Vietnamese to disengage from their Vietnameseness, to discard elements of Vietnamese culture and replace them with Khmer elements. Indeed, I detected a yearning or even desperation on the part of the ethnic Vietnamese to be considered Cambodian. They speak the Khmer language and practice Khmer religions. They remain in Cambodia in the face of physical danger. They pay fines and taxes levied especially against them. They attempt to participate in democracy by obtaining identity cards and voting. They endure police harassment — anything to avoid expulsion from Cambodia. I immediately made a parallel — the very spheres in which they are perceived to pose a threat to Khmerness (land, politics, and culture) are the de facto causes of the disappearance of Vietnameseness. To use Henri Tajfel's terminology, ethnic Khmer are a group with a rampant positive social identity, whereas ethnic Vietnamese are a clearly threatened group. Thus, "in line with a pragmatic analysis of political realities," one could conclude that the ethnic Vietnamese "have opted . . . to lie low or simply to make socially desirable responses," or culturally speaking, to disappear.[45]

The project of Vietnamese identity

Upon my first reading of the material as it was presented to me (and here I mean both in person during interviews and via printed materials), it was quite easy for me to cling to a Gordon-esque interpretation of the ethnic Vietnamese experience — that is, that the Vietnamese desired and were well on their way to assimilation. Arjun Appadurai, however, notes that perhaps the most practical way of thinking about identity is to think about it as a project:

> That is to say, one can see ethnic identity as projected, so that it has a future, without entirely giving up the idea that it is produced by histories that are marked, and that identities are particular, and cannot therefore be completely expansive. Moreover, if one looks at identity movements, and sees them as *projects* that have futures, then one has a completely different sense, first, of the question of the past in relation to those projects and second, to put it simply, of who can join. This allows a kind of openness to inclusion in the project, although not necessarily to inclusion in the history.[46]

On reviewing my material again with this in mind, I submit an alternative interpretation. While some ethnic Vietnamese wished to separate themselves from any vestiges of being Vietnamese, many others maintained that being Cambodian was a kind of hybrid existence. That they wanted to be accepted as Cambodians is unquestionable. When I encountered ethnic Vietnamese who had learned Khmer, I first assumed they had only begun the attempt to discard their cultural heritage in its entirety, rather than engaging their ethnic identity, morphing it. As I reexamined my work, I began to see the void I had left in interpreting the ethnic Vietnamese experience. True, ethnic Vietnamese individuals expressed their desire to become Cambodian — but not necessarily to become (were this possible) ethnic Khmer. As related at the beginning of this chapter, a thoughtful interpretation of Cambodian identity sees it as a site of constant contention and creation, and as such, in becoming Cambodian, ethnic Vietnamese can maintain select Vietnamese traditions and customs — and discard or change others — without becoming any less "authentic" individuals as they do so.

Thus, as I reread my material, I began to notice alternative interpretations of the stories.

During the fall of 1995, for example, I was invited to and attended a provincial wedding, in an area known to be guarded heavily by the Khmer Rouge. Many of those attending wore traditional Vietnamese dress, and the ceremony was conducted in Vietnamese. Music with Vietnamese lyrics emanated from a cassette player. Yet, many other guests in attendance were ethnic Khmer. Khmer and Vietnamese in this area, despite the Khmer Rouge influence, sustained cordial and even close everyday relationships without hostility toward each other, and Khmer participated in Vietnamese cultural practices as frequently as Vietnamese did in Khmer practices.

Back in Phnom Penh, an elderly fortune teller informed me that she was "Cambodian in every way," and in response to my questions about her lifestyle told me she followed "Buddhism just like the Khmer, ate Khmer food, wore Khmer clothes." Much later in the conversation, I noticed pictures of Catholic saints in her room, after which she admitted, smiling, that she was indeed a "follower of Jesus Christ" and attended Catholic services in a Vietnamese church. I had questioned others about their religious beliefs, and several individuals claimed that "Vietnamese Buddhism and Khmer Buddhism are the same," or "close enough." Originally, I had interpreted this to mean that they as Vietnamese had begun practicing "the same" religion as Khmer (that they were legitimizing themselves by doing "the same" as ethnic Khmer). On a second reading, perhaps they meant that their religious practices had the same significance for them as Khmer practices do for Khmer, and that the differences in the sects of Buddhism did not interfere with their experiences of being Cambodian.

In retrospect, I believe a more informed view acknowledges that the ethnic Vietnamese, in becoming Cambodians, choose and develop alternate, dialectical sites of identity, just as Cambodians have done for centuries. I have begun to truly look at Cambodian identity in "project" terms. In *Mapping the Subject: Geographies of Cultural Transformation*, Steven Pile and Nigel Thrift suggest that in "mapping" identity, it is best to think of mapping not as pinpointing an individual in time and space, which implies fixity, but rather, as "wayfinding."[47] Reframing the ethnic Vietnamese experience in this way, to be Cambodian is to be in process: changeable and changing, flexible, and transgressive, while not altogether indistinguishable nor indefinite. Cambodians of all ethnicities hold and exchange narratives about life in Cambodia; thus, the categorical construction of Cambodian identity is informed by various elements: Khmer, Vietnamese, Chinese, Cham, French, Thai, and American. As Linnekin suggests in her discussion of Pacific Islander identity, "the premise of symbolic construction leads to a complex and open-ended view of culture as an arena of negotiation and contention."[48]

Finally, as Lilley asserts, "ethnic groups are not fixed entities opposed to one another by stable internal structures and external boundaries."[49] The situation of neither the ethnic Vietnamese nor the ethnic Khmer remains stable, externally or internally. Both are affected by the environments in which they live and the feelings they have about being in these environments. One final story underscores this theme. In a small village in Kampot province there are two Vietnamese families, one of whom came to Kampot in 1979. The members of this family were neither in Cambodia prior to Pol Pot nor were they born there, but rather, as the commune chief related,

> They came because one Khmer family from this village went to Vietnam during Pol Pot and came to know this [Vietnamese] family. They knew each other and liked each other and so when the war was over and the Khmer family came back to Cambodia, they brought the other family with them. And now we are all here, together.

Identity — albeit Khmer, Vietnamese, Cambodian — can be explored, though not calcified, through the narratives told by the people themselves. We can learn much, if we listen.

Notes

1. For example, Nayan Chanda, *Brother Enemy: The War After the War: A History of Indochina Since the Fall of Saigon* (New York: Harcourt Brace Jovanovich, 1986); David Chandler, *A History of Cambodia*, 2nd ed. (Boulder, CO: Westview Press, Inc., 1993); Meng Tarr Chou, "The Vietnamese Minority in Cambodia," *Race and Class* 34 (October to December 1992), 33–48; Maurice Comte, "Rapports de Classes et Relations Inter-Ethniques Dans Le Cambodge Precolonial," *ASEMI* VII (1976); Ben Kiernan, *How Pol Pot Came to Power* (London: Verso, 1985); Sherri Prasso, *Violence, Ethnicity, and Ethnic Cleansing: Cambodia and the Khmer Rouge* (University of Cambridge, 1995); W.E. Wilmott, *The Chinese in Cambodia* (Vancouver: University of British Columbia Publications Center, 1968); to name but a few.
2. As an ethnic Khmer born and raised in the United States, I was cognizant of the animosity between Khmer and Vietnamese long before arriving on Cambodian shores.
3. Ben Kiernan, "Myth, Nationalism, and Genocide in Cambodia," Unpublished paper, cited in Prasso, *Violence*, 11.
4. Prasso, *Violence*, 17.
5. Prasso, *Violence*, 23–24.
6. Chandler, *History of Cambodia*, 13.
7. In April 1975, the communist Khmer Rouge party in Cambodia had attempted to "revolutionize" Cambodian life, removing all inhabitants of Phnom Penh and relocating them in the countryside to work, and to follow the ways of the *angkar* (organization, the vague term for the Khmer Rouge power). The Khmer Rouge forced everyone to work long days in the fields, planting and harvesting rice, ostensibly to make Cambodia a self-sufficient nation. But the Khmer Rouge effected shocking brutality and genocide. During their control, by separating parents from children and husbands from wives, destroying Buddhist temples, outlawing private property, and randomly executing any who disobeyed orders, the Khmer Rouge fractured Cambodian spirits. The Khmer rarely saw the fruits of their labors, and thousands

starved to death. The trauma suffered by both the hundreds of thousands who died as well as those who survived will never adequately be ascertained. While the Khmer Rouge were deposed by Vietnamese forces in 1979, economically, physically, psychologically, and emotionally, Cambodia was left shattered.

8. Approximately 90 to 95 percent of the Cambodian population is ethnic Khmer (*see* Steve Heder and Judy Ledgerwood, Eds., *Propaganda, Politics, and Violence in Cambodia: Democratic Transition under United Nations Peace-keeping* (London: M.E. Sharpe, 1996); Ledgerwood, *Cambodian Culture*, 10–11), with ethnic Chams (Muslims), Chinese, Vietnamese, and others comprising the remainder of the population.

9. Ledgerwood *et al.* comment that "the question of how Khmer could inflict such suffering on fellow Khmer is of particular importance." *Cambodian Culture*, 8.

10. Scholarly undertakings by Penny Edwards and Jay Jordens provide excellent analysis of who used anti-Vietnamese propaganda, when they used it, and why. To reproduce an inventory as such is beyond both the scope and the intent of this essay. Rather, I will simply reiterate that the politics of memory — the relationship between identity, remembering, and forgetting — have been used by various political factions within Cambodia throughout the 1980s and 1990s to further their own agendas. Penny Edwards, "Imaging the Other in Cambodian Nationalist Discourse Before and During the UNTAC Period," in Heder and Ledgerwood, 50–72; Jay Jordens, "Persecution of Cambodia's Ethnic Vietnamese Communities During and Since the UNTAC Period," in Heder and Ledgerwood, 134–158). Moreover, I wish to point out that while Cambodians find themselves pushed one way or another by propaganda, they are also aware that it is propaganda, and that they are being so pushed. Their figuring out and internalization of identity goes beyond blind adherence to such propaganda. In other words, it is beyond arrogant for me to assume that Cambodians are only self-reflexive if we (i.e., critics or scholars) point it out to them.

11. Mine is certainly not an exhaustive list. One could discuss in detail the perceived economic threat, as just one further example. Rather, it is my attempt to highlight some of the Khmer perceptions of Vietnamese threat as the basis for further discussion about the ethnic Vietnamese themselves. I delineated these categories after extensive discussions with Khmer about the ethnic Vietnamese.

12. A derogatory Khmer language term for Vietnamese. Chou Meng Tarr ("Vietnamese Minority," 41) argues that the term has fallen out of common parlance, but I disagree. The term is commonly heard in casual and even formal conversation or radio broadcasts, and seen in written form in newspapers and magazines.

13. *Wat Phnom News*, November 27–28, 1995.

14. *Khmer Conscience*, VII (2: 1993), 35.

15. Chou Meng Tarr, "Vietnamese Minority," 34–35.

16. Chandler, *History of Cambodia*, 94–95.

17. Throughout 1995 and 1996, various newspapers reproduced the eighteenth century story of the Khmer king Chey Chentha II, who was "seduced" into allowing Vietnamese to take Cambodian land by Cochinchine, the beautiful daughter of a Vietnamese king. Oftentimes, the same story was simply given a title that referenced current Khmer–Vietnamese tensions — "Vietnamese Policy of Taking Khmer Land Through a Prostitute War," for example — and left for readers to ponder (*Ouddamagati Khmer News*, November 30, 1995, 2–4).

18. *Nokor Phnom News*, November 14, 1995, 1.

19. In the aftermath of the Pol Pot regime and civil war of successive regimes, thousands of Khmer found themselves displaced. Those who had lived in Phnom Penh were particularly affected: many returned from the provinces and/or refugee areas to homes they once owned in the city to find them already occupied by others who had returned ahead of them. Ownership papers were lost or destroyed during the Khmer Rouge regime, and thus the legitimacy of ownership claims was difficult to verify.

20. Robin McDowell, "Gov't. to Deport 'Free Vietnam' Members," *The Cambodia Daily*, December 4, 1995: 1–2.

21. Interestingly, though, in December 1995, just days after the well-publicized "Free Vietnam" incident, King Norodom Sihanouk Varman visited North Vietnam for the first time in 22 years, in the hope of re-establishing relations between Vietnam and Cambodia. Despite assertions of the impertinence of Vietnam, the Cambodian government seems to seek to strengthen rapport between the two countries. Politically, Vietnam is too strong, too influential; to alienate it would be a very risky venture. Thus Cambodians receive a dual message: we will retain Vietnam as a necessary ally; however, ethnic Vietnamese in Cambodia are not to be respected as Cambodian nor given the rights of Cambodian citizenship.

22. International Centre of Ethnic Studies (ICES), *Minorities in Cambodia* (London: Minority Rights Group, 1995).
23 Chou Meng Tarr, "Vietnamese Minority," 35.
24 *Khmer Conscience*, March to April 1993, 25.
25. Jay Jordens, "Persecution of Cambodia's Ethnic Vietnamese," 145.
26. Penny Edwards, "Imaging the Other," 67.
27. Jay Jordens, "The Ethnic Vietnamese in Cambodia: Prospects Post-UNTAC." Unpublished lecture, University of Hawaii at Manoa: 1994, 6.
28. Khmer are also concerned that they will be categorized as Vietnamese. In Takeo, for example, a woman who claims she is *kaun-kat chen* (half-Khmer, half-Chinese), born in Cambodia, reported that police entered her village and rescinded her identity card (stating that she is ethnically Khmer), and reissued a series of papers stamped with the word "antapraves" (immigrant). Upset, angry, and terrified, she went to district and provincial officials to have herself recategorized:

> My mother is blood-Chinese and my father is Khmer, so I am Khmer. If I was Vietnamese maybe I would live in Vietnam, but I am Khmer and so I have always lived in Cambodia. I can speak French — I learned my lessons in French because during the Sihanouk regime Khmer teachers taught everything in French. That should tell you how long I've been here! I had an identity card before the war that states my Khmer nationality ... but now the police have put me in the category of "immigrant"! They looked at my face and decided that I was Vietnamese, but you can ask anyone who lives in this village — they know my mother and father ...

29. Seanglim Bit, *The Warrior Heritage: A Psychological Perspective of Cambodian Trauma* (El Cerrito, CA: published by the author, 1991), 12.
30. Sambath Kang, "A Look at an Aspect of Wartime in Cambodia," *Khmer Conscience* VII (2: 1993), 21.
31. *Utdam Keate Khmer News*, December 24–25, 1995.
32. Judy Ledgerwood, "Analysis of the Situation of Women in Cambodia: Research on Women in Khmer Society" (Phnom Penh: Cambodia: Consultancy for UNICEF, 1992), 5.
33. Chou Kim, "The Problem of Prostitution in Cambodia: Is It Normal for Khmer Society?," *Khmer Conscience* VII (2: 1993), 19.
34. *Nokor Phnom News*, November 14, 1995, translation and emphasis mine.
35. Sambath Kang, "Wartime in Cambodia," 21, emphasis mine.
36. In the areas adjacent to Wats Chak Andre Loeu and Chak Andre Krom, Vietnamese families report that young Khmer men have been attacking, possibly at the prompting of the Buddhist monks who occupy the temples (Didier Bertrand, personal communication).
37. James Kanter and Ed Madra, "Eagerly Awaited Nationality Law Approved," *Cambodia Daily*, December 8, 1995, 8.
38. Kanter and Madra, "Eagerly Awaited Nationality Law," 8.
39. *Minorities in Cambodia*, 1.
40. The arrest of the "Free Vietnam" activists occurred more than halfway through my field research. I had already returned from several of the provinces and did not have the opportunity to return to the areas I had explored throughout October and November, and therefore was unable to survey ethnic Vietnamese in these areas about their opinions vis a vis the "Free Vietnam" movement. In Phnom Penh, I conducted a very informal survey of informants which suggests that the movement was not popular with the ethnic Vietnamese who had been living in Cambodian for extended periods of time. Nearly all of the respondents had never heard of "Free Vietnam" until they read about the incident in the Newspapers, and all expressed that there were uninterested and, importantly, did not want to be involved in Vietnamese politics. I spoke to two "new" arrivals, who told me they were too involved in making ends meet economically to "worry about politics."
41. Whose cards were taken and who was recategorized as an "immigrant," moreover, was entirely *sraek tae leu chet key* (up to the discretion of the police — literally, "up to their hearts").
42. Rozanna Lilley, "Ethnicity and Anthropology," in G. Wijeyewardene, Ed., *Ethnic Groups Across Boundaries in Mainland Southeast Asia* (Singapore: Institute of Southeast Asian Studies, 1990), 178.
43. This claim is based upon countless informal discussions with Khmer acquaintances about obtaining a passport. While arguably every Cambodian has the right to obtain a passport, there are many factors involved in actually getting one, one of which being the discretion of

the officers involved in processing the applications. One friend told me, "They look at your face, ask your name at least 10 times, listen to you talk … and even if you do everything right, they can still refuse to give you what you have every right to have." I was informed that having a Khmer-sounding name would certainly heighten one's chances of "passing" the test. Examples of surnames that are typically regarded as Vietnamese include Nguyen, Le, Diep, Duc. By contrast, surnames that are understood to be Khmer include Sam, Sok, Pen, Meas.

44. *see* Prasso, *Violence, Ethnicity, and Ethnic Cleansing*, 4.
45. Henri Tajfel. *Differentiation Between Social Groups* (London: Academic Press, 1978). Cited in M. Hewstone and C. Ward, Eds., "Ethnocentrism and Causal Attribution in Southeast Asia," *Journal of Personality and Social Psychology*, 48 (3: 1985), 614.
46. Vicky Bell, "Historical Memory, Global Movements, and Violence: Paul Gilroy and Arjun Appadurai in Conversation," *Theory, Culture & Society* 16 (2: 1999), 27.
47. Steven Pile and Nigel Thrift, *Mapping the Subject: Geographies of Cultural Transformation* (London: Routledge, 1995).
48. Linnekin, "On the Theory," 251.
49. Lilley, "Ethnicity and Anthropology," 181.

Part 4
Boundaries Within

14

A Race Apart?

The Paradox of Sikh Ethnicity and Nationalism

DARSHAN TATLA

The sudden eruption of Sikh nationalism in the 1980s, especially in its most virulent form of demand for Khalistan (a Sikh homeland in the Punjab) touches on some complex issues of ethnic conflict in the postcolonial nation-building process in South Asia. While it raises issues concerning the nature of Sikh ethnicity — which in a short period of time, has transversed from group consciousness, to political community and staked a claim for a statehood — the form of conflict also calls for an examination of the emerging nature of Indian state, which despite having evolved a common framework for democratic process of political bargaining remains locked in ethnic conflicts. Some have assumed that Sikh nationalism has traveled along the route from an ethnic group toward a nation-in-the-making, yet, it has surfaced only as a reaction to certain events, and its course suggests a puzzling and inconsistent route. The eruption of Sikh nationalism in the post-1984 period as a reaction to the Indian state's invasion of the Golden Temple in Amritsar posed a serious challenge to the Indian state's borders and legitimacy. The violent insurgency lasted a decade, was suppressed brutally by the security forces, involved large-scale human rights violations, and costed over 25,000 Sikhs' lives. Many of them were executed through extrajudicial killings and a few thousand remain unaccounted for, or "disappeared" — a new term for state terror.

This paper aims to examine the nature of Sikh ethnicity, and offers some comments on the rather paradoxical behavior of Sikh ethno-nationalism in contemporary India.[1] To start with Brass who, after a careful study of Sikhs, concluded:

of all the ethnic groups and peoples of the north, the Sikhs come closest to satisfying the definition of a nationality or a nation. The Punjabi speaking Sikhs are a people objectively distinct in religion, though not in language, from other ethnic groups in the north, who have succeeded in acquiring a high degree of internal social and political cohesion and subjective awareness, and who have achieved political significance as a group within the Indian union.[2]

If this is a correct assessment, this article seeks an answer to the puzzle of Sikh nationalism: its late and sudden appearance in the 1980s. Was Sikh nationalism among those candidates for ethnic conflict who, due to diverse reasons, never "wake up" as observed by Ernest Gellner?[3] Social scientists remain perplexed by ethnicity and nationalism. Enormous efforts to understand these two interrelated phenomena still have not resolved some of the major issues: the resilience of ethnicity and diversity of nationalistic claims across the world.[4] Thus, Sikh ethnicity can be examined by referring to its shared historical past, geographical concentration, religious affiliation, language, and physical differences. Added to this definition is the self-consciousness and contrast to draw boundary between "us" and "them." Seen in this light, the Sikhs of Punjab present an interesting case study. The paper discusses the community discourse, which asserts, "Sikhs are a nation," interrogating and contrasting this against counter-claims that Sikh identity is contingent, malleable, and fluid in the context of the Indian state building project.[5] Starting with the community's origins in the fifteenth century, its evolution is highlighted in relation to its parent society, the Hindus, and that society's Other, the Muslims. While the community ancestry, religion, location, and language are considered as primordial factors shaping Sikh ethnicity, the state's role in molding and manipulating such factors are seen to be crucial to an understanding of the dynamics of ethnic mobilization.

According to the 1991 census, the population of Sikhs is about sixteen million, forming a majority community of the Indian province of Punjab, though barely two percent of India's total population. Three quarters of all Sikhs live in the Punjab, while four million are settled in other Indian provinces, and about two million are scattered across the world constituting a Sikh Diaspora, with particular concentration in Britain, Canada, and the United States. Sikh men are distinguished by turbans, their stereotyped images, and jokes about them are common. By one account, they are "simple-minded, open hearted and generous," while another set makes them "brave but fickle, fools and violent."

The making of Sikh ethnic consciousness

Like many minority communities, the Sikhs have portrayed themselves in certain ways, narrating who they are, and how they wish to be seen by the world. The answer to "who is a Sikh" is hardly standard, but some general points emerge: religion, language, history, sacred shrines, and something about the land of five rivers. This narrative, emphasizing the role of structural factors — religion, territory, and language — has gained dominance especially among Sikh academics and political leaders since the 1950s leading to an assertion that "Sikhs are a nation." This might be called as community narrative. Essentially, Sikh ethnicity revolves around three elements, namely religion, territory, and language.

Religion

Sikhs are a community of believers of a religious tradition, established as part of the Bhakti movement which swept in the Northern Indian provinces in the fifteenth and sixteenth centuries under the Mughal empire. Its founder, Nanak, was born in a Hindu family. He offered, in poetical form, profound criticism of the Hindu orthodoxy and its priestly class, while castigating Islamic clergy for their deviance from the true principles of spirituality. Punjab's lower social classes, among them the Jats (a peasantry class) in particular, eagerly embraced the new faith. The new religious tradition was nurtured by a long line of nine successors to Nanak, ending the line of gurus by a sacred book, Guru Granth installed at the center of a gurdwara (temple). Besides establishing a set of rituals, new shrines and towns were set up. Finally, the institutionalization of the community was undertaken through an initiation ceremony (*amrit*) by the last guru calling those who were baptized as the Khalsa while the community was to be called the Khalsa Panth. In 1999, 300 years of Khalsa community was celebrated with great enthusiasm across the globe.

The early history of the community, with some justification, can be portrayed as a sequence of tragedies with brief periods of relief. Besides the execution of two gurus by the Mughal authorities, faithful Sikhs almost suffered a century of persecution following the death of the last guru in 1708. The community accounts assert that Sikhs preferred to die as martyrs than lose their faith during this period. Two major battles with Afghan invaders, in 1726 and 1754, resulted in many thousand deaths; in the second battle, the Afghan armies chased them almost to a man in the plains of Malerkotla; these two events are known as *Ghallughara* (genocide). In the aftermath of this battle, many Sikhs fled into the jungle, took up arms, and formed roving bands pocketing certain areas, gradually challenging the Mughal and Afghan control over the Punjab. Again, this period — especially the martyrdom of the ninth guru at the hand of the Mughal Emperor Aurangzeb in Delhi — is interpreted as one of supreme sacrifice in defense of another faith. In this postmodernist version, the guru is seen as the exemplary human rights activist.

Geography and territory

Sikhs are a community of the Punjab — its origins and subsequent history has given them a Punjabi character, a border mentality, a temper of war-like tribes. The Punjab lies at the opening of Arabic world toward India — scene of hundreds of invaders passing through the Punjab toward the Gangetic plains, eyeing Delhi's throne or jewels. Of the ten gurus, nine were born in the Punjab. They established several towns, including the most famous, Amritsar, and subsequently, numerous historic shrines came up to commemorate their lives.

Three such places became centers of religious authority, called Takhats. By the mid-nineteenth century, they had supplemented their spiritual zeal with political will, as European travelers, English visitors to the Sikh court and witnesses to Anglo-Sikh wars were to testify. Thus Joseph Davy Cunningham in 1846 was moved by Sikhs' "nationalist spirit" during Anglo-Sikh wars. Comparing the followers of other Bhakti saints, reminded that while followers of Kabir, Gorakh, Ramanand, and others had:

> perfected forms of dissent, rather than planted the germs of nations, and their sect remain to this day as they left them. It was reserved for Nanak to perceive the true principles of reform, and to lay those broad foundations which enabled his successor Gobind to fire the minds of his countrymen with a new nationality.[6]

This religious community was transformed in 1799 as Sikhs created a sovereign Punjab under Ranjit Singh. This was a remarkable event in military terms, as they were still a small community of the Punjab. Although this majestic fabric crumbled on its fiftieth anniversary, when the East India Company replaced Sikh rule in the Punjab. However, memory of Sikh rule over the Punjab with its borders extending to the farthest limits has made an inedible print on Sikh psychology contributing to Sikhs' outlook on themselves as natural rulers of the Punjab. Moreover, the Sikh rule added to the architecture of Lahore, gold-plating of the Harimandir in Amritsar, and numerous other buildings and gardens commemorating the memory of Sikh rule. Generous to all religious institutions, with state patronage, the Harimandir in Amritsar, nevertheless, received its largest largesse from the state treasury, with a golden fracas over the temple. English visitors to the shrine coined the name Golden Temple in the 1830s.

Ethnicity and politics

Although early historical developments of the community contributed to Sikh ethnic consciousness, the community's interaction with the colonial and post-colonial rule provide a vital clue to the contemporary dynamics and of Sikh ethnic politics and its particular forms of mobilization.

The colonial era

Lasting for just a century, the colonial rule had a profound impact on the Punjab. The British administrators brought a new kind of understanding to India's social hierarchies, mainly in terms of caste and racial classification. The colonial scholar–administrators produced many fascinating tracts, books, and reports focusing on the caste as a central feature. This differentiating along caste structure had an affinity with theories of color and racial categories propounded in Europe. However, India's social structure offered a vast diversity; in North India, Brahmins occupied an unusually lowly position, while in Punjab lived "robust and warlike" Jats with "superior ethnological qualities."[7] Denzil

Ibbeston discovered that in the Punjab, the caste as a rank and purity system, could not sustain such rural yeomen, especially so in central Punjab dominated by Jat Sikhs and western districts dominated by egalitarian Muslims. These people were anything but passive "tyrannised victims of received Brahminical orthodoxies." A Punjab village was a perfect little republic, with vigorous "democratic Jats."[8] Unlike many colonial theorists, Ibbeston, however, insisted on portraying castes among Punjab's Sikhs and Muslims. From such understanding based on racial types or physiological characteristics, emerged the "martial races" theory.

A martial race?

European attempts at understanding the Indian society resulted in a detailed classification of various tribes and peoples on different criteria, including one based on their "soldiering qualities." As the East India Company's armies were reorganized in the aftermath of the 1857 uprising, such a classification came in handy for new policy of recruitment into armies. The Sikh soldiers had provided crucial support to re-establish the Company's rule in Delhi. The Jat Sikhs, along with several other Punjab tribes, classified as "martial races" were recruited on a preferential basis. By the time of World War I, proportion of Sikhs in India's armies was almost a quarter. Punjab also became an experiment for a new agrarian policy. The "Canal Colonies" projects were launched whereby surplus rivers water was diverted through specially constructed canals to Punjab's western barren lands. Thousands of Jat Sikh farmers from central districts migrated to newly irrigated areas of western districts, especially in Lyallpur and Montgomery. Gradually, a "Punjab school of administrators" emerged and advocated measures favoring peasantry against urban *bania* speculators. The colonial state's buttressing of rural interests in the Punjab, especially in banning land transfer to urban trading classes, who were mostly Hindus, meant the province had a loyal and stable political alliance until the 1940s.

Community boundaries

Punjab's newly educated urban elite under the colonial rule was actively engaged in creating community boundaries. Competition for jobs and gradual emergence of power sharing state policies led to ethnic consolidation, enforcing ambiguous boundaries into sharply defined categories. The threat posed by missionaries also mobilized three communities to propagate their respective faiths through new reformist bodies; among Hindus, the Arya Samaj emphasized the "back to Vedas" message; urbanite Sikhs responded with the Singh Sabha movement, while Muslims formed Anjumans. The new Sikh reformers called for purification of the faith by getting rid of Hindu idols and practices from its historic shrines and began a major campaign to control such shrines including the Golden Temple and birthplace of the founder, Nanakana Sahib. The colonial government, after considerable resistance, agreed to an elected body of Sikhs to manage its historic shrines; since 1925 this organization, the Shiromani Gurdwara Parbandhak Committee, has played a considerable role in institutionalization of the Sikh faith.

As the Sikh scriptures are written in Punjabi language, this language became an important constituent of Sikh ethnicity and, as we shall see later, this led to the formation of a smaller Punjabi-speaking state carved out of the Indian Punjab. However, active process of identification with Punjabi language by the Sikhs was due to elite competition during the colonial rule. Under the impact of western education, the question of written language was raised. A fierce debate over "proper" language and its "ideal" script was started. Though Punjabi was the most common medium of communication among all religious communities, the Hindu elite advocated Hindi as appropriate to the study of Vedas and other ancient Sanskrit texts; Muslims opted for Urdu for their cultural expressions. More zealots among Hindus went for the revival of Sanskrit, similarly some staunch Muslims advocated learning Arabic as common heritage of Islamic doctrine and civilization. The Sikhs chose to stick with Punjabi.

Claim over the Punjab

Unlike medieval kings and princes, who ruled by fiat, the colonial state introduced a limited franchise based on wealth and numbers. To begin with, minority groups were given limited representation in state legislatures. However, the newly established nationalist movement, Indian National Congress, dominated by Hindus, was opposed to this "communal" representation as it threatened their obvious domination. The Sikh elite gradually realized its weak bargaining power in such representative framework. After World War II, the British decided to transfer power to India's representatives. As Muslims, through the Muslim League, staked a claim for separatism, the specter of India's partition arose. The Congress leaders finally acceded to the partition in 1946. Sandwiched between the Muslims' vision of an Islamic state, and the Congress' India dominated by Hindus, the Sikh leaders faced an acute dilemma. Their leaders countered the Muslim League's demand for Pakistan by demanding an independent Punjab, proposing that boundaries be so drawn by detaching Muslim majority areas. They asserted "Sikhs are also a nation." During this crisis period, a few also proposed a rationale for a Sikh state.[9] Tara Singh, the Akali leader, declared Sikhs would not become "slaves of Pakistan or Hindustan." To the Cabinet Mission in 1946 seeking proposals on the transfer of power, the Akali Dal presented a memorandum arguing Sikhs' special claim on the Punjab:

> Whereas the Sikhs being attached to the Punjab by intimate bonds of holy shrines, property, language, traditions, and history claim it as their homeland and holy land which the British took over as a "trust" from the last Sikh ruler during his minority and whereas the entity of the Sikhs is being threatened on account of the persistent demand of [sic] Pakistan by the

Muslims on the one hand and of the danger of absorption by the Hindus on the other, the executive Committee of the Shiromani Akali Dal demands for the preservation and protection of the religious, cultural and economic and political rights of the Sikh nation, the creation of a Sikh state which would include a substantial majority of the Sikh population and their scared shrines and historical gurdwara with provision for the transfer and exchange of population and property.[10]

Although the British were sympathetic to Sikhs' special case, the community's demography defeated any special consideration. They formed only 17 percent of Punjab's population with concentration in central districts of Amritsar, Ludhiana, and Ferozepore; nowhere they commanded a majority. Punjab's Muslims formed a majority, while the rest were Hindus. More knowledgeable British officers such as Major Billy Short and Penderel Moon felt the community's best option lay in the proposed new Muslim state where they could hold the balance of power and thus save the Punjab from partition.

As the British departed, India was divided into two sovereign states. Punjab and Bengal were partitioned between India and the Islamic state of Pakistan. The newly created boundary cut through the heartland of Punjab's Sikh population forcing unprecedented migration.[11] Over twelve million people crossed the boundary; while Sikhs and Hindus left their homes in the western districts, Muslims from eastern districts migrated to the new state of Pakistan. It was a process of ethnic cleansing of horrific proportions: communal riots claimed the lives of half-a-million people.[12] The last British Viceroy, Lord Mountbatten, presiding over the transfer of power, felt anguished about Sikhs' future: "Of all the parties to the border dispute, I am particularly worried about the Sikhs — brave, fools and violent but there is something about them which makes my heart bleed for them. They would be worse off."[13]

However, the tragedy of partition proved to be mixed blessing although the Sikh peasantry lost fertile and irrigated lands in the western districts, along with 140 historic shrines including the most sacred Nankana, the birthplace of their founder, Guru Nanak. Due to forced migration, Sikhs were brought into a compact geographical unit; for the first time, they formed a majority in several districts of East Punjab.

The colonial legacy

British imperialism affected India profoundly. Above all, it brought a sense of unity to India it never had; with this emerged the idea of being an "Indian" first as an administrative category and as a distinct product of the colonial rule. While railway lines started physical integration of inaccessible regions to Delhi, loose boundaries were converted into borders, telegraphic poles conveyed news across provinces and peoples, and a Western-style education led to the emergence of an elite who could share and discuss issues through a common English language. This process of integration of diverse regional or provincial cultures into an "Indian" entity was under way and newly Western-educated Hindu intellectuals started their searches for a glorious past. This imagining of India as a civilization was substantially assisted by European Orientalist scholarship. By the turn of twentieth century, a general culture of caste (*varana*), and a host of Hindu myths and symbols were being articulated and, "the work of integrating as a collection of myths, beliefs, rituals and laws into a coherent religion and shaping an amorphous heritage into a rational faith known now as 'Hinduism' were endeavors initiated by Orientalists."[14] This Oriental construction inspired several revivalist movements in various provinces, especially in Bengal, Gujarat, and Punjab leading to an overarching "Hindu tradition." While the Indian National Congress widened its framework by adopting cultural nationalism, parallel Hindu organizations left no doubt among non-Hindu minorities about Congress' Hindu constituents and intentions.[15] Despite some Congress leaders' secular credentials, the essential spirit and mobilization appeal of the Congress was firmly entrenched in a reformed liberal Hinduism.

The distinguishing feature of imperial power, as far as minorities were concerned, was to recognize India's diversity by incorporating many layers of state structures; from princely states to tribal regions, recognition of indigenous social customs through state's legal and administrative directives. The British India was a loose federal state with imperial authority painstakingly ensuring representation of various religious and tribal communities. Its administrators harbored a somewhat natural sympathy for minorities and indigenous peoples and tribes. Moreover, for British rulers, a balance between different communities' claims was an important ethical issue. Of course, such a policy was seen and condemned by Indian nationalists (mostly Hindus) as a divide-and-rule tactic.

For the Sikhs, the imperial rule proved to be a mixed blessing. Far from disintegrating as some English observers had predicted a century earlier, the Sikhs emerged as a distinct community whose population had substantially increased through natural increase and conversion from Punjab's lower classes. They had clearly demarcated themselves as a separate community from Hindus with rituals and ceremonies sharply distinguished; with historic shrines being controlled by an elected body.

The postcolonial state

The new Indian regime adopted a unitary constitutional structure with universal franchise, scrapping the colonial system of guaranteed representation for minorities. The only exception was made for "scheduled tribes" and certain "castes."[16] The state-building and governance was to be built on three principles: (a) secularism, with freedom of worship and state non-interference; (b) economic welfare for substantive citizenship rights; and (c) democratic centralism, providing a structure of power-sharing between subnational regions and the Union state.[17] Haunted by the specter of dissolution, the principle of self-determination for regions and nationalities was fully ruled out by the Indian Constitution. Instead, it provided for the reorganization of linguistic regions while fourteen languages were recognized as state languages. Hindi was to be the official language of India along with English. In 1953, when Telegu-speakers forced a demand to reorganize their state, a States Reorganization Commission was established. By the 1980s, the Indian union consisted of twenty-two states with fifteen official languages.

However, this state-building process had a differential impact on non-Hindu communities. While the adoption of Hindi has put regional languages on the defensive — an aggressive drive toward integration and unification of personal laws smacks of Hindu hegemony. Such "integrative" policies have put Hindus, especially from Hindi-speaking regions, at an advantage over members of other communal groups.[18] It can be argued that the adoption of universal franchise has put minorities at a disadvantage, especially in ethnically divided provinces such as Punjab and the northeastern provinces. As a result, India's constitutional centralism has led to a widespread process of manipulation and repression of regional nationalisms. The second chamber of parliament has no provision for articulating and safeguarding provincial interests, a common practice in many federal polities. Some political scientists have argued India's democratic franchise is effectively for majorities, while minorities are subject to hegemonic control including spells of violent control. In such a context, the main ethnic group can effectively "dominate another through its political, economic, and ideological resources and can extract what it requires from the subordinated."[19]

With the postcolonial state dismantled those colonial rules and safeguards for fair representation of minorities, as far as minorities are concerned, the India's postcolonial state can arguably be treated as an ethnocracy.[20] The state has privileged the dominant Hindu communities by: (a) recruiting the civil and military government disproportionately from the majority ethnic group;[21] and (b) employing cultural attributes and values of the dominant ethnic community for defining its national ideology — its history, language, religion, and moral values. Thus, it can be argued that the new Indian national identity is not eth-nically neutral but derived from the Hindu world, even when it employs the language of universalism. The net result of the state's institutions, its constitu-tion, its laws, and its monopolization of power, has meant a differential impact upon various communities, while empowering the dominant ethnic commu-nity. Such characteristics run through most postcolonial states of Africa and Asia as Myron Weiner has summed up:

> in country after country a single ethnic group has taken control over the state and used its powers to exercise control over others . . . in retrospect there has been far less "nation-building" than many analysts had expected or hoped, for the process of state building has rendered many ethnic groups devoid of power or influence.[22]

Kedourie has compared such colonial and postcolonial regimes even more clearly as:

> To an imperial government the groups in a mixed area are all equally enti-
> tled to some consideration, to a national government they are a foreign
> body to be either assimilated or rejected. The national state claims to treat
> all citizens as equal members of the nation, but this fair-sounding princi-
> ple only serves to disguise the tyranny of one group over another. The
> nation must be, all its citizens must be, animated by the same spirit.
> Differences are divisive and therefore treasonable . . . to the colonial state
> they posed no threat, while the post-colonial state has been far less toler-
> ant of its various diverse nationalities. To the post-national state they are
> all insurgents.[23]

India provides a clear example typical of many Third World countries where territorial statehood and ethnic cultures differ sharply. In these countries, new nationalists' zeal to create a national community from historical boundaries and geographical regions has led to severe homeland struggles. For as many minorities who have waged successful struggles for statehood, others have been coerced into submission through forced integration. This analysis of the post-colonial regime seems justified in the case of the Indian state's policies toward the Sikhs and other minorities. Only then one can gain an understanding of the state's policies toward the Punjab, Kashmir, and the northeastern provinces. Why, for example, have the minority nationalisms of Kashmiris, Punjabis, and peoples of the northeastern states been subject to hegemonic and violent control. How can Hindu nationalism sit comfortably with Indian nationalism? Wars and aggressive postures toward its neighbors, especially Pakistan, and projection of Christians, Muslims, and in the post-1984 period, Sikhs as the "Other" are some ways the state has used to build Indian nationalism.[24]

Sikh nationalism in postcolonial India

The characteristic form of nation-building among the Sikh community has been undertaken by the Akali Dal since the 1920s. Projecting themselves as sole spokesmen for the community, Akalis have asserted that the membership of the Panth "transcends distance, territory, caste, social barriers and even race." Maintaining that the religious and political interests of the community are inseparable, it has blamed Sikhs joining Congress and other parties of compro-mising the community interests.[25] It argues that "the state must deal with [the Sikhs] as a one people, and not by atomising then into individual citizens" and that the Sikhs' loyalty to the secular state was contingent upon the state's recog-nition of the Sikhs as a collective group with a historic "theo-political status."[26] Looking at the actual history of postcolonial India, two major struggles were waged by Akali leaders. The first of these started in 1952 when the Akali Dal — the community's main political party — called for a culturally congruent Punjabi-speaking region during the first general elections in 1952:

> The test of democracy, in the opinion of the Shiromani Akali Dal, is that the minorities should feel that they are really free and equal partners in the destiny of their country . . . to bring home this sense of freedom to the Sikhs it is vital that there should a [province of] Punjabi-speaking language and culture . . . it is a question of life and death for the Sikhs for a new Punjab to be created immediately.[27]

Despite the acceptance of states' reorganization on linguistic basis elsewhere, the Indian States Reorganization Commission rejected the Akali demand for Punjab boundaries to be redrawn on a linguistic basis.[28] Citing this as an act of discrimination, Akali Dal launched an agitation for a Punjabi-speaking region in 1955.[29] This was followed by a second campaign in 1960–1961.[30] Having failed twice, a third campaign was launched in 1965, when the Akali Dal adopted another resolution arguing that Punjab was its homeland:

> This conference recalls that the Sikh people agreed to merge in a common Indian nationality on the explicit understanding of being accorded a constitutional status of co-sharers in the Indian sovereignty along with the majority community, which solemn understanding now stands cynically repudiated by the present rulers of India. Further the Sikh people have been systematically reduced to a sub-political status in their homeland, the Punjab, and to an insignificant position in their motherland, India. The Sikhs are in a position to establish before an impartial international tribunal, uninfluenced by the present Indian rulers that the law, the judicial process, and the executive action of the State of India is constitutionally and heavily weighted against the Sikhs and is administered with un-bandaged eyes against Sikh citizens. This conference therefore, resolves, after careful thought, that there is left no alternative for the Sikhs in the interest of self-preservation but to frame their political demand for securing a self-determined political status within the Republic of Union of India.[31]

The campaign was suspended as Indo-Pakistan hostilities broke out in September 1965. Impressed by Sikhs' contribution to the Indian war efforts, the central government agreed to Punjab's reorganization in 1966. As new Punjab was demarcated in November 1966, Akali leaders felt dissatisfied as several Punjabi-speaking areas, including Chandigarh, were left out while the Central government imposed its authority over Punjab's river waters. The new Punjab was Sikh majority province and elected the first Akali led coalition ministry. This provincial government was soon dismissed by the Central government.

Incomplete Punjab, frustration over sharing political power, along with new issues arising primarily due to rapid modernization of the Punjabi peasantry, set the scene for a second and more tragic confrontation between the Akalis and the central government in the 1980s. The Akalis mobilized the Sikh peasantry for a major campaign seeking a set of economic, cultural, constitutional, and religious demands based on an old charter called the Anandpur Sahib Resolution couched in the Sikh idiom. Launching their campaign under the popular name, *Dharam Yudh Morcha* (righteous struggle), in 1981, they also sought to preserve the, "distinct identity of the Sikhs," stating[32]:

> The Shiromani Akali Dal shall strive to achieve the main objective to preserve and keep alive the concept of distinct and independent identity of the Panth and to create an environment in which national sentiments and aspirations of the Sikh Panth will find full expression, satisfaction and growth.[33]

Calling for a radical shift of federal–provincial powers and an explicit recognition of India as a multinational state, the Akali Dal sought to: (a) devolve powers to provinces and create a new federal structure; (b) redraw Punjab's linguistic boundary by transferring Chandigarh and Punjabi-speaking areas into the province; (c) establish Punjab's control over river waters, farm-product prices, and an increased quota of Sikh recruitment into the armies[34]; and (d) establish an India-wide elected body of Sikhs to manage all historic shrines, along with some other religious demands including broadcast of scriptures from the Golden Temple.

During the campaign from 1981 to 1984, a new leader, Jarnail Singh Bhindranwale, emerged to tax Akalis' pragmatism.[35] The Indian Prime Minister, Indira Gandhi, eyed the Sikh unrest for her own electoral gains especially among the Hindu belt of north India by projecting the Akalis as a threat to the country's unity. After rounds of talks, she ordered armed forces to enter the Golden Temple.[36] On June 1, 1984, over 70,000 armed forces moved into the Punjab, cutting it off from the outside world and the battle began in the Golden Temple. While army tanks blasted the sacred complex, the entire Sikh community rose in rebellion against the "sacrilege," and condemned it as the third *Ghallughara* — a historical term pregnant with the community's resistance against tyrants.

Given the unprecedented army action and the destruction caused to the Akal Takhat and complex buildings, this traumatic event dramatically affected the community's duality — attachment toward the Indian state on the one hand, and membership of a Sikh ethno-political community on the other.[37] The community's loyalty toward its center of cultural power clashed with its notion of citizenship in a polity. This crucial event shifted and sharpened many Sikhs' sense of collective fate and group boundary.

The Akal Takhat — destroyed in the battle and since rebuilt — stands, both as the rival center of cultural power and as a testimony to the Indian state's callous disregard for Sikh sentiments. In the aftermath of the 1984 crisis, the predicament and social psychology of the community was admirably captured by two poets. In the pre-1984 period, the mood was relaxed as "the nation was half asleep at guru's feet."[38] Events in 1984 seared the trust [with Hindus] that had been built over centuries:

> Slowly, and surely, the wounds will heal
> broken hearts reconciled
> new agreements reached, and differences minimised
> But the unsaid trust that existed before
> has gone, and gone forever.[39]

This distrust was fuelled as the state became embroiled in repressive measures against the Sikh militants who sought revenge for the army invasion of the Golden Temple and gave a call for Khalistan, a sovereign state for the Sikhs. Anti-Sikh riots spread following the murder of Indian Prime Minister Gandhi on October 31, 1984, and as a result some 26,000 Sikh refugee families arrived in the Punjab from other parts of India, and over a thousand Hindu families moved out between 1983 and 1986.[40] Between 1984 and 1994, over 15,000 Sikhs died as the battle between militants and government security forces raged. The Punjab became not only a safe haven, but also a territory and a symbolic area that was seen to be Sikhs' own.[41] As the modern *imaginaire* of a homeland has subsumed the Hindu communities, similarly, an independent Punjab has become naturalized within the Sikh psyche.[42] A new factor emerged; the Sikh Diaspora, who like other diasporic communities, have provided finance and moral support for Sikhs in the Punjab.[43]

Then the central government brought back "democracy" by holding elections in February 1992 — with the farcical result of a Congress Party victory, while other main parties boycotted the election. A Congress ministry took charge headed by Beant Singh who was later assassinated. During the Congress regime, the security forces stepped up their hunt for militants.[44] By the summer of 1995, the Punjab resumed its normality and the central government allowed Akalis back into the political field. In the February 1997 provincial elections, a coalition of Akali Dal and Bhartiya Janata Party was voted into power. In 2002, the Congress Party defeated this coalition. The real politics of resources bargaining and distribution has returned, and the Indian state has "managed" another ethnic conflict by offering the aggrieved group some sharing of political power.

The Sikh paradox?

From a religious sect established by Baba Nanak, his followers have made a long journey towards an ethno-national community in the twentieth century. Both the colonial rule and the postcolonial regimes through complex process of interaction, have played crucial roles in transforming Sikhs' fortunes. While the colonial regime in its final phase pushed the community into a compact area, the postcolonial state, through an armed assault on the community's most sacred shrine in 1984 forced the community to imagine in terms of an independent Sikh state, Khalistan. In the post-1984 period, a yearning for Punjab independence, like other nationalist projects, became both imagined and contentious. While the powerful memory of the Punjab as a sovereign state under Ranjit Singh has been part of Sikh consciousness, other myths and memories, such as Sikhs' resistance to Mughal state were utilized to boost this self-image and drive toward freedom. Punjab holds a mysterious bond for the Sikhs, as its motherland, the home of their gurus, the site of historical gurdwaras, and as the land of five rivers. The dynamics of Sikh ethnicity and the paradoxical nature of its ethno-nationalism then need to be situated within this characteristic form of postcolonial state formation in India.

Thus, in new millennium, the Sikh elite faces a classic dilemma in its search for safeguarding the community's language, religious traditions, and culture. Having articulated the community's status as of a nation, the logical conclusion pushes them toward a sovereign state for effective political, economic, and social power. While the Indian state has aimed to mold its nationalities into a nation-state, the Sikhs would like an acknowledgement of a separate national identity, a theoretical right, not its actual resolution. However, this intention can be manipulated by the central government to project Sikhs' seeking break-up of India. Thus, the contest between the community discourse and the state's official ideology continues in numerous ways.

Community versus state discourse: competing spheres

Sikhs' image has fluctuated widely. In the 1985 elections, they were projected as extremists and disloyal people. Among the RSS, Sikhs are being propagated as *keshdhari* Hindus, a sword arm of the Hindus, and hence staunch Indian nationalists. The other image is of a disloyal and prosperous community. "There is a growing feeling that the Sikhs have always very influential and have occupied positions of privilege . . . so that the only way of dealing with them is to firmly and violently put them down."[45] In response to the Akalis' demand for acknowledging India as a multinational state, the government's statement, besides its implicit threat, is quite revealing:

> The Indian people do not accept the proposition that India is a multi-national society. The Indian people constitute one nation. India has expressed through her civilization over the ages, her strong underlying unity in the midst of diversity of language, religion etc. The affirmation of India's nationhood after a long and historic confrontation with imperialism does not brook any challenge.[46]

The community narrative, which asserts Sikhism as an independent religion with a unique message, through a set of rituals and institutions is questioned or reinterpreted by rival narratives, which emphasize its universal principles of righteousness and the equality of man underlying a theology of liberation. Perturbed by overtly political aims of the Sikh leadership, and their contemporary and past struggles for hegemony over the Punjab, much ingenuity has gone to de-emphasize the political history of the Sikh community, especially the sixth and the last guru's battles against Mughal rulers. In a major reinterpretation of traditional discourse, Oberoi demonstrates that "by the end of guru period, the category Sikh was still flexible, problematic, and substantially empty." For the modern Sikh identity to emerge, on the other hand, a "long historical period was needed before it was saturated with signs, icons, and narratives made fairly rigid by tzhe early decades of the twentieth century."[47] By separating the message from institutionalization of the faith, it is argued that contemporary discourse that equate Sikhs with the Punjab are a deviation from the original message of the gurus. A more brazen reading of this confrontation interprets the tenth guru's life as a derailment of the founder's mission, while explaining away the sixth guru's adoption of *miri piri* as a reaction to contemporary events. More serious criticism comes by way of contest about the real message of the faith. It suggests the Sikh message is to reconcile the two warring faiths, Hinduism and Islam, in the Indian subcontinent. It is argued that current Sikh nationalist rhetoric sits oddly with the original message of Sikh scriptures as contained in the Guru Granth Sahib.[48]

A section of the Sikh elite has persistently contested the Indian government's powers to define its agenda. They question the state's control over radio and TV; promotion of Hindi at the expense of Punjabi[49]; such official conventions as using terms of personal address including *Shri* and *Shrimati*, instead of the community conventions of *Sardar* and *Sardarni*; the subsumption of the Sikh marriage custom under Hindu Marriage Act of 1955; and ignoring the Sikh community's inheritance customs in favor of the provisions of the Hindu Code Bill. The Sikh community's alternative conventions compete with official expressions, such as the "national anthem," honors, and patronage of arts and literature. In particular, several domains of community building clash with Indian state nationalism. This gradually became an overarching identity against the caste, linguistic, and regional identity of individuals. For non-Hindus, this new identity also signaled danger and a contest. For Sikhs, being Indian was less important than being Punjabi; indeed, the general order of identification was likely to be: as a Sikh first, Punjabi second, and Indian third. These identities were competitive as well as overlapping, but increasingly in postcolonial India, the Hindu elite expected all non-Hindu people to shed or merge their regional and ethnic identities into an overarching Indian identity.

This is seen even more firmly in the sphere of public memory. With continuous indoctrination through media and other official channels, and also through holidays, monuments and museums, a new Indian identity was fostered among various nationalities. However, the Sikh peasantry seems to have stubbornly refused to exchange its Punjab heroes for new national heroes.[50] Thus, portraits of Punjab heroes at the Sikh museum in Amritsar contrast sharply with Indian heroes commemorated in state museums. Numerous gurdwaras in memory of Sikh martyrs act as "arresting emblems of the modern cultural nationalism."[51] Statues of Gandhi and other Indian national figures, while officially patronized, pale against the immensely popular provincial heroes Ranjit Singh, Kartar Singh Sarabha, Bhagat Singh, and others. That the Sikh minority narratives are likely to become mere footnotes in national narratives is a powerful incentive for Sikhs to gain national status.[52]

Conclusion

There is slow and perceptible rise in Sikh consciousness toward a national community, but its sudden and violent turn toward a Sikh state in the 1980s seems somewhat peculiar and an anomalous development. This short survey suggests that while Sikh ethnic identity is underpinned by structural factors, in which history, memory, regional identification, religion, and language have played their respective roles, these factors alone or in combination, are not sufficient to explain the contours of Sikh ethnicity, especially the violent ethnic conflict during the 1980s. Although an underlying thrust toward the goal "that the political and the national unit must be congruent"[53] can be detected in Sikhs' case, equally, however, this aim is compromised by pragmatic and electoral considerations. The dominant trend of the Akali Dal has been to share power at the provincial level while promoting a notion of Punjabi nationalism, by offering a coalition with Punjab's Hindus. With the experience of coalition politics in the Punjab, Sikhs' yearning for recognition could be accommodated much short of statehood through a truly federalized India. In retrospect, it can be seen that the crisis of 1984 arose mainly due to the ruling party manipulating Sikh ethnic demands for its electoral advantage by projecting them as secessionist. Thereby, a proud community of India was humiliated as the central government ordered a bungled military operation within the Golden Temple. As a reaction to this sacrilege, a violent reaction followed and a desperate cry for an independent Sikh state was made. Although the scars of this tragedy will haunt future generation of the Sikh community, the current Sikh leadership has returned to pragmatic politics of power-sharing at the provincial level. Obviously, India needs a new liberal framework where various ethno-nationalisms can find expression short of secession. Whether decolonized Indian polity is capable of such a feat involving both foresight on the part of the dominant ethnic group's elite and statesmanship eschewing partisan electoral gains, may well determine India's future as also the ultimate fate of Sikh nationalism.

Notes

1. See M.S. Chaddah, *Are Sikhs a Nation?* (Delhi: Sikh Gurdwara Parbandhak Committee, 1982); Gopal Singh, *Politics of Sikh Homeland*, 1940–1990 (New Delhi: Ajanta, 1994);

K.R. Bomball, "The Nation State and Ethno-Nationalism: A Note on the Akali Demand for a Self-Determined Political Status for Sikhs," *Punjab Journal of Politics*, 9 (1983), 166–183.

2. Paul Brass, *Language, Religion and Politics in North India* (Cambridge University Press, 1974), 277.

3. Ernest Gellner, *Nations and Nationalism* (Oxford: Blackwell, 1988). He contends that, despite shaping the contemporary world, nationalism remains "little understood."

4. *See* introductory chapter in Paul Spickard and W. Jeffrey Burroughs, eds., *We Are a People: Narrative and Multiplicity in Constructing Ethnic Identity* (Philadelphia: Temple University Press, 2000).

5. For Singh Sabhas' role in the formation of Sikh identity, *see* Harjot Oberoi, *The Construction of Boundaries: Culture, Identity, and Religious Diversity in the Sikh Tradition* (Delhi: Oxford, 1994); Richard G. Fox, *Lions of the Punjab: Culture in the Making* (Berkeley: University of California Press, 1985).

6. Joseph Davy Cunningham, *A History of the Sikhs from the Origin of the Nation to the Battle of the Sutlej* (London: John Murray, 1849), 34.

7. Susan Bayley, "Caste and 'Race' in the Colonial Ethnography of India," in *The Concept of Race in South Asia*, ed. Peter Robb (Oxford: Oxford University Press, 1995), 165–218.

8. *See* Denzil Ibbeston's portrayal of caste, tribe, and race in the Punjab, quoted in Bayly, "Caste and 'Race.'"

9. Swarup Singh, *The Sikhs Demand Their Homeland* (Lahore: Lahore Book Shop, 1946).

10. Quoted in B.R. Nayar, *Minority Politics in the Punjab* (Princeton, N.J.: Princeton University Press, 1966), 89. *See also* the memorandum by Akali Dal, March 22, 1946, reproduced in *Some Documents on the Demand for the Sikh Homeland* (1969).

11. *The Punjab Boundary Commission Report* (1947).

12. M.S. Randhawa, *Out of Ashes: An Account of the Rehabilitation of Refugees from West Pakistan in Rural Areas of East Punjab* (Chandigarh: Public Relations Department, Government of Punjab, 1954).

13. Quoted in Larry Collins and Dominique Lapierre, *Mountbatten and the Partition of India: 16 August 1947–18 June 1948* (New Delhi: Vikas, 1982). *See also* Nicholas Mensergh, ed., *Constitutional Relations between Britain and India: The Transfer of Power 1942–47*, 12 vols. (London: Her Majesty's Stationery Office, 1970–1983).

14. Quoted in Romila Thapar, "Imagined Religious Communities: Ancient History and the Modern Search for a Hindu Identity," *Modern Asian Studies*, 23.2 (1989), 209–231.

15. A reading of Nehru and Gandhi's lives could illustrate this process — one by rejecting its religious heritage, but through geography, and the other through a hegemonic liberal Hinduism — both attempting to include the "outsiders" in an "Indian community."

16. Its Minorities Sub-Committee rejected separate electorates by 26 votes to 3. Hukam Singh and four Muslims demanded that the Council of States and the House of People should be elected by proportional representation. For the House of People this was rejected. See A. Robinson, *The Constitution of India* (Oxford University Press, 1966).

17. A. Jalal, *Democracy and Authoritarianism in South Asia: A Comparative and Historical Perspective* (Cambridge University Press, 1995).

18. Cynthia H. Enloe, *Ethnic Conflict and Political Development* (Boston: Little, Brown, 1973), 143.

19. For a further discussion of hegemonic and other measures of control over minorities, *see* Brendan O'Leary and Arthur Paul, "Introduction: Northern Ireland as the Site of State and Nation-Building Failures," in *The Future of Northern Ireland*, eds. John McGarry and Brendan O'Leary (Oxford: Clarendon Press, 1990); Gurharpal Singh, *Ethnic Politics in India* (London, 2001); Sammy Smooha, "Minority Status in an Ethnic Democracy: The Status of the Arab Minority in Israel," *Ethnic and Racial Studies*, 13.3 (1990), 389–414.

20. For the definition of such a state in Southeast Asia, *see* David Brown, *The State and Ethnic Politics in Southeast Asia* (London: Routledge, 1994).

21. Simeon Dilip, "Tremors of Intent: Perceptions of the Nation and Community in Contemporary India," *Oxford Literary Review*, 16.1–2 (1994), 225–245. He argues Brahmins, with 5 percent of India's population, held 72 percent of Indian administrative posts. All scheduled castes together accounted for 10 percent of Class 1 posts in the Indian state despite 40 years of reservations.

22. M. Weiner, "Political change: Asia Africa and the Middle East", in *Understanding Political Development*, eds., M. Weiner and S. P. Huntingdon (Boston: Little, Brown, 1987), 36–37.

23. E. Kedourie, *Nationalism in Asia and Africa* (London: Frank Cass, 1970).

24. Ian Talbot, "Back to the Future? The Punjab Unionist Model of Consociational Democracy for Contemporary India and Pakistan," *International Journal of Punjab Studies*, 3.1 (1996), 65–74.

Also *see* Talbot [1995]; Veena Das, *Critical Events: An Anthropological Perspective on Contemporary India* (Delhi: Oxford University Press, 1995); Ashis Nandy, "The Discreet Charm of Indian Terrorism," *Journal of Commonwealth and Comparative Politics*, 28.1 (1990), 25–43.

25. *The Spokesman*, August 17, 1981.

26. Gurnam Singh, 1960.

27. *The Spokesman*, August 29, 1951.

28. *Report of States Reorganization Commission* (Government of India, 1955). Commenting upon the Commission's ruling that Hindi and Punjabi are similar, Hukam Singh wryly observed, "while other got States for their languages, we lost even our language"; *see The Punjab Problem*.

29. In the 1941 census, Hindus and Sikhs were 26 percent and 13 percent, respectively. In 1951, after partition, Hindus were 61 percent, Sikhs 35 percent, and Muslims just 1 percent.

30. Anit Singh Sarhadi, *Punjabi Suba: The Story of the Struggle* (Delhi, Kapur, 1970); Baldev Raj Nayar, *Minority Politics in the Punjab* (Princeton, N.J.: Princeton University Press, 1966); Nayar, "Punjab," in *State Politics in India*, ed., Marion Weiner (Princeton, N.J.: Princeton University Press, 1968), 433–502; Gurnam Singh, *A Unilingual Punjabi State and the Sikh Unrest* (New Delhi: Super Press, 1960).

31. Akali Dal Conference, *Resolution* (Ludhiana, July 4, 1965), cited in Harbans Singh, *The Heritage of Sikhs*, rev. ed. (Bombay: Asia Publishing House, 1983), 369–370. It was drawn up by Kapur Singh, a Member of Parliament, and moved by Gurnam Singh, the leader of Akali Dal in the Punjab Legislative Assembly.

32. *Raj Karega Khalsa* (Khalsa shall rule) has been part of Sikh vocabulary since the eighteenth century. In contemporary Punjabi, *quam* is commonly used for "nation" or "community," along with *des* for "the country." While *des* may convey an idea of Punjab or refer to India, the word *quam* always referred to the Sikh community. W.H. McLeod, "On the Word Panth: A Problem of Terminology and Definition," *Contributions to Indian Sociology*, 12.2 (1978), 287–295.

33. Shiromani Akali Dal, *Anandpur Sahib Resolution* (1978), 1.

34. The "martial races" idea was scrapped in 1949. In 1974, the Sikh army ratio was set at 2.5 percent, still above their portion of the population of just 2 percent. S. Cohen, "The Military and Indian Democracy," in *India's Democracy: An Analysis of Changing State-Society Relations*, ed. Atul Kohli (Princeton, NJ: Princeton University Press, 1988); Atul Kohli, *Democracy and Discontent: India's Growing Crisis of Governability* (Cambridge, U.K.: Cambridge University Press, 1990).

35. Chand Joshi, *Bhindranwale: Myth and Reality* (New Delhi: Vikas, 1984). San Bhindranwale's rise and prominence in Akali politics remains an enigma. Called a saint by many, he was subsequently painted as a demonic figure by Indian official pronouncements. His presence in the Golden Temple was used as an excuse for army action. From 1982 onward, he preached, through fiery language, religious orthodoxy, and blamed the Akali leaders for compromises. Official versions have branded him a terrorist who sent hit squads from the Golden Temple to murder his opponents. Yet, while he was alive, he was not charged with the heinous crimes that were attributed to him posthumously. For the Sikh youth who took up arms, he became a martyr.

36. Accounts of the army action in the Golden Temple and subsequent developments include: Paul Brass, *Ethnicity and Nationalism: Theory and Practice* (New Delhi: Sage); Rajiv Kapur, *Sikh Separatism: The Politics of Faith* (London: Allen and Unwin, 1986); Tatla and Talbot, *Punjab*.

37. A.D. Smith, "War and Ethnicity: The Role of Warfare in the Formation of Self-Images and Cohesion of Ethnic Communities," *Ethnic and Racial Studies*, 4 (1981), 175–197; Smith, "States and Homelands: The Social and Geopolitical Implications of National Territory," *Millennium: A Journal of International Studies*, 10 (1981), 187–202; Smith, *State and Nation in the Third World* (London: Wheatsheaf Books, 1983); Smith, *The Ethnic Origins of Nations* (Oxford: Blackwell, 1986).

38. Harinder Singh Mahboob, *Jhana Di Raat*, 1990.

39. Harbhajan Singh, *Nik Suk* (Delhi: Navyug, 1990).

40. *Facts about the Punjab Situation* (Chandigarh, 1986).

41. *India Today*, April 15, 1988.

42. Appadurai 1990; Oberoi, "From Punjab to Khalistan."

43. *See* Darshan Singh Tatla, D.S. *The Sikh Diaspora; The Search for Statehood* (London: UCL Press, 1999). Besides the classic case, the Jewish diaspora, other ethnic groups engaged in international politics include Armenians, Ethiopians, Hispanics, Irish, Lithuanians, and

Latvians, Indians, Blacks, and Europeans in America; and Chinese in East Asia and the Americas. Examples of migrant groups meddling in international politics include Bangladeshis, Muslims, and Afro-Caribbeans in Britain; Kurds, Moroccans, Algerians, and Tunisians in France; Cubans and Mexicans in America; Croats, Kurds, and Turks in Germany; Koreans in Japan; Palestinians in America and the Middle East; Tibetans in India; Vietnamese in East Asia and America. Diasporas involved in their homeland campaigns in the recent past included: Armenians, Jews, Kashmiris, Kurds, Latvians, Nagas, Palestinians, Sikhs, Tamils, Tibetans, and Ukrainians. Also *see* Robin Cohen *Global Diasporas: An Introduction* (London: UCL Press [World Diasporas Series No.1], 1997); William Safran, "Diaspora in Modern Societies: Myths of Homeland and Return," *Diaspora*, 1.1 (1991), 83–99.

44. Leaders of the Babbar Khalsa, the Khalistan Commando Force, the Khalistan Liberation Force, the Bhindranwale Tiger Force and several other groups were killed. Jaijee (1995), quoting from the "Punjab Legislative Assembly Proceedings: Reply by Chief Minister to a Starred Question," lists a total of 41,684 rewards given to policemen between January 1991 and December 1992 for killing Sikh militants. According to Vaughan (1993), "elite Indian intelligence force had received intelligence training in Israel and returned to apply its skills in Punjab."

45. R. Kothari, "Cultural context of communalism", *Economic and Political Weekly*, November 14, 1989, 83.

46. White Paper, 1984, 17.

47. Harjot S. Oberoi, "From Punjab to Khalistan: Territoriality and Metacommentary," *Pacific Affairs*, 60.1 (1987), 26–41 (*see* page 32).

48. Joyce Pettigrew, 1991, "Betrayal and Nation-Building among the Sikhs," *Journal of Commonwealth and Comparative Politics*, 19.1 (1991), 25–43. "Possessing territorial sovereignty became especially important not only because of the events of 1947 and 1984 and the feeling of humiliation that developed during and after 1984. For a nation whose primary reference had been a book rather than a land. . . . no sense of boundary was provided by their very tolerant religious scripture."

49. From the 1960s on, the issue of whether to draw on Hindi/Sanskritic origins or Urdu/Persian loan words for Punjabi language was debated among Punjabi writers and linguists.

50. J.R. Gillis, *Commemorations: The Politics of National Identity* (Princeton University Press, 1994), 8.

51. B. Anderson, *Imagined Communities: Reflections on the Origin and Spread of Nationalism* (London: Verso, 1983), 17.

52. For an alternative view, *see* Robin Jeffrey, *What's Happening to India: Punjab, Ethnic Conflict, Mrs. Gandhi's Death and Test for Federalism* (London: Macmillan, 1986); Teresa Hubel, *Whose India? The Independence Struggle in British and Indian Fiction and History* (London: Leicester University Press, 1996); Robin Jeffrey, "Grappling with History: Sikh Politicians and the Past," *Pacific Affairs*, 60 (1987), 59–72.

53. Gellner, *Nations and Nationalism.*

15

Race and Ethnicity in South Africa
Ideology and Experience

T. Dunbar Moodie

In popular understandings of Africa, race and ethnicity (often called "tribalism") tend to be sharply distinguished. On the one hand, race is held to have been a colonial import, brought from the metropolitan West to justify rule over "inferior" or "uncivilized" peoples. Racist, colonial rule on this reading was largely abolished in the 1960s when most African states attained independence. "Tribalism," on the other hand, is believed to be indigenous, peculiarly African, and at the heart of ongoing, insolvable problems that continue to haunt African nation-states to this very day. There is a widespread fear (or is it an assumption) that the achievement of African rule in South Africa in defeating racism will inevitably also lead to insurgent tribalism in a predestined scenario of African disaster.

So powerful is the grip of the "African tribal imaginary" on Western reporting about South Africa that widespread violence in the province of Natal in the four years between 1987 and 1991 (about 6,000 persons killed, 20,000 homes destroyed, and almost 100,000 refugees[1]) was hardly mentioned in the international press. This was "Zulus" killing "Zulus" and was very hard to fit into the "tribal" mode. Then, in 1990, the violence moved to the Witwatersrand where, in a short two months, nearly 1,000 persons in the townships around Johannesburg were killed in faction fights. This time it was "Zulus" killing "Xhosa." With an almost audible sigh of relief, the international press widely reported this "tribal warfare." The fact that in both places the fighting was between Inkatha and UDF/COSATU supporters[2] was hardly mentioned. In Africa "tribalism" trumps all other explanations. Thus, since successful African independence struggles against colonial rule supposedly eliminated racism, previously colonial powers have been absolved from all responsibility for African events. The conventional wisdom is that primordial tribal animosities typically have divided African states against themselves. Indeed, there are those who argue that colonial administrations kept tribalism at bay. Despite its racial basis, then, colonial rule subdued tribalism.

Virtually all scholars of Africa disagree with this conventional wisdom. "Tribalism," they argue, is as much a product of colonial domination as is racism. African tribal beliefs and movements would be inconceivable without prior colonial rule. Prior to colonization, homestead and lineage groupings, more or less loosely structured into chiefdoms (linked together by the exchange of cattle and women), were the standard forms of social organization. Larger "states" where they existed (like Zulu since the 1820s) were created by destroying chieftains and incorporating homesteads and lineages rather than excluding them on "ethnic" grounds.[3] Indeed, the formulation of indigenous ethnic consciousness gives situational expression to group identities designed to meet particular needs in the colonial context. Tribal consciousness is a colonial construct — or at least developed in response to colonial policies.

The standard work on tribalism in southern Africa, an edited collection of essays by Leroy Vail,[4] suggests that powerful tribal ethnic ideologies[5] developed in rural areas in the presence of three fundamental factors. First, Christian missionaries brought reified European conceptions of ethnic culture and schooled a new class of African intellectuals in Western ideological assumptions about language differences and "national" history. Often Bible translations standardized different dialects into separate languages. Second, colonial policies of indirect rule set up "traditional authorities," which institutionalized the articulation of customary, tribal forms through everyday practices of power. The colonial state empowered chiefs as tribal "Native Authorities," who administered "customary" justice along ethnic lines. Chiefs who interpreted custom in ways unacceptable to their colonial masters were simply deposed. If need be, the colonial state backed compliant chiefly authority with force exercised in the name of custom. If African societies were matrilineal or stateless or if chiefly power had long since been dismantled, chiefs were created for them. Since all chiefs were freed from traditional checks and balances as paid officials of the colonial state, it was hardly surprising that many rural subjects eventually rejected the "vulgarization of authority"[6] implicit in customary law. Indirect rule also provided an opportunity for missionaries and the new African intelligentsia to implement their ideological programs by forming alliances with newly recognized chiefs.

Third, tribalism arose most powerfully in southern African societies that sent out migrant men to work on the South African (or Zambian or Zimbabwean) mines or in secondary industries. Here it had popular appeal as a masculine ideology that enabled migrant men to maintain control of land and women back home. Thus, says Vail:

> Ethnicity . . . may be interpreted . . . as a form of popular male resistance to the forces that were reshaping African lives throughout southern Africa. It was for this reason also that the appeal of ethnic ideologies was strongest amongst those who were migrant labourers. . . . Men came to

think of themselves as belonging to particular ethnic groups, then . . . because the ethnic apparatus of the rural area — the chiefs, "traditional" courts, petty bourgeois intellectuals, and the systematized "traditional" values of the tribe as embodied in the ethnic ideology — all worked to preserve the very substantive interests which these men had in their home areas. . . . In those situations in which labour migrancy was not a pressing reality . . . or in areas from which men did not emigrate in large numbers, such as southern Zambia and central Malawi, the ethnic message has clearly had less popular appeal, reaching no further than the petty bourgeoisie in most cases.[7]

Opportunity hoarding by tribal groups in the migrant workplace should be added to Vail's third factor. While ethnic identity was rooted in rural networks, factional struggles often represented workplace interest groups, establishing new social networks at work that bound migrants together into ethnic solidarities.[8]

Anticolonial movements in Africa were explicitly antiracist. They made national[9] rather than ethnic appeals. Colonially nurtured ethnic sentiments were either ignored or manipulated, Africanists argue, and have thus returned to haunt African regimes to this day with the grisly specter of tribal conflict. In a recent book, Mahmood Mamdani[10] has moved this argument beyond mere beliefs or feelings by insisting that ethnic sentiments were institutionalized in the operation of postcolonial African states, legally, politically, and economically. New African rulers may have confronted racial domination at the center but ethnic divisions were built into the very structures of the states they inherited.

Although the formation of tribalism was thus situational and colonial, it gave rise to entrenched political and economic interests that have proved very difficult to overcome. South African apartheid, Mamdani argues, especially in its ethnic expression as "separate development," was also formed in this typically African colonial mode. The new South African government is thus confronted with entrenched ethnic structures that cannot be dealt with by policies of nonracialism alone. Thus, for Mamdani, recognizing the colonial construction of tribalism does not necessarily imply its irrelevance in postcolonial African politics, even in South Africa. One does not have to make essentialist or primordial assumptions to argue the centrality of tribalism (however constructed) in contemporary South Africa, despite much higher levels of industrialization and a somewhat different colonial history than the rest of Africa. What about Zulu ethnicity and the appeal of Chief Mangosuthu Buthelezi's Inkatha movement, for example?

I wish to argue in this chapter that the South African situation is far more complicated than any simple distinction between colonial racism and its ethnic or tribal fallout might imply. I shall focus on three different South African examples to point out the complex relations between race and ethnicity. The simple dichotomy between race and ethnicity is inappropriate — at least for the South African case. In the first place, in South Africa, the development of ethnic networks and sentiments was not restricted to colonized Blacks. White Afrikaners also developed their own version of an anticolonial ethnic identity that muddied the distinction between race and ethnicity. In addition, Afrikaner ethnic justifications for racial domination, early gave rise to Africanist racial consciousness among Blacks across tribal lines. In the Black Consciousness movement, opposition to racism took the guise of ethnic-style racial mobilization. Second, while ethnic differences in South Africa were certainly "made" by an uneasy combination of missionary activity, the intelligentsia it produced, migrant labor and "native affairs" administration, this did not happen in the same way everywhere. "Zulu identity" has always been something of an anomaly in South Africa. I shall examine the different experience of Xhosa-speakers in the Transkei. This is especially relevant because White South Africans, especially, often allege that the ANC government in South Africa is dominated by a "Xhosa cabal." Third, I shall use examples from the complex history of the National Union of Mineworkers (NUM) to argue that this organization (the largest labor union in South Africa) has constantly confronted ethnic differences amongst migrant workers at the same time that it fought racist management. Such a battle on two fronts was typical of the South African labor movement more generally and ultimately of the politics of the African National Congress (ANC) itself.

Afrikaner ethnicity and Black consciousness

In 1968, when I was living in Stellenbosch and beginning my research on Afrikaner civil religion,[11] I went to a lecture at the local university by A.P. Treurnicht, at that time a Dutch Reformed church minister.[12] Treurnicht spoke of the glories of Afrikaner culture, the beauty of the language, and the fundamental importance of maintaining Afrikaner values. Afterward in question time, a young man rather uncertainly explained in immaculate Afrikaans that while his mother was Afrikaans-speaking, his father was English. Where did he fit into the scheme of things? Treurnicht trembled, pointed fiercely at the questioner, and said sharply: "You don't exist." The student sat down looking stunned. Many other students in the audience nodded sagely at Treurnicht's wisdom.

If one is to understand the importance of ethnicity in South Africa, one forgets at one's peril that Afrikaners fought a drawn-out, sometimes violent, culture war against their "imperialist oppressors," the British. I have argued that the National Party election victory in 1948, which introduced apartheid, was partly a fallout from that early cultural struggle.[13] Indeed, the cultural aspect of the apartheid ideology, which soon came to be called "separate development," was rooted in the Afrikaner's own struggle for cultural survival and economic advancement. Ethnicity, tribalism if you will, was profoundly important to many Afrikaans-speaking White South Africans, and the making of Afrikaner identity was crucial to their political victory in 1948, and institutionalized in the apartheid state over against English-speaking White South Africans as well as Africans.

That said, one must not overlook the racial component to this "cultural" struggle. Apartheid was, of course, about race as well as culture. One has only to recall that many of the very first acts of the new Afrikaner nationalist government after achieving power in 1948, deliberately excluded mixed-race "Coloureds" from the vote and from White society. This was despite the fact that the majority of so-called Coloureds spoke Afrikaans and were Dutch Reformed church members. Culturally, they were Afrikaners. The Immorality Act and the ban on mixed marriages impacted these "brown Afrikaners" most profoundly. For all the talk of culture by Afrikaner idealists, and despite its undoubted political importance in the Afrikaner social movement, in the end, apartheid was essentially about race.

Ivan Evans[14] has argued convincingly that the tension between cultural and racial strands in apartheid theory was manifested within the Afrikaner state itself. W.W.M. Eiselen, the Secretary for Native Affairs in the early apartheid government, was firmly committed to cultural justifications for apartheid. His position was soon eclipsed by the racist pragmatism of H.F. Verwoerd, however, when the latter was appointed Minister of Native Affairs in 1950. Verwoerd did not hesitate to use the language of ethnicity to speak of separate development, but the practical tenor of the Native Affairs Department under his leadership had to do with racial control.

This racial state had a profound effect on the Black intelligentsia who, in the late 1960s and early 1970s, developed a cultural form of racial consciousness in response to their experience of racial oppression.[15] In 1959, the apartheid state closed traditionally White universities to Black applicants and mandated the establishment of five new "tribal" universities for various Black ethnic groups, Coloureds, and Indians. Despite claims to represent the cultural interests of different "Black" groups, however, these institutions of higher education were staffed almost entirely by White Afrikaners. Ethnic appeals to the moral integrity of "separate development" manifestly promoted the racial interests of Afrikaners. This was true across the entire spectrum of "ethnic reforms" introduced as aspects of the "cultural" policy of separate development. Practices of racial control and White self-interest overwhelmed the ethnic ideology that justified separation along cultural or customary lines. Understandably, student responses took place along a racial rather than an ethnic axis and the Black Consciousness movement was born.

The intellectual origins of Black Consciousness in South Africa are complex and obscure. Black theology, imported from the United States and transformed along the lines of Anton Lembede's 1940s Africanism,[16] was crucial, as was Black students' experience of racial condescension from White students in NUSAS, the national student organization. The new conception of Black power also included Indians and Coloureds (and, grudgingly, women) in an inclusively racial ethnic movement, the single most important ideological ingredient for Black student organizations that sparked the 1975 Soweto uprising.

Interestingly enough, as the movement matured, most of its members affiliated with the nonracial ANC. The successes of the independent union movement and the United Democratic Front in the 1980s (in a country with a Black majority) largely led to abandonment of the Black Consciousness movement's racial exclusiveness within a decade of its greatest successes among students of color. The complications of racial ethnicity were abandoned in a straightforward struggle for nonracial social justice and political power. Black Consciousness, as a movement, essentially died even as it revealed the racial core of Afrikaner ethnic policies.

South African colonialisms

The most important exception to the antitribalism represented by the ANC is Mangosuthu Buthelezi's Zulu Inkatha movement.[17] Buthelezi initially used his ethnic power-base in KwaZulu to oppose the apartheid regime, taking leadership in the Zulu bantustan reluctantly and refusing to accept self-government unless the South African state delivered on its promises of more land and greater independence. In the 1970s, the ANC was mildly supportive of cooperation with Buthelezi. Black Consciousness student organizations, however, militantly opposed him as a "sell-out." Buthelezi fought back vehemently and violently. His supporters regularly beat up students in the name of "traditional" patriarchal authority.

Drawing on the economic and political resources available to him as leader of a bantustan, Buthelezi built "hierarchical networks of clientage"[18] in KwaZulu, dispensing and withholding patronage in every part of KwaZulu through his "customary" Inkatha organization. While Inkatha had little appeal in the urban townships (except in migrant hostels), it did establish a tight lock on rural settlements and the rural intelligentsia. In this regard, Inkatha does indeed follow the pattern of colonially constructed "tribal power." Moreover, Buthelezi was a major force in the ANC's acceptance of a pluralistic federalism in South Africa — a federalism that left his patronage machine in KwaZulu intact. The Zulu ethnic movement fits right into the "tribal" mold, conjuring up a primordial Zulu identity and counterposing it to the universal rights of South African citizens.

While the majority of urban Zulu-speakers have always identified with class-based groupings as workers and citizens, there can be no denying the appeal and the political force of Buthelezi's Inkatha movement in the rural districts of KwaZulu and amongst Zulu-speaking workers who chose (or were obliged) to live in migrant hostels in the townships. Overt factional hostility between regular townspeople and hostel-dwellers is a remarkably recent phenomenon, however, often rooted in urban hostility to the South African state's introduction of urban "councillors" and the formation of the KwaZulu-based Inkatha Freedom Party (IFP) in the late 1980s. At that point, Zulu urban migrants in Johannesburg fell back on the authority of traditionalist "indunas" to represent their interests, thus, maintaining "tribal" solidarities within the urban area.

The question is whether such indunas and their "migrant" supporters represent genuine access to rural resources or merely claims to authority based on male seniority or the patronage systems of Buthelezi's Inkatha regime. Leslie Bank suggests that, at least in the Xhosa-speaking hostels of East London, traditionalist patriarchs claim despotic authority not because they have rural resources but precisely because they have lost them. Women and younger men reject patriarchal authority, as it becomes merely ideological without a material base in the countryside. Nostalgia for an eroding rural system of customary authority barely sustains such Xhosa-speaking men in the absence of ethnic patrons like Inkatha or Buthelezi's IFP. Thus, Bank suggests it is Buthelezi's power to dispense patronage (and ship in ragged mercenaries willing to use violence when patriarchal power is threatened) rather than his customary authority that maintains Zulu migrant solidarities on the Witwatersrand.[19]

Xhosa-speaking areas in South Africa, anyway, have a different history than Zululand. In the first place, it is difficult to pin down Xhosa identity, especially for men still rooted in rural life. "Xhosa" might include Mpondo (who speak Xhosa but, unlike other Xhosa-speakers, do not circumcise). They might include Ciskeians or Transkeians, whose chiefdoms include Thembu, Bomvana, Hlubi, Bhaca, Mfengu, Xesibe, and Mpondomise, as well as Mpondo among others. Often they were mixed. (My assistant, Vivienne Ndatshe, for instance, was proud to be Mpondo, but her father was Mfengu and her mother Bomvana.) Does it make sense to speak of these groups as "tribal?" In some contexts it does. On the mines, Xhosa-speakers were often all housed together, but sometimes, if numbers warranted it, the Mpondo or the Bomvana or the Bhaca would be separated out. Sometimes they fought with one another. At other times, they joined together against other "tribal" groups like Basotho or Malawians. Because of their divisions, however, traditional "Xhosa" were never able to avoid contextualizing their ethnicity.

Unlike most colonial African regimes, Xhosa-speaking areas were subject to paternalist direct rule by the Cape Native Affairs Department.[20] The territory was divided into magisterial districts, each consisting of several "locations" administered by a "headman" appointed by the magistrate (or native commissioner) and answerable to him. The headman was assisted by a district council, half of whom were elected and half appointed. It was the headman, on the authority of the magistrate, who distributed land to homestead proprietors according to the principle of usufruct. Although chiefs usually served on the district councils, were paid a stipend by the state, could continue to exercise informal power, and could be consulted by magistrates and headmen, the formal system of government bypassed them completely. There was no codified system of customary law and the chiefs were given no juridical authority.[21]

Ethnic divisions in the Xhosa-speaking areas were overlaid by a distinction between traditionalists and Christian converts, so-called "red" and "school" people,[22] which cut across chiefdoms. Educated Christian converts were more likely to immigrate to town to work in secondary industry or clerical jobs. Illiterate traditionalists chose to work on the mines where they were insulated from the attractions of town life and could defer their pay as a lump sum until the end of their contracts to buy livestock. Entire locations or sublocations tended to be either "red" or "school" in their affiliations. While they were quite critical of one another, there was considerable mutual tolerance. Generally, though, I think it can safely be said that until the apartheid era after 1948, the Xhosa-speaking areas, despite their rural aspect, were subject to direct colonial control that ignored ethnic differences amongst chiefdoms. Faction fights tended to take place within, rather than between, traditional chiefdoms.

In the 1950s, the South African Department of Native Affairs under the control of Hendrik Verwoerd forcibly reintroduced chiefly power and customary law as the means for despotic policies of rural development in both the Ciskei and the Transkei.[23] Where chiefs did not exist, they were created. When chiefs opposed development reforms, they were deposed. Headmen who objected were also removed. K.D. Matanzima, a minor chief, ruthlessly imposed his will on the western Transkei. Eastern Pondoland exploded into a revolt against the newly constituted tribal authorities. Led by a democratic council of elders called the "Kongo" (for Congress or ANC) the Mpondo revolt killed chiefs, seized livestock, and burned huts. The South African military sealed off the entire territory and bombed it into submission. Hoyce Phundulu from Lusikisiki, whom I interviewed at the mines in 1998,[24] had vivid memories of the period:

> It definitely started for me when I was a very young boy during the Mpondo Rebellion in 1960. I was very young, looking after cattle at home, fighting with sticks and so on, enjoying the very important culture for a young boy to become a man. . . . We heard guns and the old people said that people are being shot at on that mountain where they were assembling. We used to see a lot of vans driving in the mielie-fields [maize-fields], destroying the mielies as they drove. Very, very cruel, brutal people who are looking at Blacks as total animals to kill. We saw them harassing mothers, harassing old people, old mothers; we saw them arresting them. We grew up knowing many people were taken by the helicopters of the Boers. When they came to your home they kicked everything, destroyed everything in the house. So you just came to understand what the old people were talking about — the cruelties of the Whites.

As with many who became leaders in the NUM, Hoyce Phundulu brought his politics with him when he came to the mines to work in 1974. He brought with him years of commitment to a struggle that had always remained alive for him.

Phundulu's memories of the Pondoland revolt do not recall a tribal struggle against local chiefs, however. For Mpondo, at any rate, the involvement of the central state in support of their "tribal" oppression was so obvious that the struggle that had started out against the imposition of a bankrupt type of tribal authority rapidly became a struggle against White military occupation. Phundulu, remember, stressed "the cruelties of the Whites." "Definitely they were true because you could see," he told me. "It was a very terrible thing at that time. I was very young and I was definitely conscientized by it, definitely conscientized by it." The temptations of tribal identity, always present for the uncircumcised but Xhosa-speaking Mpondo, were offset by the blatantly racial and racist repression of their democratic revolt.

Although the rest of the Transkei did not rise up in the same way, there too "tribal authorities" were given little respect. The application of tribal despotism was too abrupt and violent to legitimate collaborating "tribal authorities" with the balm of "culture." The racism of Verwoerd's "indirect rule" in the Transkei was quite obvious to the youthful Phundulu growing up in Lusikisiki. Moreover, the policy of resettling workers laid off by modernizing White commercial farms (and those removed from urban townships) into huge, festering rural slums in the western Transkei fueled resentments that could in no way be assuaged by appeals to "custom" or "culture." Class divisions increased in the rural areas and they were manifestly class and not status divisions (except perhaps for increased intergenerational strife). A military coup in the Transkei at the end of the apartheid years did not lead to despotic military rule. Rather, it brought the Transkei back into the new democratic South Africa.

I do not wish to argue that the "tribal temptation" does not exist in South Africa. Buthelezi, in KwaZulu, long ago succumbed to it. Intense poverty in other rural areas has led to charges of widespread corruption in the process of the institutionalization of an ANC government. The jury is still out on the reconstruction of South Africa. Over time the ANC may break down along tribal lines but at present, race and class rather than ethnicities remain the major divides in town and countryside alike.[25] Again, Kwazulu is the exception.

Organization on the mines

In February 1985, unionized Black workers at Anglo-Vaal's Hartebeestfontein Gold Mine (colloquially called "Harties") near Klerksdorp in the Transvaal, organized a boycott of liquor outlets set up by management in the compounds. In return, management allegedly ordered an induna to bribe certain Mpondo Xhosa-speakers at #4 shaft hostel to drink at the bar and break the boycott. Whatever the actual situation, it soon deteriorated into a faction fight between Xhosa-speaking and Basotho workers. In three days, the fight had extended to four shafts and others were threatened. Faction fights were always a potential problem in ethnically segregated mine hostels and ran directly counter to the National Union of Mineworkers' (NUM) policy of racial solidarity. At Hartebeestfontein, Hoyce Phundulu, who was at #2 shaft but not yet a leader, asked permission from the union stewards on his shaft to negotiate a settlement of the faction fight. As we know, he was from a small rural Mpondo area near Lusikisiki (one of the areas in Pondoland most riven with faction fighting, but between locations not tribes) and he told the union leaders, "Let me advise you, we must stop this now. If they are defeated now, they are going to plan another action. I don't know what they are going to do, but they are going to get back at you. I have experience from activity at home. Faction fighting will not stop faction fights." He suggested negotiation. The branch committee agreed, telling him, "Go ahead, do it." Phundulu and a comrade brought together key people from different "tribes"[26] to discuss the matter. "There are in the mine people who are highly respected from their tribes because of their age, because of their popularity," he told me. "They are highly respected by their own tribe in the mine situation." He and his colleague brought together such people from each shaft and asked them, "What is the problem?" They discovered that the main grievance was that some of the shaft stewards who had led the liquor outlet boycott, had taken to selling liquor outside the hostel. Phundulu and his friend called together the shaft stewards, two per shaft, from all shafts on the mine. It was an illegal meeting but they went ahead anyway. They agreed that no union member would be allowed to sell liquor outside the hostel. People were authorized to confiscate any such liquor found and drink it free of charge. There was one other complaint. People from #4 shaft said that the tribal indunas must be dismissed because they were collaborating with management. The meeting, however, decided, "Let's not call anyone a collaborator. Let's persuade that person to become a member of the union and support the union, whether it be the induna or whatever." The following day, the faction fight ended and the liquor boycott continued. After a week, management started arresting union shaft stewards and firing them. Security forces from the mine transported them to the borders of their respective homelands and dumped them there. Security raided the hostels time and again. Mass dismissals created chaos on the mine. The union at Hartebeestfontein was totally destroyed. "Management was so very, very brutal at that time, I can tell you," said Phundulu. Union resolution of tribal conflict led promptly to direct repression from management.

There emerge from Phundulu's account the two themes we have already discovered to be fundamental for understanding race and ethnicity in South African society and history: first, the uneasy relationship between racial and ethnic categories and, second, their imbrication in power struggles. Phundulu's story is centrally about NUM resistance to racial colonial despotism in its local mine context. Such despotism enabled exploitation of Black workers along racial lines by White managers and supervisors. It was, however, reinforced by the assistance of Black indunas who presided over their own "tribal" establishments in each mine compound. For Phundulu, faction fights between tribal groups on the mines were fomented by management to undercut union action but, historically, networks of tribal solidarity had been crucial survival strategies for South African mine workers. Phundulu also recognized the independent appeal of ethnic or tribal identities for mine workers. Indeed, as we have seen, he initiated meetings with tribal representatives in order to undercut the divisive effects of ethnicity on racial unity. Appeals to racial or worker solidarity were necessarily mediated through tribal identities once ethnic conflict was under way.

On the face of it, Phundulu's story seems to sustain the argument for the importance of tribalism. Rural-based "ethnic" distinctions had always been the major basis for factional conflict on the mines. Representatives of the NUM had constantly to fight a rear-guard action against tribal divisions. Nonetheless, the union grew during the early 1980s faster than any other union in South Africa — perhaps in the world. When I interviewed Hoyce Phundulu in 1998, the NUM was well-established on Hartebeestfontein mine and he was the local regional secretary in Klerksdorp. He and his comrades who endured had maneuvered the union through the shoals of ethnic conflict and management opposition to a position of relative security on the mine. How did racial and ethnic practices actually work on the South African gold mines?

Mine management officials saw the NUM as a "Xhosa union." "Sotho" were conceived to be much more conservative and potential allies in the struggle against the union. The early union leadership at Harties was, in fact, almost entirely Basotho, however. "Sotho" on the mines are citizens of the independent state of Lesotho, a small, mountainous, land-locked, ex-British dependency, completely surrounded by South Africa. Lesotho was formed from a motley collection of lineage and language groups during the time of troubles of the early nineteenth century that also gave rise to the Zulu kingdom and eventually Zulu ethnicity. Basotho tribal identity was derived from the defensive posture of Moshoeshoe, their chief ruler, rather than the famously more offensive Zulu stance, however.[27] Dispossessed by the Orange Free State Boers of their most fertile farmland along the western reaches of the upper Caledon river, the Basotho were pushed back into the Maluti mountains, where (as refugee groups poured into the country) they became hopelessly overpopulated and increasingly dependent on migrant labor.[28] Although the British colonial government never ceded Lesotho to South African rule, Basotho migrated to South African cities in great numbers. Politically independent from Britain since 1966, Lesotho is economically dependent on South Africa.

Predictably, independence has mostly benefited chiefs and the intellectual elite, and it is they who are primarily responsible for the ideological glorification of Lesotho citizenship. Many years of migration, however, have given rise to a Basotho working class culture marvelously expressed in the *lifela* songs splendidly captured by David Coplan.[29] This form of ethnicity is wrought in the experience of migrant work ("we are the lions of the mine") where the Basotho pride themselves on their abilities as shaft sinkers[30] and lashers (rock shovelers). While such an ethnic consciousness blends in a continuum into a Basotho "national" ideology, it takes the more amorphous form of common sense[31] in everyday life at work.

In 1963, the South African government forbade employment for citizens of Lesotho in all sectors of the South African economy except mining and agriculture. On the mines, this eventually entrenched Basotho in many senior clerical and supervisory positions — a process of opportunity hoarding much resented by young, educated Xhosa-speakers who returned to the mines in great numbers during the 1970s. Meanwhile, after Lesotho obtained representative government in 1960 and independence under Chief Lebua Jonathan of the Basotholand National Party (BNP) in 1966, the Basotholand Congress Party (BCP) was elected in 1970, only to have the election abrogated by Jonathan, throwing BCP members into exile. Many BCP members established themselves on the South African gold mines whence they conducted a guerrilla war in Lesotho. Thus, in 1982 at its inauguration, the NUM found BCP leaders on the mines, already organized and eager to participate in the new union movement. The initial NUM leaders at Hartebeespoort gold mine were drawn from this group. Indeed, at Hartebeestfontein the early leadership was almost entirely Basotho. It was they who threw the local union into its disastrous confrontation with management that led to the 1985 mass dismissals Phundulu described.

Oliver Sokanyile, who had been regional chair of the union in the western Transvaal, told me that part of the problem at Harties was the recklessness of the early union leadership. (He did not even mention to me that they were all Basotho.) Phundulu agreed that this compounded the problem of an intransigent management, saying: "There was strong leadership but the strategic approach on activities and themes needed good leadership that would calculate the politics of every aspect. The people were guided by anger most of the time. So, I'm sure that was Comrade Sokanyile's argument."

The anger at Harties in 1985 was not unique. Even at Vaal Reefs, an Anglo-American mine with a supposedly more enlightened management policy, Phundulu's friend Wiseman Nobongwana experienced precisely the sort of disrespectful treatment that so aroused worker anger.[32] In 1989, he was elected chief shaft steward at Vaal Reefs South. He had just taught himself English, but was still very much a rural Mpondo traditionalist. Andy Beytell, the personnel manager and Nobongwana's boss, said he needed to see Wiseman in his office. Wiseman told me the story:

> Then, to me on that day, it was my happiest day to be called by the Personnel Manager in his office because I even don't know where it is. Then I went there, running, to see the Personnel Manager, thinking that there is something for the workers. Then he, Beytell, asked me, "What is your name?" I told him that my name is Wiseman. And your surname, Nobongwana, he said. He asked me my tribe and I told him that I am South African.

This was the standard response for a union member, confronting management's assertion of ethnic primordialism with a claim to civic allegiance. Beytell refused to be sidetracked, although he almost certainly interpreted Nobongwana's response as cheeky. He pressed on, insisting on his own crude ethnic assumptions. Having forced Nobongwana to admit that he came from Bizana, he continued: "Are you a Xhosa?" Nobongwana answered proudly, as he also told me:

> "I am a conservative one, a conservative Xhosa." After I said that he asked me, "Do you know a Xhosa?" Then I started looking at the ceiling of the

office and I said, "No, I don't know a Xhosa." He stood up and did a role-play about the Xhosa, saying that the Xhosa is a man who comes to a company requesting a job and when the manager employs him, after two weeks the Xhosa looks at everything, saying, "This and this and this is wrong. This one is right. This is wrong and so on and so on." He was moving up and down his office. He told me that that is the type of man.

Such ethnic insults were mild compared to the racist treatment that followed, however.

He went to his telephone and called in security — he was speaking Afrikaans to them — and although I was starting to learn English, he spoke Afrikaans and I didn't understand him. After ten minutes, security guys came in and I was taken out from that office in the way that I really don't know. You see the office had steps. My head was looking down and my feet were on top there. Carrying me shoulder high. Before they actually carried me, I got some fists and some kicks. Beytell said to the security that I was obstructing him in his job. Mind you, the man actually phoned and I talked to his secretary and asked directions to get to his office because I didn't even know where it was.

From 1985, the union focused its campaign against management representing such rampant intimidatory racism firmly couched in ethnic terms. Nobongwana, like Phundulu, was deeply committed to the NUM policy of understanding *ethnic* differences in order to overcome them so as to unite workers in opposition to the policy of apartheid that used tribalism as a justification for *racial* humiliation.

Many Basotho from the BCP, including the NUM president, James Motlatsi, shared the general sense of racial alienation and eagerly joined the union's commitment to fighting racism on the mines. Phundulu told me that the NUM national congress, in January 1985, decided that "each branch of the union must identify their demands and submit them to the management and start taking action so that management would meet them." This turn to the grass roots moved the union rapidly from an earlier legalistic strategy to direct confrontation with management and its black minions, like indunas and many team leaders.

The union's new policy of attacking racial exploitation and authoritarian management was fraught with difficulty, however, requiring an ability for strategic maneuver that implied disciplined understanding not only to provide solidarity but also to overcome ethnic divisions eagerly exploited by management. The new policy tapped into deep resentments of Black workers subject to intense humiliations. On the one hand, this became a powerful source of appeal for union recruitment. On the other hand, it was difficult for union leaders to negotiate successful compromises with management if "the people were guided by anger most of the time." Phundulu explained that this was "a learning stage for the union. We were putting demands because the mining industry had terrible conditions, and people were beginning to have a space to air their grievances, and people were beginning to see different ways of organizing their comrades [than the old ethnic styles of organization]."

Different management styles and tactics, especially the extent to which supervisors were willing to use ethnic differences to reinforce their rule, explain why union objectives and strategies necessarily differed from mine to mine, he said:

> In the final analysis, survival depended on solidarity across ethnic lines. Collective action was used sparingly and only when there was strong grassroots support. We were only able to take hard action when we saw that the workers were definitely together. Management wouldn't take out all the workers, otherwise they would have to close the mine. Those were the tactics that we played. So we definitely managed to survive with each other under those hard conditions.

The NUM, thus, pulled together workers from all the various ethnic groups on the mines in opposition to racial exploitation and the indignities and humiliations suffered on a day-to-day basis at the hands of White and Black supervisors. Management and the police constantly invoked ethnic categories in an effort to undermine such opposition. In the end, the union prevailed. It is difficult to imagine with that history that union leaders would resort to ethnic patronage.

In spite of management policies that actively sought to exploit ethnic divisions in the workforce, the history of the rise of the NUM challenges arguments for the inevitability of tribalism. The situation on the South African gold mines during the 1980s was more complex than Phundulu's story makes out, however, especially in regard to workers from Lesotho. Developments in Lesotho have not taken place entirely in parallel with those in South Africa. We have seen that BCP opposition to the "chiefly" rule of Lebua Jonathan provided important leadership material for the NUM in its early years. At the same time, however, Basotho workers' greater experience meant that they were substantially overrepresented in the ranks of supervisory personnel underground. To the extent that White mine managers resisted the growth of the union, they tended to recruit support not only from indunas but also from team leaders, underground supervisors, the majority of whom were "traditionalist" Basotho. To some extent, the existence of Lesotho as a "nation state," politically independent but economically totally dependent on South Africa, does reinforce "nationalist" ethnic identity. Much of the most violent opposition to the NUM in the 1980s and early 1990s came from Basotho team leaders. While such opposition was often inspired by management encouragement in the early years, it became increasingly politicized as the NUM organized strike campaigns in support of the ANC in the early 1990s.

Lesotho, however, is a far cry from KwaZulu. The country has a strong tradition of democratic opposition, and political patronage networks, while substantial, lack the unity and ruthlessness of Inkatha. There was always strong support for the NUM from many Lesotho nationals, and once the ANC came to power, the NUM returned to policies of support for all workers whatever their "national" or "tribal" origin. Despite massive downsizing on the South African gold mines (from 500,000 workers in 1987 to 240,000 today), incidents of ethnic strife have drastically diminished. Economic pressures have induced many mine workers from Lesotho to claim South African citizenship and team leaders are increasingly drawn from a wide range of workers with different origins, including some from urban townships. The structural basis for Basotho ethnic organization, both at home and in the workplace, seems to have disintegrated as the mines have established a working relationship with the union. In spite of the complications of Lesotho nationality, then, ethnic assumptions again run up against South African historical realities.

Conclusion

In this chapter, I have tried to spell out some of the complexities of race and ethnicity as social processes in South Africa. I conclude that ethnic identities are carried by social networks that share common symbols, common interests, and the institutions that sustain them over time. My own work on the history of migrant labor to the South African gold mines indeed suggests that ethnic integrities were created and sustained by conceptions of masculinity rooted in the rural economy and particular interest groupings on the mines themselves. My work also suggests, however, that as rural society broke down, the very meaning of "manhood" itself changed.[33] The structural base for traditional ethnic identities also disappeared. In fact, with the important exception of "the Zulu," ethnic identities in South Africa came to matter less and less in the 1980s and 1990s. Leslie Bank has documented a similar development amongst "lapsed migrant" hostel-dwellers in East London. He argues that generational conflict between younger and older men as well as dispossession was a fundamental part of the process.[34] On the mines, rural underdevelopment and generational conflict came together in the 1970s. Where there are still pockets of patriarchal tribalism, these depend more on the institutionalization of ethnic networks pursuing direct political interests than on a split between the central state and ethnic rural polities. To the extent that ethnic politics occurs in the future South Africa, it will look more like American ward politics than Mamdani's African model of rurally based ethnic separatism.

In contemporary South Africa, *race* still forms a useful basis for political appeal. *Ethnic* solidarities as patriarchal opportunity-hoarding reactions to urban migration are no longer a serious option, however, since senior men have lost access to the rural resources that guaranteed their previous power. Nostalgia, however violently asserted in the name of tribal allegiances, cannot be more than a rearguard action in a situation where power has come to reside in education and social class rather than old-style rural patronage networks. Of course, as South Africa continues to industrialize, processes of capitalist accumulation will increasingly lead to class divisions. These divisions may well come to be articulated by cultural entrepreneurs and other social actors in racial or ethnic terms, leading to cultural rather than class conflicts. Such tendencies, however, are typical throughout the developed capitalist world (and especially the "new capitalisms" of Eastern Europe) but they are not "tribalism" with its peculiarly African form. Analyses of South African politics in "tribal" terms should be regarded with profound suspicion. They almost always lead to misleading analogies and false conclusions. Popular understandings of race and ethnicity in Africa in terms of tribalism are usually misleading. In the case of South Africa, they are almost always wrong.

Notes

1. Martin Murray, *The Revolution Deferred* (London: Verso, 1994), 100.
2. The distinction here is between a Zulu-speaking rural and migrant patriarchal revanchist movement and a trade union and youth-based political movement against apartheid. Inkatha certainly made Zulu ethnic claims but these were eschewed by their opponents, whether Zulu- or Xhosa-speaking.
3. For South Africa, a most comprehensive and accessible discussion of precolonial social organization may be found in Carolyn Hamilton, ed., *The Mfecane Aftermath* (Johannesburg and Pietermaritzburg: Witwatersrand University Press and Natal University Press, 1995); *see also* Jean and John Comaroff, *Of Revelation and Revolution: Christianity, Colonialism and Consciousness in South Africa, Volume 1* (Chicago: University of Chicago Press, 1991), chapter 4.
4. Leroy Vail, ed., *The Creation of Tribalism in Southern Africa* (London: James Currey; Berkeley: University of California Press, 1989).
5. Following Raymond Williams' reading of Antonio Gramsci, I make a distinction here between "ideology" as a worked-out system of cultural ideas to which conscious appeal may be made and "common-sense" as those taken-for-granted assumptions that inform everyday conduct in all societies. The distinction is not dichotomous but exists on a continuum.
6. Ivan Evans, *Bureaucracy and Race: Native Administration in South Africa* (Berkeley: University of California Press, 1997), 246.
7. Vail, *Creation of Tribalism*, 15.
8. T. Dunbar Moodie, *Going for Gold: Men, Mines and Migration* (Berkeley: University of California Press; Johannesburg: Witwatersrand University Press, 1994), 182–210.
9. The anticolonial "nation" was itself, of course, a product of colonial rule.
10. Mahmood Mamdani, *Citizen and Subject: Contemporary Africa and the Legacy of Late Colonialism* (Princeton, NJ: Princeton University Press, 1996).
11. T. Dunbar Moodie, *The Rise of Afrikanerdom: Power, Apartheid and the Afrikaner Civil Religion* (Berkeley: University of California Press, 1975).
12. Treurnicht was later to become Minister of Bantu Education. It was he who precipitated the Soweto uprising in 1976 by insisting that African high school students take half their subjects through the medium of Afrikaans — a language that most of them and many of their teachers could not speak.
13. Moodie, *Rise of Afrikanerdom*.
14. Evans, *Bureaucracy and Race*.
15. For a very useful overview of the development of the Black Consciousness movement, *see* Thomas G. Karis and Gail M. Gerhart, *From Protest to Challenge: A Documentary History of African Politics in South Africa, 1882–1990* (Bloomington: Indiana University Press, 1997), 89–155. See also N. Barney Pityana *et al.*, eds., *Bounds of Possibility: The Legacy of Steve Biko and Black Consciousness* (London: Zed Press; Cape Town: David Philip, 1991).

16. Anton Lembede, who had a profound effect on the Africanist ANC Youth League in the 1940s (that included Nelson Mandela), grew up in the Orange Free State. He read and spoke Afrikaans fluently and I strongly suspect that his intellectual development was profoundly affected by the writings of Afrikaner ideologues like Nic Diederichs.

17. The best brief overview of Inkatha is Karis and Gerhart, *From Protest to Challenge*, 251–278.

18. Karis and Gerhart, *From Protest to Challenge*, 264.

19. Leslie Bank, "Men with Cookers: Transformations in Migrant Culture, Domesticity and Identity in Duncan Village, East London," *Journal of Southern African Studies*, 25 (1999).

20. Saul Dubow, "'Holding a Just Balance between White and Black': The Native Affairs Department in South Africa, c. 1920–33," *Journal of Southern African Studies*, 12 (1986).

21. For an accessible discussion of colonial governmental structures in the Transkei, *see* W.D. Hammond-Tooke, *Command or Consensus* (Cape Town: David Philip, 1975).

22. Philip and Iona Mayer, *Townsmen or Tribesmen* (Cape Town: Oxford University Press, 1961).

23. Evans, *Bureaucracy and Race*, 190–275.

24. Material from Hoyce Phundulu is based on my interview with him in Klerksdorp on November 5, 1998.

25. For a cogent analysis of class forces in contemporary South Africa, *see* Hein Marais, *South Africa: Limits to Change: The Political Economy of Transition*. Revised and expanded new edition (London: Zed Books; Cape Town: University of Cape Town Press, 2001).

26. However problematic their origins, "tribal" identities have been essentialized by (especially White but also many Black) actors in South African social situations. This is particularly true on the mines where they have come to represent genuine interest groups. Designations may vary (thus, Mpondo may sometimes be identified as members of the Xhosa tribe whereas they are given their own autonomy in other contexts) but tribal affiliations are real to the extent that they are taken as real by social actors.

27. *See* Elizabeth Eldredge, *A South African Kingdom: The Pursuit of Security in Nineteenth Century Lesotho* (Cambridge: Cambridge University Press; Johannesburg: Witwatersrand University Press, 1993).

28. For a critical account of development schemes within Lesotho, *see* James Ferguson, *The Anti-Politics Machine* (Cambridge: Cambridge University Press, 1990). Sandra Wallman, *Taking Out Hunger* (London: Athlone, 1969) also remains relevant.

29. David Coplan, *In the Time of Cannibals: The Word Music of South Africa's Basotho Migrants* (Chicago: University of Chicago Press, 1994).

30. Jeff Guy and Motlatsi Thabane, "Technology, Ethnicity and Ideology: Basotho Miners and Shaft-Sinking on the South African Gold Mines," *Journal of Southern African Studies*, 14.2 (1988).

31. Unlike Gramsci, from whom I derive my understanding of common sense, I wish to leave open the extent to which and for whom it is hegemonic.

32. I interviewed Wiseman Nobongwana in Klerksdorp on July 31, 1999.

33. Moodie, *Going for Gold*.

34. Bank, "Men with Cookers."

16

Eritrea's Identity as a Cultural Crossroads[1]

Tekle M. Woldemikael

When Eritrea formally joined the Organization of African Unity (OAU) in Cairo 1993, its newly elected president, Isaias Afworki, remarked at the summit, "indeed, the sad fact remains that the OAU has become a nominal organization that has failed to deliver on its pronounced objectives and commitments. In this regard, I must admit that we have sought membership in the organization not because we have been impressed by its achievement but, as a local proverb goes, in the spirit of familial obligation, because we are keenly aware that what is ours is ours."[2] This statement reflected a deliberate attempt on the Eritrean leader's part to invoke family relations in order to show Eritrea's kinship ties with other African states. On the other hand, the president was using the family metaphor to scold the OAU as a dysfunctional household, placing Eritrea as a new family member with a fresh vision — a family member convinced of its superiority and innocence. He invoked such an analogy, in part, to express Eritrea's frustration with most OAU members who were not supportive of the Eritrean liberation movement during its over thirty years of bitter conflict with Ethiopia. Such a feeling of disappointment makes sense when one considers that the Eritrean case was never brought up as topic for discussion on the agenda of the OAU members.[3] By making this statement, Afworki showed off his confidence as a newcomer to power, and as a man to contend with.

In the same speech, President Isaias admonished members of OAU, saying "Africa is not a place where its citizens can walk with raised heads but a continent scorned by all its partners, a continent that seems to produce endlessly the wrong manuals for economic development, democracy and political management ... That all these problems are not entirely of our making is of course apparent ... [but] we must put our act together if this continent is to be relieved from the multiple problems that have devoured it for decades."[4] This attitude reflects a sense of pride of a leader of a new nation with a determination to chart a new direction for economic development and political stability (and thus serve as a model for others to emulate), a confidence that is also embedded in the sense of difference and cultural superiority Eritreans (and Ethiopians) feel relative to other sub-Saharan Africans. This paper explores the cultural norms and ideological basis of Eritrea's self-identification as a different and a unique nation in Africa. The roots of this sense of difference are built on a long history of cultural norms and ideology that have been practiced within Eritrea and easily merged with the current western writers and journalists' perception of Eritrean cultural distinctness from other sub-Saharan Africans.

Conceptions of race and ethnicity in local contexts

Most writers have written with the assumption that the blending of populations in Ethiopia and Eritrea has produced a population that some scholars have defined as belonging to an ethno-racial group different from sub-Saharan Africa. It is assumed that this blending of peoples from Africa and the Middle East took place under historical contexts in which the lighter skinned Middle Eastern peoples subjugated local African populations, colonized their land, and established their cultural hegemony.[5] Edward Ullendroff has stated that

> Generally speaking, the predominant Ethiopian type reveals fairly close anthropometric affinities to that commonly found among the Arabs of South Arabia, i.e., medium stature, long face, and a fairly straight and thin nose — all characteristics not encountered among the neighbouring African peoples. The hair is curly or frizzy, lips are thinner and very much less protruding than is otherwise the case in Africa. The colour of the skin varies a good deal, but is generally rather light, somewhere between olive and light brown.[6]

Donald Levine, a prominent sociologist who has written extensively on Ethiopian culture and society, adds that "As a base line for reconstructing the history of Greater Ethiopia then, we may consider it plausible that by the end of the third millennium B.C. its main inhabitants were dark-skinned Caucasoid or 'Afro-Mediterranean' peoples practicing rudimentary forms of agriculture and animal husbandry and speak three branches of Afro-Asiatic — Semitic, Cushitic, and Omotic."[7] These scholars' conception of race is based on an essentialist and naturalistic view of race in which race is seen as a concept that can be usefully applied to classify human societies into clearly defined racial groups based on physical attributes.

Concepts, such as race and ethnicity are no longer seen as naturally given and essential aspects of human nature, but as socially constructed classifiers that do not adequately explain an individual's or groups' multiple identities of mixing, breaking away, and uniting, assimilating to or separating from institutionalized groups or social order. That is, scholarly knowledge of ethnicity and race has been undergoing thorough transformations, shifting our understanding of race and ethnic groups from seeing them as primordial, essentialist, and naturalized groups to socially and culturally constructed social formations.[8] This paradigm shift has challenged our ideas of racial purity and ethnic homogeneity. They have been replaced with the conception of ethnic and racial categories as socially constructed labels used to sort out human bodies into groups that are identifiable identities with signs coded with meaningful symbols based on putative common descent, claims of shared history, and symbols of peoplehood. Race and ethnicity are similar, but there are some fundamental differences as well. While ethnic groups might begin from assignment by others or might originate from self-definition, others often assign racial identity. In contrast to ethnicity, race refers more clearly to perceived physical differences and reflects an inequality of power between those who have assigned an ethnic or racial label and those who received labels. The identities assigned often signify differences in worth.[9]

The term "ethnic" is normally used to describe the socially defined differences between groups based on the cultural makeup of the social groups and the term "race" to designate the socially defined differences between groups based on the assumed physical differences between them. In this case study of Eritrea, I use the term "ethno-racial" rather than simply "ethnic" or "race" to describe the cultural and social relations among Eritreans because the two concepts are intertwined in the ways the social groups in Eritrea view and treat one another. I will describe the ideology that justifies such social relations as ethno-racial ideology when its cultural manifestation is a discourse and practice of seeing the cultural differences as something that are genetic and inherited from generation to generations through birth.[10]

Ethno-racial ideology often emphasizes the undesirability of the groups viewed as "inferior" and possessing an "undesirable" character. The idiom of ethno-race in Eritrea is expressed in terms of an ideology of honor and respect that is given to a kinship group. This ideology of honor holds that one's kinship group is of pure descent, meaning it has not been mixed with "undesirable" groups. I consider it "ethno-racial" when members of subordinated groups are excluded from intermarriage and the children born from any sexual relations are denied from establishing any kinship relations with the dominant group because of the "negative attribution given to their culture, their ethnic identity, their personality as well as 'racial' stock."[11] On the other hand, I regard a group "ethnic" when a group considers itself as different from others based on its assumed cultural heritage and kinship difference from others without necessarily implying that the group possesses superior hereditary traits and genetic makeup from others.

In the case of Eritrea, what one may classify as ethnic groups are internally seen from a naturalistic, essentialist view that assumes populations are divided into types of human bodies that share "similar blood, flesh and bone structures."[12] The foundation of Eritrean ethnic grouping share a lot in common with what is often seen as the basis for racial groupings and, thus, it hard to separate the two groupings clearly. Attributes that are considered as purely racial and also as purely ethnic are conflated into one naturalized form of identity, which I will call an ethno-racial identity. An ethno-racial identity is both an ethnic and racial identity and can be seen as a naturalized identity of groups who are seen or see themselves as culturally and racially unique people. In Eritrea, ethno-racial purity is the best and most desirable norm, while ethno-racial mixtures are not. Local people believe that the mixing of ethno-racial groups that produced the current ethno-racial groups is something that happened in some distant past and under unusual instances of conquest, slavery, subjugation, and domination. Now, intermarriage between identifiable ethno-racial groups is rare and is considered taboo. The various ethno-racial groups have an ideology of purity and maintenance of that purity through endogamy within ethno-racial groups. The rules of exogamy apply between lineages within ethno-racial groups. Since most ethno-racial groups share the same religion (with some exceptions), religious traditions set the boundaries of marriage and matrimony between ethno-racial groups.[13]

Cultural intersections and marginality

Eritrea, just like Ethiopia, Somalia, and Sudan, has been a crossroads between the Middle East and Africa. Eritrea consists of three million people speaking nine different languages. The languages are classified as part of two large, major language groups in the world, including Nilo-Saharan and Afro-Asiatic families. The Nilo-Saharans include the Nara and Kunama. The Afro-Asiatic further splits into two: Semitic, consisting of Tigrinya, Tigre, and Arabic; and Cushitic languages, consisting of Afar, Bilen, Hadareb, and Saho.[14] The present government of Eritrea considers the people who speak those languages as nationalities. It employs such classification as a way of mapping the terrains of social relations within the Eritrean population. The classifications of the language groups as ethno-racial groups, however, could be misleading if we consider languages spoken now to show survival of distinct ethno-racial groups over a long period of time. The history of the nine ethno-racial groups shows that they are socially constructed identities that have evolved and changed over time. Some of the language groups were political units, each with its own power base and political history. Some Semitic language-speaking populations are believed to have originated from Southern Arabia and to have colonized some of the earliest residents, including the Kunama and the Nara speakers, who are considered to have migrated from southern Nile Valley; and the Cushitic-speaking populations, who are thought to have come from Northern and Eastern Africa. The encounter of these diverse indigenous and migrant populations is assumed to have produced an Eritrean people that reflects a hybrid of cultures and languages that combine Semitic, Cushitic, and Nilo-Saharan influences.[15]

It is paradoxical that Eritreans maintain an ideology of ethno-racial purity and the undesirability of ethno-racial mixing, yet, they identify themselves through their oral stories and legends that assert that Eritreans are a product of some racial and ethnic mixture of light-skinned migrants from the Arabian Peninsula and the dark-skinned indigenous African populations. The fact that the Middle Eastern-based ideas of giving lower status to those who are assumed to have more "African" and/or slave ancestry have established cultural hegemony over the local African norms demonstrates that there has been a long-term, unequal encounter between the peoples of the Middle East and local African populations in Eritrea (and the rest of the Horn of Africa region). Middle Eastern peoples came to the Horn of Africa as immigrants, traders, missionaries, soldiers of invading powers, and nomadic pastoralists. The assumed different shades of complexion and physical features of Eritrea's population are held by outside observers to reflect the various mixing of people coming from the Middle East and Africa. The blending of cultures from Africa and the Middle East has left its marks on the hegemonic cultural norms and ideologies of local people. For example, some powerful light-skinned peoples from across the Red Sea are supposed to have conquered the indigenous inhabitants of Africa, resulting in a local population in Eritrea and Ethiopia who thinks of themselves as a mixed race (Habesha, otherwise known as Abyssinians), but who are hierarchically organized in ways that allow those who can claim purity and association with the more powerful Semitic languages and cultural norms to be given higher honor and status in social relationships.[16] Thus, the classifications of ethno-racial groups in Eritrea are in constant flux and their numbers and boundaries are mutable.

In terms of socially labeled races in Eritrea, on one end of the ethno-racial spectrum are Eritreans who are nomadic pastoralist Arabs who migrated from the Saudi Arabia to Eritrea in the late nineteenth century. They are considered as socially positioned on the periphery of the society because of their presumed distinct appearance and cultural goods, such as clothing, ornaments, utensils, and tools. Many Rashaidas are engaged in trade. Some of them are rich enough to own pick-up trucks, which can be parked underneath their tents. There are also Hadramuti and Yemeni Arabs who are trading merchants, owning market stalls in most of the larger towns in Eritrea. At the other end of the ethno-racial spectrum are the Kunama and Nara, who are also seen as more different from the mainstream core of the population because of their putative darker shade of skin, kinkier hair, and more "African" features than the average Eritreans. As mentioned before, Eritrea is made up of nine language groups that are part of two large, major language families in Africa, including the Nilo-Saharan and Afro-Asiatic families, that is, languages that straddle Africa and Asia. The Afro-Asiatic language speakers include two: Afro-Semitic, consisting of Tigrinya, Tigre and Arabic; and Cushitic languages, consisting of Afar, Bilen, Haadareb and Saho. The awareness of "racial" characteristics among those who identify themselves as one of the Afro-Asiatic language-speaking groups is built on the sense of honor and respect a person has in the predominantly (as opposed to the Nilo-Saharan groups, which are matrilineal) Afro-Asiatic language-speaking

Eritrean societies. The "purer" the ancestry an individual claims, that is, to have had no slave ancestry or ancestry from Nilo-Saharan language groups, the higher his or her status. Since the Afro-Asiatic language-speaking societies are predominantly patrilineal, the "purity" and "impurity" of genealogy is often traced more extensively through the male rather than the female ancestors. It should be noted here that these local "racial" classifications are based on minor distinctions and gradations, for most Eritreans are dark-skinned but exhibit skin tones that vary from very dark to light brown, and have hair texture that is rarely wavy but varies from kinky and short to curly and sometimes straight. The distinctions, however, are not based on clearly visible differences. Rather, they are based on the minor cues and oral stories about the impurity of the family history. This does not mean intermarriage among different ethno-racial and linguistic groups does not exist. In fact, Eritrean society is as much a "Creole" society as many parts of the world where ethno-racial groups are living close to one another. But, in spite of the mixing among the various ethno-racial groups over a long period of time, the ideology of purity still persists. The 20,000 or more Eritreans of mixed Italian and Eritrean ancestry who were forced to move to Italy or other locations during the postcolonial era are another evidence of Eritrea as a cultural crossroads as well as the power of the ethno-racial ideology of purity. Despite their lighter skins, they never were assimilated into the predominant society. Next, I will explore how the various ethno-racial classifications are intersected by and arranged into larger units of identification based on religion.

Religion as an idiom of cultural boundary

On the surface it would seem that since most Eritreans belong to the same group that look alike, the issue of racism would be far from their ways of thinking in relating to one another and their fellow Africans, south of the Sahara. Similar to other peoples in the Horn of Africa, including Sudan, Ethiopia, and Somalia, there is a form of racism that I would call internalized racism among Eritreans. Just like Ethiopia, Somalia, and Sudan, Eritrea is a crossroads between the Middle East and Africa. The diversity of shades of complexion and physical features reflect the various racial and ethnic mixing of the population from various parts of Africa and the Middle East. The mixing of peoples took place under circumstances in which the lighter skinned Middle Eastern populations were able to convert the local populations into their religious beliefs, including Orthodox Christianity and Islam and accept their ideology of racial superiority as legitimate and valid. Eritreans share the value system that put higher preference for Middle Eastern looking features and skin colour over the assumed African physical features and dark skin colour. In addition, the established internalized racism was reinforced when the region that we now know as Eritrea was colonized by a European state, Italy, and named the region it colonized as Eritrea. The Italians occupied Eritrea in 1886 and subsequently made it their colony from 1889 to 1941. During World War II, the British defeated the

Italians and made Eritrea their protectorate. The British ruled Eritrea from 1941 to 1952. The Italians rulers, especially under Mussolini, established an apartheid system in Eritrea by which the local populations were segregated from the European populations. Thus, the ethno-racial ideology of superiority of Europeans and Middle Eastern peoples over the local African populations was established and internalized among the people of Eritrea.

Religion is vital to the daily life of the average person in Eritrea. Along with language and legend, the local populations of Eritrea have domesticated the two major religions, Islam and Christianity, and have made them their own. The two religious identities have become a way of thinking, identifying, and relating to individuals and groups in everyday life. The two major religions have assimilated various pre-Christian and pre-Islamic cultural practices, Eritrean Christianity has, thus, developed separately from Eastern Orthodox Christianity and other Orthodox churches. The two religious communities in Eritrea remain socially separate to some extent and intermarriage is unusual. Religious identifications function almost as subnational ethnicities in the sense that individuals are identified in terms of their religious heritage regardless of the ostensible claims of individuals or the state to be secular.

The Eritrean population is fairly evenly divided between Orthodox Christians and Muslims, although Christians have historically dominated Eritrea's political economy and continue to do so. Although Eritrea is a culturally diverse land, the Tigrinya- and the Tigre-speakers make up four fifths of the population. The Tigrinya-speaking population is mostly Orthodox Christians and the Tigre-speakers are mostly Sunni Muslims. The remaining one fourth of the population is divided among seven ethnic groups, five who are predominantly Muslim (Hadareb, Afar, Saho, Rashaida, and Nara), and two ethnic groups (Bilen and Kunama), which are fairly evenly divided between Islam and Christianity. Some Kunama and Nara are followers of indigenous African religions.

Religious identities predominate over other forms of ethno-racial identifications because religion functions as a socially constructed identity that mediates between kinship based ethno-racial identities and national identity. It is an organizing principle in the context of national identity and the allocation of state resources and power. Religion is an organizing principle that has a long history in Eritrea and remains an enduring force.[17] Both the Muslim and Christian segments of the society emphasize this religious distinctiveness. Similar to other Muslims in the Horn of Africa, Muslims in Eritrea have adopted the fictive idea of being descendants of a holy family, in that they are all are related to the families of Mohammed the Prophets and/or his disciples. It is widely believed that Mohammed's disciples found refuge in Eritrea when they sought protection from their persecutors in Saudi Arabia during the seventh century, at the time when Islam was a new religion. Indeed, while the Prophet was still alive. Many Muslims see themselves as part of the Arab world and thus emphasize their connection to Islam and Arabic language.[18] The

Christians in Eritrea, together with the Amhara and Tigrayans in Ethiopia, on the other hand, claim their origins as descendants of immigrants from the Arabian Peninsula to Eritrea about 2000 years ago. They converted to Christianity in the fourth century A.D. They have their own alphabet (derived from Sabean script) used in writing their language, Tigrinya, and claim the legends of King Solomon and the Queen of Sheba (also claimed by Ethiopians) as part of their history.[19]

Hence, Eritreans associated themselves with Middle Eastern and European Christian peoples and cultures rather than their African neighbors, whom they regard as different and to some extent inferior.[20] Yet, this feeling of being distinct creates uneasiness in their relations with both the Middle Eastern and African world. Eritreans face triple marginality from these three sectors of the world: the African world that they reject; the Middle Easterners, who do not fully accept them; and Europe that does not see them as an integral part of its racial and ethno-racial identity. They are on the periphery of all three. Unlike the celebrated triple heritage of Africans, as proclaimed by the leading African scholar, Ali Mazrui, Eritreans suffer from triple alienation and exceptionalism.[21] The hybrid nature of the languages, the religions, and the people themselves has created a mélange of people who stand out culturally. And, although it is hard to clearly define them as a race, they are aware of all these differences, particularly the significance of skin color and physical features, which affect their sense of beauty and desirability for marriage, birth of children, and intimate relations.

Although the distinctions Eritreans and others significant influences such as the Europeans and Arabs make about race, ethnicity, and religion do place Eritreans on the periphery, most Eritreans seem to be unaware of this fact. Instead, they have tried to turn oppression to their advantage, by creating myths of exceptionalism that reinforce their insularity. In general, the light-skinned are preferred over dark-skinned, straight hair or wavy hair over kinky hair. Physical features that are judged as Arab or European are preferred to physical features that are deemed as African. It is not uncommon for sub-Saharan Africans to experience direct hostility and insults in Eritrea, Ethiopia, and Sudan. But, that does not mean Europeans are accepted. Even though this remark seems somewhat contradictory, given the preferences for light skin mentioned earlier, all outsiders are considered "exotic," but Europeans have been recognized as more powerful, and offering access to the international culture that dominates the globe, in this century and the last. Xenophobia or nativist impulse exists in both Eritrea and Ethiopia, but in Eritrea, it has been mixed with pragmatic acceptance of political power, especially where Europeans and Americans are concerned. They are identified as "Ferengi," meaning White or European, "Tilian," meaning Italian (who came as colonizers of Eritrea from 1889 to 1941), or "Kewaja," which also means foreigners. At the same time, they identify Middle Easterners as Arabs and as different from them. Moreover, many Middle Easterners and Europeans consider Eritreans to be Africans. And while many African nations have gained independence, more stability, and prominence, Eritrea has not. Thus, the sense of superiority built on the preexisting notion of purity and impurity of genealogy has been called into question and the people have been humbled by doubt. This has really been a process of unraveling that has gone on for a century or so. The clash between education and village/family mythology has made many Eritreans more enlightened (though certainly not more humble). There is less respect for religion-based education. There is less pride in the centuries old Orthodox Christian based traditions among the Christians and the old Islamic traditions among the Muslims. The traditional leadership based on semifeudal hierarchical power structure, the power of elders based on kinship and lineages and the power of religious leaders based on the power of religion on the society has been challenged. An attempt to chart a new direction without the guidance of existing traditional institutions makes the current generation of Eritreans less confident of the direction in which their nation is heading and their place in the African world and, therefore, they are more obsessed with asserting a unique identity that differentiates them from any other group but they are also unable to clearly explain what the basis of this uniqueness is in practice.

Self-identity and cultural ideology of belonging

If you ask individuals in Eritrea who they are, they will tell you what village their parents come from and what kinship or regional groups they belong to. They will tell their genealogy, which in turn narrates their oral history or story of their descent groups. These genealogies have been repeated orally and passed on from generation to generation, and serve as a guide to the oral history the local people tell about themselves. For instance, I have been told my own paternal and maternal genealogies. It only takes a few steps to trace my lineages to outside of my father's village. My father's village, Adi Baro, and my mother's village, Adi Guabo, are linked to two distinct, descent-based, regional genealogies, and connect to some old names of regional divisions in the society. Tracing a few generations in my father's genealogy on the patrilineal line, my lineage becomes a part of lineages of a larger oral history of the people in a region known as Logo Chewa. Logo Chewa is a region consisting of a large group of people tracing themselves to a common lineage that incorporates many villages and hamlets in the region, and also scattered in other historic regions. The Logo Chewas are believed to have the oldest written traditional laws that are still practiced until now. The name Logo Chewa signifies the mixing of two groups, Logos and Chewas, who trace their descent to Semiticised Cushitic ancestors. There are at least two narratives on the origins of the Logos, one from a written tradition that relates that the Logos are believed to have been soldiers who came from Kara, in the heartland of the Amhara region (in northwestern Ethiopia), and settled in fertile valleys of the Eritrean highlands. The second narrative comes from the oral tradition I received from my family, which differs from the story of the Logos as documented in history books.[22] My lineage starts with the name Asawer (which is neither an Islamic nor Christian name, and perhaps predates the conversion of the population to Christianity or Islam), who lived in Zula, on the eastern coastal plains near the Red Sea coast. I am twenty-seven generations from Asawer, who is remembered as the founder of my lineage. Three generations removed from Asawer the names change to Islamic ones, including Mohammed and Abdela, and these last until the sixth generation from Asawer. From the seventh to the tenth generation, the names change to traditional names. From the eleventh to my current generation, the names are consistently Christian.

On the other hand, the Chewas are believed to have come later from the Shewa province in central Ethiopia as soldiers of a king to either pacify the region or collect taxes or both. Now, the two groups, both Chewas and Logos (all of whom are peasant farmers and Orthodox Christians), live together in villages as one people. The formal distinction of being either a Logo or a Chewa has little social significance except to maintain a patrilineal kinship system and ascertain a person's belonging to either of the two through the male line. An individual has to be able to claim descent from one of the two. If one cannot claim lineage to either, then that person has no identity and cannot claim a piece of land to cultivate in the communally owned land tenure system, nor can they build a home in the village.[23]

An oral history among the Saho-speaking Cushitic population (seminomadic pasturalists whose home territory includes the Zula region) lends credence to the second narrative I heard from my family. Among the Saho speakers there is a major clan called Asawerta, who trace their ancestry to Asawer. This implies that the earlier descendants might have been nomadic herders who spoke Cushitic languages and believed in traditional African religion, then converted to Islam and later to Christianity as they migrated from the dry coastal plains to the fertile agricultural areas of highlands in search of grazing grasslands for their animals. In the highlands, the Asawerta encountered settled agriculturists, the Chewa, who were Tigrinya-speaking Afro-Semites. Here, perhaps, they were colonized by the Chewa and later assimilated into their culture, adopting their religion and way of life. What is so interesting is that even when living in villages as peasant farmers, they kept large number of animals and migrated along the Mereb River in search of pasture during the dry seasons. Although there is no overarching sense of oneness as a people, the scholarly belief that Cushitic-speaking people are related to other Cushitic-speaking people leads to assumption of kinship between Cushitic-speakers in Eritrea, Ethiopia, Sudan, and Egypt.[24]

It is believed that the Kunama and the Nara, who are Nilo-Saharans who have pre-dated the Cushitic and Afro-Semitic populations in Eritrea's interior have historically been subjected to raids and made into slaves in precolonial Eritrea.[25] Such uneven power relationships have created a cultural norm among the Cushitic and Afro-Semitic populations, which holds that any person suspected to have originated from an ethno-racial group that had a slave status implies impurity of race and ethnic heritage. This imagined "blood" impurity signifies some form of innate impurity and pollution of the kinship group.

Thus, the internal belief of purity exists in terms of genealogy, with the implication that any individual with slave heritage is "impure of blood and bone." But, because this notion of impurity is based on oral traditions, it is hard to ascertain the purity of a person's ancestry in any way. By claiming racial purity (as opposed to membership in stigmatized groups), kinship groups establish an individual's identity. This perceived racial purity also affords individuals the right to own land and access land for animal grazing.

The Kunama and Nara share similar views of their history. They believe that they were historically victimized by powerful outsiders (mostly people from whom the Afro-Semitic and Cushitic-language-speakers, including Tigrinya and Tigre speakers — among others) who attacked, raided, and enslaved them, as well as encroached upon their land. The term "Baria" (a pejorative name for Nara) in the Tigrinya and Tigre languages means "slave."[26] The Nara are now completely Muslim. Being Muslim protects them from raids and attacks because of the tradition in Muslim communities of not attacking their fellow Muslims. Although one cannot assume that the Nara became Muslims because they sought to avoid being attacked and enslaved by their more powerful Muslim neighbors, it is one of the possible reasons why they became devoted Muslims. In semifeudal, precolonial Eritrea, having a slave was seen as a status symbol. Slavery was eliminated in Eritrea with the coming of Italian colonialism. Thus, the slave status of a person's ancestor is often remembered and passed on through oral traditions and statements. It is often remembered and invoked at times of marriages and during the giving of land rights and inheritance. This form of cultural racism justifies unequal relationships between groups, using the purity of one's assumed biological heritage and kinship. If one is rich or has attained higher status in the government or other spheres, then one can erase the memory of slavery in one's family heritage, and be accepted in marriages and in creating kinship with those who are considered more proper members of society.

In summary, the cultural ideology that was produced from the ethno-racial encounters in Eritrea consisted of a value system that put higher preference for the assumed lighter skin colour and imagined more Middle Eastern-looking physical features over the supposedly darker skinned and more African features. This cultural ideology was shared among most of the ethno-racial groups in Eritrea, as well as the rest of the Horn of Africa, who still may be unaware of their bias, because it has such deep cultural roots.[27] It penetrated all aspects of social life, including respect and honor within the society, social status and ranking, rights for land and other property, inheritance, kinship, an ideal of beauty and preference for marriage, and other social relations. Even though European colonization, modernization, and urbanization have brought out some ideas of individualism and equality, they somewhat also reinforced the ethno-racial ideology and internalized racism because these modernizing influences did not penetrate deep enough into the local cultures to challenge these deeply held values. In fact, they brought their own ideology of racial superiority, thus, bestowing higher status for themselves and affirming the internalized hierarchy of power relations in society, and reinforcing the cultural ideology.

The ideology of cultural difference from Ethiopians

The elite and urban Eritrean claim of distinctiveness from Ethiopians is based on two ideological constructs. The first is rooted in the claim that Eritreans are more modern and more advanced than Ethiopians because of their experience with European colonization and subsequent exposure to modernity and urban life.[28] Moreover, the urban Muslim elites think of themselves as more cosmopolitan than their Christian compatriots and Ethiopians because of their linkage to the literate Arabic language, cultural complexity, and sophistication.[29] Eritrean nationalists argued that Eritrea was "colonized" by the Ethiopians people who were "less" modern and less cosmopolitan than them. To further understand these views, we need to put them in a historical context.

Eritrea's status as a singular entity is a relatively recent colonial invention, constructed out of a colonial boundary. Italian colonialists took control of the region in 1890, as part of the European colonization of Africa, (commonly known as "the scramble for Africa") and named their new colony Eritrea, after the Latin name for the Red Sea. They treated it as a unified colonial entity. When the Italians colonized Eritrea, they did not intend to limit themselves to Eritrea; they wanted to establish their presence throughout the Horn of Africa. If they had not encountered a strong resistance from the Ethiopian Emperor, Menelik, and had not been defeated in the battle of Adwa in 1896, the present map of Eritrea and Ethiopia would look quite different. If the Italians had defeated Menelik, they would have been able to link Italian Somaliland with Ethiopia and Eritrea to achieve their dream of an Italian East African Empire. The British victory over the Italians in 1941 ended the Italian colonization of Eritrea and made it the first colony in Africa to be liberated from a colonizer, in spite of the fact that Eritrea continued under British military rule. The United Nations federated Eritrea with Ethiopia in 1952, giving Eritrea autonomy under the sovereignty of the Ethiopian crown. With federation, the institutionalized practice of considering Eritrea to be a well-defined unit was to continue in federal form. But because Ethiopia had acquired Eritrea under a United Nations-sponsored agreement in 1952, Ethiopia then sought to centralize its control over the territory and to erode Eritrea's federal status. Ethiopia sought to integrate Eritrea not as a state in a federal relationship but as one of its provinces. It was then that some young men and women from Eritrea began to agitate to maintain the federal status and later to gain full independence. The Eritrean nationalist movement immediately emerged to challenge the intrusion of Ethiopia. Initially, that nationalist movement attempted to gain independence for Eritrea through a strategy of civil disobedience within Eritrea, and an appeal to the United Nations and the world community. When these civil and diplomatic means failed, the Eritrean nationalist movement fought the Ethiopian army on the battlefield, seeking local and international recognition for Eritrea as a nation deserving its own state. This led to more than 30 years of war, the longest war in modern African history. Eritrean nationalists fought and formally obtained their independence 1993, after the thirty years war with Ethiopia.[30]

The colonial encounter between the Italians and Eritreans was greatest among the Tigrinyaspeaking, highland Christians than in the hot, dry lowland areas, inhabited by seminomadic Muslim peoples. Thus, one can say that the impact was strongest in the Tigrinya-speaking highland Christian areas because the Italians settled and built their farms, industries, towns, and cities there. Many of the youth and children who grew up in urban areas, especially in Asmara, were exposed to a different degree of urban Italian subculture, lifestyle, dress, food, music, dance, consumption patterns, entertainment, and to some extent by the urban merchant class from Arab countries and India. These influences were reflected in the ways the youth in Asmara saw their lives as different from rural Eritrean life, especially in the way they created a creolized Tigrinya, complete with its own intonation and style of speaking. Creolized Tigrinya is a mixture of a significant amount of Italian language and, to some extent, Arabic words. In the 1950s and 1960s, creolized Tigrinya was limited to Asmara. The language of Asmara youth was hardly intelligible to rural Eritreans, and the youth invented a subculture that reflected both the Italian and Middle Eastern influences on the day-to-day life of urban culture. In urban centers in Eritrea, jokes were abundant about the backwardness of Ethiopia and the lack of sophistication of Ethiopians. A common joke told among Eritreans in Asmara was that while Addis Ababa is big village, Asmara is a small city. Through participation in guerrilla movements, mostly based in the rural areas, and a greater interaction and ease of travel to rural areas, however, the creolized Tigrinya has spread to greater parts of Eritrea and lost its geographic origins.[31]

Postindependence and cultural uniqueness

On May 24, 1993, Eritrea declared its official separation from Ethiopia and became the newest independent state in Africa; it happened to be (and is until today) the only successful case of an African country to break away from another African state. Foreign and Eritrean writers declared Eritrea different from the rest of Africa, and that the newly independent Eritrea could become a showcase for African development and recovery. The enthusiastic reception Eritrea received is partly related to the perceived malaise that most postcolonial African countries entered after their successful de-colonization. Many writers and analysts were seeking a success story from sub-Saharan Africa to set a trend for a renaissance of African progress. They believed that Eritrea could set the precedent because they were impressed with the Eritreans' show of new identity, an identity of self-sufficiency, confidence, and unity. Moreover, the idea of Eritrean uniqueness came partly because Eritrean nationalists won a war for independence in 1991, which many thought happened despite all odds. The emphasis of Eritrean difference from the rest of sub-Saharan Africa was stated in terms of Eritrea being a more advanced country and its people somewhat better than other Africans. For example, the differences that often impressed journalists was what they saw as a more advanced lifestyle when they visited the peaceful, clean, and modern style streets of Asmara, a city built by Italians when they had Eritrea under their control for sixty years. Eritrean elites and government officials also played an active role in nurturing the praises and opinions aired in the mass media about their being more advanced or better than other Africans. To illustrate this, they stressed the cleanliness of Asmara, as well as the fact that it was well-ordered and crimeless, and the ideology of self-reliance of the Eritrean government. They publicly emphasized the perceived difference of their country from other African countries, and thus its uniqueness in Africa.[32] In a short opinion article titled "Is Eritrea Better than the Rest of Africa," Tom Killion and the author of this paper addressed the continual insistence of Eritrean intellectuals, politicians, and western media on Eritrea's supposed uniqueness in relation to the rest of Africa. The article warned that "blowing one's trumpet can set oneself up for a hard fall, especially when that trumpet is being blown in a comparison to the rest of Africa, which however well intended can be misconstrued as a dismissal of African achievements, despite the knowledge that when Africa is belittled, Eritrea is diminished as well."[33] This brings us back to President Isaias' statement at the beginning of this paper.

Conclusion

This paper deals with the cultural ideology that maps the social relations within and between the nine so called ethno-racial groups in Eritrea, as well as Eritrea's relations with its neighbors and the rest of Africa. Since Eritrea is still an agrarian and a small-scale society, most of the social relations are centered on the institution of the family. Thus, a family's and an ethno-racial group's oral history of domination and subordination, interaction, migration and conquest, slavery, and enslavement of others determine that group's status in a hierarchy of social relations. Although Eritreans cannot and do not see themselves in terms of clearly defined races as in the West or the United States, the social relations between one another are based on exclusion and a mythology of purity based on family genealogy and lineages where such genealogy and lineages are said to be free from assumed "slave" lineages or membership in a caste group in society. Religion, regional belonging, and an oral history of origins determine the boundaries as well as the intermixing of the groups that evolved over a long period of time to form what we now consider ethno-racial groups. This cultural ideology of inclusion and exclusion, belonging and not belonging, also becomes an organizing principle of social relations among Eritreans and Ethiopians, Eritreans and other Africans, and others. The Eritrean identity is constructed from principles of social relations that intersect and merge with the supposed uniqueness of Eritrean history as a crossroads of the Middle East, Africa, and the antiquity of the region, as well as the recent history of Italian colonialism (1890–1941), British occupation (1941–1952), and Ethiopian federation and annexation (1952–1991). This sense of uniqueness has continued in the self-presentation of the current Eritrean state and its political leadership. However, the Eritrean cultural ideology of uniqueness hides the unresolved and unarticulated conflict of power, and the violent history of the various ethno-racial and religious groups in Eritrea. The lack of an institutionalized resolution of power conflicts and a history of violence leads to continued outbursts of violent confrontation and expression based on the mythology of uniqueness. This may be detrimental to Eritrea and Eritreans who need to live and benefit from life in a pluralistic and interdependent region. Their neighbors are also embedded in their own local mythologies, which are similar but not identical to those of the Eritreans. Thus, these myths subvert a potentially cooperative living environment across national and ethno-racial boundaries in the Horn of Africa. It should be pointed out that there is not much evidence of cooperation anywhere in the Horn of Africa. Eritrean nationalists' benign search for an identity, which they could call as their own, has led them to desire an identity based on national uniqueness. Such an identity based on Eritrean exceptionalism signifies Eritreans' sparse and weak grasp of their history. As a cultural crossroads between Africa and Middle East, Eritrea as a nation is in search of an identity that justifies its independence. Eritrea's emphasis on uniqueness is an attempt to create a primordialist, essentialist, and naturalized identity. It is also an attempt to institutionalize the new Eritrean state's initiated ethno-racial social order based on language groups that differentiates it from its surrounding countries in the Horn of Africa and the rest of Africa. On the other hand, embracing Eritrea's history of mixing and blending of its population with surrounding populations in the Horn of Africa, and the consequent hybridity of its culture and multiple identities of people, might subvert the nationalist project.

Notes

1. I would like to thank Jim Spickard and Paul Spickard for their support; John Rude, Beyan Negash, and Yosief Gebrehiwet for their critical review of this article; and the University of Redlands for providing funding for this research project.
2. "OAU Heads of State Meeting," *Eritrea Update* (July 1993), 1–2. I would like to thank John Rude, Beyan Negash, and Yosief Gebrehiwet for their critical review of an earlier version of this paper and the University of Redlands for providing funds for research support.
3. Edmond Keller, "Eritrean Self-Determination Revisited," *Africa Today* 38(1991), 7–13.
4. "OAU Heads of State Meeting," loc. cit.
5. J. Spencer Trimingham, *Islam in Ethiopia* (London: Frank Cass & Co., 1965), 1–31; Donald Levine, *Greater Ethiopia* (Chicago: University of Chicago Press, 1974), 26–39.
6. Edward Ullendroff, *The Ethiopians: An Introduction to Country and People* (London: Oxford University Press, 1973), 32.
7. Donald Levine, *Wax & Gold: Tradition and Innovation in Ethiopian Culture* (Chicago: University of Chicago Press, 1965), 28.
8. Stuart Hall, "New Ethnicities," *"Race" Culture and Difference*, eds. James Donald and Ali Rattansi (London: Sage, 1992), 252–259; Michael Omi and Howard Winant, *Racial Formation in the United States* (New York: Routledge, 1994); Paul Spickard and W. Jeffrey Burroughs, *We Are a People: Narrative and Multiplicity in Constructing Ethnic Identity* (Philadelphia: Temple University Press, 2000).
9. Stephen Cornell and Douglas Hartmann, *Ethnicity and Race* (Thousand Oaks, CA: Pine Forge Press, 1998), 35.
10. Floya Anthias and Nira Yuval-Davis, in association with Harriet Cain, *Racialized Boundaries* (London: Routledge, 1992), 12.

11. Anthias and Yuval-Davis, *Racialized Boundaries.*
12. This is a direct translation from the one of the major local languages, Tigrinya.
13. Zewde Kahsai, *Ancient and Modern Rule of Matrimony in Eritrea* (Asmara, 1966 E.C.). The book was published in 1966 Ethiopian Calender or as it sometimes is called Geez Calender, which was widely used in Ethiopia and Eritrea. In Geez Calender, the New Year starts in September and ends in August. There is about 7 or 8 years difference between Geez and Gregorian calendar. From September to December, the Geez Calender is 7 years behind the Gregorian calendar, and from January to August it is 8 years behind the Gregorian Calendar. Thus, the above-cited book might have been published in 1973 or 1974, depending on the month of its publication.
14. Kiros Frewoldu, "Linguistics and Languages in Eritrea," a paper in Tigrinya presented at the *Conference of the Eritrean Languages* in Asmara, Eritrea (August 16–18, 1996), 7–19; Aba Yishak Gebreyesus, "Languages, Written Texts and Oral Traditions in Eritrea," a paper in Tigrinya presented at the *Conference of the Eritrean Languages* in Asmara, Eritrea (August 16–18, 1996), 8.
15. *See* Mikael Hassema-Karra, *History of Eritrea,* in Tigrinya, (privately printed, 1986); and David Pool, *From Guerillas to Government* (Oxford: James Curry, 2001), for more details on the ethnic composition and mixing of people of Eritrea.
16. This account reflects my own understanding of how color, race, and ethnicity was conceived in Eritrea when I was growing up there. Since I was born and raised in Asmara, my understanding of ethnic traditions in Eritrea was derived from the predominantly Tigrinya-speaking region my family comes from, as well as what I learned from schools and oral traditions passed on to me. My perspectives, however, have been challenged and enriched by my encounter with other ways of classification and understanding of race and ethnicity in non-Tigrinya-speaking societies in Eritrea and around the world. I have acquired an understanding of race that takes into consideration more of the nuances and contexts of race and ethnic relations as I got more exposure to other ways of classification in different parts of the world, including Ethiopia, Sudan, Tanzania, Egypt, the United States, Canada, the Caribbean Islands, and many countries in Europe.
17. Most writers on Eritrean political history minimized the significance of religion on Eritrean politics. It should be emphasized that Eritrean nationalists lacked major international support partly because they were seen as motivated by religious sentiments. In order to demystify such notion, scholarly works have argued for the economic and political basis of Eritrean nationalism. *See* John Markakis, *National and Class Conflicts in the Horn of Africa* (Cambridge: Cambridge University Press, 1987); Edmond Keller, *Revolutionary Ethiopia: From Empire to People's Republic* (Bloomington: Indiana University Press, 1988); Jordan Gebre-Medhin, *Peasants and Nationalism in Eritrea* (Trenton, NJ: Red Sea Press, 1989); Ruth Iyob, *The Eritrean Struggle for Independence* (Cambridge: Cambridge University Press, 1995); Roy Pateman, *Eritrea: Even the Stones are Burning* (Trenton, NJ: Red Sea Press, 1990); and David Pool, *From Guerrillas to Government* (Oxford: James Currey, 2001).
18. *See* J. Spencer, op. cit.; Othman Saleh Sabby, *The History of Eritrea,* trans. Muhammad Fawz Al-Azam (Beirut, Lebanon: Dar Al-Masirah, 1974); Hassema-Karra, op. cit.
19. *See* Hassema-Karra, *History of Eritrea.*
20. A comprehensive study of the role of religion in current Eritrean political history has yet to be written. For a discussion on the influence of religious identification on the nationalist movements, *see* Tekle M. Woldemikael, "The Cultural Construction of Eritrean Nationalist Movements," *The Rising Tide of Cultural Pluralism,* ed. Crawford Young (Wisconsin: University of Wisconsin Press, 1993), 179–199.
21. Ali A. Mazrui, *The Africans: A Triple Heritage* (London: BBC, 1986).
22. Hassema-Karra (1986), op. cit.; Abay Gebreyesus (1962), loc. cit.
23. In the 1960s, my older brother wrote down the genealogy of my father's family after conducting interviews with some village elders. I conducted my own interview with my uncle (my mother's brother) about my mother's genealogy and wrote it down in July 2001. I have copies of both genealogies.
24. Hassema-Karra (1986), op. cit.; Abay Gebreyesus (1962), loc. cit.
25. *See* Donald Levine, *Greater Ethiopia,* op. cit., 56; and the *Representatives of the Kunama People at Home and Abroad, History of the Kunama* (August 5, 1999), http://www.ndh.net/home/kunama/History/htm. (August 18, 2000).
26. Also *see* Levine, *Greater Ethiopia,* 56; David Pool, op. cit., 10.
27. There is very little research on this topic. For the attitude of Ethiopian students in 1960 toward Africa, *see* Donald Levine, *Tradition and Innovation,* op. cit., 141–142.
28. *See* Illen Ghebrai, *Eritrea Miracleland* (Washington DC: Privately Printed, 1993), 15–16, 33, 47, 66; Jordan Gebre-Medhin, *Peasants and Nationalism in Eritrea* (Trenton, NJ: Red Sea

Press, 1989), 38; Alemseged Abbay, *Identity Jilted: Re-Imagining Identity?* (Lawrence, NJ: The Red Sea Press, 1998), 71–72.

29. I have had a lots frank conversations on this topic with many Eritrean Muslim friends.

30. To get an overview of Eritrean nationalist history read Markakis, op. cit.; Keller, op. cit.; Gebre-Medhin, op. cit.; Pateman, op. cit.; Ruth Iyob, op. cit.; Pool, op. cit.

31. This is based on my own personal experience and knowledge of the society and culture. Also *see* Tekeste Negash, *Italian Colonialism in Eritrea, 1982–1841: Policies, Praxis, and Impact* (Uppsala: Uppsala University Press, 1987).

32. *See,* for example, Michael A. Hiltzik, "Eritrea Reviving as an African Bright Spot," *Los Angeles Times,* December 28, 1991, A12; Special Correspondent in Eritrea, "Eritrea: Onion, Potatoes and T-54s," *The Economist,* March 20, 1993; Jill Hamburg, "Eritrea Showing a Lot of Promise: Free of Ethiopia, it is determined to be Africa's 'Miracle' Nation," *San Francisco Chronicle,* April 15, 1992, A16, A18; Dan Connell, "An Opening for Democracy in Eritrea," *The Christian Science Monitor,* April 30, 1993, 18; Geraldine Brooks, "Postwar Promise; Africa's Newest Nation, Little Eritrea Emerges as an Oasis of Civility," *The Wall Street Journal,* May 13, 1994, 1, A8, 52; Samir Raafat, "Where's The President," *Cairo Times,* June 10, 1999; Gordon Sato, "Eritrea is a Model for Africa," July, 2000, http:www.tamu.edu/ccbn/dewitt/manzanar/eritreamodel.htm.; Frank Smyth, "Infallible Nation? Infallible Nation?" September 24, 2001, http://www.asmarino.com/; Peter Worthington, "Eritrea is Still Africa's Last Best Hope," *Toronto Sun,* May 26, 2002.

33. "Is Eritrea Better than the Rest of Africa?" Tekle M. Woldemikael and Tom Killion, *Eritrean Studies Association Newsletter,* October 7, 1998, 4.

17

The Problem of the Color-Blind
Notes on the Discourse on Race in Italy

ALESSANDRO PORTELLI

In 1938, the Italian government became apprised that "the Eritrean subject [Eritrea was then an Italian colony] Teclehaimanot, living in Cagliari" was about to marry a young woman from Nulcis, a village in the Cagliari province of the island of Sardinia. Given the "absolute impropriety of such a marriage," the government had him deported. In the year 1938, a manifesto of Italian scientists proclaimed that "it is time for Italians to openly present themselves as racists," and the Fascist government passed the infamous racist laws discriminating against Italian citizens of Jewish origin or religion.

In spite of these precedents, Italians have long retained a self-image as "good folks" ("brava gente"), basically exempt from racist attitudes. Another story from the 1990s — also about mixed marriages — is a case in point. A student of mine, who was taking a class on African American authors, proudly announced that she had become engaged to an African boy. I congratulated her, and she went on: "The other day I had him over to meet my folks, and it all went well, without a hitch. They took to him, he took to them, everybody was happy. After he left, my father closed the door, and said: 'What a wonderful young man. On the other hand, they are a race, and we are not.'"

Finally, a news clipping from February 2001. A group of secondary school-children were suspended for peeing in the shoes of a South American classmate. The school principal said that this "is an unacceptable act that goes beyond the pale of civilized behavior." However, she added: "I exclude the interpretation that this attitude was generated by racial intolerance and spite for the color of the skin."

As the East Indian scholar Vijay Prashad said, "The Problem of the Twenty-First Century is the Problem of the Color-Blind."[1] This fits Italy perfectly. They are not a race, and racism has nothing to do with it. These are the main props of the Italian discourse on race in which denial plays an essential role. Italians believe themselves to be immune from racism because they do not see themselves as "White" but rather as "normal," as human by default (after all, in this almost solidly Catholic country, *human* and *Christian* used to be synonymous in colloquial speech: as a lady, I once interviewed in Rome, put it, "the Jews sure were persecuted, poor Christians").

Thus, jokes and songs from the colonial period never oppose a White and a Black person, but always an *Italian* and a Black. I always have to remind my students that they, too, are *White*, and that Protestants are also Christians. As in the case of my student's father, there may be no open or conscious hostility or denigration, but the line of difference between what is marked and what is unmarked is always drawn. We are *us*, and they are *the other*: there was no active and sizable Black community in Italy's past, to educate Italians to the fact that they, too, may be *other* to someone else.

We do not see our own color, or we think it is invisible or transparent. This — as we know from Olaudah Equiano onward — is exactly how Whiteness is often perceived in African eyes. A typical syndrome of African immigrants to Italy is the fear of turning White and becoming invisible. This self-reflexive color blindness explains the bewildered innocence of the curious, inquisitive, paternalistic gaze that is still often turned upon the presence of Black people as if they were some kind of nature's freaks. No offense is necessarily intended. On the other hand, there is no awareness that offense may be taken, and there is a great deal of surprise and outrage when it is.

This is due to the fact that only since the mid-1980s has Italy turned from a land of emigrants to one of immigrants. Yet, although Italy appeared and represented itself as a homogeneous country, still race was always part of their cultural discourse — albeit perhaps in the form that a group of Italian anthropologists described as "latent" racism, which only awaited an object at hand to manifest itself. In fact, when this analysis was offered in the 1960s, racism was already far from latent in the resurgence of anti-Semitic outrages.

The discourse on race culminated, as I already pointed out, with the racist laws of 1938, when the taboo about marriages and unions among Blacks and Whites made possible by the colonial expansion became, with a fascinating logical shift, the justification for the laws prohibiting intermarriage between "Aryans" and Jews: "Since Italy has conquered such a wide African territory," the preamble to the 1938 race laws went, "it has become necessary to prevent the danger of marriages between Italians and Negroes [note: "*Italians* and Negroes"!] and the consequent procreation of mulattos. . . . It is evident that the prohibition of marriages between Italian citizens of the Aryan race and persons of other races *naturally* [my italics] applies to the prohibition of marriage between an Aryan and a Jewish person."[2] This was the beginning of a process that all but excluded the Italian citizens of Jewish identity from public life and culminated in the cooperation of Italian authorities in the deportation of Jews by the Nazis.

This did not take place without paradoxes and ironies of its own. For instance, by deporting Teclehaimanot, the Italian government was protecting the "purity" of the "Italian race" as represented by Sardinian womanhood; on the other hand, for decades, leading Italian intellectuals had labeled the Sardinian people as themselves — an inferior or at least a dangerous race.[3]

Indeed, race was used in the nation-building process to rationalize internal differences and political hierarchy. As Southern Italy was being dragged, sometimes willingly and sometimes reluctantly, into an unequal national unity, difference and resistance were systematically treated in terms of race — the "accursed race" of Southern peasants. The rebellion in the Southern provinces that took the form of social banditry or *brigantaggio* was explained by a number of scholars in terms of the racial characteristics of Southerners and of peasants. Cesare Lombroso, of course, pioneered the description of Southern peasants as a separate race with distinct and measurable anthropometric features. As late as 1925, the neuropsychiatrist Levi Bianchini wrote of a "Calabrese race ... primitive but *simpatica* whose features express the historically and anthropologically primitive character of modern Calabria" as represented by "curious habits" and attitudes not unlike those he attributed to the peoples of Equatorial Africa.[4]

Like the rest of the South, Sardinia was explicitly racialized as an explanation for the social disorder in its poorer and more internal areas. In *Psicologia della Sardegna* (1896), Paolo Orano wrote that there were places in the island where "the race grows and teems like a rotten, purulent gangrene." In *La delinquenza in Sardegna* (1897), the anthropologist Alfredo Niceforo labeled these areas as "criminal zones" that emanate "pathogenic bacteria, which export blood and mayhem to other areas of Sardinia." Both Orano and Niceforo also pointed to environmental causes, such as isolation. However, as Appalachian studies in the United States have shown, isolation is precisely one of those terms that help translate environmental into biological data through the mythology of "inbreeding" and consequent genetic damage.[5]

In this context, it is significant that the partner in the forbidden marriage in Cagliari should have been an African because Africa plays a crucial role, both as a metaphor and as historical reality, in the Italian discourse on race. Italy was still in the making when the patriot Luigi Farini (1860) was writing from the South that "This isn't Italy, this is Africa — when compared to these peasants [*cafoni*], the Bedouins are models of civil virtue". Garibaldi's faithful lieutenant, Nino Bixio, described Sicily as "a land that ought to be destroyed, or at least depopulated and the people sent to Africa to be civilized." Nino Bixio is also remembered, or ought to be, for a massacre of Sicilian peasants who had thought that Garibaldi's advent would entail land reform and redistribution of the lands.[6]

The regional antagonisms of modern Italy, whether expressed as comedy in popular culture and cinema or rabidly politicized by the Northern League, are rooted in the discourse of biological racism. Levi Bianchini's assimilation of Southern Italians to Africans is part of a paradigm that goes back to the early days of national unity and remains active today. To quote an especially ugly example, during a recent soccer game in Rome in which the Naples team was playing, the organized fans of Lazio, Rome's team, shouted the following slogan: "L'Italia agli italiani/fuori i negri/e i napoletani" — Italy is for Italians, get rid of all the Negroes and Neapolitans. On the other hand, this comparison has also generated an ambiguous identification of Southern Italians with Africa. On the other hand, the Olympic gold medallist Pietro Mennea, from Puglie, explained his success by saying that Southern Italians are motivated by the same hunger as American Blacks. This did not prevent Southern Italian mobs from attacking African farm workers in the tomato fields of Campania and the tobacco fields of Puglia, and from carrying out a pogrom against a gypsy community in the Scampia neighborhood of Naples in 1999.

What counts, however, is that the identification of Southerners, peasants, bandits with Africans makes sense precisely because they are not African. As even the Benetton advertisement campaign reminds us, the most superficial biological definition of race has to do with color; thus, the fact that the objects of the discourse of race were not represented as being of another color enabled ideology to make a systematic use of race concepts and still pretend that there was no racism in Italy.

A digression may be in order here. Are Italians, indeed, White? In 1983, I was enrolling my son in elementary school in Lexington, Kentucky, and the principal was assisting us in filling the necessary form — birth date, nationality, etc. When he came to "race," he looked up from the paper and said, "White — I guess." When I saw the 1929 naturalization papers of Mattia Giurelli, an Italian immigrant from Umbria who had joined the IWW and had been active in anti-Fascist circles in Paterson, New Jersey, I noticed that the entry on "race" said: "Italian–Southern." Not only were the immigration authorities defining Italians as a "race," but they were also buying into the racial othering of Southern Italians within Italy. Incidentally, Giurelli was from Umbria, which is Central, not Southern Italy. But he had been a farm worker and, just as in Italian positivistic anthropology of the nineteenth century, race stood for class: "Southern" meant simply "rural."

The construction of color blindness is the foundation of the national myth of the "good hearted," the "kind hearted" Italian — *Italiani brava gente*. There are two narratives at the root of this myth. The first is that Italians either resisted or ignored the Fascist race laws, and that Italian citizens en masse hid out their Jewish compatriots to save them from what is represented as an exclusively German persecution. Part of the myth is the belief that Mussolini only passed the race laws to humor his ally Hitler. As late as the summer of 2003, Italy's prime minister Silvio Berlusconi claimed that Mussolini had been a "benevolent dictator" and "never killed anyone."

While there was indeed widespread solidarity and protection on the part of individuals and families, yet, the fact is that, in most cases, the Jews who were deported were denounced to the German authorities by other Italians, and delivered to them by Italian police. The German raid on the Rome Ghetto in October 1943 resulted in the deportation of 1022 persons; on the other hand, about 800 more were deported in the following months, all arrested by Italian police and turned over to the Germans. As is often said in the Jewish community in Rome, "behind each Jew who survived, there is another Italian who protected them; and beyond each Jew that was deported and killed, there is another Italian who turned them in."

The other narrative has to do with the myth of the benign Italian colonization. Remember, the psychiatrist Levi Bianchini thought that the African-like Calabresi were "primitive but *simpatici*." The stigma of inferiority is often accompanied by a paternalistic show of affection and sympathy — Italians were colonizing those Africans for their own good. Even the song that has become most closely associated with the Ethiopian war speaks to a "cute little black face, pretty Abyssinian" (*faccetta nera*) and promises that "when we come to you, we will give you another country and another king" — regardless of whether she asked for it or not.

It goes without saying that the only thing that was benign in Italian colonialism was the myth. Italians fought a twenty-year war against guerrilla resistance in Libya (indeed, the first historically known aerial bombardment was carried out by an Italian military plane in Libya in 1911). They used gas and outlawed weapons, committed massacres and retaliations. When an Ethiopian patriot wounded the head of the Italian occupying army, general Rodolfo Graziani, the Italians retaliated with a massacre of over 300 monks in the Debra Lebanos monastery and a mass deportation that raised the death toll to over 1000. In this case, the self-absolutory myth exorcises the event by saying that this was done by "Fascists" — as if the Fascists were not Italians.

There is no popular memory of the Debra Lebanos massacre; a film about Libyan resistance to the Italians, starring Anthony Quinn, was never allowed in Italian theaters. Even in the late 1990s, popular journalist Indro Montanelli attempted to deny the use of gas, which had been confirmed by official defense ministry records. The most popular high school history textbook — a progressive text that was recently the object of a fierce campaign from the right — has less than five lines on the Ethiopian war.

The combination of denial and supposed kindness about Italian colonialism is the template for the patterns of the discourse on race today: the denial that a serious problem of racism exists in Italy, a systematic effort to explain away racist actions by attributing them to other causes or claiming they are just isolated aberrations or "ignorance."

Now, ignorance does exist. While working on a project on the memory of Nazi war crimes in Rome, I interviewed a young man from the marginalized periphery of Torbellamonaca. The walls near the place where the interview was conducted were covered with soccer graffiti calling the other team's fans and players "Jews." As I asked him what he knew about racial persecutions and the extermination camps, I noticed that he used the word "Jews" very vaguely. So I asked him, "Can you tell me what this word, 'Jew,' means?"

> Jew … literally, I don't know; however, though, it's always something, say — how can I tell you — mostly, rather than a separate race, how can I tell you, it has a name, I don't remember what the name is — culturally and politically, it's something other, than the political aspect of ancient Germany and the American states and so on. So I think it must rather be something political. They were, say, people who were contrary, politically, to the concepts of, of Adolph, in other words.

I asked, "And what about religion?" He answered, "Religion? Religion, it ought to be — Catholics, I guess."

This is a remarkable example of the assumption that all humans, including Jews, are Christians, that is, Catholics (in a 2003 controversy over the exposure of crucifixes in classrooms, the current claim was that the crucifix is not just a Catholic symbol, but a universal one and, therefore, represents everybody — including Muslims and atheists). Even this young Nazi sympathizer doesn't think of Jews as a separate race; thus, racism had nothing to do with their persecution.

On the other hand, ignorance as to what exactly makes a Jew a Jew does not mean that these young people do not know how to identify their targets. Soccer fans have been identified behind attacks on Jewish businesses and theaters showing movies on the Shoah. During a game between the two major soccer teams in Rome, one team's fans raised banners saying that the other side belonged in Auschwitz and in the ovens; and the others responded with a banner that insulted, by name, the head rabbi of Rome's Jewish community. They may be ignorant, but they are well-informed, and have an unfailing instinct for the right symbols. They may not know what it means, but they systematically raise the swastika; they are never so ignorant that they raise the red flag or the hammer and sickle. When the authorities attempted to forbid "political" symbols in the stadium — note: not "racist" symbols, because of course it was denied that racism was the problem — the only banner that was actually confiscated belong to the Perugia fan club that calls itself the Red Army (after the team's colors). The only flag that made it through the police controls at the gate and was proudly waved by the fans in Rome was a confederate flag. They may not have known what it was about, but they knew which side it was on.

Racist discourse always begins in self-denial: "I'm not a racist, but . . . " This combination of denial, paternalism, and "innocence" makes possible in Italy things that would be unthinkable elsewhere. In TV advertisements, Black people are always associated with things to eat (bell hooks would have a field day on Italian commercial TV). One newspaper advertisement invited consumers to buy ladies' bags of "real Italian skin" by displaying a White woman and a Black woman side by side and saying that "sometimes it is correct to discriminate on the basis of skin."[7]

Only sometimes, however. Even the extreme right has become aware that biological racism is no longer credible, and has shifted to a more subtle position, which has been described as "differentialist racism." They speak of cultural ethnicity rather than biological race, and tie ethnicity to culture in a one-to-one relationship. Thus, the hostility to immigrants is now based not on the fact that they belong to inferior races, but on the fact that they are culturally so different that they cannot coexist with mainstream Italian culture. The assumption, of course, is that cultures are fixed and cannot change or communicate with one another. Even the Fascist regime, in fact, was never able to decide whether its anti-Semitism was based on biological racial categories or on the so-called "spiritual" racism founded on the Church's religious curse on the Jewish people. Indeed, components of the Church have resurrected this kind of spiritual and cultural racism, as the Cardinal of Bologna asked the Italian government to allow only Christian immigrants into the country because Islamic people would be inassimilable or would actually tend to take over (This was before September 11, 2001. After that date, all Arabic and Islamic people became automatically suspect.). This not only generated a number of marches and demonstrations by the Northern League, but was also seconded by articles and a book by Giovanni Sartori, a major political scientist who teaches in the United States and has been influential in projects for constitutional reform.

Now, differentialist racism comes in handy when xenophobic stereotypes are raised against groups that are, to all effects, White — such as migrants and refugees from Eastern Europe and the Balkans. Recently, after a woman and her twelve-year-old son were stabbed to death in the Northern town of Novi Ligure, the daughter testified that the crime had been committed by "two Albanians." Immediately, the Northern League prepared to march on the town and demand the ousting of all immigrants, while the Left once again keeled over to the discussion of immigration as primarily a security problem. A right-wing congressman said in parliament that Slavs are "genetically" prone to crime — a statement that would have been the end of his career in many other countries but was judged only as a gross but venial exaggeration by most of his colleagues. The massacre was not perpetrated by "Albanians," but by the daughter herself.

Another dimension is the attitude toward Rom and Sinti. Gypsies have always been accused of stealing, abducting children, begging, not washing (in camps where there is one faucet and one toilet for every five families). At this time, however, Rom and Sinti represent primarily people for whom no rights are recognized, so that anything done on their behalf becomes an insult and a deprivation to "regular," "normal" Italian citizens. The denial of all civil rights and cultural recognition to the Gypsies (their language has been excluded from the list of minority languages that may be taught in schools; on the other hand, the University of Triete has established a chair of Rom culture) becomes the differential basis upon which Italian citizens, filled with an unexplained but tangible frustration and anger, can claim what they consider their rights. Hardly anyone, aside from small Left groups, complained when the police invaded a

Gypsy camp at dawn in Rome, and deported 56 people to Bosnia, including children born on Italian soil who had always lived there. Italian citizenship, in fact, is still based on blood rather than soil: children born of foreign parents on Italian soil are not automatically Italian citizens. This is understandable in a country of emigrants, that wanted to retain a hold on its citizens who had left for other lands; but it makes no sense now that Italy has turned into a country of immigrants instead.

I would like to conclude by going back to the initial anecdote: "they" are a race, we are not. Some years ago, sociologists Enzo Campelli and Roberta Cipollini did a survey on anti-Semitism in Italy. One of their findings was that the majority of their interviewees widely exaggerated the number of Jews in the country's population. They interpreted this as a sign of paranoia: they are everywhere, we are surrounded. Indeed, the same blowing up of figures also occurred in later discourse on immigration, and partly for the same reason.

On the other hand, when I was asked by Campelli and Cipollini how many Jews lived in Italy, I said "not many, maybe 300,000." In fact, at the time they were only 35,000. I, too, had multiplied their numbers by ten. This led me to a great deal of self-scrutiny. What did I have in common with anti-Semitic paranoia? I was sure I did not feel surrounded or threatened in any way, and in fact I had prefaced my guess with the statement that I thought they were few anyway. I tried to explain it by thinking that I knew many Jews because they are relatively more numerous in intellectual professions, and — at least at the time — in the Left. But when I went to actually counting, I had to admit that, in fact, their number among my acquaintances was not overwhelming. Ultimately, I had to admit that my mistake was due to the fact that, even without any paranoia or fear, I still unconsciously made a mental note when I met a Jew (that I knew of — I do not consciously classify people by religion or descent, so I may have known Jewish people without knowing them as such). I shared, then, at least that much of the common discourse on race: the marking of the "other." The Jews were special, the others were not.

Conclusion

In conclusion, I am not out to indict my country, my culture, and my people more than they deserve. There have been intellectuals who rejected the positivistic discourse on race in the nineteenth century. Many Italians indeed risked their lives to protect Jewish compatriots. The Left and sectors of the Church, among errors and slips, have actively tried to educate their members against racism. Indeed, one of the problems in denouncing racism in this country is that often immigrants themselves participate in the absolutory explanation by ascribing the whole thing to ignorance or by telling us that it is worse in other countries. What I am trying to describe, however, is less the extent and virulence of racism than some of the specific forms it takes in a country that claims to be exempt: the attitudes of denial and of paternalism; the assumption of White and Catholic as human identities by default; the frustrating, maddening *innocence* that allows offensive acts and statements to go unchallenged and even unnoticed. These may be more subtle and less immediately violent attitudes than others that we can imagine. Yet, they are a sign that the monster is among us, and it gets uglier every day.

Notes

1. Vijay Prashad is the director of the international studies program at Trinity College in Connecticut. His talk was part of a lecture series on "Facing Racism's Pasts and Presence" at the University of Michigan, Ann Arbor (March 24, 2001).
2. Otto Klineberg, Tullio Tentori, Franco Crespi, and Vincenzo Filippone Thaulero, *Religione e pregiudizio. Analisi di contenuto dei libri cattolici di insegnamento religioso in Italia e in Spagna* (Bologna: Cappelli, 1968).
3. Gianluca Gabrielli, "Africani in Italia negli anni del razzismo di stato," in A. Burgio, *Nel nome della razza. Il razzismo nella storia d'Italia* (Bologna: Il Mulino, 1999), 201–212. I have relied on this book throughout this chapter.
4. Ferruccio Giacanelli, "Tracce e percorsi del razzismo nella psichiatria italiana della prima meta' del Novecento," in A. Burgio, *Nel nome della razza*, 389–405; Vito Teti, *La razza maledetta, Origini del pregiudizio antimeridionale* (Roma, Manifestolibri, 1993).
5. Gaetano Riccardo, "L'antropologia positivista italiana e il problema del banditismo in Sardegna. Qualche nota di riflessione," in Burgio, *Nel nome della razza*, 95–103.
6. *See* Note 4.
7. Annamaria Rivera.

Bibliography

Abbay, Alemseged. *Identity Jilted: Re-Imagining Identity?* Lawrence, NJ: Red Sea Press, 1998.

Abitbol, Michel. *The Jews of North Africa during the Second World War*. Translated by Catherine Tihanyi Zentelis. Detroit MI: Wayne State University Press, 1989.

Adams, Romanzo. *Interracial Marriage in Hawai'i*. New York: Macmillan, 1937.

Adler, Emanuel, and Michael Barnett. *Security Communities*. London: Cambridge University Press, 1998.

Ageron, Charles-Robert. *Les Algériens musulmans et la France, 1871–1919*. 2 Vols. Paris: Presses Universitaires de France, 1968.

Ahmad, Feroz. *The Making of Modern Turkey*. London: Routledge, 1993.

Alibhai-Brown, Yasmin. *Imagining the New Britain*. New York: Routledge, 2001.

All India Sikh Students Federation. *Some Documents on the Demand for the Sikh Homeland: Basic Speeches, Writings and Press Interviews by Sirdar Kapur Singh*. Chandigarh, 1969.

Almaguer, Tomás. *Racial Fault Lines: The Historical Origins of White Supremacy in California*. Berkeley, CA: University of California Press, 1994.

Altschuler, Glenn C. *Race, Ethnicity, and Class in American Social Thought, 1865–1919*. Arlington Heights, IL: Harlan Davidson, 1982.

Amson, Daniel. *Adolphe Crémieux: L'oublié de la gloire*. Paris: Éditions du Seuil, 1988.

Anderson, Benedict. *Imagined Communities: Reflections on the Origin and Spread of Nationalism*. London: Verso, 1983.

Anderson, Lisa. "Obligation and Accountability: Islamic Politics in North Africa." *Daedalus*, 120 (Summer 1991): 93–112.

Andrews, George Reid. *Black and White in São Paulo, Brazil, 1888–1988*. Madison, WI: University of Wisconsin Press, 1991.

Anthias, Floya and Nira Yuval-Davis. *Racialized Boundaries: Race, Nation, Gender, Colour, and Class and the Anti-Racist Struggle*. London: Routledge 1992.

Anzaldúa, Gloria. *Borderlands/La Frontera: The New Mestiza*. San Francisco, CA: Aunt Lute, 1987.

Appadurai, Arjun. "Disjuncture and Difference in the Global Economy," *Public Culture*, 2.2 (1990): 1–20.

Arendt, Hannah. *Elemente und Ursprünge totaler Herrschaft: Antisemitismus, Imperialismus, totale Herrschaft*. München und Zürich: Piper, 2000; orig. 1955.

Armstrong, John A. *Nations Before Nationalism*. Chapel Hill, NC: University of North Carolina Press, 1982.

Asad, Talal. "Muslims and European Identity." In *The Idea of Europe: From Antiquity to the European Union*, Ed. Anthony Pagden, 209–227. Cambridge UK: Cambridge University Press, 2002.

Asante, Molefi. *The Afrocentric Idea*. Philadelphia, PA: Temple University Press, 1987.

Asher, George, and David Naulls. *Maori Land*. Wellington: New Zealand Planning Council, 1987.

Austin, Granville. *The Indian Constitution: Cornerstone of a Nation*. Oxford: Clarendon Press, 1966.

Awatere, Donna. *Maori Sovereignty*. Auckland: Broadsheet Publications, 1984.

Baker, Houston A., Jr., Manthia Diawara, and Ruth H. Lindeborg, Eds. *Black British Cultural Studies*. Chicago, IL: University of Chicago Press, 1996.

Baker, Lee D. *From Savage to Negro: Anthropology and the Construction of Race, 1896–1954*. Berkeley, CA: University of California Press, 1998.

Balabar, Etienne, and Immanuel Wallerstein. *Race, Nation, Class: Ambiguous Identities*. London: Verso, 1991.

Ballara, Angela. *Proud to Be White? A Survey of Pakeha Prejudice in New Zealand*. Auckland: Heineman, 1986.

Balta, Paul. *Le Grand Maghreb: des indépendances à l'an 2000*. Paris: Découverte, 1990.

Bank, Leslie. "Men with Cookers: Transformations in Migrant Culture, Domesticity and Identity in Duncan Village, East London," *Journal of Southern African Studies*, 25 (1999).

Banton, Michael. *Race Relations*. New York: Basic Books, 1967.

Banton, Michael. *Racial and Ethnic Competition*. Cambridge UK: Cambridge University Press, 1983.

Banton, Michael. *Racial Theories*. Cambridge UK: Cambridge University Press, 1987.

Barbieri, William A., Jr. *Ethics of Citizenship: Immigration and Group Rights in Germany*. Durham, NC: Duke University Press, 1998.

Barcelos, Luiz Claudio. "Struggling in Paradise: Racial Mobilization and the Contemporary Black Movement in Brazil." In *Race Relations in Contemporary Brazil*, Ed. Rebecca Reichmann, 155–66. University Park, PA: Pennsylvania State University Press, 1991.

Barth, Fredrik, Ed. *Ethnic Groups and Boundaries*. Boston, MA: Little, Brown, 1969.

Bartov, Omer. *Murder in Our Midst: The Holocaust, Industrial Killing, and Representation*. New York: Oxford University Press, 1996.

Bastos, Santiago, and Manuela Camus. *Entre el Mecapal y el cielo: desarollo del movimiento maya en Guatemala*. Guatemala City: FLACSO and Cholsamaj, 2002.

Bauböck, Rainer, "Recombinant Citizenship," Institut für Höhere Studien (IHS), Wien/Institute for Advanced Studies, Vienna. Reihe Politikwissenschaft/Political Science Series No. 67. Vienna: 1999.

Bayly, Susan. "Caste and 'Race' in the Colonial Ethnography of India." In *The Concept of Race in South Asia*. Ed. Peter Robb, 165–218. Delhi: Oxford 1995.

Bayly, Susan. *Caste, Society and Politics in India from the Eighteenth Century to the Modern Age*. Cambridge UK: Cambridge University Press, 1999.

Belich, James. "Empire and Its Myth." Washington, DC: Center for Australian and New Zealand Studies, Georgetown University. Occasional papers, April 27, 2000.

Belich, James. "Maori and Pakeha, Past and Future." Waitangi Day Lecture, New Zealand Embassy, Washington, DC, February 4, 2000.

Belich, James. *The New Zealand Wars and the Victorian Interpretation of Racial Conflict*. Auckland: Penguin, 1988.

Bell, Avril. "We're Just New Zealanders: Pakeha Identity Politics." In *Nga Patai: Racism and Ethnic Relations in Aotearoa/New Zealand*, Eds. Paul Spoonley, Cluny Macpherson, and David Pearson, 144–158. Palmerston North: Dunmore Press, 1996.

Bell, David. *The Cult of the Nation in France: Inventing Nationalism, 1680–1800*. Cambridge, MA: Harvard University Press, 2001.

Bell, Vicky. "Historical Memory, Global Movements, and Violence: Paul Gilroy and Arjun Appadurai in Conversation," *Theory, Culture and Society* 16.2 (1999): 21–40.

Ben-Dor, Gabriel, and Ofra Bengio. "The State and Minorities Toward the Twenty-first Century: An Overview." In *Minorities and the State in the Arab World*, Ed. Ofra Bengio and Gabriel Ben-Dor, 191–205. London: Lynne Rienner, 1999.

Ben Jelloun, Tahar. *French Hospitality: Racism and North African Immigrants*. New York: Columbia University Press, 1999.

Bender, Gerald. *Angola Under the Portuguese*. Berkeley, CA: University of California Press, 1978.

Bengio, Ofra, and Gabriel Ben-Dor, Eds. *Minorities and the State in the Arab World*. London: Lynne Rienner, 1999.

Berezin, Mabel, and Martin Schain., Eds. *Europe Without Borders: Remapping Territory, Citizenship, and Identity in a Transnational Age*. Baltimore, MD: Johns Hopkins University Press, 2003.

Bessis, Juliette. *Maghreb: la traversée du siècle*. Paris: l'Harmattan, 1997.

Betts, Raymond F. *Assimilation and Association in French Colonial Theory, 1890–1914*. New York: Columbia University Press, 1961.

Bielefeld, Ulrich, Ed. *Das Eigene und das Fremde: Neuer Rassismus in der Alten Welt?* Hamburg: Hamburger Edition, 1998.

Biggs, Bruce G. *Maori Marriage: An Essay in Reconstruction*. Wellington: Polynesian Society, 1960.

Birnbaum, Pierre. *The Idea of France*. New York: Hill and Wang, 2001.

Bit, Seanglim. *The Warrior Heritage: A Psychological Perspective of Cambodian Trauma*. El Cerrito, CA: privately printed, 1991.

Blalock, H.M., Jr. *Toward a Theory of Minority-Group Relations*. New York: Wiley, 1967.

Blauner, Robert. *Racial Oppression in America*. New York: Harper and Row, 1972.

Blumenbach, Johann Friedrich. *The Anthropological Treatises of Johann Friedrich Blumenbach.* Boston, MA: Milford House, 1973; orig. 1865.

Bomball, K. R. "The Nation State and Ethno-Nationalism: A Note on the Akali Demand for a Self-Determined Political Status for Sikhs." *Punjab Journal of Politics,* 9 (1983):166–183.

Bonacich, Edna. "A Theory of Middleman Minorities," *American Sociological Review,* 38 (1973).

Bonner, Philip. "The Russians on the Reef 1947–1957: Urbanization, Gang Warfare and Ethnic Mobilization." In *Apartheid's Genesis, 1935–1962,* Ed. Philip Bonner, Peter Delius, and Deborah Posel. Johannesburg: Ravan, 1993.

Bonnet, Aubrey W., and G. Llewellyn Watson, Eds. *Emerging Perspectives of the Black Diaspora.* Lanham, MD: University Press of America, 1990.

Bourdieu, Pierre, *The Algerians.* Translated by Alan C.M. Ross. Boston, MA: Beacon Press, 1962.

Bowlan, Jeanne. "Polygamists Need Not Apply: Becoming a French Citizen in Colonial Algeria, 1918–1938." *Proceedings of the Western Society for French History,* 24 (1997): 110–119.

Brading, David A. "Manuel Gamio and Official Indigenismo in Mexico." *Bulletin of Latin American Research* 7.1 (1988): 75–89.

Brass, Paul, Ed. *Ethnic Groups and the State.* London: Croom Helm, 1985.

Brass, Paul, Ed. *The Politics of India Since Independence.* Cambridge UK: Cambridge University Press, 1990.

Brass, Paul, Ed. *Language, Religion and Politics in North India.* Cambridge UK: Cambridge University Press, 1974.

Brass, Paul, Ed. *Ethnicity and Nationalism: Theory and Comparison.* New Delhi: Sage, 1991.

Brathwaite, Edward. *The Development of Creole Society in Jamaica, 1770–1820.* Oxford: Clarendon Press, 1971.

Brett, Michael, and Elizabeth Fentress. *The Berbers.* Oxford: Blackwell, 1996.

Bringa, Tone. *Being Muslim the Bosnian Way: Identity and Community in a Central Bosninan Village* (Princeton, NJ: Princeton University Press, 1995.

Brisson, Jean-Paul. *Autonomisme et christianisme dans l'Afrique romaine.* Paris: E. de Boccard, 1958.

Brower, Daniel R. and Edward J. Lazzerini, Eds. *Russia's Orient: Imperial Borderlands and Peoples, 1700–1917.* Bloomington: Indiana University Press, 1997.

Brown, David. *The State and Ethnic Politics in Southeast Asia.* London: Routledge, 1994.

Brown, Leon Carl. "Changing Cultures and New Loyalties in North Africa." In *French-Speaking Africa: The Search for Identity,* Ed. William H. Lewis, 95–106. New York: Walker and Company, 1965.

Brown, Timothy C. *The Real Contra War: Highlander Peasant Resistance in Nicaragua.* Norman, OK: University of Oklahoma Press, 2001.

Brubaker, Rogers. *Citizenship and Nationhood in France and Germany.* Cambridge, MA: Harvard University Press, 1992.

Brubaker, Rogers, Ed. *Immigration and the Politics of Citizenship in Europe and North America.* Lanham, MD: University Press of America, 1989.

Brubaker, Rogers. *Nationalism Reframed: Nationhood and the National Question in the New Europe.* Cambridge UK: Cambridge University Press, 1996.

Buck, Peter H. *The Coming of the Maori.* Wellington: Maori Purposes Funds Board, 1958.

Buffington, Robert. *Criminal and Citizen in Modern Mexico.* Lincoln, NE: University of Nebraska Press, 2000.

Buick, T. Lindsay. *The Treaty of Waitangi: Or How New Zealand Became a British Colony.* 3rd ed. New Plymouth: Capper Reprint, 1976; orig. 1936.

Bunge, Carlos Octavio. *Nuestra América.* Buenos Aires: Casa Vaccaro, 1918.

Burdick, John. *Blessed Anastácia: Women, Race, and Popular Christianity in Brazil.* New York: Routledge, 1998.

Burdick, John. "Brazil's Black Consciousness Movement." *North American Congress on Latin America Report on the Americas,* 25.4 (February 1992): 23–27.

Burdick, John. "The Lost Constituency of Brazil's Black Movement," *Latin American Perspectives,* 25.1 (January 1988): 136–155.

Burgio, A. *Nel nome della razza. Il razzismo nella storia d'Italia.* Bologna: Il Mulina, 1999.

Bushnell, O. A. *The Gifts of Civilization: Germs and Genocide in Hawai'i.* Honolulu: University of Hawai'i Press, 1993.

Butler, Kim. *Freedoms Given, Freedoms Won: Afro-Brazilians in Post-Abolition São Paulo and Salvador.* New Brunswick, NJ: Rutgers University Press, 1998.

Camarillo, Albert. *Chicanos in a Changing Society: From Mexican Pueblos to American Barrios in Santa Barbara and Southern California, 1848–1930.* Cambridge, MA: Harvard University Press, 1979.

Campbell, Mavis. *The Maroons of Jamaica, 1655–1796*. Granby, MA: Bergin and Garvey, 1990.

Campt, Nina, and Michelle Wright, Eds. *Reading the Black German Experience*, special issue of *Callaloo* 26.2 (2003).

Chaddah, M.S. *Are Sikhs a Nation?* Delhi: Sikh Gurdwara Parbandhak Committee, 1982.

Chaker, Salem. "Berbères: question nationale? question culturelle?" *L'Evénement Européen*, 16 (October 1991): 191–203.

Chaker, Salem. "La langue berbère dans le champ politique maghrébin. Le cas algérien: rupture ou continuité?" In *Langues et Pouvoir: de l'Afrique du Nord à l'Extême-Orient*, Ed. Salem Chaker, 25–40. Aix-en-Provence (France): Edisud, 1998.

Chaker, Salem. "La question berbère dans l'Algérie indépendante: la fracture inévitable?" *Revue du Monde Musulman et de la Méditerranée*, 65 (1992): 97–105.

Chaker, Salem. "L'affirmation identitaire berbère à partir de 1900: constantes et mutations (Kabylie)." *La Revue de l'Occident Musulman et de la Méditerranée*, 44 (1987): 13–33.

Chaker, Salem. *Berbères aujourd'hui*. Paris: L'Harmattan, 1989.

Challener, Richard D. *The French Theory of the Nation in Arms, 1866–1939*. New York: Columbia University Press, 1955.

Chanda, Nayan. *Brother Enemy: The War After the War: A History of Indochina Since the Fall of Saigon.* New York: Harcourt Brace Jovanovich, 1986.

Chandler, David. *A History of Cambodia*. 2nd edition. Boulder, CO: Westview, 1993.

Chapin, Mac. *La población indígena de El Salvador*. San Salvador: Ministerio de Educación, Dirección de Publicaciones e Impresos, 1990.

Ching, Erik, and Virginia Tilley. "Indians, the Military, and the 1932 Rebellion in El Salvador." *Journal of Latin American Studies* 30 (1998).

Chou, Meng Tarr. "The Vietnamese Minority in Cambodia," *Race and Class* 34.2 (1991): 33–48.

Chouraqui, André. *Between East and West. A History of the Jews of North Africa*. Translated by Michel M. Bernet. Philadelphia, PA: Jewish Publication Society of America, 1968.

Cohen, Abner, Ed. *Urban Ethnicity*. London: Tavistock, 1974.

Cohen, David, and Jack P. Greene, Eds. *The Freemen of African Descent in the Slave Societies of the New World*. Baltimore: Johns Hopkins University Press, 1972.

Cohen, R. 1988. "The Military and Indian Democracy." In *India's Democracy: An Analysis of Changing State-Society Relations*, Ed. Atul Kohli, 125–145. Princeton, NJ: Princeton University Press.

Cohen, Robin. *Global Diasporas: An Introduction*. London: UCL Press, 1997.

Collier, David, Ed. *The New Authoritarianism in Latin Ameirca*. Princeton, NJ: Princeton University Press, 1979.

Comaroff, John L. and Jean. *Of Revelation and Revolution: The Dialectics of Modernity on a South African Frontier*, Vol. 2. Chicago, IL: University of Chicago Press, 1997.

Comte, Maurice. "Rapports de Classes et Relations Inter-Ethniques Dans Le Cambodge Precolonial," *ASEMI* 7.1 (1976).

Confer, Vincent. *France and Algeria: The Problem of Civil and Political Reform, 1870–1920*. Syracuse, NY: Syracuse University Press, 1966.

Cook, Larry, and Randall Johnson. Eds. *Black Brazil, Culture Identity, and Social Mobilization*. Los Angeles, CA: UCLA Latin American Studies Center, 1999.

Coplan, David. *In the Time of Cannibals: The Word Music of South Africa's Basotho Migrants* Chicago, IL: Chicago University Press, 1994.

Cornell, Stephen, and Douglas Hartmann. *Ethnicity and Race.* Thousand Oaks, CA: Pine Forge Press, 1998.

Cox, Lindsay. *Kotahitanga: The Search for Maori Unity*. Auckland: Oxford University Press, 1993.

Cox, Oliver C. *Caste, Class, and Race*. New York: Modern Reader, 1970; orig. 1948.

Cunningham, Joseph Davy. *A History of the Sikhs from the Origin of the Nation to the Battle of the Sutlej*. London: John Murray, 1849.

da Costa, Emília Viotti. *The Brazilian Empire: Myths and Histories*. Chicago, IL: University of Chicago Press, 1985.

Daniel, G. Reginald. *More Than Black? Multiracial Identity and the New Racial Order*. Philadelphia, PA: Temple University Press, 2001.

Daniel, G. Reginald. "Converging Paths: Race Relations in Brazil and the U.S." Paper presented at Winter Colloquium Series, UCLA Center for African American Studies, 1989.

Daniel, G. Reginald. "Multiracial Identity in Brazil and the United States." In *We Are a People: Narrative and Multiplicity in Constructing Ethnic Identity*, Ed. Paul Spickard and W. Jeffrey Burroughs, 153–178. Philadelphia, PA: Temple University Press, 2000.

Daniel, G. Reginald. "Multiracial Identity in Global Perspective: The United States, Brazil, and South Africa." In *Racially Mixed People in America*, Ed. Maria P.P. Root, 247–286. Newbury Park, CA: Sage, 1992.

Daniel, G. Reginald. "Passers and Pluralists: Subverting the Racial Divide." In *Racially Mixed People in America*, Ed. Maria P.P. Root, 91–107. Newbury Park, CA: Sage, 1992.

Das, Veena. *Critical Events: An Anthropological Perspective on Contemporary India*. Delhi: Oxford University Press, 1995.

Dávila, Jerry. *Diploma of Whiteness: Race and Social Policy in Brazil, 1917–1945*. Durham, NC: Duke University Press, 2003.

Davis, Darien. *Avoiding the Dark: Race and the Forging of National Culture in Modern Brazil*. Aldershot U.K.: Ashgate, 1999.

Davis, F. James. *Who Is Black? One Nation's Definition*. University Park, PA: Pennsylvania State University Press, 1991.

Dawson, Alexander S. "From Models for the Nation to Model Citizens: *Indigenismo* and the 'Revindication' of the Mexican Indian, 1920–1940." *Journal of Latin American Studies* 30 (1998): 279–308.

Degler, Carl N. *Neither Black nor White: Slavery and Race Relations in Brazil and the United States*. Madison, WI: University of Wisconsin Press, 1986.

de la Cadena, Marisol. *Indigenous Mestizos: The Politics of Race and Culture in Cuzco, Peru, 1919–1991*. Durham, NC: Duke University Press, 2000.

Deora, M.S. *Akali Agitation to Operation Bluestar and Aftermath*. 4 Vols. New Delhi: Ammol Publications, 1991–1992.

Deringil, Selim. *The Well-Protected Domains: Ideology and the Legitimation of Power in the Ottoman Empire, 1876–1909*. London: I.B. Tauris, 1998.

De Vos, George A., and Willliam O. Wetherall. Updated by Kaye Stearman. *Japan's Minorities: Burakumin, Koreans, Ainu and Okinawans*. London: Minority Rights Group, 1983.

Diamond, Larry, Juan J. Linz, and Seymour Martin Lipset, Eds. *Democracy in Developing Countries: Latin America*. Boulder, CO: Lynne Rienner, 1989.

Dikötter, Frank. *The Discourse of Race in Modern China*. Stanford, CA: Stanford University Press, 1992.

Dirks, Nicholas B. *Castes of Mind: Colonialism and the Making of Modern India*. Princeton, NJ: Princeton University Press, 2001.

Domingues, Regina. "The Color of a Majority Without Citizenship." *Conexões: African Diaspora Research Project*, Michigan State University, 4.2 (November 1992): 6–7.

Donald, James, and Ali Rattansi, Eds. *"Race", Culture and Difference*. London: Sage, 1992.

Dubow, Saul. "'Holding a Just Balance between White and Black': The Native Affairs Department in South Africa, c. 1920–1933," *Journal of Southern African Studies*, 12 (1986): 217–239.

Dzidzienyo, Anani. *The Position of Blacks in Brazilian Society*. London: Minority Rights Group, 1971.

Dzidzienyo, Anari. "Brazil." In *International Handbook on Race and Race Relations*, Ed. Jay A. Sigler, 23–42. New York: Greenwood Press, 1987.

Edwards, Penny. "Imaging the Other in Cambodian Nationalist Discourse Before and During the UNTAC Period." In Steven Heder and Judy Ledgerwood, Eds., *Propaganda, Politics, and Violence in Cambodia: Democratic Transition under United Nations Peace-keeping*. London: M.E. Sharpe, 1996.

Eldredge, Elizabeth. *A South African Kingdom: The Pursuit of Security in Nineteenth Century Lesotho*. Cambridge UK: Cambridge University Press,1993.

Elliott, Mark C. *The Manchu Way: The Eight Banners and Ethnic Identity in Late Imperial China*. Stanford, CA: Stanford University Press, 2001.

Enloe, Cynthia H. *Ethnic Conflict and Political Development*. Boston: Little, Brown, 1973.

Enloe, Cynthia H. "The Politics of Constructing the American Woman Soldier." In *Women Soldiers: Images and Realities*, Eds. Elisabetta Addis, Valeria E. Russo, and Lorenza Sebesta. New York: St. Martin's Press, 1994.

Epstein, A.L. *Ethos and Identity*. London: Tavistock, 1978.

Evans, Ivan. *Bureaucracy and Race: Native Administration in South Africa*. Berkeley, CA: University of California Press, 1997.

Eze, Emmanuel Chukwudi, Ed. *Race and the Enlightenment*. Oxford UK: Blackwell, 1997.

Favell, Adrian. *Philosophies of Integration: Immigration and the Idea of Citizenship in France and Britain*. 2nd ed. Basingstoke, UK: Palgrave, 2001.

Favret, Jeanne. "Relations de dépendance et manipulation de la violence en Kabylie." *L'Homme*, 8 (1968): 18–44.

Federal Government's Commissioner for Foreigners' Issues. "Facts and Figures on the Situation of Foreigners in the Federal Republic of Germany." 19th ed. Berlin and Bonn. October 2000.

Feldblum, Miriam. *The Politics of Nationality Reform and Immigration in Contemporary France*. Albany NY: State University of New York Press, 1999.

Feliu Cruz, Guillermo. *Un esquema de la evolución social en Chile en el siglo XIX*.[Santiago?] Editorial Nascim, 1941.

Ferguson, James. *The Anti-Politics Machine*(Cambridge UK: Cambridge University Press, 1990).

Fleras, Augie. "Tuku Rangatiratanga: Devolution in Iwi Government Relations." In *Nga Take: Ethnic Relations and Racism in Aotearoa/New Zealand*. Eds. Paul Spoonley, David Pearson, and Cluny Macpherson, 171–193. Palmerston North: Dunmore Press, 1991.

Fleras, Augie, and Paul Spoonley. *Recalling Aotearoa: Indigenous Politics and Ethnic Relations in New Zealand*. Auckland: Oxford University Press, 1999.

Flory, Thomas. "Race and Social Control in Independent Brazil." *Journal of Latin American Studies*, 9.2 (November 1977): 199–224.

Foley, Neil. *The White Scourge: Mexicans, Blacks, and Poor Whites in Texas Cotton Culture*. Berkeley, CA: University of California Press, 1997.

Fontaine, Pierre-Michel, Ed. *Race, Class and Power in Brazil*. Los Angeles, CA: UCLA African American Studies Center, 1985.

Fontaine, Pierre-Michel. "Transnational Relations and Racial Mobilization: Emerging Black Movements in Brazil." In *Ethnic Minorities in a Transnational World*, Ed. John F. Stack, 1–162. Westport, CT: Greenwood, 1981.

Fortune, Stephan Alexander. *Merchants and Jews: The Struggle for British West Indian Commerce, 1650–1750*. Gainesville, FL: University of Florida Press, 1984.

Foucault, Michel. *The Archaeology of Knowledge and the Discourse on Language*. New York: Pantheon, 1972.

Fraser, Nicholas. *The Voice of Modern Hatred: Encounters with Europe's New Right*. London: Picador, 2000.

Fredrickson, George M. *Black Liberation: A Comparative History of Black Ideologies in the United States and South Africa*. New York: Oxford, 1995.

Fredrickson, George M. *Racism: A Short History*. Princeton, NJ: Princeton University Press, 2002.

Fredrickson, George M. *White Supremacy: A Comparative Study in American and South African History*. New York: Oxford, 1981.

Freyre, Gilberto. *The Masters and the Slaves*. Trans. Harriet de Onís. New York: Knopf, 1963.

Freyre, Gilberto. *Order and Progress*. Trans. and Ed. Rod W. Horton. New York: Knopf, 1970.

Freyre, Gilberto. *The Mansions and the Shanties*. Trans. Harriet de Onís. New York: Knopf, 1963.

Fujitani Takashi. *Tenno no pejento: Kindai nihon no rekishi minzoku-shi kara*. Tokyo: Kyokai shuppankai, 1994

Fukuoka Yaunori. *Zainichi kankoku-chosen jin: wakai sedai no aidentiti*. Tokyo: Chuokoronsha, 1993.

Gamio, Manuel. *Forjando Patria*. Mexico: Editorial Porrúa, 1960; orig. 1916.

Gann, Lewis H. "Marginal Colonialism: The German Case." In *Germans in the Tropics*, Ed. Arthur J. Knoll and Lewis H. Gann, 1–18. New York: Greenwood, 1987.

Gates, Henry Louis, Jr., Ed. *"Race," Writing, and Difference*. Chicago, IL: University of Chicago Press, 1986.

Gavida, Francisco. "El Porvenir de la América Latina." *La Quincena* 1: 1 (August 1903).

Gebre-Medhin, Jordan. *Peasants and Nationalism in Eritrea*.Trenton, NJ: Red Sea Press, 1989.

Gebreyesus, Aba Yishak. "Languages, Written Texts and Oral Traditions in Eritrea," Paper in Tigrinya presented at the *Conference of the Eritrean Languages* in Asmara, Eritrea (August 16–18, 1996).

Gelbin, Cathy S., Kader Konuk, and Peggy Piesche, Eds. *AufBrüche: Kulturelle Produktionen von Migrantinnen, Schwarzen und Jüdischen Frauen*. Königstein/Taunus: Ulrike Helmer Verlag, 1999.

Gellner, Ernest. *Nations and Nationalism*. Oxford UK: Blackwell, 1988.

Gellner, Ernest, and Charles Micaud, Eds. *Arabs and Berbers: From Tribe to Nation in North Africa*, London: Duckworth, 1973.

Ghebrai, Illen. *Eritrea Miracleland*.Washington, DC: privately printed, 1993.

Gillette, Aaron. *Racial Theories in Fascist Italy*. London: Routledge, 2001.

Gillis, F.R. *Commemorations: The Politics of National Identity*. Princeton, NJ: Princeton University Press, 1994.

Gilroy, Paul. *The Black Atlantic: Modernity and Double Consciousness*. Cambridge, MA: Harvard University Press, 1993.

Gilroy, Paul. *"There Ain't No Black in the Union Jack": The Cultural Politics of Race and Nation*. Chicago, IL: University of Chicago Press, 1991.

Gladney, Dru C. *Ethnic Identity in China*. Fort Worth TX: Harcourt Brace, *1998*.

Gladney, Dru C. *Making Majorities: Constituting the Nation in Japan, Korea, China, Malaysia, Fiji, Turkey, and the United States*. Stanford, CA: Stanford University Press, 1998.

Gobineau, Joseph Arthur, comte de. *The Inequality of Races*. New York: H. Fertig, 1915; orig. 1856.

Gomez, Michael. *Exchanging Our Country Marks: The Transformation of African Identities in the Colonial and Antebellum South*. Chapel Hill, NC: University of North Carolina Press, 1998.

Gong, Gerrit W. *The Standard of "Civilization" in International Society*. Oxford U.K.: Clarendon Press, 1984.

González, Lelia. "The Unified Black Movement: A New Stage in Black Mobilization." In *Race, Class and Power in Brazil*, Ed. Pierre-Michel Fontaine, 120–134. Los Angeles, CA: UCLA Center for African American Studies, 1985.

Gordon, David C. *North Africa's French Legacy 1954–1962*. Cambridge MA: Harvard University Press, 1962.

Gordon, Milton. *Assimilation in American Life*. New York: Oxford, 1964.

Gossett, Thomas F. *Race: The History of an Idea in America*. New York: Schocken, 1965.

Gould, Jeffrey L. *To Die in This Way: Nicaraguan Indians and the Myth of Mestizaje, 1880–1965*. Durham, NC: Duke University Press, 1998.

Gould, Jeffrey. "'Vana Ilusión!' The Highlands Indians and the Myth of Nicaragua Mestiza, 1880–1925," *Hispanic American Historical Review* 73.3 (1993):393–429.

Gould, Stephen Jay. *The Mismeasure of Man*. Rev. Ed. New York: Norton, 1996.

Government of India. *The Punjab Boundary Commission Report*. Delhi, 1947.

Government of India. *White Paper on the Punjab Agitation*. Delhi, 1984.

Government of Punjab. *Facts about the Punjab Situation*. Chandigarh, 1986.

Graves, Joseph L., Jr. *The Emperor's New Clothes: Biological Theories of Race at the Millennium*. New Brunswick, NJ: Rutgers University Press, 2001.

Greenland, Hauraki. "Maori Ethnicity as Ideology." In *Nga Take: Ethnic Relations and Racism in Aotearoa/New Zealand*. Eds. Paul Spoonley, David Pearson, and Cluny Macpherson. Palmerston North: Dunmore Press, 1991.

Guibernau, Monserrat, and John Rex, Eds. *The Ethnicity Reader*. Cambridge UK: Polity Press, 1997.

Guterl, Matthew Pratt. *The Color of Race in America, 1900–1940*. Cambridge, MA: Harvard University Press, 2001.

Gutiérrez, Ramón. *When Jesus Came, the Corn Mothers Went Away: Marriage, Sexuality, and Power in New Mexico, 1500–1846*. Stanford, CA: Stanford University Press, 1991.

Gutiérrez, Ramón, and Richard J. Orsi, Eds. *Contested Eden: California Before the Gold Rush*. Berkeley, CA: University of California Press, 1998.

Guy, Jeff, and Motlatsi Thabane, "Technology, Ethnicity and Ideology: Basotho Miners and Shaft Sinking on the South African Gold Mines," *Journal of Southern African Studies*, 14.2 (1988):257–278.

Haas, Lisbeth. *Conquests and Historical Identities in California, 1769–1936*. Berkeley, CA: University of California Press, 1995.

Haberly, David T. "Abolitionism in Brazil: Anti-Slavery and Anti-Slave," *Luso-Brazilian Review*, 9.2 (1972): 30–46.

Habib, Salah. "Fusion et confusion des cultures et des identités." *Passerelles*, 11 (Winter 1995/96): 41–63.

Hachi, Slimane. "Note sur la politique berbère de la France." *Tafsut*, 1 (1983): 29–33.

Hale, Charles R. "*Mestizaje*, Hybridity, and the Cultural Politics of Difference in Post-Revolutionary Central America." *Journal of Latin American Anthropology* 2.1 (1996).

Hale, Charles R. *Resistance and Contradiction: Miskitu Indians and the Nicaraguan State, 1894–1987*. Stanford, CA: Stanford University Press, 1994.

Hale, Grace Elizabeth. *Making Whiteness: The Culture of Segregation in the South, 1890–1940*. New York: Pantheon, 1998.

Hall, Catherine, Ed. *Cultures of Empire: Colonizers in Britain and the Empire in the Nineteenth and Twentieth Centuries*. New York: Routledge, 2000.

Hall, Stuart. "Minimal Selves." In *Black British Cultural Studies*, Ed. Houston A. Baker, Jr., Manthia Diawara, and Ruth H. Lindeborg, 114–119. Chicago, IL: University of Chicago Press, 1996.

Hall, Stuart. "New Ethnicities." In *"Race," Culture and Difference*, Ed. James Donald and Ali Rattansi. London: Sage, 1992.

Hamashita Takeshi. *Okinawa nyumon—ajia o tsunagu kaiiki koso*. Tokyo: Chikumashobo, 2000.

Hamilton, Charles V., Lynn Huntley, Neville Alexander, Antonio Sergio Guimarães, and Wilmot James, Eds. *Beyond Racism: Race and Inequality in Brazil South Africa, and the United States*. Boulder, CO: Lynne Rienner, 2001.

Hanagan, Michael, and Charles Tilly, Eds. *Extending Citizenship, Reconfiguring States*. Lanham, MD: Rowman and Littlefield, 1999.

Hanchard, Michael George. *Orpheus and Power: The Movimento Negro of Rio de Janeiro and São Paulo, Brazil, 1945–1988*. Princeton, NJ: Princeton University Press, 1994.

Hanihara Kazuo and Omoto Keishi. *Nihonjin wa doko kara kita ka shiriizu: Karada kara nihonjin no kigen o saguru*. Tokyo: Fukutake shoten, 1986.

Hannaford, Ivan. *Race: The History of an Idea in the West*. Washington: Woodrow Wilson Center Press, 1996.

Harada Tomohiko. *Hisabetsu burakumin no rekishi*. Tokyo: Asahi shinbunsha, 1975.

Harbi, Mohamed. "Nationalisme algérien et identité berbère." *Peuples Méditérranéens*, 11 (avril-juin 1980): 31–37.

Hargreaves, Alec G. *Immigration, "Race" and Ethnicity in Contemporary France*. London: Routledge, 1995.

Hargreaves, Alec G., and Jeremy Leaman, Eds. *Racism, Ethnicity and Politics in Dontemporary Europe*. Aldershot, U.K.: Edward Elgar, 1995.

Harrell, Stevan. *Ways of Being Ethnic in Southwest China*. Seattle, WA: University of Washington Press, 2001.

Hasenbalg, Carlos A. "O Negro nas Vésperas do Centenário." *Estudos Afro-Asiáticos*, 13 (Março de 1987): 79–86.

Harenbalg, Carlos A. "Race and Socioeconomic Inequalities in Brazil." In *Race, Class, and Power in Brazil*, Ed. Pierre-Michel Fontaine, 25–41. Los Angeles: UCLA Center for African American Studies, 1985.

Hasenbalg, Carlos A., Nelson do Valle Silva, and Luiz Claudio Bracelos. "Notas Sobre Miscegenação no Brasil," *Estudos Afro-Asiaticos*, 6 (1989): 189–197.

Hassema-Karra, Mikael. *History of Eritrea*. Privately printed, 1986.

Hazen, William E. "Minorities in Assimilation: The Berbers of North Africa." In *The Political Role of Minority Groups in the Middle East*, Ed. Ronald McLaurin, 135–155. New York: Praeger, 1979.

Hechter, Michael. *Internal Colonialism: The Celtic Fringe in British National Development, 1536–1966*. Berkeley, CA: University of California Press, 1975.

Heckmann, Friedrich. "Ethnos, Demos und Nation, oder: Woher stammt die Intoleranz des Nationalstaats gegenüber ethnischer Minderheiten?" In *Das Eigene und das Fremde*, Ed. Ulrich Bielefeld, 51–78. Hamburg: Hamburger Edition, 1998.

Heder, Steven, and Judy Ledgerwood, Eds. *Propaganda, Politics, and Violence in Cambodia: Democratic Transition under United Nations Peace-keeping*. London: M.E. Sharpe, 1996.

Hewstone, Miles, and Colleen Ward. "Ethnocentrism and Causal Attribution in Southeast Asia." *Journal of Personality and Social Psychology* 48.3 (1985): 614–623.

Hinz, Manfred O., Helgard Patemann, and Arnim Meier, Eds. *Weiss auf Schwarz: Kolonialismus, Apartheid und afrikanischer Widerstand*. Berlin: Elefanten Press, 1986.

Hobsbawm, E.J., *Nations and Nationalism since 1780*. Cambridge UK: Cambridge University Press, 1990.

Hobsbawm, E.J. and Terence Ranger, Eds. *The Invention of Tradition*. Cambridge UK: Cambridge University Press, 1983.

Hoetink, Hartimus. *Slavery and Race Relations in the Americas: Comparative Notes on Their Nature and Nexus*. New York: Harper and Row, 1973.

Hohepa, P. "Maori and Pakeha: The One People Myth." In *Tihe Mauri Ora: Aspects of Maoritanga*, Ed. Michael King, 98–111. Auckland: Methuen, 1978.

Holzberg, C.S. *Minorities and Power in a Black Society: The Jewish Community of Jamaica*. Lanham, MD: North-South Publishing, 1987.

Horrocks, David, and Eva Kolinsky, Eds. *Turkish Culture in German Society Today*. Providence, RI: Berghahn, 1996.

Horsman, Reginald. *Race and Manifest Destiny: The Origins of American Racial Anglo-Saxonism*. Cambridge, MA: Harvard University Press, 1981.

Howard, Michael C. *Fiji: Race and Politics in an Island State*. Vancouver: UBC Press, 1991.

Hubel, Teresa. *Whose India? The Independence Struggle in British and Indian Fiction and History*. London: Leicester University Press, 1996.

Huber-Koller, Rose-Marie. "Schwarze Deutsche: Zwischen 'Ethnos' und 'Demos' im historischen Spannungsgeld unterschiedlicher Legitimationsgrundlagen und Techniken politischer Herrschaft." In *Vom Ausländer zum Bürger: Problemanzeigen im Ausländer–, Asyl– und Staatsangehörigkeitsrecht*. Festschrift für Fritz Franz und Gert Müller, 126–180. Baden-Baden: Nomos Verlagsgesellschaft, 1994.

Hügel-Marshall, Ilka. *Daheim unterwegs: Ein deutsches Leben*. Berlin: Orlanda, 1998.

Husbands, Christopher T. " 'They must obey our laws and customs!': Political Debate about Muslim Assimilability in Great Britain, France and the Netherlands." In *Racism, Ethnicity and Politics in Contemporary Europe*, Eds. Alec G. Hargreaves and Jeremy Leaman, 115–130. Aldershot, UK: Edward Elgar, 1995.

Hutchinson, John, and Anthony D. Smith, Eds., *Ethnicity*. Oxford UK: Oxford University Press, 1996.

Ingenieros, José. "La Formación de una Raza Argentina," *R. de Filosofia* 11 (1915).

Ingenieros, José. *Sociologia Argentina*.Buenos Aires: Editorial Losada, 1946.

Ingenieros, Jose. *Por la Unión Latino Americana*.Buenos Aires: L.J. Rosso y Cia, 1922.

International Centre for Ethnic Studies. *Minorities in Cambodia*. London: Minority Rights Group, 1995.

Ishizawa Yasuharu. *Nihonjinron-nihonron no keifu*. Tokyo: Maruzen, 1997.

Iyob, Ruth. *The Eritrean Struggle for Independence*. Cambridge U.K.: Cambridge University Press, 1995.

Jaijee, I.S. *Politics of Genocide*. Chandigarh: Baba Publications, 1995.

Jeffrey, Robin. "Grappling with History: Sikh Politicians and the Past," *Pacific Affairs*, 60 (1987): 59–72.

Jeffrey, Robin. *What's Happening to India: Punjab, Ethnic Conflict, Mrs Gandhi's Death and Test for Federalism*. London: Macmillan, 1986.

Johnson, Ollie A., III. "Racial Representation and Brazilian Politics: Black Members of the National Congress, 1983–1999," *Journal of Interamerican Studies and World Affairs* 40.4 (Winter 1998): 112–113

Jordens, Jay. "The Ethnic Vietnamese in Cambodia: Prospects Post-UNTAC." Unpublished lecture. University of Hawai'i at Manoa, 1994.

Jordens, Jay. "Persecution of Cambodia's Ethnic Vietnamese Communities During and Since the UNTAC Period." In *Propaganda, Politics, and Violence in Cambodia: Democratic Transition under United Nations Peace-keeping*, Ed. Steven Heder and Judy Ledgerwood, 134–158. London: M.E. Sharpe, 1996.

Jørgensen, Vibeke Heide. *Allahs piger*. [*Allah's Girls*.] Copenhagen: Ascheoug, 1996.

Kahsai, Zewde Kahsai. *Ancient and Modern Rule of Matrimony in Eritrea*. Asmara: EC, 1966.

Kamakau, Samuel. *Ka Po'e Kahiko*. Honolulu: Bishop Museum, 1991.

Kame'eleihiwa, Lilikalā. *Native Land and Foreign Desires*. Honolulu: Bishop Museum, 1992.

Kang, Sambath. "A Look at an Aspect of Wartime in Cambodia." *Khmer Conscience*, 7.2 (1993).

Karis, Thomas, and Gail M. Gerhart. *From Protest to Challenge: A Documentary History of African Politics in South Africa, 1882–1990*. Bloomington: Indiana University Press, 1997.

Kawharu, I.H., Ed. *Waitangi: Maori and Pakeha Perspectives of the Treaty of Waitangi*. Auckland: Oxford, 1994.

Kayali, Hasan. *Arabs and Young Turks: Ottomanism, Arabism, and Islamism in the Ottoman Empire, 1908–1918*. Berkeley, CA: University of California Press, 1997.

Heilbronner, Kay Günter Renner, and Christine Kreuzer. *Staatsangehörigkeitsrecht. Kommentar*. München: Beck, 1998.

Kedourie, Elie, Ed. *Nationalism in Asia and Africa*. London: Frank Cass, 1970.

Keller, Edmond. *Revolutionary Ethiopia: From Empire to People's Republic*. Bloomington, IN: Indiana University Press, 1988.

Kelsey, Jane. "Legal Imperialism and the Colonisation of Aotearoa." In *Tauiwi*, Ed. Paul Spoonley, *et al*. Palmerston North: Dunmore Press, 1984.

Kerber, Linda K. "May All Our Citizens Be Soldiers and All Our Soldiers Citizens: The Ambiguities of Female Citizenship in the New Nation." In *Women, Militarism, and War: Essays in History, Politics, and Social Theory*, Eds. Jean Bethke Elshtain and Shelia Tobias, 89–103. Savage, MD: Rowman and Littlefield, 1990.

Khader, Naser. *Ǽligre og Skam*. [*Honor and Shame*.] Copenhagen: Borgen, 1996.

Khader, Naser. *khader.dk. Sammenførte erindringer*. [*khader.dk. Joint Memories*.] Copenhagen: Ascheoug, 2000.

Kiernan, Ben. *How Pol Pot Came to Power*. London: Verso, 1985.

Kikuchi Isao. *Ainu minzoku to nihonjin: Higashi ajia no nakano ezochi*. Tokyo: Asahi shinbunsha, 1994.

Killion, Tom. *Historical Dictionary of Eritrea*. Lanham, MD: Scarecrow Press, 1998.

Kim, Chou. 1993. "The Problem of Prostitution in Cambodia: Is it Normal for Khmer Society?" *Khmer Conscience*, 7.2 (1993).

King, James C. *The Biology of Race*. 2nd ed. Berkeley, CA: University of California Press, 1981.

King, Michael. *Being Pakeha*. Auckland: Hodder and Stoughton, 1985.

King, Michael. "New Zealandness: Towards a Prescription." Waitangi Day Address, New Zealand Embassy, Washington, DC February 6, 2001.

King, Michael, Ed. *Tihe Mauri Ora: Aspects of Maoritanga*. Auckland: Methuen, 1978.

Klein, Herbert S. *African Slavery in Latin America and the Caribbean*. New York: Oxford University Press, 1986.

Klein, Herbert. "Nineteenth-Century Brazil." In *Neither Slave Nor Free: The Freemen of African Descent in the Slave Societies of the New World*, Ed. David Cohen and Jack P. Greene, 309–334. Baltimore MD.: Johns Hopkins University Press, 1972.

Klineberg, Otto, Tullio Tentori, Franco Crespi, and Vincenzo Filippone Thaulero. *Religione e pregiudizio. Analisi di contenuto di libri cattolici di insegnamento religioso in Italia e in Spagna*. Bologna: Cappelli, 1968.

Knoll, Arthur J., and Lewis H. Gann, Eds. *Germans in the Tropics. Essays in German Colonial History*. New York: Greenwood Press, 1987.

Kohli, Atul. *Democracy and Discontent: India's Growing Crisis of Governability*. Cambridge UK: Cambridge University Press, 1990.

Kohli, Atul, Ed. *India's Democracy: An Analysis of Changing State-Society Relations*. Princeton, NJ: Princeton University Press, 1988.

Kokuritsu Kokkai Toshokan. *Dokyumento sengo no nihon — shinbun nyuusu ni miru shakaishi daijiten — dai 19 kan, ainu minzoku to okinawa mondai*. Vol. 15 (Vol.1–50) Tokyo: Taikusha, 1995.

Koshiro Yukiko. *Trans-Pacific Racisms and the US Occupation of Japan*. New York: Columbia University Press, 1999.

Kudo Takashi. *Yamato shosu minzoku bunkaron*. Tokyo: Taishukan, 1999.

Kuper, Adam. *Changing Jamaica*. London: Routledge and Kegan Paul, 1976.

Lal, Victor. *Fiji: Coups in Paradise: Race, Politics and Military Intervention*. London: Zed, 1990.

Landau, Jacob M. *Pan-Turkism: From Irredentism to Cooperation*. Bloomington, IN: Indiana University Press, 1995.

Laroui, Abdallah. *L'Histoire du Maghreb: un essai de synthèse*. Paris: Maspero, 1970.

Laskier, Michael. *North African Jewry in the Twentieth Century: The Jews of Morocco, Tunisia, and Algeria*. New York: New York University Press, 1994.

Ledgerwood, Judy. *Analysis of the Situation of Women in Cambodia: Research on Women in Khmer Society*.Phnom Penh, Cambodia: Consultancy for UNICEF, 1992.

Ledgerwood, Judy, May M. Ebihara, and Carol A. Mortland, Eds. *Cambodian Culture Since 1975: Homeland and Exile*. Ithaca, NY: Cornell University Press, 1994.

Lehning, James R. *To Be a Citizen: The Political Culture of the Early French Third Republic*. Ithaca, NY: Cornell University Press, 2001.

Lesser, Jeffrey. *Negotiating National Identity: Immigrants, Minorities, and the Struggle for Ethnicity in Brazil*. Durham, NC: Duke University Press, 1999.

Levine, Donald. *Greater Ethiopia*. Chicago, IL: University of Chicago Press, 1974.

Levine, Donald. *Wax and Gold: Tradition and Innovation in Ethiopian Culture*. Chicago, IL: University of Chicago Press, 1965.

Levitt, Peggy, and Mary C. Waters, Eds. *The Changing Face of Home: The Transnational Lives of the Second Generation*. New York: Russell Sage, 2002.

Lewis, Martin D. "One Hundred Million Frenchmen: The Assimilationist Theory in French Colonial Policy." *Comparative Studies in Society and History*, 4.2 (1962): 129–153.

Lewis, William H., Ed. *French-Speaking Africa: The Search for Identity*. New York: Walker and Company, 1965.

Lie, John. *Mutiethnic Japan*. Cambridge, MA: Harvard University Press, 2001.

Lilley, Rozanna. "Ethnicity and Anthropology." In *Ethnic Groups Across Boundaries in Mainland Southeast Asia*, Ed. G. Wijeyewardene. Singapore: Institute of Southeast Asian Studies, 1990.

Lind, Andrew W., Ed. *Race Relations in World Perspective*. Honolulu: University of Hawai'i Press. 1955.

Linger, Daniel Touro. *No One Home: Brazilian Selves Remade in Japan*. Stanford, CA: Stanford University Press, 2001.

Linnekin, Jocelyn. "On the Theory and Politics of Cultural Construction in the Pacific." *Oceania*, 62 (1992): 249–263.

Lovell-Webster, Peggy. "The Myth of Racial Equality: A Study of Race and Mortality in Northeast Brazil," *Latinamericanist*, (May 1987): 1–6.

Lovell-Webster, Peggy and Jeffrey Dwyer. "The Cost of Being Nonwhite in Brazil," *Sociology and Social Research*, 722 (1988): 136–138.

Lowenthal, David. *West Indian Societies*. London: Oxford, 1972.

Lyons, D.P. "An Analysis of Three Maori Prophet Movements," In *Conflict and Compromise*, Ed. I.H. Kawharu. Wellington: Reed, 1975.

Ma, Laurence, and Carolyn Cartier, Eds. *The Chinese Diaspora*. Lanham, MD: Rowman and Littlefield, 2003.

Macpherson, Cluny, Paul Spoonley, and Melani Anae, Eds. *Tangata O Te Moana Nui: The Evolving Identities of Pacific Peoples in Aotearoa/New Zealand*. Palmerston North: Dunmore Press, 2001.

Maddy-Weitzman, Bruce. "The Berber Question in Algeria: Nationalism in the Making?" In *Minorities and the State in the Arab World*, Eds. Ofra Bengio and Gabriel Ben-Dor, 31–52. London: Lynne Rienner, 1999.

Mahé, Alain. *Histoire de la Grande Kabylie: XIX–XXe siècles*. Paris: Editions Bouchène, 2001.

Malik, Kenan. *The Meaning of Race*. New York: New York University Press, 1996.

Mallon, Florencia E. "Constructing *Mestizaje* in Latin America: Authenticity, Marginality, and Gender in the Claiming of Ethnic Identities," *Journal of Latin American Anthropology*, 2.1 (1996).

Malo, David. *Hawaiian Antiquities*, 2nd ed., trans. Nathaniel Emerson. Honolulu: Bishop Museum, 1951; orig. 1898.

Mamdani, Mahmood. *Citizen and Subject: Contemporary Africa and the Legacy of Late Colonialism* (Princeton, NJ: Princeton University Press, 1996).

Manz, Beatrice, Ed. *Central Asia in Historical Perspective*. Boulder, CO: Westview Press, 1994.

Marais, Hein. *South Africa: Limits to Change: The Political Economy of Transition*. Revised and Expanded New Edition. London: Zed, 2001.

Marçais, Philippe W. "Peoples and Cultures in North Africa." *The Annals of the American Academy of Political and Social Science*, 298 (March 1955): 21–29.

Marcílio, Maria Luisa. "The Population of Colonial Brazil." In *Colonial Latin America, The Cambridge History of Latin America*, vol. 2, Ed. Leslie Bethell. Cambridge, U.K. Cambridge University Press, 1984.

Margolis, Mac. "The Invisible Issue: Race in Brazil." *Ford Foundation Report*, 23.2 (Summer 1992).

Markakis, John. *National and Class Conflicts in the Horn of Africa*. Cambridge UK: Cambridge University Press, 1987.

Marks, Jonathan. *Human Biodiversity: Genes, Race, and History*. New York: Aldyne de Gruyter, 1995.

Marks, Jonathan. *What It Means to Be 98% Chimpanzee: Apes, People and Their Genes*. Berkeley, CA: University of California Press, 2002.

Marks, Shula. *The Ambiguities of Dependence in South Africa: Class, Nationalism, and the State in Twentieth-Century Natal*. Johannesburg: Ravan Press, 1986.

Martin, Claude. *Les Israélites algériens de 1830–1902*. Paris: Editions Herakles, 1936.

Marx, Anthony. *Making Race and Nation: A Comparison of the United States, South Africa, and Brazil*. New York: Cambridge University Press, 1998.

Masferrer, Alberto. *Paginas escogidas*. San Salvador: Ministerio de Educación Departamento Editorial (1961; orig. 1923).

Mason, Philip. *Patterns of Dominance*. London: Oxford University Press, 1971.

Massaquoi, Hans J. *Destined to Witness: Growing Up Black in Nazi Germany*. New York: Morrow, 1999.

Mayer, Philip and Iona. *Townsmen or Tribesmen*. Cape Town: Oxford University Press, 1961.

McHugh, P.G. "Constitutional Theory and Maori Claims." In *Waitangi: Maori and Pakeha Perspectives of the Treaty of Waitangi*, Ed. I.H. Kawharu. Auckland: Oxford University Press, 1994.

McLaurin, Ronald. *The Political Role of Minority Groups in the Middle East*. New York: Praeger, 1979.

McLeod, W.H. "On the Word Panth: A Problem of Terminology and Definition," *Contributions to Indian Sociology*, 12.2 (1978): 287–295.

McLeod, W.H. *Who is a Sikh? The Problem of Sikh Identity*. Delhi: Oxford University Press, 1989.

McMillen, Neil R. *Dark Journey: Black Mississippians in the Age of Jim Crow*. Urbana, IL: University of Illinois Press, 1989.

McNeill, William H. *Polyethnicity and National Unity in World History*. Toronto: University of Toronto Press, 1986.

Mecheril, Paul, and Thomas Teo. *Andere Deutsche*. Berlin: Dietz Verlag, 1994.

Melber, Henning. *Der Weißheit letzter Schluß: Rassismus und kolonialer Blick*. Frankfurt: Brandes und Apsel, 1992.

Mélia, Jean. *L'Algérie et la guerre (1914–1918)*. Paris: Plon-Nourrit, 1918.

Memmi, Albert. *The Colonizer and the Colonized*. Boston: Beacon, 1967; orig. 1956.

Memmi, Albert. *Racism*. Trans. Steve Martinot. Minneapolis, MN: University of Minnesota Press, 2000.

Menchaca, Martha. *Recovering History, Constructing Race: The Indian, Black, and White Roots of Mexican Americans*. Austin: University of Texas Press, 2001.

Mensergh, Nicholas, Ed. *Constitutional Relations between Britain and India: The Transfer of Power 1942–47*. 12 Vols. London: Her Majesty's Stationery Office, 1970–83.

Merimée, J. *De l'accession des Indochinois à la qualité de citoyen français*. Toulouse: Imprimerie Andrau et La Porte, 1931.

Metge, Joan. *A New Maori Migration: Rural–Urban Relations in Northern New Zealand*. LSE Monographs on Social Anthropology. London: Athlone, 1964.

Meynier, Gilbert. *L'Algérie révélée: La guerre de 1914–1918 et le premier quart du XXe siècle*. Geneva: Droz, 1981.

Miller, John. *Early Victorian New Zealand: A Study of Racial Tension and Social Attitudes, 1839–1852.* London: Oxford University Press, 1958.

Mires, Fernando. *El discurso de la indianidad.*Quito, Ecuador: Ediciones Abya-Yala, 1991.

Mitchell, Michael. "Blacks and the Abertura Democrática." In *Race, Class and Power in Brazil,* Ed. Pierre-Michel Fontaine, 120–134. UCLA Center for African American Studies, 1985.

Mizuno, Takaaki. "Ainu, The Invisible Minority." *Japan Quarterly* 34 (1987): 143–148

Molina Enríquez, Andrés. *Los grandes problemas nacionales.*Mexico: Ediciones Era, 1978; orig. 1909.

Monroy, Douglas. *Thrown Among Strangers: The Making of Mexican Culture in Frontier California.* Berkeley, CA: University of California Press, 1990.

Montagne, Robert. *The Berbers: Their Social and Political Organization.* Trans. David Seddon. London: Frank Cass, 1973.

Montagu, Ashley. *Man's Most Dangerous Myth: The Fallacy of Race.* New York: World, 1964.

Moodie, T. Dunbar. *The Rise of Afrikanerdom: Power, Apartheid and the Afrikaner Civil Religion.* Berkeley, CA: University of California Press, 1975.

Moodie, T. Dunbar. *Going for Gold: Men, Mines and Migration.* Berkeley, CA: University of California Press; 1994.

Mosse, George L. *Towards the Final Solution: A History of European Racism.* New York: Howard Fertig, 1978.

Nandy, Ashis. "The Discreet Charm of Indian Terrorism," *Journal of Commonwealth and Comparative Politics*, 28.1 (1990): 25–43.

Nantambu, Kwame. "Pan-Africanism versus Pan-African Nationalism: An Afrocentric Analysis," *Journal of Black Studies*, 28.5 (1998): 561–574.

Nascimento, Abdias do. *Mixture or Massacre?: Essays on the Genocide of a Black People.* Trans. Elisa Larkin Nascimento. Buffalo, NY: Puerto Rican Studies and Research Center, State University of New York, 1979.

Nayar, Baldev Raj. *Minority Politics in the Punjab.* Princeton, NJ: Princeton University Press, 1966.

Nayar, Baldev Raj. "Punjab." In *State Politics in India,* Ed. Myron Weiner, 433–502. Princeton, NJ: Princeton University Press, 1968.

Negash, Tekeste. *Eritrea and Ethiopia: The Federal Experience.* New Brunswick: NJ: Transaction Publishers, 1997.

Negash, Tekeste. *Italian Colonialism in Eritrea, 1882–1941.* Uppsala: Uppsala University Press, 1987.

Nettleford, Rex. *Identity, Race and Protest in Jamaica.* New York: Morrow, 1972.

Nettleford, Rex. "Race, Identity and Independence on Jamaica." In *Caribbean Freedom: Economy and Society from Emancipation to Present,* Ed. Hilary Beckles and Verene Shepherd. Princeton, NJ: Markus Wiener, 1993.

Nicholls, David, "The Syrians of Jamaica," *Jamaican Historical Review*, 15 (1986).

Nobles, Melissa. *Shades of Citizenship: Race and the Census in Modern Politics.* Stanford, CA: Stanford University Press, 2000.

Noiriel, Gérard. *The French Melting Pot: Immigration, Citizenship, and National Identity.* Minneapolis, MN: University of Minnesota Press, 1996.

Norris, Kathleen. *Jamaica: The Search for an Identity.* London: Oxford, 1962.

Oberoi, Harjot. "From Punjab to Khalistan: Territoriality and Metacommentary," *Pacific Affairs*, 60.1 (1987): 26–41.

Oberoi, Harjot. *The Construction of Boundaries: Culture, Identity, and Religious Diversity in the Sikh Tradition.* Delhi: Oxford University Press, 1994.

O'Donnell, Guillermo, and Philippe C. Schmitter. *Transitions from Authoritarian Rule: Tentative Conclusions about Uncertain Democracies.* Vol. 4. Baltimore, MD: Johns Hopkins University Press, 1986.

Oguma Eiji. *Tan'itsu minzoku shinwa no kegen: "Nihonjin" no jigazo no keifu.* Tokyo: Shinyosha, 1995.

Oguma Eiji. *Nihonjin no kyokai: Okinawa, Ainu, Taiwan, Chosen shokuminchi shihai kara fukki undo made.* Tokyo: Shinyosha, 1998.

Oguntoye, Katharina, May Opitz, und Dagmar Schulz, Eds. *Farbe bekennen. Afro-Deutsche Frauen auf den Spuren ihrer Geschichte.* Berlin: Orlanda, 1986.

Ohnuki-Tierney, Emiko. "A Conceptual Model for Historical Relationship Between the Self and the Internal and External Others: The Agrarian Japanese, the Ainu, and the Special-Status People." In *Making Majorities: Constituting the Nation in Japan, Korea, China, Malaysia, Fuji, Turkey, and the United States,* Ed. Dru C. Gladney, 31–51. Stanford, CA: Stanford University Press, 1998.

O'Leary, Brendan, and John McGarry, Eds. *The Future of Northern Ireland.* Oxford: Clarendon Press, 1990.

Oliver, William H. *Claims to the Waitangi Tribunal*. Wellington: Waitangi Tribunal Division, Department of Justice, 1991.

Omi, Michael, and Howard Winant. *Racial Formation in the United States: From the 1960s to the 1990s*. New York: Routledge, 1994.

Orange, Claudia. "An Exercise in Maori Autonomy: The Rise of the Maori War Effort Organisation," *New Zealand Journal of History*, 21 (1987): 156–172.

Orange, Claudia. *The Treaty of Waitangi*. Wellington: Allen and Unwin, 1989.

Ortiz, Fernando. *Cuban Counterpoint*. Trans. Harriet de Onís. New York: Knopf, 1947; orig. 1940.

Osorio, Jonathan. *Dismembering Lāhui: A History of the Hawaiian Nation to 1887*. Honolulu: University of Hawai'i Press, 2002.

Ostendorf, Berndt. "Why is American Popular Culture so Popular? A View from Europe." *Amerikastudien — American Studies*, 46.3 (2001): 339–366.

Owens, Joseph. *Dread: The Rastafarians of Jamaica*. Exeter, NH: Heinemann, 1976.

Padmore, George. *Pan-Africanism or Communism: The Coming Struggle for Africa*. New York: Anchor, 1972.

Pan, Lynn. *Sons of the Yellow Emperor: A History of the Chinese Diaspora*. Boston, MA: Little, Brown, 1990.

Park, Robert Ezra. *Race and Culture*. New York: Free Press, 1950.

Pateman, Roy. *Eritrea: Even the Stones are Burning*. Trenton, NJ: Red Sea Press, 1990.

Pettigrew, Joyce. "Betrayal and Nation Building among the Sikhs," *Journal of Commonwealth and Comparative Politics*, 29.1 (1991): 25–43.

Pierson, Donald. *Negroes in Brazil: A Study of Race Contact at Bahia*. Chicago, IL: University of Chicago Press, 1942.

Pile, Steven, and Nigel Thrift. *Mapping the Subject: Geographies of Cultural Transformation*. London: Routledge, 1995.

Pimentel, Francisco. *Memoria sobre las causas que han originado la situación actual de la raza indígena de México y medios de remediarla*, reprinted in *Dos Obras de Francisco Pimentel*. Xoco, CP, Mexico: Consejo Nacional Para la Cultura y las Artes, 1995.

Pitt, Leonard. *The Decline of the Californios: A Social History of the Spanish-Speaking Californians, 1846–1890*. Berkeley, CA: University of California Press, 1966.

Pityana, N. Barney, *et al.* Eds. *Bounds of Possibility: The Legacy of Steve Biko and Black Consciousness*. London: Zed, 1991.

Pool, David. *From Guerrillas to Government*. Oxford: James Currey, 2001.

Porch, Douglas. *The March to the Marne: The French Army, 1871–1914*. Cambridge UK: Cambridge University Press, 1981.

Powell, T.G. "Mexican Intellectuals and the Indian Question, 1876–1911," *Hispanic American Historical Review* (February 1969).

Prado, Caio, Jr. *The Colonial Background of Modern Brazil*. Trans. Suzette Macedo. Berkeley, CA: University of California Press, 1969.

Prasso, Sherri. *Violence, Ethnicity, and Ethnic Cleansing: Cambodia and the Khmer Rouge*. Cambridge UK: University of Cambridge, 1995.

Ralston, Caroline. "'Polyandry,' 'Pollution,' 'Prostitution': The Problems of Eurocentrism and Androcentrism in Polynesian Studies." In *Crossing Boundaries: Feminism and the Critique of Knowledges*, Eds. Barbara Caine, E.A. Groz, and Marie de Lepervanche. Sydney: Allen and Unwin, 1988.

Randhawa, M.S. *Out of Ashes: An Account of the Rehabilitation of Refugees from West Pakistan in Rural Areas of East Punjab*. Chandigarh: Public Relations Department, Government of Punjab, 1954.

Rarrbo, Kamel. "Les jeunes Algériens: entre chômage et quête identitaire." *Passerelles*, 11 (Winter 1995/96): 140–146.

Rashid, Rushy. *Et løft a sløret*. [*Lifting the Veil*.] Copenhagen: Gyldendal, 2000.

Rattansi, Ali. "'Western' Racisms, Ethnicities and Identities in a 'Postmodern' Frame." In *Racism, Modernity and Identity: On the Western Front*, Eds. Ali Rattansi and Sallie Westwood, 15–79. Cambridge UK: Polity Press, 1994.

Raureti, M. "The Origins of the Ratana Movement." In *Tihe Mauri Ora: Aspects of Maoritanga*, Ed. Michael King, 42–59. Auckland: Methuen, 1978.

Ravitch, Norman. "Your People, My People, Your God, My God: French and American Troubles Over Citizenship." *The French Review*, 70.4 (1997): 515–527.

Reed-Anderson, Paulette. *Berlin und die Afrikanische Diaspora: Rewriting the Footnotes. Berlin and the African Diaspora*. Die Ausländerbeauftragte des Berliner Senats. Berlin: Verwaltungsdruckerei, 2000.

Reichmann, Rebecca. "Brazil's Denial of Race," *North American Congress on Latin America Report on the Americas*, 28.6 (1995): 35–42.

Reichmann, Rebecca, Ed. *Race Relations in Contemporary Brazil*. University Park, PA: Pennsylvania State University Press, 1991.

Rex, John, and David Mason, Eds. *Theories of Race and Ethnic Relations*. Cambridge UK: Cambridge University Press, 1986.

Ribbat, Christoph, " 'Ja, ja, deine Mudder!'American Studies und deutsche Populärkultur." In *Kulturwissenschaftliche Perspektiven in den Nordamerikastudien*, Ed. Friedrich Jäger. Tübingen: Stauffenburg, 2002.

Ribbat, Christoph. "How Hip Hop Hit Heidelberg: German Rappers, Rhymes, and Rhythms". In *"Here, There and Everywhere": The Foreign Politics of American Popular Culture*, Ed. Reinhold Wagnleitner and Elaine Tyler May, 207–216. Hanover, NH: University Press of New England, 2000.

Robb, Peter, Ed. *The Concept of Race in South Asia*. Delhi: Oxford, 1995.

Roberts, Hugh J.R. "The Economics of Berberism: the Material Basis of the Kabyle Question in Contemporary Algeria." *Government and Opposition*, 19 (1983): 218–235.

Roberts, Kenneth M. "Beyond Romanticism: Social Movements and the Study of Political Change in Latin America." *Latin American Research Review*, 32.2 (1997).

Robinson, Lori S. "The Two Faces of Brazil; A Black Movement Gives Voice to an Invisible Majority," *Emerge* (October 1994): 38–42.

Rodinson, Maxime. *Les Arabes*. Paris: Presses Universitaires de France, 1979.

Rodríguez, Clara E. *Changing Race: Latinos, the Census, and the History of Ethnicity in the United States*. New York: NYU Press, 2000.

Roland, Edna. "The Soda Cracker Dilemma." In *Race Relations in Contemporary Brazil: From Indifference to Inequality*, Ed. Rebecca Reichmann, 195–207. University Park PA: Pennsylvania State University, 1991.

Root, Maria P. P. *Racially Mixed People in America*. Newbury Park, CA: Sage, 1992.

Ross, J. O. "Busby and the Declaration of Independence," *New Zealand Journal of History*, 14 (1980): 18–39.

Rowe, Irving. *The Tainos: Rise and Decline of the People Who Greeted Columbus*. New Haven, CT: Yale University Press, 1992.

Ruedy, John. *Modern Algeria: The Origins and Development of a Nation*. Bloomington, IN: Indiana University Press, 1992.

Russell-Wood, A.J.R. "Colonial Brazil." In *Neither Slave Nor Free: The Freemen of African Descent in the Slave Societies of the New World*, Eds. David Cohen and Jack P.Greene, 84–133. Baltimore MD: Johns Hopkins University Press, 1972.

Sabby, Othman Saleh. *The History of Eritrea*, trans. Muhammad Fawz Al-Azam. Beirut: Dar Al – Masirah, 1974.

Said, Edward. *Culture and Imperialism*. New York: Knopf, 1993.

Said, Edward. *Orientalism*. New York: Pantheon Books, 1978.

Safran, William. "Diaspora in Modern Societies: Myths of Homeland and Return. *Diaspora*, 1.1 (1991): 83–99.

Sansone, Livio. *Blackness Without Ethnicity: Constructing Race in Brazil*. New York: Palgrave Macmillan, 2002.

Sarabia, Justina, Ed. *José Vasconcelos*.Madrid: Ediciones de Cultura Hispánica, 1989.

Sarhadi, A.S. *Punjabi Suba: The Story of the Struggle*. Delhi: Uttar Chand Kapur, 1971.

Sawada Yotaro. *Okinawa to Ainu: Nihon no minzoku mondai*. Tokyo: Shinsensha, 1996.

Schermerhorn, R.A. *Comparative Ethnic Relations*. Chicago, IL: University of Chicago Press, 1970.

Schmokel, Wolfe. *Dream of Empire: German Colonialism, 1919–1945*. New Haven, CT: Yale University Press, 1964.

Shaw, Karena. "Indigeneity and the International: Repoliticizing Decolonization," Unpublished paper, International Studies Association Annual Meeting, Chicago, 2001.

Sheffer, Gabriel, Ed. *Modern Diasporas in International Politics*. London: Croom Helm, 1986.

Sherlock, Philip, and Hazel Bennett. *The Story of the Jamaican People*. Princeton, NJ: Markus Wiener, 1998.

Sherrif, Robin. *Dreaming of Equality: Color, Race, and Racism in Urban Brazil*. New Brunswick, NJ: Rutgers University Press, 2001.

Shryock, Andrew. *Nationalism and the Genealogical Imagination: Oral History and Textual Authority in Tribal Jordan*. Berkeley, CA: University of California Press, 1997.

Siddle, Richard. "Ainu: Japan's Indigenous People," in *Japan's Minorities: The Illusion of Homogeneity*. Ed. Michael Weiner. New York: Routledge, 1997.

Silva, Nelson do Valle. "Updating the Cost of Not Being White in Brazil." In *Race, Class, and Power in Brazil*, Ed. Pierre-Michel Fontaine, 25–41. Los Angeles: UCLA Center for African American Studies, 1985.

Silva, Nelson do Valle and Carlos A. Hasenbalg, "Race and Educational Opportunity in Brazil." In *Race Relations in Contemporary Brazil: From Indifference to Inequality*, Ed. Rebecca Reichmann. University Park, PA: Pennsylvania State University, 1991.

Silverman, Maxim. *Deconstructing the Nation: Immigration, Racism and Citizenship in Modern France*. London: Routledge, 1992.

Silverman, Maxim. *Facing Postmodernity: Contemporary French Thought on Culture and Society*. London: Routledge, 1999.

Simeon, D. "Tremors of Intent: Perceptions of the Nation and Community in Contemporary India," *Oxford Literary Review*, 16.1–2 (1994): 225–245.

Singh, Gopal. *Politics of Sikh Homeland, 1940–1990*. New Delhi: Ajanta, 1994.

Singh, Gurharpal. *Ethnic Politics in India: A Case Study of Punjab*. London: Macmillan, 2001.

Singh, Gurnam. *A Unilingual Punjabi State and the Sikh Unrest*. New Delhi: Super Press, 1960.

Singh, Harbans. *The Heritage of Sikhs*. Rev. ed. Bombay: Asia Publishing House, 1983.

Singh, Harbhajan. *Nik Suk*. Delhi: Navyug, 1990.

Singh, Hukam. *The Punjab Problem: An Education*. Amritsar: Shiromani Akali Dal, n.d.

Singh, Swarup. *The Sikhs Demand Their Homeland*. Lahore: Lahore Book Shop, 1946.

Skidmore, Thomas A. *Black into White: Race and Nationality in Brazilian Thought*. New York: Oxford University Press, 1974.

Skidmore, Thomas A. "Bi-Racial U.S.A. vs. Multi-racial Brazil: Is the Contrast Still Valid?" *Journal of Latin American Studies*, 25 (1993): 383–386.

Skidmore, Thomas A. "Race and Class in Brazil: A Historical Perspective." In *Race, Class and Power in Brazil*, Ed. Pierre-Michel Fontaine, 11–24. Los Angeles: UCLA Center for African American Studies, 1985.

Skidmore, Thomas A. "Race Relations in Brazil." *Camões Center Quarterly*, 4.3–4 (Autumn and Winter 1992–1993): 49–57.

Slezkine, Yuri. "The USSR as a Communal Apartment, or How a Socialist State Promoted Ethnic Particularism," *Slavic Review* 53 (Summer 1994): 414–452.

Small, Stephen. *Racialised Barriers: The Black Experience in the United States and England in the 1980s*. London: Routledge, 1994.

Smedley, Audrey. *Race in North America*. 2nd ed. Boulder, CO: Westview, 1999.

Smith, Anthony D. *The Ethnic Origins of Nations*. Oxford: Blackwell, 1986.

Smith, Anthony D. *Nations and Nationalism in a Global Era*. Cambridge UK: Polity Press, 1995.

Smith, Anthony D. *State and Nation in the Third World*. London: Wheatsheaf Books, 1983.

Smith, Anthony D. "States and Homelands: The Social and Geopolitical Implications of National Territory." *Millennium: A Journal of International studies*, 10 (1981): 187–202.

Smith, Anthony D. "War and Ethnicity: The Role of Warfare in the Formation of Self-Images and Cohesion of Ethnic Communities." *Ethnic and Racial Studies*, 4 (1981): 375–397.

Smith, M.G. *The Plural Society in the British West Indies*. Berkeley, CA: University of California Press, 1965.

Smooha, Sammy. "Minority Status in an Ethnic Democracy: The Status of the Arab Minority in Israel," *Ethnic and Racial Studies*, 13.3 (1990): 389–414.

Sohal, H.S. "The East Indian Indentureship System in Jamaica, 1845–1917." Ph.D. dissertation, University of Waterloo, 1979.

Sollors, Werner. *Beyond Ethnicity: Consent and Descent in American Culture*. New York: Oxford, 1986.

Sollors, Werner. "The Idea of Ethnicity." In *The Truth About the Truth: De-Confusing and De-Constructing the Postmodern World*, Ed. Walter Truett Anderson, 58–65. New York: Tarcher/Putnam, 1995.

Sollors, Werner. *Theories of Ethnicity*. New York: New York University Press, 1996.

Song, Miri. *Choosing Ethnic Identity*. Cambridge UK: Polity Press, 2003.

Sorrenson, M.P.K. "Towards a Radical Reinterpretation of New Zealand History: The Role of the Waitangi Tribunal." In *Waitangi: Maori and Pakeha Perspectives of the Treaty of Waitangi*, Ed. I.H. Kawharu. Auckland: Oxford University Press, 1994.

Spickard, Paul. "The Illogic of American Racial Categories." In *Racially Mixed People in America*, Ed. Maria P.P. Root, 12–23. Newbury Park, Calif.: Sage, 1992.

Spickard, Paul. *Japanese Americans: The Formation and Transformations of an Ethnic Group*. New York: Twayne, 1996.

Spickard, Paul and W. Jeffrey Burroughs, eds. *We Are a People: Narrative and Multiplicity in Constructing Ethnic Identity*. Philadelphia: Temple University Press, 2000.

Spickard, Paul, and G. Reginald Daniel, Eds. *Racial Thinking in the United States: Uncompleted Independence.* Notre Dame, IN.: University of Notre Dame Press, 2004.

Spickard, Paul, and Rowena Fong. "Ethnic Relations in the People's Republic of China: Images and Social Distance between Han Chinese and Minority and Foreign Nationalities." *Journal of Northeast Asian Studies* (Fall 1994).

Spickard, Paul, and Rowena Fong. "Pacific Islander American Multiethnicity: A Vision of America's Future?" *Social Forces*, 73.4 (1995): 1365–1383.

Spickard, Paul, Joanne L. Rondilla, and Debbie Hippolite Wright, Eds. *Pacific Diaspora: Island Peoples in the United States and Across the Pacific.* Honolulu: University of Hawai'i Press, 2003.

Spoonley, Paul. "Constructing Ourselves: The Post-Colonial Politics of Pakeha." In *Justice and Identity: Antipodean Practices*, Eds. Margaret Wilson and Anna Yeatman. Wellington: Bridget Williams Books, 1995.

Spoonley, Paul. "Pakeha Ethnicity: A Response to Maori Sovereignty." In *Nga Take: Ethnic Relations and Racism in Aotearoa/New Zealand*, Eds. Paul Spoonley, David Pearson, and Cluny Macpherson, 154–170. Palmerston North: Dunmore, 1991.

Spoonley, Paul, *et al.*, Eds. *Tauiwi: Racism and Ethnicity in New Zealand.* Palmerston North: Dunmore, 1984.

Spoonley, Paul, Cluny Macpherson, and David Pearson, Eds. *Nga Patai: Racism and Ethnic Relations in Aotearoa/New Zealand.* Palmerston North: Dunmore, 1996.

Spoonley, Paul, David Pearson, and Cluny Macpherson, Eds. *Nga Take: Ethnic Relations and Racism in Aotearoa/New Zealand.* Palmerston North: Dunmore, 1991.

Stabb, Martin S. "Indigenism and Racism in Mexican Thought: 1857–1911," *Journal of Inter-American Studies* 1 (1959): 405–424.

Stack, John F. *Ethnic Minorities in a Transnational World.* Westport, CT: Greenwood, 1981.

Starn, Orin. "Missing the Revolution: Anthropologists and the War in Peru," *Cultural Anthropology* 6.1 (1991): 65–93.

Staunæs, Dorthe. *Transitliv. Andre perspektiver på unge flygtninge.* [*Life of Transit. Other perspectives of young refugees.*] Copenhagen: Politisk Revy, 1998.

Steinberg, Stephen. *The Ethnic Myth: Race, Ethnicity, and Class in America.* Boston: Beacon, 1981.

Stoecker, Helmut, and Peter Sebald. "Enemies of the Colonial Idea." In *Germans in the Tropics.* Ed. Arthur J. Knoll and Lewis H. Gann. New York: Greenwood Press, 1987.

Stoecker, Helmut, and Peter Sebald. "The Position of Africans in the German Colonies." In *Germans in the Tropics.* Ed. Arthur J. Knoll and Lewis H. Gann, 119–130. New York: Greenwood, 1987.

Subtelny, Maria Eva. "The Symbiosis of Turk and Tajik." In *Central Asia in Historical Perspective*, Ed. Beatrice Manz. Boulder CO: Westview, 1994.

Sundiata, Ibrahim K. "Late Twentieth-Century Patterns of Race Relations in Brazil and United States," *Phylon*, 47 (1987): 62–76.

Suny, Ronald G. *The Revenge of the Past: Nationalism, Revolution, and the Collapse of the Soviet Union.* Stanford, CA: Stanford University Press, 1992.

Taira, Koji. "Troubled National Identity: The Ryukyuans/Okinawans." In *Japan's Minorities*, Ed. Michael Weiner. New York: Routledge, 1997.

Tajfel, H. *Differentiation Between Social Groups.* London: Academic Press, 1978.

Takaki, Ronald. *A Different Mirror: A History of Multicultural America.* Boston, MA: Little, Brown, 1993.

Talbot, Cynthia. "Inscribing the Other, Inscribing the Self: Hindu–Muslim Identities in Pre-Colonial India," *Comparative Studies in History and Society*, 37 (1995): 692–722.

Talbot, Ian. "Back to the Future? The Punjab Unionist Model of Consociational Democracy for Contemporary India and Pakistan," *International Journal of Punjab Studies*, 3.1 (1996): 65–74.

Tatla, D.S. 1999. *The Sikh Diaspora: The Search for Statehood.* London: UCL Press.

Tatla, D.S. and Ian Talbot. *Punjab.* Oxford UK: Clio Press, 1995.

Taylor, Charles. *Multiculturalism and the Politics of Recognition.* Princeton, NJ: Princeton University Press, 1992.

Taylor, Quintard. "Frente Negra Brasileira: The Afro-Brazilian Civil Rights Movement 1924–1937," *Umoja*, 2.1 (1978): 30.

Te Poata-Smith, Evan S. "He Pokeke Uenuku I Tu Ai: The Evolution of Contemporary Maori Protest." In *Nga Patai: Racism and Ethnic Relations in Aotearoa New Zealand.* Ed. Paul Spoonley, Cluny Macpherson, and David Pearson. Palmerston North: Dunmore, 1996.

Telles, Edward E. "Racial Distance and Region in Brazil: Intermarriage in Brazilian Urban Areas," *Latin American Research Review* (1992): 141–162.

Telles, Edward E. *Racismo à Brasileira: Uma Nova Perspectiva Sociolgica.* Rio de Janiero: Relume Dumará, 2003.

Telles, Edward E. "Residential Segregation by Skin Color in Brazil," *American Sociological Review*, 57 (April 1992): 186–197.

Terkessidis, Mark. *Migranten*. Hamburg: Europäische Verlagsanstalt/Rotbuch, 2000.

Terkessidis, Mark. *Psychologie des Rassismus*. Opladen/Wiesbaden: Westdeutscher Verlag, 1998.

Tessler, Mark, Linda Hawkins, and Jutta Parsons. "Minorities in Retreat: The Jews of the Maghreb." In *The Political Role of Minority Groups in the Middle East*, Ed. Ronald McLaurin, 188–220. New York: Praeger, 1979.

Teti, Vito. *La razza maledetta, Origini del pregiudizio antimeridionale*. Rome: Manifestolibri, 1993.

Thapar, Romila. "Imagined Religious Communities: Ancient History and the Modern Search for a Hindu Identity," *Modern Asian Studies*, 23.2 (1989): 209–231.

Tilly, Charles. *Durable Equality*. Berkeley, CA: University of California Press, 1998.

Tilley, Virginia. *Seeing Indians: A Study of Race, Nation, and Power in El Salvador*. Albuquerque: University of New Mexico Press, 2005.

Tilley, Virginia. "New Help or New Hegemony? The Transnational Indigenous Peoples' Movement and 'Being Indian' in El Salvador," *Journal of Latin American Studies* (2002).

Toplin, Robert Brent. *Freedom and Prejudice: The Legacy of Slavery in The United States and Brazil*. Westport, CT: Greenwood, 1981.

Torpey, John. *The Invention of the Passport: Surveillance, Citizenship and the State*. Cambridge UK: Cambridge University Press, 2000.

Trimingham, J. Spencer. *Islam in Ethiopia*. London: Frank Cass, 1965.

Tucker, William H. *The Science and Politics of Racial Research*. Urbana, IL: University of Illinois Press, 1994.

Turner, J. Michael. "Brown into Black: Changing Racial Attitudes of Afro-Brazilian University Students." In *Race, Class and Power in Brazil*, Ed. Pierre-Michel Fontaine, 73–94. Los Angeles, CA: UCLA Center for African American Studies, 1985.

Twine, France Winddance. *Racism in a Racial Democracy: The Maintenance of White Supremacy in Brazil*. New Brunswick, NJ: Rutgers University Press, 1997.

Ueda Masaaki. *Nihon no shinwa o kangaeru*. Tokyo: Shogakukan, 1994.

Ugarte, Manuel. *The Destiny of a Continent*. New York: Knopf, 1925.

Ullendorff, Edward. *The Ethiopians: An Introduction to Country and People*.London: Oxford University Press, 1973.

Umesao Tadao. *Nihonjin towa nani ka: Kindai nihon bunmei no keisei to hatten*. Tokyo: Nihon hoso shuppan kyokai, 1986.

Vail, Leroy, Ed. *The Creation of Tribalism in Southern Africa*. Berkeley, CA: University of California Press, 1989.

Valente, Ana Lúcia E.F. *Política e Relações Raciais: Os Negros e As Eleições Paulistas de 1982*. São Paulo: Fundação de Amparo a Pesquisa do Estado de São Paulo, 1986.

Vasconcelos, José. "Prólogo a la obra 'Breve historia de México.' " In *José Vasconcelos*, Ed. Justina Sarabia. Madrid: Ediciones de Cultura Hispánica, 1989.

Vasconcelos, José. "Indología." In *José Vasconcelos*, Ed. Justina Sarabia. Madrid: Ediciones de Cultura Hispánica, 1989.

Vasconcelos, José. "La raza cósmica." In *José Vasconcelos*, Ed. Justina Sarabia. Madrid: Ediciones de Cultura Hispánica, 1989.

Vasconcelos, José, and Manuel Gamio. *Aspects of Mexican Civilization*. Chicago, IL: University of Chicago Press, 1926.

Vayda, Andrew P. *Maori Warfare*. Wellington: Polynesian Society, 1960.

Verlan, Sascha, und Hannes Loh. *20 Jahre Hiphop in Deutschland*. Höfen: Hannibal Verlag, 2000.

Wagnleitner, Reinhold. "'No Commodity Is Quite So Strange As This Thing Called Cultural Exchange': The Foreign Politics of American Pop Culture Hegemony." *Amerikastudien – American Studies* 46.3 (2001): 443–470.

Wagnleitner, Reinhold, and Elaine Tyler May, Eds. *"Here, There and Everywhere": The Foreign Politics of American Popular Culture*. Hanover, NA: University Press of New England, 2000.

Waldinger, Renée, Philip Dawson, and Isser Woloch, Eds. *The French Revolution and the Meaning of Citizenship*. Westport, CT: Greenwood Press, 1993.

Walker, Ranginui. *Ka Whawhai Tonu Matou: Struggle without End*. Auckland: Penguin, 1990.

Walker, Sheila S. "Africanity Versus Blackness: The Afro-Brazilian/Afro-American Identity Conundrum." In *Introspectives: Contemporary Art by Americans and Brazilians of African Descent*, Ed. Nancy McKinney, 17–21. Los Angeles, CA: California Afro-American Museum, 1989.

Wallman, Sandra. *Taking Out Hunger*. London: Athlone, 1969.

Ward, Alan. *A Show of Justice: Racial "Amalgamation" in Nineteenth Century New Zealand*. Auckland: Auckland University Press, 1995.

Warren, Kay. *Indigenous Movements and Their Critics*. Princeton, NJ: Princeton University Press, 1999.

Watanabe Shoichi. *Nihon no shinzui — Kodai-kizoku shakai hen: Raisanyo no "nipppon gakufu" o yomu*. Tokyo: PHP, 1992.

Weiner, Myron. "Asian-Americans and American Foreign Policy," *Revue Europeene des Migrations Internationales*, 5.1 (1989): 10–22.

Weiner, Myron. "Bad Neighbors, Bad Neighborhoods: An Inquiry into the Causes of Refugee Flows," *International Security*, 21.1 (1996): 5–42.

Weiner, Myron, Ed. *Japan's Minorities*. New York: Routledge, 1997.

Weiner, Myron, and Samuel P. Huntington, Eds. *Understanding Political Development*. Boston, MA: Little, Brown, 1987.

Wijeyewardene, G., Ed. *Ethnic Groups Across Boundaries in Mainland Southeast Asia*. Singapore: Institute of Southeast Asian Studies, 1990.

Williams, David. "Te Tiriti O Waitangi: Unique Relationship between the Crown and Tangata Whenua?" *Waitangi: Maori and Pakeha Perspectives of the Treaty of Waitangi*, Ed. I.H. Kawharu, 64–91. Auckland: Oxford University Press, 1989.

Williams, Robert G. 1994. *States and Social Evolution: Coffee and the Rise of National Governments in Central America*. Chapel Hill NC: University of North Carolina Press, 1994.

Wilmott, W.E. *The Chinese in Cambodia*. Vancouver: University of British Columbia Publications Center, 1968.

Winant, Howard. *Racial Conditions: Politics, Theory, Comparisons*. Minneapolis, MN: University of Minnesota Press, 1994.

Woldemikael, Tekle M. "Political Mobilization and Nationalist Movements: The Case of the Eritrean People's Liberation Front." *Africa Today*, 38.2 (1991): 31–42.

Woloch, Isser. *The New Regime: Transformations of the French Civic Order, 1780–1820s*. New York: W.W. Norton, 1994.

Wood, Charles H., and José Alberto Magno de Carvalho. *The Demography of Inequality in Brazil*. New York: Cambridge University Press, 1994.

Yamakawa Tsutomu. *Meijiki ainu minzoku seisaku-ron*. Tokyo: Miraisha, 1996.

Yatsugi Kunio. *Tenno to nihon no kindai (jo), Kenpo to arahitogami: Tenno to nihon no kindai (ge), Kyoiku chokugo no shiso*. 2 Vols. Tokyo: Kodansha, 2001.

Yinger, J. Milton. *Ethnicity*. Albany: SUNY Press, 1994.

Young, Crawford, Ed. *The Rising Tide of Cultural Pluralism*. Madison, WI: University of Wisconsin Press, 1993.

Young, Robert J.C. *Colonial Desire: Hybridity in Theory, Culture and Race*. London: Routledge, 1995.

Zaimoglu, Feridan. *Koppstoff: Kanaka Sprak vom Rande der Gesellschaft*. Hamburg: Rotbuch Verlag, 1999.

Zaimoglu, Feridan. *Kanak Sprak: 24 Mißtöne vom Rande der Gesellschaft*. Hamburg: Rotbuch Verlag, 1995.

Zips, Werner. *Black Rebels: African Caribbean Freedom Fighters in Jamaica*. Princeton, NJ: Markus Wiener, 1999.

Zürcher, Erik J. *Turkey: A Modern History*. London: I.B. Tauris, 1993.

Index

A

Abdülhamid II, 242–243
Abel, Jean-Baptiste, 188
Abu-Lughod, Janet, 4
Adams, Romanzo, 77–84
affirmative action, in Brazil, 105–107
Africa Conference in Berlin, 196
Africa, sub-Sahara, 337–351
African Diaspora, The, 6
African National Congress (ANC), 322, 323, 324, 326
Africanism, 323
Africanization, re-Africanization, 162
Afrikaans, 321, 322
Afrikaners, 322
Afrocentrism, 165
Afworki, Isaias, 337
Agentes de Pastoral Negro (the African Brazilian Pastoral movement), 93
Ainu, 15, 18, 116, 118–121, 126–127, 128
Akalis, Akali Dal, 304–305, 308–311, 312, 314
Akashi Yasushi, 279
Akcura, Yusuf, 242
Aktar, Ayhan, 248
Albanians, 244, 249, 361
Algeria, 135–153, 171–191
ali'i, 70–71
Almohades dynasty, 140
amalgamation, 220–221
amarelos, 103–104
Americanization, 207
Americans, 77
Anandpur Sahib Resolution, the, 310
Anatolia, 246, 247, 251, 252
Anjumans, 303
anti-Semitism, 144, 197, 199, 203, 356, 361, 362
Anzaldúa, Gloria, 20

Aoeteroa, 215–236
apartheid, 21, 321, 322–323
Appadurai, Arjun, 291
Arabs, 3, 18, 135, 138–141, 146, 247, 338, 340, 343–344
Arabism, Arabization, 149–150, 152
Arai Hakuseki, 122–123
Arendt, Hannah, 197
Arikirangi, Te Kooti, 222
Armenia and Armenians, 243–244, 245, 261
Armstrong, Richard, 74
Arya Samai, 303
Aryans, 197, 199, 224, 356
Asante, Molefe, 165
assimilation, 17, 78–83, 90, 147, 172–177, 183, 190–191, 205, 207, 224, 247, 252, 291. and immigration, 78–83, 190–191, 205, 207, and race, 78–84
assimilation model, 82–83
assimilationism, 172–177, 190–191, 234–235, 247, 254
Atsız, Nihal, 252
Aulard, Alphonse, 185
aupuni, 69
Ausländer, 196, 202, 204, 205, 206
Awatere, Donna, 228
Azerbaijan, 250

B

Balkans, 244, 247, 249
Ballara, Angela, 220, 224
Balta, Paul, 138
Baluchis, 261
Bandini, Don Juan, 37
Bank, Leslie, 325, 333
Banton, Michael, 5
Barbieri, William, Jr., 202–203
Basotho, 329–331

Basotholand Congress Party, 330
Basotholand National Party, 330
Batchelor, John, 126
Baubóck, Rainer, 208
Beckles, Colin, 164
Belich, James, 216, 222, 224
Bella, Ben, 149
Bentley, Jerry, 4
Berbers, 18, 135–153
Berlusconi, Silvio, 358
Besatzungerkinder, 201
Bey, Rasih, 246
Beytell, Andy, 330–331
Bhartiya Janata Party, 311
Bhindranwale, Jarnail Singh, 310
Bianchini, Levi, 357
biculturalism, 215–216, 220, 230–231,
    233–234, 236
biethnic, 288
bilingual, 288
Birnbaum, Pierre, 189
Bixio, Nino, 357
Black Atlantic, the, 156–157, 164
Black Bookshop movment, the, 164–165
Black collectivity, 160, 163
Black Consciousness movement, the, 21,
    92–98, 100–101, 165, 322–324
Black nationalism, 160–163, 165
Black Power movement, the, 22, 161–163
Black Soul movement, the, 92–93
Black supremecy, 161
*Blackness in Latin America and the
    Caribbean*, 6
Blackness, 3, 21–22, 44–45, 88, 91, 102, 156,
    162, 200, 207
Blumenbach, Johann, 125
Bogardus, Emory, 78, 79
Bogle, Paul, 163
Bolsheviks, 258, 262–264, 268
Bosnians, 249, 254
Brahmin, 302
Braithwaite, Edward, 159
brancos, 87–88, 97, 103–104
Brass, Paul, 299–300
Brazil, 21, 87–108
Britain, 164
Brubaker, Roger, 174
Bryce-Laporte, Roy Simon, 157
Bucareli, Antonio María, 36
Buddhism, 117–118, 273, 289, 292,
    Theravada, 282
Buddhist Liberal Democratic Party (BLDP),
    279
Burdick, John, 99,101
Byzantines, 138

C

Cakmak, Fevzi, 253
California, 33–50
Californios, 33–50
Cambodia and Cambodians, 273–293
Campelli, Enzo and Roberta
    Cipollini, 362
Canal Colonies, 303
candomblé, 93
Cape Native Affairs Department, 325
carnival, 164
Carroll, Sir James, 225
caste, 302–303, 306
Catholicism, 12–13, 33–50, 93, 189, 282,
    289, 292
Celâl Nuri Bey, 249
Central America, 59
Central Asia, 257–268
centralism, democratic or constitutional,
    306–307
*Centro de Articulação de Populações
    Marginalizadas* (the Center for
    Marginalized Populations), 94
Centro de Estudos Afro-Asiáticos (the Center of
    Afro-Asiatic Studies), 94
China, 1, 14, 17–18
Chinese, 1, 75–76, 83, 116, 158–159
Chodïrs, 259
Christianity, in Brazil, 93, in Cambodia, 282, in
    Eritrea, 343–345, in Hawai'i, 73–74, in
    North Africa, 139, 141, in South Africa,
    320, 325, in Turkey, 243–244, 253
Christianization, 137
chuncheat Vietnam, 285
Circassians, 249, 252
citizenship, 8, 16, 69–84, 143–145, 171–191,
    196–200, 203–206, 240, 249–254, 267,
    285–287, 306, 310, 362, and race, 69–84,
    and religion, 171–191, 241, 243
civilization and race, 45–46
claramente mulato, 90
Clarke, John Henrik, 160
class and race, 83, 96, 108
Clemenceau, Georges, 185
Cliff, Jimmy, 165
Collegium for African American
    Research, 6
Colombia, 3
colonialism, 8, 14–16, 155, 319–320, Chinese,
    1–2, British, 157, 215–224, 302–306,
    342–343, 348, French, 141–148, 153,
    171–191, 278, German, 195–208, Italian,
    342–343, 348, 359, Russian, 261–262,
    South African, 324–327, Vietnamese, 277
color-blindness, 355–363

Coloureds, 322
Commission Interministeriel des Affaires Musulmanes (CIAM), 181–185
comparability, question of, 4
conjuncture, 166
Cook, James, 218
cosmic race, 20, 35
counter-hegemonic, 164–165
Cox, Lindsay, 225
Cox, Oliver, 4
Creolization, 159
Criola, 94
Croats, 254
Crosby, Alfred, 4
cultural identity and religion, 342–345
cultural ideology of uniqueness, 349–351
cultural nationalism, 306, 313
culturelessness, 287
Cunningham, Joseph Davy, 302
Curtin, Philip, 4

D

Dana, Richard Henry, 41, 47–48
Debra Lebanos massacre, the, 359
degeneration, 224
Degler, Carl, 89
demos, 17, 35b, 200, 204–205
Depont, Octave, 184
Deringil, Selim, 241, 243
descent, 199–201, 242, 259, 261, 263–264, 273, 339, 345
Dharam Yudh Morcha, 310
dhimmis, 144–145
Dia de la Raza, 60
diaspora, African, 156, 160, 162, 167, 200, Afro-Caribbean, 156, 160, 162–163, 167, Sikh, 300, 311
die Asylantenflut, 203
differentialist model, 174
disease, 37–38, 73, 218, 223
diversity, cultural, 253, ethnic, 139, 246, 251, 257, 306, linguistic, 140, 246, 254, 307, 340, racial, 108, social, 139
Doizy, Henri, 183–184, 187
Doutté, Edmond, 184
Drake, St. Clair, 5
Du Bois, W. E. B., 22
Dufour, Bishop Charles, 165
Durán, Padre Narciso, 37, 38, 40, 41
Durant, Will, 4

E

East India Company, 303
East Indians, in Jamaica, 157–158

Ebert, Friedrich, 199
economic location
egalitarian pluralism, 108
egalitarianism, 80–81, 191
Eiselen, W.W.M., 323
El Salvador, 59, 65
Elias, Norbert, 198
El-Tayeb, Fatima, 197
Entine, Jon, 11
Equiano, Olauda, 356
Eritrea, 22, 23, 337–351, 355
Ersarïs, 259, 260
essentialism, 101, 321, 338–339, 351
Ethiopians, 22, 160, 337, 340, 342, 344, 348–349
ethnic cleansing, 305
ethnic conflict, 264, 274, 299–300, 314
ethnic consciousness, 300–302
ethnic groups, 10, 20
ethnic mobilization, 300, 322
ethnic patronage, 332
ethnic separatism, 333
ethnicity, and identity, 149, 261, 273–293, 273–293, 313, 321, and language, 135, 273, 300, 304, 341–342, and nationalism, 299–314, and politics, 302–311, and religion, 301, 344, and statehood, 259, and territory, 301–302, Black, 157, theory, 5
ethnicity and race, as social and cultural constructs, 338–339, as social processes, 333, contrasted, 3, 12, 53, Eritrea, 338–340, Hawai'i, 69–84, India, 299–314, South Africa, 319–334
ethnicization, 53, 67, 147, 157
ethnocracy, 307
ethno-nationalism, 299, 311
ethno-racial ideology, 339–340
ethnos, 17, 35, 200, 204–205
Eurocentric, 215
Evans, Ivan, 323
Ewlad, 260
exceptionalism, 197, 344, 351
exclusion, 151, 253

F

Fahreddin, Iskander, 251
family and race, 45
Farbe bekennen, 200
Farini, Luigi, 357
Federal Republic, 201, 204
Feldblum, Miriam, 190
Fiji, 12
Filipino, 76

Fischer, Joschka, 195
Flandin, Etienne, 177
Fleras, Augie, 231
foreignness and foreigners, 70–77
France, 13, 15, 17
Frank, Andre Gunder, 4
Fredrickson, George, 5
Free Coloreds, 88–89
Free Vietnam, 277, 285
Frente Negra Brasileira (the Black Front),
    94, 100
Freyre, Gilberto, 87, 90
Front des Forces Socialistes, 151
Fujii Teikan, 122
Fukuzawa Yukichi, 124–125

G
Gagauz, 253
Gamio, Manuel, 57–58, 63
Gamio, Manuel, *Forjando Patria*, 57–58
Gandhi, Indira, 310–311
Garibaldi, 357
Garvey, Marcus, 22
Garveyism, 161
Gastarbeiter, 202, 205
Geledés, 94
Gellner, Ernest, 10, 300
genealogy, 200, 257–268, 342, 345–348
gente de razón, 38–39, 41, 44
German Colonial Society, 199
German Democratic Republic,
    203–204
German Southwest Africa, 196, 199
Germans, 358–359
Germanness, 197–198, 200, 203,
    207–208
Germany, 18, 174, 195–208
Ghallughara, 301, 310
Gilroy, Paul, 156, 164, 198
Giuerlli, Mattai, 358
Glazer, Nathan, 16
Glick, Clarence, 78
Golden Temple, the, or Akal Takhat, 303,
    310–311
Gordon, Derek, 156
Gordon, George William, 163
Gould, Jeff, 65
Greek Orthodox, 248
Greeks, 244, 248
Grupo Cultural Afro-Reggae (the Afro-Reggae
    Cultural Group), 94
Guatamala, 66
gul, 260
Gülhane Rescript, the, 241–242
gypsies, 252, 361–362

H
Hall, Stuart, 166
Hamelin, Jules, 181
Haole, 70–77
Hartebeestfontein Gold Mine, 327–333
Harties, 327–333
Haut Conseil à l'Intégration, 190
Hawai'i and Hawaiians, 15, 21, 23, 69–84
Heke, Hone, 225
Hereros, 198
Herrnstein, Richard, 11
heterogeneity, 203
heterogeneity, theories of, 122–124, 126–127
hierarchies, cultural, 348, ethnic, 268, geneo-
    logical, 267, racial, 2–3, 12, 54–55, 63, 69,
    78, 84, 89, 115–128, 199, 240, 302–303,
    social, 257–268, 302–303
Hindu Code Bill, 313
Hindu Marriage Act of 1955, 313
Hindus and Hinduism, 300, 303, 304, 306, 312,
    313
Hine, Darlene Clark and Jacqueline McLeod,
    Crossing Boundaries, 6
hip-hop, 165, 206–207
Hisabetsu Burakumin, 116, 128
Hohepa, Pat, 229
Hokkaido, 118–121
Holocaust, the, 198
homeland, 263, 267, 299, 308–309, 311
homogeneity, cultural and political, 197–98,
    ethnic and racial, 339, 356, theories of,
    122–124, 126–127
Hormann, Bernhard, 78
Hozumi Hassoku, 124
Huber-Koller, Rose Marie, 201
Hügel-Marshall, Ika, 201
Hüseyin Avni Bey, 248
hybridity, 20, 207, 291, 340, 351
hybridization, 125

I
Ibbleston, Denzil, 302–303
identity, and ethnicity, 149, 261, 273–293,
    273–293, 313, 321, and language, 261, 267,
    273, 287–289, 341–342, and race, 10, and
    region, 313, and religion, 261, 289, 343,
    African Brazilian, 92–108, Afrikaner,
    322–324, Cambodian, 273–293, cultural,
    281–282, 287–288, 337–351, ethnic,
    273–293, ethnonational, 196, ethno-racial,
    337–351, Māori, 234, mapping, 292,
    Pākehā, 234, political, 240, racial, 103, 239,
    social, 291, Zulu, 324
identity movements as projects, 291
identity politics, 95

ig, 260
immigration, 78–83, 190–191, 195, 200–203,
  205–208, and assimilation, 78–83,
  190–191, 205, 207
Immorality Act, the, 322
imperialism, British, 305–306, 322,
  Vietnamese, 276
İnan, Afet, 251
inclusion, 253
India and Indians, 157–158, 205, 299–314
India, post-colonial, 306–311
Indian National Congress, 304, 306
Indian problem, 55–58
Indian-ness, 3, 56, 61
Indians, North American, 33–50
Indigenas, 104
indigènes, 171
indigenization, 265
indo-mestizaje, 58, 63, 66
indunas, 324
Ingenieros, José, 60
Inkatha Freedom Party, 324
Inkatha movement, 321, 324–325
Inländer, 196
Instituto de Pesquisas Afro-Brasileiras
  (the Institute of Afro-Brazilian
  Research), 94
interculturalism, 195
intermarriage, 236, 267, 290, 322, 340, 342,
  355, 356
internationalism, Marxist or Soviet,
  262, 266
interracial marriage, 78–83
Iran, 250
Islam, 13, 139–141, 145, 171–191, 241–254,
  313, 343, 345, 361
Islamism, 242
Islamization, 139–141
Israel, 3, 146
Italian brava gente, 358
Italy, 355–363
Italy, Southern, 357–358
Itō; Hirobumi, 125
Ittihad ve Terakki Cemiyeti (Committee for
  Union and Progress), 243–244

J

Jackson, Helen Hunt, *Ramona*, 45–46
jadids, 261–262, 265
Jamaica, 22, 155–167
Jamaican Labor Party, 160
Japan, 18, 23, 115–128
Japanese, 1, 15, 76, 115–128
Japanese Brazilians, 117
Jats, 301, 302, 303

Jews, 3, 10,138, 141–146, in Algeria, 142–144, in
  Germany, 201, 203, in Italy, 356, 358–360,
  362, in Jamaica, 159, in Morocco, 144–145,
  in Tunisia, 144, in Turkey, 244, 253
Jonathan, Chief Lebua, 330
Jonnart Law, the, 186–188
Jonnart, Charles, 185–188
Jordens, Jay, 279
Judaism, 13, 138
jus sanguinis, 174, 190, 196, 198
jus soli, 174–175, 190, 196

K

Kabyle, Kabylians, 147, 150
Kalakaua, David, King of Hawai'i, 77
Kampuchea Krom, 276, 282, 283
Kampuchea, 273–293
kānaka maoli, 69
Kanter, James and Ed Madra, 285
Kashmiris, 308
Katahitanga, or Unity, 223
Kazakhs, 259, 261, 265
Kedourie, E., 308
Kelsey, Jane, 222
Kemal, Mustafa, 246–247
keshdhari Hindus, 312
Khalistan, 299, 311, 312
Khalsa Panth, 301
Khmer Rouge, 274–275, 279, 283–284, 289,
  290, 292
Khmers, 273–293
Khmerness, 273, 275, 287–288, 291
Kida Sadakichi, 123
Ki-ki mythology, 117–122, 127
Kilic, Hilmi, 253
Killion, Tom, 350
King, Michael, 234
King, T. Butler, 42
kinship, 259–260, 267, 339, 343, 345
Kirisci, Kemal, 249–250
Kojiki, 117–122
kokutai-ron, 123–124
Koreans, 76
Koreans, in Japan, 116, 128
Kulturkampf, 206
Kuper, Adam, 156
Kurds, 248, 251–252, 253, 261
KwaZulu, 324

L

la guerra de las razas, 48
la raza cosmica, 20, 65
la raza, 59–60, 64
Lam, Margaret, 78

Lambede, Anton, 323
language, and ethnicity, 135, 273, 300, 304, 341–342, and identity, 261, 267, 273, 287–289, 341–342, and nationality, 262–263, 265, 309
Lasuén, Padre Fermín, 36, 37
Latimer, Sir Graham, 229
Latin American, 58–60, 66–67
latins, 61, 63, 64
latino-mestizaje, 61–63, 66
Lausanne Conference, the, 247–249
le Printemps Berbère, 150–151
Ledgerwood, Judy, May Ebihara, and Carol Mortland, 274
legal imperialism, 215, 222, 223
Leitkultur, 206, 208
Lenin, 263, 268
Lesotho, 329–330, 333
levee en masse, 175
Levine, Donald, 338
Lewis, Bernard, 246
Lewis, Gordon, 159
Lewis, Rupert, 156
Libya, 359
Lili'uokalani, Queen of Hawai'i, 77
Lilley, Rozanna, 293
Lind, Andrew, 78
lineage, 345–348
linguistic imperialism, 265
Linnekin, Jocelyn, 293
locals, 83
Lombroso, Cesare, 357
Lowenthal, David, 156
Lugo, José del Carmen, 41
Lugones, Leopoldo, 60
Lula da Silva, Luiz Inácio, 105
Lutaud, Charles, 181–185, 188, 189

M
Machada, Juana, 40
Maghreb, 135–53
Mahmud II, 240
maka'āinana, 70, 72
Mamdani, Mamood, 321, 333
Mammeri, Mouloud, 151
Mana Motuhake, 229
mana, 71–72, 217, 228–229, 233
Manatu Māori, 231
Mangosothu Buthelezi, 321, 324–325
Manley, Norman, 163
Māori, 15, 16, 215–236
Māori Battalion, the, 226
Māori Congress, the, 232
Māori Sovereignty, 228–229
marginality, marginalization, 151, 207, 223, 344, 359

Marley, Bob, 165
Maroons, 160–161, 165
martial races theory, 303
Marx, Anthony, 5
Marxism, 258, 262–264
masculine ideology, 320, 333
Masferrer, Albert, 60, 64–65
Mason, Philip, 6
Massaquoi, Hans-Jürgen, 200
Masuoka Jitsuichi, 78
Matanza, 65
Matanzima, K. D., 326
Matlatsi, James, 331
Mboya, Tom, 163
McHugh, P.G., 219, 230
McNeill, William H., 4
Meiji, 118–122
membership, 195–208, 240, 242
Mennea, Pietro, 358
Menzie, Archibald, 71
Mercier, Gustave, 188–189
mestizaje, 20–21, 34–35, 54–55, 58, 59, 63–66
mestizo, 3, 38–40, 57–58, 64
metaphors, national, 244, 254, racial, 252
Mexicans, 33–50
Mexico, 55–66
Middle East, Middle Easterners, 338, 342, 344
Middleman Minorities, 159
migrant labor, 320–321, 322, 324–325, 333
migrant, 227
Mikaere, Buddy, 233
military participation and power, 171–178, 226
Miller, John, 218–219
Millerand, Alexandre, 177, 181
Milliès-Lacroix, Raphaël, 189
minority groups, 9, 106, Indian, 307–308, Japanese, 115–128
minority nationalisms, 307–308
minzoku, 123–124
miscegenation, 49, 56, 89–91, 99, 105
Mischlinge, 201
Mistral, Gabriela, 60
Mitchell, Samuel Augustus, 125
Molina, Enríquez, 56–57
monoculturalism, monoculture, 215–216, 230, 233–234
Montanelli, Indro, 359
Moon, Penderel, 305
Morant Bay Rebellion, 163
Moroccans, Morocco, 135–153, 201, 207
Mountbatten, Lord, 305
Moutet, Marius, 184–185, 191
Movimiento Negro Unificado (the Unified Black Movement), 93–97, 99
Mpondo Rebellion, the, 326
mulato claro, 90

mulatto escape hatch, 89, 98, 102
mulattoes, 3, 88–89, 97, 107
multiculturalism, 108, 150, 190, 204, 207
multiethnic, 259
multinational, 310, 312
multiracialism, multiracial identity, 89, 95, 98, 155, 157
Murray, Charles, 11
Muslim family customs, 182–186
Muslim League, the, 304
Muslims, in Algeria, 171–191, in Eritrea, 343–345, in India, 300, 303, 304, in North Africa, 141–148, in Turkey, 241–254
Mussolini, Benito, 343, 358
Myanmar, 4
myths, mythology, 8, 116–122, 196–197, 234, 251, 358–359
mythology of inbreeding, 357

N

Namas, 198
Namibia, 198
Nanak, Baba, 301, 305, 311
narratives, community, 300–301, 313, 314, national, 117–122, 126, 196–198, 258, 314, 340, racial and ethnic, 22–23, 117–122, 273–274, 293, 340, 345–348
Nascimento, Abdias do, 94
Nash, Gary, 20
nation, 10, 257–268, and race, 10–11, 239–254, as historical construct, 258, Stalinist definition, 263
national identity, and religion, 261, 299–314, Berbers and, 150–151, Brazilian, 87–108, , Cambodian, 273–293, Eritrean, 343, French, 171–191, German, 204, Japanese, 115–128, nationality and race, 115–128, 155–167, New Zealand, 219, Turkey, 239–254, Turkmen, 257–268
National Socialism, 197, 198
national sovereignty, 266
National Union of Mineworkers, 322, 326–333
nationalism, 11, 16–18, 65, 155–167, 240, 257, and ethnicity, 299–314, African, 321, African diasporic, 166, Arab, 150, Basotho, 329, Hindu, 308, Indian, 304, 306, 308, Lesotho, 329–330, 333, Muslim, 247, Punjabi, 314, Russian, 247, Sikh, 299–314, Turkish, 239–254, Turkmen, 257–268, 265
nationality, 20, 143, 145, 171, 174, 258, 285, and language, 262–263, 265, 309, and territory, 262, 300, titular, 262, 266
nationalizing, 264
nation-building, 53, 56–68, 196–197, 243, 356, Jamaica, 160, Mexico, 53, 56–58

nationhood, 8, 155–167, 172, 189, 196, 249, 254, 258–259, 263–264, 265, 268
nation-making, 8–9
Native Americans, 15, 17, 33–50
Native Schools movement, the, 224
natives, 15, 70–77
naturalization, 175–176, 178–191
Nazis, 359–360
negro, 88, 99–104
neonationalism, 204
Nettleford, Rex, 156, 161
New Zealand, 15, 16, 215–236
New Zealand Company, 218–220
Ngata, Sir Apirana, 225
Nicaragua, 59, 65
Niceforo, Alfredo, 357
Nihon minzoku, 124
Nihon shoki, 117–122
Nihon-ron, or *Nihonjin-ron*, 127–128
Niyazov, Saparmurad, 268
Nkrumah, Kwame, 22
Nobongwana, Wiseman, 330–331
nonracialism, 156–157, 160, 162, 163, 167, 321
Nordic, 197
Norinaga, Motoori, 123
North Africa, 15, 135–153, 171–191, 203, 206
Northern League, the, 357, 361
Nuremberg Laws, 199, 201

O

Obuchi Keizō, 127
Oguma Eiji, 122–124
Oguntoye, Katharina, May Opitz, and Dagmar Schultz, 200
Ogus-Khan, 259
Oguz, 267
Okinawans, 116, 121–122, 126, 128
Shigenobu, Ōkuma, 123
Oliver, William H., 229
one-drop rule, 13, 101
Orano, Paolo, 357
Organization of African Unity (OAU), 337
Orientalism, 306
Osio, Antonio María, 41
Ottomanism, 240–245
Özkaya, Nuri, 253

P

Pākehā, 215–236
Pakistan, 304, 309
pan-Africanism, 22, 160, 162, 163–164, 167

Panth, 308
pan-tribalism, 222, 233
pardos, 87, 97–104
Park, Robert, 9, 79
Parthians, 267
partition, Indian, 304–305
Pasha, Emir, 246–247
paternalism, 360, 362
patrias, 56, 63
Payeras, Mariano, 37
Pentecostalism, 93
People's National Party, 160
People's Political Party, 161
Persians, 261
Peru, 3
Petain, Philippe, 146
Peters, Carl, 199
Phillips, D.L., 49
Phoenicians, 135–136
Phundulu, Hoyce, 326–332
Pile, Steven, and Nigel Thrift, 292
pluralism, plurality, 100–101, 189
pluralistic federalism, 324
Pol Pot, 279, 293
political participation and power, 93–97,
    185–186, 222–225, 228, 231–233, 279,
    285–287, 306–307, 308–311
political status, 285–287
politics and ethnicity, 302–311
polygamy, 172, 182–186, 187, 189
Pope, J.H., 224
Potatau I, 222
power and race, 2, 10, 12
Prashad, Vijay, 355–356
Prenderast, Chief Judge, 230
pretos, 87–88, 97–104
primordialism, primordialization,
    258–259, 268, 300, 319, 321,
    324, 339, 351
pseudoscience, 11
Puketapu, Kara, 229
Punjab and Punjabi, 299–314

R

race (racial) consciousness, 79, 155, 161, 165,
    322, 323
race, and assimilation, 78–84, and citizenship,
    69–84, and civilization, 45–46, and class,
    83, 96, 108, and family, 45, and identity,
    10, and nation, 10–11, 239–254, and
    national identity, nationality, 115–128,
    155–167, and power, 2, 10, 12, and
    religion, 12, 13–14, 33–50, 93,
    117–118, 344, 359, and the
    body, 2, 12

race and ethnicity, as social and cultural
    constructs, 338–339, as social processes,
    333, contrasted, 3, 12, 53, Eritrea, 338–340,
    Hawai'i, 69–84, India, 299–314, South
    Africa, 319–334
race relations cycle, 9, 78–83
race, theory, 5, 239–254, as a process, 12, as a
    social construct, 116, defined, 2–3,
    metaphors of, 239–254, sociological theory
    of, 78–84
racial and ethnic systems, 1–4, 23
racial democracy, 87, 89–92, 93, 95, 98
racial distance quotients, 79
racial moment, 2, 11–12
racial multiplicity, 20–21
racial nationalism, 54
racial pluralism, 100–101, 159
racial project, binary, 87–88, 92–98, 108,
    ternary, 87–92, 102,108
racial superiority, 342
racial thinking, 36–50, 239–240, 254
racialization, 116, 128, 157, 165
racism, biological, 357, 360, cultural, 347,
    denial of, 355–363, differential, 361, inter-
    nalized, 342
Ramos, Guerrero, 94
Ranariddh, Prince, 280
Ranjit Singh, 302, 312, 314
*Rassemblement pour la Culture et la
    Démocratie*, 151
Rastafarianism, 22, 160–161
Ratana, 222
re-Africanization, 93
re-ethnicization, 206
reggae, 22, 160, 162, 165, 206–207
region and identity, 313
regional nationalisms, 307–308
Reich, 197–200
religion, and citizenship, 171–191, 241, 243,
    and cultural identity, 342–345, and
    ethnicity, 301, 344, and identity, 261, 289,
    343, and national identity, 261, 299–314,
    and race, 12, 13–14, 33–50, 93, 117–118,
    344, 359
religion, Algeria, 171–191, Eritrea, 342–345,
    Hawai'i, 71, India, 299–314, Jamaica,
    158–159, Japan, 117–118, North Africa,
    138–153, Turkey, 241–254
Ribbat, Chrisoph, 207
Richmond, J.C., 221
Ringatu, 222
Ripoll, Padre, 38
ritual drama, 43
Riza Nur Bey, 248
Rodney, Walter, 161–162, 163

Rom, 361
Romania, 253
Romans, 136–137
Roy, Oliver, 266
Rushton, J. Philippe, 11
Russians, 261, 265, 266
Ryukyu, 121–122

S

Sahib, Nanakana, 303
sajones, 60
Salïrs, 259
Salzmann, Ariel, 242
Samih Rifat Bey, 249
Samrin, Heng, 279, 289
Sandinistas, 65–66
Sardinia, 355, 357
Sarïks, 259
Sarkozy, Nicholas, 190–191
Scheinasylanten, 203
Schlesinger, Arthur, Jr., 16
Schroeder, J., 234
Schutzgebiete, 197
scientific racism, 197, 239–240, 253
Scott, David, 166–167
Searanke, M, 229
secularism, 306
Selassie, Haile, 22, 160
self-determination, 232, 307
self-identity, 345
Sen, Hun, 279, 280
separatism, 151
Serbs, 254
Serra, José, 105
Serra, Padre Junipero, 41
settlers, settler-colonialism, 19, 54, 215–223
shame, 40
Sherlock, Philip S., and Hazel B. Bennet, 158
Shinto, 117–118, 126–127
Shiromani Gurdwara Parbandhak
    Committee, 304
Short, Major Billy, 305
Sihanouk, Norodom, King, 280
Sikh, 299–314
Silverman, Max, 174
Singh, Bhagat, 314
Singh, Beant, 311
Singh, Sabha, 303
Singh Sarabha, Kartar, 314
Sinophobia, 65
Sinti, 361
Skidmore, Thomas A., 89
Smith, Anthony D., 10
Smith, Carlson, 78
Smith, M.G., 156

snhcheat khmaer, 285
social Darwinism, 125–126
social distance, theory of, 79–83
socialism, 262
Sokanyile, Oliver, 330
solidarity, racial and ethnic, 327, 333
Somalia, 340, 342
Sorrenson, M.P.K., 230
South Africa, 15, 16, 19–20, 21, 23, 216,
    319–334
South Asia, 299–314
Southeast Asia, 273–293
Soviet Union, 257, 266
Soweto uprising, 323
Spaniards, 33–50
Spencer, Herbert, 125
Stalin, Joseph, 258, 262, 263
state-building, India, 300, 306–308
statehood and ethnicity, 259
statut musulman, 179, 185
statut personnel, 172, 178–186, 188–189
Stone, Carl, 156, 161
Story of the Jamaican People, The, 158
Sudan, 340, 342, 344
suffrage, 279, 285–287
Sumer Kızı, 251
Suphi (Tanröver), Hamdullah, 249,
    252, 253
Syrians, 159

T

Tajfel, Henri, 291
Takaki, Ronald, 76
Tara Singh, 304
Tarr, Chou Meng, 276
Tasman, 218
Tatars, 261
Te Kingitanga (King Movement), 222
Te Puni Kokiri, 232
te Tira Ahu Iwi, 231–232
Teatro Experimantal do Negro (Black
    Experimental Theater), 100
Tekes, 259, 261, 262
territory and ethnicity, 301–302
territory and nationality, 262, 300
Tesal, Resat, 252
Tesujirō, Inoue, 124
the body and race, 2, 12
theology of liberation, 313
theo-political status, 308
Thomson, Gaston, 187
Thornton, John, 4
Tibet, 14
Tigrinya, 349
Tilley, Virginia, 8, 11, 20

Tokugawa, 118–119
Torū Ryūzō, 123
Tosh, Peter, 162, 165
Touré, Sékou, 22
Toynbee, Arnold, 4
transcultural process, 90
transnational identities, 166, 208
transnationalism, 156, 160, 162, 163, 167
transracial process, 90
Treaty of Waitangi, the, 216, 220–221, 223,
    228–235
Tregear, Edward, 224
Treurnicht, A.P., 322
tribes and tribalism, 19, 217–218, 223–224,
    227, 232–233, 235, 257–261, 267–268, 306,
    323–322, 325, 326, 329, 332, 334
troupes indigènes, 171–191
Tsuboi Shōgorō, 123
Tunisia, 135–153, 201
Turanism, 246
Turkey and Turks, 201–202, 203, 206, 207,
    239–254
Turkification, 244, 247
Turkish Republic, the, 245–254
Turkishness, 245, 247, 252
Turkism, 242
Türkkan, Reha Oğuz, 252
Turkmenistan, 257–268
Turkmenness, 257, 263, 264
Turpan, 1

U

Überfremdung, 202
Ullendroff, Edward, 338
umbanda, 93
União de Negros pela Igualidade (United Blacks
    for Equality), 94
United Democratic Front, 324
United Nations Transitional Authority in
    Cambodia, 274, 279, 283–284
universal franchise, 307
universalism, 191
University of Hawaiʻi, 77–78
urbanization, 226–228
Uygurs, 1, 14
Uzbeks, 259, 261, 265, 268
Uzbekistan, 260, 268

V

Vail, Leroy, 320–321
Vandals, 137–138
Vargas, Getúlio, 94
Varona, Enríque Jose, 60
Vasconcelos, José, 20, 60–63, 65
Venegas, Padre, 37
Verwoerd, Hendrik F., 323, 326
Vietnamese, in Cambodia, 273–293
Vietnameseness, 283–285, 291
Viollette, Maurice, 183
Volk, 196–197, 200, 204, 208
Von Langsdorff, Georg, 45

W

Waitangi Tribunal, the, 216, 229–230, 233
Wakefield, Edward Gibbon, 218–220
Walker, Ranginui, 229
Wallerstein, Immanuel, 4
Ward, Alan, 220, 222
Weber, Max, 46
Weiner, Myron, 307
White supremacy, 5
Whiteness, 88–89, 91, 102, 200,
    203, 356
Whitening, 56, 90–91, 98
world history, 4–5
xenophobia, 344

X

Xhosa, 319, 322, 325–327, 329–331

Y

Yamamuro Shin'ichi, 124–125
Yamato, 116, 122, 126
Yemen, 244, 249
Yildiz, Ahmet, 245
Yomuts, 259
Young Māori Party, 225
Young Turks, 243–244
Yugoslavia, 254

Z

Zalvidea, Padre, 43
Zionists, Zionism, 10, 244
Zulus, 319–322, 324, 333